Era of the
AMERICAN
REVOLUTION

Clio Bibliography Series 4

Abstracts from the periodicals data base of the
American Bibliographical Center

Eric H. Boehm, Editor

Users of the Clio Bibliography Series may refer to current issues of
America: History and Life *and* Historical Abstracts
*for continuous bibliographic coverage of the subject areas
treated by each individual volume in the series.*

1.
The American Political Process
Dwight L. Smith and Lloyd W. Garrison
1972   LC 72-77549   ISBN 0-87436-090-0

2.
Afro-American History
Dwight L. Smith
1974   LC 73-87155   ISBN 0-87436-123-0

3.
Indians of the United States and Canada
Dwight L. Smith
1974   LC 73-87156   ISBN 0-87436-124-9

4.
Era of the American Revolution
Dwight L. Smith
1975   LC 74-14194   ISBN 0-87436-178-8

Era of the

AMERICAN REVOLUTION

A Bibliography

DWIGHT L. SMITH

Editor

RICHARD B. MORRIS

Introduction

TERRY A. SIMMERMAN

Assistant Editor

Santa Barbara, California
Oxford, England

A B C - CLIO Inc. ®

Z
1238
E7
1975

Library of Congress Catalog Card Number 74-14194
ISBN Clothbound Edition 0-87436-178-8

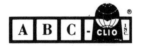

American Bibliographical Center—Clio Press, Inc.
2040 Alameda Padre Serra
Santa Barbara, California

European Bibliographical Center—Clio Press
Woodside House, Hinksey Hill
Oxford OXI 5BE, England

Design by Barbara Monahan, from an 1768 engraving by
Paul Revere of British troops landing at Boston.
Printed and bound in the United States of America

CONTENTS

PREFACE

The observance of the Bicentennial of the American Revolution will take many forms. The world of scholarship continues to study the momentous history of that quarter-century to uncover information to fill some of the blanks on the pages of history, to furnish data for synthesis, and to confirm or modify old interpretations or suggest fresh ones.

While the years of the Bicentennial observance will produce a literal plethora of scholarly research publication, there is already a significant body of literature. This bibliography is designed to alert the user to some of these publications and thus to suggest what needs to be done. As the Bicentennial commemoration progresses, hopefully a sufficiently funded project will be launched to prepare an exhaustive series of bibliographies on the American Revolution. Meanwhile, there are efforts already published or in progress that are significant steps in that direction.

Era of the American Revolution, the fourth contribution to the open-ended *Clio Bibliography Series* of special reference volumes published by the American Bibliographical Center, is concerned specifically with the literature which has appeared in the world's historical and related social science and humanities periodicals of the last two decades. The 1401 entries consist of classified bibliographic citations and descriptive abstracts for each.

America: History and Life is the data bank or source of the entries. Its worldwide coverage of about 2000 periodicals in some thirty languages makes it the most comprehensive source of bibliographic information available. Updating of the entries of this bibliography on the American Revolution can thus be achieved by consulting subsequent issues of *America: History and Life,* commencing with Volume XI (1974).

I assumed the editorial responsibility for this bibliography while on assignment as consultant to the American Bibliographical Center during the summers of 1973 and 1974. Lloyd W. Garrison, executive vice president, helped me in the conceptual stage and served as a sounding-board throughout the project. I am especially grateful to Terry A. Simmerman, assistant editor of the *Clio Bibliography Series.* She and I edited, classified, and indexed the abstract entries in the volume. Simmerman also supervised the production and served as liaison with the subcontractors. Joyce Duncan Falk, director of the American

Bibliographical Center, was a helpful source of editorial advice. And the several members of the editorial and production staffs contributed their special skills and expertise throughout the project.

It is our good fortune that Richard B. Morris, distinguished historian of the American Revolution at Columbia University as well as chairman of the Bicentennial Committee of the American Historical Association and president-elect of the association, accepted our invitation to write the introductory essay for this bibliography. His remarks give context and perspective and hence greater utility to the volume.

The broad foundation upon which *Era of the American Revolution* is built are the volunteer abstracts written by hundreds of historians throughout the world. Their names appear with each abstract and in a special listing at the end of the volume. We acknowledge our indebtedness to them.

DWIGHT L. SMITH

Miami University
Oxford, Ohio

INTRODUCTION

Richard B. Morris, Columbia University

Anticipation of the commemoration of the Bicentennial of the American Revolution has spurred renewed interest on the part of historians in analyzing the personages, forces, and events shaping that notable era. Over the past generation the American Revolution — its causes, conduct, and consequences — has been reexamined, the impact of that epoch on America and on the rest of the world reappraised, many older views modified, discarded, or rehabilitated and new approaches have opened enlarged vistas for the professional historian, the teacher, and the student.

To this reappraisal periodical literature contributes significantly, but many relevant articles published in historical periodicals here and abroad and written in a variety of foreign languages may not be readily available to the researcher. We are fortunate indeed that the American Bibliographical Center has for the past two decades devoted itself to making available the scholarship of periodical literature in its abstracts publications dealing with history and the behavioral sciences. The coverage is comprehensive and the abstracting of the articles is done with meticulous care and objectivity and at sufficient length for the researcher to determine their relevance for his purposes.

On the eve of the Bicentennial it is especially appropriate that the era of the American Revolution is the subject of a volume in the Clio Bibliography Series, the special abstracts bibliographies on major topics published by the Center. We now have a comprehensive conspectus of contemporary scholarship on this era and on this country's national origins.

Era of the American Revolution: A Bibliography has not only unearthed a wealth of scholarly contributions in the periodical literature but organizes them according to a logical scheme in eleven specific areas. The opening section deals with the historiography of the era and with the philosophical background of the Revolution. Section two discusses general aspects of the Revolution including its impact on the economy and on religious groups, notably the pacifist Quakers. It also surveys affairs in the Continental Army and Navy such as logistics, discipline, and medical and sanitary conditions. The biographical material in section three focuses on the involvement of personalities in the Revolution. Section four treats the pre-Revolutionary controversy through the First Continental Congress. Sections five through seven deal with the shooting war, not only the military events from Lexington to Yorktown, but also the regional fighting, notably in the West, and the diplomatic struggle to gain aid and recognition. Section eight recognizes that the American Revolution was also a civil war, with the Loyalists representing perhaps twenty percent of the population, and with many neutrals and fence-sitters. The amount of attention paid by article writers to the Tories is a tribute to the ability of historians today to transcend earlier prejudices and treat imperial issues and the loyal opposition in America with objectivity and understanding. Parts nine and ten deal with the Confederation and the Constitution, while the concluding section treats socioeconomic developments, focusing on the states and localities.

The investigators whose articles are herein abstracted range over the whole spectrum of the issues of the period 1763-89. In their consideration of the complex character of the American Revolution they find common ground in renouncing any simplistic political interpretation of the causes of the War for Independence. Nor have they embraced in its place any simplistic economic interpretation. We see a flight from determinism, a realistic recognition of the complexity of the issues precipitating the conflict. While old explanations are reexamined and redefined, new approaches are advanced. Some, like Daniel Boorstin, Edmund Morgan, and Bernard Bailyn reaffirm the view that the American Revolution was a constitutional struggle. Not only was the constitutional relation of Crown to colonies altered, but the internal constitutional structure of the separate colonies underwent transformations that helped account for the increasing friction with royal authorities. Jack Greene attributes that friction in no small measure to the increased power of the colonial legislatures, which royal governors were unable to curb. Bailyn sees also a moral and an ideological basis for that friction, a fear on the part of the colonists of the corrupting influence of government and a conviction that a conspiracy existed to deprive them of rights long asserted. Statistical and administrative studies seek to determine how much, if anything, the enforcement of mercantilism contributed to that friction, but the results are inconclusive.

Recent scholars, following the trail blazed by George Rudé, E. P. Thompson, and other innovators, devote considerable attention to analyzing the popular bases of the American Revolution — the organization of the Sons of Liberty and Committees of Safety — and focus on the inarticulate members of preindustrial society. They contend that the crowd was both well organized and highly disciplined, that attacks on property were rarely indiscriminate, rather the demonstrations were purposeful and the objects of the crowd's wrath chiefly confined to those charged with enforcement of unpopular British measures. The seamen are one group singled out among the working-class constituency of Patriotic protest. The mariner's special grievances arising from impressment practices in pre-Revolutionary years are noted, their war service studied, and their behavior in British prisons during wartime investigated.

The renewed attention to the common man has spawned a variety of demographic studies, using the tools of cliometrics to determine the distribution of wealth, the extent of vertical mobility and the effect of demographic change on town settlement patterns and land policies in the Revolutionary era.

Numerous articles examine Carl Becker's seminal thesis that the American Revolution was fought both to obtain home rule and to decide who should rule at home. Some describe divisions of power on the basis of family politics, as in New

York, and stress the formation of parties in pre-Revolutionary alignments; others emphasize socioeconomic divisions.

Investigators continue to grapple with the issue raised more than half a century ago by J. Franklin Jameson. To what extent did the American Revolution have social overtones? If it was not directly a social revolution, could it be considered as a social movement? Was there resistance to large-scale land concentration, of tenants to landlords? Were the Regulators on the frontier a mistreated agricultural class? Was there a general revolution in expectations? Did the Revolution result in the emergence of new men in the seats of power and in the augmentation of the political influence of the back country? Was the American Revolution in fact a people's revolution? The articles abstracted here provide a variety of answers.

One of the cruel paradoxes of the American Revolution was that the leadership professed its attachment to freedom and equality, but generally confined these objectives to white society. Few were prepared to liberate the slave population or to provide equality for the free blacks. A number of articles abstracted examine this signally ambiguous character of the Revolution, review the posture of the British government in offering freedom to slaves who deserted their masters, consider the treatment of black Tory refugees in Nova Scotia, evaluate the impact of the Revolution in the North in effecting immediate or gradual emancipation and contrast the situation there with the Southern states where the impact of the Revolutionary ideology on the slave issue was more muted.

Numerous articles review the overseas dimension of the American Revolution, the terms of the French alliance, the special part Spain played, and the contribution of foreign soldiers to the winning of American independence. The American Revolution touched off a world war fought in the English Channel, along the West African coast, and in India, as well as in North America. It involved a struggle for the West Indies and for Gibraltar. The peace objectives of the United States were shaped not only by the course of the war but also by the war aims of its ally France, and by those of Spain, a nation allied to France, which refused to recognize the rebellious American states and was grudging with its secret aid. The neutral nations had a considerable impact on the war, both as suppliers of contraband goods to America and as members of a League of Armed Neutrality ostensibly formed for protection from England's violation of neutral rights.

The American Revolution had a profound impact on European intellectuals. From France to Poland the American state constitutions were carefully scrutinized and their virtues and defects analyzed. They served as models then and later for constitution-making in revolutionary Europe and Latin America. Republicanism, federalism, egalitarianism, civil liberties were all caught up in the winds that blew throughout the world in that other revolutionary era commencing in 1789.

Numerous articles address themselves to the historiographic issues as to whether the years of the Confederation interlude constituted a "critical Period." To what extent did the states resolve their fiscal problems? Had the economic decline in America been arrested by the time of the calling of the Federal Convention; indeed, was an economic upswing already in progress? Did Shays' Rebellion trigger the move for revision of the Articles of Confederation or were there deep underlying factors which made such a move inevitable? What issues precipitated the rise of parties and factions in the Confederation era? What role did debts owing British merchants play in exposing the weakness of the central authority? What was the effect of the continued confiscation of Loyalist property in derogation of the Treaty of Peace with Great Britain? How much was the determination to strengthen the central government precipitated by the weak posture of America toward the rest of the world, notably her failure to consummate a commercial treaty with Great Britain, to settle outstanding grievances with Spain, or to curb piratical depredations on American shipping by the Barbary states? Answers to these and other central questions of the Confederation period are found here, along with an evaluation of the constructive role played by the Congress of the Confederation in the settlement of interstate boundary and land title disputes, in Indian relations, and in the organization of the Northwest.

The issues at the Federal Convention are examined and the role of individual leaders and factions in the ratification of the Federal Constitution dissected. Investigators seem to have settled the authorship of the *Federalist* papers, but their contemporary influence still seems moot. Numerous so-called compromises of the Constitution are reconsidered, such as the three-fifths compromise, which, as one writer sees it, was not a compromise over slavery, but rather one between nationalists, who espoused popular sovereignty, and antifederalists, who championed states' rights. Historians and behavioral scientists continue to explore the geographic, economic, and ideological ties of the framers and ratifiers, with Orrin G. Libby's stress on geography standing the test of time perhaps better than Charles A. Beard's simplistic economic determinism.

The Treaty of Paris of 1783 ended the war, but it did not mark a watershed in the evolving cultural, religious, and social patterns on the North American continent. Reviewed are trends in public and higher education, in journalism, and in science and medicine. Also examined is the special role of Baptists and Methodists in contributing to the constitutional principle of separation of church and state and to bolstering safeguards for religious liberty. Experienced leaders, freed of wartime responsibilities, sought to reassert a political leadership which new personalities had in some cases successfully challenged on the state and local level.

This bibliography reveals new methodological techniques utilized by contemporary investigators of the American Revolutionary era and opens a variety of original source material. One finds inventories of public records, notably court records, so fruitful for the social historian, of diplomatic archives, church records, private diaries, journals, muster rolls, business papers and accounts, and sources for vital statistics. An examination of these abstracts not only will bring the reader abreast of innovative approaches but will suggest new tools and untilled fields to quicken his or her investigative zeal.

Era of the
AMERICAN
REVOLUTION

LIST OF ABBREVIATIONS

A	Author-Prepared Abstract	*IHE*	Indice Histórico Espanol
Acad.	Academy, Academie, Academia	*Illus.*	Illustrated, Illustration
Agric.	Agriculture, Agricultural	*Inst.*	Institute, Institut, Instituto, Institution
AIA	Abstracts in Anthropology	*Internat.*	International
Akad.	Akademie	*J*	Journal-Prepared Abstract
Am.	America, American	*J.*	Journal
Ann.	Annals, Annales, Annual	*Lib.*	Library, Libraries
Anthrop.	Anthropology,	*Mag.*	Magazine
	Anthropological	*Mus.*	Museum, Musée, Museo
Arch.	Archives	*Natl.*	National, Nationale, Nacional,
Archeol.	Archaeology, Archaeological		Nazionale
Assoc.	Association, Associate	*Phil.*	Philosophy, Philosophical
Asst.	Assistant	*Photo.*	Photograph
Biblio.	Bibliography, Bibliographical	*Pol.*	Politics, Political, Politique, Político
Biog.	Biography, Biographical	*Pres.*	President
Bull.	Bulletin	*Pro.*	Proceedings
Can.	Canada, Canadian, Canadien	*Pub.*	Publication
Cent.	Century	*Q.*	Quarterly
Coll.	College	*R.*	Review, Revue, Revista, Rivista
Com.	Committee	*Res.*	Research
Comm.	Commission	*S*	Staff-Prepared Abstract
Dept.	Department	*Sci.*	Science, Scientific
Dir.	Director, Direktor	*Secy.*	Secretary
Econ.	Economy, Economic,	*Soc.*	Society, Société, Sociedad, Societa
	Économique, Económico	*Sociol.*	Sociology, Sociological
Ed.	Editor	*Tr.*	Transactions
Educ.	Education, Educational	*Trans.*	Translator
Geneal.	Genealogy, Genealogical,	*U.*	University, Université, Università,
	Généalogique		Universidad, Universidade,
Grad.	Graduate		Universität
Hist.	History, Historical, Histoire,	*U.S.*	United States
	Historia, Historische	*Y.*	Yearbook

Abbreviations also apply to feminine and plural forms.
Abbreviations not noted above are based on *Webster's Third International Dictionary*
and the *United States Government Printing Office Style Manual.*

1

INTERPRETING THE REVOLUTION: THE HISTORICAL VIEW

Historiography of the Revolution

1. Adams, Willi Paul. DAS GLEICHHEITSPOSTULAT IN DER AMERIKA-NISCHEN REVOLUTION [The postulate of equality in the American Revolution]. *Hist. Zeitschrift [West Germany] 1971 212(1): 59-99.* Relying on the concepts developed by Charles Merriam and Harold Lasswell in *A Study of Power* (Glencoe, Ill.: Free Press, 1950), the author asks, "How did the postulate of equality become so important in the political rhetoric of the American revolution?" Without giving a simple answer, the author presents nine different theses derived from various historical writings. 110 notes.   G. H. Davis

2. Bardolph, Richard. REVIEW OF NORTH CAROLINA NONFICTION, 1968-1969. *North Carolina Hist. R. 1970 47(2): 145-151.* North Carolina has fallen upon evil days, as little nonfiction was issued in 1968-69. Most of this meager output came from university professors prodded by the imperious expectations of their profession to be productive. John R. Alden's *History of the American Revolution* (New York: Alfred A. Knopf, 1969) is a notable contribution in correcting romantic and filiopietistic views; Harry Golden's *The Right Time* (New York: G. P. Putnam's Sons, 1969) is a warm autobiography. Praises university presses for keeping scholarly production alive in America. Illus.
                    H. M. Rosen

3. Billias, George A. THE AMERICAN REVOLUTION: A MEASURE OF AMERICA'S MATURITY. *New England Social Studies Bull. 1964 22(1): 7-9.* As the main speaker at the spring meeting of the New England Teachers' Association held at the American Antiquarian Society in Worcester, the author traced treatment of the American Revolution by historians. Five periods are described. 1) Until about 1830 the Revolution was looked upon as essential to the separation of America from the corruption of the Old World so that the United States could serve as the "glorious renovator of the world"; 2) The nationalist school, 1830-80,

viewed the Revolution as a step forward in the divinely-ordained march of liberty; 3) The imperial historians, beginning in the 1890's, emphasized the constitutional problem and the conflict between the governing power at the center of the Empire and the colonies that had long enjoyed increasing autonomy; 4) During the early 20th century the economic interpretation of the Revolution developed, accompanied by emphasis upon the Revolution as a social movement; 5) The current trend is to treat the Revolution as the result of American efforts to defend their traditional rights as Englishmen against the radical extension of controls by the British Government.   W. D. Metz

4. Bonner, Thomas N. AMERIKAS KRIEGE UND IHRE URSACHEN IN DER SICHT DER HISTORIKER [America's wars and their causes as viewed by historians]. *Deutsche Rundschau [West Germany] 1959 85(3): 212-219.* An analysis of changing historical opinion about the causes of America's wars. Historical thought in each instance has progressed through three distinct phases: 1) acceptance by historians of the contemporary, official interpretation of the reasons for America's involvement in war, 2) a sharp revision of the early interpretation in the light of new knowledge or insights or more critical points of view, and 3) a partial return to the earlier views of the causes of war. Based on a study of the secondary historical literature concerning each of America's wars.   A

5. Cartwright, William H. BRAINWASHING AND THE AMERICAN REVOLUTION. *Social Educ. 1965 29(1): 32-34.* Examines one charge made in E. Merrill Root's *Brainwashing in the High Schools* (New York: Devin-Adair, 1958). This charge is that the American Revolution was not a dual revolution, that is, a civil war and a social revolution, and that high school textbooks saying it was are guilty of gross error. Cartwright states that the dual revolution concept has much validity in fact and that it was first put forth by John McCulloch in his *A Concise History of the United States,* published in Philadelphia in 1795.
                                                      F. Rotondaro

6. Cary, John. STATISTICAL METHOD AND THE BROWN THESIS ON COLONIAL DEMOCRACY, WITH A REBUTTAL BY ROBERT E. BROWN. *William and Mary Q. 1963 20(2): 251-276.* Challenges Brown's conclusions in *Middle-Class Democracy and the Revolution in Massachusetts, 1691-1780* (Ithaca: Cornell U. Press, 1955), that Massachusetts was democratic before the Revolution and that the war was caused by British attempts to subvert that democracy. Cary asserts that Brown's samples are too limited, especially in his analyses of wills and tax records, that he studies structures but ignores ideas, and that he uses the word democracy anachronistically. In rebuttal, Brown stresses that he used the word only with respect "to those areas where the colonists *did* have a voice in their affairs," that the statistical evidence was intended not as a fair sample, but to provide examples, and that one must consider what men believed to be true as well as the facts themselves.   E. Oberholzer, Jr.

7. Craig, G. M. SOME RECENT BOOKS IN AMERICAN HISTORY. *Can. Hist. R. 1954 35(2): 140-151.* A critical review of 10 books on the history of America which have appeared in the past two years. The opening critique is of

the first volumes in the "New American Nation" series, one of which is John R. Alden's *The American Revolution, 1775-1783* (New York: Harper and Row, 1954). Considerable attention is paid to the series of essays on Charles A. Beard as a historian, as well as to the new publication by Gerald Stourzh *Franklin and American Foreign Policy*. A list of the books reviewed is appended to the article.

J. Erickson

8. Cullen, Maurice R. MIDDLE-CLASS DEMOCRACY AND THE PRESS IN COLONIAL AMERICA. *Journalism Q. 1969 46(3): 531-535.* Catherine Drinker Bowen's *Miracle at Philadelphia* (Boston, Mass.: Little, Brown and Co., 1966) should be of concern to historians of journalism. In it she found the Constitutional Convention to be the work of a strong and deeply concerned middle class. The class-struggle concept of the Constitution and Revolutionary War is not supported by primary sources. Three fundamental aspects must be explored from primary sources to determine the causes of the Revolutionary War and the role of leadership pursued by the colonial press. These areas are economic opportunity, extent of democracy, and literacy. The evidence is extensive for a democratic, literate middle class. The campaign waged by early journalists was for political separation from England. However, the debate continues; one side maintains that the press was involved in a class war involving illiterates, and the other that colonial journalism's vitality stemmed from the ability of the citizens to read and be moved to action. Based on secondary sources; 19 notes.

K. J. Puffer

9. Cunningham, John T. HISTORIAN ON THE DOUBLE. *Am. Heritage 1968 19(4): 54-64, 78-81.* Benson John Lossing was a pioneer in the use of visual effects to supplement and clarify scholarly research. The technique seems to have begun with his interest in Revolutionary history. He was a talented artist and wood engraver, possessed a deep sense of historical accuracy, and had the gift of being able to interview people. His travels and work often resulted in a 16-hour day. Lossing began his quest for unique and often humanistic historical data at Greenwich, Connecticut, in 1848 when he interviewed, by chance, General Ebenezer Mead of the Connecticut militia. Lossing became so excited with assorted pieces of information about the Revolution that he traveled throughout New England, the Middle States, and the South in pursuit of data which had been neglected by his more orthodox peers. The imaginative researcher transformed his notes, sketches, and pictures into a 700-thousand-word manuscript, refined his rough field sketches, prepared an elaborate index, and produced a number of beautiful wood engravings. The result was a two-volume edition of the *Pictorial Field-Book of the Revolution* (1852). It contained 1,450 pages and 1,100 woodcuts. The book was so successful that similar works followed. Lossing continued to preserve the past in this manner until his death in 1891. Based on primary and secondary sources; 22 illus.

J. D. Born, Jr.

10. Dixon, Max. HISTORY AND THE AMERICAN REVOLUTION. *Social Studies 1968 59(2): 67-70.* Questions the dichotomous nature of the historical record and asserts that the history we read is the interpretation given by the victors of the situation, i.e., the ones whose privilege it is to write the historical

account of the situation. Some prejudice, resulting from value judgments, may be involved. Concludes that "the key to understanding the past is always in the future." 2 notes.   L. Raife

11. Egnal, Marc and Ernst, Joseph. AN ECONOMIC INTERPRETATION OF THE AMERICAN REVOLUTION. *William and Mary Q. 1972 29(1): 3-32.* The authors analyze Progressive and neo-whig American historians and their interpretations of the economic causes of the Revolution. Both schools have not delved into essential questions. A new interpretation may be gleaned from probing the growth of a self-conscious colonial elite, the involvement of lower classes, and the broad economic changes transforming the Atlantic community—the latter of which the authors concentrate on. Direct dealings by British firms bypassing colonial merchants in the American market antagonized the merchant class. Contraction of colonial business aggravated various economic problems. The authors comment on trade—intercolonial and Atlantic—and the economic changes in urban centers. 78 notes.   H. M. Ward

12. Greene, Jack P. THE FLIGHT FROM DETERMINISM: A REVIEW OF RECENT LITERATURE ON THE COMING OF THE AMERICAN REVOLUTION. *South Atlantic Q. 1962 61(2): 235-259.* Reviews the conflicting interpretations of the causes of the American Revolution, contrasting the imperial school, led by Charles M. Andrews, George Louis Beer and Lawrence H. Gipson, and the socioeconomic or "progressive" group, including Carl Becker, Arthur Schlesinger, Sr., J. F. Jameson and Merrill Jensen, with the more recent work of Edmund S. Morgan, Oliver M. Dickerson, Bernhard Knollenberg, Carl Ubbelohde, and John R. Alden on the whole colonial scene, and of many others who have dealt with individual colonies. This more recent group, discussed in greater detail, has shown the colonies drawing away from the Empire. The author concludes that this is no simple return to the interpretations of George Bancroft, but a realistic recognition of the complexities of the situation.
                                                                         C. R. Allen, Jr.

13. Greene, Jack P. THE PLUNGE OF LEMMINGS: A CONSIDERATION OF RECENT WRITINGS ON BRITISH POLITICS AND THE AMERICAN REVOLUTION. *South Atlantic Q. 1968 67(1): 141-175.* A review essay of recent literature on British politics in the 18th century. Most recent writing is Namieristic, and in Sir Lewis Namier's terms, the structure of British politics made the American Revolution inevitable. The demise of the First British Empire was the necessary result of its own structural failure. This conclusion, so evident in British writing, runs counter to recent American interpretations of the Revolution which stress human rather than structural failures. Recent British literature stresses the consensus in Britain on Parliamentary sovereignty and other fundamentals, at least among politically relevant segments of society. It was almost impossible for Britons to comprehend the American constitutional arguments. The American Revolution was not the result of a failure of vision, but the product of the weight of British ideational tradition.   J. M. Bumsted

14. Gründorfer, Willi. VON JEFFERSON BIS EISENHOWER [From Jefferson to Eisenhower]. *Tagebuch [Austria] 1955 10(14): 4.* A favorable review of Marie Rapp's *Von Jefferson bis Eisenhower* (Wien: Stern Verlag, 1954), which castigates American bourgeois historical writings for subverting the noble origins of the Revolutionary and Civil Wars in order to whitewash present-day hypocritical and aggressive American imperialism.   R. Mueller

15. Higginbotham, Don. AMERICAN HISTORIANS AND THE MILITARY HISTORY OF THE AMERICAN REVOLUTION. *Am. Hist. R. 1964 70(1): 18-34.* Surveys the contributions to the military history of the American Revolution from 1775 to the present. There have been three periods of investigation. In the first period, lasting to about 1900, the military histories were very patriotic and uncritical. The second period, up to World War II, saw a new class of graduate school, professional historians who were either very critical of revolutionary military history or completely ignored it. Since World War II, works on military history have been more realistic. 41 notes.   W. A. Buckman

16. Imazu, Akira. AMERIKA-KAKU-MEI-SHI NO REKISHI [Research history of the American Revolution]. *Shirin [Japan] 1959 42(2): 153-190.* Historical survey of two basic problems: 1) the main causes of the American Revolution, and 2) how the movements for independence of the 13 colonies were related to the sociopolitical tension within the colonies. The author supports E. S. Morgan's view: "We must not expand particular insights into a complete explanation. We must continue to ask, for we still do not fully know, what the Revolution was."   T. Kage

17. Jensen, Merrill. THE AMERICAN PEOPLE AND THE AMERICAN REVOLUTION. *J. of Am. Hist. 1970 57(1): 5-35.* Finds a resemblance between his traditional views on the Revolution and the position taken by some "new left" historians that the event should be seen more "from the bottom up" than from the exclusive standpoint of the "elite." Recognizing the difficulty of such an approach, the author notes the hostility toward democracy and the rule of the people expressed at the Constitutional Convention of 1787. This hostility had its roots in the actions and words of large numbers of the common people in the period from 1763 on, as revealed in mobs, mass meetings, newspapers, antibusiness animus, local political struggles, rule over committees on a local level, attacks on private property, pressure for much more democratic State governments, and the overturn of established leaders in many colonies. These "democrats" did not succeed everywhere, but they convinced many that the Revolution was, in part, a "people's revolution." 93 notes.   K. B. West

18. Kaplan, Sidney. *THE HISTORY OF NEW-HAMPSHIRE:* JEREMY BELKNAP AS LITERARY CRAFTSMAN. *William and Mary Q. 1964 21(1): 18-39.* Discusses the literary qualities of Belknap's works, noting that for him history "was a literary art." In his treatment of the Revolution, Belknap combines the features of scientific historian with "a village oracle who dispenses morality in the manner of Cotton Mather."   E. Oberholzer, Jr.

19. Kessel, Eberhard. RANKES AUFFASSUNG DER AMERIKANISCHEN GESCHICHTE [Ranke's concept of American history]. *Jahrbuch für Amerikastudien [West Germany] 1962 7: 19-52.* Gives a detailed analysis of the meaning of the "individual character of America" within the framework of Ranke's concept of world history. The two aspects of American history that were essential to Ranke were the English colonization and the American Revolution with the setting up of an independent nation. Unconcerned with 19th-century American history, Ranke seems to have been preoccupied with such relationships as idea and reality; revolution and tradition; freedom and necessity; the English, American, and French revolutions. Traces the sources of Ranke's concept of American history and compares it with the view of American history of such contemporaries as Bancroft, Jacob Burckhardt, Tocqueville, Hegel, Droysen. Based on the manuscripts of Ranke's historical lectures.   G. P. Bassler

20. Kluxen, Kurt. REVIEW ESSAY OF BERNARD BAILYN *PAMPHLETS OF THE AMERICAN REVOLUTION 1750-1776* (CAMBRIDGE: HARVARD U. PRESS, 1965). *Hist. and Theory 1967 6(1): 96-105.* Emphasizes the importance for the ultimate success of the American Revolution of the active process of communication and the inner dynamism of the Atlantic and European worlds. The revolutionary age saw the formation of a new category typical of the age, namely the bourgeois general public. This thesis of an Atlantic civilization and revolution emphasizes that aspect which alone makes intelligible the American Revolution. The Revolution, in a word, was less a social debate than an ideological-constitutional struggle.   L. V. Eid

21. Lewis, Merrill. ORGANIC METAPHOR AND EDENIC MYTH IN GEORGE BANCROFT'S *HISTORY OF THE UNITED STATES. J. of the Hist. of Ideas 1965 26(4): 587-592.* "Bancroft's profuse and sometimes elaborate use of figurative language furnishes the argument as well as the rhetoric for this assertion—that in Bancroft's *History of the United States* (10 volumes, published between 1834-74) the idea of Eden cannot be separated from the pastoral imagery of the garden. The revolt of the colonies from England was the result of an 'alliance of God and nature.' 'Heaven and earth' together aided the resolution of the Americans to be free....Such statements were, for Bancroft, not merely rhetorical claims, but matters of historical fact—necessary and universal truths."   W. H. Coates

22. Lokken, Roy N. THE CONCEPT OF DEMOCRACY IN COLONIAL POLITICAL THOUGHT. *William and Mary Q. 1959 16(4): 568-580.* A reexamination of the George Bancroft-Charles M. Andrews controversy in the light of R. E. Brown's *Middle-Class Democracy and the Revolution in Massachusetts, 1691-1780* (Ithaca, 1955). Lokken notes that in colonial thought, pure democracy, patterned on the Greek polis, was distinguished from mixed, or constitutional democracy. In *The Rights of Man,* Paine expressed his preference for the latter. In the 18th century colonial thought favored a closer approximation of the English constitution, regarded as the ideal form of mixed democracy. Insofar as

the colonial assemblies were the counterpart of the Commons, the democratic part of a mixed government, democracy existed in the colonies.

E. Oberholzer, Jr.

23. Lucas, Paul. A NOTE ON THE COMPARATIVE STUDY OF THE STRUCTURE OF POLITICS IN MID-EIGHTEENTH-CENTURY BRITAIN AND ITS AMERICAN COLONIES. *William and Mary Q. 1971 28(2): 301-309.* Takes a middle ground in the debate between Bernard Bailyn and Jack Greene as to the reason for the breakdown of British authority over the Colonies. Greene contends that the increased power of the legislatures was the cause, whereas Bailyn postulates the rise of individualism and the fear of the corrupting influence of the Governor. The answer rests in a comparative study of English and American politics; especially in America new men were challenging the "court" party. Greene, therefore, is more correct in emphasizing politics than is Bailyn in suggesting a fundamental cultural change. 2 notes.

H. M. Ward

24. Main, Jackson Turner. THE RESULTS OF THE AMERICAN REVOLUTION RECONSIDERED. *Historian 1969 31(4): 539-554.* Historians have not given much attention to analyzing the results of the American Revolution because the known facts are few and controversial. The author summarizes and assesses what we do know about economic, social, political, and ideological changes in the new United States. 18 notes.

N. W. Moen

25. Malagodi, Giorgio O. LA RIVOLUZIONE AMERICANA [The American Revolution]. *Storia e Politica [Italy] 1967 6(2): 350-361.* Reviews the causes of the American Revolution as expounded in the work of Charles Howard McIlwain, *American Revolution: A Constitutional Interpretation,* written in 1923 and translated into Italian in the *Collezione di Storia Americana* in 1966. The reviewer states that, according to McIlwain, the American Colonies owed allegiance and fealty to the king but not to Parliament, especially since they had no representation in that Parliament. It is also brought out that the Colonists were not fighting to gain the right to run their own affairs, but to retain those rights which they had long had.

H. O. Nelli

26. Marshall, Peter. RADICALS, CONSERVATIVES AND THE AMERICAN REVOLUTION. *Past and Present [Great Britain] 1962 23: 44-56.* This essay surveys recent American studies of the nature and causes of the American Revolution, and recent reappraisals of Charles Beard's *Economic Interpretation of the American Revolution.* Concludes that the economic and social aspects of the Confederation period require further investigation before we can decide whether any genuine revolution occurred.

A. W. Coats

27. Marshall, Peter. THE BRITISH EMPIRE AND THE AMERICAN REVOLUTION. *Huntington Lib. Q. 1964 27(2): 135-145.* Vincent T. Harlow's thesis that a conscious ambition after 1763 to open new fields of commerce in the East represented a new concept of empire contrasts sharply with the earlier views of C. M. Andrews which stressed the territorial imperialism of the period. Recently available data on trade tend to validate Andrews' distinction between the old

mercantilism and the new imperialism, but in any event a geographical division of interests does not in fact reflect the behavior of contemporaries. The imperialist drives of the period of the American Revolution saw enterprise and capital going wherever there was opportunity. Meanwhile political and administrative decisions for the rapidly expanding empire were hampered by a combination of inertia, bewilderment, and conventions.   H. D. Jordan

28. Mason, Bernard. THE HERITAGE OF CARL BECKER: THE HISTORI-OGRAPHY OF THE AMERICAN REVOLUTION. *New-York Hist. Soc. Q. 1969 53(2): 127-147.* Carl Becker's significant monograph, *The History of Political Parties in the Province of New York, 1763-1776,* appeared in 1909. Since that time, Becker's thesis that the Revolution resulted from two interacting movements—the move for home-rule and independence and the growth of democracy in society and politics—has provoked much debate among historians and has resulted in a vast body of literature on the subject. The author discusses some of the historians who have disputed the Becker thesis and concludes that, although the monograph has been discredited in part, it will remain of considerable significance for some time to come. Primary and secondary sources; 5 illus., 37 notes.
                                                                          C. L. Grant

29. Middleton, Richard. BRITISH HISTORIANS AND THE AMERICAN REVOLUTION. *J. of Am. Studies [Great Britain] 1971 5(1): 43-58.* After the Revolution, British historians (notably John Andrews and George Chalmers) were resigned but bitter about the loss of the American empire; a few, especially William Gordon, applauded the American cause. Next the "Tory school"—John Leycester Adolphus and Robert Bisset were leading exponents—dominated British writing on the Revolution. After 1830, Whig interpretations, influenced heavily by Edmund Burke and Sir Robert Walpole, appeared in the histories of Philip Henry Stanhope and the classic works of John Richard Green and Sir George Otto Trevelyan. The Tory viewpoint, meanwhile, persisted in the writings of William Massey and William Edward Hartpole Lecky. Whig and Tory histories had one common facet: almost total concern with British politics and relegation of the American Colonies to the periphery of events. After World War I, Hugh Edward Egerton and Sir Lewis Bernstein Namier encouraged new scholarship on the Revolution, but British historians continued to eliminate America from view. Since the 1950's Britons have developed stronger tastes for American subjects. Based on secondary sources; 70 notes.   H. T. Lovin

30. Morgan, Edmund S. THE AMERICAN REVOLUTION: REVISIONS IN NEED OF REVISING. *William and Mary Q. 1957 14(1): 3-15.* A discussion of the imperial, socioeconomic and Namierist revisions of the Whig historians which concludes that none of these offer a consistent and adequate explanation of the causes of the Revolution. The answer may be found in a study of the local institutions which gave the patriot leaders their political experience.
                                                                    E. Oberholzer, Jr.

31. Morris, Richard B. CLASS STRUGGLE AND THE AMERICAN REVO-LUTION. *William and Mary Q. 1962 19(1): 3-29.* Reviews the historiography

of the American Revolution, compares and contrasts the American with the French Revolution, and challenges the Populist-Progressive views of Carl L. Becker, Charles A. Beard, John F. Jameson, and Merrill Jensen and the Marxist interpretations of Louis Hacker, Hans Simons and Herbert Aptheker. Not a "clearcut class war because too many members of the different classes are found on both sides," the Revolution was "a classic instance of a civil war," in which the truly revolutionary political changes directly due to the war must be distinguished from the socioeconomic by-products. The Declaration of Independence shifted the ground from unconstitutional relations to an emphasis on social contract and natural rights.   E. Oberholzer, Jr.

32. Mowat, C. L. A STUDY OF BIAS IN BRITISH AND AMERICAN HISTORY TEXTBOOKS. *British Assoc. for Am. Studies Bull. [Great Britain] 1965 (10): 31-39.* A preliminary report on a study sponsored by three British and American historical associations and two foundations. A committee of five scholars examined 14 American and 22 English secondary history texts for bias in their treatment of the American Revolution, the War of 1812, and the First World War. "The main forms of bias found were inaccurate statements, omissions, weighted language, and lack of proportion." Undocumented.

D. J. Abramoske

33. Murrin, John M. THE MYTHS OF COLONIAL DEMOCRACY AND ROYAL DECLINE IN EIGHTEENTH-CENTURY AMERICA: A REVIEW ESSAY. *Cithara 1965 5(1): 53-69.* Examines Robert E. Brown and B. Katherine Brown, *Virginia, 1705-1786: Democracy or Aristocracy?* (East Lansing: Michigan State U. Press, 1964); Lucille Griffith, *Virginia House of Burgesses, 1750-1774* (Williamsburg: Colonial Press, 1963); and Jack P. Greene, *The Quest for Power: The Lower Houses of Assembly in the Southern Royal Colonies, 1689-1776* (Chapel Hill: U. of North Carolina Press, 1963). All of these books, especially that by the Browns, force their research into a false interpretive framework. "Each interprets the eighteenth century in the light of a Revolution yet to come, a Revolution which no one desired, predicted or sought before 1765." In fact, royal power grew in 18th-century America, and colonial politics were aristocratic. "The Revolution began as a typical old-regime quarrel between different corporations, disputing the boundaries of their respective privileges and authority. Significantly, not the success of America's assemblies, but their inability to succeed as eighteenth-century corporate bodies, marked the transformation of the struggle from a constitutional conflict of the old regime into a genuine democratic revolution...." Documented.

Brown, Katherine and Brown, Robert E. COMMUNICATIONS, 1966 5(2): 86-87. The Browns argue that Murrin himself misinterprets the sources, for example, Richard Henry Lee.   D. M. Fahey

34. Newmyer, R. Kent. A NINETEENTH-CENTURY VIEW OF THE HISTORIOGRAPHY OF THE AMERICAN REVOLUTION: A FOOTNOTE ON PLAGIARISM. *Papers of the Biblio. Soc. of Am. 1964 58(2): 164-169.* Summarizes Francis Markoe's "Documentary History of the American Revolution" which in September 1835 appeared in Robert Walsh's *American Quarterly*

Review. Markoe, an honorary member of the Georgia Historical Society, attempted to persuade readers of the possibility of an objective history of the Revolution if documents were available. To complement his plea he alleged that 36 Revolution histories were plagiarized from the *Annual Register* and William Gordon's *The History of the Rise, Progress, and Establishment of the Independence of America (1788-1794).* Markoe briefly documented many instances of plagiarism—a pioneering venture in historical criticism.   C. A. Newton

35. Newmyer, R. Kent. CHARLES STEDMAN'S *HISTORY OF THE AMERICAN WAR. Am. Hist. R. 1958 63(4): 924-934.* "The reputation of this work is not fully warranted by the facts and...its present high evaluation must be severely qualified....Although [Stedman] has not been guilty of the wholesale plagiarism employed by several of his contemporaries, he has resorted to that practice to a sufficient degree to cast doubt upon the value of his entire work." As in similar cases of plagiarism involving histories of the American Revolution, the main source of the plagiarized information was the *Annual Register.*
R. C. Raack

36. Newton, Craig A. LOUIS GIRARDIN'S REPUBLICAN VIEW OF THE AMERICAN PAST. *Radford R. 1966 20(1): 5-17.* Girardin (d. 1823), the author of most of volume 4 of John D. Burk's *History of Virginia* (1816), narrated the Revolutionary years in Virginia with a distinctly Jeffersonian interpretation. Victory in 1781 was the result of the American adherence to natural rights ideals; during the war, the creation of key institutions in Virginia was the culmination of colonial progress toward popular government. Girardin favored temporary restraints upon popular responsibility, noted that shortcomings abridging the proper exercise of popular will were often of popular origin, and was critical of basic human nature. But like Jefferson, with whom he disagreed on the subject of the Bank of the United States, he preferred minimum restraint upon, and maximum effort in behalf of, the common welfare. While he was his own historian, Girardin "expressed the best hopes of the age of Jefferson in 1816." Documented.   A

37. Persons, Stow. THE CYCLICAL THEORY OF HISTORY IN EIGHTEENTH CENTURY AMERICA. *Am. Q. 1954 6(2): 147-163.* Modifies the earlier thesis of Carl Becker that the idea of progress was a direct secularization of the millenialist interpretation of history. The American reaction to the millennialism of the Great Awakening was the development of a conservative cyclical theory of history, which held that empires have a natural rise and fall within a static historical continuum. This view was generally accepted by the dominant social classes until the Revolution, when it was gradually transformed into the doctrine of inevitable American progress. This third philosophy of history incorporated the millenial hope of the religious enthusiasts but retained the moralism of the cyclical theory, along with a conviction that Europe faced inevitable decline and decadence. The thesis that a cyclical theory served such a mediating function is documented with source material from sermons and the writings of many individuals.   D. Davis

38. Pocock, J. G. A. VIRTUE AND COMMERCE IN THE EIGHTEENTH CENTURY. *J. of Interdisciplinary Hist. 1972 3(1): 119-134.* A review-essay of works "re-evaluating the character and role of ideology in the American Revolution." Emphasizes Gordon S. Wood's *The Creation of the American Republic, 1776-1787* (Chapel Hill: U. of North Carolina Press, 1969) and Gerald Stourzh's *Alexander Hamilton and the Idea of Republican Government* (Stanford: Stanford U. Press, 1970). Recent historiography of the American Revolution, especially in the works of Bernard Bailyn, has emphasized the ideological roots of the transformation from colony to independent republic. Oppositional political ideology in the 18th-century Anglo-American world pitted a "Court" and a "Country" ideology against one another. The "Country" ideology was rooted in the tradition of classical republicanism and civic humanism, and was a contemporary reaction against growing commercialization and professionalization in the 18th-century world. (Thus, "Country" *virtue* is oppositional to "Court" *commerce.*) Wood shows how Federalist theory instigated a new political vocabulary for the checks and balances of government *power* without a "classical mode of conceiving of the 'people.' " This new theory emphasized a romantic-kinetic ideology instead of the classical-organic model: now interest groups might change without the government structure altering. Stourzh's book offers a study of Hamilton as a "Court" thinker opting for a government run by interest groups, accepting the focus on commerce as both necessary and good. 24 notes.

A. H. Pfeiffer

39. Pole, J. R. THE AMERICAN PAST: IS IT STILL USABLE? *J. of Am. Studies [Great Britain] 1967 1(1): 63-78.* Surveys American historical writing and argues that historical scholarship in the United States is becoming more sophisticated. Present-minded historians like George Bancroft and Charles Beard structured the past simplistically, virtually overlooking the pluralistic nature of American life. The alternative to the Whig interpretations of such historians as George Bancroft, Charles Beard, Vernon Louis Parrington, and Arthur M. Schlesinger, Jr., "begins with a fundamental respect for the integrity of the past" as demonstrated in the studies of Carl Bridenbaugh, Perry Miller, and Samuel Eliot Morison. The last 20 years of American historical scholarship—work of George F. Kennan, John M. Blum, and Ernest R. May on American diplomacy, for example—have produced indications of a kind of expertise that "is refreshing in its coolness, its liberation from the favoured American illusions, and its tone of sceptical pragmatism." The gains to scholarship resulting from this mood are traced in such widely different fields as the American Revolution, the character of politics in the age of Andrew Jackson, and the motives and achievements of the several interests in Reconstruction. The author concludes with a discussion of the subtle division between those who believe in the primacy of mind—historians like Richard Hofstadter and Louis Hartz—and those like Frederick Jackson Turner and Daniel J. Boorstin who believe in the primacy of fact. Documented.

D. J. Abramoske

40. Procacci, Giuliano. RIVOLUZIONE AMERICANA E STORIOGRAFIA ITALIANA [The American Revolution and Italian historiography]. *Rassegna Storica del Risorgimento [Italy] 1954 41(2/3): 565-571.* Italian historiography of the late 18th and early 19th centuries, influenced by French publications, passed

a variety of judgments on the American Revolution. Some interpreted it as an internal struggle between England and her American colonies, resulting in an organization of states similar to that of antiquity (Carlo Botta *Storia della guerra di indipendenza degli Stati Uniti d'America,* Florence: reprinted, 1857). Others regarded the Revolution as progress on the road toward democratization (e.g., G. Compagnoni *Storia dell'America in continuazione del compendio della Storia universale del Sig. Conte di Ségur,* Milano, 1821-23).

                                                                W. E. Heydendorff

41. Sellers, Charles G., Jr. THE AMERICAN REVOLUTION: SOUTHERN FOUNDERS OF A NATIONAL TRADITION. *Writing Southern History: Essays in Historiography in Honor of Fletcher M. Green (Baton Rouge: Louisiana State U. Press, 1965): 38-66.* Finds the origins of American Revolutionary historiography in the work of David Ramsay of Charleston, South Carolina (works published 1778-1819). A southern historiography of the Revolution never existed; rather there was much writing by southerners about the American Revolution and about the events and leaders of the period in the South. At the end of the 19th century, scholars trained at Johns Hopkins University began producing a substantial body of professional scholarly monographs, but the golden age of scholarly publications about the South during the Revolution began in 1940. The only observable trend in interpretation was that which viewed the Revolution "as a struggle over constitutional principles and home rule." 56 notes.

                                                                E. P. Stickney

42. Shimizu, Hiroshi, Tomita, Torao, Yasuko, Ichihara, Nishikawa, Susumu, and Ohara, Yuko. DOKURITSU-KAKUMEI SHI NO SHIGAKU-TEKI SAI KENTŌ [The American Revolution reconsidered: historiographical studies]. *Shien [Japan] 1962 23(1): 35-85.* Examines historical writings on the American Revolution, the Confederation and the establishment of the U.S. Constitution, with a special emphasis on the studies in Japan on the history of the American Revolution. Two different views are recognized in the interpretation of the historical process from the Revolution to the establishment of the Constitution: one emphasizing the significance of the conflict between the conservative and radical political forces within American society, and the other assuming a negative attitude toward it. The authors point out that the difference should not be considered as a result of the self-development of the studies per se, but should be attributed to the differences in the practical stand toward actual problems of individual historians. Hence alternative judgment is not advisable. Both views may be scrutinized and developed from an angle aiming at the analysis of the bourgeois revolution.   T. Miyake

43. Smith, Page. DAVID RAMSAY AND THE CAUSES OF THE AMERICAN REVOLUTION. *William and Mary Q. 1960 17(1): 51-77.* A historiographical essay. The author discusses the views of Ramsay, who ascribed the Revolution to misunderstanding, of George Bancroft, "an unconscious mythmaker," who first saw "a conscious plan to subvert liberty," of the "scientific" historians Sidney George Fisher and Arthur M. Schlesinger, Sr., and of Claude Van Tyne, Charles M. Andrews, Lawrence H. Gipson, and Edmund and Helen

Morgan, whose position is essentially that of Ramsay. The first generation of Revolutionary historians was more objective than the later ones; the "most extreme distortions" were committed by those who claimed to be scientific, disguising their presuppositions as objective findings based on research.

E. Oberholzer, Jr.

44. Smith, Paul H. CHARLES THOMSON ON UNITY IN THE AMERICAN REVOLUTION. *Q. J. of the Lib. of Congress 1971 28(3): 158-172.* Thomson, Secretary of the Continental Congress, wrote a 17-page letter dated 4 November 1786 to David Ramsay in criticism of the manuscript of volume one of *The History of the American Revolution.* This letter, reproduced here, had considerable direct influence on Ramsay's work which was published in 1789. The letter differs in many respects from the previously published version of the letter. It testifies to Thomson's concern for correctly relating how leaders of the Revolution achieved American unity in 1774. Illus., 21 notes.   E. P. Stickney

45. Spector, Robert M. THE AMERICAN REVOLUTION: SOMETHING BEYOND THE CAUSES. *Social Studies 1971 62(3): 99-106.* Historians have overworked the causes of the American Revolution and other events without properly emphasizing basic issues. Suggests restudy to clarify misunderstood aspects of the relations between Great Britain and the Colonies. 25 notes.

L. Raife

46. Streirer, William F., Jr. CONFLICT OR CONSENSUS? RECENT TRENDS IN THE HISTORIOGRAPHY OF THE AMERICAN REVOLU-TION. *Pro. of the South Carolina Hist. Assoc. 1967: 32-42.* In an examination of the historiography of the American Revolution since the late 1940's the author classifies the historians as to taking either the conflict or the consensus approach. Almost every major historian of the American Revolution is covered and classified. The author lists the seven major areas of disagreement between the conflict and consensus historians. It is the author's belief that the consensus approach has been more popular the last few years because of "the perpetual atmosphere of suspicion, distrust and emotionalism" caused by the Cold War and the fact that Americans do not want "to be reminded of strife and violence," and thus represents a social need just as earlier the conflict approach had. Among the historians whose work was classified were Edmund S. Morgan, Clinton Rossiter, Louis B. Hartz, Daniel Boorstin, Charles A. Beard, Bernhard Knollenberg, J. Franklin Jameson, Merrill Jensen, R. R. Palmer, and Bernard Bailyn.

J. W. Thacker, Jr.

47. Tolles, Frederick B. THE AMERICAN REVOLUTION CONSIDERED AS A SOCIAL MOVEMENT: A RE-EVALUATION. *Am. Hist. R. 1954 60(1): 1-12.* Through four lectures given at Princeton in 1925 and published in 1926 as *The American Revolution Considered as a Social Movement,* J. Franklin Jameson became one of the founders of American cultural and social history. Recent research, however, has suggested: 1) that the Revolution made less difference in the status of persons in America than Jameson believed; 2) that there was less diffusion or democratization of land ownership resulting from the break-up of

large estates than Jameson supposed; 3) that Jameson perceived clearly that the Revolution loosed potent new forces in the American economy, forces whose relation to the social and political democracy still remain to be studied; and 4) that Jameson deserves credit for bringing American church history, intellectual democracy, and cultural nationalism within the purview of American historians. Despite some oversights and overstatements in his lectures, Jameson's "thesis" that the American Revolution involved more than political, democratic, and military history remains sound.   W. C. Langsam

48. Upton, L. F. S. REVIEW ARTICLE: BAILYN, ED., *PAMPHLETS OF THE AMERICAN REVOLUTION,* VOLS. XI AND XII. *Can. J. of Hist. 1968 3(1): 95-99.* Bailyn focuses on the ideological ferment ("the Contagion of Liberty") which swept the colonies in the decades before the Revolution. When his collection is completed, he will have published 72 pamphlets. Gipson approaches the Revolution from the wider perspective of British imperial organization and imperial problems. Nevertheless, both concur in the view that the Revolution was above all else an ideological-constitutional struggle.   F. J. McDonald

49. Van Tassel, David D. HENRY BARTON DAWSON: A NINETEENTH-CENTURY REVISIONIST. *William and Mary Q. 1956 13(3): 319-341.* A biographical and historiographical study of an early critic of traditional interpretations of the American Revolution, based chiefly on his writings.
E. Oberholzer, Jr.

50. Venturi, Franco. UN GRANDE STORICO: SIR LEWIS NAMIER [A great historian: Sir Lewis Namier]. *Il Ponte [Italy] 1957 13(7): 1046-1055.* Notes some similarities and differences between the roles of Namier and the Italian historian Gaetano Salvemini. Namier can be termed a "radical" Tory; Salvemini, a "right-wing" socialist. The author discusses at some length Namier's works—especially those dealing with the period of George III and the American Revolution, and concludes by calling Namier the Polybius of our century. Based partly on the author's broadcast over the "third program" of the RAI, 12 June 1957, in honor of the English historian.   C. F. Delzell

51. Ver Steeg, Clarence L. THE AMERICAN REVOLUTION CONSIDERED AS AN ECONOMIC MOVEMENT. *Huntington Lib. Q. 1956/57 20(4): 361-372.* Historians have stressed the social and political, while neglecting the economic, effects of the Revolution. Much study is needed on this, for the Revolution effected enormous changes in such areas as mineral rights, farming and land policy, the routes and character of trade, business organization, money and its supply, manufacturing, and foreign investments. Its economic were even greater than its social consequences.   H. D. Jordan

52. Williams, David A. THE TWO AMERICAN REVOLUTIONS. *Virginia Q. R. 1965 41(4): 624-627.* Reviews the first volumes in two major documentary series on the American Revolution. *Pamphlets of the American Revolution, 1750-1776: Volume I., 1750-1765* (Cambridge: Harvard U. Press, 1965) edited

by Bernard Bailyn contains a 200-page introduction and 14 pamphlets. Bailyn sees the Revolution as an ideological-constitutional struggle. *Naval Documents of the American Revolution, Volume I., 1774-1775* (Washington: Government Printing Office, 1964) edited by William B. Clark promises much. The first of 15 projected volumes indicates need for a clear selective policy and improved editing standards if it is to be a definitive edition. O. H. Zabel

53. Wood, Gordon S. RHETORIC AND REALITY IN THE AMERICAN REVOLUTION. *William and Mary Q. 1966 23(1): 3-32.* Trying to find a middle ground between idealism and behaviorism in the historiography of the American Revolution, this résumé of the last 50 years' writing on the Revolution argues the need for a Tory perspective to balance the "Neo-Whig" interpretations of recent historians. From the rhetoric of the patriots, which was not mere propaganda but "ideas with real personal and social significance," a definite "revolutionary syndrome" is evident. H. M. Ward

54. Wright, Esmond. RECENT INTERPRETATIONS OF THE AMERICAN REVOLUTION. *Jahrbuch für Amerikastudien [West Germany] 1968 13: 43-52.* The significance of the American Revolution lies in its being "the central event in America, and indeed in world history." It marked the beginning of an independent state which then produced a nation; it was a declaration of faith in mankind and its rights; it marked a total breach with the traditions of an aristocratic society; and it was a daring experiment in federalism which succeeded largely because this revolution recognized its limitations and stopped at its own frontiers. A survey of the historiography on the American Revolution concludes with the author's idea of "what really happened" in the American Revolution, namely that the British Government failed to govern when discontent in the colonies increased and George Washington became the symbol of a new nation. A paper read at the annual meeting of the Deutsche Gesellschaft für Amerikastudien in Göttingen. Undocumented. G. P. Bassler

Comparative Revolutions

55. Barrow, Thomas C. THE AMERICAN REVOLUTION AS A COLONIAL WAR FOR INDEPENDENCE. *William and Mary Q. 1968 25(3): 452-464.* A new evaluation of historiographical controversies over the American Revolution. The author seeks to define the American Revolution and stresses similarities of the American Revolution with other colonial wars for independence. 20 notes. H. M. Ward

56. Cobban, Alfred. THE AGE OF THE DEMOCRATIC REVOLUTION. *History [Great Britain] 1960 45(155): 234-239.* A review article of R. R. Palmer's *The Age of the Democratic Revolution: A Political History of Europe and*

America, 1760-1800, Vol. 1, *The Challenge,* in which the reviewer suggests that the method of comparing European revolutions with the American Revolution is possibly carried a little too far.   **W. D. McIntyre**

57. Córdoba-Bello, Eleazar. INDEPENDENCIA DE LAS COLONIAS AN-GLOAMERICANAS. CAUSAS. INFLUENCIA QUE EJERCIO EN OTROS EVENTOS REVOLUCIONARIOS EUROPEOS Y AMERICANOS [Independence of the English colonies in America. Causes. Influence it exercised on other revolutionary events in Europe and America]. *R. de Hist. [Venezuela] 1960 1(4): 57-95.* After stating the basic difference between the English and Spanish systems of colonization of America—the absence of mixed marriage on a large scale in the English colonies—gives the ideological and economic reasons for the difference, and then describes the influence of the American Revolution on Belgium, France and Spanish America. The author concludes by drawing attention to the historical similarities between the North American and Latin American revolutions. Based on documents from the Royal Archives in Brussels and on published works.   **B. T. (IHE 38971)**

58. Echeverria, Durand, trans. and ed. CONDORCET'S "THE INFLUENCE OF THE AMERICAN REVOLUTION ON EUROPE." *William and Mary Q. 1968 25(1): 85-108.* The Marquis de Condorcet's essay, first published in 1786, is considered to be the most forceful presentation of the idea that the American Revolution served as the inspiration of the French Revolution. The many ideas of Condorcet revealed in his other writings also appear here, such as the theory of progress, republicanism, egalitarianism, pacifism, the doctrine of separation of powers, and physiocratic economic and tax theories. The essay is reproduced. 7 notes.   **H. M. Ward**

59. Godechot, J. LES COMBATTANTS DE LA GUERRE DE L'INDEPEND-ANCE DES ETAT-UNIS ET LES TROUBLES AGRAIRES EN FRANCE DE 1789 A 1792 [The combatants of the War of Independence of the United States and agrarian troubles in France from 1789 to 1792]. *Ann. Historiques de la Révolution Française [France] 1956 28(3): 292-294.* Examines the suggestion of Professor Forrest McDonald of Texas University (expressed in an article in *Agricultural History,* October, 1951) that French soldiers who fought in the American Revolution might have played an important part in the French Revolution because of certain influences they received from some aspects of American agricultural orientation. The author hesitates to accept as conclusive Professor McDonald's attempt to prove this thesis by spotting a map of France with the place of origin of such soldiers, and comparing it with a map showing those areas in France where the greatest amount of rural agitation took place. The author suggests that the correlation in the maps may be due to the fact that the provinces shown on the maps were among the most poverty-stricken and burdened in France.   **J. Gagliardo**

60. Kirk, Russell. FRIEDRICH GENTZ ON REVOLUTIONS. *Contemporary R. [Great Britain] 1956 190(1091): 283-287.* An article occasioned by a recent reprint of Gentz's *Origin and Principles of the American Revolution, Compared*

with the Origin and Principles of the French Revolution, which was originally translated into English by John Quincy Adams. Both Gentz and Adams were disciples of Edmund Burke, and both claimed that the two revolutions were essentially different, or rather that the American Revolution was no revolution at all.   J. G. Gazley

61. Manning, Clarence A. THE AMERICAN AND UKRAINIAN REVOLUTIONS. *Ukrainian Q. 1967 23(1): 65-74.* Compares the Ukrainian Revolution (1917-20) with the American Revolution and the establishment of the United States and finds many parallels. The author recalls that T. Shevchenko, a Ukrainian poet, had appealed for a "new Washington with a new and righteous law."   Y. Slavutych

62. Middleton, R. THE HUBRIS AND NEMESIS OF POWER. *Royal United Service Inst. J. [Great Britain] 1969 114(654): 70-72.* Investigates the comparison between the Vietnam War and the War of American Independence, suggesting that Britain after 1769 and the United States after 1945 both felt conscious of their enormous power. They were morally and materially over-confident and then failed, when faced with overseas insurgents, to estimate correctly the tenacity of the enemy and to mobilize effectively the goodwill of the masses. In both cases the military failure overlay a political failure, but the predictions of British extinction if she lost the Colonies were not fulfilled; neither need America's withdrawal from Vietnam produce dire consequences.   D. H. Murdoch

63. Palmer, R. R. THE AMERICAN REVOLUTION IN A COMPARATIVE LIGHT. *Jahrbuch für Amerikastudien [West Germany] 1968 13: 34-42.* A paper read at the annual meeting of the Deutsche Gesellschaft für Amerikastudien in Göttingen on 19 May 1967. The author assesses the similarities and differences between the American Revolution and later revolutions, and its possible effects on revolutionary developments outside America. On the one hand, the American Revolution can be and has been viewed as a revolt against British control, as a conservative counterreform, as a conspiracy or as the prelude to a long European revolutionary period. For the latter, if interpreted as bourgeois revolutions in a Marxist sense, the American experience was of little significance. As a precedent for revolutions aiming at national liberation and independence, on the other hand, the American example has been widely followed, except in cases where this type of revolution merged with the category known as revolt against the West. The relevancy of the American Revolution for the ensuing Western and later anticolonialist revolutions is discussed in more detail. Undocumented.   G. P. Bassler

64. Rudolph, Lloyd I. THE EIGHTEENTH CENTURY MOB IN AMERICA AND EUROPE. *Am. Q. 1959 11(4): 447-469.* Reiterates the thesis that during the 18th century property had less to fear from "the mob" in America than in Europe. The author sees in the Gordon Riots in England and the events of the French Revolution illustrations of how the "debased" masses of Europe were moved less by the spirit of liberty than by "a spirit of revenge and destruction." Conversely, the American "mob" of revolutionary times usually confined itself

to pursuing the limited, middle-class objectives of its leaders. In brief, "America...
was...spared from the mob in the European sense of the word."

W. M. Armstrong

65. Santovenía, Emeterio S. UNIVERSALIDAD DE DOS AMERICANOS
[Universality of two Americans]. *J. of Inter-Am. Studies 1962 4(1): 33-51.*
Benjamin Franklin (1706-90) and José Julián Martí (1853-95) were two men who
contributed to the independence of America at two different times. Franklin was
a participant in the beginning of American independence in the 18th century,
while Martí aided Cuban independence at the conclusion of the 19th century. The
entire period encompassed by the lives of these two leaders might be considered
an independence era. Both men recognized the universality of ideas and both
wanted to raise the level of America to world prominence. They dedicated their
lives to their countries and were men of creative genius. Undocumented.

J. R. Thomas

66. Sokol, Irene M. THE AMERICAN REVOLUTION AND POLAND: A
BIBLIOGRAPHICAL ESSAY. *Polish R. 1967 12(3): 3-17.* Discusses the influence of American revolutionary and constitutional thought on the shapers of
Poland's destiny between the two partitions. Since Polish newspapers were few,
any dissemination of ideas was limited. The American Constitution was frequently cited by the Poles who drew from it what suited their purposes. Documented.

S. R. Pliska

67. Stourzh, Gerald. WILLIAM BLACKSTONE: TEACHER OF REVOLU-
TION. *Jahrbuch für Amerikastudien [West Germany] 1970 15: 184-200.* Stresses
the significance of William Blackstone's interpretation of the Glorious Revolution for the revolutionary reasoning of the American colonists. A revealing
passage of Blackstone's *Commentaries on the Laws of England* was used in 1769
in a South Carolina newspaper debate by a virtually forgotten planter-politician,
John McKenzie, and not by Christopher Gadsden as has been widely assumed.
McKenzie's former opponent, William Henry Drayton, published the debate in
a hitherto-unknown volume, *The Letters of Freeman, etc.* (London: 1771), which
was never reprinted in America. This and related sources suggest that a "Black-
stonian" way of interpreting the Glorious Revolution was more important in
1775-76 than a "Lockean" way.

G. P. Bassler

68. Wood, Gordon S. A NOTE ON MOBS IN THE AMERICAN REVOLU-
TION. *William and Mary Q. 1966 23(4): 635-642.* Examines the views of George
Rudé who contends that American mob action was of middle-class character and
thus differs from European mob action. The author upholds Rudé's theory that
European crowds were usually rational and seldom indiscriminate. Yet the variation in results between Europe and America derived from differences in historical
and social situation. In American riots, the weakness of constituted authority and
the democratic character of legislative policies dampened the threat of serious
social eruption.

H. M. Ward

Political Theory & the Revolution

69. Bailyn, Bernard. POLITICAL EXPERIENCE AND ENLIGHTENMENT IDEAS IN EIGHTEENTH CENTURY AMERICA. *Am. Hist. R. 1962 67(2): 339-351.* "Major attributes of enlightened politics had developed naturally, spontaneously, early in the history of the American colonies, and they existed as simple matters of social and political fact on the eve of the Revolution. New developments, however gradual, were suspect by some, resisted in part, and confined in their effects. This divergence between habits of mind and belief on the one hand and experience and behavior on the other was ended at the Revolution. A rebellion that destroyed the traditional sources of public authority called forth the full range of advanced ideas. Precisely because so many social and institutional reforms had already taken place in America, the revolutionary movement there, more than elsewhere, was a matter of doctrine, ideas and comprehension." M. Berman

70. Buell, Richard, Jr. DEMOCRACY AND THE AMERICAN REVOLUTION: A FRAME OF REFERENCE. *William and Mary Q. 1964 21(2): 165-190.* Attempts to interpret the relationship of the Revolution to democracy in the light of the colonial leaders' "common experience within the British imperial system" and their reliance on the British dissenting tradition. The author examines the colonial leaders' use of the contract theory of government, their philosophical justification of disobedience, and the theory and practice of representation and the elective franchise. E. Oberholzer, Jr.

71. Carson, Clarence B. THE FOUNDING OF THE AMERICAN REPUBLIC. *Freeman 1971 21(8): 451-459, (9): 524-535, (10): 621-634, (11): 667-677, (12): 731-742.* Part I. Deals with the beginnings of the United States. Criticizes the professional historians who have failed to recognize the unitary history of that seminal period of 1760-1800 because of their preoccupation with its parts. 2 notes. Part II. No matter how they altered it and however ambiguous their attitude toward it, the new people of America did not reject their English heritage. 11 notes. Part III. Reviews the socioreligious experiences of the American colonists and claims that one reason for the nonrevolutionary character of the American Revolution was that by the late 18th century Americans "were chastened by their experiences with attempts at reconstructing society, by the use of government to achieve some religious end." 8 notes. Part IV. Although theirs were limited experiences in self-government, no people save the English people were so well prepared to govern themselves as were the American colonists on the eve of the Revolution. 9 notes. Part V. Once the break with Great Britain occurred the American colonists had to seek a new rationale for government other than that of the English Constitution. They found that ideology in the natural law philosophy which historically was the veritable underpinning of Western civilization.3 notes. D. A. Yanchisin

72. Cecil, Robert. OLIGARCHY AND MOB-RULE IN THE AMERICAN REVOLUTION. *Hist. Today [Great Britain] 1963 13(3): 197-204.* American society in the 18th century was modeled upon English society; in particular the colonies were ruled by their respective oligarchies. The closely knit legislatures and the governors monopolized political and economic power. By the time of the Boston "Tea Party" and the "Intolerable Acts" the Committees set up by Samuel Adams came into action. He had understood that "a revolution cannot subsist on anarchy" but requires an organization with communications and propaganda. "If the mobs were at first the sinews, the Press and the Committees [of Correspondence] were the nerves of the Revolution..." Undocumented. Illus.

E. P. Stickney

73. Chapin, Bradley. COLONIAL AND REVOLUTIONARY ORIGINS OF THE AMERICAN LAW OF TREASON. *William and Mary Q. 1960 17(1): 3-21.* English law, based on the statutes of 25 Edward III and 7 and 8 William III, was followed throughout the colonial period. During the Revolution, treason became "an incident of battle and an act, not a state of mind." Grand juries were reluctant to indict; defendants were accorded full legal rights, and many persons convicted were pardoned. The Revolutionary period provided the link between the English law of treason and its reformulation to meet republican conditions. Based on case law, with a table of cases.

E. Oberholzer, Jr.

74. Colbourn, H. Trevor. THOMAS JEFFERSON'S USE OF THE PAST. *William and Mary Q. 1958 15(1): 56-70.* Relying chiefly on the Whig historians, for whose position he also found support in Cornelius Tacitus and Sir William Blackstone, Jefferson studied the past in search of guidance for the future. American rights, he believed, derived from Saxon times; because America had not been subject to the Norman Conquest, it was not subject to feudal land tenure. Americans, Jefferson felt, must rely on their Saxon heritage and repudiate subsequent usurpations of their rights.

E. Oberholzer, Jr.

75. Dion, Léon. NATURAL LAW AND MANIFEST DESTINY IN THE ERA OF THE AMERICAN REVOLUTION. *Can. J. of Econ. and Pol. Sci. 1957 23(2): 227-247.* Discusses the impact of the idea of manifest destiny on American history. The author demonstrates that it was not the religiously determined belief in manifest destiny of the early Puritan settlers, but the idea of Natural Law that had a lasting effect. During the revolutionary period it was held that America was to become the last stronghold of European liberties and the realization of Natural Law. This idea helped to shape the American nation and bound the 13 colonies together, even though they had very divergent interests. To the revolutionaries, it seemed that America was in the fortunate position to create the best state humanly possible. It had to be an example to the world, the home of freedom, culture and morals. In this way, America became a cause, which led to both isolationism and expansionism as a consequence of the limitless space to be opened up.

D. van Arkel

76. Green, Fletcher M. CYCLES OF AMERICAN DEMOCRACY. *Mississippi Valley Hist. R. 1961 48(1): 3-23.* Reviews the progress of democracy in America

since 1776. "The developments of the nineteenth and twentieth centuries have been the working out of principles first enunciated as the tenets of American democracy during the Revolutionary era." From that era can be dated the beginnings of a series of cycles in the growth of American democracy. During the first cycle (1776-1800) "the people assumed authority to establish the governments by which they were to be governed." During the second (1800-60) "the several states, acting as agents for the people, were responsible for democratic advance. During the latter third of the nineteenth century the Congress exercised a controlling influence...and the judiciary served as a check to slow down progress. During the early years of the twentieth century, as the fourth cycle began, the executive seemed destined to replace the Congress as the leader, but since the 1930's the judiciary has been in the ascendency." D. R. Millar

77. Hawke, David F. THE AMERICAN REVOLUTION—WAS IT A REAL ONE? *Am. Book Collector 1967 17(7): 27-29, 31-32.* Contrary to the contention of some historians that the American Revolution did not result in any fundamental changes in America, the war produced a completely different outlook on life, a republican rather than a hierarchial view of politics and society. This was brought about by the frustration of talented young men in America when they found they could advance so far and no further in society as it was then organized. It was reflected in the constitutions of the various States written between 1775 and 1776. But neither this frustration nor the flood of political pamphlets was enough to cause the Revolution. Military and independent-minded men manipulated events in the colonies to create favorable conditions. The Revolution succeeded so well in establishing equality that a visiting Frenchman after the war found only one thing which distinguished persons one from another—money. Undocumented, illus. D. Brockway

78. Hudson, Winthrop S. JOHN LOCKE—PREPARING THE WAY FOR REVOLUTION. *J. of Presbyterian Hist. 1964 42(1): 19-38.* Contends that Locke's political thought was basically a restatement of familiar principles worked out by the Puritan Independents during the English Civil Wars. "...Locke and Sidney and Calvin were representatives of a single tradition." Furthermore, "it is impossible to discover a single significant difference" between the arguments on behalf of toleration set forth by Roger Williams and those later advanced by Locke. For both, the "basic assumptions were Puritan assumptions, assumptions that were derived from Geneva," and, by the time Locke wrote, assumptions accepted in England by all dissenting parties. W. D. Metz

79. Jacobson, Norman. POLITICAL SCIENCE AND POLITICAL EDUCATION. *Am. Pol. Sci. R. 1963 57(3): 561-569.* "Two varieties of political thought contended for the allegiance of the American people at the founding of the new nation....One was notable for its expression of friendship and brotherhood, for its insistence upon individual spontaneity and uniqueness, and for its disdain for material concerns; it was intuitive and unsystematic in temper." A proponent of this view was Thomas Paine. Much of the basis of this thought can be found in the writings of Rousseau. The Declaration of Independence and the Articles of Confederation are expressions of it. "The other displayed a preoccupation with

social order, procedural rationality, and the material bases of political association and division; it was abstract and systematic in temper." Hamilton and Madison were the champions of this view which found its expression in the Constitution. Eric Bentley and John Dewey are 20th-century exponents. "Our political science has succeeded to the extent that the Constitution has performed its supreme function, the political education of the citizens." It has worked a gigantic self-fulfilling prophecy on the American polity.   B. W. Onstine

80. Jensen, Merrill. DEMOCRACY AND THE AMERICAN REVOLUTION. *Huntington Lib. Q. 1956/57 20(4): 321-341.* States the case for believing that the American Revolution was a genuinely democratic movement in its results, though not in its origins.   H. D. Jordan

81. Kammen, Michael. THE MEANING OF COLONIZATION IN AMERICAN REVOLUTIONARY THOUGHT. *J. of the Hist. of Ideas 1970 31(3): 337-358.* The historical reconstruction of their original purpose in colonizing that best suited American revolutionaries on the eve of independence was that they had emigrated "to seek or preserve civil and religious liberties." This was naturally thought to be a distorted view by American Tories.   W. H. Coates

82. Kenyon, Cecilia M. REPUBLICANISM AND RADICALISM IN THE AMERICAN REVOLUTION: AN OLD-FASHIONED INTERPRETATION. *William and Mary Q. 1962 19(2): 153-182.* Rejecting dichotomous analyses of groups and movements of the period, and ascribing them to the influence of the Populists and Charles A. Beard, the two-party-system, and the lack of precise terminology, the author reexamines the extent to which the Revolution was radical or conservative, using such labels in clearly defined senses. Starting as a conservative protest, and never losing certain conservative features, the Revolution acquired a radical aspect as attitudes toward republican governments changed. The modification of John Locke's philosophy was also radical. The "most truly radical" event was the development of the federal system as expressed in the Constitution of 1787.   E. Oberholzer, Jr.

83. Livingston, William S. EMIGRATION AS A THEORETICAL DOCTRINE DURING THE AMERICAN REVOLUTION. *J. of Pol. 1957 19(4): 591-615.* Examines, against the background of the American Revolution, the "doctrine of emigration," whereby a citizen could revoke his consent to the social contract and leave a community, abandoning loyalty and obligation to it, in order to see how closely theory and practice fit in this particular controversy. The fit is close, but not perfect. Partly by means of an examination of the causes and nature of the emigration during the Revolution, the author shows that the outlook of the revolutionary era was sympathetic to such a theory, but not more than that.   C. A. LeGuin

84. McCormick, Richard. POLITICAL ESSAYS OF WILLIAM PATERSON. *J. of the Rutgers U. Lib. 1955 18(2): 38-49.* Incorporates five essays by William Paterson (1745-1806), with a biographical introduction and appraisal. Paterson,

a member of the Constitutional Convention, later served as Senator from New Jersey, Governor of New Jersey, and Associate Justice of the Supreme Court of the United States. The essays reveal Paterson as an ultra-Federalist who believed that the American Revolution was carried out for the purpose of protecting traditional rights of person and property that had been violated under British tyranny. R. E. Wilson

85. Nelson, William H. THE REVOLUTIONARY CHARACTER OF THE AMERICAN REVOLUTION. *Am. Hist. R. 1965 70(4): 998-1014.* The American Revolution was two-sided in nature: it was both affirmation and denial. The severance of ties with Britain in certain respects spelled impoverishment for America; not only institutionally, ideologically, and economically, but psychologically, for Americans long remained poorer Englishmen because of their alienation and remoteness from the centers of English life. But the Revolution also meant liberation. Through the Revolution, dissent was transformed into a new system, positive and lawful, one of political individualism. The Revolution's most visible achievement was the new sense of nationhood embodied in the Constitution which, though attacked, has stood firm. The spirit of the Revolution survives with more than a trace of revolutionary zeal that has never let the descendants of the founding fathers forget that a revolutionary society lives by its principles and by their deliberate propagation from age to age and to the world beyond their borders. Based on a paper read at the 1964 Anglo-American Conference of Historians in London. 44 notes. E. P. Stickney

86. Pole, J. R. HISTORIANS AND THE PROBLEM OF EARLY AMERICAN DEMOCRACY. *Am. Hist. R. 1962 67(3): 626-646.* Critically examines recent discussions of the role of democracy in America in the years before and after the American Revolution, and proposes an alternate hypothesis. "The alternative view, which I want to suggest, does not confine itself merely to rejecting the 'democratic' interpretation by putting in its place a flat, antidemocratic account of the same set of institutions. What it does, I think, is to see the democratic elements in their proper perspective by adding a further dimension without which the rest is flat, incomplete, and, for all its turbulence, essentially lifeless. This is the dimension of what Cecilia Kenyon has called 'institutional thought.' " M. Berman

87. Pole, J. R. THE CREATION OF THE AMERICAN REPUBLIC. *Hist. J. 1970 13(4): 799-803.* A review article based on Gordon S. Wood, *The Creation of the American Republic, 1776-1787* (Chapel Hill: U. of North Carolina Press, 1969). The period between the revolt of the American Colonies against the Stamp Act (1765) and the making of the Constitution was vital in the history of American society and politics. Wood explains the intellectual character of the political transformation which took place as a result of the American Colonies' break with England. One prominent problem, influenced by the predominantly Whiggish thought of the colonists, was the transformation to a more open democracy. Overintellectualization, however, tends to distort the enlargement of suffrage and

representation by the new State constitutions. The conflict between Federalists and Anti-Federalists is an important factor in the study of American political and social developments.
L. Brown

88. Preston, Paula Sampson. THE SEVERED HEAD OF CHARLES I OF ENGLAND: ITS USE AS A POLITICAL STIMULUS. *Winterthur Portfolio 1970 6: 1-13.* Discusses the symbolic use in paintings and political cartoons of the head of Charles I (1600-49). During the years leading to the American Revolution, the severed head of Charles I became a political theme. Patrick Henry (1736-99) and Thomas Paine (1737-1809) are but two who used the theme. Prints appearing as late as 1782 implied that the rights of Englishmen must be protected. The recurring theme, in varying degrees of subtlety, was that the English monarch must suffer the fate of Charles I if the individual rights of the American colonists were to survive. Interestingly, American patriotic artists such as Joseph Wright (1756-93) did not refrain from exhibiting paintings with this theme in London. Based on primary and secondary sources; 15 photos, 13 notes.
N. A. Kuntz

89. Ripley, Randall B. ADAMS, BURKE AND EIGHTEENTH-CENTURY CONSERVATISM. *Pol. Sci. Q. 1965 80(2): 216-235.* Proposes that the leading literature on conservative thought in England and in America, having caught some of the similarity in temperament between Edmund Burke and John Adams, has missed the real differences in their thought because it failed to examine in enough detail the two societies in which they lived and wrote. Burke and Adams came to similar conclusions only when they were confronted with events which involved a third country—France—or which involved English-American relations. When confronted with wholly national questions they arrived at divergent conclusions. Burke could be totally anti-Enlightenment and still affect the course of English politics profoundly. Adams had to be an Enlightenment figure in order to have a real impact on the America of his time. Documented.
Sr. M. McAuley

90. Savelle, Max. NATIONALISM AND OTHER LOYALTIES IN THE AMERICAN REVOLUTION. *Am. Hist. R. 1962 67(4): 901-923.* "The concept of an 'American empire,' or nation, which replaced the image of the British imperial society to which men had given their loyalty before 1775 in their minds and hearts, was the product of a slow intellectual and emotional growth....It was many years before the image of the British empire-nation of the colonial era was fully and perfectly replaced in the minds of all Americans by the image of a genuine, integral American nation. The war years, 1776-1783, constituted what might be called the period of its gestation and, toward the end of the war, its birth."
M. Berman

91. Tate, Thad W. THE SOCIAL CONTRACT IN AMERICA, 1774-1787: REVOLUTIONARY THEORY AS A CONSERVATIVE INSTRUMENT. *William and Mary Q. 1965 22(3): 375-391.* Although Americans evolved a "distinctive constitutional method" from ideas of the social contract, they also retained a limited view of contractual government. The social contract was called

into being in order to justify the separation from Great Britain; no efforts were made to broaden it beyond a rationalization to establish government. That the people remained in a state of nature and could resist lawful government was not admitted. As a conservative doctrine the contract sought merely to legitimize a revolutionary course of action while at the same time it tended to discourage revolutionary thought. H. M. Ward

92. Varg, Paul A. THE ADVENT OF NATIONALISM, 1758-1776. *Am. Q. 1964 16(2, part 1): 169-181.* When English officials offended American colonists' sense of equal status, they violated the colonists' long standing identification with English political tradition. Reared as they had been in an atmosphere of liberty and an awareness of their own importance, the colonists augmented their feeling of national separateness by engaging in controversy with the English government. To accept "subject" status meant renunciation of cherished English traditions such as "consent"; it also signalled contentment with inferiority. Many colonists could not eat humble pie. Instead, in true nascent nationalist tradition, they came to regard themselves as "chosen people" with a separate historical existence. R. S. Pickett

93. Washburn, John L. TWO MEANINGS OF THE TERM CONSTITU- TION: A COMMENT ON "CONSTITUTIONALISM IN AMERICAN THOUGHT." *Pennsylvania Hist. 1969 36(4): 419-423.* Theorists of the 17th and 18th centuries distinguished between two social contracts: one which formed a society and the other which resulted in legitimate government. The first was a mutual contract between equals; the second was one in which the individual essentially surrendered powers and consented to be governed. These distinctions were often blurred. After 1763 Americans rediscovered the first type of social contract. They learned that "men through mutual agreements could in fact structure their own political existence." 5 notes. D. C. Swift

94. Werner, James M. DAVID HUME AND AMERICA. *J. of the Hist. of Ideas 1972 33(3): 439-456.* Hume believed that by 1775 the American colonies had sufficiently matured to be worthy of independence. Thus, although Hume's *History of England* was too nonpartisan to be fully appreciated by the Whig-inclined colonists, many Americans were well disposed toward Hume's historical and political writings. Among Americans who drew on Hume were Charles Carroll of Carrollton, Josiah Quincy, Jr., Thomas Paine, Alexander Hamilton, and, most importantly, Benjamin Franklin and James Madison. W. H. Coates

2

GENERAL HISTORY OF THE REVOLUTION: LEXINGTON TO YORKTOWN

General

95. Billias, George Athan. ELBRIDGE GERRY'S LETTER CODE. *Manuscripts 1968 20(4): 3-13.* The need for secrecy during the Revolutionary War often led to the use of various ciphers in correspondence. These ciphers have presented a problem to modern scholars. The letter code of Elbridge Gerry (1744-1814), a member of the Continental Congress from Massachusetts, has not been deciphered. The text of one of Gerry's coded letters is reproduced. Based on MSS deposited at the Massachusetts Historical Society; illus., photos.

P. D. Thomas

96. Boyd, Julian P. A PEOPLE DIVIDED. *North Carolina Hist. R. 1970 47(2): 161-175.* The American Revolutionary heritage stressing the inevitability of discord and the legitimacy of opposition is the lifeblood of American institutions and is the best assurance of progress. The Revolution, America's first and most deeply divisive issue, was of prime import for the human race. The Revolution was a watershed: born in a society ruled by one set of social assumptions, America created for itself and the world another set. America's crucial decade did not come in the 1780's but rather in the 1790's, when the right of opposition was tested. The authentic voice of the revolution of 1800 elevating Jefferson to power reiterated the implications of 1776: dissent and debate, within the framework of "a common allegiance," would be the Nation's cornerstone.

H. M. Rosen

97. Brown, Wallace. NEGROES AND THE AMERICAN REVOLUTION. *Hist. Today [Great Britain] 1964 14(8): 556-563.* An analysis of British and colonial American usage of Negroes in the revolutionary war. The Negroes were

utilized more in the civilian services and the navy than in the army, and they received few tangible benefits from their participation. Illus.

L. A. Knafla

98. Coad, Oral S. PINE BARRENS AND ROBBER BARONS. *New Jersey Hist. Soc. Pro. 1964 82(3): 185-199.* The Pine Robbers were desperadoes from both inside and outside of New Jersey who pretended to be pro-British in sympathy and attempted to justify their raids against patriots during the Revolutionary War on the ground of loyalty to the king. The literary use that has been made of these characters is surveyed. The most notorious of these bandit leaders were Jacob Fagan, Lewis Fenton, and John Bacon. 14 notes.

E. P. Stickney

99. Fleming, E. McClung. THE AMERICAN IMAGE AS INDIAN PRINCESS, 1765-1783. *Winterthur Portfolio 1965 2: 65-81.* Traces the evolution of the allegorical figure used to represent "America" and later the United States. From 1765 to 1783, the symbol was an Indian princess. Portrayed at first as the dependent daughter of Britannia, the princess frees herself from British fetters of taxation and finally gains liberty through the Revolution. Before 1776 the daughter-mother relationship included every kind of affection, alienation, and reconciliation. The American image sought liberty during these years, while England's chief concern was trade. Various artists, both abroad and at home, portrayed the princess in headdress, with bow and arrow. The symbol evolved slowly into a Greek goddess, and finally into Uncle Sam in the 19th century. Based on primary and secondary sources; 13 photos, 26 notes.

N. A. Kuntz

100. Gibbs, Richard F. IN QUEST OF A SPIRITUAL RENAISSANCE. *North Carolina Hist. R. 1970 47(2): 138-144.* Explains the role of "commemoration" as a means to an end. Celebration of the Revolution is analogous to the Christian Eucharist. As the Eucharist is a ritual which symbolically recreates and reenacts events and circumstances attending the liberation of man's soul from eternal damnation, the Revolutionary commemoration will serve to keep before America her legacy of liberty with its concomitant obligation to perpetuate this blessing whatever the risk. To achieve its goal, the commission envisions its prime role as that of educator, informing America of its heritage and fostering a patriotic renaissance.

H. M. Rosen

101. Gowans, Alan. PRESERVATION. *J. of the Soc. of Architectural Historians 1965 24(3): 252-253.* A plea for the consideration, by architectural historians, of preserving ancient buildings, with some examples of how restorers' tastes have changed. "The criterion of a good restoration is not its archaeological accuracy, but how well it conveys historic 'meaning.' " The author cites Independence Hall, Philadelphia, as an admirable example, where a building was not restored to its original state but to "its state in the great days of 1776." Undocumented.

W. D. McIntyre

102. Haarmann, Albert W. and Holst, Donald W. THE FRIEDRICH VON GERMANN DRAWINGS OF TROOPS IN THE AMERICAN REVOLU-

TION. *Military Collector and Historian 1964 16(1): 1-9.* Discusses and describes the 13 colored single-figure drawings of American, British, and German troops during the American Revolution. All of these drawings by Von Germann are in the Print Room of the New York Public Library and are reproduced in black and white in this article. The authors believe that these primitive but detailed drawings are based largely on secondary sources. Illus., 13 notes.   C. L. Boyd

103. Hamer, Elizabeth E. and Rutland, Robert A. THE COMING BICENTEN-NIAL OF THE UNITED STATES. *Scholarly Publishing 1971 2(2): 139-147.* The bicentennial of the signing of the Declaration of Independence approaches; such national anniversaries provide excellent opportunities to serve scholarship. Aware of this situation, the Library of Congress has made plans to utilize this event to acquaint scholars with its holdings and also to provide historical information of interest to the general public. A general reading bibliography of the American Revolution has already appeared. Other projects, including a guide to relevant manuscript collections and a revision of Edmund Burnett's *Letters of Members of the Continental Congress,* are under way. Already the work of the advisory committee to the Library of Congress has unearthed much previously unknown manuscript material. When completed, the work of the Library of Congress in connection with the bicentennial promises to be of lasting service to scholarship.   J. A. Casada

104. Hancock, Harold B., ed. LETTERS TO AND FROM CAESAR ROD-NEY. *Delaware Hist. 1966 12(1): 54-76, (2): 147-168.* Part I. Reprints letters to and from Rodney (1728-84) during 1765-77. Of special interest are two letters by Rodney describing the Stamp Act Congress in New York and his own role in the examination of persons connected with a Tory uprising in Sussex County. Also of interest are several letters from Dennys deBerdt, agent for the Lower Counties in England, in which deBerdt relates his efforts to win repeal of the Stamp Act and Townshend Act and cautions patience on the part of the colonists. John Haslet and James Tilton provide Rodney with a detailed account of Delaware troops in action at White Plains, and Haslet writes of his disgust with the politics of the Delaware State Convention. Other letters relate a sighting of a large British fleet off Lewes in 1777, the suppression of the Sussex insurrection, and the commissioning of various individuals. The letters come from 19 historical societies and archives as well as one private owner, and they represent a supplement to previously published Rodney correspondence. 25 notes. Part II. Letters to and from Caesar Rodney, 1777-81.   R. M. Miller

105. Harper, Lawrence A. AMERICAN HISTORY TO 1789. *J. of Econ. Hist. 1959 19(1): 1-24.* Calls attention to about four hundred titles appearing since 1945. They range from problems of imperial planning, the Indian economy, the frontier and defense; through trade, industry, labor, agriculture, the professions, arts and education, money and banking; to accounts of population, immigration, travel and colonial diseases. The survey is supplemented by regional and bibliographical references and discussions of the era of the Articles of Confederation and the Constitution.   A

106. Kenney, Alice P. THE ALBANY DUTCH: LOYALISTS AND PATRI-OTS. *New York Hist. 1961 42(4): 331-350.* The Revolution divided the Dutch in New York, as it did other groups. This division resulted in the shattering of the ethnic unity of the Dutch as a group. After the war, they were no longer able to maintain their culture as a separate way of life.   A. B. Rollins

107. Lacy, Harriet S. THE LANGDON PAPERS, 1716-1841. *Hist. New Hampshire 1967 22(3): 55-65.* Description and list of about a thousand items of commercial papers, deeds, and correspondence of the Langdons of Portsmouth, New Hampshire, chiefly of the Atlantic trading voyages of the brothers Woodbury and John from 1762 to 1775. John outfitted privateers and attended the Continental Congress during the Revolution, later attended the Constitutional Convention, and became a governor and a senator.   T. D. S. Bassett

108. Lee, Ronald F. INDEPENDENCE NATIONAL HISTORICAL PARK. *Historic Preservation 1966 18(5): 184-187.* The uses made of the Independence Park, which contains Independence Hall, Congress Hall, and Carpenters' Hall are discussed. The author comments also on the plan for preservation and renewal of the area around the park, Old Philadelphia or "Society Hill." Illus.
                 J. M. Hawes

109. Logan, Gwendolyn Evans. THE SLAVE IN CONNECTICUT DURING THE AMERICAN REVOLUTION. *Connecticut Hist. Soc. Bull. 1965 30(3): 73-80.* Discusses laws pertaining to the emancipation and military service of the six thousand Negroes in Connecticut during the American Revolution. The author concludes that, despite movements to end the slave trade and gradually free Negroes, severe black codes and other restrictions limited the freedom of Connecticut blacks. It is not clear how many Negroes who served in the Revolutionary armies received their freedom as a result. "That the ideals of the American Revolution and the practical...needs for fighting strength had helped bring about the emancipation of the Negro in Connecticut is not justified by the evidence." Biblio.   L. R. Murphy

110. Main, Jackson Turner. GOVERNMENT BY THE PEOPLE: THE AMERICAN REVOLUTION AND THE DEMOCRATIZATION OF THE LEGISLATURES. *William and Mary Q. 1966 23(3): 391-407.* Analyzing newspaper opinion and legislative structure, the author observes three phenomena: continual control by local elites, widening of public participation in politics, and the emergence of a defense of popular government. Liberalization may be attributed to new leadership arising during the Revolution and the augmented power of the back country.   H. M. Ward

111. Martin, James Kirby. MEN OF FAMILY WEALTH AND PERSONAL MERIT: THE CHANGING SOCIAL BASES OF EXECUTIVE LEADERSHIP SELECTION IN THE AMERICAN REVOLUTION. *Societas: A R. of Social Hist. 1972 2(1): 43-70.* Executives during the Revolution "were more dependent upon personal initiative and drive, rather than family wealth and

standing in working their way into the political arena." Many colonial executives became Loyalists, thus partially clearing the road to the top. When executives became not appointed but elective, freemen turned to men with modest amounts of wealth, Maryland being the exception where 70 percent of high officials were men of great family wealth. By the time of state constitution-making, those who felt a prerogative to govern clearly felt threatened. "The state constitutions were a small beginning for the emerging conception that men of virtue and talent, even those with common social origins, could hold high political offices." 6 tables, 37 notes.   E. P. Stickney

112. Mohrt, Michel. LA GUERRE DE L'INDEPENDANCE AMERICAINE [The American War of Independence]. *R. de Paris [France] 1965 72(4): 44-57.* Discusses the causes of the American Revolution and the composition of the patriot cause and its ideological position. Time after time the British government underestimated the strength and singleness of purpose of the Americans.
                                                                J. A. Clarke

113. Murray, Eleanor. MOUNT INDEPENDENCE IN TIME OF PEACE, 1783-1960. *Vermont Hist. 1967 35(2): 109-119.* Mount Independence, on the Vermont shore of Lake Champlain, was so named by the troops stationed there when the Declaration of Independence was read to them on 28 July 1776. It served as one of the most significant fortresses of the Revolution. However, its later history is hidden by an "enveloping fog." Because of its inaccessibility it never became a tourist attraction. The land around Mount Independence, as well as the mount itself, was shown to be a rich field for archaeologists by some work done there in the 1930's by the Museum of the American Indian. "The science of archeology will tell properly the story Mount Independence has kept hidden all these years."   R. S. Burke

114. Peckham, Howard H. DOCUMENTS OF FREEDOM. *Am. Heritage 1965 16(4): 65-73.* Significant documents on the American Revolution are reproduced in facsimile, from the British order that started the war to the surrender of Cornwallis as he conveyed it to Sir Henry Clinton. Helpful background information is provided, using quotes from the documents. All the selections are in the Clements Library at the University of Michigan.   J. D. Filipiak

115. Reed, John F. REVOLUTIONARY RARITIES. *Manuscripts 1967 19(4): 21-25.* Lists and classifies autographs of the Revolutionary period, not concerned with content, format, or condition, but only the autographs per se. They are divided into categories: excessively rare, exceedingly rare, very rare, and rare. A further division into nationalities is established.   C. J. Allard

116. Reynolds, Thomas H. MOUNT INDEPENDENCE UNDER THE AEGIS OF THE VERMONT BOARD OF HISTORIC SITES. *Vermont Hist. 1967 35(2): 120-131.* In 1959 a movement was initiated to develop Mount Independence. The author surveyed the site that summer, and a year later the state of Vermont bought the rest of the mount not owned by the Ticonderoga Associates.

Using the Twiss-Wintersmith map of 1777 and student help in the summers of 1964-66, the author identified the construction it showed. The 1966 legislative session permitted the creation of a private, nonprofit corporation, the Mount Independence Associates, for custody and development. In spite of continued pilfering, the site is unusually undisturbed and ready for restoration.

T. D. S. Bassett

117. Shaffer, Janet. NEW LONDON. *Virginia Cavalcade 1966 15(3): 22-29.* A history of the town of New London, Virginia, emphasizing the importance of the town during the Revolutionary War. Undocumented, illus.   R. B. Lange

118. Thompson, Mack E. THE WARD-HOPKINS CONTROVERSY AND THE AMERICAN REVOLUTION IN RHODE ISLAND: AN INTERPRE- TATION. *William and Mary Q. 1959 16(3): 363-375.* Refutes the thesis that in their struggle for political supremacy Samuel Ward and Stephen Hopkins repre- sented Southern mercantile and Northern agrarian interests, respectively, and that the Northern radicals brought Rhode Island into the Revolution. The expla- nation of the Ward-Hopkins conflict lies in the rise of Providence as a commercial center. By the eve of the Revolution, the old agrarian groups had disintegrated and leadership was shared by the mercantile interests of Newport and those of Providence. Opposition to British rule was led by the merchants of both areas; the farmers followed the leadership of the merchants. The class conflict did not emerge until after the Revolution.   E. Oberholzer, Jr.

119. Woods, John A., ed. THE CORRESPONDENCE OF BENJAMIN RUSH AND GRANVILLE SHARP, 1773-1809. *J. of Am. Studies [Great Britain] 1967 1(1): 1-38.* Reproduces a selection of unpublished letters exchanged between the English reformer, Granville Sharp, and Dr. Benjamin Rush of Philadelphia. Rush initiated the correspondence as a result of his acquaintance with Anthony Bene- zet, a pioneer opponent of slavery who had been writing to Sharp. The correspon- dents discussed three subjects at length: slavery and the slave trade, relations between England and America, and religion. Rush was especially interested in the "influence of physical causes upon the moral faculty." As for slavery, Sharp, for example, proposed a detailed scheme for compensated emancipation in the colonies. The events leading to the American Revolution were treated in some detail, both men condemning British policy. After the Revolution views were exchanged on the proper method of strengthening the American Episcopal Church. Such topics as the founding of Dickinson College, the danger of standing armies in America, and the personalities of George Washington, Thomas Jeffer- son, and James Madison were also discussed. The Rush-Sharp manuscripts an- notated by the editor are in the possession of the Historical Society of Pennsylvania and Miss Lloyd-Baker of Hardwicke Court and were written in 1773-75, 1783-86, 1797, 1799, 1801, and 1809.   D. J. Abramoske

120. —. THE MECHANICS. *Labor Hist. 1964 5(3): 215-224; 225-246; 247-276.* Revised versions of papers given at the Mississippi Valley Historical Association

Annual Convention at Omaha, Nebraska, May 1963. The three articles describe the role of the city artisan or "mechanic" in New York city politics during the last quarter of the 18th century.

AFTER CARL BECKER: THE MECHANICS AND NEW YORK CITY POLITICS, 1774-1801. The introduction seeks to define the term "mechanic," whom Carl Becker in a study on New York politics published in 1909 defined as a revolutionary democrat.

Lynd, Staughton. THE MECHANICS IN NEW YORK POLITICS, 1774-1788. The mechanics, who organized a committee in 1774, favored independence in 1776, popular ratification of the state constitution, the secret ballot, annual elections, rotation of office, and popular election of all local officials. Throughout the war the Committee of Mechanics was actively supporting the war against the British. During the 1780's candidates were nominated in the annual elections. In 1788 the mechanics joined the merchants in supporting ratification of the Constitution.

Young, Alfred. THE MECHANICS AND THE JEFFERSONIANS: NEW YORK, 1789-1801. At the opening of the decade the mechanics staunchly supported the Federalists. During the 1790's the mechanics, nationalistic and democratic in their outlook, switched their support to the Republicans, although many remained Federalists even after 1800. The author concludes that the "mechanics did not always behave as one unified class in politics."

J. H. Krenkel

Journalism, Literature & the Revolution

121. Christadler, Martin. POLITISCHE DISKUSSION UND LITERARISCHE FORM IN DER AMERIKANISCHEN LITERATUR DER REVOLUTIONSZEIT [Political discussion and literary form in the American literature of the Revolutionary era]. *Jahrbuch für Amerikastudien [West Germany] 1968 13: 13-33.* The political essay allowing for the simultaneous expression of daily interests and eternal principles became the literary form most adequate to the Revolutionary situation in America and its problems. The most characteristic antithetic features of the political essay and related literary forms of the period are discussed and their function and literary quality are shown. Many sermons, memoirs, and political and other writings are quoted.   G. P. Bassler

122. Hixson, Richard F. FOUNDING OF NEW JERSEY'S FIRST PERMANENT NEWSPAPER. *Journalism Q. 1963 40(2): 233-235.* New Jersey was the last of the 13 American colonies to have its own newspaper, because New York and Pennsylvania newspapers circulated widely into the state. As the Revolutionary War reached its most critical point, with New Jersey its "cockpit," delivery of those newspapers became difficult and the cities were for a large part of the

time in the hands of the enemy. Governor William Livingston, General George Washington, and the state printer Isaac Collins, corresponded on the subject. Livingston persuaded the Legislature toward the end of 1777 to subsidize the *New Jersey Gazette,* of which 446 issues were published in the following nine years.

S. E. Humphreys

123. Leithead, J. Edward. THE REVOLUTIONARY WAR IN DIME NOVELS. *Am. Book Collector 1969 19(8/9): 14-21.* A listing and brief description of the various series of dime novels about the American Revolution which appeared at the end of the 19th and beginning of the 20th century. Illus.

D. Brockway

124. Litto, Fredric M. ADDISON'S *CATO* IN THE COLONIES. *William and Mary Q. 1966 23(3): 431-449.* Discusses the popularity and influence in America of Joseph Addison's play *Cato,* first produced in London in 1713. Cato's stand for liberty against the tyranny of Caesar found a sympathetic reception among the colonists. During the Revolutionary era it became an effective instrument of propaganda. The author comments on theatrical groups in America and the use of "Cato" as a pseudonym for notable colonists.

H. M. Ward

125. Osborne, William S. JOHN PENDLETON KENNEDY'S *HORSE-SHOE ROBINSON:* A NOVEL WITH "THE UTMOST HISTORICAL ACCURACY." *Maryland Hist. Mag. 1964 59(3): 286-296.* In the preface to the first edition of his *Horse-Shoe Robinson* (1835), Kennedy wrote: "The events narrated in the following pages came to my knowledge in the process of my [research] into the personal history of some of the characters who figure in the story. I thought them worth being embodied into a regular narrative...because they serve to illustrate the temper and character of the War of our Revolution." Later, in the introduction to the second edition, Kennedy revealed Horse-Shoe Robinson's "personal history," Robinson being the hero of "the first significant tale of the Revolution in the South."

W. L. Fox

126. Pickering, James H. ENOCH CROSBY, SECRET AGENT OF THE NEUTRAL GROUND: HIS OWN STORY. *New York Hist. 1966 47(1): 61-73.* In a book called *The Spy,* which was published during 1821, James Fenimore Cooper presented a thrilling story of revolutionary warfare on the neutral ground of New York's Westchester and Dutchess counties. Many readers came to believe that the hero of this volume, Harvey Birch, actually lived under another name. Because of a book by H. L. Barnum, most of the speculation soon focused upon Enoch Crosby, who lived in the Putnam County town of Carmel, New York. Cooper refused to comment on these assertions, but Crosby applied for a Federal pension in 1832 and confessed that he had been the secret agent of a Committee for Detecting and Defeating Conspiracies in the period between September 1776 and May 1777. The editor here reprints the full text of the story contained in Crosby's application and adds a series of explanatory notes.

B. T. Quinten

127. Pickering, James H. NEW YORK IN THE REVOLUTION: COOPER'S *WYANDOTTE. New York Hist. 1968 49(2): 121-141. Wyandotté* (1843) was one of James Fenimore Cooper's more successful historical novels. Analyzing the nature of the historical sources used by Cooper as background for his novel, the author finds that he displayed excellent historical judgment. Drawing on a large volume of family papers, and relying on the oral testimony of participants, Cooper rejected the prevailing Whig interpretation of the Revolution as a struggle between virtuous patriots and unprincipled Tories, in favor of a more realistic view which saw the Revolution as a traumatic event which set father against son and brother against brother. Based on Cooper's personal papers and published writings, and on primary and secondary sources; 9 illus., 24 notes.

G. Kurland

128. Skaggs, David C. EDITORIAL POLICIES OF THE *MARYLAND GA-ZETTE,* 1765-1783. *Maryland Hist. Mag. 1964 59(4): 341-349.* "From the passage of the Stamp Act to the signing of the Treaty of Paris, the *Maryland Gazette's* weekly issues both influenced and reflected local thought." Among the arguments were those concerning the established church; whether coercion should be used to enforce the Articles of Association; arguments for and against Thomas Paine's *Common Sense;* and the question of the confiscation of Loyalist property. Throughout the War of Independence, the newspaper printed notices of military action in a manner designed to encourage the rebels. The *Gazette's* publishers saved their highest accolade for the victor of Yorktown when he visited Annapolis in November 1781. Long Maryland's only newspaper, the *Gazette* helped to construct American democracy. 32 notes.   E. P. Stickney

129. Smith, Julian. HAWTHORNE'S *LEGENDS OF THE PROVINCE HOUSE. Nineteenth-Cent. Fiction 1969 24(1): 31-44.* The *Legends* (1838-39) are rarely discussed as a group; yet, taken together, they are Hawthorne's "only successful use of the framing tale device." They are also "the only fiction...in which he deals with the American Revolution." The "moral balance" between Republican and Loyalist forces reflected in the *Legends* suggests Hawthorne's lack of interest "in the obvious political advantages of the Revolution for the colonists." Hawthorne reminds his readers of the pain of the Revolution and "of the guilt they inherited with their independence." 13 notes.

C. L. Eichelberger

130. Stickle, Warren E., III. STATE AND PRESS IN NEW JERSEY DURING THE AMERICAN REVOLUTION. *New Jersey Hist. 1968 86(3): 158-170, (4): 236-250.* Part I. An account of the trials and tribulations of New Jersey's two patriot newspapers during the American Revolution. Not satisfied with the Philadelphia and New York City revolutionary journals, New Jersey subsidized but did not regulate the *New Jersey Gazette* and the *New Jersey Journal.* The papers flourished but were often plagued by a shortage of printers, post riders, and supplies. 36 notes. Part II. Stresses the most pressing financial problem faced by these journals—that of nonpayment by subscribers. 28 notes.   T. H. Brown

131. Teeter, Dwight L. BENJAMIN TOWNE: THE PRECARIOUS CAREER OF A PERSISTENT PRINTER. *Pennsylvania Mag. of Hist. and Biog. 1965 89(3): 316-330.* Discusses the journalistic and printing activities of Benjamin Towne (d. 1793), publisher of the chameleonic *Pennsylvania Evening Post.* Towne's newspaper first appeared in January 1775 and appears to have been backed by conservative elements in the community. Prior to the British occupation of Philadelphia, the *Evening Post* was "loyal to the cause of the Revolution," but after General Howe arrived Towne printed "an orthodox Tory newspaper." Following the British evacuation, the Supreme Executive Council of Pennsylvania labeled Towne a traitor to the state, but the *Evening Post* again became loyal to the American cause and the treason proceedings were ultimately called off. The decline and eventual failure of the newspaper is also described. Based principally on contemporary newspapers and secondary sources; 69 notes.

D. P. Gallagher

Religion & the Revolution

132. Akers, Charles W. "NEW LIGHT" ON THE AMERICAN REVOLUTION. *New-York Hist. Soc. Q. 1967 51(3): 283-291.* Alan Heimert's *Religion and the American Mind from the Great Awakening to the Revolution* (Cambridge: Harvard U. Press, 1966) is reviewed in this essay. Although the reviewer feels that the book tends toward religious determinism, he feels that it may be an important contribution which may lead to more detailed examinations of religious forces as causes of the Revolution. 15 notes.   C. L. Grant

133. Applegate, Howard L. ANGLICAN CHAPLAINS SERVING IN THE AMERICAN REVOLUTIONARY ARMY, 1775-1783. *Hist. Mag. of the Protestant Episcopal Church 1961 30(2): 138-140.* A list of 17 chaplains known to have been Anglicans and of 14 whose denominational affiliation is unknown.

E. Oberholzer, Jr.

134. Bamsted, J. M. ORTHODOXY IN MASSACHUSETTS: THE ECCLESIASTICAL HISTORY OF FREETOWN, 1683-1776. *New England Q. 1970 43(2): 274-284.* The town of Freetown in Massachusetts Bay was settled under a Plymouth patent in 1683. Throughout its history it remained a persistent source of resistance to Puritan ecclesiastical orthodoxy. It never laid rates to pay the minister's salary, tolerated adult baptism, and in 1747 called as minister one Silas Brett, who while not a "Separate" was a religious enthusiast without a university education. His induction into the church was irregular, but for nearly 30 years he preached and struggled with poverty. The final culmination of intransigence came in 1776, when many in town remained Loyalists, although Brett, like most New England Puritan clergymen, was a patriot. Accordingly, Brett was dismissed. 35 notes.   K. B. West

135. Bayles, Thomas R. EARLY YEARS OF SOUTH HAVEN CHURCH. *Long Island Forum 1970 33(6): 112-115.* The South Haven Church was founded in 1740. During the period of the American Revolution, David Rose (1736-99) was minister of South Haven's Presbyterian Church as well as a leader of the Patriot faction. A 1760 graduate of Yale, Rose felt threatened by the recently founded Anglican church and feared that it would challenge his Presbyterian church as the established religion of South Haven. Rose fought in the Battle of Long Island and, after Washington abandoned the island, he fled to Connecticut where he spent the duration of the war. Besides Rose, South Haven also produced William Floyd, a signer of the Declaration of Independence, and Judge William Smith who helped draft New York's first constitution. Undocumented, 3 illus.
G. Kurland

136. Bradley, A. Day. NEW YORK FRIENDS AND THE CONFISCATED LOYALIST ESTATES. *Quaker Hist. 1972 61(1): 36-39.* No Friends organized off Long Island before 1783, except in Westchester County, where, during part of the Revolution, meetings could not gather without crossing army lines. Friends there suffered raids, removal and imprisonment because they would not take sides. For a dozen years after the war, Friends were disowned for dealing in confiscated Tory land. Zephaniah Birdsall and Abraham Underhill, members of Chappaqua meeting and tenants of Phillips Manor, lost 1,400 pounds' worth of improvements between them because they refused to bid when this estate was sold in 1785. The New York Meeting for Sufferings investigated, found they did not need relief, and declined to record their faithfulness to the peace testimony because of delinquencies not explained in the record. 10 notes.
T. D. S. Bassett

137. Bridenbaugh, Carl. CHURCH AND STATE IN AMERICA, 1689-1775. *Pro. of the Am. Phil. Soc. 1961 105(6): 521-524.* A preliminary report on a study to determine the role of religion in bringing on the American Revolution. Concludes that religion was a fundamental cause of the Revolution.
N. D. Kurland

138. Buchanan, John G. DRUMFIRE FROM THE PULPIT: NATURAL LAW IN THE COLONIAL ELECTION SERMONS OF MASSACHUSETTS. *Am. J. of Legal Hist. 1968 12(3): 232-244.* From 1661 to the 1760's an annual sermon was given on the morning of the election of the higher officials of Massachusetts. Analyzes these sermons, concentrating on the development of the expression of natural law concepts. The original focus was "mixed government— a mingling of monarchy, aristocracy, and democracy. Obedience to a constitutional theory which demanded separation of the spheres of governmental activity and delimitation of power and responsibility." But with the coming of the Revolution rationalism affected the interpretation of natural law. The scope widened to include the reason of things and the nature of man in addition to God's will on the shape and structure of man's institutions. 51 notes.   L. A. Knafla

139. Buchanan, John G. PURITAN PHILOSOPHY OF HISTORY FROM RESTORATION TO REVOLUTION. *Essex Inst. Hist. Collections 1968*

104(4): 329-348. Analyzes clerical thought in the Bay Colony as expressed in election sermons from 1661 to the American Revolution with emphasis on the complex theory of history enunciated by the clerics. This theory emphasized a belief in divine direction and original sin. This led sometimes to chiliastic visions but usually was expressed in terms of a cyclical view of world history in which the golden age was in the past. As the Revolution drew closer, chiliasm and cyclicism merged into a view that freedom from British oppression would bring a new age to God's chosen people. 79 notes, mostly from published sermons.

J. M. Bumsted

140. Campbell, Agnes H. "IN THIS TIME OF COMMOTION." *Quaker Hist. 1971 60(2): 120-123.* Quotes a letter from New York Friends to Philadelphia Friends asking advice on what to do with rent paid by the British Army for storage space in the meetinghouse basement. Philadelphia advised returning the money because Friends ought not to rent space for military purposes—and it might convert the British. The Commissary General refused the money, but London Friends eventually paid the Exchequer. Based on official Quaker sources; 9 notes.

T. D. S. Bassett

141. Ervin, S. THE ANGLICAN CHURCH IN NORTH CAROLINA. *Hist. Mag. of the Protestant Episcopal Church 1955 25(2): 102-161.* Surveys the organizational problems of the Anglican Church in colonial North Carolina. The reasons for the Church's inability to withstand the shock of the Revolution were the lack of an episcopate, clergy shortage, lack of zeal, indifference of the proprietors and royal governors, and opposition of Nonconformists. Based on material from colonial records; appendix.

E. Oberholzer, Jr.

142. Ervin, S. THE ESTABLISHED CHURCH IN MARYLAND. *Hist. Mag. of the Protestant Episcopal Church 1955 24(3): 232-292.* Though mainly concerned with the colonial period, also treats the years from 1776 to about 1810. The Revolution had a disastrous effect on the Church, partly because of its dependence in the colonial period on secular authorities. Discusses the creation and early legislation of the Diocese of Maryland and shows the interaction of civil and ecclesiastical legislation, with special reference to the Vestry Act of 1779 and its amendments.

E. Oberholzer, Jr.

143. Foster, Stephen. A CONNECTICUT SEPARATE CHURCH: STRICT CONGREGATIONALISM IN CORNWALL, 1780-1809. *New England Q. 1966 39(3): 309-333.* Discusses the schism within the First Congregational Church of Cornwall, Connecticut, during the years 1780-1809, a situation similar to that of a number of towns in the State. Religion itself was not really one of the various issues between the Reverend Hezekiah Gold and the Litchfield Consociation, the ecclesiastical establishment for the county, on the one hand and the people of Cornwall on the other. Though certain of Gold's theological points and his lackluster performance dismayed the townspeople, the dispute began over money. During the Revolution soaring taxes worked financial hardship upon the town; the citizens wished to discontinue the salary to their already wealthy minister and subsequently to remove him altogether. These unfulfilled demands

led to the establishment of an independent and separate congregation. The economic dispute had become a political one, and efforts to unite the two churches failed, ultimately resulting in a geographical division of the town into two ecclesiastical societies. Based on various state and local records, printed sources, and secondary works; 83 notes.   W. G. Morgan

144. Fox, Dixon Ryan, ed. MINUTES OF THE PRESBYTERY OF NEW YORK, 1775-1776. *New York Hist. 1969 50(4): Supplement, 22-43.* The Presbyterian church was particularly strong in the middle colonies. Democratic in organization, fearing Episcopal control, and drawing support from the middle class, it was an early advocate of American independence. The minutes of the New York Presbytery, reproduced from the scarce first issue of the *Quarterly Journal of the New York State Historical Association* (October 1919), documents the church's reaction to the coming of the American Revolution. Based on primary and secondary sources; 39 notes.   G. Kurland

145. Govan, Thomas P. THE HISTORIAN AS PARTISAN, PROSECUTOR, AND JUDGE. *Hist. Mag. of the Protestant Episcopal Church 1963 32(1): 49-56.* Refutes the thesis advanced by Carl Bridenbaugh, in *Mitre and Sceptre* (New York: Oxford U. Press, 1962), that the question of the American episcopate was "a fundamental cause of the American Revolution." The author notes that Bridenbaugh overlooks the fact that non-episcopal churches also engaged in religious persecution and falsely identifies religious freedom with republicanism. "Condemning here and giving absolution there," Bridenbaugh "stands the risk of being 'generally devoid of historical sense.' "   E. Oberholzer, Jr.

146. Hanley, Thomas O'Brien. THE STATE AND DISSENTERS IN THE REVOLUTION. *Maryland Hist. Mag. 1963 58(4): 325-332.* "The current state of scholarship points to one clear area where conscience was very much alive during the Revolution. Such pacifists as the Quakers provide the more striking instances. Others had a much more complex adjustment of principles to make." The Maryland Assembly established in 1775 the right of religious dissent. The author confines his study to Maryland.   W. L. Fox

147. James, Sydney V. THE IMPACT OF THE AMERICAN REVOLUTION ON QUAKERS' IDEAS ABOUT THEIR SECT. *William and Mary Q. 1962 19(3): 360-382.* An examination of changing doctrines of the church in Quakerism. The creation of state governments and the coming of loyalty oaths, conscription, and arbitrary anti-Quaker legislation raised problems of conscience unknown before the Revolution and resulted in greater discipline of members and greater uniformity among the meetings. After the war, which they saw as a punishment for slavery and drunkenness, the Quakers, giving up the principle of separation from society at large, became active in social reforms and politics.
                                                                    E. Oberholzer, Jr.

148. Mackie, Alexander. GEORGE DUFFIELD, REVOLUTIONARY PATRIOT. *J. of the Presbyterian Hist. Soc. 1955 33(1): 3-22.* Describes the life of

the Reverend George Duffield (1732-90), Presbyterian pastor. Duffield actively supported American independence and was appointed chaplain of the Continental Congress in 1776. Based on church records and published sources.   S

149. McLoughlin, William G. ESSAY REVIEW: THE AMERICAN REVOLUTION AS A RELIGIOUS REVIVAL: "THE MILLENNIUM IN ONE COUNTRY." *New England Q. 1967 40(1): 99-110.* In reviewing Alan Heimert's *Religion and the American Mind from the Great Awakening to the Revolution* (Cambridge: Harvard U. Press, 1966), agreement is expressed with the central theme that evangelical Protestantism of the Great Awakening provided the radical American nationalism that prompted the Revolution. Awakening preachers sought to review God's covenant with America and to repudiate the materialistic, acquisitive, corrupt world of an affluent colonial society. The source of this corruption lay in England, and a severance of the ties with the mother country would result in a rededication of America to the making of God's Kingdom. However, Heimert is criticized for not recognizing the differences between educated and uneducated evangelists, and for not recognizing the significance of Separate-Baptists and Methodists. The reviewer also sees evangelicals as representing a distinctive pietistic quality constantly reaffirmed in American history.
K. B. West

150. Mixon, Harold D. BOSTON'S ARTILLERY ELECTION SERMONS AND THE AMERICAN REVOLUTION. *Speech Monographs 1967 34(1): 43-50.* An examination of the contribution to the revolutionary spirit of 47 sermons presented (between 1672 and 1774) on "artillery election day" to the Ancient and Honorable Artillery Company of Boston. The author concludes, contrary to the opinion of Justin Winsor in *The Memorial History of Boston* (1880-81), that these particular sermons were guarded and often vague in reference to ideas of revolutionary import and thus precluded any significant contribution to the fomenting of revolutionary spirit. 45 notes.
D. R. Richardson

151. Morgan, Edmund S. THE PURITAN ETHIC AND THE AMERICAN REVOLUTION. *William and Mary Q. 1967 24(1): 3-43.* Contains a discussion of the meaning of "Puritan Ethic." Though not causative, Puritan ideas influenced policies and the overall understanding of the American patriots. The sense of austerity, mission, morality, and constitutionality in events leading up to and during the war are treated. Party divisions during the war are cited as varying degrees of embracing the "Puritan Ethic." Also commented on is the Puritan contribution in economic theory on framing the Constitution.
H. M. Ward

152. Nichols, John Hastings. JOHN WITHERSPOON ON CHURCH AND STATE. *J. of Presbyterian Hist. 1964 42(3): 166-174.* No other American clergyman was more conspicuous or influential in public affairs in the Revolutionary years and immediately thereafter than Witherspoon. President of the College of New Jersey, Witherspoon also served in the New Jersey Legislature and the Continental Congress, and was a signer of the Declaration of Independence. In

his lectures to students, Witherspoon showed himself "in all essentials an exponent of John Locke's views on government and toleration." When the American Presbyterian Church was organized in 1786, Witherspoon apparently drafted the preface to the new *Form of Government*. In it he asserted the universal inalienable right of private judgment in religion and repudiated special aid to churches by civil power. In so doing he was reaffirming the position taken by the colonial Presbyterian Church in 1729 in adopting the Westminster Confession of Faith with a declaratory statement rejecting any control by civil magistrates over the synods and any power in the civil government "to persecute any for their religion." The primary concern of Witherspoon and the Presbyterian Church was clearly religious liberty; separation of church and state was valued as a means to that end.   W. D. Metz

153. Parramore, Thomas C. JOHN ALEXANDER, ANGLICAN MISSIONARY. *North Carolina Hist. R. 1966 43(3): 305-315.* The Church of England faced numerous obstacles in colonial America and was never able to recruit sufficient priests for the colonies. One North Carolina missionary who survived was John Alexander, a Scotch-Irish Presbyterian who took Anglican orders in 1766. Alexander's difficulties in obtaining ordination; his clashes with dissenters; his battles against poverty, disease, and balky vestries; and his loyalty to Britain during the American Revolution were "all relatively common problems with Anglican clergy." 60 notes.   J. M. Bumsted

154. Sappington, Roger E. NORTH CAROLINA AND THE NON-RESISTANT SECTS DURING THE AMERICAN WAR OF INDEPENDENCE. *Quaker Hist. 1971 60(1): 29-47.* A few Mennonites (including Amish) and more Dunkers or Brethren, Quakers, and Moravians or United Brethren, constituted the nonresistant sects in late 18th-century North Carolina. Moravians were in some ways like the Reformed and Lutheran Germans, but they had been exempt from military service by British statute of 1749. Some scared Indians away with arms and stockades, and some (like some Quakers, who were disowned) served in the militia, but the official Moravian position remained nonresistant. They objected to taking an oath of abjuration because they might have to undertake missions under British rule. The 1779 legislature adopted a way of affirming loyalty which satisfied Moravians and Brethren. All peace groups paid triple taxes or fines in lieu of military service, but Quakers, to whom the 1779 law was unsatisfactory, paid fourfold and sometimes sevenfold fines by distraint. Mennonites behaved like Friends on these issues. Dunkers had been massacred in the French and Indian War. They would not pay for substitutes nor resist military tax collection by distraint, but they had no scruples about oath-taking. The legislature showed tolerance, respect for useful citizens, and restraint in dealing, though tardily, with these nonconformists.   T. D. S. Bassett

155. Sappington, Roger E. TWO EIGHTEENTH CENTURY DUNKER CONGREGATIONS IN NORTH CAROLINA. *North Carolina Hist. R. 1970 47(2): 176-204.* By 1800, the Dunkers (Church of the Brethren) had established six settlements in North Carolina. Two survived to the 20th century. The oldest is the Fraternity Church of the Brethren, six miles southwest of Winston-Salem.

The congregation was founded in 1775 by Jehu Burkhart. Many problems beset this early community, especially the American Revolution. As pacifists the Dunkers refused to participate on either side. Generally, North Carolina officials took a tolerant attitude, exempting Dunkers from service on the payment of a 25-pound fine. Treatment here was much more lenient than in States with a larger number of these people. The major reason for the church's survival was the strong leadership provided by Jacob Pfau and his son Isaac until 1835. Other problems which beset the Fraternity were emigration of leaders westward, discord with the Moravians, and more prominently, a threat from the tenets of Universalism. To prove its potency, Universalism permanently destroyed thriving Dunker congregations in South Carolina. Naturally, acceptance of this heresy by a Dunker elder, John Ham, aroused anxiety. Ham was eventually excommunicated. Pfau succeeded in keeping the congregation loyal to accepted doctrines. The second surviving Dunker congregation is a remnant of early westward migration. A group of Dunker emigrants stopped at the New River in Wilkes County in western North Carolina. Surviving difficulties of birth, the congregation is today the Flat Rock Church of the Church of the Brethren. Four other Dunker congregations broke up due to emigration, death of leaders, and absorption into other churches. Fraternity and Flat Rock made possible the permanence of the Dunkers in North Carolina. H. M. Rosen

156. Schattschneider, A. W. THE MORAVIAN CHURCH AT NEW DORP, STATEN ISLAND, NEW YORK. *Moravian Hist. Soc. Trans. 1965 20(pt. 1): 197-225.* Explores the life of the New Dorp congregation from 1742, when David Bruce (the Moravian evangelist for New York City) preached his first sermon on Staten Island, to 1962 when Charles Adams was installed as pastor. Generous quotes from church records refer to early members and clergy as well as to episcopal visits. The role of the Moravian Church in the American Revolution and the development of the physical aspects of the New Dorp church and cemetery are discussed. J. G. Pennington

157. Sengel, William R. REBELLION IN THE MEETING HOUSE. *Virginia Cavalcade 1964 14(1): 34-39.* An account of the agitation for independence by members of the Old Presbyterian Meeting House in Alexandria, Virginia. It is based largely on the diary of Nicholas Cresswell (New York: Dial Press, 1924), an Englishman who lived in Virginia from 1774 to 1777. Illus.
R. B. Lange

158. Smylie, James H. PRESBYTERIAN CLERGY AND PROBLEMS OF "DOMINION" IN THE REVOLUTIONARY GENERATION. *J. of Presbyterian Hist. 1970 48(3): 161-175.* Discusses the theme of dominion as it was understood in the revolutionary generation. Beginning with Bernard Bailyn's definition of the term in *The Ideological Origins of the American Revolution* (Cambridge, Mass.: Harvard U. Press, 1967), the author argues that "dominion" incorporated theological connotations and interpretations. Presbyterians and other religious groups contributed substantially to the development of revolutionary and constitutional principles by their construction and application of the term "dominion." The concept of dominion, as used by Presbyterians, embodied four

dimensions. The first was expressed by John Witherspoon in "The Dominions of Providence Over the Passions of Men" in which he argued that a supreme power was irresistible unless it operated in a tyrannical fashion. Under such circumstances an attempt might be made to overthrow the power, with God determining the outcome. A second meaning of dominion appeared in the Westminster Confession's statement that no man is equal to or above God and that political dominion must be exercised to thwart human aspirations to attain Godlike status. Another dimension is revealed in the Confession's conception of God as the lord of conscience. A balance between church and state preserving liberty of conscience was therefore required. Finally, dominion was seen as a judgment by God which required a special mission for the people of the United States. God was understood to have a plan for America and was expected to judge Americans in terms of their success or failure in implementing God's plan. The author concludes with a call for further research into theological contributions to the thought and history of the revolutionary era. Based largely on secondary sources; 56 notes.   S. C. Pearson, Jr.

159. Stokes, Durward T. HENRY PATTILLO IN NORTH CAROLINA. *North Carolina Hist. R. 1967 44(4): 373-391.* Biographical sketch of the life of one of the outstanding religious leaders in 18th-century North Carolina. Pattillo was born in Scotland in 1726, came to Virginia in 1740, studied for the Presbyterian ministry with the "venerable Samuel Davis" and was ordained in 1758 following a series of careful examinations of his learning and orthodoxy. He soon moved to North Carolina where he spent the remainder of his life. Pattillo supported the Revolution, although he had opposed the Regulator movement; he even served as a delegate to the first Provincial Congress in 1775. In later years he wrote a *Geographical Catechism* and published collected sermons (which supported Christian unity and Calvinism while opposing Deism). He was an ardent American nationalist, arguing that American independence "has, to a vast extent of continent, secured those civil and religious liberties, which are unknown in any other part of the globe." 86 notes.   J. M. Bumsted

160. —. [THE REVEREND PRICE DAVIES]. *Virginia Mag. of Hist. and Biog. 1971 79(2): 153-166.*
   Evans, Sir David. PRICE DAVIES, RECTOR OF BLISLAND PARISH: TWO LETTERS, 1763, 1765, pp. 153-161. Reprints for the first time letters from Davies, whose parish was on the York River near Williamsburg, to the Reverend William Conway at Stoughton. They are the only documents of American origin in the Wigfair Collection of manuscripts in the National Library of Wales at Aberystwyth. Includes a biographical introduction. 16 notes.
   Jennings, John Melville. FURTHER NOTES ON THE REVEREND PRICE DAVIES, pp. 162-166. Comments particularly on Davies' economic and social success, suggesting that his patriotism during the Revolution came readily for reasons not all political. 24 notes.   C. A. Newton

Economic Considerations

161. Bowman, Larry G. THE SCARCITY OF SALT IN VIRGINIA DURING THE AMERICAN REVOLUTION. *Virginia Mag. of Hist. and Biog. 1969 77(4): 464-472.* Records in detail the largely unsuccessful efforts of Virginia to cope with the wartime salt crisis. Prices soared as salt became scarce, and efforts on the part of the Continental Congress to relieve the shortage fell pitiably short: so too did attempts to evaporate the saline water of the Chesapeake Bay, to exploit privately owned salt works, or to stimulate importation by the payment of bounties. By 1779 the state assumed control over all salt privately imported, but regulation produced no discernible increase in the salt supply. However, the paradox of government control in a revolution to abolish British imperial orders indicates the pragmatic quality of the Revolution. Notes.   C. A. Newton

162. Coleman, Elizabeth Dabney. GUNS FOR INDEPENDENCE. *Virginia Cavalcade 1963 13(3): 40-47.* An account of the activities of Fielding Lewis and Charles Dick to keep the State Manufactory of Arms in Fredericksburg, Virginia operating during the Revolutionary War. Undocumented.   R. B. Lange

163. Evans, Emory G. PRIVATE INDEBTEDNESS AND THE REVOLUTION IN VIRGINIA, 1776 TO 1796. *William and Mary Q. 1971 28(3): 349-374.* How to deal with debts due British subjects was a divisive issue in Virginia. The act for sequestering British property permitted Virginians to discharge debts to British merchants by paying depreciated currency to the loan office; but very few did. Examines arguments, and the persons involved, for and against payment of the debts. War damage, British refusal to return slaves, the scarcity of money, and economic depression all contributed to postponement of settlement with British creditors. Analyzes votes in the legislature in reference to legislators' occupations and districts. Relates the issue to sides taken at the time of the ratification of the Constitution. Mentions final success in payment of the debts. 48 notes.   H. M. Ward

164. Ferguson, E. James. BUSINESS, GOVERNMENT, AND CONGRESSIONAL INVESTIGATION IN THE REVOLUTION. *William and Mary Q. 1959 16(3): 293-318.* A study of profiteering by public officials during the Revolution. As de facto manager of foreign procurement, Robert Morris diverted large sums to his own purposes, and most of the agents of the Committee of Trade were in commercial alliance with Morris. Silas Deane's indiscretions were but a part of the common practice. Other figures discussed included William Bingham, Benedict Arnold, Nathanael Greene and Jeremiah Wadsworth. The rise of Congressional investigations beginning in 1778 led to large-scale resignations. The underlying problem was the lack of distinction between public and private functions and the merger of the two in the same persons.
E. Oberholzer, Jr.

165. Graewe, Richard. THE AMERICAN REVOLUTION COMES TO HANNOVER. *William and Mary Q. 1963 20(2): 246-250.* From records in the Saxon archives at Hannover, concludes that "North German trade rose tremendously during the American Revolution" in spite of George III's efforts to cut off trade with the colonies. E. Oberholzer, Jr.

166. Hecht, Arthur. LEAD PRODUCTION IN VIRGINIA DURING THE SEVENTEENTH AND EIGHTEENTH CENTURIES. *West Virginia Hist. 1964 25(3): 173-183.* Traces lead production in Virginia from its earliest discovery near Jamestown through the 18th century. Mining in Virginia was of little importance during most of the period because individuals with investment capital regarded such a venture as less respectable than agriculture. The American Revolution increased the need for lead and caused the governor to promote its production. After the Revolution the Virginia mines continued to produce for several years, but by 1796 Moses Austin found them no longer productive. Based largely on previously published sources. D. N. Brown

167. Herndon, G. Melvin. A WAR-INSPIRED INDUSTRY: THE MANUFACTURE OF HEMP IN VIRGINIA DURING THE REVOLUTION. *Virginia Mag. of Hist. and Biog. 1966 74(3): 301-311.* While hemp was a major crop in the Valley of Virginia before the Revolution and some weaving had been carried on, it remained for the nonimportation agreements and the war to bring about a rapid development of linen weaving. Many factories and ropewalks operated in Virginia during the Revolution but most closed after the war as the production of flax and hemp ceased, except in the valley. Based on printed and manuscript sources. 75 notes. K. J. Bauer

168. Hollowell, M. Edgar, Jr. THE POINT OF FORK ARSENAL. *Military Collector and Historian 1970 22(1): 11-13.* Located about 45 miles from Richmond, the Point of Fork Arsenal served as a major producer and distributor of war material to the Continental Army and the Virginia militia. Destroyed in 1781, the arsenal resumed operations and was able to produce siege equipment for use at Yorktown and later to serve as a depot for military supplies needed on the frontier. D. C. Oliver

169. Mason, Bernard. ENTREPRENEURIAL ACTIVITY IN NEW YORK DURING THE AMERICAN REVOLUTION. *Business Hist. R. 1966 40(2): 190-212.* Many businessmen in New York benefited from the American Revolution. Extensive expenditures by the Continental Army and the state government provided most of the new business. The export of agricultural products to neighboring states, illegal trade with the British, and privateering also played a part in increasing business for the merchants and landowners. J. H. Krenkel

170. Reynolds, Donald E. AMMUNITION SUPPLY IN REVOLUTIONARY VIRGINIA. *Virginia Mag. of Hist. and Biog. 1965 73(1): 56-77.* After failing in efforts to produce gunpowder domestically in 1775-76, Virginia successfully turned to foreign sources. Since she possessed sizable lead mines, the state had

relatively little problem with its supply. Nevertheless, Virginia had difficulties meeting all the demands on her for munitions during the Southern campaigns of 1778-81, particularly after Benedict Arnold's January 1781 raid on Richmond. Based on printed documents.   K. J. Bauer

171. —. [THE AMERICAN REVOLUTION AND AMERICAN AGRICUL-TURE]. *Agric. Hist. 1969 43(1): 107-127.*
     Jensen, Merrill. THE AMERICAN REVOLUTION AND AMERICAN AGRICULTURE, pp. 107-124. Most economic histories of the Revolutionary era distort the picture by giving insufficient attention to agriculture. Colonial exports were primarily products of farms, forests, and the sea. This pattern continued after the war, though some crops, such as indigo, became unimportant. The farmers' economic problems partially determined state financial policy in the post-Revolutionary period and were a factor in the adoption of the Constitution. Based on published sources; table, 20 notes.
     Rasmussen, Wayne D. THE AMERICAN REVOLUTION AND AMERICAN AGRICULTURE: A COMMENT, pp. 125-127. Agrees with Jensen's conclusions. British land policy created resentment among farmers and was a factor in the Revolution. The Revolution brought few changes in American agriculture apart from shifts in trade and a more liberal land policy. There seem to have been no great advances in productivity during or after the war.
                                                                     D. E. Brewster

Military & Naval Affairs

172. Alexander, John K. FORTON PRISON DURING THE AMERICAN REVOLUTION: A CASE STUDY OF BRITISH PRISONER OF WAR POL-ICY AND THE AMERICAN PRISONER RESPONSE TO THAT POLICY. *Essex Inst. Hist. Collections 1967 103(4): 365-389.* Attempts a balanced picture of British prison policy and American response by employing both British official records and American official records and prisoner accounts. Much of the mistreatment of American prisoners was on the prison ships and not in the land prisons. At Forton near Portsmouth, England, the prisoners were generally well-treated and fed, thanks largely to subscriptions among the British populace. The death rate at Forton was fairly low. Nevertheless, the prisoners thought largely of escape or exchange, and disliked their captivity. While more research is needed, "this much is sure: Forton was no Andersonville." 125 notes.
                                                                     J. M. Bumsted

173. Alexander, John K. JONATHAN HASKINS' MILL PRISON *DIARY:* CAN IT BE ACCEPTED AT FACE VALUE? *New England Q. 1967 40(4): 561-564.* Many entries in Haskins' diary, published in the *New England Quarterly* 1944 18(2,3), are almost word-for-word identical with entries in two other diaries: those of Samuel Cutler and Charles Herbert. Internal evidence would

seem to indicate that Haskins plagiarized from Herbert. This does not mean the diary is valueless since at least half of it is not so tainted. However, it must be used with care.   K. B. West

174. Anderson, Olive. AMERICAN ESCAPES FROM BRITISH NAVAL PRISONS DURING THE WAR OF INDEPENDENCE. *Mariner's Mirror [Great Britain] 1955 41(3): 238-240.* The high number of successful escapes by American sailors was not due solely to their audacity, but also the lax way in which they were guarded, and the support they enjoyed from British sympathizers. Moreover, some of the escapes were merely shams, prisoner and guard sharing the reward for recapture. Based on British Admiralty Archives.
                                                                        J. A. S. Grenville

175. Anderson, Olive. THE TREATMENT OF PRISONERS OF WAR IN BRITAIN DURING THE AMERICAN WAR OF INDEPENDENCE. *Bull. of the Inst. of Hist. Res. [Great Britain] 1955 28(77): 63-83.* Shows that despite contemporary and later charges of barbarity, the treatment of prisoners of war was relatively humane. Attributes the enlightened policies to the desire to ensure survival of prisoners for exchange against British prisoners in enemy hands, to the general tendency of administrative reform, and to the humanitarianism of the period. Based on published sources and documents in the Public Record Office, especially the records of the Commissioners for Sick and Hurt Seamen and the Exchange of Prisoners of War.   P. H. Hardacre

176. Baer, Mabel Van Dyke. REVOLUTIONARY WAR PENSION APPLICATIONS; STITES, GLASGOW, BRYAN, CORNELL, DAVIS. *Natl. Geneal. Soc. Q. 1963 51(1): 49-59.* Discusses war pensioners and their service between 1777 and 1782. Lists eight veterans and gives data from their applications —length of service, location of war service, and the officers served under. All pensions were applied for under the Pension Act of 7 June 1832. Undocumented.
                                                                        D. H. Swift

177. Bonnel, Ulane. QUELQUES PUBLICATIONS AMERICAINES RECENTES INTERESSANT L'HISTOIRE NAVALE [Some recent American publications concerning naval history]. *R. d'Hist. Econ. et Sociale [France] 1967 45(1): 119-128.* Discusses 15 recent publications on American maritime history. Works of special importance published by the U.S. Naval History Division in Washington, D.C., are William B. Clark, ed., *Naval Documents of the American Revolution,* vol. 1 (1964); *Dictionary of American Naval Fighting Ships* (2 vols., 1959-1963); and several biographies of American naval commanders. Notable books issued by the U.S. Naval Institute at Annapolis include Carl C. Cutler, *Greyhounds of the Sea; The Story of the American Clipper Ship* (1960); Robert E. Johnson, *Thence Round Cape Horn: The Story of United States Naval Forces on Pacific Station* (1963); Vaughan W. Brown, *Shipping in the Port of Annapolis, 1748-1775* (1965); and Robert H. Rankin, *Uniforms of the Sea Services: A Pictorial History* (1962). 15 notes.   J. R. Vignery

178. Bowers, Ray L., Jr. THE AMERICAN REVOLUTION. A STUDY IN INSURGENCY. *Military R. 1966 46(7): 64-72.* Discusses the American Revolution as an example of insurgency warfare. Drawing implicit parallels with modern-day insurgency and the American experience, discusses extensive use by the Colonies of the propaganda weapon; the counterinsurgency psychology of the British (the Revolution as a test of British determination); partisan warfare techniques; and the use of improvised weapons during the American Revolution. Concludes that these weapons are as difficult to counter now as they were yesterday.   G. E. Snow

179. Brown, Ralph Adams. NAVAL RECORDS OF THE AMERICAN REVOLUTION: AN ESSAY REVIEW. *New York Hist. 1972 53(2): 195-200.* Discusses problems in producing, and describes the contents of, the first five volumes of the *Naval Documents of the American Revolution,* published under the auspices of the Historical Research Section of the Navy Department. Praises the completeness of the series and lauds the editorial and bibliographical skill that went into the production. William Bell Clark edited Volumes I-IV. William James Morgan edited Volume V. 2 notes.   G. Kurland

180. Cary, John. *A CONTRARY WIND AT SEA AND CONTRARY TIMES AT HOME* —THE SEA LOGS OF FRANCIS BOARDMAN. *Essex Inst. Hist. Collections 1965 101(1): 3-26.* Analysis of the sea logs of Francis Boardman of Salem, Massachusetts, covering the years 1763-88 and preserved in the Essex Institute, Massachusetts. The Boardman logs provide much evidence of the lore and knowledge of 18th-century American mariners, including the practical learning, sea chanties, and social amenities. The petty incidents and worries of a captain on long voyages are revealed, as is the monotony of daily life. The logs demonstrate that the "captain of an eighteenth-century merchantman was as much itinerant trader as mariner," especially in the West Indies trade. Boardman was not above smuggling, and he paid little heed to the currents of revolution except when captured by the British in 1775. Documented from unpublished manuscripts in the Essex Institute.   J. M. Bumsted

181. Cometti, Elizabeth. DEPREDATIONS IN VIRGINIA DURING THE REVOLUTION. *The Old Dominion: Essays for Thomas Perkins Abernethy (Charlottesville: The U. Press of Virginia, 1964), pp. 135-151.* Tidewater Virginia was particularly vulnerable to the predatory ships of the enemy. In 1776 Norfolk was destroyed by Governor John Dunmore and his Loyalist followers. Other depredations followed, and in 1781 Benedict Arnold established a British base at Portsmouth from which raids continued. The march of Cornwallis ("the scourge") to Yorktown resulted in losses of three million pounds. Instead of bolstering naval forces to keep the British from landing, those in authority placed too much reliance upon untrained militia. Had a strong executive office not been suspect at the time, governors might have been willing to exceed their limited authority and might have mitigated some of the disasters. 54 notes.
                                                                E. P. Stickney

182. Craighead, Alexander McC. MILITARY ART IN AMERICA, 1750-1914. *Military Collector and Historian 1963 15(2): 35-40, 15(3): 73-79, 1964 16(1): 10-13, (2): 42-45, 1965 17(2): 42-48, and 17(3): 76-80.* Parts I and II discuss 18th- and 19th-century military artists and their work. Part III is concerned with combat artists during the Civil War. Part IV. The work of another type of combat artist in the Civil War—the artist who made sketches at the front and later incorporated them in oil paintings—is discussed. Part V. Concerns such artists and their military works as Archibald M. Willard, *Yankee Doodle,* more commonly known as the Spirit of '76; Cassilly Adams, *Custer's Last Fight, the Battle of the Little Big Horn on June 25, 1876;* Charles Schreyvogel, *My Bunkie;* and Frederic Remington, *Cutting the Lemon, Indians Making Smoke Signals, Troops Guarding Train.* Part VI. Combat artists and their works during the Spanish-American War are discussed. Illus.   C. L. Boyd

183. Hargreaves, Reginald. NORTH AMERICAN TAPESTRY. *Royal United Service Inst. J. [Great Britain] 1964 109(635): 251-252.* A theme of abiding interest to successive generations is the story of Britain's love-hate relationship with her 13 North American colonies, culminating in the War of Independence. In commenting on *The War for America: 1775-1783* by Piers Mackesy (London: Longmans, 1964) it notes that the collapse of the Canada-Hudson-New York strategy recommended by Burgoyne resulted in the entrance of France; analyzes the weakness of the Royal Navy; and regrets the utter lack of firm central control. "In the final analysis independence meant more to the leaders of the revolt than did reconquest and military occupation to the British."   E. P. Stickney

184. Hatch, Charles E., Jr. MEDAL OF HONOR OF THE REVOLUTION. *Virginia Cavalcade 1963 13(2): 14-17.* A history of the Badge of Military Merit (Purple Heart), established by George Washington during the Revolution as an award for "singularly meritorious action." Undocumented.   R. B. Lange

185. Holst, Donald. REGIMENTAL COLORS OF THE CONTINENTAL ARMY. *Military Collector and Historian 1968 20(3): 69-73.* Attempts to establish the system of regimental flags used by the Continental Army. The author concludes that the most common practice involved carrying three or more stands of colors per regiment. It is not clear just how widespread the custom was, but it is possible to suggest the general pattern of these standards. 3 illus., 24 notes.   D. C. Oliver

186. Jenrich, Charles H. THE OLD *JERSEY* PRISON SHIP. *U.S. Naval Inst. Pro. 1963 89(2): 168-171.* Description of the inhumane conditions on board the British prison hulk *Jersey* in New York harbor during the American Revolution. Undocumented.   W. C. Frank

187. Kennedy, William V. L'ARMEE AMERICAINE [The American Army]. *Etudes [France] 1964 321(November): 507-524.* Examines the extent and the nature of the influence of the military on American life. The author gives a brief history of the American Army since the Battle of Louisbourg (Nova Scotia) in

1745, and concludes that the experience of the colonial period and of the War for Independence permanently fixed the idea that persuasion, rather than authoritarianism, was the key to success in commanding American troops. The author looks at the later arguments for a Prussian-style military establishment in America and examines the role of the various branches of the services.

R. I. Giesberg

188. Leach, MacEdward. NOTES ON AMERICAN SHIPPING BASED ON RECORDS OF THE COURT OF THE VICE-ADMIRALTY OF JAMAICA, 1776-1812. *Am. Neptune 1960 20(1): 44-48.* Draws attention to the records of the Court of the Vice-Admiralty in Jamaica, housed in the Public Archives at Spanish Town for the years just preceding and following the American Revolution. Of major interest are the papers of vessels seized during the Revolution and before the War of 1812. These papers consist of ships' logs, commissions, manifests, registry documents, and business and personal letters. The testimony of American and British officers also on file here contains much important information bearing on the time.

A

189. Lutz, Paul V. A STATE'S CONCERN FOR THE SOLDIERS' WELFARE: HOW NORTH CAROLINA PROVIDED FOR HER TROOPS DURING THE REVOLUTION. *North Carolina Hist. R. 1965 42(3): 315-318.* North Carolina provided well for her troops in the American Revolution. They received cash bounties, after 1780 a slave "or the value thereof," clothing, food, and land (after 1782 from 640 to 1,200 acres depending on rank). The State attempted to mitigate against inflation in its compensation by valuing paper money in relation to specie. 11 notes.

J. M. Bumsted

190. Lutz, Paul V. HISTORY DEPICTED BY COMMISSIONS. *Manuscripts 1965 17(2): 27-32.* Four New England commissions of the Revolutionary War are illustrated on these pages. They are for officers who fought on behalf of New Hampshire, Massachusetts, Vermont, and Great Britain. A fifth commission from the State of Connecticut, dated after the Revolution, is discussed, but not shown. The author outlines a brief story of each of these items and he demonstrates the fun a collector can have in studying and researching his material. Illus.

C. J. Allard

191. Lutz, Paul V. LAND GRANTS FOR SERVICE IN THE REVOLUTION. *New-York Hist. Soc. Q. 1964 48(3): 221-235.* Both the states and the Continental Congress had programs to reward service during the Revolutionary War; however, unlike 20th-century wars, the reward usually was made as an inducement to enlistment. Both cash and land grants were used. The efforts of the states and Congress in the use of land grants, generous in view of then current conditions, are described in some detail.

C. L. Grant

192. Lutz, Paul V. THE OATH OF ABSOLUTION. *Georgia Hist. Q. 1969 53(3): 330-334.* Describes a document in the author's collection which contains a petition sent by an American prisoner of war to Gen. Anthony Wayne. The

prisoner appealed for release, claiming that the British had forced him to serve with them. The author contends that the Revolution placed innumerable Americans in the similar position of taking false oaths of loyalty, even double oaths, under compulsion. Based on secondary sources; 9 notes.   R. A. Mohl

193. Martin, Joseph Plumb. PRIVATE YANKEE DOODLE. *Am. Heritage 1962 13(3): 33-48.* A contemporary account by a private in the American Revolutionary Army recorded and published in 1830. This is a selection from the edition which George F. Scheer edited and republished, and deals with a variety of military episodes and anecdotes.   C. R. Allen, Jr.

194. Maurer, Maurer. MILITARY JUSTICE UNDER GENERAL WASHINGTON. *Military Affairs 1964 28(1): 8-16.* Military law was "one of the most powerful instruments available to Washington for establishing and maintaining discipline." The article discusses procedures under the Continental Articles of War and the punishments inflicted.   K. J. Bauer

195. McCusker, John J., Jr. THE CONTINENTAL SHIP *ALFRED. Nautical Res. J. 1965 13(2/3): 37-68.* Attempts to gather all the extant information about this merchant ship (formerly known as the *Black Prince* of Philadelphia) which the Continental Congress purchased and converted into the flagship of the first American fleet. The author estimates the ship's dimensions using a comparative method based on tonnage and discusses the contemporary comments on sailing qualities. Several drawings and paintings which are supposed to represent this ship are evaluated with the conclusion that they are all inaccurate. Based on a wide range of archival sources, both British and American. Illustrations include three 18th-century ship plans and a drawing of the *Alfred* based on the author's conclusions done by naval artist Phillips Melville.   A

196. McMaster, Fitzhugh. ST. HELENA VOLUNTEERS, SOUTH CAROLINA MILITIA. *Military Collector and Historian 1965 17(3): 92-93.* Describes the dress of this early Revolutionary force. The South Carolina Council of Safety approved the formation of the St. Helena Volunteer Company of Militia on 20 October 1775. The dress included a beaver cap with a silver crescent on which were the words, "Liberty or Death." Illus., 10 notes.   C. L. Boyd

197. Morgan, Madel. MISSISSIPPI STATE AUDITOR'S WARRANTS ISSUED TO REVOLUTIONARY WAR PENSIONERS. *J. of Mississippi Hist. 1970 32(1): 75-80.* In 1839 Mississippi "granted to soldiers of the American Revolution residing within the state who were not on the U.S. pension rolls a pension of one hundred dollars per annum," and also exempted them from State and county taxes. The author reprints data regarding warrants issued to 12 individuals during the period 1839-48. During the years 1843-50 the State paid out more than ten thousand dollars to Revolutionary soldiers. Based on materials deposited in the Mississippi Department of Archives and History.
          J. W. Hillje

198. Morton, Louis. THE ORIGINS OF AMERICAN MILITARY POLICY. *Military Affairs 1958 22(2): 75-82.* Describes the formation and development of colonial militia, particularly in Massachusetts and Virginia.   K. J. Bauer

199. Owen, Lewis F. THE TOWN THAT WAS ROBBED. *New Jersey Hist. Soc. Pro. 1963 81(3): 164-180.* Though a vital post during the Revolutionary War, the name Snedens Landing will not be in the records of the Revolutionary War. Known to the army as "Dobbs Ferry on the west side of the Hudson," it was later named Rockland and is now called Palisades. "It saw the grimmest days of '76 and at the end was chosen to witness the symbolic end of the entire conflict." Its history goes back to 1687. In 1776 when Washington tried in vain to close the Hudson to the British, cannon were mounted at both ends of the ferry crossing, and it was abandoned to the British. By 1782 Snedens Landing was Washington's intelligence center and there occurred the first British salute to our colors. Beginning in 1830 the railroads began to siphon off its chief excuse for existence. Documented.   E. P. Stickney

200. Parramore, Thomas C. THE GREAT ESCAPE FROM FORTEN GAOL: AN INCIDENT OF THE REVOLUTION. *North Carolina Hist. R. 1968 45(4): 349-356.* One of the major escape attempts from Britain's Forten Gaol (a military prison) during the American Revolution was led by officers and men from the brig *Fair American.* 40 notes.   J. M. Bumsted

201. Peterson, Harold L. WEAPONS OF THE REVOLUTIONARY WAR. *Am. Hist. Illus. 1968 2(10): 27-46.* Discusses shoulder weapons and guns used by the Continental Army during the Revolutionary War. There was no such thing as a single standard weapon. However, "of all the types of individual firearms, the musket was by far the most important." Americans used the British musket, the Brown Bess, particularly during the beginning of the war. One reason for this was that "Americans had grown familiar with the British arms during the colonial period." Other types of weapons were musketoons, carbines, rifles, fusils, pistols, and wall guns. Excerpted from the author's *The Book Of The Continental Soldier* (Harrisburg, Pa.: Stackpole Books, 1968). 17 illus.   R. V. McBaine

202. Salisbury, William. JOHN PAUL JONES AND HIS SHIPS: THE NEED FOR MORE RESEARCH. *Am. Neptune 1968 28(3): 195-205.* Discusses American naval vessels during the Revolutionary period. The author calls for additional research not simply of naval encounters themselves but of the ships which fought them. Specifications of individual ships are presented. Note.   M. Svanevik

203. Shy, John W. A NEW LOOK AT THE COLONIAL MILITIA. *William and Mary Q. 1963 20(2): 175-185.* Suggests that the militia, usually considered a static institution, "varied from province to province" and with time. Concentrating on Massachusetts and Virginia, the author shows how environmental differences and changed conditions affected the militia. With the decline of the Indian danger, the militia also declined. In the 18th century, the militia had more social than military significance.   E. Oberholzer, Jr.

204. Small, Edwin W. SALEM MARITIME NATIONAL HISTORIC SITE: A PHYSICAL REMINDER OF DEPARTED SEAFARING GLORY. *New England Social Studies Bull. 1955 12(4): 7-14, 27.* Describes the Salem, Massachusetts, Maritime National Historic Site and the part played by Salem as a center of seafaring activity in the late colonial, Revolutionary, and early national periods. During the Revolution, it was important mainly for the privateering activity of such merchants as Elias Hasket Derby. The heyday of Salem's world trade was just before the Embargo and the War of 1812, when 126 vessels engaged in deep-sea shipping made it their home port. When the size of vessels began to increase after the War of 1812, the port gradually lost its importance as it could not accommodate vessels drawing over 12 feet.   W. D. Metz

205. Stowe, Gerald C. and Weller, Jac. REVOLUTIONARY WEST POINT: "THE KEY TO THE CONTINENT." *Military Affairs 19(2): 81-98.* A discussion of the strategic importance of the defenses of the Highlands centering on West Point from 1775 to 1783. Attention is also given to the strategic use of this position by Washington.   G. J. Stansfield

206. Unsigned. A TREASURY OF EARLY SUBMARINES (1775-1903). *U.S. Naval Inst. Pro. 1967 93(5): 97-114.* Pictorial essay describing the development of the submarine during its earliest experimental stage, 1775-1903. Designs and craft from France, the Netherlands, Spain, Sweden, and the United States are shown. 33 illus. and plans with captions. Undocumented.   W. C. Frank

207. Unsigned. NAVAL ACTION IN THE AMERICAN REVOLUTION. *U.S. Naval Inst. Pro. 1955 81(2): 204-211, (4): 444-451, and (6): 688-695.* Reproductions of watercolors, depicting naval action in the Revolutionary War, from the Bailey Collection of the Mariners' Museum, Newport News, Virginia. The artist may have been Charles Turner Warren (1767-1823) or his son, Alfred William Warren.   H. M. Madden

208. Wheeler, E. Milton. DEVELOPMENT AND ORGANIZATION OF THE NORTH CAROLINA MILITIA. *North Carolina Hist. R. 1964 41(3): 307-323.* Reviews development of the militia system from the Carolina Charter of 1663 through the American Revolution. The institution developed in trial and error response to various exigencies of the 18th century, notably Indian attacks and the wars with France and Great Britain. Detailed treatment, particularly of the militia acts of 1715, 1756, and the Revolutionary period, is based on published colonial and state records.   L. R. Harlan

209. White, Joseph. THE GOOD SOLDIER WHITE. *Am. Heritage 1956 7(4): 74-79.* A reproduction of a pamphlet written and printed by White, *A Narrative of Events as They Occurred from Time to Time in the Revolutionary War...* (Charlestown, Massachusetts, 1833). This pamphlet is a contemporary account of experiences in General George Washington's army, 1775-77, and includes

specific accounts of the Battle of Trenton and the Battle of Princeton. The author also notes experiences under General Anthony Wayne and General Israel Putnam.   C. R. Allen, Jr.

210. Zlatich, Marko. NEWSPAPER EXTRACTS DESCRIBING MILITARY AND NAVAL DRESS OF THE AMERICAN REVOLUTIONARY WAR, 1775-1783. *Military Collector and Historian 1969 21(3): 69-79, 21(4): 116-120.* Part I. Supplements and corrects Charles M. Leffert's *Uniforms of the American, British, French and German Armies in the War of the American Revolution* with deserter descriptions published in American newspapers. The article covers the Continental army and navy, as well as the Connecticut, Maryland, Massachusetts, and New York regiments and naval units. 7 notes. Part II. Describes dress of the Pennsylvania Armed Boats, Philadelphia Associators, Virginia Regiments of the Continental Line, French navy and marines, British army, British navy and marines, Loyalists forces, and German mercenaries. 10 notes.

D. C. Oliver and D. J. Engler

Foreign Relations & Attitudes

211. Baker, Donald S. CHARLES WESLEY AND THE AMERICAN WAR OF INDEPENDENCE. *Methodist Hist. 1966 5(1): 5-37.* Charles Wesley believed that the Christian had responsibilities for obedience before he had rights of individual judgment. He was sympathetic to the American Loyalists and critical of the conduct of the war by Sir William Howe. His views were colored by his predominant high church Toryism and his fanatical adherence to the person of the king. To him the peace settlement in 1783 was a calamity from which Britain would not or could not ever recover. To illustrate Wesley's views on the war and the peace settlement, the author quotes verses from two Wesley manuscripts, "Hymns and Verses on Modern Patriotism, & the American Rebellion and Independency Miscellaneous Poems" and "The American War under the Conduct of Sir William Howe." 45 notes.   H. L. Calkin

212. Baker, Donald S. CHARLES WESLEY AND THE AMERICAN WAR OF INDEPENDENCE. *Pro. of the Wesley Hist. Soc. [Great Britain] 1964 34(7): 159-164.* Examines the attitudes of Charles Wesley (1707-88) to the American War of Independence and summarizes the events. Stresses Wesley's poems "The American War under the conduct of Sir William Howe" and "Hymns and Verses on Modern Patriotism and the American Rebellion and Independency, Miscellaneous Poems." To Wesley the war was not war but rebellion against God personified or rather symbolized by George III, and he strongly attacked the conduct of British Commander-in-Chief Sir William Howe. Wesley regarded the peace of 1783 as a catastrophe and condemned it as the final blasphemy of British politics.

L. Brown

213. Ballesteros Gaibrois, Manuel. PARTICIPACION DE ESPAÑA EN LA INDEPENDENCIA DE ESTADOS UNIDOS [Spain's participation in the independence of the United States]. *R. Cubana [Cuba] 1957 31(3/4): 29-48.* Deals with: European politics before the War of Independence; the military and diplomatic aspects of the war; French aid; Spanish economic, military and diplomatic aid, relations between Spain and the United States after the War of Independence; and the influence of the war on the Spanish American colonies.

B. T. (IHE 27879)

214. Barton, H. A. SWEDEN AND THE WAR OF AMERICAN INDEPENDENCE. *William and Mary Q. 1966 23(3): 408-430.* Swedish reaction to the American Revolution was mixed. Backers of the crown considered the war a usurpation of legitimate authority. Opponents of the king, and men of the Enlightenment thought that the American cause was a stroke for liberty. Nonideological reasons also accounted for support: Sweden's pro-French alliance, continental resentment of Britain, and the opportunity afforded to merchants to trade with anti-British powers. A number of Swedes fought for American independence. Discusses the League of Armed Neutrality and the effects of the war upon Swedish politics.

H. Ward

215. Bennett, Nolan J. A BRITISH EDITOR REPORTS ON THE AMERICAN REVOLUTION WITH CURIOUS SIDELIGHTS ON BENJAMIN FRANKLIN. *Pennsylvania Mag. of Hist. and Biog. 1956 80(1): 92-112.* Excerpts from the files of a provincial English newspaper.

D. Houston

216. Crick, Bernard R. SECOND LIST OF ADDENDA TO A GUIDE TO MANUSCRIPTS RELATING TO AMERICA IN GREAT BRITAIN AND IRELAND. *Bull. of the British Assoc. for Am. Studies 1963 (7): 55-64.* An annotated list of additional holdings in 34 libraries, record offices, and private collections. Although there are a few references to Canada and the West Indies, almost all the material deals with the 13 colonies and the United States and dates from the 18th and 19th centuries. A wide variety of political, economic, and cultural topics is covered by the letters, diaries, business documents, and other manuscripts. Many of the items are of value for the period of the American Revolution. The Acts of Court of the Mercers' Company, however, begin in 1453 and "contain such things as orders made for the investment in money in the early 17th century Virginia ventures." This list follows the one published in the *Bulletin* 1962 (5).

D. J. Abramoske

217. Crick, Bernard R. THIRD LIST OF ADDENDA TO "GUIDE TO MANUSCRIPTS RELATING TO AMERICA IN GREAT BRITAIN AND IRELAND." *British Assoc. for Am. Studies Bull. [Great Britain] 1966 (12/13): 61-77.* An annotated list of manuscripts in private and public archives of England, Wales, Scotland, and Northern Ireland. A wide variety of political, economic, and cultural topics are covered by the letters, diaries, business records, military papers, and other documents. Although there are references to Canada, most of the material deals with the Thirteen Colonies and the United States and dates from the 17th through the 19th centuries. Some 20th-century documents

are also listed. The final item in the guide is an extensive list of emigrant letters and records found in a variety of collections. Previous lists of addenda were published in the *Bulletin,* New Series, Nos. 5 and 7. D. J. Abramoske

218. Dabney, William M. LETTERS FROM NORFOLK: SCOTTISH MERCHANTS VIEW THE REVOLUTIONARY CRISIS. *The Old Dominion: Essays for Thomas Perkins Abernethy (Charlottesville: The U. Press of Virginia, 1964), pp. 109-121.* To the Scottish merchants in Norfolk in 1769 the future for their prosperous community looked bright. By 1774 patriot mobs loomed larger in the correspondence which merchants James Parker and William Aitchison carried on with Charles Steuart whose business they handled after his return to Scotland. As conditions became worse, Aitchison and Parker did not leave for Great Britain as did many Scottish merchants, since their wives were Virginians and their personal commitment was to their colony. However, when the moment of decision came, Parker became a captain in the royal service and never returned; Aitchison stayed on but his property was confiscated. Based on microfilm of the Charles Steuart Papers at the Institute of Early American History and Culture, Williamsburg. 44 notes. E. P. Stickney

219. Douglass, Elisha P. GERMAN INTELLECTUALS AND THE AMERICAN REVOLUTION. *William and Mary Q. 1960 17(2): 200-218.* Far from remaining aloof, German intellectuals, familiar with Voltaire and Rousseau, generally identified themselves with the colonial aims. Johann Schiller and Johann Voss protested the sale of German troops to Britain, and Georg Jacobi, Christoph Wieland and Christian Schubart regarded the Revolution as "a call for national regeneration." Reacting against violence, August Schlözer and Matthias Sprengel, who supported the Loyalists, favored reform of existing institutions. Jakob Mauvillon, Christian von Dohm and Johann Christian Schmöhl sought to rebut the arguments of Schlözer and Sprengel: they reflected the position of the Whigs whereas Schlözer and Sprengel reflected that of the Tories.

E. Oberholzer, Jr.

220. Gallardo, Guillermo. EL TERCER CONGRESO INTERNACIONAL DE HISTORIA DE AMERICA Y SUS ECOS EN CHILE [The Third International Congress on the history of America and its repercussions in Chile]. *Historia [Argentina] 1960 4(21): 253-279.* Information on the congress, held in Buenos Aires in 1960. The names of participants are given, together with the titles and authors of the works presented, which are classified under the following headings: the ideological, political, social and economic factors of the American Revolution; the revolution in the New World; the May Revolution in general; antecedents and development; repercussions of the May Revolution in the provinces and abroad. There is also a copy of a commentary on the congress, published in the *Diario Illustrado* in Santiago, Chile. C. B. (IHE 40294)

221. Gonda, Eugene. MITTELEUROPA UND DIE GESCHICHTE AMERIKAS [Central Europe and the history of America]. *Aussenpolitik [West Germany] 1961 12(11): 771-782.* In order to prove that isolation has never been a real alternative for the United States, the author examines the War of Indepen-

dence, the Louisiana Purchase, the Monroe Doctrine, and the Civil War—all of which were caused or at least promoted by Central European crises related to the "Missouri problem of Europe": the domination over the Danube valley. Franklin D. Roosevelt did not recognize this geopolitical law, that demonstrates the necessity of a European balance of power, and therefore could not prepare a lasting peace.   G. Schoebe

222. Greenway, John. THE AUSTRAMERICAN WEST. *Am. West 1968 5(1): 33-37, 75-79.* Australia was an "invention" that was mothered by the necessity of the American Revolution. It served England's need of a place where the thousands of "criminals" that glutted her jails and prison hulks during the Revolution could be dumped. Australia was nurtured and supplied by American whalers, sealers, and merchantmen during its first two desperate decades. The resultant historical friendship of the Australians and Americans smoothed the course of "environmental determinism," i.e., "when other factors are equal, similar organisms will react to similar environments in similar ways." The author's thesis is that the history of both countries is similar: principally the history of both is that of frontier conquest. Further, Americans and American influence are ubiquitous throughout Australian history. The author illustrates his argument with such items as gold rushes, treatment of natives, public land policy, folklore, and settlement patterns. 8 illus., biblio. note.   D. L. Smith

223. Gruber, Ira D. LORD HOWE AND LORD GEORGE GERMAIN: BRITISH POLITICS AND THE WINNING OF AMERICAN INDEPEN-DENCE. *William and Mary Q. 1965 22(2): 225-243.* Links the political enmity between the brothers Howe (supported by Lord North) and Lord Germain, the colonial secretary (backed by the majority of the ministry), with the indecisive British policies of treating the American rebellion as both a military and a political conflict. With the recall of the Howes, after the waning British fortunes in 1777, the British government faced up to the military realities of the war.
                                                                    H. M. Ward

224. Gruber, Ira D. THE AMERICAN REVOLUTION AS A CONSPIRACY: THE BRITISH VIEW. *William and Mary Q. 1969 26(3): 360-372.* Charges that the colonies conspiring for rebellion found little reception outside the British ministry before April 1775. After that date, with fighting now a fact, officials in America saw the Revolution as the result of a long-standing conspiracy. This belief explains much of British strategy, based on the assumption that substantial elements of the American populace were loyalist. Speeches of members of Parliament and various officials are cited as evidence. 33 notes.   H. M. Ward

225. Hancock, Harold, ed. HISTORICAL RECORDS RELATING TO DELA-WARE IN THE BRITISH ISLES. *Delaware Hist. 1963 10(4): 321-360.* Publishes samples of manuscript material relative to Delaware which are in various depositories in England. The items published relate to the tobacco trade of the Lower Counties in the 17th century; the continuing colonial problems of smuggling, privateering, and piracy; a list of the men raised by Captain Samuel Jenkins for King George's War; a letter of Robert Quary attacking William Penn's

administration; an item by the Reverend Philip Reading on the status of Negroes in 1748; several items on customs affairs during the Revolutionary period; an account of the clash between American and British vessels near "Wilmington Creek" in 1776; and a description of the state of manufactures in Delaware in 1789, by the British consul in Philadelphia. Based on documents in the Public Record Office, London, and the House of Lords Library; 27 notes.

R. M. Miller

226. Holland, L. M. JOHN WESLEY AND THE AMERICAN REVOLU-TION. *J. of Church and State 1963 5(2): 199-213.* An examination of Wesley's political creed which meant "loyalty to his king and his church" and his support of the British king and his policies during the American Revolution. Wesley's political tracts and pamphlets are discussed. 62 notes.   D. F. Rossi

227. Kahn, Robert L. GEORG FORSTER AND BENJAMIN FRANKLIN. *Pro. of the Am. Phil. Soc. 1957 102(1): 1-6.* A study of the relations of Georg Forster (1754-94), German author and scientist, with Franklin. Forster met Franklin in Passy in 1777 and remained an ardent admirer of his for the rest of his life. He wrote to Germans and in German publications about Franklin. Excerpts from those statements are included here. Documented.

N. Kurland

228. Labaree, Benjamin W. THE IDEA OF AMERICAN INDEPENDENCE: THE BRITISH VIEW, 1774-1776. *Pro. of the Massachusetts Hist. Soc. 1970 82: 3-20.* English public opinion lent support to the coercive measures adopted by the London government regarding colonial grievances. The outbreak of violence at Lexington and Concord provided evidence to many Englishmen that the Americans had been conspiring all along to free themselves from the mother country. Based on British newspapers and pamphlets; 25 notes.

J. B. Duff

229. MacCarthy, M. Dugue. REFLECTIONS ON WAR OF INDEPEN-DENCE. A FRENCH VIEW. *Military R. 1966 46(7): 19-25.* Discusses reasons behind the favorable reception of the American insurrection in France. The author lists as the strongest reasons mutual strategy, mutual opposition to the British, and ideological compatibilities.   G. E. Snow

230. Miller, Ralph N. AMERICAN NATIONALISM AS A THEORY OF NATURE. *William and Mary Q. 1955 12(1): 74-95.* George Buffon's *Histoire naturelle* and Denis Diderot's *Encyclopédie* contained a fantastic amount of misinformation on America. Buffon's theory that America was geologically too young to develop men and institutions was taken over by other European writers, including William Robertson, whose moderate views were exploited by extreme Tories in England during the Revolution. American writers reacted, first by defending America against the distortions, and later by exalting American quali-ties and arguing that the new Nation was created in accord with natural princi-ples.   E. Oberholzer, Jr.

231. Murphy, Orville T. THE AMERICAN REVOLUTIONARY ARMY AND THE CONCEPT OF "LEVEE EN MASSE." *Military Affairs 1959 23(1): 13-20.* Discusses the influence on French thought of the American militia system and its supposed success during the American Revolution. Based on contemporary French sources.   K. J. Bauer

232. Murphy, Orville T. THE FRENCH PROFESSIONAL SOLDIER'S OPINION OF THE AMERICAN MILITIA IN THE WAR OF THE REVOLUTION. *Military Affairs 1969 32(4): 191-198.* Although the picture of the American militia created in France by French and American propaganda was highly favorable, that reported by French professional soldiers was more balanced. Based on contemporary accounts and memoirs; 44 notes.
          K. J. Bauer

233. O'Neil, James E. COPIES OF FRENCH MANUSCRIPTS FOR AMERICAN HISTORY IN THE LIBRARY OF CONGRESS. *J. of Am. Hist. 1965 51(4): 674-691.* Report on the Library of Congress' copying program of French manuscripts dealing with American history. Most of the manuscripts reproduced date from the 17th and 18th centuries and relate to the Mississippi Valley, Canada, and the West Indies. The subjects covered include "discovery, exploration, colonization, the diplomatic and military struggles with Britain, the American Revolution, and French-American diplomatic and cultural relations...."
          H. J. Silverman

234. Plumb, J. H. READING, WRITING, AND HISTORY: DOVES AND HAWKS, 1776. *Am. Heritage 1968 19(2): 97-101.* Examines British public opinion before and during the American Revolution. Nobility and commoners alike were sympathetic to the Americans during the early stages, but became increasingly disenchanted with their war aims by 1776. Britons were critical of George III's policies after he came to power in 1760. Many wanted the same freedoms which Americans demanded—religious toleration, a broader franchise, and the "rationalization of law and authority." Their leaders included radicals and moderates such as James Watt, Erasmus Darwin, Junius, Lord Pembroke, and Josiah Wedgwood. These people resented high taxes, the repressive acts of the ministry, and the lack of a program of social reform. Merchants, however, grew to fear that English radicals might become powerful, diminish profits from American trade, increase local taxes, and destroy the traditional sovereignty of crown and parliament. A whiplash effect with conservative reaction followed. The Revolution vitiated a "widespread middle-class intellectual radicalism" which was beginning to develop social, political, and economic equality for all Britons.
          J. D. Born, Jr.

235. Ratcliffe, D. J. THE BRITISH AND NORTH AMERICA: ILLUSTRATIVE MATERIALS AT DURHAM. *Durham U. J. [Great Britain] 1970 63(1): 19-38.* An exhibition of books, maps, and pictures illustrating the relationship between the British and North America was produced in 1968 by Durham University Library to mark the beginning of American Studies at the university. Describes the nature of this material in a survey of Britain's connection with

America from 1480 to 1870. The sections into which the survey is divided are: the period of colony foundation, the "Anglo-American nation" of the period *ca.* 1650 to the Revolution, the era of "informal Empire" after 1783 to the end of the Civil War, and the antislavery movement in Britain and America. Based on MS. and secondary sources; 71 notes.   D. H. Murdoch

236. Renwick, John, ed. MARMONTEL ON THE GOVERNMENT OF VIRGINIA (1783). *J. of Am. Studies [Great Britain] 1967 1(2): 181-189.* Publishes, exactly as it was written in the original French, "Observations d'un ami des Américains sur le Gouvernement de la Virginie" by Jean-François Marmontel, a long-established member of the philosophical party, the Historiographe du Roi, and, significantly, a good friend of Benjamin Franklin. The document, written in 1783 in response to a paper from Philip Mazzei, Jefferson's factotum in Europe, sheds light on "the similarities that existed between the political and social theories of the new independent Americans...and those of the liberal-minded French under the Ancien Régime." Most striking are the close parallels between Marmontel's thought and "Jefferson's political and social views as presumably found in the manuscript which was later to be published under the title *Notes on the State of Virginia.*   D. J. Abramoske

237. Robertson, M. L. SCOTTISH COMMERCE AND THE AMERICAN WAR OF INDEPENDENCE. *Econ. Hist. R. [Great Britain] 1956 9(1): 123-131.* "The American War of Independence, and the consequent failure of the lucrative colonial trade, set in motion a train of events which were in time to alter the pattern of Scottish economic life....The Declaration of Independence seemed to rock the whole precarious structure of Scottish commerce." Glasgow's tobacco trade spectacularly collapsed between 1775 and 1777, but the prudence of Scottish merchants in collecting the bulk of outstanding debts before the outbreak of war and the search for new trade, particularly West Indian, reduced the effects of Glasgow's loss. The war, in the long run, had the result of accelerating the development of the first of Scotland's great industries, "which established the country's economy on a more solid foundation and led to its emergence as a predominantly industrial rather than a predominantly trading nation."
                                                        J. A. S. Grenville

238. Tharp, Louise Hall. NEW ENGLAND UNDER OBSERVATION. *New England Galaxy 1964 6(2): 3-9.* Based upon accounts of German soldiers of the British army in colonial America. Most of the observations are from letters describing the people, with many descriptions of women and their social role. Illus.   S

239. Van Alstyne, Richard W. GREAT BRITAIN, THE WAR FOR INDEPENDENCE, AND THE "GATHERING STORM" IN EUROPE, 1775-1778. *Huntington Lib. Q. 1964 27(4): 311-346.* Approaches the American Revolution from the British side and stresses the extensive and accurate intelligence available to London concerning aid given the Americans from the Continent. Well-informed but curiously passive, the British government from as early as 1775 watched the building up of a great system of trade and privateering that was little

short of war against it. By September 1777 the situation was clearly getting out of hand. Not Burgoyne's surrender, but the cumulative procrastinations and decisions of several governments over several years explain the drift toward Franco-American alliance and formal war.   H. D. Jordan

240. Voltes Bou, Pedro. REPERCUSIONES ECONOMICAS DE LE INTER-VENCION ESPAÑOLA EN LA GUERRA DE INDEPENDENCIA DE LOS ESTADOS UNIDOS [Economic repercussions of Spain's intervention in the U.S. War of Independence]. *Hispania [Spain] 1961 (81): 49-150.* The article includes in its entirety the work by the same author of "Estudio estadístico de durante el reinado de Carlos III," *Documentos y Estudios* 1961 6: 5-46. The rest, particularly in the third part, is a literal copy of excerpts of the works by A. Ruiz y Pablo, "Historia de la Junta de Comercio de Cataluña" (Barcelona, 1919, pp. 214-218); M. Danvila Collados, "El reinado de Carlos III" (Madrid, 1891, cf. III, p. 496, and V, pp. 41-59, 124-125, 479); J. Carrera Pujal, "Historia de la economía española" (cf. III, pp. 137-138, 517, 555-556, 561, 563-565; IV, pp. 61-65, 78, 82-83, 119-120, 123, 125-126, 235, 249, 254-255, 273-274, 325-328, 331-333, 335, 344, 349-350, 352; V, pp. 262, 312, 323-324, 336-338), "Historia política y económica de Cataluña" (cf. II, pp. 476-477, 479-480, 483-485; 111, pp. 62, 83-85, 88, 239-240, 284-285, 452-454, 461, 514; IV, pp. 157, 448-449) and "La Barcelona del siglo XVIII" (Barcelona, 1951, cf. I, p. 82), whose archive references it gives as sources. Otherwise, the article follows Alexander Hamilton's works on the economy of the period, together with anecdotal information.

E. G. (IHE 39933)

3

PARTICIPANTS IN THE REVOLUTION: PERSONALITIES & BIOGRAPHY

General

241. Bailey, James H. GEORGE NICHOLAS, VIRGINIA PATRIOT. *Virginia Cavalcade 1965 15(2): 23-33.* A short biography of George Nicholas, a Virginian who fought in the Revolutionary War and was active in both Virginia and Kentucky politics. He was instrumental in Virginia's decision to ratify the Constitution. Illus.   R. B. Lange

242. Bayles, Thomas R. WILLIAM FLOYD, THE SIGNER. *Long Island Forum 1972 35(5): 102-104.* Floyd (1734-1821) was born on a four-thousand-acre estate at Mastic, became a Major General in the Revolutionary War, served in the Continental Congress where he was an early advocate of American independence, and served as a New York State Senator. After the Revolution, he led the life of a country squire. He was an elector in every presidential election up to 1820. Undocumented, 2 illus.   G. Kurland

243. Bumsted, John M. NEW ENGLAND'S TOM PAINE: JOHN ALLEN AND THE SPIRIT OF LIBERTY. *William and Mary Q. 1964 21(4): 561-570.* John Allen, who authored political pamphlets in pre-Revolutionary Boston, was an advocate of an American parliament as a counterpoise to the British Parliament. He was also a persistent critic of conditions in America ranging from slavery to religious taxation. Liberty and equality, to Allen, were derived fundamentally from the Scriptures.   H. M. Ward

244. Charles, Steven T. JOHN JONES, AMERICAN SURGEON AND CONSERVATIVE PATRIOT. *Bull. of the Hist. of Medicine 1965 39(5): 435-449.* A discussion of five letters written by Jones and "addressed to James Duane (1733-1797), a conservative Whig jurist, born in New York City and a resident there much of his life, who tried to quell the Stamp Act riots." Jones was born in Jamaica, Long Island, New York, on 10 March 1729. "He was known through-

out the American colonies for his surgical skill, especially in lithotomy, and he is remembered by medical historians because he wrote the first surgical book published in America, a monograph entitled: *Plain Concise Practical Remarks on the Treatment of Wounds and Fractures: To Which is Added a Short Appendix on Camp and Military Hospitals; Principally Designed for the Use of Young Military Surgeons in North America.* This book, published in 1775 and reprinted in 1776, was used extensively during the Revolutionary War." The letters are dated 20 June, 18 July, and 7 December 1775; 14 April 1776, and 16 January 1778. "Like Duane, Jones opposed armed revolution and hoped for reconciliation, but the continued stubbornness of George III and growing popular unrest made independence inevitable, whatever its means. In his 1776 and 1778 letters, Jones' dedication to his country's cause is clearly stated; though he disapproved of the method used in gaining freedom, he was still willing to serve in his country's military establishment." 2 figs., 48 notes.   D. D. Cameron

245. Coles, Robert R. THE SANDS FAMILY BURYING GROUND. *Long Island Forum 1971 34(9): 196-201.* History of the Sands family, who were among the earliest settlers at Cow Neck (now Port Washington), Long Island. Arriving in the late 17th century, the Sands family produced 10 members who participated in the American Revolution, as well as two members who served in the Provincial Congress of New York. The family's burying ground, now in a state of neglect, has many gravesites dating back to the early 18th century. 2 illus.

                                                                    G. Kurland

246. Condit, William W. CHRISTOPHER LUDWIG, PATRIOTIC GINGER-BREAD BAKER. *Pennsylvania Mag. of Hist. and Biog. 1957 81(4): 365-390.* Discusses the valiant efforts of baker Ludwig in supplying Washington's army with bread during the Revolution. Based on colonial documents and other primary sources.   W. Hunsberger

247. Coulter, E. Merton. NANCY HART, GEORGIA HEROINE OF THE REVOLUTION: THE STORY OF THE GROWTH OF A TRADITION. *Georgia Hist. Q. 1955 39(2): 118-151.* Reviews the growth, during the last 170 years, of the Nancy Hart tradition, which is now well-established in Georgia.

                                                                    C. F. Latour

248. D'Innocenzo, Michael and Turner, John. THE PETER VAN GAASBEEK PAPERS: A RESOURCE FOR EARLY NEW YORK HISTORY, 1771-1779. *New York Hist. 1966 47(2): 153-159.* As merchant, military officer and politician, Peter Van Gaasbeek lived in the Ulster County, New York, community of Kingston from his birth in 1754 until his death in 1797. Having surveyed some ten thousand items in the Van Gaasbeek collection at Kingston, the authors demonstrate the potential value of these papers for accounts of the Revolutionary War, the ratification of the Federal Constitution, and late 18th-century politics at both the state and national levels.   B. T. Quinten

249. Dickoré, Marie. THE CORNELIUS SNIDER FAMILY OF HAMILTON COUNTY, OHIO. *Cincinnati Hist. Soc. Bull. 1964 22(3): 195-197.* Presents historical data and extracts from the family Bible records of Cornelius Snider I (1762-1822), his wife, Mary Felter Snider (1763-1828) whom he married on 3 September 1783 in Orange County, New York, and of their eight children. Cornelius Snider brought his family from Orange County, New York, to the Sycamore township of Hamilton County, Ohio, in 1795. Although very young, he served in the militia and in the army in the American Revolutionary War (1775-1783). Also given are the details of land purchased by Cornelius Snider in 1796, of his will, which he made in 1822, and of burial records in the Hopewell Cemetery. Documented from records in the Snider family Bible and from the Hamilton County, Ohio, courthouse.   D. D. Cameron

250. Doan, Daniel. THE ENIGMATIC MOODY BEDEL. *Hist. New Hampshire 1970 25(3): 26-36.* A land speculator who developed a settlement in present-day Pittsburg, New Hampshire, Moody Bedel (1764-1841) served as orderly for his father, Colonel Timothy, during the invasion of Canada, 1775-76. He inherited about seven thousand pounds, mostly in wild land around Haverhill, New Hampshire, developed the town of Coventry (Benton), New Hampshire, built the first toll bridge to South Newbury, Vermont, invested in sawmills, organized a Masonic lodge, trained the militia, served in the legislature, and sired 18 children. In 1814 Bedel led a sortie out of Fort Erie which ended its siege, and was promoted to colonel. His land company bought all of New Hampshire north of Bath and Ossipee for 3,100 dollars from the Saint Francis Indians, in violation of federal statutes. The Eastman land company of Concord had another Indian deed to the same area. Bedel was taxed for 53,333 acres in 1819. He merged with his rivals in 1830, sold his share for four thousand dollars, and died landless. His heirs ultimately realized two thousand dollars from his land claims and a quarter-section of Minnesota land for his Revolutionary War service. Based on manuscripts in the New Hampshire Historical Society; illus., photo.
                    T. D. S. Bassett

251. Hamer, Philip M. HENRY LAURENS OF SOUTH CAROLINA—THE MAN AND HIS PAPERS. *Massachusetts Hist. Soc. Pro. 1965 77: 3-14.* A biographical sketch of Henry Laurens, describing the location of the main groups of the Laurens Papers and the impending publication of 12 volumes of them, the first of which is scheduled for publication in the spring of 1967. Based on the Laurens Papers and the biography by D. D. Wallace, 18 notes.
                    J. B. Duff

252. Hawke, David Freeman. DR. THOMAS YOUNG—"ETERNAL FISHER IN TROUBLED WATERS." *New-York Hist. Soc. Q. 1970 54(1): 6-29.* A brief account (subtitled "Notes for a Biography") of the revolutionary activities of Thomas Young called "the most unwritten about man of distinction of the American Revolution." His activities took him to New York, Massachusetts, Rhode Island, and Pennsylvania, and he was associated with most of the best known revolutionary leaders. Also, he was a very successful physician. Quite

likely his lack of fame may be attributed to his unpredictable behavior and his untimely death early in the Revolution. Based on primary sources; 5 illus., 50 notes.

C. L. Grant

253. Hendricks, J. Edwin. JOSEPH WINSTON: NORTH CAROLINA JEF-FERSONIAN. *North Carolina Hist. R. 1968 45(3): 284-297.* Not even residents of Winston-Salem have much knowledge of Joseph Winston, after whom the city was named. Winston was an important Revolutionary leader and local politician three times elected to Congress. For his time he was a liberal humanitarian and in Congress was a good Jeffersonian who voted against a military establishment and for limited government. 51 notes.

J. M. Bumsted

254. Herndon, G. Melvin. GEORGE MATTHEWS, FRONTIER PATRIOT. *Virginia Mag. of Hist. and Biog. 1969 77(3): 307-328.* Prior to the Revolution, George Matthews amassed a sizable fortune, served as an Indian fighter, and became a local political figure in Augusta County, Virginia. During the war he fought with distinction until he was badly wounded and captured in 1777. Later exchanged, he saw little further service and in 1784 secured a tract of land in Georgia. He was elected Governor of Georgia in 1787 and 1793 and to Congress in 1789, but was ruined politically by his connection with the Yazoo lands scandal. In 1797 he moved to Mississippi Territory and the following year was nominated as territorial governor but the Senate refused confirmation. In 1810 he acted as a secret agent during the seizure of West Florida, although later he was repudiated by the American Government. Based on materials in the Draper Collection, Wisconsin Historical Society, and printed sources; 76 notes.

K. J. Bauer

255. Hixson, Richard F. SIMEON DE WITT, CLASS OF 1776. *J. of the Rutgers U. Lib. 1966 29(3): 65-73.* Biographical sketch of the Rutgers alumnus, Simeon De Witt, 1756-1834, who served successively as topographer and geographer to the Continental Army under the Confederation; surveyor general of New York State November 1783-1834 (in which capacity he helped survey the Erie Canal); vice-chancellor and chancellor of the University of the State of New York, 1819-34. 15 notes, including references to materials in various manuscript and map collections in which De Witt papers constitute important sources.

H. J. Graham

256. Howard, Cary. JOHN EAGER HOWARD. *Maryland Hist. Mag. 1967 62(3): 300-317.* Howard (1752-1827) was an officer in the Revolutionary War who had a brilliant record, rising from captain to colonel during battles from Virginia and Maryland to South Carolina. He served in the Maryland General Assembly and was Governor for three terms (1787-91). He served in the U.S. Senate from 1796 to 1803. Howard followed the programs and policies of the Federalist Party. He was survived by six of his nine children. Two children served in the military, two in public service, and one became a physician. 108 notes.

D. H. Swift

257. Kammen, Michael G. INTELLECTUALS, POLITICAL LEADERSHIP, AND REVOLUTION. *New England Q. 1968 41(4): 583-593.* Reviews Clifford K. Shipton's *Biographical Sketches of Those Who Attended Harvard College in the Classes 1756-1760, With Bibliographical and Other Notes By Clifford K. Shipton* [Sibley's Harvard Graduates, Vol. XIV] (Boston: Massachusett Hist. Soc., 1968). Kammen suggests that the biographical sketches of many figures who were to be of real importance in the Revolutionary era might serve as a good place to begin a scholarly study of the relationship between intellectual leadership and the Revolution. Men like Joseph Warren (1741-75), John Avery, and James Lovell (1737-1814) were intellectuals who were unable to find an autonomous life of their own in a developing nation. Thus, they threw themselves intensely into political activity and moved from the rejection of one traditional authoritarian collectivity into a new, alternative, revolutionary collectivity. The scholarly work of Edward Shils is cited as useful theoretical underpinning for such a study. 13 notes.
K. B. West

258. Klein, Randolph Shipley. MOSES BARTRAM (1732-1809). *Quaker Hist. 1968 57(1): 25-34.* The second son of botanist John Bartram became a leading Philadelphia druggist. His correspondence and papers show an independent scientific interest in ocean currents, locusts, silkworms, and other natural history, mercantile ability, and fertility. As a member of the American Society for the Promotion of Useful Knowledge from 1766 he helped arrange a merger into the American Philosophical Society in 1769. During the Revolution he looked after the families of soldiers, suffered property damage by British occupation, was disowned for accepting military service, and joined the Free Quakers.
T. D. S. Bassett

259. Longley, R. S. LORD STIRLING: TITLED WHIG OF THE AMERICAN REVOLUTION. *Tr. of the Royal Soc. of Can. 1962 56(Section II): 11-22.* Biographical sketch of William Alexander, who claimed to be the only titled colonial who espoused the American side in the Revolution. Alexander, a wealthy merchant of New York, married a member of the politically powerful Livingston family and became associated with Governor William Shirley of Massachusetts in the latter's abortive expedition against Fort Niagara in the French and Indian War. Going to Scotland, Alexander prevailed upon a jury to declare him the sixth Earl of Stirling. At least one other individual had a better claim to the title, though apparently no inclination to press it. The House of Lords refused to recognize his claim, but Alexander returned to America and assumed the title. Failure to succeed in politics may account for his joining the rebel cause. As an officer in the American army, he performed well on occasion, but his addiction to the bottle prevented his being entrusted with major responsibilities.
D. F. Warner

260. Mayo, Bernard. THE ENIGMA OF PATRICK HENRY. *Virginia Q. R. 1959 35(2): 176-195.* Using "the recent scholarship, impressive in range and quality, on the men and events of Henry's Revolutionary Epoch," critically compares the popular image of Patrick Henry with that presented by scholars. The flesh and blood Henry is not found to be "avaricious and rotten hearted,"

as Thomas Jefferson once described him; but instead, "he continues to be, as he was in his own day, the unequaled and ever-inspiring orator of liberty."

W. E. Wight

261. McCorison, Marcus Allen. AMOS TAYLOR. A SKETCH AND BIBLI-OGRAPHY. *Pro. of the Am. Antiquarian Soc. 1959 69(1): 37-55.* Taylor, an itinerant teacher, poet, publisher and bookseller, was born in Groton, Massachusetts on 7 September 1748, served in the Revolutionary War, farmed and taught in Vermont, and finally moved into New York State before 1813. Biblio.

W. D. Metz

262. Morrissey, Charles T., ed. THE DIARY OF PHINEHAS SPAULDING: A PIONEER'S LIFE IN THE CHAMPLAIN VALLEY. *Vermont Hist. 1971 39(2): 113-115.* A notebook owned by a descendant records the family vital statistics of a Panton proprietor from Connecticut who settled by mistake in Addison in 1767. Father and three sons fought in the Revolution; three were captured and escaped, one was recaptured, and one died of smallpox.

T. D. S. Bassett

263. Robinson, Thomas P. and Leder, Lawrence H., eds. GOVERNOR LIVINGSTON AND THE "SUNSHINE PATRIOTS." *William and Mary Q. 1956 13(3): 394-397.* Publication of an affectionate letter from Governor William Livingston to his brother, denying Philip Schuyler's request to return from his self-imposed refuge in Loyalist New York to New Jersey.

E. Oberholzer, Jr.

264. Ross, Emily. JOHN HANCOCK, THE FORGOTTEN PATRIOT. *Daughters of the Am. Revolution Mag. 1971 105(2): 101-103, 144, 170.* Details Hancock's youth, rise in the Boston shipping industry, and growing involvement in the pre-Revolutionary resistance movement. Hancock personally abhorred the violence attendant upon the movement, which explains his occasional hesitance in supporting the activities of more radical figures such as Samuel Adams. Analyzes Hancock's flight from Boston and his involvement in the Second Continental Congress. Stresses his efforts on behalf of debtors during his terms as Governor of Massachusetts, and his support of the Constitution in 1787. Hancock's rapport with the "indifferent masses" was instrumental in the development of American democracy. Illus., biblio.

D. A. Sloan

265. Russell, Helen H. THE LIFE AND TIMES OF HENRY ANTES. *Now and Then 1965 14(11): 325-344.* Gives an account of Henry Antes, a member of a prominent Pennsylvania German landholding family, who was active in the work of the Moravian Church, and who played host to Bishop Henry Melchior Muhlenberg and several other "Great Awakening" ministers. The author also describes the activities of Colonel John Antes, Henry's son, who commanded the Pennsylvania militia in the area around Muncy during the Revolutionary War. Wills of three Antes as well as a genealogy of the Antes family are included. Partial documentation.

H. Ershkowitz

266. Silverman, E. H. PAINTER OF THE REVOLUTION. *Am. Heritage 1958 9(4): 40-51, 95-97.* Discusses the role of John Trumbull as an American patriot and creator of historical paintings of the American Revolution. Illus.

C. R. Allen, Jr.

267. Stokes, Durward T. THOMAS HART IN NORTH CAROLINA. *North Carolina Hist. R. 1964 41(3): 324-337.* Treats in detail the North Carolina career of Hart for the 20 years after 1757. Unpublished and published local and state records are utilized to describe his success as planter, merchant, and rope and nail manufacturer, his political role as opponent of the Regulators and supporter of the American Revolution, and his promotional venture as partner of the Transylvania Company. Hart's later business career in Maryland and Kentucky, where his rope and hemp business was of national scope, is briefly treated.

L. R. Harlan

Military & Naval Personnel

268. Alexander, John K., ed. JONATHAN CARPENTER AND THE AMERICAN REVOLUTION: THE JOURNAL OF AN AMERICAN NAVAL PRISONER OF WAR AND VERMONT INDIAN FIGHTER. *Vermont Hist. 1968 36(2): 74-90.* Farmer boy, apprentice carpenter, militiaman (1775-77) on the privateer *Reprisal* out of Boston, captured after two months, Carpenter spent a year in Forton prison (19 June 1778-2 July 1779) near Portsmouth, England. In May 1780 he settled in Pomfret, Vermont, and scouted during the Indian-Tory raids on Barnard and Royalton that year. This diary is in the Vermont Historical Society.

T. D. S. Bassett

269. Cook, Fred J. ALLAN MC LANE: UNKNOWN HERO OF THE REVOLUTION. *Am. Heritage 1956 7(6): 74-77, 118-119.* Describes the exploits of McLane, a prosperous Philadelphian, during the American Revolution as a scout, dashing fighter, and romantic trooper with Washington's armies. Illus.

C. R. Allen, Jr.

270. Danachair, Caoimhín O. GENERAL STEPHEN MOYLAN. *Irish Sword [Ireland] 1958 3(12): 159-161.* Stephen Moylan (1737-1811) was secretary and aide-de-camp to George Washington and later quartermaster general during the American Revolution. This brief biographical sketch deals principally with his activities from 1775 to 1783.

H. L. Calkin

271. Fleming, Thomas J. THE "MILITARY CRIMES" OF CHARLES LEE. *Am. Heritage 1968 19(3): 12-15, 83-89.* Recounts the testimony offered in the military court-martial of Charles Lee (1731-82), brilliant but eccentric former British officer who retired to a Virginia estate but espoused the cause of the

American Revolution and was appointed second in command to George Washington. Lee believed guerrilla warfare was the best possible American strategy. He was captured in December 1776 and remained a British prisoner until exchanged in 1778 in time for the Battle of Monmouth. Lee was accused of failure to follow orders, "disrespect to the Commander-in-Chief," and conducting a "shameful and disorderly retreat." The tribunal, composed of a large number of Washington's friends, found Lee guilty of all charges. He was suspended from the service for a year. The vitriolic general reacted by submitting an article to the Pennsylvania *Packet* which contained an attack on the generalship of Washington. With this unfavorable publicity, the dallying Congress confirmed the decision of the court. Lee never returned to military duty. The case, however, did not end until 1925 when certain papers of General Henry Clinton substantiated Lee's allegations that he had to retreat in the face of a superior British army. Lee died a bitter and unhappy man who believed that he was a victim of the court and Washington's friends. Based on the Lee and Clinton papers; illus.

J. D. Born, Jr.

272. Furlong, William B. THE FATHER OF OUR NAVY. *New York Times Mag. 1956 16(September): 66-67.* Surveys the life of Commodore John Barry, a naval hero of the American Revolution and first senior officer of the U.S. Navy.

D. Houston

273. Gerlach, Don R. PHILIP SCHUYLER AND "THE ROAD TO GLORY": A QUESTION OF LOYALTY AND COMPETENCE. *New-York Hist. Soc. Q. 1965 49(4): 341-386.* Throughout his Revolutionary War career General Philip Schuyler's patriotism and military competence were often questioned. Evidence presented here indicates that such questions were without foundation and that, instead, Schuyler deserves more credit for the defeat of John Burgoyne's army than does General Horatio Gates. After acquittal by a court-martial, Schuyler's vindication was complete when he was made president of the Continental Congress.

C. L. Grant

274. Greene, Wallace M., Jr. REMARKS OF GENERAL WALLACE M. GREENE, JR., USMC AT LAUNCHING OF U.S.S. *NATHANAEL GREENE* (SSBN), U.S. NAVAL SHIPYARD, PORTSMOUTH, NEW HAMPSHIRE 12 MAY 1964. *Rhode Island Hist. 1964 23(4): 97-101.* Briefly analyzes Nathanael Greene's role as a military strategist during the Revolutionary War.

P. J. Coleman

275. Hawes, Lilla M., ed. THE PAPERS OF LACHLAN MC INTOSH, 1774-1799. *Georgia Hist. Q. 1955 39(1): 52-68, (2): 172-186, (3): 253-268, (4): 356-375, 1956 40(1): 65-88, and (2): 152-174.* Presents various letters and papers from the personal records of a Georgia officer during and after the American Revolution.

C. F. Latour

276. Herr, Remly. MAD ANTHONY WAYNE—PATRIOT. *Indiana Hist. Bull. 1970 47(3): 25-27.* A biography of Wayne (1745-96) and a description of

his service to America during the American Revolution. A lengthy quotation from the Lebanon (Indiana) *Pioneer* notes that Wayne is "buried" in two locations at opposite ends of Pennsylvania. Illus.   D. H. Eyman

277. McDonald, Hugh. A TEEN-AGER IN THE REVOLUTION. *Am. Hist. Illus. 1966 1(2): 25-34 and (3): 38-47.* Part I. Discusses the adventures of Hugh McDonald, a boy of 14 years who left home and joined the Continental army during the Revolutionary War. Young Hugh kept a journal of his daily adventures, and part of that journal is reproduced here. His company marched through his home state of North Carolina to Philadelphia where it joined General Washington. Although many of his discussions concern personal matters, he does reflect many of the various attitudes toward the war. 5 illus. Part II. Describes the small skirmishes with the British as his unit marched through Pennsylvania. A number of anecdotes are noted concerning General Washington and his relationship with his men. The journal ends abruptly with an account of two U.S. officers who had been dismissed from the army for misconduct and had returned to North Carolina. 5 illus.   M. J. McBaine

278. Mebane, John. JOSEPH HABERSHAM IN THE REVOLUTIONARY WAR. *Georgia Hist. Q. 1963 47(1): 76-83.*

279. Moyne, Ernest J. WHO WAS COLONEL JOHN HASLET OF DELAWARE? *Delaware Hist. 1969 13(4): 283-300.* Decries the lack of study on Colonel John Haslet (1727-77), Revolutionary War hero from Delaware who died at Princeton. Haslet, an immigrant from Scotland and a physician by training, was early a Whig and a longtime friend and political ally of Caesar Rodney in the struggle for American independence. Haslet was active in public affairs before he served with the Delaware Continentals. Includes eulogies of Haslet and sketches of his relatives. 20 notes.   R. M. Miller

280. Murphy, W. S. FOUR SOLDIERS OF THE AMERICAN REVOLUTION. *Irish Sword [Ireland] 1962 5(20): 164-174.* Biographical sketches, with emphasis on their military careers, of Major-Generals Henry Knox, Anthony Wayne, Richard Butler and John Sullivan.   H. L. Calkin

281. Rudulph, Marilou Alston. MICHAEL RUDULPH, "LION OF THE LEGION." *Georgia Hist. Q. 1961 45(3): 201-222.* Examines the life of Michael Rudulph, focusing on his daring career as an officer in the American Revolution, his residence in Georgia, and his return to military service as a disgruntled officer on the Northwest frontier in the 1790's. In 1793, after resigning from the army, he sailed on a vessel destined for the West Indies and was never heard from again.   R. Lowitt

282. Rudulph, Marilou Alston. THE LEGEND OF MICHAEL RUDULPH. *Georgia Hist. Q. 1961 45(4): 309-328.* Examines the growth of the Rudulph-Ney

legend throughout the 19th century, according to which Michael Rudulph, a hero of the American Revolution and Adjutant-General of the United States Army was in reality Napoleon's famous marshal, Michel Ney.   R. Lowitt

283. Scheer, George F. THE ELUSIVE SWAMP FOX. *Am. Heritage 1958 9(3):* *40-47, 111.* Reexamines the legend of Francis Marion, the Swamp Fox, in the American Revolution, and concludes that reality is in this case not far from the legend. Undocumented; illus.   C. R. Allen, Jr.

284. Shapiro, Darline. ETHAN ALLEN: PHILOSOPHER-THEOLOGIAN TO A GENERATION OF AMERICAN REVOLUTIONARIES. *William and Mary Q. 1964 21(2): 236-255.* Allen provided a philosophical justification, strongly Lockean in orientation, for the rule of the Green Mountain Boys. His religious views were the consequence of his political philosophy. The author suggests that Allen's *Reason the Only Oracle of Man* (1784) was "an application for admission to the city of the eighteenth century philosophes."
E. Oberholzer, Jr.

Foreign Participants

285. Aylott, F. G. LT. COL. PATRICK FERGUSON 71ST REGT. *Bull. of the Military Hist. Soc. [Great Britain] 1959 9(35): 58-59.* An account of the development of the Ferguson rifle by its inventor, Lieutenant Colonel Patrick Ferguson, who raised the Light Infantry Company and equipped it with his rifle; briefly describes his campaigns during the War of American Independence. Undocumented.   J. A. S. Grenville

286. Berendt, Bohdan. KOŚCIUSZKO W ŚWIETLE DOKUMENTÓW WOL-NOMULARSKICH [Kościuszko in the light of Masonic publications]. *Teki Historyczne [Great Britain] 1969-71 16: 103-106.* The question of whether Thaddeus Kościuszko was a Freemason is still a point of interest for Polish and American historians. After reviewing the literature of Polish and American Masons, the author concludes that there is definitely no evidence that Kościuszko was formally a member of a Masonic lodge.   C. M. Nowak

287. Brock, Peter. THE SPIRITUAL PILGRIMAGE OF THOMAS WATSON: FROM BRITISH SOLDIER TO AMERICAN FRIEND. *Quaker Hist.* *1964 53(2): 81-86.* Fatherless coal miner at seven, orphan sailor, Watson enlisted in the British army and came to New York in 1773. Soon after fighting in the battle of Germantown (October 1777) he became a conscientious objector and deserted in March 1778. He married in Rhode Island, attended Baptist and then Quaker worship, and became a Quaker in 1785. As a farmer in Bolton, Massachusetts toward 1798 he was active among local Friends, recorded as a minister in

1801, and traveled during his last decade, especially among Methodists and Baptists. Drawn from *The Life...of Thomas Watson...of Bolton, Massachusetts. Written by Himself* (New York, Daniel Cooledge, 1836; 2nd ed. 1861), and from local meeting minutes. T. D. S. Bassett

288. Budka, Metchie J. E. "WHAT CAME FIRST—KOŚCIUSZKO OR THE AMERICAN REVOLUTION?" *Polish R. 1966 11(4): 134-139.* Basically a review of two small books dealing with Thaddeus Kościuszko: Zofia Libiszowska, *Opinia polska wobec rewolucji Amerykanskiej* [The American Revolution in contemporary Polish public opinion] and Krystyna Sreniowska, *Kosciuszko. Ksztaltowanie pogladow na bohatera narodowego* [The formation of the images of a national hero]. The reviews throw light on Kościuszko and his role in both revolutions, the American and the Polish. S. R. Pliska

289. Fitzpatrick, Paul J. GENERAL EDWARD HAND AND ROCK FORD. *Social Sci. 1969 44(1): 3-11.* "American historians have generally neglected General Edward Hand in their treatment of various engagements of the War of the Revolution, his name being relegated to footnotes and the index. Hand was a very capable general whom Washington greatly admired and trusted for his military exploits. Moreover, since very little information has appeared so far about the nature of Rock Ford, the general's fine mansion, which was opened to the public on May 2,1960, it is fitting that some description of the home should be included. "Hand left his native Ireland for this country, on May 20, 1767." J

290. Fleming, Thomas J. THE ENIGMA OF GENERAL HOWE. *Am. Heritage 1964 15(2): 6-11, 96-103.* Every time he met Washington in battle he soundly beat him, yet Sir William Howe never followed up his advantage so as to end the American Revolution. This article discusses the proposed reasons for Howe's failure to do so. Fleming suggests that the answer, at least in part, is that Howe should never have been given his post as he was not completely sympathetic with the British position. Well illustrated but not documented. C. R. Allen, Jr.

291. Hargreaves, R. "GOOD-NATURED BILLY." *Army Q. and Defence J. [Great Britain] 1967 93(2): 177-190.* A biographical account of the career of Sir William Howe, with particular emphasis on his military activities in America (1759-77) and the battles of Quebec, Bunker Hill, Brandywine, and Germantown. 15 notes. D. H. Murdoch

292. Holland, J. D. AN EIGHTEENTH-CENTURY PIONEER: RICHARD PRICE, D.D., F.R.S. (1723-1791). *Notes and Records of the Royal Soc. of London [Great Britain] 1968 23(1): 43-64.* An authority on public finance and author of one of the first major treatises in the field of life insurance, Richard Price was so sympathetic to the cause of the American colonists that he published *Observations on the Nature of Civil Liberty, the Principles of Government, and the Justice and Policy of the War with America* (1776). Price relayed intelligence from London to the colonists, passed on information received from them, and was

given code number 176 by the Committee of Secret Correspondence which was organized in 1775 and which included Benjamin Franklin among its members. The author views details of the opening phases of the American Revolution from a British perspective. Based largely on secondary sources and papers in the archives of the Royal Society; biblio.   N. W. Moen

293. Innes, R. A., ed. JEREMY LISTER, 10TH REGIMENT, 1770-1783. *J. of the Soc. for Army Hist. Res. [Great Britain] 1963 41(166): 59-73.* Eleven letters and the journal of an ensign in the 10th Regiment of Foot, covering the period 1770-83. The first four are from Canada, the remainder from Boston.
          K. James

294. Johnston, Edith. THE CAREER AND CORRESPONDENCE OF THOMAS ALLAN, 1767-85. *Bull. of the Irish Com. of Hist. Sci. [Ireland] 1956 (75): 2-3.* A study of the career of Thomas Allan, Lord Nash, when he was agent of the Lord Lieutenant of Ireland, advisor to the British Government on Irish affairs, and acted as an unofficial undersecretary for Ireland. Allan's correspondence contains information relating to: the North administration, Irish affairs, the American Revolution, the Wilkes Case, and 18th-century administration. Based on manuscripts and documents in Somerset House, Richmond Parish church and the Bank of England Record Office.   K. Eubank

295. Kendal, John Charles. WILLIAM TWISS: ROYAL ENGINEER. *Duquesne R. 1970 15(1): 175-191.* Discusses the professional career of William Twiss (1745-1827), a British military engineer, concentrating on his activities in the Royal Army during the American Revolution. Attention is focused on his accomplishments in directing the construction of fortifications and other facilities in the St. Lawrence River area, and on his rise to "Commanding Engineer in Canada." Based on private papers in the Public Archives of Canada; 60 notes.
          M. R. Strausbaugh

296. Lane, Nicholas. LIFE INSURANCE AND THE WAR OF INDEPENDENCE. *Hist. Today [Great Britain] 1959 9(8): 560-564.* A biographical sketch of the life and influence of Richard Price, the Welsh Nonconformist minister who was distinguished for the variety of his interests, ranging from religion, philosophy, mathematics, life insurance, the problems of population, to the cause of the American colonists and the revolutionary movement in France. He made a profound contribution to the development of life insurance in Britain. His pamphlet *Observations on Civil Liberty* outlines both the Commonwealth ideal and the federal principle upon which the United States were to be established and was one of the inspirations of the Declaration of Independence. He declined on grounds of old age an invitation by the American Congress to set the new government's finances in order.   B. Waldstein

297. Morice, Joseph. THE CONTRIBUTIONS OF CHARLES W. F. DUMAS TO THE CAUSE OF AMERICAN INDEPENDENCE. *Duquesne R. 1961 7(1): 17-28.* Lists the valuable services of this Hollander in the diplomatic employ

of the American colonies during the Revolutionary War and explains why his initial enthusiasm for the colonials had all but evaporated by the end of the conflict.   L. V. Eid

298. Parsons, Lynn H. THE MYSTERIOUS MR. DIGGES. *William and Mary Q. 1965 22(3): 486-492.* Was Thomas Attwood Digges of Warburton, Maryland, a double agent for the British during the American Revolution and in the 1790's when, as patron of the United Irishmen in America, he went to Ireland supposedly to work for Irish independence? Digges is acquitted by the author of the first charge, but evidence on the second charge incriminates Digges as an informer on the Irish leader, Theobald Tone. 16 notes.   H. M. Ward

299. Quarles, Benjamin. LORD DUNMORE AS LIBERATOR. *William and Mary Q. 1958 15(4): 494-507.* Dunmore's proclamation granting freedom to slaves joining the Loyalist forces, which caused about 800 slaves to join the British side at the time and set the example for thousands of others, made him infamous in the eyes of the Patriots and a hero of the slaves.   E. Oberholzer, Jr.

300. Whitworth, Rex. FIELD-MARSHAL LORD AMHERST, A MILITARY ENIGMA. *Hist. Today [Great Britain] 1959 9(2): 132-137.* Lord Amherst (1717-97) was the hero of the Seven Years' War in America, but he was reluctant to return there either as Governor of Virginia, or as commander of the British military forces during the American Revolution. The author discusses several possible reasons for this enigma, but decides that the answer will only be found by further research.   L. D. Johnson

301. Wyatt, Frederick and Wilcox, William B. SIR HENRY CLINTON: A PSYCHOLOGICAL EXPLORATION IN HISTORY. *William and Mary Q. 1959 16(1): 3-26.* A collaborative study, by a historian and a psychologist, designed to determine the causes of Clinton's enigmatic conduct during the American Revolution. Inner tensions arising from "an unconscious conflict over authority," rather than the external situation, determined Clinton's behavior. The author discusses the methods of psychological history and biography. Research in this field must be collaborative; neither the historian nor the psychologist can do it alone.   E. Oberholzer, Jr.

John Adams

302. Andrews, Robert Hardy. JOHN ADAMS: THE FIRST ANGRY MAN IN THE WHITE HOUSE. *Mankind 1969 2(1): 12-15, 44-49.* Adams (1735-1826) was a man of principle who because of a temperament that made him unpopular was relegated to second place several times in his political career. Lacking the facility to play politics, Adams accepted difficult, unpopular, lonely roles. He ably

defended the British soldiers who killed Crispus Attucks; he was on the committee to discuss a declaration of independence, but deferred to Jefferson in the drafting of the document. His plight was symbolically summed up in his adherence to the opinion that 2 July, not 4 July, was the true Independence Day: "Wrong by two days, he continued to err just sufficiently to keep him in second place." Thus as a minister plenipotentiary, he took orders from Franklin; he was Vice-President to Washington; as President he was but a nominal Federalist while Hamilton ruled the faction; in the election of 1800 he had to sit by while Jefferson and Burr vied for the office he held. Afterwards, he read much and continued his pungent stream of commentaries, directing them toward the writers he studied. In the end he died on the day others called Independence, but he finally accepted it, willfully accepting second place to a Jefferson he believed still to live, yet who ironically died the same day. 8 illus.   A. H. Pfeiffer

303. Breen, Timothy H. JOHN ADAMS' FIGHT AGAINST INNOVATION IN THE NEW ENGLAND CONSTITUTION, 1776. *New England Q. 1967 40(4): 501-520.* The key to understanding the political thought of John Adams is seen in the New England heritage of republican institutions as preserved most closely in Connecticut. Britain was denounced as a malicious "innovator" threatening New England traditions with admiralty courts, a despotic royal governor, and Parliamentary taxation. In 1775, Adams wanted to preserve as much of the traditional political framework of Massachusetts as possible—the charter government with the royal element removed. By 1776 the urgency for a formal constitution for Massachusetts was clear. However, Adams was disturbed about the mania for innovation displayed by many of the "levelling citizens" of the State. His disenchantment reached a peak in the summer of 1776, when the militia seemed to exclude men of quality from leadership, and Americans showed an unexpected addiction to corruption. He retained faith in a balanced, three-part legislature as the *summum bonum* of political virtue. Documented from Adams' *Works.*   K. B. West

304. Butterfield, L. H. THE PAPERS OF THE ADAMS FAMILY: SOME ACCOUNT OF THEIR HISTORY. *Pro. of the Massachusetts Hist. Soc. 1953-57 71: 328-356.* Describes how the famous collection of original manuscripts of the Adams family, accumulated from the early 18th to the late 19th century, were collected, and are being published. Based on letters to and from the Adams family in the Massachusetts Historical Society.   N. Callahan

305. Ellsworth, John W. JOHN ADAMS: THE AMERICAN REVOLUTION AS A CHANGE OF HEART? *Huntington Lib. Q. 1965 28(4): 293-300.* A gradualist, psychological interpretation of the Revolution can be found in Adams' postpresidential writings and has been of some influence. But careful examination of Adams' attitudes in the 15 years before 1776 shows his later generalizations as too simple, for in fact his responses were mainly brought out by the actual course of events.   H. D. Jordan

306. Garrett, Wendell D. THE PAPERS OF THE ADAMS FAMILY: A NATURAL RESOURCE OF HISTORY. *Hist. New Hampshire 1966 21(3): 28-37.*

Historical editing changed from patriotic, eulogistic distortion to a science with the work done on the sources of the Revolutionary era by Worthington C. Ford, Max Farrand, and E. C. Burnett in the early 20th century. "After World War II a fresh generation of scholars added a new dimension to historical editing." The author cites the Adams Papers—a documented chronicle of the family over four generations—to show the value of such raw material. These "natural resources" for history serve as a perennial "natural resource" of our country.

R. S. Burke

307. Hayes, Frederic H. JOHN ADAMS AND AMERICAN SEA POWER. *Am. Neptune 1965 15(1): 35-45.* Views Adams as statesman-founder of American naval power, who through his whole career recognized its importance as a factor in American defense. On the Marine Committee of the Continental Congress, as a diplomat and as president, he remained interested and involved in naval affairs, finally presiding over the creation of a permanent Navy Department. He saw naval power as an essential in foreign policy to protect trade, attack enemy commerce, defend the coast and force respect for American vessels. He understood the actual and the theoretical value of naval power. Main source: Adams Papers.   J. G. Lydon

308. Knollenberg, Bernhard. JOHN DICKINSON VS. JOHN ADAMS: 1774-1776. *Pro. of the Am. Phil. Soc. 1963 107(2): 138-144.* Traces the deterioration of relations between John Adams and John Dickinson from the convening of the First Continental Congress through the debate over adoption of the Declaration of Independence. Dickinson opposed immediate adoption of the Declaration, a stand which cost him political popularity, because the colonies had not yet decided on the proper relations which should exist between themselves and because the French court had not yet indicated what assistance would be given to the Americans. "On balance...Dickinson's arguments were sound." In any event, his moral courage was admirable. Based on the correspondence of both men, Adams' diary, and other primary source material.   R. G. Comegys

309. Morgan, Edmund S. JOHN ADAMS AND THE PURITAN TRADITION. *New England Q. 1961 34(4): 518-529.* A review article on the four volumes of the *John Adams Papers,* which publish a new edition of Adams' diary and autobiography. The new edition, edited by Lyman Butterfield and others, is more complete and useful than the older one of Charles Francis Adams. Adams' writings reveal more facets of his character as well as his lack of broad learning in such areas as art, architecture and science, his excessive vanity, his Puritan roots, and combination of political ambition and disinterested service which led him to serve so well the colonial cause and the new nation which he had helped to found.   L. Gara

310. Mugridge, Donald H. THE ADAMS PAPERS. *Am. Archivist 1962 25(4): 449-454.* There is an essential difference between the publication of the projected 80-volume Adams Papers and all similar projects. Namely, the Adams Papers will show the successes and failures of three or four generations of a family instead of one individual. The Adams Papers will appear in three main divisions: Series

One, will contain the diaries and autobiographies of the three statesmen; Series Two, selected inter-family correspondence, 1767-1859; Series Three, a selection of correspondence, public papers, and speeches of the three statesmen.

G. M. Gressley

Benjamin Franklin

311. Aldridge, Alfred Owen. CHARLES BROCKDEN BROWN'S POEM ON BENJAMIN FRANKLIN. *Am. Literature 1966 38(2): 230-235.* Describes the circumstances surrounding some eulogistic verses on Benjamin Franklin by Charles Brockden Brown (1771-1810) which were published in the *State Gazette of North Carolina* in 1789. The blundering printer, either from zeal or ignorance, substituted the name of Washington for Franklin. "Instead of 'An Inscription for Benjamin Franklin's Tomb Stone' the title read 'An Inscription for General Washington's Tomb Stone,' and in the opening stanza 'the Shade of great Newton' yielded most inappropriately 'Philosophy's throne' to Washington instead of to Franklin." Brown's verses were clearly modeled after a widely known attack upon Franklin which was probably written by Jonathan Odell, the wittiest of the Loyalist writers, and which was circulated in Philadelphia and elsewhere during the American Revolution. "Charles Brockden Brown, as an acquaintance and strong admirer of the philosopher of Philadelphia, undoubtedly condemned these verses and wrote his own tribute to Franklin as a means of repudiating them or counteracting their influence." 12 notes.   D. D. Cameron

312. Aldridge, Alfred Owen. FORM AND SUBSTANCE IN FRANKLIN'S AUTOBIOGRAPHY. *Essays on American Literature in Honor of Jay B. Hubbell (Durham: Duke U. Press, 1967), pp. 47-62.* Franklin's autobiography is flawed in order and structure, but "the self-revelation and realistic view of life in his memoirs...elevate his work to a higher plane than the didactic one he recognized." Although "Franklin was virtually forced to live up to his reputation as a diverting stylist," the major value of his memoirs is "psychological rather than artistic." 26 notes.   C. L. Eichelberger

313. Aldridge, Alfred Owen. THE FIRST PUBLISHED MEMOIR OF FRANKLIN. *William and Mary Q. 1967 24(4): 624-628.* Comments on a brief article, "Authentic Memoir of Dr. Franklin," published in the *London Chronicle* for 1 October 1778, reputed to be the first segment of Franklin's autobiography to be published. Discrepancies are found when it is compared with the later published *Autobiography* (1791). The contradictory versions of Franklin's arrival at Philadelphia may be attributed to his greater concern for a philosophy of life rather than interest in details. 10 notes.   H. M. Ward

314. Amacher, Richard E. THE GROWING SHELF OF FRANKLINANA. *Am. Q. 1965 17(2, Part 1): 261-265.* Book reviews of the following: William S. Hanna, *Benjamin Franklin and Pennsylvania Politics* (Stanford: Stanford U. Press, 1964) receives high credit as a fresh and frank portrayal of Franklin, the political opportunist; Bruce I. Granger, *Benjamin Franklin: An American Man of Letters* (Ithaca: Cornell U. Press, 1964) is less helpful, although it makes some useful distinctions concerning Franklin's writing; Robert F. Sayre, *The Examined Self: Benjamin Franklin, Henry Adams, Henry James* (Princeton: Princeton U. Press, 1964) is a contribution to understanding Franklin as an autobiographer and to autobiography per se; Leonard W. Labaree, Ralph L. Ketcham, Helen C. Boatfield, and Helene H. Fineman, ed., *The Autobiography of Benjamin Franklin* (New Haven: Yale U. Press, 1964) is regarded as less useful than the high quality collection of memoirs being put together by Yale; and Leonard W. Labaree, Whitfield J. Bell, Jr., Ralph L. Ketcham, Helen C. Boatfield, and Helene H. Fineman, ed., *The Papers of Benjamin Franklin, Vols. I-VII* (New Haven: Yale U. Press, 1959-63) covers the period of Franklin's life for the years 1706-58 and constitutes valuable source material for a variety of subjects.

R. S. Pickett

315. Bell, Whitfield J., Jr. "ALL CLEAR SUNSHINE": NEW LETTERS OF FRANKLIN AND MARY STEVENSON HEWSON. *Pro. of the Am. Phil. Soc. 1956 100(6): 521-536.* After a brief description of the collections in which the letters exchanged between Benjamin Franklin and his friend Mary Stevenson Hewson can be found, gives a summary of the contents of the correspondence. Passages of some letters are quoted. Documented.

N. Kurland

316. Beloff, Max. BENJAMIN FRANKLIN: INTERNATIONAL STATES-MAN. *Memoirs and Pro. of the Manchester Literary and Phil. Soc. [Great Britain] 1955/56 97: 13-30.* Commemorates the 250th anniversary of Franklin's birth by tracing his contribution to the development of a foreign policy specifically suited to American needs. Originally devoted to the British connection, Franklin was by 1776 advocating complete independence; during the Revolution, as America's chief diplomatic agent abroad, he was faced with the dilemma of finding a way to take advantage of the hostility of France and Spain to Britain while avoiding falling into a new, unbreakable dependence upon either of these allies. A realist in his outlook, a believer in America's "manifest destiny," and flexible in his methods, he (aided by John Jay) successfully charted a course whereby French assistance was used to gain independence, then Britain's position as a counterweight was used to maintain it. Thus was evolved the foreign policy compounded partly of idealism and partly of realism which, being suited to the peculiar condition of a newly enfranchised state, has subsequently served as a model for a great variety of emergent nations, both in and out of the Common-wealth.

R. G. Schafer

317. Berti, G. *BENJAMIN FRANKLIN AND ITALY. Studi Storici [Italy] 1959/60 1(2): 365-372.* Reviews a book by Antonio Pace (Philadelphia: Am.

Philosophic Soc., 1958) which is part of a collection dealing with America's cultural impact upon the rest of the world. Pace's book examines Benjamin Franklin's influence in Italy, tracing it to the present day.   D. F. Rossi

318. Bushman, Richard. ON THE USES OF PSYCHOLOGY: CONFLICT AND CONCILIATION IN BENJAMIN FRANKLIN. *Hist. and Theory 1966 5(3): 225-240.* Undertakes the task of showing how the historian can use the insights of psychology. A study of the role of conflict and conciliation in Benjamin Franklin's *Autobiography* illustrates some possible methods for developing facility in fully utilizing psychological techniques in biographical work.

L. V. Eid

319. Commager, Henry Steele. FRANKLIN STILL SPEAKS TO US. *New York Times Mag. 1955 15(February): 19, 74, 76.* Sketches the personal characteristics and basic ideas of Benjamin Franklin that have made him "survive" as a truly representative American.   R. F. Campbell

320. Couve de Murville, Maurice. BENJAMIN FRANKLIN: THE DIPLO-MAT AND JOURNALIST. *Pro. of the Am. Phil. Soc. 1956 100(4): 316-325.* Franklin combined the traditional art of diplomacy with skillful manipulation of public opinion to win a brilliant diplomatic success in France during the American Revolution. He won French sympathy as a symbol of the free and self-made man and wrote letters and pamphlets to stir up public opinion in France and England. Franklin's restraint and skill brought France into the war on the American side and helped carry the allies through the war together without an open break.   N. Kurland

321. Cullen, Joseph P. BENJAMIN FRANKLIN: "THE GLORY OF AMER-ICA." *Am. Hist. Illus. 1971 6(1): 4-11, 40-47.* Born of humble parents in Boston in January 1706, Franklin learned the printing trade under an apprenticeship with his brother. He ran away to New York and later to Philadelphia at age 17. He owned the *Pennsylvania Gazette* at 24, and published the first *Poor Richard's Almanac* two years later and continued it for 25 years. He retired to "philosophical studies and amusements" at 42, but in reality served the public for an additional 42 years—initially in the service of Pennsylvania and later as Special Agent to Parliament for four colonies, as a member of the Continental Congress, and from 1776 to 1785 as U.S. diplomat in France. He returned to the United States in 1785 and was a conciliatory spirit at the Constitutional Convention of 1787. Franklin was industrious and frugal; but most of all, he was a great diplomat with men, women, and nations. Based on secondary sources; 16 illus.

D. Dodd

322. Dijksterhuis, E. J. BIJ DE 250e HERDENKING VAN BENJAMIN FRANKLIN'S GEBOORTEDAG [On the occasion of the 250th anniversary of the birth of Benjamin Franklin]. *Gids [Norway] 1956 119(1): 24-36.* Biography of Benjamin Franklin (1706-90). The author stresses the importance of his discoveries in the field of electricity, stating that the lightning rod should be considered

a major invention, for it was in keeping with the ideas of the Enlightenment on man's control over nature. Franklin was popular in France not only because he was minister of an allied nation but also because he was an intellectual and a champion of liberty and equality. D. van Arkel

323. Golladay, V. Dennis. THE EVOLUTION OF BENJAMIN FRANKLIN'S THEORY OF VALUE. *Pennsylvania Hist. 1970 37(1): 40-52.* Describes the evolution of Franklin's concept of value from an emphasis on the importance of labor to a position which joined labor and land as prime determinants of value. In "A Modest Inquiry into the Nature and Necessity of a Paper Currency," Franklin defended paper currency over specie because precious metals vary in value according to supply and demand. The value of a paper currency, he argued, would rest upon the amount of labor in a colony. In other writings, he emphasized the relationship between the availability of inexpensive land and high wages. Contact with the French Physiocrats, who found land and husbandry the true sources of value, enabled Franklin to merge his ideas on importance of labor and land in determining value. To him, the only source of value was the labor of a farmer. Manufactured goods were valued not according to the hours of labor put into them but rather according to how much food the laborer consumed as a result of the application of his skills to manufacture an article. 38 notes.
D. C. Swift

324. Kahn, Robert L. ADDENDUM CONCERNING A LOST FRANKLIN-RASPE LETTER. *Pro. of the Am. Phil. Soc. 1956 100(3): 279.* Text of, and brief comment on, a letter written by Benjamin Franklin from Passy on 4 May 1779.
N. Kurland

325. Kahn, Robert L. AN ACCOUNT OF A MEETING WITH BENJAMIN FRANKLIN AT PASSY ON OCTOBER 9, 1777: FROM GEORG FOR-STER'S ENGLISH JOURNAL. *William and Mary Q. 1955 12(3): 472-474.* A fragment from the journal, describing Benjamin Franklin at a dinner; contains an introduction by the editor. E. Oberholzer, Jr.

326. Kahn, Robert L. FRANKLIN, GRIMM, AND J. H. LANDOLT. *Pro. of the Am. Phil. Soc. 1955 99(6): 401-404.* A casual relationship led to an encounter between Landolt and Franklin which produced a description of Franklin in old age. Based on a letter in the Society's collection and on the unpublished diaries of Landolt. C. B. Joynt

327. Katcham, Ralph L. BENJAMIN FRANKLIN AND WILLIAM SMITH: NEW LIGHT ON AN OLD PHILADELPHIA QUARREL. *Pennsylvania Mag. of Hist. and Biog. 1964 88(2): 142-163.* In April 1755 William Smith wrote a pamphlet on the colony of Pennsylvania bitterly attacking the Quakers. He was devoted to the Penn family and had the typical political and social outlook of the Anglican orthodoxy of the day. He was born to controversy and published dozens of polemical pamphlets. The personalities of Smith and Franklin were deeply at odds. The former disdained Franklin's patient negotiating, while Franklin was

disgusted with Smith's flamboyant indiscretions. Smith's views were those of influential Englishmen; Franklin spoke for the "new man" in the colonies. Their quarrel in its persistence and bitterness thus foreshadowed in microcosm the break between Britain and her colonies. Based on the Penn Papers, Franklin Papers, pamphlets and newspapers. 57 notes.   E. P. Stickney

328. Labaree, Leonard W. IN SEARCH OF "B. FRANKLIN." *William and Mary Q. 1959 16(2): 188-197.* Relates the experiences of an editor in search of Benjamin Franklin manuscripts. Some turned up in East Germany and Moscow, and others proved to be forgeries.   E. Oberholzer, Jr.

329. Labaree, Leonard W. and Bell, Whitfield J., Jr. THE PAPERS OF BENJAMIN FRANKLIN: A PROGRESS REPORT. *Pro. of the Am. Phil. Soc. 1957 101(6): 532-534.* Approximately 27 thousand surviving letters and other writings of Franklin and all letters to him have been photocopied and catalogued in preparation for the publication of a comprehensive edition of Franklin papers under the sponsorship of Yale University and the American Philosophical Society. There are about five thousand duplicate items, and about six thousand of the remainder are by Franklin. This new edition will have about three times as many documents by Franklin as the most recent previous edition by Albert Henry Smyth, published in 1905-07.   N. Kurland

330. Lingelbach, William E. [BENJAMIN FRANKLIN AND THE AMERICAN PHILOSOPHICAL SOCIETY]. *Pro. of the Am. Phil. Soc.*
  BENJAMIN FRANKLIN'S PAPERS AND THE AMERICAN PHILOSOPHICAL SOCIETY. 1955 99(6): 359-380. With the cooperation of Yale University, the Philosophical Society and other institutions with large Franklin holdings, an edition of Franklin's papers is in preparation. The author describes the relations of the Society with Franklin papers over the last century and a half.
  BENJAMIN FRANKLIN AND THE AMERICAN PHILOSOPHICAL SOCIETY IN 1956. 1956 100(4): 354-368. Includes a survey of the celebrations in honor of Franklin's birthday in 1776, 1806, 1856 and 1906 with indications of the various ways Franklin has been honored since his death.
                                    C. B. Joynt and N. Kurland

331. Miles, Richard D. THE AMERICAN IMAGE OF BENJAMIN FRANKLIN. *Am. Q. 1957 9(2): 117-143.* An extensive survey of the literature, mostly American, on Benjamin Franklin. In the years immediately following his death, Franklin's reputation fell upon evil days. His political enemies systematically emphasized the less attractive aspects of his character and minimized his achievements. The pattern thus laid down was retained until mid-century, when the first real attempts were made to paint a broader portrait of this many-sided man. Franklin's "rags to riches" career had a natural attraction in the intellectual climate of the post-Civil War period, and he became "the patron saint of getting on," a role that he has not yet lost. The xenophobia of the period also affected the image of Franklin in that his prudential philosophy appeared less an expression of selfishness than a means of achievement expressive of the best in the

American national character. The late 19th century also saw the beginning of real Franklin scholarship, and today the various aspects of Franklin's genius are receiving due recognition. "Whatever the place of Poor Richard in the real Franklin, it is losing its importance as the many specialized studies of Franklin's other aspects are completed." The task of present-day scholarship is to reveal a nobler, more heroic Franklin. D. Houston

332. Ward, John William. "WHO WAS BENJAMIN FRANKLIN?" *Am. Scholar 1963 32(4): 541-553.* "One need only consider in retrospect how swiftly Franklin moved upward through the various levels of society to see the openness, the fluidity of his world." If there is much of our national character implied in his career it is because he is an early representative of a response to the "rapid social change that has remained about the only constant in American society." Part I of his autobiography was intended for his son but the other parts were written after the Revolution in full consciousness "that he was offering himself to the world as a representative type, the American." E. P. Stickney

333. Weaver, Glenn. BENJAMIN FRANKLIN AND THE PENNSYLVANIA GERMANS. *William and Mary Q. 1957 14(4): 536-559.* Pre-revolutionary relations between Franklin and the Pennsylvania Germans were cool. By the eve of the Revolution, however, the "church" Germans had joined with the Scotch Irish in opposition to the neutralist coalition of Quakers and "sect" Germans; Franklin, observing their Americanization, found them to be useful tools in setting up the extra-legal machinery of the Revolution. The article also discusses the founding of the German Lutheran and Reformed school, Franklin College, in which Benjamin Rush was influential. E. Oberholzer, Jr.

334. Wright, Esmond. BENJAMIN FRANKLIN: A TRADESMAN IN THE AGE OF REASON. *Hist. Today [Great Britain] 1956 6(7): 439-447.* A brief biographical sketch and character analysis. W. M. Simon

335. Zimmerman, John J. BENJAMIN FRANKLIN AND THE *PENNSYL-VANIA CHRONICLE. Pennsylvania Mag. of Hist. and Biog. 1957 81(4): 351-364.* Shows how the *Pennsylvania Chronicle,* even though Franklin had no official or business connection with it, served as a channel for his ideas and as a result convinced his critics of his loyalty to the colonists' cause. W. Hunsberger

336. —. BENJAMIN FRANKLIN ISSUE. *Pennsylvania Mag. of Hist. and Biog. 1956 80(1): 5-91.* A special issue devoted to Benjamin Franklin.
Sellars, Charles C. FRANKLIN'S LAST PORTRAIT, pp. 5-11.
Wolf, Edwin. FRANKLIN AND HIS FRIENDS CHOOSE THEIR BOOKS, pp. 11-37.
Hoopes, Penrose R. FRANKLIN ATTENDS A BOOK AUCTION, pp. 37-46.
Mulcahy, James M. CASH TO DR. FRANKLIN, pp. 46-74. Excerpts from the account books of Franklin's business agent.

Mulcahy, James M. CONGRESS VOTING INDEPENDENCE: THE TRUMBELL AND PINE-SAVAGE PAINTINGS, pp. 74-91.

D. Houston

Alexander Hamilton

337. Adair, Douglass, ed. CHANCELLOR KENT'S *BRIEF REVIEW OF THE PUBLIC LIFE AND WRITINGS OF GENERAL HAMILTON. Historian 1956/57 19(2): 182-202.* The representation of the best sketch of Hamilton by a contemporary, here identified as the work of Chancellor James Kent.

E. C. Johnson

338. Mitchell, Broadus. "IF HAMILTON WERE HERE TODAY": SOME UNANSWERED QUESTIONS. *South Atlantic Q. 1963 62(2): 288-296.* Alexander Hamilton's biographer poses certain questions about Hamilton's life and actions which are left unanswered by the surviving record. These range from his early life and education through a number of actions and decisions of his later career.

C. R. Allen, Jr.

339. Panagopoulos, E. P. HAMILTON'S NOTES IN HIS PAY BOOK OF THE NEW YORK STATE ARTILLERY COMPANY. *Am. Hist. R. 1957 62(2): 310-325.* In 1776 Alexander Hamilton was commander of the Artillery Company of New York State. At the same time, he was a student at King's College and used the back pages of the company paybook as a student's note book. These notes reveal how early Hamilton developed his interest in economics and statesmanship and shed some light on his scholastic background. They also disclose ideas that recur years later in several of his important papers. The notes are concerned with numerous economic subjects, "political arithmetic," extracts from classical authors, and jottings on miscellaneous matters. Evidence is cited showing that he referred to these notes in later life.

D. Houston

340. Syrett, Harold C. and Cooke, Jacob E. THE PAPERS OF ALEXANDER HAMILTON. *Historian 1956/57 19(2): 168-181.* A summary of the work being done by Columbia University Press editors under a grant from Time, Inc., and the Rockefeller Foundation. The editors have found useful the work of Hamilton's widow, Elizabeth, in collecting, and that of John Church Hamilton in editing his papers. The most extensive collections of Hamilton papers are those in the Library of Congress and the National Archives.

E. C. Johnson

341. Wright, Esmond. ALEXANDER HAMILTON: FOUNDING FATHER. *Hist. Today [Great Britain] 1957 7(3): 182-189.* Investigates why Hamilton, though "perhaps the most creative figure thrown up by the American Revolution," has not become the focus of a legend, and has even been relatively neglected

by historians. The answer lies partly in his obscure and foreign beginnings, and partly in his reactionary political and economic ideas, but above all "Hamilton's failure was a failure of personality": he was inconsistent, he was quarrelsome, and he was ambitious.   W. M. Simon

John Paul Jones

342. Balderston, Marion. THE FLAG JOHN PAUL JONES REALLY FOUGHT UNDER. *Huntington Lib. Q. 1969 33(1): 77-83.* The colors flown by vessels of the Revolutionary Navy were unstandardized. The author gives a history of the flags John Paul Jones sailed under during his career, in order to verify or dispel Jones's statement, "My hand first hoisted the American flag." Jones's famous *Ranger* flew the 13 red and white stripes as its ensign, with stars in a pennant which was flown from the topmast. At no time did he combine the stars and stripes.   H. D. Jordan

343. Cullen, Joseph P. JOHN PAUL JONES: A PERSONALITY PROFILE. *Am. Hist. Illus. 1966 1(1): 12-19.* Discusses the colorful military career and complex character of John Paul Jones. Born in Scotland in 1747, Jones settled in Virginia about 1773 and was commissioned into the Continental Navy in 1775. His naval career was virtually unnoticed until 1780 when he became the darling of Europe for his capture of the British frigate *Serapis.* Perhaps the greatest hindrance to his advancement in the U.S. Navy was his "tendency to criticize his superiors and withhold praise and credit from his subordinates." He was extremely egotistical and had an explosive temper. He did not succeed in ingratiating himself with Congress or with his naval superiors and thus missed opportunity for advancement. After the Revolution, when Congress discontinued the Navy, Jones was out of a job. He traveled in Europe for several years and then entered the Russian Navy as a rear admiral. Relieved of his command, he returned to Paris, where he died in 1792. His remains now rest in the crypt of the chapel at the U. S. Naval Academy at Annapolis.   M. J. McBaine

344. Morison, Samuel Eliot. THE ARMS AND SEALS OF JOHN PAUL JONES. *Am. Neptune 1958 18(4): 301-305.* Refers to heraldry as a key to a man's ambition and character. John Paul, a Scot, took the name of John Paul Jones when a commissioned officer in the U.S. Navy, 1775, and adopted the arms of a Welsh Jones family quartered with those of the English Pauls. To this he added a coronet when made Chevalier de l'Ordre du Mérite Militaire by Louis XVI.
                                                          A

345. Morison, Samuel Eliot. THE WILLIE JONES-JOHN PAUL JONES TRADITION. *William and Mary Q. 1959 16(2): 198-206.* From a reexamination of the evidence, concludes that the tradition that John Paul added the name "Jones"

in gratitude to Willie Jones resulted from the false identification of one Paul Jones, a grantee of land held by Willie Jones' parents-in-law, with John Paul Jones. The naval hero added the "Jones" as an alias while a fugitive from prosecution for killing a man in self-defense. E. Oberholzer, Jr.

346. Warner, Oliver. JOHN PAUL JONES IN BATTLE. *Hist. Today [Great Britain]* 1965 15(9): 613-618. John Paul Jones was a Scottish gardener who learned his seamanship on a slave ship and went to Virginia to take over his dead brother William's estate in 1773. The author describes the marauding ventures of Jones from Europe to America, 1778-80, concentrating on his strategy and tactics. It concludes with some mention of Jones' service in the Russian navy in the last decade of his life. Illus. L. A. Knafla

Marquis de Lafayette

347. Maurois, André. NEW LIGHT ON AN OLD FRIEND. *New York Times Mag.* 1956 19(August): 24f. Some recently discovered letters of the Marquis de Lafayette furnish the occasion for this article. The letters, found at Château de la Grange, France, cover most of his public career, from his days in America up to 1824. A short survey of Lafayette's career is included. D. Houston

348. Unsigned. HOW A FRENCH NOBLEMAN'S "HEART WAS EN-ROLLED" IN THE AMERICAN REVOLUTION. *Freedom and Union* 1957 12(9): 16-18. A biographical sketch of the Marquis de Lafayette, commemorating the bicentenary of his birth. Lafayette's dedication to the ideals of the revolution of the American colonies was awakened by the Duke of Gloucester, brother of George III, during his visit to France. The Marquis' laborious efforts to obtain a commission in the Continental Army after his arrival in Philadelphia in 1777 are praised. The American government and population greatly honored Lafayette when he visited the United States again in 1824-25. R. Mueller

349. Whitridge, Arnold. LAFAYETTE GOES TO AMERICA. *Hist. Today [Great Britain]* 1970 20(8): 527-533. Marie Joseph Paul Yves Roch Gilbert du Motier, later Marquis de Lafayette, was a young French nobleman who sailed out of Bordeaux for America in the spring of 1777 to avenge his father's death at the hands of the British. Describes the way in which Lafayette came to make the decision to throw his life into the American War for Independence, and the problems he had in leaving France. Based on contemporary letters and memoirs; illus. L. A. Knafla

350. Wright, Esmond. LAFAYETTE: HERO OF TWO WORLDS. *Hist. Today [Great Britain]* 1957 7(10): 653-661. A reexamination of the life of Lafayette on the occasion of the celebration in France and the United States of the bicentenary

of his birth. His role in the American Revolution and his subsequent failures as a leader in his own country are discussed. Lafayette has become far more important as a symbol of Franco-American friendship than as a contributor to American independence. E. D. Johnson

Thomas Paine

351. Brunel, Adrian. THOMAS PAINE. *Contemporary R. [Great Britain] 1955 188(1075): 52-56.* A favorable account of Paine's career, his early years in England as an exciseman, his role in the American and French Revolutions and tragic later life. J. G. Gazley

352. Gimbel, Richard. THE RESURGENCE OF THOMAS PAINE. *Pro. of the Am. Antiquarian Soc. 1959 69(2): 97-111.* Thomas Paine, one of the most effective propagandists of all time, contributed mightily to the establishment of the United States as an independent nation through his *Common Sense* and *The American Crisis.* Later he helped support the revolutionary cause in France and defended human freedom in England in his *Rights of Man.* In *The Age of Reason* he sought to save France from atheism, urging the acceptance of a religion agreeable to the rational nature of man. He spent his last years in the United States, attacked violently by all the forces of conservatism and traditional religion. Since his death in 1809, however, hostility toward him has gradually disappeared, and public appreciation increased. Illustrative of the continuing interest in his works is the recent reprinting of the *Age of Reason* in an edition of 100,000 and the translation of the *Rights of Man* into Russian. W. D. Metz

353. Gimbel, Richard. THOMAS PAINE FIGHTS FOR FREEDOM IN THREE WORLDS: THE NEW, THE OLD, THE NEXT. CATALOGUE OF AN EXHIBITION COMMEMORATING THE ONE HUNDREDTH ANNIVERSARY OF HIS DEATH. YALE UNIVERSITY LIBRARY, OCTOBER 1959. *Pro. of the Am. Antiquarian Soc. 1961 70(2): 397-492.* Brief descriptions of a rich and varied selection of items from the Paine Collection of Richard Gimbel, arranged under the following headings: Paine's separate works, letters, manuscripts; collected works (1791-1827); portraits and engravings; caricatures; tokens; and celebrations. A total of 427 items is included. In many cases, the descriptions include not only the contents of the items but important background information as well. W. D. Metz

354. Gummere, Richard M. THOMAS PAINE: WAS HE REALLY ANTI-CLASSICAL? *Pro. of the Am. Antiquarian Soc. 1965 75(2): 253-269.* Focuses on Thomas Paine the journalist rather than Paine the patriot or the world reformer. Analyzing his attitude toward the Greek and Latin classics leads to the conclusion that he made as many references to the classic writers as did his

contemporaries. The major difference, however, was that Paine, in contrast to his contemporaries, relied on translations rather than the originals for his knowledge, in the conviction that good translations saved the scholar's time from the work of translation. Tracing his reluctance to study languages to his early education leads to the discovery that he was sometimes superficial in his reading and to the conclusion that his attitude was more one of respect than of real admiration for the Greek and Roman thinkers. 43 notes.   R. V. Calvert

355. Hinz, Evelyn J. THE "REASONABLE" STYLE OF TOM PAINE. *Queen's Q. [Canada] 1972 79(2): 231-241.* Instead of exemplifying rational common sense, the prose style in Thomas Paine's works is essentially demagogic. Examines Paine's major works, *Common Sense* (1776), *The Rights of Man* (1791-92), and *The Age of Reason* (1794-96), to demonstrate how each "invokes" common sense while Paine "asserts" that he is utilizing reason; in short, reason is not being used as a persuasive force to sway readers. 6 notes.
                                                                    J. A. Casada

356. Ihde, H. THOMAS PAINES WEG ZUM REVOLUTIONÄR [Thomas Paine's development as a revolutionary]. *Wissenschaftliche Zeitschrift der Humboldt-U. zu Berlin [East Germany] 1966 15(5): 635-640.* Reviews Paine's development as a revolutionary pamphleteer and theorist. Using numerous quotes from Paine's writing and letters, the author shows that Paine was a typical representative of the petty bourgeoisie dedicating his life to the struggle against feudalism.   D. Visser

357. Schroeder, Theodore. THOMAS PAINE: APOSTLE OF LIBERTY. *J. of Human Relations 1963 11(2): 210-220.* Extols Paine and his role in the American and French Revolutions. This "biographical statement" was adapted from the pamphlet *Thomas Paine,* now out of print, published by Promoting Enduring Peace, Inc., Woodmont, Connecticut. Undocumented.   D. J. Abramoske

George Washington

358. Bernath, Stuart L. GEORGE WASHINGTON AND THE GENESIS OF AMERICAN MILITARY DISCIPLINE. *Mid-Am. 1967 49(2): 83-100.* An examination of George Washington as a military disciplinarian shows that as a colonel in the French and Indian Wars and as commander in chief of the Continental army, "the germ of discipline unfolded." Although problems persisted, Washington's positive and negative approaches to discipline bore fruit in victories. 91 notes.   L. D. Silveri

359. Boller, Paul F., Jr. GEORGE WASHINGTON AND THE QUAKERS. *Bull. of Friends Hist. Assoc. 1960 49(2): 67-83.* An account of the relations

between Washington and the Quakers. Washington came gradually to respect, but not to share, the principles of the Friends. He did not sympathize with their pacifism during the Revolution: but he treated them with fairness and decency. After the war his sympathy increased, although he objected to their vigorous agitation on the antislavery issue. He approved of their efforts on behalf of the Indians. On the issue of war with France, he had a disagreement with the Quaker George Logan. Documented. N. D. Kurland

360. Bragdon, Henry W. GEORGE WASHINGTON: MONUMENT OR MAN? *Am. Hist. Illus. 1967 1(10): 34-42.* Starting from the premise that George Washington remains an "unknown man" because of the tendency to deify him, the author attempts to portray a man who speaks to our age in terms we can understand. Comments of British and French observers form the basis for this new look at an old hero. F. J. Stachowski

361. Jackson, Donald. THE PAPERS OF GEORGE WASHINGTON. *Manuscripts 1970 22(1): 2-11.* Discusses the forthcoming edition of the George Washington Papers. Calls for the cooperation of private collectors and provides case examples of their compliance. Lists the advisory committee to the papers and discusses automated techniques used in collating material. Shows a computer print-out from the list of Washington items. 3 photos. D. A. Yanchisin

362. Knowlton, John D. "PROPERLY ARRANGED AND SO CORRECTLY RECORDED." *Am. Archivist 1964 27(3): 371-374.* Lt. Col. Richard Varick was appointed by George Washington as recording secretary, May 1781, to classify and transcribe the papers of the commander in chief. The work was done in Poughkeepsie, New York. Thirty-seven folio volumes were produced, under the following classifications: government officers, military officers, governors, foreigners, enemy, councils of war, and personal. Account based on Washington papers in Library of Congress. D. C. Duniway

363. Mason, Julian. DAVID HUMPHREYS' LOST ODE TO GEORGE WASHINGTON, 1776. *Q. J. of the Lib. of Congress 1971 28(1): 28-37.* The manuscript of this 1776 poem to Washington, apparently never before made public, was acquired by the Library of Congress in March 1970. Reproduces the manuscript. The circumstances of its composition are detailed, its literary qualities evaluated, and its later history told. Illus., 23 notes. E. P. Stickney

364. Maurois, André. WASHINGTON, FONDATEUR DES ETATS-UNIS [Washington, founder of the United States]. *Historia [France] 1956 20(117): 123-127.* A study of French opinion on George Washington at different times in history. Before the French Revolution, his prestige, thanks mostly to Lafayette, was very great in France. He was viewed with some hostility by French leaders after 1793 but was popular again after Bonaparte's coup d'état. Forgotten after 1815, his popularity was revived during World War I. H. Monteagle

365. Morris, Richard B. CLUES TO THE WASHINGTON PARADOX. *New York Times Mag. 1959 22(February): 12, 43 and 45.* Contrasts George Washington's basic conservatism as a man of great holdings with his natural adventurous spirit and daring, to show how the leader of American independence used his military position to hold the Revolution to limited objectives and to make it what it was, a war for political independence.	R. J. Marion

366. Scribner, Robert L. FARMER WASHINGTON. *Virginia Cavalcade 1964 13(4): 4-9.* Focuses on George Washington engaged in his favorite occupation, that of the farmer of Mount Vernon. Undocumented.	R. B. Lange

367. Sterett, Larry S. A PAIR OF PISTOLS BEQUEATHED BY WASHINGTON TO LAFAYETTE. *J. of the Arms and Armour Soc. [Great Britain] 1963 4(7): 105-106.*

368. Wall, Cecil. GEORGE WASHINGTON: COUNTRY GENTLEMAN. *Agric. Hist. 1969 43(1): 5-6.* Within the environment of Mount Vernon, George Washington modeled his life after that of an English country gentleman. He realized early that row crops were poorly adapted to Mount Vernon's soil, and began experimenting with money crops other than tobacco. There is a rich source of unexplored documents about Washington's career as a farmer.	D. E. Brewster

369. Wright, Esmond. WASHINGTON: THE MAN AND THE MYTH. *Hist. Today [Great Britain] 1955 5(12): 825-832.* A brief survey of the early hero-worship of George Washington, of the "swing of the pendulum from iconography to something like iconoclasm" under the impact of the New History, and of the partial return to a "central position" with D. S. Freeman. A rounded appraisal of Washington has been difficult because of the restrained character of his writings. "The root of his triumph in war and his skill in peace" is found in his integrity and his capacity for organizing.	W. M. Simon

4

DECADE OF CONTROVERSY, 1763-1775: DETERIORATION OF COLONIAL ADMINISTRATION

General

370. Bailyn, Bernard. THE ORIGINS OF AMERICAN POLITICS. *Perspectives in Am. Hist. 1967 1: 9-120.* The bearing of certain 18th-century British political ideas on the realities of politics in pre-Revolutionary America provides sufficient background for understanding why there was a Revolution. British political thought, the structure of British politics, and the impact on colonial thought of the writings of English opponents of the royal government are discussed in detail. "Threats to free government, it was believed, lurked everywhere, but nowhere more dangerously than in the designs of ministers in office to aggrandize power by the corrupt use of influence, and by this means ultimately to destroy the balance of the constitution. Corruption...was as universal a cry in the colonies as it was in England, and with it...the same belief that tyranny, already dominant over most of the earth, was continuing to spread its menace and was threatening even that greatest bastion of liberty, England itself." In the colonies the executive was legally far stronger than in England, but circumstances —such as inflexible royal instructions, encroachments on the governors' patronage, the more democratic nature of colonial politics, the impermanency of the governors' tenure, and the possibility of going over the governors' heads and appealing directly to authorities in England—worked to reduce radically the influence of the colonial governors. With an indeterminate leadership, an unstable economic structure, and the exertion by colonial governments of creative power unknown to 18th-century England, the colonial political system was troubled, contentious, even explosive, evoking, as it did, both the belief that faction was seditious and the fear that the government was corrupt and threatened the survival of liberty. English constitutional theory offered "a mode of comprehension of such an inflamed, anomalous politics; and it is this mode of understanding... that forms the background of the American Revolution." The author's thesis is

also illustrated with an examination of the politics of individual colonies. Based on secondary works, newspapers, and other published primary sources.

D. J. Abramoske

371. Barrow, Thomas C. A PROJECT FOR IMPERIAL REFORM: "HINTS RESPECTING THE SETTLEMENT FOR OUR AMERICAN PROVINCES," 1763. *William and Mary Q. 1967 24(1): 108-126.* Interpretation of the motives and assumptions in writing the "Hints," published 25 February 1763 and probably written by William Knox after his return from colonial service in Georgia. The document's mercantilist bias and its antagonism toward the colonies are explained. The "Hints," reproduced in full here, delves into three areas: general, civil, and military.

H. M. Ward

372. Blassingame, John W. AMERICAN NATIONALISM AND OTHER LOYALTIES IN THE SOUTHERN COLONIES, 1763-1775. *J. of Southern Hist. 1968 34(1): 50-75.* Southern colonists were loyal to England during this period, but became aware of common interests and lives which they shared with other citizens of the American English colonies. Between 1763 and 1775 English actions weakened the loyalty of Southerners, who developed a sense of devotion toward America as a country. They demanded greater freedom from England as they became convinced of the true destiny of the colonies. By 1775 they had reluctantly decided that they could be loyal to England or to America, but not to both. While seeking to resolve their conflict of loyalties, the colonists gradually accepted the de facto Continental Congress as a sovereign government. Based on letters, papers, and books; 107 notes.

K. P. Davis

373. Calhoon, Robert M. "UNHINGING FORMER INTIMACIES": ROBERT BEVERLEY'S PERCEPTION OF THE PRE-REVOLUTIONARY CONTROVERSY, 1761-1775. *South Atlantic Q. 1969 63(2): 246-261.* Little has been written about those men who were uncertain of their stand as to the looming American revolution. A good many were uncommitted. Few left much personal testimony on their attitudes. An exception is Robert Beverley of Virginia who tried to remain outside the emotions of politics. He criticized from without, and the hostility this engendered from his contemporaries confirmed his suspicions about the corroding effect of politics on men of good will. Beverley tried to make a virtue of indecision, but his relative lack of information hindered anything constructive which he tried to say. He refused to recognize that the debate had passed "the stage of a conversation between gentlemen." Based mainly on contemporary sources; 38 notes.

J. M. Bumsted

374. Calhoon, Robert M. WILLIAM SMITH JR.'S ALTERNATIVE TO THE AMERICAN REVOLUTION. *William and Mary Q. 1965 22(1): 105-118.* William Smith's "Thoughts upon the Dispute between Great Britain and her Colonies" is printed here with introductory comments. The lack of coordination in the imperial relations between New York and Great Britain, as Smith saw it, was due to flaws in the imperial structure. His chief recommendation is the establishment of an agency of arbitration to settle imperial-colony disputes.

H. M. Ward

375. Calhoon, Robert M., ed. "A SORROWFUL SPECTATOR OF THESE TUMULTUOUS TIMES": ROBERT BEVERLEY DESCRIBES THE COMING OF THE REVOLUTION. *Virginia Mag. of Hist. and Biog. 1965 73(1): 41-55.* Reprints, with introduction and notes, Beverley's letter to William Fitzhugh of 20 July 1775. "A helter-skelter compilation of episodes from the revolutionary controversy" by a critic of the Revolution, this letter expresses thoughts which "differed sharply with the opinions of most Virginia planters." The original letter is in Beverley's letter book in the Library of Congress.

K. J. Bauer

376. Carson, Clarence B. THE FOUNDING OF THE AMERICAN REPUBLIC. *Freeman 1972 22(2): 112-124, (3): 147-159, (4): 232-244.* Part I. The colonial opposition to British policy culminating in the American Revolution was marked by the ascendancy of George III. It was this monarch's determination to rule and the decision of his ministers to stop conciliating the American colonists for the benefit of English merchants that precipitated the initial crisis of 1763-66 leading to American independence. 21 notes. Part II. Traces the conflict between the British Parliament and the North American colonies from 1766 to the denouement of the so-called Intolerable Acts. 16 notes. Part III. Describes the colonial reaction to the Intolerable Acts leading to independence. 17 notes.

D. A. Yanchisin

377. Champagne, Roger J. LIBERTY BOYS AND MECHANICS OF NEW YORK CITY, 1764-1774. *Labor Hist. 1967 8(2): 115-135.* Studies the social origins and political behavior of the Liberty Boys (Sons of Liberty) of New York City who were drawn from the lower social and economic strata of society. Rent by internal divisions, loyal to leaders as well as political principles, involved in local politics, the Liberty Boys were a "complex lot" whose alliances with the aristocracy shifted in response to personality clashes and factionalism. They were suffered by the aristocracy because they were useful in political struggles since they formed the largest single group in the city's electorate. By 1774 full-blown political opposition to aristocratic leadership had emerged from the Sons of Liberty. The author presents tables showing the adult male electorate, identifies mechanic voters by occupation, and the distribution of mechanics' votes in the election of the Assembly in 1768 and 1769. Based on the collections of the New-York Historical Society and the New York Public Library. 60 notes.

L. L. Athey

378. Corner, Betsy Copping. DR. JOHN FOTHERGILL AND THE AMERICAN COLONIES. *Quaker Hist. 1963 52(2): 77-89.* Dr. Fothergill (1712-80) served as official correspondent between Philadelphia and English Friends from 1743 to his death. He recruited the historian Robert Proud and other teachers for William Penn Charter School and the medical department of the College of Philadelphia, sent books and teaching aids to the Pennsylvania Hospital, and financed John Bartram's travels. He aided Benjamin Franklin as agent of Pennsylvania, and with him and the Quaker banker, David Barclay, produced in the winter of 1774-75 a "Plan [for]...a permanent union between Great Britain and

her colonies." Through his patients, Lord Dartmouth and Lord Hyde, this proposal reached Lord North, who rejected it as impractical.

T. D. S. Bassett

379. Curtis, Thomas D. LAND POLICY: PRE-CONDITION FOR THE SUCCESS OF THE AMERICAN REVOLUTION. *Am. J. of Econ. and Sociol. 1972 31(2): 209-223.* "This summary article examines the effects which England's colonial land policies had upon the major economic interest groups in North America from 1763 to 1775. Completely excluded from this study is an examination of the effects which England's land policies had upon economic interest groups within the mother country. For the most part, the reaction of the colonial merchants toward changing imperial policies has been dealt with only in cursory fashion. The thesis is that Great Britain altered her land policies after the Seven Year[s'] War and so brought the many diffused interest groups in the colonies into a configuration of opposition. The coming together of the Southern planters, Northern merchant land speculators, backwoods farmers, the fur interest, and frontiersmen was a necessary precondition for a successful revolution."   J

380. Day, Alan and Day, Katherine. ANOTHER LOOK AT THE BOSTON "CAUCUS." *J. of Am. Studies [Great Britain] 1971 5(1): 19-42.* Obscurity surrounds the Boston North End Caucus because its proceedings were secret, its surviving records are brief, and its members were closely associated with commercial organizations, with Boston's complex system of social clubs, and with revolutionary bodies (among them the Sons of Liberty and the Committee of Correspondence). Caucus officers and members included such prominent figures in pre-Revolutionary Massachusetts as John and Samuel Adams, James Otis, John Hancock, and Joseph Warren. The best-documented activity of the caucus was its success in nominating and electing its candidates to public office. Its relationships with the commercial sector in Boston and its revolutionary activities in the 1770's remain partly concealed. Provides details about the membership of the North End Caucus. Based on published collections of primary sources and secondary works; map, 3 tables, 88 notes.   H. T. Lovin

381. Evans, Emory G. PLANTER INDEBTEDNESS AND THE COMING OF THE REVOLUTION IN VIRGINIA. *William and Mary Q. 1962 19(4): 511-533.* Rejecting the views of Beard, Harrell, and Gipson, maintains that planter indebtedness was not a cause of the Revolution. Indebtedness was as endemic as extravagance and optimism, and not all Virginia debtors favored independence. The closing of the courts after the Coercive Acts of 1774 prevented the collection of debts, and as late as 1775 nonpayment of debts was used as a tool in the hope of securing concessions from Britain.   E. Oberholzer, Jr.

382. Fiore, Jordan D. SIR FRANCIS BERNARD, COLONIAL GOVERNOR. *New England Social Studies Bull. 1954 12(1): 13-18.* A biographic sketch of the British Governor of Massachusetts, Sir Francis Bernard (1711-79), who showed himself incapable of mastering the critical situation in Boston and was recalled

after nine years of activity (1760-69). Extensive material on the period of his service as Governor of Boston is available in the Houghton Library at Harvard.

S

383. Fitzpatrick, Paul J. ROYAL GOVERNORS' RESIDENCES IN THE ORIGINAL 13 AMERICAN COLONIES. *Social Sci. 1971 46(2): 71-78.* "Because very little has been written about the existence and nature of the royal governors' residences in the original 13 American colonies, this research paper is an exploratory effort to ascertain whether the British Crown or the particular colony ever built a residence for its royal governor. The paper points out certain social, political, and economic conditions in each colony during the period preceding the War of the American Revolution, 1720-1770. No other writer is known to have explored this area and period. Each of the colonies is treated separately."

J

384. Frese, Joseph R. SOME OBSERVATIONS ON THE AMERICAN BOARD OF CUSTOMS COMMISSIONERS. *Massachusetts Hist. Soc. Pro. 1969 81: 3-30.* Discusses two aspects of the customs service: one, the controversy involving merchants, shippers, customs collectors, and customs commissioners in Great Britain and America over fees; the other, the efforts of Henry Hulton, a customs official in Boston, to collect a tax levied on the wages of all British mariners to support the royal hospital for disabled seamen in Greenwich, England. Based on primary and secondary sources; 138 notes. J. B. Duff

385. Goebel, Dorothy Burne. THE "NEW ENGLAND TRADE" AND THE FRENCH WEST INDIES, 1763-1774: A STUDY IN TRADE POLICIES. *William and Mary Q. 1963 20(3): 331-372.* A detailed analysis of French trading regulations, and of the trade of the French West Indies. The variance between mercantile interests and the concerns of the French colonies created a vacillating policy and considerable contraband trade. British trade with St. Lucie centered in Dominica, while New England benefitted from the trade with St. Domingue. If French regulations failed to diminish foreign trade, they benefitted both French and British colonies, and the contacts between New England and the French West Indies had implications for the American Revolution.

E. Oberholzer, Jr.

386. Greene, Jack P. BRIDGE TO REVOLUTION: THE WILKES FUND CONTROVERSY IN SOUTH CAROLINA, 1769-1775. *J. of Southern Hist. 1963 29(1): 19-52.* In December 1769, the Commons House of the South Carolina colony, without the consent of either the council or of the lieutenant governor (the governor was absent from the colony), ordered the colonial treasurer to advance, pending a later appropriation, 1,500 pounds sterling to the Bill of Rights Society in London to support John Wilkes, British radical and foe of the ruling Tory ministry in Great Britain. The Board of Trade, with the backing of attorney general and the Privy Council, instructed the colonial Commons House to limit its appropriations to local purposes and the governor to approve only such appropriations. The legislature refused to comply and despite several dissolutions and new elections an impasse was created. No annual tax bill was passed in South

Carolina, no legislation at all after February 1771. For practical purposes royal government broke down. With the exception of parliamentary taxation, no other issue was so important in persuading South Carolinians they could expect no sympathetic treatment of their grievances from London and in making revolutionaries of them.   S. E. Humphreys

387. Greene, Jack P. POLITICAL MIMESIS: A CONSIDERATION OF THE HISTORICAL AND CULTURAL ROOTS OF LEGISLATIVE BEHAVIOR IN THE BRITISH COLONIES IN THE EIGHTEENTH CENTURY. *Am. Hist. R. 1969 75(2): 337-360.* Argues that British colonial legislative behavior during the 18th century was initially and deeply rooted in the 17th-century English tradition of opposition to the Crown which developed out of the repeated clashes between the first two Stuarts and their Parliaments and the Whig opposition to Charles II and James II. The article tries to identify and explain the nature of that opposition—the sources and ways through which it may have been transmitted to the colonies, the intellectual and institutional imperatives required of the adherents of opposition, the internal social and political circumstances that contributed to the acceptance and perpetuation of opposition in the colonies long after it had spent much of its force in England, and the extent to which it continued to inform and shape colonial legislative behavior right down to the American Revolution.   A

388. Greene, Jack P. THE GADSDEN ELECTION CONTROVERSY AND THE REVOLUTIONARY MOVEMENT IN SOUTH CAROLINA. *Mississippi Valley Hist. R. 1959/60 46(3): 469-492.* Governor Thomas Boone arrived in South Carolina in 1761. All might have gone well for the new governor had he not chosen to contest the Commons House of Assembly to determine the validity of the election of one of its own members, Christopher Gadsden. The Commons, after a bitter two-year struggle, won the contest. Several benefits accrued to the pre-Revolutionary movement. It offered an opportunity to South Carolina to develop leadership potential and political techniques which were utilized in the subsequent struggle for political and civil rights. It forged a common bond among South Carolinians which were useful in the struggle against England.   G. M. Gressley

389. Guttridge, G. H. THOMAS POWNALL'S *THE ADMINISTRATION OF THE COLONIES:* THE SIX EDITIONS. *William and Mary Q. 1969 26(1): 31-46.* Considers the six editions of Pownall's work in the light of changing constitutional crises between Great Britain and the colonies. Pownall was searching for a natural harmony in a medieval and Newtonian sense. He advocated a strong, centralized system of control, and in 1768, endorsed the old requisition system of revenue rather than direct taxation. In the 1768 edition and afterwards, a representative American union and maintenance of the old colonial system as it existed before 1763 is favored. 45 notes.   H. M. Ward

390. Kammen, Michael G. THE COLONIAL AGENTS, ENGLISH POLITICS, AND THE AMERICAN REVOLUTION. *William and Mary Q. 1965 22(2): 244-263.* The colonial agents acquired new significance after 1763. Caught

between inflexible constituencies and an increasingly hostile ministry, the agents sided fully with the colonists. Their role became essentially that of "plenipotentiaries from a sovereign state," thus forming a nucleus of a foreign service of the later American nation.   H. M. Ward

391. Keller, Hans Gustav. PITTS "PROVISIONAL ACT FOR SETTLING THE TROUBLES IN AMERICA." DAS PROBLEM DER EINHEIT DES BRITISCHEN REICHS [Pitt's "Provisional Act for Settling the Troubles in America." The problem of the unity of the British Empire]. *Hist. Zeitschrift [West Germany] 1962 194(3): 599-645.* Examines the efforts of William Pitt the Elder to prevent the loss of the American colonies by creating a new and lasting relationship between the Old World and the New World. Pitt hoped his proposal would establish a "Magna Charta" of the British Empire. Included is the text in English of Pitt's "Provisional Act for Settling the Troubles in America," dated 1 February 1775.   G. H. Davis

392. King-Hall, Stephen, Sir. THE PARTING OF THE WAYS. *Parliamentary Affairs [Great Britain] 1955 8(2): 192-204, (3): 318-333.* A descriptive survey, with much quotation from parliamentary debates, of the taxation and coercion issues between England and the American colonies in the decade 1765-75.   H. D. Jordan

393. Land, Aubrey C., ed. THE FAMILIAR LETTERS OF GOVERNOR HORATIO SHARPE. *Maryland Hist. Mag. 1966 61(3): 189-209.* A summary of the years 1753-69 in the colonial history of Maryland. The letters show Governor Sharpe (1718-73) to have been a conscientious administrator, careful and well-informed. Letters discussed were to his brothers John, William, Gregory, Philip, and Joshua. They were the progenitors of the permanent civil servant who gave stability and continuity to British public life in the 19th and 20th centuries. 50 notes.   D. H. Swift

394. Lemisch, Jesse. JACK TAR IN THE STREETS: MERCHANT SEAMEN IN THE POLITICS OF REVOLUTIONARY AMERICA. *William and Mary Q. 1968 25(3): 371-407.* Looks at a neglected figure, the New England sailor, considers the lure of going to sea, and the perils to a clean-cut young farm boy. The admiralty laws were harsh. There was controversy in the colonies over the impressment policies of the Royal Navy, including riots and political consequences. The author comments on the duties and loyalties of the seaman. 139 notes.   H. M. Ward

395. Lovejoy, David S. RIGHTS IMPLY EQUALITY: THE CASE AGAINST ADMIRALTY JURISDICTION IN AMERICA, 1764-1776. *William and Mary Q. 1959 16(4): 459-484.* A study of admiralty jurisdiction as a cause of political discontent. Historians have failed to stress that the means of enforcing tax legislation were as novel as the taxes themselves. Recognizing the jurisdiction of admiralty courts in cases of prizes, wrecks, salvage, and seamen's wages, the colonists objected to the extension of admiralty jurisdiction in the colonies. The

demand for equality and Jefferson's "All men are created equal" were intended to mean that the colonists had equal rights with Englishmen, rather than in a socioeconomic sense.   E. Oberholzer, Jr.

396. Maier, Pauline. JOHN WILKES AND AMERICAN DISILLUSION-MENT WITH BRITAIN. *William and Mary Q. 1963 20(3): 373-395.* Believing that Wilkes "could effect reforms calculated to check monarchical encroachment," the colonists followed the developments in Britain with interest. Wilkes's expulsion from Parliament "left its mark by forcing the first lasting instance of colonial disillusionment with British government.   E. Oberholzer, Jr.

397. Maier, Pauline. POPULAR UPRISINGS AND CIVIL AUTHORITY IN EIGHTEENTH-CENTURY AMERICA. *William and Mary Q. 1970 27(1): 3-35.* Discusses the constitutional significance of the popular uprisings of the 18th century. The mobs contributed to the evolution of the idea in America that authority should be controlled by popular action. Two kinds of mobs are considered: those acting as an extralegal arm of the community and those protesting imperial policies. The author comments on the mechanisms of law enforcement and riot legislation. The character of mobs in the colonies is compared with that of mobs in Europe. The lesson learned in the Revolutionary period was that the will of the people could be despotic; however, the republicanism of political institutions provided stability and discouraged mob action during this period. 57 notes.   H. M. Ward

398. Merritt, Richard L. THE COLONISTS DISCOVER AMERICA: ATTENTION PATTERNS IN THE COLONIAL PRESS, 1735-1775. *William and Mary Q. 1964 21(2): 270-287.* A quantitative analysis of a sampling of newspapers shows "a high degree of correlation between levels of interest in America" and the more dramatic events of the time. After the French and Indian War, "American symbols" became more prominent than "British symbols," and in the months before the Revolution, the shift in emphasis was marked. The papers of Massachusetts and South Carolina led in giving more attention to American events.   E. Oberholzer, Jr.

399. Merritt, Richard L. THE EMERGENCE OF AMERICAN NATIONALISM: A QUANTITATIVE APPROACH. *Am. Q. 1965 17(2, Part 2): 319-334.* Describes and illustrates how symbol analysis can determine when the colonists lost their British identification and began to refer to themselves as Americans. Through trend analysis of the colonial press, a cyclical development with increasingly higher peak years, i.e., 1740, 1756, 1769 and 1775 (or later), is revealed. Although regional variations show up, 1764 represents the dividing line when the balance of self-referent symbols shifted from British to American. Documented.   R. S. Pickett

400. Meyerson, Joel D. THE PRIVATE REVOLUTION OF WILLIAM BOLLAN. *New England Q. 1968 41(4): 536-550.* From 1766 to 1774 Bollan (1710-82) authored several pamphlets which reveal his increasing disenchantment with

English authority and political institutions, his growing concern with corruption in English society, and a progressive expansion of the power of colonial assemblies. By 1774 he had reached a position in which he envisioned Parliament as simply one legislature in a multistate empire headed by the Crown. This intellectual revolution was brought about in part by Bollan's consistent concern for the development of a harmonious empire which he saw increasingly threatened by British malfeasance, and also by his private uncertainty due to his repudiation by Governor Thomas Hutchinson, his earlier break with the radicals in the Massachusetts General Assembly, and, above all, his failure to get a hearing from the Duke of Newcastle or from MP's in the House of Commons. 21 notes.

K. B. West

401. Morton, W. L. THE LOCAL EXECUTIVE IN THE BRITISH EMPIRE, 1763-1828. *English Hist. R. [Great Britain] 1963 78(308): 436-457.* Examines the relationship between crown, ministers, and Parliament in Britain, Ireland, and North America before and after the American Revolution. While the British American provinces were working out the consequences of the "principle of assimilation" after 1791, a few individuals in the Canadas were slowly developing the idea of provincial cabinet government which had sprung from the Irish revolution and which led to responsible government. A. H. Lawrance

402. Nadelhast, Jerome J. POLITICS AND THE JUDICIAL TENURE FIGHT IN COLONIAL NEW JERSEY. *William and Mary Q. 1971 28(1): 46-63.* The contest over the right of the crown to appoint judges only "during pleasure" came to a climax in New Jersey during Gov. Josiah Hardy's administration (1761-63). Hardy (fl. 1715-63) upheld the appointment of Robert Hunter Morris (ca. 1700-64) for "good behavior," and was replaced by William Franklin (1731-1813). A small, unpopular faction carried the day; most colonists were unconcerned with the constitutional principle involved. The author looks into the background of the conflict in the administrations of Lewis Morris (1738-46), Jonathan Belcher (1746-57), Francis Bernard (1758-60), and Thomas Boone (1760-61). The proprietors wanted to dominate the royal governors through the judiciary in order to protect their lands from trespass. 57 notes.

H. M. Ward

403. Nash, George H., III. FROM RADICALISM TO REVOLUTION: THE POLITICAL CAREER OF JOSIAH QUINCY, JR. *Pro. of the Am. Antiquarian Soc. 1969 79(2): 253-290.* By examining only fragments of Josiah Quincy's life, historians may have obscured the reasons for his change of thought in the years 1767-75, from a position of strong opposition to British policy to one of acceptance of the necessity for total separation from Great Britain. Quincy's activities during these years reveal not a gradual process of orderly transformation but, rather, a series of waverings between restraint and radicalism—a pattern which may have had implications for his contemporaries. Four significant factors in Quincy's erratic career are as follows: 1) an uneasiness about mobs seemed to influence his "moderate" tendencies; 2) a reluctance to view bloodshed as the only means to liberty restained his radicalism; 3) his distrust of Thomas Hutchinson, as the source of all evil as far as the colonists were concerned, was an important

moderating influence; and 4) Quincy's own impressionable personality was the major reason for his political vacillations. It is possible that somewhat similar causes and motives influenced some of Quincy's contemporaries. In the years 1765-75 he was acting out an erratic although progressive estrangement from Great Britain—a painful transformation being experienced by thousands of others and thereby producing the American Revolution. Based on printed material; 56 notes. R. V. Calvert

404. Olton, Charles S. PHILADELPHIA'S MECHANICS IN THE FIRST DECADE OF REVOLUTION 1765-1775. *J. of Am. Hist. 1972 59(2): 311-326.* Contrary to the views of some progressive historians, the mechanics of Philadelphia were never extreme radicals. Those who organized politically were artisan entrepreneurs and employers, not conscious of themselves as a dependent "have-not" class doing battle with a "have" aristocracy. Their position reflected a relative openness in Philadelphia's society. Mechanics often did define themselves in opposition to merchants. This was especially the case with regard to nonimportation agreements which mechanics tended to favor as a device to facilitate the growth of native manufactures. Merchants did not favor them, and in the crisis of 1774 were able to overcome the mechanics' desire to implement a complete suspension of commercial intercourse with Great Britain. Artisans did continue to strive for a share of political power and were never part of a "general consensus" including merchants. Concludes that "social class and social change were essential ingredients of the Revolution." 67 notes. K. B. West

405. Pierce, Arthur D. A GOVERNOR IN SKIRTS. *New Jersey Hist. Soc. Pro. 1965 83(1): 1-9.* The first royal governor of New Jersey, Lord Cornbury (Edward Hyde), Queen Anne's cousin, was often resplendent in feminine attire. He took bribes, exploited religion for his private purposes, was crude in his political methods. Queen Anne and her successors were remote physically; when most of the appointed governors inspired hostility and disrespect, the British throne "became an increasingly fragile symbol of authority." When the testing time for loyalty to the King came, the wonder is that there were so many loyalists considering "how little the Crown had done to earn the respect and fealty of Jerseymen." Illus. E. P. Stickney

406. Rea, Robert R. THE TROUBLE AT TOMBECKBY. *Alabama R. 1968 21(1): 21-39.* An account of the occupation by the British in 1763, abandonment in 1764, reoccupation in 1766, and final abandonment in 1767 of the fort called Tombeckby, but officially named York. Based on the Gage Papers in the William L. Clements Library, Ann Arbor, Michigan; 48 notes. D. F. Henderson

407. Reese, Trevor Richard. COLONIAL AMERICA AND EARLY NEW SOUTH WALES: INTRODUCTORY NOTES TO A COMPARATIVE SURVEY OF BRITISH ADMINISTRATIVE POLICIES. *Hist. Studies [Australia] 1959 9(33): 74-84.* Colonial America in the 18th century and the Australian colonies of the early 19th century had similar relations with Britain. In both instances the home authorities controlled councils, regarded colonial assemblies as a privilege, retained the power of disallowing laws, insisted on a faithful grant

of the civil list, and removed judges at will. Yet, when these issues came to a head in Australia, liberal views about colonies and colonial administration gained ground in Britain, and the Australian colonies were to be conceived in a new way. A new concept of empire, a form of friendly and equal association, replaced the 18th-century approach.   G. D. Bearce

408. Riggs, A. R. ARTHUR LEE, A RADICAL VIRGINIAN IN LONDON, 1768-1776. *Virginia Mag. of Hist. and Biog. 1970 78(3): 268-280.* In light of current emphasis on the intellectual origins of the American Revolution and significance of the pamphlet and journalists in coverting debate into conflict, the place of Arthur Lee is reevaluated. While in London he composed over 250 pieces complaining of a British conspiracy against America, placing the majority in two daily newspapers as well as publishing at least nine pamphlets. Each highlight of the controversy called Lee to reiterate the existence of "a monolithic and trans-oceanic conspiracy," although he argued revolution only as the necessary resort of an unheard people pleading for a Bill of Rights, a *"Magna Carta Americana."* Extensive notes.   C. A. Newton

409. Sachs, William S. INTERURBAN CORRESPONDENTS AND THE DE-VELOPMENT OF A NATIONAL ECONOMY BEFORE THE REVOLU-TION: NEW YORK AS A CASE STUDY. *New York Hist. 1955 36(3): 320-335.* Describes the growing business contacts among merchants of various colonial cities during the 1750's and 1760's which helped to build up a national feeling and group rapport important to the revolutionary struggle. Based largely on contemporary journals, letters, and account books.   A. B. Rollins

410. Schlesinger, Arthur Meier. POLITICAL MOBS AND THE AMERICAN REVOLUTION. *Pro. of the Am. Phil. Soc. 1955 99(4): 244-250.* Mob violence played a key role at every important turning point leading up to the War of Independence. Some violence was deliberately engineered in advance by Whig leaders and some was spontaneous. Violence represented the seeds of revolution.   C. B. Joynt

411. Shade, William G., ed., Gipson, Lawrence H., Nichols, Roy F., Main, Jackson Turner, and Stauffer, Jean M. LAWRENCE HENRY GIPSON: FOUR DIMENSIONS. *Pennsylvania Hist. 1969 36(1): 7-79.* In his autobiographical essay, Gipson answers the question "How did you become involved in writing your history, *The British Empire before the American Revolution?"* Nichols discusses Gipson's role as a founder and active member of the Pennsylvania Historical Association. Main provides a volume by volume critical overview of Gipson's magnum opus. He also holds that Gipson's heavy reliance on British sources led him to view the colonists as would a British administrator. "We are left," Main writes, "with an adolescent demanding freedom from a kindly par-ent...." In *The Coming of the American Revolution,* Gipson offered too many details and exaggerated his case. The final articles are a collection of reviews of *The British Empire before the American Revolution* and a bibliography of Gip-son's works.   D. C. Swift

412. Shammas, Carole. CADWALLADER COLDEN AND THE ROLE OF THE KING'S PREROGATIVE. *New-York Hist. Soc. Q. 1969 53(2): 102-126.* Cadwallader Colden served as acting governor of the colony of New York from 1760-65 after a long career as a colonial official. During those years he attempted to exercise the authority vested in the office and thereby aroused the enmity of the people, who were accustomed to little interference from the Crown. As a result Colden became, in colonial eyes, typical of the British official who wished to assert the King's prerogative and thus helped to condition the colonial mind for the acceptance of the idea of separation. Primary sources; 5 illus., 32 notes.
C. L. Grant

413. Shephard, James F. A BALANCE OF PAYMENTS FOR THE THIR-TEEN COLONIES, 1768-1772: A SUMMARY. *J. of Econ. Hist. 1965 25(4): 691-695.* Concludes that capital flows of a long-term nature between Great Britain and the colonies were very small or nonexistent during the period 1768-72. 10 notes.
D. F. Rossi

414. Shepherd, James F. COMMODITY EXPORTS FROM THE BRITISH NORTH AMERICAN COLONIES TO OVERSEAS AREAS, 1768-1772: MAGNITUDES AND PATTERNS OF TRADE. *Explorations in Econ. Hist. 1970 8(1): 5-76.* Corroborates the thesis that overseas trade played a significant role in the economic development of the American Colonies. Estimates the quantitative magnitudes involved in the trade and examines its composition. Estimates from surviving evidence the value of commodity exports, by colony of origin and overseas area of destination. Concludes that, with the exception of the African trade, the usual historical description of the colonial export trade seems consistent with the estimates. Since exports to Africa averaged less than one percent of total export value, the author suspects that the emphasis placed on this trade by historians has been due to its "immoral" and "inhumane" aspects. Based on primary and secondary sources; 8 tables, 50 notes.
C. J. Pusateri

415. Skaggs, David Curtis. MARYLAND'S IMPULSE TOWARD SOCIAL REVOLUTION: 1750-1776. *J. of Am. Hist. 1968 54(4): 771-786.* In the period from 1771 to 1776 Maryland was controlled by a landholding elite which monopolized political and ecclesiastical office and dominated a heterogeneous population, 40 percent of whom were disfranchised. Battles were fought increasingly with an irresponsible absentee proprietor and the royal government in which mobs of the landless were engaged, and certain changes came upon the political scene: extralegal political organization and decline in traditional deference to authority. The "mob" threatened to escape control of the elite when demands were made for universal suffrage, legislative supremacy, and a shift in the tax base. These demands reached a peak in the elections to the constitutional convention in 1776. Conservatives were able to draft a constitution which protected the power of the property-holding elite, but demands for a more democratic social, political, and economic order persisted.
K. B. West

416. Stout, Neil R. GOALS AND ENFORCEMENT OF BRITISH COLONIAL POLICY, 1763-1775. *Am. Neptune 1967 27(3): 211-220.* Discusses Brit-

ish naval policy following the Treaty of Paris in 1763. Pointed out are the three goals of the British government: defense of the empire, stricter central control of the colonies, and increased revenues from the colonies. The author discusses the size and disposition of the British fleet in North American waters and the problems encountered in enforcing imperial regulation. It is concluded that the new enforcement procedures failed and that British policy after 1763 was no departure from the past except in the attempts to bring about enforcement. Sources include both primary and secondary works as well as British government material; 42 notes.   M. Svanevik

417. Stout, Neil R. MANNING THE ROYAL NAVY IN NORTH AMERICA, 1763-1775. *Am. Neptune 1963 23(3): 174-185.* In early 1763 the second largest element of the Royal Navy was assigned to the North American coast to aid in enforcing the customs laws. The major difficulty faced was the steady drain of desertions, sometimes actively encouraged by American merchants, which often kept vessels in port. The doubtful legality of impressment and poor results of enlistment campaigns hampered naval operations. The Admiralty was aware that impressment could provide men but could not authorize its use. Though no seizures were made ashore, hundreds were impressed at sea. Vague instructions saw impressment widely used in 1764-65, resulting in violent incidents in New York, Massachusetts, and Rhode Island. The most important effect of the manpower shortage was the limitation on customs control. Main source is Admiralty correspondence.   J. G. Lydon

418. Surrency, Erwin. REVISION OF COLONIAL LAWS. *Am. J. of Legal Hist. 1965 9(3): 189-202.* Explores the efforts of the British government to require the colonies to provide a collection of colonial statues for the use of British public officials. Using state records and archival materials, the author discusses the various attempts to write down colonial laws and to review their legislation.
                                                                       N. Brockman

419. Tate, Thad W. THE COMING OF THE REVOLUTION IN VIRGINIA: BRITAIN'S CHALLENGE TO THE RULING CLASS, 1763-1776. *William and Mary Q. 19(3): 323-343.* Examines Virginia's strong revolutionary leadership in view of the fact that other colonies were more adversely affected by British policy. Rejecting the Parson's Cause, planters' debts, the Currency Act, and the Proclamation of 1763 as serious causes, the author finds that constitutional questions induced the planters, who had a monopoly on power, to espouse the Revolution. In Virginia, where local power and native loyalism were lacking, the threats to constitutional rights were as influential in promoting revolutionary ferment as local conditions were elsewhere.   E. Oberholzer, Jr.

420. Thomas, Robert Paul. A QUANTITATIVE APPROACH TO THE STUDY OF THE EFFECTS OF BRITISH IMPERIAL POLICY UPON COLONIAL WELFARE: SOME PRELIMINARY FINDINGS. *J. of Econ. Hist. 1965 25(4): 615-638.* A study of the extent of burdens imposed upon the thirteen colonies due to imperial regulation of foreign commerce. The Navigation Acts are examined, since they were the main regulatory force imposed upon foreign com-

merce. Membership of the thirteen colonies in the British Empire after 1763 did not amount to a "significant hardship." Tables of commerce, 55 notes.

D. F. Rossi

421. Walett, Francis G. GOVERNOR BERNARD'S UNDOING: AN EAR-LIER HUTCHINSON LETTERS AFFAIR. *New England Q. 1965 38(2): 217-226.* Some letters to government offices in London from Francis Bernard, unpopular governor of Massachusetts from 1760 to 1769, fell into the hands of the Sons of Liberty. The colonists, contending that the letters misrepresented conditions and actions in the colony, blamed Bernard for their difficulties with the home government. The letters were published in colonial newspapers and were the subject for action by the Council and the House of Representatives. Bernard returned to England in 1769, at the time the charges over the letters were rife. He did not return to Massachusetts and in 1770 the lieutenant governor, Thomas Hutchinson, was appointed governor. Thus was tested the pattern of treatment which was to force Hutchinson out of office later. 27 notes to printed letters, official papers, and other records.   A. Turner

422. Walton, Gary M. THE NEW ECONOMIC HISTORY AND THE BUR-DENS OF THE NAVIGATION ACTS. *Econ. Hist. R. [Great Britain] 1971 24(4): 533-542.* Surveys the differing methods of studying, and conclusions concerning, the effects of the 17th- and 18th-century Navigation Acts on Great Britain's relations with its American colonies, especially the forced rerouting of commodities through England, as found in such works as Lawrence A. Harper's "The Effect of the Navigation Acts on the Thirteen Colonies," in Richard B. Morris, ed., *The Era of the American Revolution* (New York, 1959), 3-39; Peter D. McClelland, "The Cost to America of British Imperial Policy," *American Economic Review,* Papers and Proceedings LIX (May 1969), 370-381; and Robert P. Thomas, "A Quantitive Approach to the Study of the Effects of British Imperial Policy of Colonial Welfare: Some Preliminary Findings," *Journal of Economic History* 1964 25(4): 615-638. Concludes that if the new economic history has improved on Harper's early studies, these improvements have been modest and are found primarily in the study by Thomas. Harper's general conclusion still holds: not exploitation, but friction created by continued changes in regulation 1763-75, urged revolt.   B. L. Crapster

423. Warden, G. B. THE PROPRIETARY GROUP IN PENNSYLVANIA, 1754-1764. *William and Mary Q. 1964 21(3): 367-389.* An analysis of the status and influence of the proprietary group, noting its disproportionate influence in the council and other public positions, in city administration, and in commerce and landholding. The lessons learned in the 1750's enabled the proprietary men to gain control in 1766 and made it impossible for the assembly to regain its power. The author observes that the first popular demonstrations against English colonial policies were led by the proprietary group, which won the following of the under-represented frontiersmen and the nonvoters of the city.

E. Oberholzer, Jr.

424. Waters, John J. and Schutz, John A. PATTERNS OF MASSACHUSETTS COLONIAL POLITICS: THE WRITS OF ASSISTANCE AND THE RIVALRY BETWEEN THE OTIS AND HUTCHINSON FAMILIES. *William and Mary Q. 1967 24(4): 543-567.* Puts the Otis-Hutchinson controversy into the perspective of total interaction between the two families and describes the rise of the two families into the elite. Behind-the-scenes politics and legalities of the Writs of Assistance Case (1761) are discussed. New interpretations are from the recently opened Otis Papers now in the Columbia University Library. 55 notes.
H. M. Ward

425. Wickwire, Franklin B. JOHN POWNALL AND BRITISH COLONIAL POLICY. *William and Mary Q. 1963 20(4): 543-554.* Traces the influence of Pownall (1724 or 1725-95) on the Lords of Trade and Board of Trade. Rising from a clerk to undersecretary of state for the American Department, Pownall influenced the decisions of the colonial administrators in Whitehall, helped draft the Proclamation of 1763 and the Quebec Act, drew up the papers in the *Gaspee* case, and influenced the recall of Governor Thomas Hutchinson.
E. Oberholzer, Jr.

426. Younger, Richard D. GRAND JURIES AND THE AMERICAN REVOLUTION. *Virginia Mag. of Hist. and Biog. 1955 63(3): 257-268.* Relates the struggles between colonial grand juries and royal chief justices during the period 1768-74, and the assistance rendered by the grand juries to the revolutionary colonial governments, with emphasis on Massachusetts and South Carolina.
C. F. Latour

427. Zimmerman, John J. CHARLES THOMSON, "THE SAM ADAMS OF PHILADELPHIA." *Mississippi Valley Hist. R. 1958 45(3): 464-480.* A study of the emergence of Thomson as the leader of the Philadelphia radicals in the decade prior to 1774. A brief biographical sketch of Thomson's early activities as a teacher, secretary at several Indian conferences, and merchant is included. During the Stamp Act crisis Thomson stood out as the only Quaker Party supporter who actively opposed the Act. A significant result of the crisis was the entente formed between Thomson and Benjamin Franklin, then Pennsylvania's colonial agent in London. The cooperation between the two during the Townshend crisis (1767-70) led to Thomson's leadership of the radicals when the First Continental Congress met.
A

The Grenville Program

428. Barrow, Thomas C. BACKGROUND TO THE GRENVILLE PROGRAM, 1757-1763. *William and Mary Q. 1965 22(1): 93-104.* The professed concern of the Grenville ministry for solving the problems of finance and defense

was only an excuse for the real intent of reorganizing imperial administration and curtailing illicit trade, especially trade with the French in time of war with France. The Grenville program, which led to the Sugar Act, reflected English discontent with the commercial independence of the colonists.　　H. M. Ward

429. D'Innocenzo, Michael and Turner, John J., Jr. THE ROLE OF NEW YORK NEWSPAPERS IN THE STAMP ACT CRISIS, 1764-66. *New-York Hist. Soc. Q. 1967 51(3): 215-231, 51(4): 345-365.* Part I. As was the case in other colonies, the three New York City newspapers led the resistance to the British colonial policies during the pre-Revolutionary period. Early in 1764 the papers began to question the changes in imperial policies and concentrated in particular on the slogan "no taxation without representation." This article traces the development of the protests in the three journals and notes that they pursued a negative policy without proposing possible alternatives. Primary sources, 5 illus., 40 notes. Part II. Gradually the press assumed leadership and, by late 1765, was committed to open defiance of the act. Undoubtedly the newspapers played a significant role in molding public opinion. Based primarily on newspapers, 5 illus., 36 notes.
　　　　　　　　　　　　　　　　　　　　　　　　　　　　　　　C. L. Grant

430. Ernst, Joseph A. GENESIS OF THE CURRENCY ACT OF 1764: VIRGINIA PAPER MONEY AND THE PROTECTION OF BRITISH INVESTMENTS. *William and Mary Q. 1965 22(1): 33-74.* Germane to the currency question were the interests of London merchants who wanted their sterling investments in the colonies protected, the Virginia planters who considered paper money a protection against insolvency and confiscation, and the Glasgow merchants who did not fear legal tender currency as long as it would maintain its value in relation to sterling. The act, a compromise trying to please everyone in that legal tender paper was banned only for private debt payments, eventually pleased no one.　　　　　　　　　　　　　　　　　　　　　　H. M. Ward

431. Ernst, Joseph A. THE CURRENCY ACT REPEAL MOVEMENT: A STUDY OF IMPERIAL POLITICS AND REVOLUTIONARY CRISIS, 1764-1767. *William and Mary Q. 1968 24(2): 177-211.* Looks into the problems of Parliamentary taxation and the quest of Great Britain for American revenue. Benjamin Franklin's currency scheme, colonial petitions, the lobby of London merchants, and business and trade conditions in the colonies relative to the need for currency are discussed. The author treats the pressures for repeal of the Currency Act and describes the role of the colonial agencies of the period. 99 notes.　　　　　　　　　　　　　　　　　　　　　　　　　　　H. M. Ward

432. Fowler, William M., Jr. WILLIAM ELLERY: MAKING OF A RHODE ISLAND POLITICIAN. *Rhode Island Hist. 1971 30(4): 125-135.* Analyzes Ellery's (1727-1820) career as merchant and later as lawyer, his association with the Ward faction in Rhode Island politics in 1765, and his emergence as a leading Whig in the Stamp Act crisis and subsequent crises in imperial relations. Ellery served his apprenticeship in factional politics during the decade beginning in 1765. By 1776 he was ready to take his place on the national level. Based on MSS. and on secondary sources.　　　　　　　　　　　　　　　　　P. J. Coleman

433. Frieberg, Malcolm. AN UNKNOWN STAMP ACT LETTER. *Massachusetts Hist. Soc. Pro. 1966 78: 138-142.* Prints an anonymous and undated letter, probably written on 15 August 1765, attacking Andrew Oliver, the recently appointed stamp distributor for Massachusetts. The letter reinforces our knowledge about the Stamp Act protest particularly concerning upper-class participation in the demonstrations in Boston 14 August 1765. 17 notes.

J. B. Duff

434. Gerlach, Don R. A NOTE ON THE QUARTERING ACT OF 1774. *New England Q. 1966 39(1): 80-88.* Attempts to present the content and purpose of the Quartering Act of 1774 more precisely than have prior treatments. After scrutinizing the specific provisions of the act and examining the precedents and historical context, the author concludes that numerous textbooks and monographs have judged the statute much too harshly since they often suggest that the law was a gross imposition on American privacy and/or a significant violation of colonial constitutional rights. It is felt that such inaccurate discussions of the act perpetuate a myth of British tyranny. Based on printed sources and utilizes various secondary works for comparative analysis, 23 notes.

W. G. Morgan

435. Greene, Jack P. and Jellison, Richard M. THE CURRENCY ACT OF 1764 IN IMPERIAL-COLONIAL RELATIONS, 1764-1776. *William and Mary Q. 1961 18(4): 485-518.* Not an explosive issue, the Currency Act nevertheless was a major grievance and had the important psychological effect of reminding the colonial population of their subordination to the desires of Whitehall. The southern colonies, unable to resolve the financial problems caused by the act, may have induced the First Continental Congress to cite the act as a grievance.

E. Oberholzer, Jr.

436. Greene, Jack P., ed. "NOT TO BE 'GOVERNED' OR 'TAXED' BUT BY ...OUR REPRESENTATIVES": FOUR ESSAYS IN OPPOSITION TO THE STAMP ACT BY LANDON CARTER. *Virginia Mag. of Hist. and Biog. 1968 76(3): 259-300.* Reprints, with an introduction, four essays by Carter. The earliest, dated 3 June 1764, was a dramatic but suppressed attempt to call the colonists' attention to the "anticonstitutional" nature of the Stamp Act. The second, written in September 1765 but not published until May 1766, expounded Carter's concept of the constitutional relationship between Britain and her colonies. The third was a pamphlet-length constitutional argument intended for publication in London but apparently never printed. The fourth, dated March 1766, attacked both the Stamp Act and Parliament's establishment of a colonial postal system. Based on materials in various manuscript collections and printed works; illus., 53 notes.

K. J. Bauer

437. Harlan, Robert D. DAVID HALL AND THE STAMP ACT. *Papers of the Biblio. Soc. of Am. 1967 61(1): 13-37.* David Hall (1714-72) "was the proprietor of a leading Philadelphia bookshop, the publisher of one of the most popular newspapers in the colonies *[Pennsylvania Gazette]*, and a partner of Benjamin Franklin." Prior to 1764 his business was, at worst, solvent, and usually it

prospered, but the shortage of currency and the tightening of credit that followed 1763 created an anxiety that the announcement of the Stamp Act converted to desperation. The proposed taxes increased costs. Debtors remained indifferent to Hall's pleas to settle up, the increase threatened to wipe out his small profits, and subscribers would not accept a price hike. Subscriptions declined sharply even before November 1765. Despite Hall's effort to obey the Stamp Act in both letter and spirit, or perhaps because of his obedience, his business suffered irrevocably. "By 1766...in a formerly loyal subject the British government now had an enemy." Documented.   C. A. Newton

438. Johnson, Allen S. BRITISH POLITICS AND THE REPEAL OF THE STAMP ACT. *South Atlantic Q. 1963 62(2): 169-188.* Recounts in detail the role of internal British politics in the repeal of the Stamp Act, 1765-66, and concludes that "the primary fact in the political situation appears to be the weakness of the Rockingham administration, which was created without substantial parliamentary support because the political eccentricities of George III and Earl Temple forbade any other settlement. This...made the ministers unduly solicitous of Pitt's support, and prevented...an independent course or revision, partial repeal, or other action." Such weakness kept them from following Pitt's advice. They had to follow a course of compromise and expediency and satisfied no one.
C. R. Allen, Jr.

439. Johnson, Herbert A., and Syrett, David. SOME NICE SHARP QUILLETS OF THE CUSTOMS LAW: THE *NEW YORK* AFFAIR, 1763-1767. *William and Mary Q. 1968 25(3): 432-451.* Discusses the seizure of the merchant ship *New York,* bound for New York City from Port au Prince, which refused to surrender its cargo for customs inspection. But eventually the ship was seized and illegal goods found. The court case and the effectiveness of the old Acts of Trade and Navigation are examined, and the status of civil liberties in common law versus admiralty jurisdiction are revealed with citations of pertinent cases. Goods are defined and classified under the Staple Act of 1663. The case called attention to the need of controlling the colonies through statutory alteration and revision. 57 notes.   H. M. Ward

440. Lee, Lawrence. DAYS OF DEFIANCE: RESISTANCE TO THE STAMP ACT IN THE LOWER CAPE FEAR. *North Carolina Hist. R. 1966 43(2): 186-202.* In North Carolina, reaction to the Stamp Act centered on the Lower Cape Fear area because the principal port, Brunswick, and the governor's residence were there. "In their actions, however, the people of the Lower Cape Fear represented all the people of North Carolina." The province had not been represented at the Stamp Act Congress because the assembly had not been called into session to choose delegates. Demonstrations against the act began in October of 1775. Since the province had not received official notification of the act, it was not at first enforced. After the Cape Fear people forced the resignation of the stamp distributor, Governor William Tryon offered to seek exemption for the province. By February 1766, however, the act was in force and the ports were closed. An armed mob forced the opening of the port and frightened the officials charged with enforcing the act into swearing there would be no enforcement.

Opposition in North Carolina was led by "sober and responsible citizens" who did not seek to hide their identity from those they were defying. 53 notes.

J. M. Bumsted

441. Lemay, J. A. Leo. ROBERT BOLLING AND THE BAILMENT OF COLONEL CHISWELL. *Early Am. Literature 1971 6(2): 99-142.* Reconstructs the political controversy in colonial Virginia precipitated by the poet Robert Bolling's anonymous charge in the *Virginia Gazette* (20 June 1766) that Colonel John Chiswell had murdered Robert Routledge. More significantly, Bolling revealed that Chiswell, having been denied bail by the Cumberland County Court, was intercepted by three members of the General Court—William Byrd III, Presley Thornton, and John Blair—who thereupon granted a motion for bailment. The widespread tendency to credit Bolling's charges of favoritism and malfeasance against the judges was encouraged by simultaneous revelations of blatantly self-serving and frequently illegal acts of the ruling oligarchy. The Chiswell affair tended to divide the House of Burgesses along the same lines which formed in response to the Virginia Stamp Act Resolves: John Robinson, Peyton Randolph, John Randolph, and George Wythe attacked the Resolves and defended the judges; Patrick Henry, Thomas Jefferson, Richard Henry Lee, Arthur Lee, and George Mason supported the Resolves and denounced the judges. The refusal of a grand jury to indict Bolling on a charge of libel brought by William Byrd III effectively broke the Governor's hold on the press. Based on primary and secondary sources; 44 notes, 2 appendixes.

D. P. Wharton

442. Lemisch, L. Jesse. NEW YORK'S PETITIONS AND RESOLVES OF DECEMBER 1765: LIBERALS VS. RADICALS. *New-York Hist. Soc. Q. 1965 49(4): 313-326.* An account of the origins of the Petitions and Resolves adopted by the New York Assembly during the Stamp Act crisis. These protests proved to be typical of those passed by other colonial legislatures. As in other colonies, the leadership in New York agreed to the protests as a means of blocking the passage of more radical proposals.

C. L. Grant

443. Matthews, John C. TWO MEN ON A TAX: RICHARD HENRY LEE, ARCHIBALD RITCHIE, AND THE STAMP ACT. *The Old Dominion: Essays for Thomas Perkins Abernethy (Charlottesville: The U. Press of Virginia, 1964), pp. 96-108.* Richard Henry Lee applied early for a stamp distributorship. When the General Assembly, of which he was a member, met in Williamsburg in November 1764, the majority of the burgesses was strongly opposed to the Stamp Act. Lee, reflecting on his application, was struck by "the impropriety of an American being concerned in such an affair." He prepared the first draft of the address and memorials urging that the colonies be permitted to tax themselves and later was responsible for the mock hanging of Virginia's stamp agent. When Archibald Ritchie tried to clear his warehouse of stamped paper, Lee was a leader in forming the Westmoreland Association which succeeded in forcing Ritchie to change his position. 27 notes.

E. P. Stickney

444. Minchinton, Walter E. THE STAMP ACT CRISIS: BRISTOL AND VIR-
GINIA. *Virginia Mag. of Hist. and Biog. 1965 73(2): 145-155.* Not until about
six months after the passage of the Stamp Act did the merchants of Bristol,
England become concerned. Then as their trade with the American colonies
declined as a result of the nonimportation agreements, they appealed to Parliament for a modification or repeal of the act. Documented.   K. J. Bauer

445. Newcomb, Benjamin H. EFFECTS OF THE STAMP ACT ON COLO-
NIAL PENNSYLVANIA POLITICS. *William and Mary Q. 1966 23(2): 257-
272.* Studies political behavior in reaction to the Stamp Act. The Proprietary
Party, fearful of loss of charter rights, instigated riots to discredit Benjamin
Franklin's Quaker Party, which favored the Crown's taking over the colony. The
Proprietary Party specialized in libel; the Assembly Party in politics. In the
election of 1-3 October 1765, the loss of seats by the Proprietary Party demonstrated that the electorate favored moderate resistance to the Stamp Act enforcement. Emphasized is the conciliatory influence of Joseph Galloway.
                                                                  H. M. Ward

446. Richards, David Alan. NEW HAVEN AND THE STAMP ACT CRISIS
OF 1765-66. *Yale U. Lib. Gazette 1971 46(2): 67-85.* Delineates stages of opposition in New Haven to the Stamp Act (1765). Concentrates on the role of editor
Benjamin Mecom and his newly established (1765) *Connecticut Gazette.* A
controversy in the newspaper between Connecticut's radicals and conservatives
precipitated by Naphtali Daggerr's ("Cato") personal attack on the locally prominent Stamp-Master, Jared Ingersoll ("Civis"), assumed intercolonial significance. While the Stamp Act crisis was marked by orderliness in New Haven, it
was a significant developmental phase in that political-theological cleavage peculiar to Connecticut. 34 notes.   D. A. Yanchisin

447. Sosin, Jack M. IMPERIAL REGULATION OF COLONIAL PAPER
MONEY, 1764-1773. *Pennsylvania Mag. of Hist. and Biog. 1964 88(2): 174-198.*
The wars of the 18th century led colonial legislatures to issue paper money which
inevitably depreciated since it was far in excess of the needs of peacetime transactions. This practice brought forth complaints from British creditors who sought
redress of their grievances. The House of Commons passed the Currency Act of
1764 which established rules for enforcing the retirement of bills; it was a compromise effected by the Commissioners of Trade, the British merchants, and the
colonial agents. In 1773 the Currency Act of 1764 was amended allowing colonial
assemblies to issue notes deemed legal tender at colonial treasuries for duties and
taxes. Since this paper could be redeemed at the provincial treasury, it would
circulate at face value. Paper currency had been secured by the colonial agents
by the tacit acknowledgement of the authority of Parliament. Based on papers
in the Colonial Office, Public Record Office, 43 notes.   E. P. Stickney

448. Stout, Neil R. CAPTAIN KENNEDY AND THE STAMP ACT. *New
York Hist. 1964 45(1): 44-58.* Examines the activities of Captain Archibald

Kennedy, commander of British naval ships in New York during the Stamp Act crisis of 1765, and describes his later attempts to vindicate his action and reestablish his suspended naval career.   A. B. Rollins

449. Surrency, Erwin. THE LAWYER AND THE REVOLUTION. *Am. J. of Legal Hist. 1964 8(2): 125-135.* Discussing the role of lawyers in the American Revolution, the author emphasizes their reaction to the Stamp Act, which they regarded as a threat to the legal profession. Based mainly on secondary sources.
N. Brockman

450. Thompson, Mack. MASSACHUSETTS AND NEW YORK STAMP ACTS. *William and Mary Q. 1969 26(2): 253-258.* Probes the causes and effects of the early stamp acts of two colonies. The view that the stamp acts were short-lived and unpopular is not fully accurate. Little criticism was levelled against the acts, which were passed upon the requests of royal governors to meet military emergencies. A probable reason for the discontinuance of the taxes was increased revenue from excise and other taxes. Opposition to the stamp taxes came from the people most affected and not from any general discontent. 16 notes.   H. M. Ward

451. Watson, D. H. BARLOW TRECOTHICK. *British Assoc. for Am. Studies Bull. [Great Britain] 1960 (1): 36-49, 1961 (2): 29-39.* An account of the agitation, on behalf of the American colonies, of Barlow Trecothick (1720-75), the Boston-born merchant of London, who acted as agent for New Hampshire, and became Member of Parliament for London in 1768. Emphasizes his role as chairman of the pressure group which helped to secure the repeal of the Stamp Act. Based on English manuscript sources such as the Wentworth Woodhouse Papers and the Newcastle Papers, and British and Colonial printed sources.
W. D. McIntyre

452. Young, Henry J. AGRARIAN REACTIONS TO THE STAMP ACT IN PENNSYLVANIA. *Pennsylvania Hist. 1967 34(1): 25-30.* The Stamp Act affected the Pennsylvania countryside by causing German and Swiss farmers to hasten in obtaining naturalization papers as the fees connected with these documents were to be increased by the act. Naturalization was sought because citizenship carried with it certain advantages in land transactions. As the Stamp Act would also make land transactions more costly, all elements of Pennsylvania society participated in a land boom that, once begun, continued after the crisis. Based on primary sources; 10 notes.   D. C. Swift

The Townshend Administration

453. Brown, Richard D. THE MASSACHUSETTS CONVENTION OF TOWNS, 1768. *William and Mary Q. 1969 26(1): 94-104.* Finds participation and nonparticipation of towns was related to local politics and, where friends of the Crown were influential after the Stamp Act crisis, these towns were not represented in the convention. The convention itself did not enjoy wide popular support. Included is an amended version of Robert Treat Paine's list of delegates to the convention. 21 notes.   H. M. Ward

454. Chaffin, Robert J. THE TOWNSHEND ACTS OF 1767. *William and Mary Q. 1970 27(1): 90-121.* Discusses the formulation of the Townshend Acts, the various alternatives proposed, and the conditions in England which necessitated such taxes. Townshend's actions were for the most part independent of the ministry. Townshend also sought to strengthen customs administration in America. The Duke of Grafton blocked most of Townshend's schemes. The East India Company effectively lobbied for commercial advantages to be accrued by further monopolizing the selling of tea to the colonists. Political shuffling over the passage of a colonial revenue led to a delay in the final enactment, which was eventually accomplished by the Rockinghamites whose maneuver was a return to power. 118 notes.   H. M. Ward

455. Fowler, William M., Jr. A YANKEE PEDDLER, NONIMPORTATION, AND THE NEW YORK MERCHANTS. *New-York Hist. Soc. Q. 1972 56(2): 147-154.* In the midst of attempts to uphold a New York nonimportation agreement adopted following the passage of the Townshend Acts, an itinerant Massachusetts peddler, David Hill, tried to sell imported goods in New York. After local merchants persuaded Hill to withhold his goods from sale, radicals publicly burned the merchandise. Hill then sued the merchants for damages, and won. The episode widened the breach between the radicals and the merchants, because the merchants suffered for a crime of which they were innocent. None of the five merchant-defendants later actively supported the revolutionary cause. Based on secondary sources and Rhode Island court records; illus., 25 notes.
                                    C. L. Grant

456. Hutson, James H. AN INVESTIGATION OF THE INARTICULATE: PHILADELPHIA'S WHITE OAKS. *William and Mary Q. 1971 28(1): 3-25.* Cites fraternity of ship carpenters of the post-Stamp Act crisis period as a good example of an "inarticulate" group in the American Colonies. The White Oaks were a law-and-order group with a special fondness for positions espoused by Benjamin Franklin, such as opposition to the Paxton boys, to Germans and to proprietors. The author disagrees with earlier historians of colonial Pennsylvania, who have postulated a tie between frontiersmen and urban workingmen in furthering democracy. The White Oaks were usually conservative, though they

supported nonimportation in opposition to the Townshend duties. While from the lower class, they were not alienated; nor did they seek goals through violence. 77 notes. H. M. Ward

457. Jacobson, David L. THE PUZZLE OF "PACIFICUS." *Pennsylvania Hist. Q. 1964 31(4): 406-418.* Considers two letters of July 1768 concerning the Townshend Acts, their effects on Pennsylvania politics, and that colony's reactions to British taxation. The first letter, by Joseph Galloway, attacked the recent actions of the Pennsylvania Assembly. The author discusses the authorship of the second letter. Pacificus II suggested a stronger stand when petitions and complaints failed to solve colonial problems. 11 notes. D. H. Swift

458. Kaestle, Carl F. THE PUBLIC REACTION TO JOHN DICKINSON'S "FARMER'S LETTERS." *Pro. of the Am. Antiquarian Soc. 1968 78(2): 323-359.* In writing 12 letters signed "A Farmer" which appeared in 19 of the 23 colonial English-language newspapers in 1767 and 1768, John Dickinson boldly attempted to clarify and strengthen the colonists' claims. All duties not for regulation were really taxes, he argued, and any taxation by Parliament was unconstitutional. Although the distinction was not new, Dickinson made it more comprehensive than had been done previously, opening new theoretical dimensions, and providing controversialists with needed ammunition. In many ways, the "Letters" were well contrived. Making use of familiar Whig conceptions, Dickinson in his choice of a pseudonym also appealed to a widespread belief about the good life of the soil. His self-description suggested the farmer-scholar qualities of detachment, scholarship, virtuous leisure, moderate wealth, and humility. Popular success of the "Letters" was due partly to Dickinson's skill as a publicist and partly to their promotion by the Whig press. A small group of Whigs with effective control of the press emphasized the positive reaction to the "Farmer's Letters" while English opinion was distorted. Response indicated that Dickinson's convictions were matched by those of his readers. Based mainly on colonial newspapers; 4 appendixes, 59 notes. R. V. Calvert

459. Thomas, P. D. G. CHARLES TOWNSHEND AND AMERICAN TAXATION IN 1767. *English Hist. R. [Great Britain] 1968 83(326): 33-51.* The view that Townshend pledged himself to obtain a revenue from America to satisfy popular demand among Members of Parliament and that he intended to do this by exploiting what was believed to be the colonial distinction between internal and external taxation has undergone considerable modification. New evidence permitting an examination of the introduction and passage of the Townshend Duties suggests further review. Townshend's motive in 1767 was not primarily to raise colonial revenue; the duties were a token to popular and parliamentary opinion. His real aim was to start to free the administration of government in America from dependence on colonial assemblies. It is possible that it was his deliberate strategy in 1767 to overcome the resistance of his ministerial colleagues (all pro-American) by announcing his plan for taxation first and the underlying purpose later. The evidence indicates however that his basic policy had not been

pursued with sustained purpose since 1754, when he first stated it. Documented from the Newdigate MSS, Warwickshire County Record Office, the Harrowby MSS, and printed sources.   D. H. Murdoch

460. Watson, Derek. THE ROCKINGHAM WHIGS AND THE TOWN-SHEND DUTIES. *English Hist. R. [Great Britain] 1969 84(332): 561-565.* The article by P. D. G. Thomas, "Charles Townshend and American Taxation in 1767," in the *English Historical Review* 83(326): 33-51 underestimates the complexities of the time; it was for Rockingham (Charles Watson Wentworth, 2d Marquis of Rockingham) and his supporters much more than "the simple issue of a vote on the question of the principle and expediency of taxing the American colonies." Reasons for the Rockinghamites' abstention from voting in January and February 1767 should be sought in the attempted Rockingham rapprochement with the Grenvilleites in order to reduce the Land Tax, which made inexpedient a full-scale discussion of American taxation. Townshend's taxation proposals of May-June coincided with discussion of New York's resistance to the Mutiny and Quartering Act; Rockinghamite opposition to the duties might have led to the challenging of Parliamentary supremacy over America. Finally, since Rockingham wished it known that he believed in the principles he had laid down during his first administration, he could not organize opposition to the Townshend duties without inviting the charge of inconsistency. Based partly on the Newcastle Papers, British Museum.   D. H. Murdoch

461. —. [THE WHITE OAKS]. *William and Mary Q. 1972 29(1): 109-142.*
    Lemisch, Jesse and Alexander, John K. THE WHITE OAKS, JACK TAR, AND THE CONCEPT OF THE "INARTICULATE," pp. 109-134. The authors dispute James H. Hutson's "An Investigation of the Inarticulate: Philadelphia's White Oaks," *William and Mary Quarterly* 1971 28(1): 3-25. "Hutson fails to demonstrate similarity between the White Oaks and the 'inarticulate'... Hutson never establishes with any clarity who or what the White Oaks were." The inarticulate were composed of "unlike groups." The authors criticize Hutson's viewpoint and use of sources. 59 notes.
    Crowther, Simeon J. SIMEON J. CROWTHER'S NOTE, pp. 134-136. Though the White Oaks probably were in the upper echelon of the mechanics, "the interests of the ship carpenters were certainly not in conflict with those of their fellow mechanics during nonimportation." Rising shipbuilding output during the period meant that "economic self-interest" was not part of the issue for shipbuilders. 12 notes.
    Hutson, James H. JAMES H. HUTSON'S REBUTTAL, pp. 136-142. "In the White Oaks of Philadelphia I discovered a group of inarticulate ship carpenters whose political activities during a crucial pre-Revolutionary period could be clearly followed. Since they proved to be the very opposite of a radical, protorevolutionary group, their story appeared to be worth telling. My purpose was to demonstrate to skeptical students that the inarticulate were not always radical." 8 notes.   S

Crises of Friction:
Boston Massacre, *Gaspee,* Tea Party

462. Brown, Richard D. MASSACHUSETTS TOWNS REPLY TO THE BOS-
TON COMMITTEE OF CORRESPONDENCE, 1773. *William and Mary Q.*
1968 25(1): 22-39. The towns' reply—consisting of a statement of rights, a list
of grievances, and a "Letter of Correspondence"—and its significance as a product of local democratic action are analyzed. Though the document said nothing
new in political theory, the recataloging of American rights had propaganda
value, and the cooperative response of the towns furthered the cause of the
Revolution. Local politics, town meeting democracy, and the leadership of the
Boston Committee of Correspondence are commented on. 57 notes.

H. M. Ward

463. Bryant, Samuel W. HMS *GASPEE*—THE COURT-MARTIAL. *Rhode*
Island Hist. 1966 25(3): 65-72. Briefly describes the burning of the *Gaspee* and
reproduces the record of the court-martial of her commander, Lieutenant William Dudingston. Based on a copy of the trial record in the Rhode Island
Historical Society.

P. J. Coleman

464. Bryant, Samuel W. RHODE ISLAND JUSTICE—1772 VINTAGE. *Rhode*
Island Hist. 1967 26(3): 65-71. Describes the trial in a Rhode Island court of
Lieutenant William Dudingston, commander of HMS *Gaspee,* in a suit to recover
the value of rum and sugar belonging to Rhode Island merchants which Dudingston had seized and shipped to Boston as smuggled goods. Dudingston paid over
300 pounds in damages and costs. Based on local and state archives, documents
in the Public Record Office (London), and a published contemporary legal treatise.

P. J. Coleman

465. Daniell, Jere. REASON AND RIDICULE: TEA ACT RESOLUTIONS
IN NEW HAMPSHIRE. *Hist. New Hampshire 1965 20(4): 23-28.* Edits resolutions of the Hinsdale March (1774) meeting, probably written by Daniel Jones,
judge and Loyalist, and an 18 February *New Hampshire Gazette* piece, satirizing
agitation against the Tea Act.

T. D. S. Bassett

466. Dickerson, Oliver M. USE MADE OF THE REVENUE FROM THE TAX
ON TEA. *New England Q. 1958 31(2): 232-243.* Maintains that revenue from
the tax on tea, as well as other American taxes, was used by Lord North for
purposes of political patronage rather than for colonial defense, for which it was
supposedly earmarked. Based on a study of official British Treasury records.

L. Gara

467. Gerlach, Larry R. CHARLES DUDLEY AND THE CUSTOMS
QUANDARY IN PRE-REVOLUTIONARY RHODE ISLAND. *Rhode Island*

Hist. 1971 30(2): 52-59. Reproduces and annotates a letter of 12 June 1773 from Dudley, the collector of customs for Rhode Island, to Frederick Smyth, chief justice of New Jersey and a member of the Commission of Inquiry into the *Gaspee* affair, urging the extension of the investigation to earlier attacks on royal vessels. Includes a short introduction to the incident and the document. Based on a manuscript in the Smyth Papers in the American Philosophical Society Library, Philadelphia, published documents, and secondary accounts.

P. J. Coleman

468. Knollenberg, Bernhard. DID SAMUEL ADAMS PROVOKE THE BOS-TON TEA PARTY AND THE CLASH AT LEXINGTON? *Pro. of the Am. Antiquarian Soc. 1961 70(2): 493-503.* Seeks to correct the view set forth by various writers who have based their statements on an assertion by Thomas Hutchinson, made about 1778, that Samuel Adams and the Boston Committee of Correspondence forced the tea ships in December 1773 to tie up at the Boston wharves and then prevented their return to England. By reference to documents contemporary with the Tea Party, including some by Hutchinson himself, the author shows that the Whigs in fact tried to have the tea sent back to England, provided it could be done without payment of duty, and that Governor Hutchinson must bear the ultimate responsibility for preventing this action. Likewise, but without extensive discussion, the author questions the belief that Adams was responsible for the decision of the Minute Men to confront the British troops at Lexington.

W. D. Metz

469. Lord, Donald C. and Calhoon, Robert M. THE REMOVAL OF THE MASSACHUSETTS GENERAL COURT FROM BOSTON, 1769-1772. *J. of Am. Hist. 1969 55(4): 735-755.* For three years during what has been described as a "quiet" period in the colonial protests against British actions, an acrimonious but inconclusive dispute was waged between the Massachusetts General Court and governors of the province over the legality or "rightness" of an executive order removing the General Court to Cambridge from its traditional rest at Boston. In the controversy, Governor Thomas Hutchinson relied on a right of the Crown through the prerogative to instruct and bind the governor in matters not only concerning the Court, but also in garrisoning Castle William and other matters. Alarmed at the potential threat from an expanded use of prerogative rule, the Court argued for the governor's discretion in following instructions and sought to restrain prerogative by asserting it could not be used contrary to the "public good" as interpreted by the representative assembly. 48 notes.

K. B. West

470. Morton, Mary Beth, ed. A RECENTLY DISCOVERED THOMAS HUTCHINSON LETTER. *Pro. of the Massachusetts Hist. Soc. 1970 82: 105-109.* Reprints a letter written in September 1771 by Hutchinson, then Royal Governor of Massachusetts, to Joseph Sewall, at the time both Attorney General of Massachusetts and judge of the vice-admiralty court at Halifax. This document, discovered in 1970 during the demolition of a building in London, is an interesting commentary on the intricacies of preferment politics in the British Empire of the 18th century. 9 notes.

J. B. Duff

471. Quarles, Benjamin. CRISPUS ATTUCKS. *Am. Hist. Illus. 1970 5(7): 38-42.* Describes the role of Attucks, a runaway slave and mulatto, in the "Boston Massacre" of 5 March 1770 and chronicles the historical significance of the act from 1770 to 1970. Attucks was in the front ranks of the party which taunted the soldiers; was the first to die, being "killed instantly"; may have been the leader of the group and was likely the most aggressive; was the victim referred to most often in the murder trial of the British soldiers; and had a monument in his honor erected in 1888 on historic Boston Common. His name has become familiar to 10 generations of black Americans—particularly in Boston, where for years 5 March was celebrated as Crispus Attucks Day. Based on primary sources; 5 illus.

D. Dodd

472. Steedman, Marguerite. CHARLESTOWN'S FORGOTTEN TEA-PARTY. *Georgia R. 1967 21(2): 244-259.* Describes Charlestown's (now Charleston) tea-party of November 1774, quoting from the contemporary *South-Carolina Gazette.* Charlestown always felt close ties with Boston and went to Boston's relief after the Boston Port Bill. Charlestown had boycotted tea with the third duty since December 1773, but on 3 November 1774, "an Oblation was made to NEPTUNE, of the seven said Chests of Tea" by three merchants to whom the consignment had been made. On 7 November "a MAGNIFICENT exhibition of EFFIGIES" was held, the whole city decrying "Popery," loyalism, and Lord North's government. In 1776 the boycotted tea was removed from the exchange, sold, and drunk.

T. M. Condon

473. Stout, Neil R. THE *GASPEE* AFFAIR. *Mankind 1967 1(1): 48-51, 89-92.* Survey of the background of the burning of the British armed schooner *Gaspee* on 9 June 1772 by Rhode Island patriots. The *Gaspee* was a symbol of Britain's claim that she had the right to tax the American colonies without their consent. The burning of the *Gaspee* was an American statement that the colonies did not recognize the British right of taxation. Illus., biblio.

P. D. Thomas

474. Unsigned. THE FIRST OVERT ACT OF THE REVOLUTION. *Newport Hist. 1972 45(2): 36-40.* The burning of the British sloop *Liberty* in July 1769 was the first overt act of the Americans against British customs demands. Reproduces part of a contemporary account of the burning of the *Liberty.*

D. P. Peltier

475. Upton, L. F. S. PROCEEDINGS OF YE BODY RESPECTING THE TEA. *William and Mary Q. 1965 22(2): 287-300.* This anonymous narrative from the Sewell Papers, Public Archives of Canada, Ottawa, sheds light on the arguments of the patriots during their meetings at the Old South Church between 29 November and 16 December 1773. The narrator, a moderate Tory, reveals a sense of history. The narrative is reproduced.

H. M. Ward

476. Watson, D. H. JOSEPH HARRISON AND THE *LIBERTY* INCIDENT. *William and Mary Q. 1963 20(4): 585-595.* The text of a hitherto unpublished letter by the collector of customs at Boston to Rockingham, dated 17 June 1768,

with an introduction by the editor. The letter tells of the incarceration of the customs agent on the *Liberty* and describes the sentiments of the Bostonians of the time. The letter tends to refute the suggestion that the *Liberty* incident was part of a concerted effort to harass John Hancock.   E. Oberholzer, Jr.

477. Zobel, Hiller B. NEWER LIGHT ON THE BOSTON MASSACRE. *Pro. of the Am. Antiquarian Soc. 1968 78(1): 119-128.* A passage in Governor Thomas Hutchinson's third volume of his history of Massachusetts (published posthumously in 1828), when compared with his journal entry for 5 December 1770, reveals that the governor knew much more than he was willing to tell about the so-called Boston Massacre participants' trial proceedings. The happy outcome of the case (acquittal of seven of the soldiers and convictions for nonpunishable manslaughter for two others) apparently tempered Hutchinson's account before it was published. Largely ignored (in the British Museum), the Hutchinson journal account leaves the reader with the uncomfortable conclusion that defense counsel for the accused soldiers, John Adams, in trying to do what he considered justice to Boston, came shockingly close to sacrificing his clients for the good of his constituency. Although the John Adams-Josiah Quincy defense of the soldiers has long been considered the apogee of the American legal profession, Hutchinson declares in his journal entry that Adams's "bias to the general conduct of the Town appeared very strong." Based partly on unpublished documents; 41 notes.
R. V. Calvert

The Coersive Acts

478. Adams, Thomas R. THE BRITISH PAMPHLETS OF THE AMERICAN REVOLUTION FOR 1774: A PROGRESS REPORT. *Massachusetts Hist. Soc. Pro. 1969 81: 31-103.* Analyzes the British pamphlets as bibliographic entities rather than as interpretative problems. For 1774, the prototype pamphlet was printed anonymously in London, was issued by booksellers-publishers in an octavo format for one shilling, and was printed in an edition of 500 copies. The author's bibliography is almost complete for the year 1774 and also contains six titles which appeared before 1774 but which had editions printed in that year. 10 notes, biblio.   J. B. Duff

479. Bargar, R. D. MATTHEW BOULTON AND THE BIRMINGHAM PETITION OF 1775. *Willian and Mary Q. 1956 13(1): 26-39.* Discusses the roles of Lord Dartmouth and Edmund Burke in the matter of James Watt's condenser patent, in which Boulton had a two-thirds interest. Seeking to induce Dartmouth to intercede on his behalf, and with Dartmouth's approval, Boulton instigated a counter-petition, asking for the strict enforcement of the Coercive Acts of 1774. This paper reached Parliament ahead of the merchants' petition, asking conciliation with America, which it sought to counteract.   E. Oberholzer, Jr.

480. Marion, Séraphin. L'ACTE DE QUEBEC, CONCESSION MAG-
NANIME OU INTERESSEE? [The Quebec Act: generous or calculated concession?]. *Cahiers des Dix [Canada] 1963 28: 147-177.* Reviews the numerous
interpretations for the Quebec Act of 1774: that it was brought about by a British
desire to create a strong military base in the event of trouble in the southern
colonies, to prevent French-Canadian support for France in any future war, to
pacify the Indians, and to prevent a mass exodus which would destroy the
newly-conquered province. The conquerors found that the French Canadians
were useful in strengthening their empire. Concludes that it would be puerile to
thank the British authorities for benefits decreed by a guiding Providence.
L. F. S. Upton

481. Radoff, Morris L. AN ELUSIVE MANUSCRIPT—THE *PROCEED-
INGS OF THE MARYLAND CONVENTION OF 1774. Am. Archivist 1967
30(1): 59-65.* Presents evidence concerning the history of the missing manuscript
copy of the *Proceedings of the Maryland Convention* (1774), which met three
times that year after the passage of the Boston Port Act. The manuscript was
published in the Maryland *Gazette* and was apparently retained by the editor,
Frederick Green. His grandson Jonas Green evidently used the manuscript for
the 1836 printed edition, and it is assumed from the Maryland State Library
catalog of 1837 that the manuscript was given to the State library. It is not further
identified in the library records. In 1846 and 1882, State records were transferred
temporarily to the Maryland Historical Society and returned to the State in 1934.
The manuscript appears in the society's 1854 catalog, as well as in the annual
reports of the Land Office as a record at the Historical Society under the provisions of the 1882 act. It may have been sold by the Commissioner of the Land
Office in 1889. Documented. D. C. Duniway

482. Sosin, Jack M. THE MASSACHUSETTS ACTS OF 1774: COERCIVE OR
PREVENTIVE? *Huntington Lib. Q. 1962/63 26(3): 235-252.* The four acts
which were the response of the British Government to the tea crisis in Boston
were limited in aim. Their purpose was to provide a legal basis on which the
constituted civil officers could arrest a revolutionary challenge to authority. The
intent was not to eliminate the democratic part of colonial government, but to
restore the balance of a "mixed" government such as already existed in the other
royal provinces. H. D. Jordan

The First Continental Congress

483. Bowman, Larry. THE VIRGINIA COUNTY COMMITTEES OF
SAFETY, 1774-1776. *Virginia Mag. of Hist. and Biog. 1971 79(3): 322-337.*
Virginians formed 49 Committees of Safety by the end of 1775 to enforce the
boycott commanded by the First Continental Congress in article 11 of the Continental Association. Despite occasional overzealousness the committees per-

formed ably. They were realistic, dedicated to fairness within absolute justice and swift punishment, and thorough in their vigilance. When Virginia's new constitution went into effect, the committees quickly dissolved in the summer of 1776. Based primarily on secondary sources; 81 notes. C. A. Newton

484. Chase, Theodore. THE ATTACK ON FORT WILLIAM AND MARY. *Hist. New Hampshire 1963 18(1): 20-34.* John Langdon and John Sullivan led several hundred in bloodless assaults on the delapidated "Castle" on Great Island at the mouth of the Piscataqua, 14-15 December 1774. They captured about a hundred barrels of gunpowder, small arms, small cannon and shot, used later by the revolutionaries. Three days later, British vessels and troops regained control. T. D. S. Bassett

485. Collier, Christopher. SILAS DEANE REPORTS ON THE CONTINENTAL CONGRESS: A DIARY FRAGMENT: OCTOBER 1-6, 1774. *Connecticut Hist. Soc. Bull. 1964 29(1): 1-8.* Scholars are still debating Silas Deane's place in the politics of the American Revolution. He was a delegate to the First Continental Congress that opened in Philadelphia on 5 September 1774. He missed no opportunity of censuring his fellow delegates from Connecticut, Eliphalet Dyer and Roger Sherman. The fragment of a diary here published is in the Deane Papers at the Connecticut Historical Society. It is perhaps the only report extant of certain aspects of the First Continental Congress. The "Loyal Address" to the king declared that 13 parliamentary acts passed since 1763 violated American rights. Illus. E. P. Stickney

486. Wolf, Edwin, 2nd. THE AUTHORSHIP OF THE 1774 ADDRESS TO THE KING RESTUDIED. *William and Mary Q. 1965 22(2): 189-224.* Examines the authorship of this address, which John Dickinson assumed that he had written but could not recall. Dickinson probably made changes in and rewrote an original draft by Richard Henry Lee. Documents reproduced here: drafts by Lee, Patrick Henry, and Dickinson, Dickinson's letter to Charles Thomson, and the engrossed copy sent to England. H. M. Ward

5

THE WAR FOR RIGHTS:
BEFORE THE
DECLARATION OF INDEPENDENCE

General

487. Betts, John L. A CONVERSATION IN A PHILADELPHIA INN, 1775. *Hist. Teacher 1972 5(3): 9-20.* Describes a teacher's presentation of a fictional conversation in order to highlight the economic and political complaints of Americans from all sections of the Colonies and to give the British position in response. Appendix.   P. W. Kennedy

488. Copeland, Peter F. and Zlatich, Marko. THE MINUTE BATTALION OF CULPEPER COUNTY, VIRGINIA, 1775-1776. *Military Collector and Historian 1965 17(2): 52-54.* Describes the dress of the battalion which consisted of at least 10 companies from Culpeper, York and James City counties in Virginia. Based on contemporary eyewitness accounts and manuscripts from the Virginia State Library, illus., 4 notes.   C. L. Boyd

489. Copeland, Peter F. and Simpson, J. P. 11TH NEW HAMPSHIRE PRO-VINCIAL REGIMENT, 1774-1775. *Military Collector and Historian 1969 21(1): 16-18.* Describes the organization and uniforming of the 10th, 11th, and 12th New Hampshire infantry regiments which were enrolled just prior to the Revolution. Their brief existence provided some military training for men later active in the struggle for independence. Most notable of these was Benjamin Thompson—spy, Loyalist officer and later a count of the Holy Roman Empire.
D. C. Oliver

490. J. E. WINSTON CHURCHILL AND BENJAMIN FRANKLIN: TWO VISITS TO CRAVEN STREET. *British Survey 1956 (82): 1-4.* The negotiations between Lord Chatham and Benjamin Franklin to find a compromise in the

quarrel between the mother country and the colonies are briefly discussed in conjunction with a visit of Sir Winston Churchill to the former Franklin quarters on Craven Street, now headquarters of the British Society for International Understanding. Sir Winston was there to receive an American medal.

G. Rehder

Lexington & Concord

491. Barnes, Eric W. ALL THE KING'S HORSES...AND ALL THE KING'S MEN. *Am. Heritage 1960 11(6): 56-59, 86-87.* Recounts the episode in which the British troops crossed North River Bridge, Salem, Massachusetts, a center of American Patriot activity, in February 1775. There the first American blood was shed, nearly two months before Lexington and Concord. The author concludes that this, perhaps, was the first blow of the American Revolution. Undocumented.   C. R. Allen, Jr.

492. Barton, John A. LEXINGTON: THE END OF A MYTH. *Hist. Today [Great Britain] 1959 9(6): 382-391.* Deals with the problems of 1) the reason for the presence of American troops at Lexington, and 2) who fired the first shot. The author shows that American troops were not justified in defending Lexington and attributes the blame to an unidentified American who unwittingly fired the first shot and set the machinery of war in motion.   L. D. Kasparian

493. Cohen, Joel A. LEXINGTON AND CONCORD: RHODE ISLAND REACTS. *Rhode Island Hist. 1967 26(4): 97-102.* Describes the internal conflict in Rhode Island, particularly the response of different factions to the call for troops, and emphasizes the lack of unanimity. The defeat of Governor Joseph Wanton by the legislature is discussed. Based on primary and secondary sources and government documents.   P. J. Coleman

494. Cullen, Joseph P. BATTLES, LEADERS, AND ISSUES OF THE REVOLUTION: TO ARMS: THE WAR HAS BEGUN. *Am. Hist. Illus. 1967 2(3): 4-11.* A detailed account of the dramatic events marking the opening of the American Revolution. Illustrated with maps and reproductions of paintings and sketches made by contemporaries.   F. J. Stachowski

495. McCurry, Allan J. THE NORTH GOVERNMENT AND THE OUTBREAK OF THE AMERICAN REVOLUTION. *Huntington Lib. Q. 1971 34(2): 141-157.* After the Coercive Acts of 1774 and the meeting of the refractory Americans in a general congress, the British Government rapidly concluded that submission must be compelled by force even if that should lead to war. Efforts at conciliation, one unofficial and revolving around Benjamin Franklin, the other a formal proposal by Lord North, were not serious. These efforts and the discus-

sion of an offer of pardons were intended primarily to divide the colonists. Ministerial planning during the four or five months before arrival of the news of Lexington and Concord focused on the use of military power against the New Englanders. 80 notes.   H. D. Jordan

496. Quimby, Ian M. G. THE DOOLITTLE ENGRAVINGS OF THE BAT-TLE OF LEXINGTON AND CONCORD. *Winterthur Portfolio 1968 4: 83-108.* Deals with the controversy over the authorship of the original paintings that inspired Amos Doolittle (1754-1832) to produce four engravings shortly after the battles of Lexington and Concord. The engravings are the best pictorial record of the events of 19 April 1775. The author also discusses the role of John Warner Barber (1798-1885) and Ralph Earl (1751-1801). Traces various reprints and uses of the original engravings. Gives a concise history of the battles in order to show the accuracy of the engravings. Based on primary and secondary sources; 17 photos, 62 notes.   N. A. Kuntz

497. Scott, Kenneth. TIMOTHY WALKER'S ACROSTIC ON DANIEL THOMPSON. *Hist. New Hampshire 1966 21(1): 27-29.* Two versions of a patriotic rhyme about a minuteman killed by a grenadier on a march to or from Concord on 19 April. A sketch of the acrostic's author, later paymaster of New Hampshire troops besieging Boston, is included. Based on the Walker Papers in The New Hampshire Historical Society and family histories.
                                                  T. D. S. Bassett

498. Wright, Geneva Aldrich. THE SHOT HEARD ROUND THE WORLD, APRIL 19, 1775. *Daughters of the Am. Revolution Mag. 1971 105(4): 393-394, 464, 472.* Remarks the colonial reluctance to move toward independence, and analyzes the impact of the Boston Port Act of 1774 upon the separatist movement in New England. Discusses General Gage's plans to stop the revolutionary movement by seizure of arms and arrest of leaders, rebel countermoves, the confrontations at Lexington and Concord, and colonial harassment of British troops during the return march to Boston. The events of 19 April 1775 have been fundamental to all American accomplishments since that time. Illus.   D. A. Sloan

Military Campaigns

499. Abernethy, Thomas J. CRANE'S RHODE ISLAND COMPANY OF AR-TILLERY, 1775. *Rhode Island Hist. 1970 29(2/3): 46-51.* Reconstructs the roster of the unit commanded by Major John Crane (1744-1805) of Providence, Rhode Island, which served in the siege of Boston in May 1775. Based on records in the Rhode Island, Massachusetts, and National Archives.
                                                  P. J. Coleman

500. Bradford, Sydney S., ed. THE COMMON BRITISH SOLDIER. *Maryland Hist. Mag. 1967 62(3): 219-253.* A journal by Thomas Sullivan, an enlisted man of the 49th Regiment of Foot. Contains the seldom-recorded experiences and observations of a common soldier. The diary covers 1775-76. Lists the departure of the unit from Ireland and service in the New England Colonies. Describes the Battle of Bunker Hill, with the number of British dead and wounded. Pictures Boston and locality, including the economic life of the city. The chronicle for 1776 includes the organization of field tactics against the rebels in Massachusetts. 114 notes.   D. H. Swift

501. Collier, Christopher. INSIDE THE AMERICAN REVOLUTION; A SILAS DEANE DIARY FRAGMENT APRIL 20 TO OCTOBER 25, 1775. *Connecticut Hist. Soc. Bull. 1964 29(3): 86-96A.* This fragment of Silas Deane's diary is in two parts; 20 April to 24 July and 10 May to 25 October 1775. It was found among the Deane Papers in the Connecticut Historical Society. In it are references to Ethan Allen's Ticonderoga expedition which was largely organized by Silas Deane and financed through Deane's efforts by the Connecticut Committee of Safety. The notes on the transactions of the Continental Congress begin with 10 May 1775.   E. P. Stickney

502. Collins, J. Richard. THE *HANNAH-NAUTILUS* AFFAIR. *Essex Inst. Hist. Collections 1968 104(1): 34-41.* The first vessel commissioned by George Washington upon his assumption of command of the Continental Army in 1775 was the 78-ton schooner *Hannah.* The American vessel was intercepted by a British sloop, the 316-ton *Nautilus,* on 10 October 1775 outside the Beverly, Massachusetts, harbor and was run aground by her captain. While attempting to destroy the *Hannah,* the *Nautilus* ran aground herself and was caught in an American crossfire, suffering one fatality. This was "certainly the first documented naval engagement of the Revolutionary War." 45 notes.
                                                                    J. M. Bumsted

503. Cullen, Joseph P. MOORE'S CREEK BRIDGE. *Am. Hist. Illus. 1970 4(9): 10-15.* The little-known action in February 1776 at Moore's Creek Bridge may have saved North Carolina for the Americans. To the South this action meant what Lexington meant to the North. "So much military ardor was kindled among the country folk that in fifteen days 10,000 volunteers turned out for the militia and the Continental line." Illus.   E. P. Stickney

504. Davis, Kenneth S. "IN THE NAME OF THE GREAT JEHOVAH AND THE CONTINENTAL CONGRESS." *Am. Heritage 1963 14(6): 65-77.* Recounts the legend and history of Ethan Allen during the revolutionary years, with emphasis on the battle of Ticonderoga. Illus. Undocumented.
                                                                    C. R. Allen, Jr.

505. Ditsky, John. THE YANKEE INSOLENCE OF ETHAN ALLEN. *Can. R. of Am. Studies 1970 1(1): 32-38.* Discusses *A Narrative of Colonel Ethan Allen's Captivity,* first published in 1779. Characterizes the prison behavior of

Allen (1738-89) as "out-Englishing the English," which showed that "the conditions of American life had accomplished a quickening of the characteristics generally ascribed to the British national character." Allen's behavior helped to establish "a new national spirit" in both Canada and the United States, a spirit the author labels "Yankee insolence." 12 notes.   J. M. Hawes

506. Dowdell, Vincent S. THE BIRTH OF THE AMERICAN NAVY. *U.S. Naval Inst. Pro. 1955 81(11): 1251-1257.* George Washington, facing a shortage of ammunition, ordered John Glover to charter ships and man these with soldiers familiar with sea life, in order to seize British supply ships. The first ship to set sail was the *Hannah,* on 5 September 1775; others followed. The valuable services these ships rendered stimulated Congressional action. A naval committee came into being and consequently, the U.S. Navy. The author holds that 5 September 1775 was its date of birth.   D. van Arkel

507. Hagelin, Wladimir and Brown, Ralph A., eds. CONNECTICUT FARMERS AT BUNKER HILL: THE DIARY OF COLONEL EXPERIENCE STORRS. *New England Q. 1955 28(1): 72-93.* Completely reprinted diary, covering 21 November 1774-28 June 1775. It includes an account of meetings of the Connecticut Assembly, the reaction to the news of Concord and Lexington, the march to Cambridge, and the battle of Bunker Hill, in which the colonel, however, was not an active participant.   G. Rehder

508. Jones, Newton J. THE WASHINGTON LIGHT INFANTRY AT THE BUNKER HILL CENTENNIAL. *South Carolina Hist. Mag. 1964 65(4): 195-204.* Shows the significance of South Carolina participation in a national event at the end of Reconstruction. Chiefly newspaper and secondary sources.
V. O. Bardsley

509. Ketchum, Richard M. "THE DECISIVE DAY IS COME." *Am. Heritage 1962 13(5): 80-93.* A selection from the author's forthcoming book *The Battle for Bunker Hill,* this article details the battle and preparations for it. Undocumented; map.   C. R. Allen, Jr.

510. Lajoie, John. A HISTORY OF THE GREEN MOUNTAIN BOYS. *Vermont Hist. 1966 34(4): 235-240.* This article tied for first prize in an essay contest. Summarized from six texts.   T. D. S. Bassett

511. Maguire, J. Robert. HAND'S COVE: RENDEZVOUS OF ETHAN ALLEN AND THE GREEN MOUNTAIN BOYS FOR THE CAPTURE OF FORT TICONDEROGA. *Vermont Hist. 1965 33(4): 416-437.* Scrutiny of

Shoreham, Vermont, deeds, proprietors' records, petitions, and other sources establishes the pre-Revolutionary presence of Bemans, Rowleys, Moores and others, and suggests that the Hand's Cove property Rufus Herrick bought in 1783 had a one-room, square-timbered house built before Ethan Allen took Fort Ticonderoga. Map, 74 notes.   T. D. S. Bassett

512. Manders, Eric I. NOTES ON TROOP UNITS IN THE CAMBRIDGE ARMY, 1775-1776. *Military Collector and Historian 1971 23(3): 69-74.* After the Lexington alarm, four New England governments reorganized the various troops at Boston into the so-called Cambridge Army. Shortly after the Battle of Breeds Hill ("Bunker Hill," 17 June 1775) the force was adopted by the Continental Congress and its structure again was modified. Describes both of these organizational patterns, classifying regiments by number, place of origin, and name of the commander. Based on primary sources; 2 tables, 7 notes.
                                                                          D. C. Oliver

513. Moomaw, W. Hugh. THE BRITISH LEAVE COLONIAL VIRGINIA. *Virginia Mag. of Hist. and Biog. 1958 66(2): 147-160.* British colonial government was ended in Virginia in June 1775 when the Governor, Lord Dunmore, fled. For the next 14 months Dunmore attempted to carry on military and naval operations from a small flotilla anchored off the coast. The complete failure of these efforts was due in large measure to a lack of cooperation between departments of government and to friction between the civil authorities and the military commanders. These problems plagued British administration throughout North America and are illustrated in the case of Virginia by the bitter conflict between Dunmore and Captain Andrew Hammond, the local naval commander.   D. Houston

514. Page, Elwin L. WHAT HAPPENED TO THE KING'S POWDER? *Hist. New Hampshire 1964 19(2): 28-33.* Of the 98 100-pound barrels of gunpowder taken from Fort William and Mary, 14-15 December 1774, almost half was probably dealt out to militia joining Washington at Cambridge after the battles of Lexington and Concord; but about 54 barrels remained in New Hampshire after the battle of Bunker Hill. The disposal of this remainder is traced from published archives and local histories.   T. D. S. Bassett

515. Smith, Philip C. F. and Knight, Russell W. IN TROUBLED WATERS: THE ELUSIVE SCHOONER *HANNAH. Am. Neptune 1970 30(2): 86-116.* Utilizing extensive documents, the authors reveal a variety of misconceptions

about *Hannah* and contend that much of the published research about the vessel is "wrong, questionable, or based on circumstantial evidence." *Hannah* was allegedly the first of General Washington's armed schooners used during the Revolution. However, little is known of her construction, ownership, appearance, size, conversion for battle duty, or actual use during the Revolution. There is a paucity of evidence regarding her wartime activities. After 200 years, *"Hannah* still sails on Troubled Waters." Photos, 58 notes.   J. D. Born, Jr.

Canada and the War

516. Beirne, Francis F. MISSION TO CANADA: 1776. *Maryland Hist. Mag. 1965 60(4): 404-420.* A detailed account of a diplomatic mission to Canada to unite Quebec with the American Colonies. The military mission to Canada failed to accomplish its purpose. The author describes the activities and people of the mission in their attempt to entice the Canadians away from British rule. It took another war before the United States learned the futility of uniting the two countries by force. The lesson learned has resulted in a century and a half of peaceful coexistence. 41 notes.   D. H. Swift

517. Cecil, Robert. WHEN CANADA DID NOT CHOOSE FREEDOM. *Hist. Today [Great Britain] 1963 13(8): 511-519.* The peoples of the northernmost colonies did not rally to the cause of the Thirteen because they were exposed to British seapower, because they retained commercial advantages from nonparticipation, and because grievances in the north were less acute than farther south. Though the Thirteen were fighting in the name of liberty, they at once embarked on an invasion of their northern neighbors, partly out of fear of uprising if the Indians were inflamed by their enemies, partly misled by the early achievements of Ethan Allen. No later invasion was attempted after France had joined openly in the war, because of the terrible prospect of a midwinter invasion with inadequate forces, and because France did not wish to see the new republic extend over much of the continent. Undocumented. Illus.   E. P. Stickney

518. Cohen, Sheldon S. LIEUTENANT JOHN STARKE AND THE DEFENCE OF QUEBEC. *Dalhousie R. [Canada] 1967 47(1): 57-64.* Publishes "The Case of Lieutenant John Starke of His Majesties Navy" from the archives of the National Maritime Museum, Greenwich, England, insofar as it describes the siege of Quebec in 1775-76. Starke's brief account corroborates lengthier descriptions by other defenders of Quebec.   L. F. S. Upton

519. Coleman, John M. HOW "CONTINENTAL" WAS THE CONTINENTAL CONGRESS? *Hist. Today [Great Britain] 1968 18(8): 540-550.* Puts forward the thesis that the Continental Congress was not continentally oriented

because it had no sincere desire to incorporate French Canadians into the new republic. While the Continental Congress struggled to expand its basis of support from the Thirteen Colonies to a wider area, two plans for an invasion of Canada were considered but never adopted. Lafayette both spoke and wrote to convince French Canadians in the 1770's to join the colonies in their revolt against British tyranny. Benjamin Franklin, as late as 1782, attempted to negotiate with Britain a cession of Canada. In the end, "the French Canadians had no intention whatever of changing their culture, or of submitting themselves to the American melting pot; and the success of the American experiment, if it was to be a success, depended on the melting pot." Portraits, maps.   L. A. Knafla

520. Craig, G. M. LETTERS IN CANADA: 1965. SOCIAL STUDIES, LOCAL AND REGIONAL. *U. of Toronto Q. [Canada] 1966 35(4): 472-477.* Survey of works published in 1965 which concern particular sections of Canada and some which do not fit into local or regional classifications. Topics discussed in the local and regional books include: a visitor's impressions of Newfoundland; a history of the maritime provinces, 1712-1857; a biography of Frontenac; descriptions of Montreal; events in Quebec during the 1960's; Toronto under French rule; a diary of the wife of Upper Canada's first lieutenant governor for the years 1791-96; a biography of a pioneering figure in the settlement of southwestern Ontario; a study of Scottish "Loyalists" from New York who came to Ontario during the American Revolution; the 1837 rebellion in Upper Canada; a social history and pictorial record of Toronto in the 19th century; public welfare administration in Ontario, 1791-1893; a history of Manitoba; accounts of homesteading in Saskatchewan and Alberta; the credit union movement in Saskatchewan; scenic descriptions of the British Columbia coast, six major Canadian mountain peaks and two rivers. Subjects covered by the nonlocal and nonregional books include: a history of Canada's flag; the history of Canada prior to federation; a history of the Jews in Canada to 1900; Canadian-American boundary disputes; Canada's role in the race to build the atom bomb during the Second World War; and biographies of certain Canadian political, literary, artistic, and scientific figures.
W. L. Bowers

521. Greening, W. E. FORT LENNOX: A HISTORIC GATEWAY TO CANADA. *Can. Geographical J. 1969 78(2): 48-53.* Fort Lennox, on Ile aux Noix on the Richelieu River south of Montreal, lies in the path of the historic invasion route to Canada. The first fort was begun in 1759, late in the French and Indian War. When the fort fell in 1760, British occupation of Montreal and all Canada became inevitable. Traces the fort's history through the American Revolution, the War of 1812, and the Fenian difficulties after the Civil War. The fort was abandoned in 1870 and lay in disrepair until 1921 when it was acquired by the National Parks branch of the Department of Interior. 6 illus.
R. D. Tallman

522. Greening, W. E. THE HISTORIC KENNEBEC ROAD. *Can. Geographical J. 1967 75(5): 162-167.* The route of the old Kennebec Road runs south from Quebec City to Skowhegan and Augusta, Maine. It was one of the battlegrounds in the struggle between the British and French for domination of eastern North

America. Along this route the Jesuit missionaries worked among the Abnaki Indians, who became allies of the French in raids on frontier settlements in southern Maine and New Hampshire. The New Englanders eventually destroyed the Jesuit mission and forced the Abnaki northward. Benedict Arnold and his men used this path in his trek from Boston to attempt the capture of Quebec in 1775. Illus., map. C. J. Allard

523. Huston, James A. THE LOGISTICS OF ARNOLD'S MARCH TO QUE-BEC. *Military Affairs 1968 32(3): 110-124.* Despite the energetic leadership of its commander Benedict Arnold, the American column which moved through the Maine wilderness in the fall of 1775 nearly perished from starvation. The difficulties can be traced to the hurry with which the expedition was mounted and the use of bateaux rather than canoes to carry supplies. Based on printed documents and monographs; 11 notes. K. J. Bauer

524. Leland, Marine. FRANÇOIS-JOSEPH CUGNET (1720-1789). *R. de l'U. Laval [Canada] 1965 20(2): 143-150, (3): 267-274.* I. Specific detail of the reception of Cugnet's publications between 15 February and 13 May 1775 is not known, although there is evidence in the correspondence of Pierre Guy and François Baby of the general discontent and chaotic atmosphere of Canada at the time. Guy directed his criticism of the Quebec Act in terms of the Canadian seigneurs and the preference Carleton showed them. While men like Guy and Baby were quietly complaining, Cugnet fulfilled the function of French secretary to the governor with zeal, reporting suspected enemies of the Quebec Act to the governor. At the same time Cugnet continued his involvement in land speculation in the province. II. Ironically, Governor Carleton of Quebec responded to the outbreak of the American Revolution with a restoration of the ancient militia which had been abolished by royal proclamation. Doubtless, Carleton believed that the seigneurs could control the inhabitants, although he knew that they were not as a class likely to relish commanding a bare militia. Carleton discovered that the plan was not enthusiastically received by habitants suspicious of a despotic and hypocritical government, and that the clergy and nobility had lost their influence with the people. After the Americans were driven out of the province, and before he was replaced by Burgoyne as commander in chief, Carleton reestablished the ancient institution of *Foi et Hommage* which had lapsed after the Conquest. This had long been a suggestion of Cugnet, who was appointed "Clerk for the Adjustment of the Land Roll" in 1777. J. M. Bumsted

525. Neatby, Hilda. FRENCH CANADIAN NATIONALISM AND THE AMERICAN REVOLUTION. *Centennial R. 1966 10(4): 505-522.* Discusses whether separation has been a possibility in Canada since the beginning of British rule. The British unintentionally irritated the French into an intransigent nationalism. The American Revolution destroyed the possibility of anglicization and produced "strong and lasting" effects on Canada. During the American Revolution Sir Guy Carleton set up two hierarchies under his direct control—the clerical under the Catholic Church and the secular under the seigneurs. In doing so, Carleton "accentuated the social differences which already existed in French Society." The Church was preserved as the "greatest unifying influence in French

Canada." The final blow to anglicization came from the influx of ill-humored and ill-mannered Loyalists during and after the American Revolution.

A. R. Stoesen

526. Rawlky, George A. THE AMERICAN REVOLUTION AND NOVA SCOTIA RECONSIDERED. *Dalhousie R. [Canada] 1963 43(3): 378-394.* Discusses the varying tides of public opinion prevalent in the maritime colonies in regard to the American Revolution, with special attention to the views held by settlers who had emigrated from New England, many of whom are named. Suggests reasons why sentiment favorable to the revolting colonies failed to result in abandonment of neutrality.   M. B. Rex

527. Ritchie, C. I. A. LIEUTENANT STARKE AT THE SIEGE OF QUEBEC. *Notes and Queries [Great Britain] 1959 204(11): 385-387.* A document in the National Maritime Museum, Greenwich, intended by its author to back up a claim for promotion, provides a useful account of the siege of Quebec, 1775-76.

W. D. McIntyre

528. Roche, John F., ed. QUEBEC UNDER SIEGE, 1775-1776: THE "MEMORANDUMS" OF JACOB DANFORD. *Can. Hist. R. 1969 50(1): 68-85.* An English civilian's diary of the siege of Quebec (November 1775-May 1776) by rebel forces from the Thirteen Colonies under Benedict Arnold and Richard Montgomery. Danford, an employee of the Board of Ordnance, noted all major incidents and provided details as to emplacement and fire of the artillery of attackers and defenders not given in other siege journals. An introduction to the diary outlines its history before it was brought to light in England in 1948 and deposited with the British Museum.   A

529. Smith, Ronald D. AGENT MC LANE: LONE REVOLUTIONARY IN CANADA. *Rocky Mountain Social Sci. J. 1970 7(2): 73-82.* Narrates the story of David McLane, an American citizen who allegedly conspired to overthrow British authority in Canada and who was hanged and decapitated in Quebec in 1797. McLane was convicted of treason after several co-conspirators testified against him. He maintained that he had merely relocated in Canada and had used false names to foil creditors. 12 notes.   A. P. Young

530. Trudel, Pierre. L'ATTITUDE DU GOUVERNEUR LOUIS-FREDERIC HALDIMAND A L'EGARD DES CANADIENS FRANÇAIS (1778-1781) [The attitude of Governor Louis Frederick Haldimand to the French Canadians, 1778-81]. *R. de l'U. d'Ottawa [Canada] 1966 36(1): 5-14.* Sir Frederick Haldimand's governorship of Quebec has often been represented as oppressive, but he had many real problems to deal with and he took a moderate line. The American Revolution generated much sympathy among the clergy and habitants of Quebec and, once France and England were at war, the allegiance of French Canadians to their new masters was open to doubt. Haldimand acted promptly when need arose, but always with prudence. Based on the Haldimand Papers, Public Archives of Canada.   L. F. S. Upton

531. Whitridge, Arnold. CANADA: THE STRUGGLE FOR THE 14TH STATE. *Hist. Today [Great Britain] 1967 17(1): 13-21.* A sketch of American views on Canada, and the major clashes between the two countries from colonial times to 1848. The views of Samuel Adams, George Washington, Benjamin Franklin, Henry Clay, and John Quincy Adams are taken as representative of American opinion. The author focuses on the American invasion of 1775 and the heroics of Benedict Arnold, Richard Montgomery, and Governor Sir Guy Carleton. Illus. L. A. Knafla

Movement toward Independence

532. Champagne, Roger J. NEW YORK'S RADICALS AND THE COMING OF INDEPENDENCE. *J. of Am. Hist. 1964 51(1): 21-40.* Considers the role of radical leadership in New York during the critical years of 1775 and 1776, focusing primarily on Isaac Sears, John Lamb, and Alexander McDougall, leaders since 1765 of New York's Sons of Liberty. By the time independence was declared, these three leaders who, more than any others, had paved the way for New York's independence, were out of public life, with the consequence of depriving New York's lower class of a political voice and of giving the Robert R. Livingston faction virtually a free hand in establishing New York's independence. H. J. Silverman

533. Gemmill, John K. THE PROBLEMS OF POWER: NEW HAMPSHIRE GOVERNMENT DURING THE REVOLUTION. *Hist. New Hampshire 1967 22(2): 27-38.* New Hampshire provincials evolved a government after Governor John Wentworth left on 23 August 1775. They secured congressional permission and in 1776 drafted the first of four revolutionary constitutions. The provincial assembly was reapportioned according to the 1775 census and several times adjusted, but still the Connecticut Valley towns complained. The executive was intended to be weak; the legislature was weak through high turnover; but the Committee of Safety, led by Meshech Weare, Josiah Bartlett, and Ebenezer Thompson was strong. It administered a loyalty oath to nearly nine thousand men; 773 refused to take it. Based on a Columbia University M. A. thesis using *New Hampshire Provincial Papers* and other published documents. T. D. S. Bassett

534. Klingelhofer, Herbert E. THE CAUTIOUS REVOLUTION: MARYLAND AND THE MOVEMENT TOWARD INDEPENDENCE: 1774-1776. *Maryland Hist. Mag. 1965 60(3): 261-313.* A study of the provincial convention

which met in June 1774 to cooperate with other colonies. It sent delegates to the Continental Congress and was the only representative assembly in Maryland. Discusses the events and local feeling about independence during 1775-76. Explains the vote for independence cast by Maryland delegates to the Continental Congress. A new State government was formed and a Declaration of Rights written in September 1776. 142 notes. D. H. Swift

535. McCurry, Allan J. JOSEPH HEWES AND INDEPENDENCE: A SUGGESTION. *North Carolina Hist. R. 1963 40(4): 455-464.* Disputes John Adams' theory that two distinct factions, the independence group and the "cold party" group, existed within the Second Continental Congress. There were three factions: conciliationists, moderates, and militants. Examines Joseph Hewes' attitude toward independence. Hewes was in the moderate camp although his instructions from North Carolina advised a vote for independence. Hewes favored reconciliation until England left no other choice but independence. Illus., 21 notes. D. H. Swift

536. Meistrich, Herbert A. LORD DRUMMOND AND RECONCILIATION. *New Jersey Hist. Soc. Pro. 1963 81(4): 256-277.* Discusses Lord Drummond's attempts to reconcile the differences between England and the colonists in 1774-76. Although Drummond's project failed, "it was important because it revealed the true nature of the dispute and the motivation behind the essentially ineffectual proposals offered by each side." Drummond's failure was due to the following causes: "British unwillingness to forward any proposals which would have been acceptable to the colonies, their obstinacy in refusing to invest any one with the requisite power to negotiate, and their stress on honor and the ability of the Mother Country to crush rebellion helped precipitate the insurrection...[and] build-up of the American desire for independence; Drummond's tactlessness, his failure to meet the real leaders of Congress," and Washington's interception of a Drummond letter. Based primarily on the Drummond Papers. A. Birkos

537. Sanders, Jennings B. *THE CRISIS* OF LONDON AND AMERICAN REVOLUTIONARY PROPAGANDA, 1775-1776. *Social Studies 1967 58(1): 7-12.* Relates the paradox that a pro-American periodical published in England from January 1775 to October 1776 has found no place in American history. The probable editor of *The Crisis* of London was William Moore. The author quotes extensively from *The Crisis,* and one could readily conclude that many aspects of Anglo-American relations might be better understood if knowledge of *The Crisis* of London were widely disseminated in America. Quotations show rather critical comments directed at King George III and his ministers with a general pro-American bias. 47 notes. L. Raife

Declaration of Independence

538. Angermann, Erich. STÄNDISCHE RECHTSTRADITIONEN IN DER AMERIKANISCHEN UNABHÄNGIGKEITSERKLÄRUNG [Traditions of the rights of the estates in the American Declaration of Independence]. *Hist. Zeitschrift [West Germany] 1965 200(1): 61-91.* Examines the origins and ideas of the American Declaration of Independence, especially the sections that indict King George III for wrongdoing. Compares these complaints with similar complaints in the Dutch Declaration of Independence of 1581, the trial of Charles I of England in 1649, and the English Bill of Rights of 1689. In each case a "tyrannis-syndrome" depicts the monarch as violating rights which stem not from natural law but from older concepts of rights associated with feudal estates.

G. H. Davis

539. Detweiler, Philip F. THE CHANGING REPUTATION OF THE DECLARATION OF INDEPENDENCE: THE FIRST FIFTY YEARS. *William and Mary Q. 1962 19(4): 557-574.* Neither the Constitutional Convention nor the *Federalist Papers* nor the ratifying conventions showed much interest in the philosophy of the document, and early State constitutions relied more on the Virginia Declaration of Rights than on the Declaration of Independence. Through the 1780's, orators put more emphasis on the fact of independence than on the Declaration, but between 1790 and 1820 the principles contained within the Declaration assumed more importance in political oratory.

E. Oberholzer, Jr.

540. Healey, George H. LIBRARY NOTES: THE NOYES MANUSCRIPT OF BUTTON GWINNETT. *Cornell Lib. J. 1969 8: 57-62.* Button Gwinnett (1735-77) is considered by many to be the signer of the Declaration of Independence whose autograph is the hardest to obtain. In 1927 one collector paid 51 thousand dollars for his signature. Gives a brief biography of Gwinnett, who was killed in a duel. Cornell University has his autograph as part of its complete set of signers of the Declaration of Independence in the Marguerite and Nicholas H. Noyes Collection of Americana. Illus.

M. M. Williamson

541. Howell, Wilbur Samuel. THE DECLARATION OF INDEPENDENCE AND EIGHTEENTH-CENTURY LOGIC. *William and Mary Q. 1961 18(4): 463-484.* An analysis of the logic and rhetoric of the Declaration of Independence. Although the document did not conform to principles of classical rhetoric, which emphasized analysis, it was in conformity with the newer principles of synthesis which were expounded by William Duncan, George Campbell and Joseph Priestley. Thomas Jefferson must have been familiar with Duncan's *Elements of Logic,* which, influenced by John Locke's reliance on mathematical methods, relied heavily on the importance of self-evident axioms.

E. Oberholzer, Jr.

542. Hutson, James H. THE PARTITION TREATY AND THE DECLARA-
TION OF AMERICAN INDEPENDENCE. *J. of Am. Hist. 1972 58(4): 877-896.* It is conjectured that as a result of the intrigues of a defrocked Jesuit and double agent, Pierre Roubaud, a number of influential Americans, both Whigs and Tories, became convinced that England intended to partition America with France and Spain in return for their assistance in crushing the American Revolution. Such a belief fitted in with their views of English and French capabilities, and with what they alleged to be the purpose of French troop movements to the West Indies. Such a fear may have been relatively baseless, but it was real and provided incentive for an immediate declaration of independence. The fear persisted even after independence and was not thus a "congress contrivance." 63 notes.   K. B. West

543. Malone, Dumas. THE MEN WHO SIGNED THE DECLARATION. *New York Times Mag. 1954 4(July): 6, 26, 27.* Describes with pertinent individual examples the group of men who signed the American Declaration of Independence. These men were of diverse backgrounds and talents. Most of them, however, were men of some wealth with experience in public life who were willing to stake their future on American independence.   R. F. Campbell

544. Miller, William B. PRESBYTERIAN SIGNERS OF THE DECLARA-
TION OF INDEPENDENCE. *J. of the Presbyterian Hist. Soc. 1958 36(3): 139-180.* Demonstrates that 12 of the 56 signers of the Declaration were either members of the Presbyterian Church or related to the Presbyterian Church to a significant degree. Brief biographical sketches giving the evidence underlying this claim as well as the record of their political activites are given of Benjamin Rush, James Smith, George Taylor, James Wilson, Abraham Clark, Richard Stockton, John Hart, John Witherspoon, Philip Livingston, William Floyd, Mathew Thornton, and Thomas McKean.   W. D. Metz

545. Schaar, John H. ...AND THE PURSUIT OF HAPPINESS. *Virginia Q. R. 1970 46(1): 1-26.* Examines happiness and concludes that there is little agreement or clarity in its definition. Although Jefferson, in the Declaration of Independence, placed the pursuit of happiness as an end of government, there were at least four major answers in early America as to what that pursuit was: the Puritan view that one should mix prosperity with service to the Lord, "straightforward materialism," friendship, and living a socially virtuous and useful life. The last was the dominant view of the Founders, including Franklin and Jefferson whose philosophical interpretations of happiness are analyzed. The author suggests that today "we have produced a three-sided conception of happiness of our own with little help from history or philosophy." Happiness is bountiful consumption; happiness is having fun; happiness is self-realization. The author points out the limitations of these conceptions and concludes by suggesting that "the pursuit of happiness may be a goal unworthy of a great nation or a great man."   O. H. Zabel

546. Sturm, Douglas. ON LAWFUL REVOLUTION: THE SPIRIT OF 1776 REVISITED. *Bucknell R. 1972 20(1): 117-140.* A philosophical and historical inquiry into the legal justification for revolution from 1776 to 1970 based on

natural law jurisprudence. An examination of natural law reveals that there is no contradiction in the concept of "legal revolution," because whenever a given political and legal form violates its purpose for being, the people have a right under the natural law to effect a radical change in a given legal and political organization. The Declaration of Independence is the embodiment of this universal law, but scientific, philosophical, political, economic, and social developments in the 19th and 20th centuries reduced acceptability of revolution in the United States. Based on secondary sources; 21 notes.   S. Prisco

547. Tourtellot, Arthur Bernon. ...WE MUTUALLY PLEDGE TO EACH OTHER OUR LIVES, OUR FORTUNES AND OUR SACRED HONOR. *Am. Heritage 1962 4(1): 36-41.* Traces the subsequent careers of the 56 signers of the Declaration of Independence in terms of their losses under the pledge they made. Undocumented; illus.   C. R. Allen, Jr.

548. Wishy, Bernard. JOHN LOCKE AND THE SPIRIT OF '76. *Pol. Sci. Q. 1958 73(3): 413-425.* Reexamines the relations of the ideas of government suggested in the Declaration of Independence to the political theory of John Locke, staying close to the texts of Locke and the Declaration and analyzing what they actually say. Though it seems clear that Thomas Jefferson did assert a doctrine of popular sovereignty, as did Locke, the signers of the Declaration never settled the theoretical limits of popular power, and the ambiguous relation of majority rule to individual rights still besets liberal political theory. Utilizes Willmoore Kendall's controversial *John Locke and the Doctrine of Majority Rule* (Illinois Studies in the Social Sciences, XXVI, Urbana, Illinois, 1941), in addition to the works of Locke and Jefferson.   Sr. M. McAuley

6

THE WAR FOR INDEPENDENCE: AFTER THE DECLARATION OF INDEPENDENCE

General

549. Coles, Robert R. HISTORICAL HEMPSTEAD HARBOR. *Long Island Forum 1970 33(8): 160-164.* During the American Revolution, South Hempstead and Oyster Bay were strong Loyalist centers, while North Hempstead was a Patriot citadel. After Washington's defeat at the Battle of Long Island, Hempstead Harbor was occupied by the British for the duration of the war and the residents suffered from the heavy requisitions of supplies made by the English. The cost of quartering both British and Hessian troops also proved onerous. In 1790 Washington visited Hempstead Harbor during his tour of Long Island. Steamboat service to New York City was begun in 1827 and, in the 1860's, the Long Island Railroad linked Hempstead to Brooklyn. Undocumented, 2 illus.
G. Kurland

550. Copeland, Peter F. CLOTHING OF THE 4TH PENNSYLVANIA BATTALION, 1776-1777. *Military Collector and Historian 1966 18(3): 69-74.* Describes the uniforms of the 4th Pennsylvania Battalion which served for one year and was originally commanded by Colonel Anthony Wayne. Documented with memoirs of Brigadier General John Lacey, who was a captain under Wayne, and various contemporary records from the National Archives and the Pennsylvania Archives; illus., 24 notes.
C. L. Boyd

551. Copeland, Peter F. and Zlatich, Marko. THE *HERO* GALLEY, VIRGINIA STATE NAVY, 1776-1778. *Military Collector and Historian 1964 16(4): 114-116.* Describes the dress of the officers and crew of the *Hero,* a 90-foot row galley which patrolled Virginia waters from 1776 until she was dismantled and sold in July 1779. Based largely on secondary sources. Illus., 8 notes.
C. L. Boyd

552. Copeland, Peter F. and Holst, Donald W. 16TH (QUEENS) REGIMENT OF LIGHT DRAGOONS, 1776-1778. *Military Collector and Historian 1963 15(4): 116-118.* Describes the dress of the British Mounted Royal Regiment while it was in the newly declared independent United States. Illus., 6 notes.

C. L. Boyd

553. Downey, Fairfax. FROM PLUMES TO BUCKSKIN. *Montana 1963 13(1): 18-24.* Recounts the procedures taken by the Revolutionary Dragoons to shape their hard-bitten cavalrymen, and reviews in detail the many campaigns of these units. Revised from a chapter in Downey's forthcoming book, *Indian Wars of the U.S. Army, 1776-1865,* to be published by Doubleday in 1963.

L. G. Nelson

554. Downey, Fairfax. THE GIRLS BEHIND THE GUNS. *Am. Heritage 1956 8(1): 46-48.* Brief description of the characters and roles of Molly Corbin, who manned a cannon beside her husband as others fell at Ft. Washington in northern Manhattan, 15 November 1776, and of Molly Hays (known as Molly Pitcher, because she brought water to soldiers in the field), who replaced her fallen husband at his cannon at the Battle of Monmouth, 28 June 1778. The author describes their subsequent careers and treatment by the government. Illus.

C. R. Allen, Jr.

555. Haarmann, Albert W. NOTES ON THE BRUNSWICK TROOPS—IN BRITISH SERVICE DURING THE AMERICAN WAR OF INDEPENDENCE 1776-1783. *J. of the Soc. for Army Hist. Res. [Great Britain] 1970 48(195): 140-143.* By a treaty with Britain in January 1776, Karl I, the Duke of Brunswick (1713-80), agreed to provide 4,300 men for service in North America. The agreement provided for the furnishing of a regiment of dragoons, four infantry regiments, a grenadier battalion, and a light infantry battalion. Gives details of these units, including the chief of the unit, its commander, field commanders, organization, and uniform. Illus., 8 notes.

D. H. Murdoch

556. Haarmann, Albert W. THE ARMY OF BRUNSWICK AND THE CORPS IN NORTH AMERICA, 1776-1777. *Military Collector and Historian 1964 16(3): 76-78.* Outlines the reorganization of the small Brunswick army in British service after representatives of the North German Duchy of Brunswick-Wolfenbüttel and Great Britain signed a treaty on 9 January 1776. The article contains a list of Brunswick units that served in North America in 1776-77, which includes the names of their chiefs, commanders and, where appropriate, field commanders. Secondary sources, some of which are of German origin, are cited. Illus., 7 notes.

C. L. Boyd

557. Haarmann, Albert W. THE 3RD WALDECK REGIMENT IN BRITISH SERVICE, 1776-1783. *J. of the Soc. for Army Hist. Res. [Great Britain] 1970 48(195): 182-185.* Under a treaty signed in April 1776, the Prince of Waldeck agreed to hire a regiment of infantry, with a small artillery train, to Britain for

service in America. The Third Waldeck Regiment was raised specifically for British service. Gives details of its establishment, field officers' uniform, and service in America. Lists MS. and other sources.   D. H. Murdoch

558. Hayes, John T. THE CONNECTICUT LIGHT HORSE, 1776-1783. *Military Collector and Historian 1970 22(4): 109-112.* This militia unit was periodically called to serve in various northern campaigns of the Revolution. Composed of yeoman farmers and businessmen, the Light Horse were said to have performed adequately by the standards of the time.   D. C. Oliver

559. Holst, Donald W. and Zlatich, Marko. DRESS AND EQUIPMENT OF PULASKI'S INDEPENDENT LEGION. *Military Collector and Historian 1964 16(4): 97-103.* A description of Count Pulaski's Continental cavalry which was a prototype of his more significant Independent Legion. Itemized lists of clothing, "Horse Furniture," and weapons for Pulaski's forces are included. The authors have carefully documented with contemporary records and "believe they have exhausted the resources in the Washington, D.C. area." Illus., 24 notes.   C. L. Boyd

560. Jameson, Hugh. SUBSISTENCE FOR MIDDLE STATES MILITIA, 1776-1781. *Military Affairs 1966 30(3): 121-134.* One of the greatest factors in the failure of the militia to develop into an effective field force during the Revolution was the inability of the States to solve the problem of adequately subsisting the militia when in either State or Continental service. After 1777 the middle States attempted to establish systems for feeding the troops but the nature of the campaigns, lack of magazines and commissaries in the combat zones, and want of foresight made the efforts "hasty, unsystematic, and wholly inadequate." Based on printed records and monographs, 124 notes.   K. J. Bauer

561. Londahl-Smidt, Donald M. NOTES CONCERNING THE UNIFORM OF THE DELAWARE BATTALION IN 1776. *Military Collector and Historian 1967 19(1): 9-11.* Intends "to lay the legends to rest" that have arisen concerning the uniform worn by Colonel John Haslet's Delaware battalion in 1776. Evidence suggests that members of the battalion did not wear leather caps in 1776, rather they wore felt hats. Other aspects of the uniform are discussed also. Documented with published sources, manuscripts in the National Archives, and the account book of Colonel John Haslet, 1776; 3 illus., 19 notes.   C. L. Boyd

562. Lynd, Staughton. THE TENANT RISING AT LIVINGSTON MANOR, MAY 1777. *New-York Hist. Soc. Q. 1964 48(2): 163-177.* In the belief that they could expect aid in obtaining ownership of the land from the British, about five hundred tenants on Livingston Manor took up arms in the spring of 1777. Although the uprising was quickly put down, the episode illustrated how Livingston authority had weakened. Also, it indicated that the manor families could no longer politically take tenants for granted but must modify their methods in order to command the tenant vote.   C. L. Grant

563. McBarron, H. Charles and Simpson, James P. COLONEL JOHN HAS-LET'S DELAWARE REGIMENT, 1776 (DELAWARE BLUES). *Military Collector and Historian 1965 17(2): 49-51.* Describes the colorful uniforms of the Delaware regiment which Hessian officers praised for its courage, appearance, and fine arms. Cites Delaware archival material, illus., 15 notes.

C. L. Boyd

564. Morrissey, Charles T., ed. ACTION IN VERMONT DURING THE REV-OLUTIONARY WAR: DAN KENT'S NARRATIVE. *Vermont Hist. 1971 39(2): 107-112.* An affidavit for a pension, before the Clerk of Fair Haven Probate Court, dated 10 August 1832 (in the National Archives), narrates the service, 1776-79, of Dan Kent (1758-1835), with notes added from another version provided by Anna Vaughn of Arlington, Vermont. Kent, the 18-year-old son of a Dorset tavernkeeper, served a total of six to nine months. He scouted out of Pittsford in June-July 1776, retreated from Ticonderoga with Warner, and was among those who defeated Breymann at Bennington in July-August 1777. He went to the rescue of the Shelburne blockhouse in the winter of 1778 and defended Castleton late in 1779. He became Benson's Congregational minister, 1791-1835.

T. D. S. Bassett

565. Mulligan, Luciel M. HERCULES MULLIGAN, SECRET AGENT. *Daughters of the Am. Revolution Mag. 1971 105(3): 232-235, 320.* Account of the career of Mulligan, American espionage agent during the American Revolution. A well-to-do New York City businessman and an early patron of Alexander Hamilton, Mulligan developed a secret courier system to shuttle information gained from British officers who patronized his tailoring shop in British-occupied New York City to the headquarters of General Washington. Mulligan may have been instrumental in foiling a plot to murder Washington. Suspicions that he was a collaborator were ended when Washington breakfasted with him after the British withdrawal from New York City. A plaque is being erected in his honor in New York City. Includes a short account of the activities of the British spy Ann Bates. Illus.

D. A. Sloan

566. Ray, Frederick E., Jr. and Elting, John R. THE BRUNSWICK INFAN-TRY REGIMENT VON RHETZ. *Military Collector and Historian 1965 17(2): 49-51.* Describes the movements and dress of the Regiment von Rhetz as part of the contingent which the British Government secured from the Duke of Brunswick. The regiment's movements in North America are described for the period 1776-78. Illus., 3 notes.

C. L. Boyd

567. Ritchie, Carson I., ed. A NEW YORK DIARY OF THE REVOLUTION-ARY WAR. *New-York Hist. Soc. Q. 1966 50(3): 221-280, 50(4): 401-446.* Contains the first part of a diary written during the period when Brigadier General James Pattison of the British Royal Artillery served as commandant of New York. In a lengthy introduction, the editor discusses Pattison's career and describes the military actions surrounding the writing of the diary. The author-

ship is unknown although it was probably either General Pattison or a member of his staff. The material in the diary sheds much light on the military activities of the British during the months covered by the entries.   C. L. Grant

568. Sanders, Jennings B. AFTER YORKTOWN, WHAT? *Social Studies 1965 56(1): 9-17.* Asserts that much confusion is involved in the two-year period of American history following the surrender of Lord Cornwallis to American and French forces at Yorktown, 19 October 1781. Primary historical sources relative to this period are lacking, and this would suggest a dire need for historical research. Concludes with a short summary of the history, particularly military, of the United States during this period. 50 notes.   L. Raife

569. Schmidt, H. D. THE HESSIAN MERCENARIES: THE CAREER OF A POLITICAL CLICHE. *History [Great Britain] 1958 43(149): 207-212.* Traces the reaction to the use of Hessian mercenaries by Great Britain in the American Revolutionary War, and its propaganda exploitation from 1776 to the present, chiefly in Germany but also in France, Britain and the United States. The cliché has excited, and has been deliberately used to excite, passions in both domestic and international politics.   W. M. Simon

570. Starr, Raymond. LETTERS FROM JOHN LEWIS GERVAIS TO HENRY LAURENS, 1777-1778. *South Carolina Hist. Mag. 1965 66(1): 15-37.* A series of letters from Gervais, a German immigrant who rose to partnership with Henry Laurens, member of the Continental Congress, which explore the business and social world of Charleston in this difficult period. Names of prominent men introduced. Chiefly secondary sources, Laurens Papers, newspapers.
                                                                        V. O. Bardsley

571. Stutesman, John H., Jr. NEW JERSEY'S "FOREIGN LEGION." *New Jersey Hist. 1967 85(1): 66-71.* "In the fall of 1776, foreign adventurers were landing on the shores of America...most were men-at-arms, out of work in Europe, who came seeking, above all, employment." Among them was a veteran of Frederick the Great's wars, Baron Nicholas Dietrich von Ottendorff. He was quickly commissioned a captain, and General Washington authorized him to enlist German-speaking men from the immigrants who had paid their passage to America by indenturing themselves. Ottendorff arranged for part of the servant's pay to go to the master of each German worker who was willing to bear arms, and the United States promised 13 acres of land to each such soldier when peace should be declared. The autobiography of one such soldier, Johann Carl Buettner, tells of his enlistment and of some of the hardships endured in the army. The work begun by Ottendorff had good results despite the fact that he himself in 1780 joined the forces of the traitor Benedict Arnold. Undocumented.
                                                                        E. P. Stickney

572. Waterbury, Jean Parker. THE WANDERINGS OF COLLEGIATE SCHOOL. *Halve Maen 1966 40(4): 11-13.* When the British occupied New York City in September 1776, the Dutch Reformed Church was forced to close its

Collegiate School. The British left New York in December 1783, and the school then resumed operations at the old location. In response to enrollment changes, curriculum modernizations, and other developments, the school was moved to 11 different locations during the following century but settled permanently in 1892. At this final location, the school developed a reputation for excellence and attracted the support of many New Yorkers. B. T. Quinten

573. Wildemuth, Larry. HESSIANS AND THE CITIZENS OF READING. *Hist. R. of Berks County 1970 35(2): 46-49, 66-75.* During seven years of the American Revolution, Reading, Pennsylvania, served as one of the places to keep Hessian prisoners of war. Examines the relationship between the prisoners and the townspeople. Since the Hessians had been sold by German princes to Great Britain, the mercenaries did not like to fight and preferred to be taken prisoner. To get good treatment they lived peacefully and caused little trouble. On the other hand, Reading's population disliked paying the bill to care for Hessians and feared having such a large number (more than one thousand) in their neighborhood. Fear and misunderstanding dominated the relationship of the two groups. Based on primary sources; 42 notes. H. B. Powell

574. Zlatich, Marko. UNIFORMING THE FIRST REGIMENT OF CONTINENTAL LIGHT DRAGOONS 1776-1779. *Military Collector and Historian 1968 20(2): 35-39.* Originally raised by the Commonwealth of Virginia, this regiment entered Continental service in January 1777. The author has attempted to determine the exact components of the unit's uniform and equipment. Diligent archival research has provided a fairly complete picture of the costume and some idea of the failings of the Continental supply system. Photo, 23 notes. D. C. Oliver

575. Zlatich, Marko and Copeland, Peter F. THE VIRGINIA STATE NAVY 1776-1780. *Military Collector and Historian 1968 20(2): 50-52.* Details are given of the dress of the sailors in Virginia's own Revolutionary War naval forces. The authors' diligent searching of archival materials makes it plain that Virginia attempted to provide some standardization of uniforms for her sailors without much success. Drawing. D. C. Oliver

Military Campaigns to Saratoga

576. Barrows, June. SETH WARNER AND THE BATTLE OF BENNINGTON: SOLVING A HISTORICAL PUZZLE. *Vermont Hist. 1971 39(2): 101-106.* Edward Everett (1794-1865) asked Hiland Hall (1795-1885) in 1883 how Warner's troops at Manchester could have been sent for on 13 August 1777, how Warner could accompany Stark to reinforce Gregg on 15 August, and yet how Warner's troops could enter the battle late on 16 August and repulse Breymann,

as the documents seem to show. Hall replied that from talking to survivors he found that Warner was in Bennington the 13th and accompanied Stark; and that Warner's troops were largely out of camp when ordered to Bennington, started through the rain the 14th, and spent most of the 16th six miles from the battle-field, drying arms and equipment, and arriving in time to repulse Breymann.

T. D. S. Bassett

577. Bemis, Samuel Flagg. SECRET INTELLIGENCE, 1777: TWO DOCU-MENTS. *Huntington Lib. Q. 1961 24(3): 233-249.* The two letters, one to Admi-ral Lord Howe from Lord North, and the other a summary of intelligence by William Eden, show the British government as exceedingly well informed on the efforts of the Americans to obtain assistance from Europe. These documents shortly predate knowledge in England of Burgoyne's surrender.

H. D. Jordan

578. Billias, George A. MARBLEHEADERS SAVE THE DAY AT KIP'S BAY. *New England Social Studies Bull. 1957/58 15(1): 21-23.* Describes the critical role played by the Fourteenth Regiment of the Continental Army, com-manded by Colonel John Glover and composed largely of men from Marblehead, Massachusetts, in preventing the capture of the American army still in New York City, by stopping the rout of the American troops facing the British who had made a landing midway between New York City and Harlem (15 September 1776).

W. D. Metz

579. Cohen, Sheldon S. THE DEATH OF COLONEL THOMAS KNOWL-TON. *Connecticut Hist. Soc. Bull. 1965 30(2): 50-57.* A detailed description of the Battle of Harlem Heights, emphasizing the role of the Rangers led by Lieuten-ant Colonel Thomas Knowlton. A native of Connecticut, Knowlton had left home to join the military during the French and Indian War, playing a minor role in the capture of Fort Ticonderoga. After a short stint at farming, he joined the American forces soon after Lexington and Concord and displayed notable bravery in the Battle of Breed's (Bunker) Hill. In the Battle of Harlem Heights he led 230 Rangers in a vain attempt to stop a British invasion and received a fatal wound. Illus. map.

L. R. Murphy

580. Elosua, J. THE END OF A DREAM: THE BATTLE OF SARATOGA. *Daughters of the Am. Revolution Mag. 1971 105(1): 21-26.* Discusses the tactics employed by both sides, emphasizing the use of Loyalist and Indian forces (with stress upon Indian atrocities), and the successful delaying tactics employed by the Americans. Concentrates on the personalities of British and American officers. Criticizes Horatio Gates and praises Philip John Schuyler. The death of Simon Fraser and the heroic, if disobedient, actions of Benedict Arnold were the two turning points of the battle. Concludes that Saratoga was important because this defeat of the British forces ended the threat of a "southward" advance and led to the creation of the French-American Alliance of 1778. Based largely on sec-ondary sources; 2 illus., 10 notes.

D. A. Sloan

581. Falkner, Leonard. A SPY FOR WASHINGTON. *Am. Heritage 1957 8(5): 58-64.* An account of the role played by John Honyman, a "Loyalist," in supplying information to Washington before the Battle of Trenton, Christmas night, 1776. Undocumented; illus.   C. R. Allen, Jr.

582. Falkner, Leonard. CAPTOR OF THE BAREFOOT GENERAL. *Am. Heritage 1960 11(5): 28-31, 98-100.* Describes the successful scheme, executed by Lieutenant Colonel William Barton, a hatter of colonial Rhode Island, to capture Major General Richard Prescott, commander in chief of the British at Newport, Rhode Island, in 1777, during the American Revolution. Prescott was kidnapped from his bedroom. Later, as a result of land speculation, Barton got into debt and was imprisoned until, in 1824, Lafayette paid his debts, which Barton continued to maintain were unjust. Illus.   C. R. Allen, Jr.

583. Farnham, Charles W. CREW LIST OF THE PRIVATEER *INDEPENDENCE,* 1776. *Rhode Island Hist. 1967 26(4): 125-128.* Summarizes the articles of agreement made between the owners, officers, and men of the *Independence* in September 1776 prior to a cruise of the armed sloop "for the purpose of capturing British ships." Also included is a crew list. Based on original papers in the Court of Common Pleas suits on file at the Providence, Rhode Island, County Court House.   P. J. Coleman

584. Hargreaves, Reginald. BURGOYNE AND AMERICA'S DESTINY. *Am. Heritage 1956 7(4): 4-7, 83-85.* A reexamination of the events leading to the Battle of Saratoga (17 October 1777), which proved to be the turning point of the war more by virtue of the fact that "it was a defeat of the British, rather than the victory of the Americans, at Saratoga, which turned the French sympathy for the colonist's cause from a secretive gesture into an active policy." Undocumented; illus.   C. R. Allen, Jr.

585. Hargreaves, Reginald. THE MAN WHO DIDN'T SHOOT WASHINGTON. *Am. Heritage 1955 7(1): 62-65.* A sketch of British army officer, Patrick Ferguson, who developed a lighter, breech-loading rifle which was effective at three hundred yards and capable of firing four rounds a minute. On 7 September 1776, near Brandywine, Pennsylvania, Ferguson and some of his troops had an opportunity to shoot George Washington, who was making a reconnaissance. Still influenced by the old "Chivalric code," Ferguson refused "a shot at a setting bird,"—though he had no idea of the American general's identity.   A. W. Thompson

586. Huxley, Elspeth. HOW THE DEVIL GOT INTO BENEDICT ARNOLD: A FOLKTALE FROM THE CHAMPLAIN VALLEY. *Vermont Hist. 1970 38(3): 207-213.* While stopping at Ticonderoga during a spring vacation from Cornell in 1928, Huxley drove past Crown Point, Vermont, and had tea near Arnold's Bay in Panton, Vermont. She finally persuaded a caricature of an old Vermonter to tell the legend of how a Loyalist fur trader led Benedict Arnold's men around an Indian ambush to Crown Point after they were defeated at

Valcour Island. Arnold killed a chipmunk belonging to a Dutch witch, and nothing went right with him afterward. Reprinted from Huxley's *Love Among the Daughters* (New York: William Morrow and Co., 1968).

T. D. S. Bassett

587. Jones, G. AN EARLY AMPHIBIOUS OPERATION: DANBURY 1777. *J. of the Soc. for Army Hist. Res. [Great Britain] 1968 46(187): 129-131.* A note on the expedition to destroy supplies at Danbury, Connecticut, in 1777, showing that amphibious operations could be successful up to 20 miles inland. 5 notes.

D. H. Murdoch

588. Lawrence, Alexander A., ed. JOURNAL OF MAJOR RAYMOND DEMERE. *Georgia Hist. Q. 1968 52(3): 337-347.* A travel account and diary of military activities. In 1777 Major Raymond Demere, an officer in the Continental Army, was sent with dispatches from General McIntosh in Georgia to General Washington in New Jersey. Demere's account describes the dangers of travel, the dissensions among Americans, and the details of skirmishing between American and British troops in northern New Jersey in 1777. Undocumented.

R. A. Mohl

589. Lobdell, Jared C., ed. THE REVOLUTIONARY WAR JOURNAL OF SERGEANT THOMAS MC CARTY: AUGUST 23, 1776-FEBRUARY 16, 1777. *New Jersey Hist. Soc. Pro. 1964 82(1): 29-46.* The journal of Sergeant McCarty, 8th Virginia Regiment, covers the periods 23 August to 25 September 1776 and 23 November 1776 to 16 February 1777. Place names are identified in footnotes. McCarty reports atrocities by the British in an engagement near New Brunswick on 1 February. The editor gives other sources supporting the report of this behavior. Otherwise the diary consists largely of details of march, food and drink, and sickness in camp. Printed from the Draper MS. at the State Historical Society of Wisconsin. Illus.

E. P. Stickney

590. Lutnick, Solomon. THE AMERICAN VICTORY AT SARATOGA: A VIEW FROM THE BRITISH PRESS. *New York Hist. 1963 44(2): 103-127.* Detailed description from *The Morning Post, The Packet, St. James' Chronicle, The Gazetter, The Evening Post, Gentleman's Magazine, The Morning Chronicle, Adams' Weekly Courant,* and others.

A. B. Rollins

591. Luzader, John F. THE ARNOLD-GATES CONTROVERSY. *West Virginia Hist. 1966 27(2): 75-84.* Details the reasons for the controversy which developed between General Horatio Gates and Benedict Arnold during and after the American victory at Saratoga. The first serious conflict between the two arose when Gates did not give Arnold specific credit in his report on the fighting at Freeman's Farm. Relations between the two worsened when Gates removed Morgan's Corps of Riflemen from Arnold's division. Arnold took this as a personal affront and Gates considered Arnold's manner and language insubordinate. There is no evidence that Gates accused Arnold of any crime. Richard Varick and Henry Livingston, Arnold partisans, kept Philip Schuyler informed

of Arnold's position. They hoped Gates would be discredited and Schuyler vindicated. They applauded Arnold's threat to leave the department, but he remained long enough to seriously wound a leg in the closing day of the campaign. Based on printed primary sources. D. N. Brown

592. McCusker, John J., Jr. THE AMERICAN INVASION OF NASSAU IN THE BAHAMAS. *Am. Neptune 1965 25(3): 189-217.* Emphasizes that the American attack on Nassau forced heavy commitments by the British Admiralty to the American theater thus relaxing controls over French units at Toulon and elsewhere and allowing their escape to sea in 1778. The amphibious assault on Nassau in March 1776 was the key to this problem. Commodore Esek Hopkins, commanding eight vessels and about a thousand men, assigned to clear the coasts of British naval forces, instead directed his force against the Bahamas. Though warned of the raid the islanders offered only a token defense, all of which is carefully detailed. The raid roused fears of like attacks on other West Indian islands. Based on government MSS. in England and the United States. Illus.
J. G. Lydon

593. Melville, Phillips. ELEVEN GUNS FOR THE GRAND UNION. *Am. Heritage 1958 9(6): 58-64.* Records an incident in the American Revolution when Johannes de Graaff, the Governor of the Dutch island Saint Eustatius, saluted the Continental Brigantine *Andrew Doria,* in 1776, at a time when the revolutionary United States needed friends. Undocumented; illus.
C. R. Allen, Jr.

594. Melville, Phillips. *LEXINGTON*—BRIGANTINE-OF-WAR, 1776-1777. *U.S. Naval Inst. Pro. 1960 86(4): 51-59.* Tells how the merchantman *Wild Duck* was converted to the Continental warship *Lexington* in 1776. The operations of this warship against England under Captains John Barry, William Hallock, and Henry Johnson are discussed and evaluated. Benjamin Franklin's interest in embroiling England and France in a war by basing American ships in French ports is discussed. Undocumented. A. Birkos

595. Melville, Phillips. SALUTE AT 'STATIA. *U.S. Naval Inst. Pro. 1961 87(6): 70-75.* Describes the first salute given the "Stars-and-Stripes" by a foreign power, the Dutch, at St. Eustatius, Dutch West Indies, 16 November 1776.
P. L. Saltsman

596. Moomaw, W. H. THE DENOUEMENT OF GENERAL HOWE'S CAMPAIGN OF 1777. *English Hist. R. [Great Britain] 1964 79(312): 498-512.* The responsibility for the British strategic defeat at Saratoga in October 1777 has been the subject of controversy by both contemporaries and historians. Burgoyne, advancing southward from Canada toward Albany, clearly realized General Howe's main effort was directed at Philadelphia, but by degrees came to expect support from Howe. Responsibility for Burgoyne's surrender could be assigned to Howe, if it could be proved the latter could have completed the Philadelphia campaign sooner. Howe's decision to abandon landing his forces in Delaware Bay

and to transfer them to Chesapeake Bay had been traditionally attributed to the intelligence, supplied by Captain Sir Andrew Snape Hammond, that Washington's army had crossed the Delaware and was prepared for the British landing. Though long known that this intelligence was incorrect, study of the Hammond Papers reveals that Captain Hammond strenuously opposed the change of objective and that the responsibility for it and the subsequent delays were General Howe's. Based on the Hammond Papers, Tracy W. MacGregor Library, University of Virginia.   D. H. Murdoch

597. Murphy, Orville T. "LA GUERRE ET L'AMOUR": A FOOTNOTE TO THE STORY OF WASHINGTON'S DEFEAT AT LONG ISLAND. *Am. Q. 1966 18(3): 543-547.* Reveals the *cherchez la femme* historical explanation of George Washington's defeat at the Battle of Long Island. The most explicit source, probably a projection of a vivid and sympathetic Gallic imagination, described Washington as the victim of a belle named Gibbon [no given name available] whose British sympathies led her to betray the gallant general. The two sources cited are "Variétés," in *Gazette des Deux Ponts,* 3 March 1777, and Hilliard d'Auberteuil's *Essais Historiques et politiques sur la Revolution de l'Amerique Septentrionale,* II, Part I, 4-24; 2 notes.   R. S. Pickett

598. Nelson, Paul David. THE GATES-ARNOLD QUARREL, SEPTEMBER 1777. *New-York Hist. Soc. Q. 1971 55(3): 235-252.* Unfortunately, the campaign which culminated in the surrender of General John Burgoyne's army to American forces at Saratoga was marred by a continuing quarrel between Horatio Gates and Benedict Arnold, both major generals. Arnold was convinced that he was not receiving adequate recognition and promotion, while Gates believed that Arnold's supporters were actively working against Gates and in behalf of his predecessor, Philip Schuyler. The result was a bitter exchange, largely by letter, between Gates and Arnold, and the resignation of the latter. Before leaving camp, however, Arnold took part with great distinction in the Battle of Bemis Heights during which he received a severe leg wound. Eventually, of course, all of these factors would enter into Arnold's decision to abandon the American cause. Although Gates was not without fault, Arnold must be accorded the greater blame in beginning and continuing the quarrel. Based on primary and secondary sources; 3 illus., 25 notes.   C. L. Grant

599. Pike, Robert E. NOTE ON GENERAL STARK. *Vermont Hist. 1965 33(2): 349-350.* Discusses the trophies General John Stark sent from the Battle of Bennington to the legislatures of Massachusetts, New Hampshire, and Vermont, whose troops participated. The author points out that Massachusetts resolved to present Stark with a suit of clothes.   T. D. S. Bassett

600. Reed, John F. RED TAPE AT VALLEY FORGE. *Manuscripts 1968 20(2): 20-27.* The Paymaster Department of the Continental Army had many difficulties during the Revolutionary War. Problems were often compounded by the hazards and uncertainties of war. The methods and correspondence utilized by Thomas Wooster to collect the back pay of his deceased father General David Wooster are examined.   P. D. Thomas

601. Smith, Milford K., Jr. VICTORY IN DEFEAT. *Vermont Hist. 1965 33(4): 463-468.* Second prize in an essay contest, on the Battle of Hubbardton (7 July 1777).   T. D. S. Bassett

602. Squires, James Duane. OLD NUMBER FOUR: YESTERDAY AND TO-DAY. *New England Social Studies Bull. 1959 16(2): 11-14.* Describes the colonial and Revolutionary history of Fort Number Four on the Connecticut River in Charlestown, New Hampshire. The author also describes the construction in 1759-60 of the military road between the fort and Crown Point. In the Revolution the fort and the road played important parts in the preparations for the Battle of Bennington.   W. D. Metz

603. Tucker, Louis L. "TO MY INEXPRESSIBLE ASTONISHMENT": ADMIRAL SIR GEORGE COLLIER'S OBSERVATIONS ON THE BATTLE OF LONG ISLAND. *New York Hist. Q. 1964 48(4): 293-305.* Concerns the failure of Sir William Howe, supreme commander of British forces during the Battle of Long Island, to pursue the American forces before they could retreat to Manhattan in August 1776. Abstracts from the journal of Admiral Sir George Collier, a naval commander on Howe's staff, are reproduced. Collier's reaction to the unhindered escape of the American forces was one of "baffled amazement."
                                                    C. L. Grant

604. Vivian, Frances. A DEFENCE OF SIR WILLIAM HOWE WITH A NEW INTERPRETATION OF HIS ACTION IN NEW JERSEY JUNE 1777. *J. of the Soc. for Army Hist. Res. [Great Britain] 1966 44(178): 69-83.* Howe served brilliantly under James Wolfe and, although he is better remembered for his valor in being the first to scale the Plains of Abraham than for his skill in training the newly formed light infantry, it is the latter which had the more important effect on the development of the Regular Army. It was his influence which led to the permanent establishment of a light infantry company to every battalion. Documented from the letters of Howe and George Sackville Germain, Public Record Office, London; 50 notes.   K. James

605. Weller, Jac. GUNS OF DESTINY: FIELD ARTILLERY IN THE TRENTON-PRINCETON CAMPAIGN 25 DECEMBER 1776 TO 3 JANUARY 1777. *Military Affairs 1956 20(1): 1-15.* Describes the field artillery of the Continental Army and its use in the Trenton-Princeton campaign.   K. J. Bauer

606. Willcox, William B. TOO MANY COOKS: BRITISH PLANNING BEFORE SARATOGA. *J. of British Studies 1962 2(1): 56-90.* Calls the campaign of 1777 the worst of the long series of British blunders during the War for American Independence, and places responsibility upon Burgoyne and Howe, the field commanders, and Lord George Germain, secretary of state for the American colonies. The commanders concentrated upon their respective objectives of Albany and Philadelphia, oblivious to the advantages of coordination. Germain failed to supervise the planning and to heed the warnings of Sir Henry Clinton, Howe's second in command, who alone appeared to anticipate disaster, and who,

at the end, displayed generalship superior to that of the other two. Based primarily upon the Germain and Clinton Papers in the Clements Library at Michigan.

N. W. Moen

607. Williams, John. MOUNT INDEPENDENCE IN TIME OF WAR, 1776-1783. *Vermont Hist. 1967 35(2): 89-108.* In July 1776 Fort Ticonderoga which had been designed against attack from the south and west was in ruins. Mount Independence, a 200-foot bluff on the opposite shore, was developed to block British invasion. Mount Independence accomplished its purpose by preventing the British from attacking or laying siege to it in 1776. And in 1777 it provided the Americans with time to assemble and train the troops which brought about the decisive defeat of General Burgoyne at Saratoga. Later the fort was evacuated, to be reoccupied only for bivouac and assembly of raiders against the British. George Washington paid a visit in 1783. Based on officers' published journals and secondary accounts.

T. D. S. Bassett

From Saratoga to Yorktown

608. Alexander, John K. "AMERICAN PRIVATEERSMEN IN THE MILL PRISON DURING 1777-1782": AN EVALUATION. *Essex Inst. Hist. Collections 1966 102(4): 318-340.* A critique of Howard Lewis Applegate's article "American Privateersmen in the Mill Prison During 1777-1782" *(Essex Institute Historical Collections* 1961 97(4): 303-320). Applegate failed to compare conditions in the Mill prison with other British prisons, and failed to refer to official British sources. He treated all prisoner accounts as if they were of equal value, although they varied in length, contemporaneity, and, most significantly, were frequently plagiarized from other accounts. The author discusses three sets of plagiarism in the Mill prison sources. Applegate also misread the Mill sources, citing contradictory evidence, referring to prisoner accounts which disprove his assertions, and employing events that did not occur at Mill as proof of conditions there. It is concluded that the Applegate article is unsatisfactory and cannot be cited by historians without reservation. 128 notes.

J. M. Bumsted

609. Aussaresses, Paul. L'ARTILLERIE FRANÇAISE AU SIEGE DE YORKTOWN (1781) [French artillery at the siege of Yorktown (1781)]. *R. Historique de l'Armée [France] 1970 26(2): 34-42.* Describes the role of Col. François Marie d'Aboville (1730-1817), artillery commander in Rochambeau's French Expeditionary Corps at the siege of Yorktown, Virginia, in 1781. Outlines the progress of that operation on a day-to-day basis, claiming that it was Franco-American artillery superiority which ultimately forced Cornwallis to surrender. Based on American secondary sources at the library of the U.S. Infantry School at Fort Benning, Georgia; 12 illus., 4 maps.

A. Blumberg

610. Bartenstein, Fred, Jr. N. J. BRIGADE ENCAMPMENT IN THE WIN-
TER OF 1779-1780. *New Jersey Hist. 1968 (3): 135-157.* Discusses a historical
research project undertaken in 1966 to ascertain the exact location of the New
Jersey brigade which fought with George Washington during the winter of 1779-
80. Through intensive research the author pinpointed the exact location of the
campsite in the hills and valleys south of Morristown, New Jersey. 5 maps.

T. H. Brown

611. Bass, Robert D. THE LAST CAMPAIGN OF MAJOR PATRICK FER-
GUSON. *Pro. of the South Carolina Hist. Assoc. 1968: 16-28.* Using the unpublished correspondence of Lord Cornwallis and Lyman C. Draper's *Kings
Mountain and Its Heroes* (Cincinnati, 1881) as his main sources, the author
discusses the last campaign of Major Patrick Ferguson in 1780, which culminated
in the Battle of Kings Mountain and his death. Due to mistakes on the part of
the British, the American forces were able to surround and virtually annihilate
Major Ferguson and his command.

J. W. Thacker, Jr.

612. Bell, Whitfield J., Jr. THE COURT MARTIAL OF DR. WILLIAM SHIP-
PEN, JR., 1780. *J. of the Hist. of Medicine and Allied Sci. 1964 19(3): 218-238.*
A study of the disorganized and inefficient medical service of the Continental
Army during the Revolutionary War, culminating in the court martial of the
third director-general, William Shippen, Jr. The author devotes considerable
space to the conflict between Shippen and his predecessor, John Morgan, who
also served as prosecutor during the trial. Although Shippen was acquitted, the
three major participants in the affair—Morgan, Shippen, and Benjamin Rush—
did not come out with untarnished honor. The hardest hit victim of the episode
was the entire medical department of the army, because of the adverse effect upon
the rank and file. 48 notes.

G. N. Grob

613. Bill, Alfred Hoyt. DRILL MASTER AT VALLEY FORGE. *Am. Heritage
1955 6(4): 36-39, 100.* Description of how Baron von Steuben used a tough winter
at Valley Forge to create a well-organized, trained and disciplined army out of
a collection of untrained volunteers.

A. W. Thompson

614. Bogert, Frederick W. MARAUDERS IN THE MINNISINK. *New Jersey
Hist. Soc. Pro. 1964 82(4): 271-282.* An area from the Delaware Water Gap to
a point just west of Kingston, New York, is called the Minnisink, which includes
parts of New Jersey, Pennsylvania, and New York. During the Revolution this
was the scene of devastating raids by British and Indians. 40 notes.

E. P. Stickney

615. Bonnel, Ulane Zeeck. THE DOBREE PAPERS AT NANTES. *Q. J. of the
Lib. of Congress 1971 28(4): 253-259.* The archival sources at Nantes are impor-
tant for the study of the French effort in the American Revolution, because
Nantes occupied a key position in the complex supply network to channel Fran-

ce's logistic support to the "Insurgents" in America. The personal papers of the Dobrée Collection are being microfilmed for the Library of Congress. Illus., 3 notes.   E. P. Stickney

616. Bradford, S. Sydney. HUNGER MENACES THE REVOLUTION, DE-CEMBER, 1779-JANUARY, 1780. *Maryland Hist. Mag. 1966 61(1): 1-23.* Describes the severe winter which caused a food shortage for the Continental Army encamped near Morristown, New Jersey. Only the enforced cooperation of the people of New Jersey in providing grain and cattle prevented the dissolution of the army. The letters and actions by Congress and the various States are mentioned in detail. Maryland was the only State which requisitioned specific items and vigorously collected them for the soldiers, even though the cash available for payment was in short supply. 89 notes.   D. H. Swift

617. Bradley, A. Day. NEW YORK FRIENDS AND THE LOYALTY OATH OF 1778. *Quaker Hist. 1968 57(2): 112-114.* For refusing to take the oath of allegiance to the State of New York required by an act of 1778, two Quakers were sent to Long Island, according to Quaker records. John Green of Chappaqua, New York, spent six years (1778-84) in Flushing. Joseph Mabbett spent one, being returned to Dutchess County from Westbury in 1783.
                                                                          T. D. S. Bassett

618. Brown, Richard C. HOW WASHINGTON DEALT WITH THE CRISIS OF 1780. *Hist. Teacher 1971 5(1): 44-54.* By 1780 the patriot position in the American Revolution was very weak. The British approached Benedict Arnold to surrender West Point, so they could control the Hudson River and separate New England from New York. Major John André met with Arnold and on his return to the British lines was intercepted by three American patriots. In a circuitous fashion Washington then learned of Arnold's treason, which he had not suspected. Washington, in his reaction to the plot, showed that he had a firm grasp of the principles of mass psychology. He handled the case in such a way as to check the spread of the conspiracy and in the process he provided a villain (Arnold), a victim (André), and three heroes (André's captors). Washington by his adroit moves won the support of the yeomanry for the American cause in the Revolution. Illus., biblio.   P. W. Kennedy

619. Butterfield, L. H. HISTORY AT ITS HEADWATERS. *New York Hist. 1970 51(2): 127-146.* An address delivered at the dedication of the New York State Historical Association's library at Cooperstown, New York. The author discusses the obligation of the research library to preserve, seek out, and make available the raw materials of history. As a case in point, he cites the more than 40 journals compiled by members of the ill-fated Sullivan Expedition (1779) which attempted to capture Fort Niagara from the British. All but forgotten, the journals were not made available to the historical community until the 1870's and 1880's when amateur historians and local historical societies resurrected them and had them published. This, he declares, is the primary purpose of the research library. Undocumented, 5 illus.   G. Kurland

620. Campbell, Randolph B. THE CASE OF THE *THREE FRIENDS:* AN INCIDENT IN MARITIME REGULATION DURING THE REVOLU-TIONARY WAR. *Virginia Mag. of Hist. and Biog. 1966 74(2): 190-209.* The *Three Friends,* a British trading schooner, was seized 19 February 1782 by two American privateers in North Carolina waters and taken to Virginia. Although flying a flag of truce, the schooner's real intention was to land a cargo of contraband at Edenton, North Carolina. Governor Thomas Burke of North Carolina protested the seizure as a violation of the flag of truce and an insult to the state. Before Governor Benjamin Harrison of Virginia could intervene, the prize and her cargo had been sold by the Virginia Court of Admiralty. Although he did not do so, Burke also threatened to seize the two privateers and carry off the schooner after she had reported to North Carolina authorities. The case pointed up the general problem of control over privateers during the Revolution and the difficulties in preventing smuggling under the cover of flags of truce. Documented.

K. J. Bauer

621. Cantor, Milton. TRIALS AND LOVES OF A NEW ENGLAND POET. *New England Galaxy 1965 6(4): 12-20.* Influences on Joel Barlow, the literary figure, are found in Pope's vindictive satire, *The Dunciad,* and in Timothy Dwight, then a tutor at Northampton, for whom Barlow worked one summer. In 1779 Barlow decided to go into the ministry, and was assigned as chaplain to the Massachusetts Fourth Brigade. Shortly after he rode into camp came the treason of Benedict Arnold and the capture of Major André. Barlow's "flaming political sermon" was said to have brought him great honor and led to a dinner invitation with General Washington. His courtship of Ruth Baldwin and their elopement in 1781, though begun in secret, flowered into an ideal marriage. Illus.

E. P. Stickney

622. Castries, Armand Charles. DANS L'ARMEE DE LAFAYETTE, SOUVE-NIRS INEDITS DU COMTE DE CHARLUS [In Lafayette's army, unpublished memoirs of the Count of Charlus]. *R. de Paris [France] 1957 64(7): 94-110.* A hitherto unpublished journal of the Count of Charlus (later and better known as the Duke of Castries), relating his experiences in the Franco-American forces from 7 April to 27 September 1780.

J. A. Clarke

623. Clark, William B. THAT MISCHIEVIOUS *HOLKER:* THE STORY OF A PRIVATEER. *Pennsylvania Mag. of Hist. and Biog. 1955 79(1): 27-63.* An account of the activities of the brig *Holker,* a Pennsylvania privateer, 1779-83. Based on log books, admiralty records, and newspapers.

D. Houston

624. Coker, C. F. W. JOURNAL OF JOHN GRAHAM, SOUTH CAROLINA MILITIA, 1779. *Military Collector and Historian 1967 19(2): 35-47.* John Graham served in the army of General Benjamin Lincoln which was dispatched to reconquer British-held Georgia in February 1779. A diary which Graham kept between February and July presents a good picture of the special character of the southern campaigns of the War of Independence. The Battle of Stono Ferry at the Stono River is described. Illus., map, 23 notes.

D. C. Oliver

625. Copeland, Peter F. and Zlatich, Marko. CAPTAIN DE LA PORTE'S FRENCH COMPANY, VIRGINIA STATE FORCES, 1777-1778. *Military Collector and Historian 1966 18(1): 17-19.* Describes the elaborate dress of the troops which the Virginia Council of State authorized Decrome de la Porte to raise in 1777. Documented with published original sources, illus., 3 notes.
C. L. Boyd

626. Copeland, Peter F. and Zlatich, Marko. COLONEL CHARLES DABNEY'S VIRGINIA STATE LEGION, 1782-1783. *Military Collector and Historian 1966 18(1): 18-19.* Describes the dress of the last force of State regulars raised by Virginia during the American Revolution. Documented with archival material from the Virginia State Library, illus., 5 notes.   C. L. Boyd

627. Copeland, Peter F. and Zlatich, Marko. [MILITARY DRESS OF VIRGINIA TROOPS]. *Military Collector and Historian 1965 17(3): 82-83, 85-86.*
JOSEPH CROCKETT'S WESTERN BATTALION, VIRGINIA STATE TROOPS, 1780-1783, pp. 82-83. Description of the dress and weapons of the state troops which were distinct from the Virginia Continental Line. The Thomas Jefferson and George Rogers Clark Papers are cited. Illus., 7 notes.
2ND VIRGINIA REGIMENT OF THE CONTINENTAL LINE, 1779-1781, pp. 85-86. Description of the dress of this regiment which was commanded by Colonel Christian Febiger, a former Danish officer. Based on original source material from the National Archives, Library of Congress, Pennsylvania Historical Society, and the Virginia State Library. Illus., 9 notes.   C. L. Boyd

628. Copeland, Peter F. and Haarmann, Albert W. THE PROVISIONAL CHASSEUR COMPANIES OF HESSE-CASSEL DURING THE REVOLUTIONARY WAR. *Military Collector and Historian 1966 18(1): 11-13.* Points out that there were four German Chasseur companies raised in Philadelphia, Newport, and New York between 1777 and 1780 which were not the traditional Jägers. The clothing, equipment, and tactical employment of the companies of "hand-picked volunteers" who acted as light infantry for specific campaigns are described. Documented with published diaries, letters, and journals; illus., 6 notes.   C. L. Boyd

629. Dabney, Virginius. JACK JOUETT'S RIDE. *Am. Heritage 1961 13(1): 56-59.* Retells the story of Captain John (Jack) Jouett's 40-mile ride from Cuckoo Tavern in Louisa County to Monticello and Charlottesville to save Governor Thomas Jefferson and the Virginia legislature from capture at the hands of the British Colonel Banastre Tarleton, 3-4 June 1781. The author concludes that this ride was more significant than Revere's, but the lack of a Longfellow has kept the feat obscure.   C. R. Allen, Jr.

630. Dearden, Paul F. THE SIEGE OF NEWPORT: INAUSPICIOUS DAWN OF ALLIANCE. *Rhode Island Hist. 1970 29(1/2): 17-35.* Examines the Franco-American efforts to drive the British from Newport during the American Revolution, particularly the campaign in the summer of 1778. Concludes that mutual

recriminations hampered the effort, as did the unwillingness of French and American land and naval commanders to coordinate their strategy and to work together. Based on published letters, diaries, and records, and on secondary accounts.   P. J. Coleman

631. Echeverria, Durand and Murphy, Orville T. THE AMERICAN REVOLU-TIONARY ARMY: A FRENCH ESTIMATE IN 1777. *Military Affairs 1963 27(1): 1-7, (4): 153-162.* Reprints, with an introductory note, a translation of *Voïage au Continent américan par un françois en 1777. Et Réflexions philosophiques sur ces nouveaux Républicains,* believed to be by the French artillery officer Louis de Récoicourt de Ganot. Part I describes the uniforms, tactics, and character of the American soldier. Part II describes the personnel, especially the militia and the French officers who joined the army, and the discipline.

K. J. Bauer

632. Fisher, Darlene Emmert. SOCIAL LIFE IN PHILADELPHIA DURING THE BRITISH OCCUPATION. *Pennsylvania Hist. 1970 37(3): 237-260.* Discusses the cultural and social life of Philadelphia (1777-78) when the city was occupied by General Howe's forces. Most active Whigs had left the city before the arrival of the British. While the Loyalists accorded the occupation forces a warm welcome, the Quakers adhered to their policy of neutrality. The brief occupation period saw the theater flourish and a number of elaborate balls. Dislocations included the necessity of quartering officers in private homes and some plundering of private property by British soldiers. Discusses food and fuel supplies, care of the poor, British treatment of prisoners, sanitation regulations, and educational activities. Based on letters, journals, and newspapers; 120 notes.

D. C. Swift

633. Fleuriot de Langle, Y. CONTRIBUTION DE LA MARINE FRANÇAISE A LA VICTOIRE DE YORKTOWN [The French navy's contribution to the victory at Yorktown]. *R. Maritime [France] 1970 (273): 177-183.* Victory for the forces of General George Washington was nowhere in sight until the French squadron under Admiral François Joseph Paul de Grasse made up the naval deficiency of the United States by sailing to Chesapeake Bay where the French squadron repulsed a British squadron, thus isolating Lord Cornwallis and forcing him to surrender to Washington and the Comte de Rochambeau. Undocumented; photo, chart.   J. S. Gassner

634. Furlong, Patrick J. A SERMON FOR THE MUTINOUS TROOPS OF THE CONNECTICUT LINE, 1782. *New England Q. 1970 43(4): 621-631.* Abraham Baldwin (1754-1807), later to win fame as a political leader in Georgia, was in 1782 a chaplain in the Connecticut Line of the Continental Army. In that year there was a threat of mutiny among Connecticut troops. It came to nothing and was little noted by contemporaries. However, it provided an occasion for Baldwin to deliver a nonreligious sermon to the troops, expounding on their long and loyal service, the dangers to the revolutionary cause, and the need to endure a while longer, and appealing to their loyalty to their officers, especially George Washington. Baldwin believed that, although the troops had suffered deprivation,

the impetus to mutiny must have been British intrigue. There is no way of measuring the impact of the sermon. Reproduces the text of the sermon. 10 notes.

K. B. West

635. Furlong, Patrick J. AN EXECUTION SERMON FOR MAJOR JOHN ANDRE. *New York Hist. 1970 51(1): 63-69.* British Major John André was executed without benefit of clergy on 2 October 1780 at Tappan, New Jersey. Abraham Baldwin, a Connecticut chaplain, wrote an execution sermon for André, which for some unknown reason was never delivered. Included is a reproduction of the text of the execution sermon, which reveals a strong sympathy for André. Based on primary and secondary sources; 4 illus., 6 notes.

G. Kurland

636. Gerlach, Don R. AFTER SARATOGA: THE GENERAL, HIS LADY, AND "GENTLEMAN JOHNNY" BURGOYNE. *New York Hist. 1971 52(1): 5-30.* Commander of the Northern Department, Philip Schuyler (1733-1804) was blamed for the evacuation of Fort Ticonderoga (5-6 July 1777) by General Arthur Saint Clair (1737-1818), and was stripped of his command by Congress. Not until October 1778 did Congress clear Schuyler's name and restore his reputation. After the battle of Saratoga (1777), Schuyler used his personal credit to supply Continental troops, gathered intelligence information, and advised the expeditions against the Indians which avenged the Wyoming and Cherry Valley massacres. The British attempted to kidnap him in 1781. Although unjustly blamed for the loss of Fort Ticonderoga, Schuyler continued to work for the success of the Patriot cause. Based on primary and secondary sources; 7 illus., 64 notes.

G. Kurland

637. Greaves, Percy L., Jr. FROM PRICE CONTROL TO VALLEY FORGE: 1777-78. *Freeman 1972 22(2): 81-84.* Price controls are not a viable means of bolstering an economy. They constitute a form of economic slavery. They almost cost the United States its independence when reverted to in 1777-78 as compensation for lavish issues of fiat money. Reprinted from *Christian Economics* (20 May 1952).

D. A. Yanchisin

638. Griffiths, David M. AN AMERICAN CONTRIBUTION TO THE ARMED NEUTRALITY OF 1780. *Russian R. 1971 30(2): 164-172.* Shows how the capture of eight ships by an American privateer off Norway was the initial motivating factor behind the armament of the Russian fleet in 1779. It was then just a step from protection of neutral coasts to protection of neutral shipping. Based on primary sources; 24 notes.

R. B. Valliant

639. Haarmann, Albert W. THE ANSPACH-BAYREUTH TROOPS IN NORTH AMERICA, 1777-1783. *Military Collector and Historian 1967 19(2): 48-49.* Describes the organization and uniforms of the German troops furnished by the Margrave of Brandenburg-Anspach-Bayreuth for service with the British in the War of Independence. These troops served in New York, Pennsylvania, Rhode Island and Virginia. 18 notes.

D. C. Oliver

640. Haarmann, Albert W. and Holst, Donald W. THE HESSE-HANAU FREE CORPS OF LIGHT INFANTRY, 1781-1783. *Military Collector and Historian 1963 15(2): 40-42.* Describes an agreement of 15 January 1781 between British Major General William Faucitt and the ministers of Count William of Hesse-Hanau "whereby a corps of light infantry would be raised for British service in America." From August 1781 until July 1783, when it returned to Germany, the Free Corps had an uneventful tour of duty in the vicinity of New York. Some original source material is used. Illus., 13 notes.   C. L. Boyd

641. Hale, Richard W., Jr. NEW LIGHT ON THE NAVAL SIDE OF YORK-TOWN. *Pro. of the Massachusetts Hist. Soc. 1953-57 71: 124-133.* Author's conception of what might have happened if a signal had not been bungled on 5 September 1781, among the British naval forces before Yorktown. Undocu-mented.   N. Callahan

642. Hammes, Doris D. THE ROAD TO GLORY AND GREAT POSSES-SIONS. *Virginia Cavalcade 1969 19(2): 12-19.* An account of the difficulties encountered by Baron Friedrich Wilhelm von Steuben (1730-94), a Prussian officer in the service of the Continental Army, in obtaining the cooperation of the Virginia government and citizens against the British in the years 1780-81. The author depicts this situation as Prussian authoritarianism clashing with the demo-cratic ideas of Virginia under the governorship of Thomas Jefferson (1743-1826). However, the stern discipline of von Steuben proved of value to the unseasoned American troops. Von Steuben's unfulfilled hopes for glory and land as rewards from the American government are also related. Undocumented, illus.
                                                        N. L. Peterson

643. Heisley, John W., ed. and trans. EXTRACTS FROM THE DIARY OF THE MORAVIAN PASTORS OF THE HEBRON CHURCH, LEBANON, 1755-1815. *Pennsylvania Hist. 1967 34(1): 44-63.* Many entries for the years 1755 to 1758 center on repeated Indian attacks and the burials of murdered settlers. On one occasion, four bodies were sent to Philadelphia for the governor to view them. The entries for the Revolutionary War include an account of the quartering of Hessian troops in the village from August 1777 to March 1778. The pastor, a patriot, reported a rumor that when French troops arrived in Philadelphia, "all...are to swear allegiance to the king of France and, those who do not, will be...stabbed to death." News of the Battle of Yorktown was greeted with bell ringing and the shooting of guns throughout the day. It appears that people attended religious services in the nearest church, and there is evidence of Luther-ans and Mennonites taking communion in this Moravian church. A typed copy of this diary is in the Moravian Church Archives at Bethlehem. 84 notes.
                                                            D. C. Swift

644. Holst, Donald W. and Zlatich, Marko. A RETURN OF SOME CONTI-NENTAL REGIMENTAL COLORS OF 1778. *Military Collector and His-torian 1967 19(4): 109-115.* In 1778 Major Jonathan Gastelowe composed a list of 13 sets of colors newly issued to the Continental Army. The authors have reconstructed the design of one of these flags with the aid of a fragment now in

the possession of the U.S. National Museum. Seven other designs correspond to the devices used on Continental money. While the authors have been able to authenticate Gastelowe's list and reconstruct the designs, it is not yet known which regiments carried these colors. Some suggestions are made in this regard. 6 illus., photo, 5 notes.   D. C. Oliver

645. Hoyt, Edward A., ed. A REVOLUTIONARY DIARY OF CAPTAIN PAUL BRIGHAM: NOVEMBER 19, 1777-SEPTEMBER 4, 1778. *Vermont Hist. 1966 34(1): 2-30.* Six months' active service near Peekskill, in the Battle of Germantown and in the defense of Fort Mifflin, preceded the opening of this terse record. It reveals the cold and deprivations of the Valley Forge winter, mitigated for Brigham by a furlough to Connecticut (18 January-14 March 1778) and by the privilege of boarding out of camp. He mentions the Battle of Monmouth in five lines; also the weather, discipline, drill, sickness and deaths, desertion and movements. Brigham (1746-1824) resigned because of ill health in April 1781 and took his wife and four children from Coventry, Connecticut to Norwich, Vermont. Here he lived as an esquire, land speculator, and perpetual officeholder (lieutenant governor, 1796-1812, 1815-19). His portrait (on the cover) with his wife's (frontispiece) are from the Frick Art Reference Library. Verbatim transcription of mutilated MS. in the Vermont Historical Society Library, which has two other pieces.   T. D. S. Bassett

646. Hrobak, Philip A. THE SLOVAKS WERE THERE: MAJOR JOHN L. POLERECKÝ FOUGHT FOR AMERICA'S INDEPENDENCE. *Slovakia 1957 7(3/4): 83-87.* John Polerecký, a native of Polerieka, Slovakia, was a member of General Rochambeau's French Hussars, which participated in the War of Independence. The British under General Cornwallis surrendered their arms at Yorktown to Polerecký. Based on the research of Joseph Cincík.   J

647. Kennett, Lee, ed. CHARLESTON IN 1778: A FRENCH INTELLIGENCE REPORT. *South Carolina Hist. Mag. 1965 66(2): 109-111.* Discusses the fortifications around the city and the attitude of the people toward foreign officers. Based on a report in the French archives.   V. O. Bardsley

648. Ketchum, Richard M., ed. NEW WAR LETTERS OF BANASTRE TARLETON. *New-York Hist. Soc. Q. 1967 51(1): 61-81.* Five letters written by a young British officer, Banastre Tarleton, during the campaigns against American forces. The letters, covering military movements of the British during these years, were recently acquired by the New-York Historical Society. The editor has written an introduction to each. 4 illus.   C. L. Grant

649. Kleber, Louis C. JONES RAIDS BRITAIN. *Hist. Today [Great Britain] 1969 19(4): 277-282.* An analysis of John Paul Jones's landing of the *Ranger* at Whitehaven, Cumberland, England, on the night of 22 April 1778. While the raid did comparatively little material damage (between 250 and 1,250 pounds sterling), the shock to official and public sensitivities was enormous. Illus.   L. A. Knafla

650. Klotz, Edwin F. AN AMERICAN PATRIOT IN SPAIN: 1781. *Social Studies 1966 57(3): 124-126.* Recounts the story of the American patriot John Trumbull, the youngest son of the governor of Connecticut, whose voyage from England to La Coruna, Spain in 1781 became eventful when he was allowed passage to America on a British packet boat that was captured by Captain Hill, the master of the *Cicero.* Trumbull had studied portrait painting in England under Benjamin West. He had served on Washington's military staff and had proven himself a brave soldier in combat previous to his trip to England. He later became a portrait painter of great renown. L. Raife

651. Kyte, George W. GENERAL WAYNE MARCHES SOUTH, 1781. *Pennsylvania Hist. 1963 30(3): 301-315.* In 1781 General Anthony Wayne (1745-96) was responsible for reorganizing the Pennsylvania Continental Line which only a few months earlier had been shattered by mutiny. As soon as the troops were ready he was ordered to Virginia to assist the Marquis de Lafayette (1757-1834) against the army of Cornwallis. A summary is given of the campaign between the troops of Lafayette and those of Wayne and Cornwallis. Wayne's forces played an important part in the campaign, particularly in the saving of the stores at Albermarle Old Court House. After the British withdrawal from Georgia and the Carolinas, Wayne's troops returned to Pennsylvania in 1783. Based on primary and secondary sources; illus., 25 notes. M. J. McBaine

652. Kyte, George W. STRATEGIC BLUNDER: LORD CORNWALLIS ABANDONS THE CAROLINAS, 1781. *Historian 1960 22(2): 129-144.* Shows that even had there been no Yorktown, Cornwallis "would have been charged with responsibility for the disasters suffered by the British" as a consequence of his disregard for the security of the forces in the deep South when he marched into Virginia. Ignoring Clinton's instructions to protect Charleston, Cornwallis left the scattered British posts in Georgia and the Carolinas under Lord Rawdon with his efficient, but depleted, crack combat troops to withstand the American offensive led by Nathanael Greene. Based on the Nathanael Green Papers and the Sir Henry Clinton Papers in the Clements Library, University of Michigan, and the Baron von Steuben Papers held by the New-York Historical Society. Sr. M. McAuley

653. Lacy, Harriet S. NATHANIEL PEABODY PAPERS, 1767-1815. *Hist. New Hampshire 1967 22(2): 39-46.* Nathaniel Peabody, a revolutionary politician, doctor and speculator in Grafton County land, is represented in this collection by a 354-page volume of copies of Army Headquarters Supply Committee documents, April-August 1780, and 125 loose items, arranged chronologically (most of them 1780-96). Alphabetical lists of correspondents are included. T. D. S. Bassett

654. Langle, Fleuriot de. LE MARECHAL DE CASTRIES ET LA GUERRE D'INDEPENDANCE AMERICAINE [Marshal de Castries and the American War of Independence]. *Miroir de l'Hist. [France] 1956 7(81): 311-318.* Marshal de Castries (ancestor of Christian de Castries, general at Dien Bien Phu) served as naval minister under Louis XVI after October 1780. In that capacity, he helped

plan de Grasse's naval campaigns in support of the Americans and La Pérouse's expedition into Hudson Bay. Later, with Louis XVI, he laid plans for a world cruise led by La Pérouse and the chevalier de Langle.   R. C. Delk

655. Larrabee, Harold A. A NEAR THING AT YORKTOWN. *Am. Heritage 1961 12(6): 56-64, 69-73.* Describes in some detail the Battle of Chesapeake Bay, which began 5 September 1781 and ended with the French fleet in control of the entrance to the Bay on 13 September. It was the decisive battle of the American Revolution, because it permitted the encirclement of Lord Cornwallis at Yorktown, Virginia. The British fleet was under the command of Admiral Graves and the French, under Admiral de Grasse. Illus; maps.   C. R. Allen, Jr.

656. Leliepvre, Eugene and Baldet, Marcel. SOME FRENCH REGIMENTS AT SAVANNAH, SEPTEMBER 1779. *Military Collector and Historian 1964 16(4): 111-113.* Describes some of the regimental dress distinctions in the varied French forces commanded by Admiral d'Estaing at the siege of Savannah—First Lieutenant, Régiment du Cap; mulatto drummer, Régiment d'Armagnac; Grenadier, Régiment d'Haynault; and Fusilier, Régiment de Champagne. Based largely on secondary French sources. Illus., 2 notes.   C. L. Boyd

657. Lutnick, Solomon M. THE DEFEAT AT YORKTOWN: A VIEW FROM THE BRITISH PRESS. *Virginia Mag. of Hist. and Biog. 1964 72(4): 471-478.* Discusses the British press commentary on the Yorktown campaign and the surrender of Cornwallis.   K. J. Bauer

658. Lutz, Paul V. REBELLION AMONG THE REBELS. *Manuscripts 1967 19(3): 10-16.* On Monday the first of January 1781 occurred the largest and most orderly mutiny of the American Army. The soldiers of the Pennsylvania line, ably led and disciplined by their sergeants, demanded back pay, discharge, food, and clothing in accordance with the promises they claimed had been made to them upon enlistment. Eventually the Congress and the soldiers reached a compromise which included most of the mutineers' demands. General Anthony Wayne was senior officer of the Pennsylvania line at the time and a copy of one of the discharges signed by him is herein reproduced. The mutiny did have the effect of improving the lot of the American soldier generally and their morale was better by the time the troops faced the British at Yorktown. Illus.   C. J. Allard

659. Luvass, Jay. BARON VON STEUBEN: WASHINGTON'S DRILLMASTER. *Am. Hist. Illus. 1967 2(1): 4-12.* Biographical sketch of the man reputed to have transformed the Continental forces from "a rabble into a disciplined army." While admitting that von Steuben misrepresented his qualifications to the Continental Congress, the author stresses his organizational accomplishments. Von Steuben's *Regulations of the Order and Discipline of the Troops of the United States* (1778-79) was accepted as the official training manual for American troops.   F. J. Stachowski

660. MacMaster, Richard K., ed. NEWS OF THE YORKTOWN CAMPAIGN: THE JOURNAL OF DR. ROBERT HONYMAN, APRIL 17-NOVEMBER 25, 1781. *Virginia Mag. of Hist. and Biog. 1971 79(4): 387-426.* Honyman (1747-1824) gathered the highly accurate materials for his journal for 1781 from travelers, his neighbors in Hanover County where he practiced medicine, and General Thomas Nelson. The journal is in the Library of Congress. 102 notes.

C. A. Newton

661. Mahler, Michael D. 190TH ANNIVERSARY—THE BATTLE AT COWPENS. *Military R. 1971 51(1): 56-63.* Describes the military background and troop disposition of the battle at Cowpens, South Carolina, in 1781. The American victory there resulted primarily from General Daniel Morgan's ability to compensate for the weaknesses of his situation. His choice of terrain, his detailed preparation for the battle, his organization for combat, and his conduct of the battle all combined to give the British forces one of their most decisive defeats during the Revolutionary War. Moreover, Morgan's choice of Cowpens as the place to give battle resulted in an accidental psychological advantage—the terrain encouraged British commander Banastre Tarleton to make a frontal assault without stopping to evaluate the open terrain. Also, Tarleton relied in this instance exclusively on the bravery of his troops, was too impatient of delay, and was too confident of success. The resultant impetuous frontal attack not only contributed to Tarleton's defeat, but affected the remaining course of the Revolutionary War in that it deprived the British Army of the major portion of its light troops during the remainder of the campaign in the Carolinas.

G. E. Snow

662. Mansinne, Andrew, Jr. THE WEST POINT CHAIN. *Am. Hist. Illus. 1966 1(3): 23-26.* During the Revolution the Hudson River was recognized by both the British and the Americans as a strategic waterway. There were several attempts to block the river to British passage, but each failed until the building of the West Point chain in 1778. This chain was 500 yards long and made of iron. On 30 April 1778 the chain was finally laid across the Hudson. The British never attempted to challenge the chain and the Hudson River was safe from encroachment. Undocumented, 3 illus., map.

M. J. McBaine

663. McCowen, George S. THE CHARLES TOWN BOARD OF POLICE, 1780-1782: A STUDY IN CIVIL ADMINISTRATION UNDER MILITARY OCCUPATION. *Pro. of the South Carolina Hist. Assoc. 1964: 25-42.* With the conquest of Charleston in May 1780, the British established a Board of Police as an interim government to function until the reestablishment of normal civil government. Headed by an intendant, the government functioned until the British withdrew in December 1782. The author concludes that the intendants were mainly prominent citizens who hoped to secure office later, while preserving a continuity of civil administration.

J. W. Thacker, Jr.

664. McKinney, Francis F. THE INTEGRITY OF NATHANAEL GREENE. *Rhode Island Hist. 1969 28(2): 53-60.* Argues that Greene's reputation for integrity tipped the scales in favor of the restoration of civil rights to Edward Fenwick,

Jr., a South Carolina planter who had accepted a commission in the British Army. Apparently, in the closing phase of the Revolution, Fenwick sought to prevent the confiscation of his property by acting as a spy for Greene. In return, Greene agreed to use his influence to protect Fenwick's property and to have him readmitted to citizenship. Based on documents in the South Carolina Archives Department and on secondary sources.   P. J. Coleman

665. Meyer, P. DEUTSCHE HILFSTRUPPEN IN FREMDEN HEEREN [German auxiliary forces in foreign armies]. *Militärpolitisches Forum [West Germany] 1955 4(4): 26-33 and (5): 31-36.* Part I. An account of the German military manpower contribution to foreign armies from the 16th century to the American Revolution. Part II. Discusses German military engagement at Yorktown and in the Napoleonic Wars.   F. B. M. Hollyday

666. Montross, Lynn. AMERICA'S MOST IMITATED BATTLE. *Am. Heritage 1956 7(3): 35-37, 100-101.* A discussion of the place held by the Battle of Cowpens (January 1781), the victory of the Americans under Brigadier General Daniel Morgan over the superior British forces of Lieutenant Colonel Banastre Tarleton, in military history. The author describes the imaginative use of untrained militiamen to fire volleys, retreat and reattack, after circling to the rear, thus taking advantage of the lack of persistence so characteristic of the militia. He notes the reuse of this strategy by General Nathanael Greene later in the American Revolution and by the militia Brigadier General Jacob Brown at the battle of Sackett's Harbor in 1813. Undocumented; illus.

C. R. Allen, Jr.

667. Morgan, Marshall. ALEXANDRE BERTHIER'S JOURNAL OF THE AMERICAN CAMPAIGN: THE RHODE ISLAND SECTIONS. *Rhode Island Hist. 1965 24(3): 77-88.* A translation of the relevant portions of *Alexandre Berthier Journal de la Campagne d'Amérique 10 Mai 1780-26 Août 1781,* transcribed with a foreword by Gilbert Chinard (Institut Français de Washington, 1951). In letters to a friend in France, Berthier described conditions in Rhode Island at scattered times in 1780 and 1781, commented on the progress of the War for Independence, and paid particular attention to shipping movements, including the activities of naval vessels and privateers. The original journal is in the possession of the Princeton University Library.   P. J. Coleman

668. Morris, Richard B. THE REVOLUTION'S CAINE MUTINY. *Am. Heritage 1960 11(3): 10-13, 88-91.* Recounts the story of the mutiny aboard the *Alliance* against the egotistic Captain Pierre Landais (1779). Undocumented; illus.   C. R. Allen, Jr.

669. Moyne, Ernest J. THE REVEREND WILLIAM HAZLITT: A FRIEND OF LIBERTY IN IRELAND DURING THE AMERICAN REVOLUTION. *William and Mary Q. 1964 21(2): 288-297.* Letters by Hazlitt, printed in Cork newspapers in 1782, describe the poor treatment of American prisoners of war in Ireland.   E. Oberholzer, Jr.

670. Murphy, Orville T. THE BATTLE OF GERMANTOWN AND THE FRANCO-AMERICAN ALLIANCE OF 1778. *Pennsylvania Mag. of Hist. and Biog. 1958 82(1): 55-64.* Shows that misleading reports received in France concerning the Battle of Germantown, fought two weeks before the defeat of Burgoyne, and the condition of Washington's army, played an important role in the making of the Franco-American alliance of 1778.   H. W. Currie

671. Murphy, W. S. THE IRISH BRIGADE OF FRANCE AT THE SIEGE OF SAVANNAH, 1779. *Irish Sword [Ireland] 1955 2(6): 95-102.* Description of the role of the Irish Brigade in the siege. The author considers the tactics employed and the reason for the failure of the expedition. He provides biographical data concerning some of the officers of the Brigade and notes that the enlisted men were mostly of Continental nationalities. Based largely on contemporary accounts of the siege.   H. J. Gordon, Jr.

672. Nilsen, Halkild. FRIGIVELSEN AV TRE AMERIKANSKE PRISESKIP I BERGEN 1779, OG AMERIKANERNES KRAV OM ERSATNING [Release of three American prize ships at Bergen in 1779 and American demands for compensation]. *Historisk Tidsskrift [Denmark] 1(1): 64-106.* During the American Revolution, Andreas Bernstorff, Foreign Minister of Denmark, formulated regulations regarding American privateers and their prizes, as well as shipping of both Danish and American bottoms, with restrictions on sale of munitions and contraband. The group of privateers under John Paul Jones took three prizes into Bergen where the British were soon given possession. The American demands for compensation covered not only the ships and their cargoes but damages for the welfare of the sailors and crews of the prize ships who were held at Bergen. The case dragged on through the 19th century until, in 1844, the last report was made in the House of Representatives. Benjamin Franklin in Paris was involved in an extensive correspondence on the subject, as were his successors, notably Thomas Jefferson. John Paul Jones was never given compensation for his share of the prizes (as he was not for his assistance to the American cause). English summary.
R. E. Lindgren

673. Norris, John M. BENEDICT ARNOLD'S PLAN FOR PRIVATEERING, 1782. *William and Mary Q. 1956 13(1): 94-96.* The letters ask for subsidies for the construction of a frigate and throw light on Arnold's financial distress. Two letters from the Shelburne Papers, with an introduction and notes.
E. Oberholzer, Jr.

674. Perry, James M. DISASTER ON THE DELAWARE. *U.S. Naval Inst. Pro. 1962 88(1): 84-92.* Describes the unsuccessful attempt of the Continental forces to oust the British from Philadelphia by cutting off contact between that city and the British fleet at sea, in the fall of 1777. The Americans controlled the Delaware River below Philadelphia with the forts of Mercer, Mifflin and Billingsport, and had a river fleet of galleys, half-galleys, floating batteries, frigates, brigs, sloops and schooners. They successfully repelled a Hessian assault on Fort Mercer and destroyed the British vessel *Augusta* on 21 October. But service rivalry, mistrust and indecisiveness on the part of the undisciplined Continental officers and men

prevented a sustained and coordinated defensive campaign. The result was a disastrous defeat for the Americans and the consolidation of the British position at Philadelphia on 21 November.　　　　　R. E. Wilson

675. Pugh, Robert C. THE REVOLUTIONARY MILITIA IN THE SOUTH-ERN CAMPAIGN, 1780-1781. *William and Mary Q. 1957 14(2): 154-175.* Seeks to refute the traditional allegations that the militia was incompetent, by analyzing its role in the Carolinas. The British victory at Camden was due to Horatio Gates' poor leadership, not to the incompetence of the militia. At Cowpens, General Daniel Morgan displayed great tactical skill and made full use of the militia as a complement to regular troops, and the rash Sir Banastre Tarleton blundered into a disastrous defeat. The consequence was increased confidence of regulars and militiamen in each other.　　　　　E. Oberholzer, Jr.

676. Rathbun, Frank H. RATHBUN'S RAID ON NASSAU. *U.S. Naval Inst. Pro. 1970 96(11): 40-47.* The author is a collateral descendant of Captain John Peck Rathbun, whose daring raid on Nassau, New Providence Island, in the Bahamas, in January 1778 is unrivaled, for sheer audacity, in U.S. naval history. Captain Rathbun had served in the Navy since its creation in late 1775, and for more than a year had been John Paul Jones' first lieutenant. In April 1777 he was promoted to captain and given command of the sloop *Providence,* in which he had served as a lieutenant during a successful 1776 attack on Nassau by an American fleet. In 1778, Rathbun's plan was to capture Nassau using only the 50 men from his own ship, and then take as prizes any ships in the harbor. His Marine detachment, commanded by Captain John Trevett, was successful in seizing the two forts on the island, and Rathbun managed to capture three prize vessels. As it turned out, the expedition from a financial standpoint was unsuccessful, because there were few prize dollars, after all had been settled, for Rathbun and his crew. 2 illus., 2 maps.　　　　　A. N. Garland

677. Reed, John F. PURSUIT. *Manuscripts 1967 19(4): 26-27.* Relates the pursuit of a twice-sold manuscript of an Oath of Fidelity taken at Valley Forge resulting in the purchase from its owner.　　　　　C. J. Allard

678. Ristow, Walter W. THE MAPS OF THE AMERICAN REVOLUTION: A PRELIMINARY SURVEY. *Q. J. of the Lib. of Congress 1971 28(3): 196-215.* In 1777 Washington complained of the lack of accurate maps, and recommended that Robert Erskine be commissioned Geographer and Surveyor-General of the Continental Army, a recommendation approved by Congress. The author describes in detail a large number of maps of the period, and naval charts for the harbors. These *Atlantic Neptune* charts are preserved in bound volumes, no two identical; the collections of the Geography and Map Division include 19 of these sets in one to three volumes each. Among the collections are the maps of the Comte de Rochambeau, general of the French Army in America. The British Army's cartographic resources were superior. The largest group of British headquarters maps in the United States is in the William L. Clements Library, University of Michigan. Illus., 26 notes.　　　　　E. P. Stickney

679. Rogers, George C. LETTERS OF CHARLES O'HARA TO THE DUKE OF GRAFTON. *South Carolina Hist. Mag. 1964 65(3): 158-180.* Six letters, full of the names and events of the period, present a frank view of the position of the British.   V. O. Bardsley

680. Rutledge, Archibald. THE BATTLE OF KINGS MOUNTAIN. *Am. Hist. Illus. 1966 1(1): 22-30.* Discusses the strategy and consequences of the battle between Tories and Whigs at Kings Mountain. Prior to this confrontation of 7 October 1780, the South and West had not really become involved in the war. However, when the Tory Major Patrick Ferguson marched his 1,100 men through the Carolinas, the "overmountain men" of the backwoods country decided it was time to gather in force for the right of self-government. Major Ferguson decided to wait for the Whigs at Kings Mountain in South Carolina. Although he was a highly trained, expert British officer, there were two major flaws in his strategy: he anticipated that the enemy would attack in solid lines as the British Army did and he had chosen a heavily wooded area which was the natural environment of the Whig soldiers. The battle lasted only one hour and the Tory army was completely overcome as soon as Major Ferguson was killed. Once the battle had ended, the Whig army melted back into the mountain country. This was a most important event in the American Revolution because "it turned the tide of the war in the South, and broke the Tory influence in the Carolinas for all time." 10 illus., 2 maps.   M. J. McBaine

681. Scheer, George F. THE SERGEANT MAJOR'S STRANGE MISSION. *Am. Heritage 1957 8(6): 26-29, 98.* Describes the efforts of Sergeant Major John Champe in October 1780, acting under the orders of George Washington, to pretend to desert in an effort to capture the traitor Benedict Arnold in British-occupied New York. Undocumented; illus.   C. R. Allen, Jr.

682. Sherman, Constance D. CAPTAIN DIEMAR'S REGIMENT OF HUSSARS ON LONG ISLAND. *J. of Long Island Hist. 1965 5(3): 1-16.* Captain Frederick von Diemar, who had formerly served with the 16th British Regiment, found a number of unattached Brunswick soldiers in New York in March 1779 and decided of his own accord to raise a volunteer Hussar force. Between 1779 and 1781, Diemar raised 180 men plus equipment for service with the British Army under General Henry Clinton. Contains a list of the 180 men and their fates when ascertainable.   J. Judd

683. Shipton, Nathaniel N. GENERAL JOSEPH PALMER: SCAPEGOAT FOR THE RHODE ISLAND FIASCO OF OCTOBER 1777. *New England Q. 1966 39(4): 498-512.* Examines the role of General Joseph Palmer in the unsuccessful attempt by an American force under the command of General Joseph Spencer to invade Newport, Rhode Island, in October of 1777. Palmer was appointed one of the two leaders of a force of militia raised for October of 1777 by Massachusetts; these troops were to serve with others under Spencer. The author recounts the frustrating false starts of the expedition and ultimately the unsuccessful attempts to effect the invasion. After a court of inquiry by Massachusetts, Rhode Island, and Connecticut, the participating States, Massachusetts

ordered the court martial trial of Palmer as the man to be blamed for the failure. But the Continental Congress voted to take over the matter and appointed three commissioners to investigate. Consideration of the evidence led to Palmer's being cleared, though historians have since accepted the charges as valid. Using new evidence in the form of the Robert Treat Paine Papers in the Massachusetts Historical Society, as well as printed sources, the author concludes that the blame should not be placed upon Palmer. 62 notes.   W. G. Morgan

684. Sifton, Paul G., ed. LA CAROLINE MERIDIONALE [SOUTH CARO-LINA]: SOME FRENCH SOURCES OF SOUTH CAROLINA REVOLU-TIONARY HISTORY, WITH TWO UNPUBLISHED LETTERS OF BARON DE KALB. *South Carolina Hist. Mag. 1965 66(2): 102-108.* Gives the location "of manuscript sources, in French repositories, of South Carolina history during the period of the American Revolution." De Kalb's letters, written during the arrival of Lafayette's volunteers in Charleston in 1777, describe personnel and fortifications.   A. Birkos

685. Stapleton, Darwin H. GENERAL DANIEL ROBERDEAU AND THE LEAD MINE EXPEDITION, 1778-1779. *Pennsylvania Hist. 1971 38(4): 361-371.* In 1778, the Continental forces were in great need of lead for bullets. General John Armstrong suggested to the Pennsylvania Council that an expedition be sent to Sinking Spring Valley in order to mine lead. This suggestion was acted upon by General Daniel Roberdeau (1727-95), a brigadier in the Pennsylvania Associa-tors. A member of the Continental Congress, Roberdeau was a Philadelphia merchant of Huguenot background. He and unknown partners obtained from the Pennsylvania legislature the right to extract lead from the Sinking Spring deposit, but they did not receive title to the land which was owned by the Penn family. The State promised to purchase the lead and to indemnify Roberdeau for any loss he might incur. Fort Roberdeau was erected in April 1778, and the mine was operated until late summer or early fall 1779. There is some evidence that the force was comprised largely of English deserters who had mining experience. Only half a ton of lead was refined and shipped from Sinking Spring. The abandonment of the operation was due to the small lead output, Indian raids, and the assurance of adequate munition supplies from France as provided by the treaty of alliance in 1778. There is no evidence that Pennsylvania paid Roberdeau for the lead or his losses. Based largely on archival material; 50 notes.
D. C. Swift

686. Sterling, David L., ed. AMERICAN PRISONERS OF WAR IN NEW YORK: A REPORT BY ELIAS BOUDINOT. *William and Mary Q. 1956 13(3): 376-393.* An editorial introduction and the text of Boudinot's objective report to the Board of War, following his inspection of the British prisons in February 1778, with appendices on prisoners charged with specific crimes, clothing fur-nished to prisoners, and the purchase of provisions for prisoners.
E. Oberholzer, Jr.

687. Sturgill, Claude C., ed. ROCHAMBEAU'S MEMOIRE DE LA GUERRE EN AMERIQUE [Rochambeau's memoir of the war in America]. *Virginia Mag.*

of Hist. and Biog. 1970 78(1): 34-64. Reviews already printed variants of Rochambeau's 1781 report. Supplies a translation of the original dispatch of 1781.
44 notes. C. A. Newton

688. Turner, Eunice H. AMERICAN PRISONERS OF WAR IN GREAT
BRITAIN 1777-1783. *Mariner's Mirror [Great Britain] 1959 45(3): 200-206.*
Although American prisoners of war were generally treated with tolerance and
good sense and committed to special prisons set up for their reception, mistakes
made by magistrates, confused by the situation, were not always rectified. The
author gives examples of this state of affairs and a detailed account of the life and
treatment of American prisoners of war. Based on unpublished Admiralty material. J. A. S. Grenville

689. Unsigned. BRITISH, HESSIAN AND PROVINCIAL TROOPS AT
PAULUS HOOK, 18TH-19TH AUGUST, 1779. *J. of the Soc. for Army Hist.
Res. [Great Britain] 1967 45(183): 177-183.* An analysis of the units taking part
in the British defense of Paulus Hook in 1779 corrects several errors in W. H.
Richardson and W. P. Gardner's *Washington and the Enterprise Against Paulus
Hook.* Based on printed sources; 20 notes. K. James

690. Unsigned. NEWS FROM THE UNITED STATES IN THE *GENEVA
HISTORICAL AND POLITICAL JOURNAL,* IN THE YEAR 1779. *Notes
and Queries [Great Britain] 1958 203(2): 75-80.* An examination of the *Journal
Historique et Politique de Genève* as a "test case" of the role of French newspapers in keeping up enthusiasm for the Franco-American alliance. Using as its
sources a correspondent in America, the British press, and news from French and
Spanish ports, the *Journal* carefully selected its news with the aim of "writing
up the alliance with the American revolutionaries and the insistent proclamation
of the undying gratitude and friendship of the Americans toward their new
allies." British victories were played down and British atrocities alleged, while the
revolutionary principles of the Americans were avoided. W. D. McIntyre

691. Unsigned. "THE DRUM BEATS TO ARMS..." TWO LETTERS FROM
YORKTOWN AND A MISSING MAP. *Princeton U. Lib. Chronicle 1970
31(3): 209-213.* The transcription of two letters at Princeton Library by Elias
Dayton (1737-1807), a Colonel of the Second New Jersey Regiment, to his son
Elias B. Dayton, describing the siege and surrender of Cornwallis at Yorktown.
The first letter refers to a map of the locations of the two armies, but it is missing.
D. Brockway

692. Valentine, Harriet G. THE YOUNG MAJOR ANDRE. *Long Island
Forum 1971 34(10): 210-213.* Describes the capture and execution of Major John
André (1751-80). Reproduces his last will and testament, and an anonymous 1857
poem (apparently written by a Long Islander) which commemorates his execution. 4 illus., biblio. G. Kurland

693. Vivian, Frances. THE CAPTURE AND DEATH OF MAJOR ANDRE. *Hist. Today [Great Britain] 1957 7(12): 813-819.* Describes the events leading up to the arrest of Major John André as a British spy by the American Army in September 1780, and his subsequent trial and execution.   E. D. Johnson

694. Voltes Bou, Pedro. BARCELONA Y LA INDEPENDENCIA DE LOS ESTADOS UNIDOS [Barcelona and the American War of Independence]. *Barcelona [Spain] 1956 2(15): 94-98.* Notes on Barcelona's participation in the pirate war against England during the American War of Independence (1777-81). Documents from the Historical Archive of the City of Barcelona.

J. Cabestany Fort (IHE 16953)

695. Warner, Oliver. H.M.S. *VICTORY* 1765-1965. *Hist. Today [Great Britain] 1965 15(5): 306-312.* A description of the ship and mention of a few of the famous battles in which she participated during the American Revolution and the Napoleonic Wars, 1778-1812.   L. A. Knafla

696. Warner, Oliver. THE ACTION OFF FLAMBOROUGH HEAD. *Am. Heritage 1963 14(5): 42-49, 105.* This account forms a chapter of the author's *Great Sea Battles* (Macmillan, 1963) and deals with John Paul Jones' encounter in the *Bonhomme Richard* with HMS *Serapis* off the English coast in 1779. Illus. Undocumented.   C. R. Allen, Jr.

697. Weller, Jac. IRREGULAR BUT EFFECTIVE: PARTISAN WEAPONS TACTICS IN THE AMERICAN REVOLUTION, SOUTHERN THEATRE. *Military Affairs 1957 21(3): 118-131.* Warfare south of the Dan River differed in many respects from that to the north. In particular, the southern partisans applied different weapons tactics. The northern battles generally followed the basic European pattern while the southern ones tended to be fought by Indian fighters or hunters who carried only their personal weapons. They were inseparable from their horses and fought in a land which by European and northern standards was largely wilderness. The southern partisans were the only American troops to make important use of rifles in combat and stressed surprise to a degree unknown in the north. The southerners developed guerilla operations and improvisation to a high degree, but it remained for Daniel Morgan to combine them with regular troops into the unbeatable combination which won the Battle of the Cowpens.   K. J. Bauer

698. Weller, Jac. REVOLUTIONARY WAR ARTILLERY IN THE SOUTH. *Georgia Hist. Q. 1962 46(3): 250-273, (4): 377-387.* A technical analysis of the various types of artillery operative in the American Revolution, followed by a discussion of their use in the five major pitched battles in the South and in Southern actions or sieges where relatively heavy caliber guns were engaged. In the Southern Department conditions were not ideal for its use, but, nevertheless, artillery was important in many actions.   R. Lowitt

699. Weller, Jac. THE IRREGULAR WAR IN THE SOUTH. *Military Affairs* *1960 24(3): 124-136.* At the outbreak of the American Revolution the patriots in the South formed a relatively small percentage of the population. Their ulti- mate victory was accomplished by a combination of military and political war- fare.   K. J. Bauer

700. Wells, Thomas L. AN INQUIRY INTO THE RESIGNATION OF QUARTERMASTER GENERAL NATHANAEL GREENE IN 1780. *Rhode Island Hist. 1965 24(2): 41-48.* Analyzes Greene's motives, the circumstances surrounding the event, and Congressional and other reactions. Based on pub- lished letters and memoirs and secondary accounts.   P. J. Coleman

701. Whitridge, Arnold. THE MARQUIS DE LA ROUËRIE, BRIGADIER GENERAL IN THE CONTINENTAL ARMY. *Mass. Hist. Soc. Pro. 1967 79: 47-63.* Discusses the unusual career of the Marquis de la Rouërie, known as Colonel Armand, who succeeded Pulaski as chief of cavalry in the Continental Army and later became a leader of the counterrevolutionary Breton conspiracy during the French Revolution. Armand impressed Washington with his character and military ability. Based chiefly on manuscript collections and *Writings* of Washington; 24 notes.   J. B. Duff

702. Whitridge, Arnold. TWO ARISTOCRATS IN ROCHAMBEAU'S ARMY. *Virginia Q. R. 1964 40(1): 114-128.* The careers of the Chevalier de Chastellux and Duc de Lauzun in America are reviewed with emphasis on their impressions of America. The contributions and importance of these men are often forgotten or minimized in favor of the better publicized but possibly less signifi- cant Lafayette.   C. R. Allen, Jr.

703. Wiener, Frederick Bernays. THE MILITARY OCCUPATION OF PHIL- ADELPHIA IN 1777-1778. *Pro. of the Am. Phil. Soc. 1967 111(5): 310-313.* Discusses the British occupation of Philadelphia, 1777-78. Emphasis is placed on the military government implemented by the occupation forces. Based on the author's book, *Civilians Under Military Justice: The British Practice Since 1689, Especially in North America* (Chicago: U. of Chicago Press, 1967); note.
                                                                                                      W. G. Morgan

704. Wyllie, John Cook, ed. NEW DOCUMENTARY LIGHT ON TAR- LETON'S RAID: LETTERS OF NEWMAN BROCKENBROUGH AND PE- TER LYONS. *Virginia Mag. of Hist. and Biog. 1966 74(4): 452-461.* Reprints from the Richmond *Virginia Gazette* of 1784, with introduction and notes, two letters written that year relating to the capture of Brockenbrough and Lyons during British Colonel Banastre Tarleton's raid on Charlottesville in June 1781. 19 notes, chiefly genealogical.   K. J. Bauer

705. Yeager, Henry J., trans. THE FRENCH FLEET AT NEWPORT, 1780- 1781. *Rhode Island Hist. 1971 30(3): 87-93.* Annotated translation of the relevant portions of the published memoirs of Thomas Chevalier de Villebresme, *Souve-*

nirs du Chevalier de Villebresme, mousquetaire de la garde du roi, 1772-1816 (Paris: Berger-Levrault et Cie, 1897), who served with the French fleet and expeditionary force which occupied Newport, Rhode Island, in the summer of 1780.   P. J. Coleman

706. Zlatich, Marko. THE 1ST AND 2ND VIRGINIA STATE LEGIONS, 1781-1783. *Military Collector and Historian 1965 17(2): 35-37.* Discusses the efforts to bring these two legions commanded by Brigadier General Alexander Spotswood into the service of the Virginia state government. "Spotswood's Legions simply were ignored out of existence by Virginia, heavily in debt and preoccupied with the settlement of veterans' accounts and the maintenance of a legion which actually served." Archival material from the Virginia State Library is cited. Illus., 5 notes.   C. L. Boyd

707. —. [FRANCE AND THE AMERICAN REVOLUTION]. *R. Historique de l'Armée [France] 1957 13(2): 11-70.*
Cossé-Brissac, de. LA FRANCE ET LA GUERRE DE L'INDEPEND-ANCE [France and the War of Independence], pp. 11-21.
Montross, Lynn. FRANÇOIS-LOUIS DE FLEURY, FORT-MIFFLIN 1777, STONY-POINT 1779, pp. 21-29.
Paul, Pierre. LES ANCETRES ET LE BERCEAU DE LAFAYETTE [The ancestors and cradle of Lafayette], pp. 29-37.
Fabre, Marc-André. LE LIEUTENANT-GENERAL COMTE D'ES-TAING, pp. 37-43.
des Cilleuls, Jean. LE SERVICE DE L'INTENDANCE A L'ARMEE DE ROCHAMBEAU [Rochambeau's army commissariat service], pp. 43-62.
Finke, H. and Todd, Frederick P. L'INFLUENCE FRANÇAISE SUR LES PREMIERS UNIFORMES DES ETATS-UNIS [French influence on the first uniforms of the U.S.], pp. 62-68.
Fabre, Marc-André. UNE MISSION FRANÇAISE AUX ETATS-UNIS POUR LE CENTENAIRE DE YORKTOWN [A French mission to the Yorktown centenary—1881], pp. 68-70.
These seven articles on the American War of Independence pay tribute to French military, naval and economic assistance from 1777 to 1783, emphasizing the monetary sacrifices of the French Government and Rochambeau. Based on documents from the resources of the Archives of the Historical Service of the Army; illus.   H. M. Adams

The Diplomatic Front

708. Bail, Hamilton Vaughan. A LETTER TO LORD GERMAIN ABOUT VERMONT. *Vermont Hist. 1966 34(4): 226-234.* Joshua Locke, veteran of the French and Indian Wars and Massachusetts Loyalist, asked the Secretary of State for the Colonies Lord George Germain to guarantee New Hampshire land titles

and accept independent Vermont as a province, extending its western boundary to the Hudson River as far south as the northern Connecticut line. The author relates this proposal to the contemporary negotiations of some Vermont leaders with General Frederick Haldimand, commander at Quebec.

T. D. S. Bassett

709. Boiteux, L. A. UN MEMOIRE PROPHETIQUE DE TURGOT SUR LA REVOLUTION D'AMERIQUE (1776) [A prophetic memoir of Turgot on the American Revolution (1776)]. *R. d'Hist. Diplomatique [France] 1959 72(3): 231-239.* Reviews the struggle in Louis XVI's cabinet over the wisdom of aiding the American colonists. Vergennes and the military chiefs saw an opportunity to weaken Britain and to protect France's remaining colonial holdings. Turgot insisted that France's financial situation demanded economy and peace. American success would be a bad example for opponents of monarchical authority in France. He also believed that the commercial growth of an independent America would endanger the other colonies of the mercantilistic powers.

J. H. Jensen

710. Boyd, Julian P. SILAS DEANE: DEATH BY A KINDLY TEACHER OF TREASON? *William and Mary Q. 1959 16(2): 165-187, (3): 319-342, and (4): 515-550.* An analysis of the relations of Silas Deane, first emissary from the United States to a foreign state; Edward Bancroft, double-spy who sold his services both to the British cabinet and to the American agents in Paris during the American Revolution; and Thomas Jefferson, minister from the United States to France 1784-89. The author raises questions as to Bancroft's responsiblity for Deane's death and attempts to assess the effect of their treasonable activities on the American move for independence. Examines the death of Deane against the background of his relations with Edward Bancroft. The author considers Bancroft's sale of the stolen Deane papers to Thomas Jefferson. In 1789 Deane was eager to return to the United States, confident that he would find acceptance at home. Rejecting the suicide theory, the author concludes that Bancroft poisoned Deane as an act of charity toward the hapless spy and for the self-preservation of his master.

A and E. Oberholzer, Jr.

711. Brown, Marvin L., Jr. AMERICAN INDEPENDENCE THROUGH PRUSSIAN EYES: A NEUTRAL VIEW OF THE NEGOTIATIONS OF 1782-1783. *Historian 1955/56 18(2): 189-201.* Shows the failure of the Prussians to understand the significance of the American Revolution, which they regarded as a largely unimportant phase of the imperial struggle. When Frederick the Great realized that American independence was inevitable, he still failed to believe that the American Union could endure.

E. C. Johnson

712. Duyverman, J. P. AN HISTORIC FRIENDSHIP. *Halve Maen 1965 40(3): 11-12, 15.* Jean Luzac was editor of the *Gazette de Leyde,* the best known of all Dutch newspapers during the American Revolution. When John Adams went to Europe in 1779 to represent the revolting American colonies, he decided that Luzac could be a valuable friend for the new United States. Luzac had long been publishing news about America, and he readily welcomed a warm friendship with

Adams. Luzac further encouraged this friendship by serving as a tutor for John Quincy Adams, translating memoranda for the elder Adams to the States General and by leading a movement to recognize the independence of the United States.

B. T. Quinten

713. Griffiths, David M. NIKITA PANIN, RUSSIAN DIPLOMACY, AND THE AMERICAN REVOLUTION. *Slavic R. 1969 28(1): 1-24.* Explains changes in the Russian Government's attitude toward the American Revolution by referring both to Panin's replacement and to Catherine the Great's adoption of expansionist plans.

H. K. Rosenthal

714. Gunther, Hans Karl. FREDERICK THE GREAT, THE BAVARIAN WAR OF SUCCESSION AND THE AMERICAN WAR OF INDEPEN- DENCE. *Duquesne R. 1971 16(2): 59-74.* The diplomatic posture of Frederick II (Frederick the Great) toward the United States during the American Revolu- tion, while favorable, was not as positive as it might have been if Prussia had not had to resist Austrian efforts to annex Bavaria. The ensuing War of the Bavarian Succession (1778-79) forced Prussia to concern itself with continental diplomacy which was in a state of flux because of these conflicts. Frederick continued to villify the British, but his maritime and commercial interests, which were a positive force in his attitude toward the United States, were forced to the back- ground because of European developments. Based on diaries, diplomatic dis- patches, and letters; 83 notes.

M. R. Strausbaugh

715. Haffner, Gerald O. CAPTAIN CHARLES ASGILL: AN ANGLO- AMERICAN INCIDENT, 1782. *Hist. Today [Great Britain] 1957 7(5): 329- 334.* An Anglo-American incident in the handling of prisoners of war during the 18th century arose in 1782 out of the partisan warfare of the War of Indepen- dence. A British officer, prisoner of war, was to be hanged for retaliatory purposes by the Americans. England, the United States, France and Holland were soon involved. World opinion spoke out against retaliation. The British officer was liberated eventually, and the newly established United States avoided the shed- ding of innocent blood. Based on private and official letters, journals, diplomatic correspondence, government records, and historical recollections and chronicles.

A

716. Henderson, H. James. CONGRESSIONAL FACTIONALISM AND THE ATTEMPT TO RECALL BENJAMIN FRANKLIN. *William and Mary Q. 1970 27(2): 246-267.* Looks at the behind-the-scenes politics that led to a recall motion in Congress to remove Franklin from his European mission. The main reason for the motion was the belief that Franklin was neglecting his duties rather than the factionalism of the Lee-Deane controversy. The anti-Lee faction was willing to sacrifice Franklin, even though he was amenable to Silas Deane's supporters, as a price to bring Arthur Lee back home. The author discusses debates over the issue in Congress—largely following a New England versus Southern States alignment. Table of votes per man on 11 different questions, 47 notes.

H. M. Ward

717. Henderson, Robert. IRA ALLEN AND HIS DEALINGS WITH THE BRITISH. *Vermont Hist. 1966 34(1): 31-35.* Third prize winner in high school essay contest. The conspiracy with Haldimand bought time and prevented English invasion.   T. D. S. Bassett

718. Kirk, Grayson. THE UNITED STATES IN THE FAMILY OF NATIONS. *Pro. of the Am. Phil. Soc. 1956 100(4): 289-295.* An account of Benjamin Franklin's mission to France, 1777-85, and an analysis of the diplomatic methods by which he won French support for the American cause.   N. Kurland

719. Kittredge, T. B. NATIONAL PEACE OBJECTIVES AND WAR AIMS FROM 1775 TO 1955. *Marine Corps Gazette 1956 40(7): 8-19.* Discusses the meaning and implication of such terms as war and peace, policy and strategy, national peace objectives and war aims, prior to reviewing America's past experience in seeking foreign policy objectives through military action. The author concludes that sound future U.S. policy must include the considered opinion of the military leaders.   G. A. Mugge

720. Lopez, Claude A. BENJAMIN FRANKLIN, LAFAYETTE, AND THE *LAFAYETTE. Pro. of the Am. Phil. Soc. 1964 108(3): 181-223.* A narrative, much of which involves a transport renamed the *Lafayette,* concerning the diplomatic, financial, and transportational difficulties connected with an effort to purchase and ship military supplies from France to America, 1779-81. The article, based on hitherto unexploited manuscript sources, includes much incidental information concerning the life and personal relationships of Franklin, Lafayette, the French merchant Jacques-Donatien Leray de Cahumont, and many others.
                                                                R. G. Comegys

721. Morales, Victor Lezcano. DIPLOMACIA Y POLITICA FINANCIERA DE ESPAÑA DURANTE LA SUBLEVACION DE LAS COLONIAS INGLESAS EN AMERICA: 1775-1783 [Diplomacy and financial policy of Spain during the rebellion of the English colonies in America: 1775-1783]. *Anuario de Estudios Americanos [Spain] 1969 26: 507-564.* Rebellion of the 13 British Colonies upset the British hegemony that Europe had not been able to challenge since the Treaty of Utrecht, but France and Spain quickly seized the opportunity to defeat the mistress of the seas. All Europe was affected, but these two powers felt the impact most keenly. While the nations were establishing varied responses to the developing crisis caused by the American Revolution, the independent merchant-trader supplied the tie between peoples of the maritime powers, and through them a general readjustment of the Atlantic trading area was achieved. The struggle resulted in the exhaustion of the European combatants, of repeated budgetary failures, the increase of national debts, and the consequent issue of a flood of paper money that dragged down all the trading currencies. The 13 Colonies, also bankrupted in the struggle, served as a catalyzer as a result of their direct involvement in the conflict. 5 charts, 2 tables, 107 notes, appendix.
                                                                T. B. Davis

722. Morris, Richard B. JOHN JAY AND NEW ENGLAND CONNECTION. *Massachusetts Hist. Soc. Proc. 1968 80: 16-37.* Analyzes the relations between John Jay and New Englanders throughout his long career. At first, as President of Congress in 1778, Jay aroused the antagonism of John Adams and the New England faction. Later, however, Jay's tough and independent stance as minister to Spain (1779) and as a member of the American Peace Commission (1782) won him the respect of Adams and his section. A strong feeling of goodwill continued for the remainder of Jay's life. Based on several manuscript collections; 72 notes.
J. B. Duff

723. Morris, Richard B. THE JAY PAPERS...MISSION TO SPAIN. *Am. Heritage 1968 19(2): 8-21, 85-96.* Documents John Jay's efforts to secure financial aid and diplomatic recognition for the young republic from Charles III of Spain. Jay and his wife Sarah, accompanied by a party of four, including his secretary, William Carmichael, arrived at Cadiz in February 1780 after a tempestuous voyage. The party journeyed 400 miles to Madrid by mule-drawn carriage where Jay tried to negotiate a loan and secure aid from the Bourbon power. A series of meetings with Spanish officials yielded scanty gains for the Americans. Charles III was not available, the Count of Floridablanca was evasive, and the Count's representative, Don Diego de Gardoqui, had no power. The Spanish court, plagued with intrigues such as the English-inspired Hussey-Cumberland mission, offered no respite for Jay, but he refused to waive any American claims to navigate the Mississippi. Therefore, no real American gains were accomplished. Based on hitherto unpublished collections of Jay's papers in the Columbia University Library; illus.
J. D. Born, Jr.

724. Rabb, Reginald E. THE ROLE OF WILLIAM EDEN IN THE PEACE COMMISSION OF 1778. *Historian 1958 20(2): 153-178.* Relates the activities of William Eden, later Baron Auckland, as key member of the unsuccessful British peace commission which visited the American colonies in 1778-79 in an unsuccessful and belated attempt to get the colonies to accept measures short of independence. Based on a study of the Auckland Papers in the British Museum.
E. C. Johnson

725. Radovskii, M. I. AVTOGRAF VENIAMINA FRANKLINA [An autograph of Benjamin Franklin]. *Istoricheskii Arkhiv [USSR] 1956 (4): 259-260.* A Russian translation and a photocopy of a letter addressed to Richard Rache and written on 2 March 1778 during Franklin's mission in France. The letter is kept in the Saltykov-Shchedrin State Library in Moscow.
G. Lovas

726. Rasch, Aage. FORBUDET AF 4. OKTOBER 1775 MOD EKSPORT AF VÅBEN TIL DE AMERIKANSKE OPRØRE [Prohibition of 4 October 1775 against export of weapons to the American rebels]. *Historisk Tidsscrift [Denmark] 1961 (Series 11) 6(4): 467-482.* The prohibition of shipments of arms and other contraband resulted from English pressures upon the European powers. Shipments prior to the outbreak of the revolt showed that Denmark shared with the Netherlands in shipments, with three and a half times the amount of cargo in 1777 over the previous year. Until the French entered the war, the Dutch

directly or indirectly supplied the largest amounts of munitions from Europe to the Colonies. After 1776 Andreas Peter Bernstorff (1735-97) sought to placate the British and to prevent any disturbance of Anglo-Danish relations or of the Danish trade in the West Indies, where smuggling and illicit trade furnished a profitable business. In 1776 he sent a proclamation to the West Indian Danish islands but application was left to the discretion of the governor, with the natural consequence that he disregarded both Danish and English prohibitions. A mystery arose in 1782 over the sale of several cannon and munitions to a Danish ships' captain and the destination of the cargo, ostensibly the American Colonies.

R. E. Lindgren

727. Sánchez Mantero, Rafael. JOHN JAY EN ESPAÑA [John Jay in Spain]. *Anuario de Estudios Americanos [Spain]* 1967 24: 1389-1431. The mission of John Jay to Spain during the American Revolution usually has been considered a failure. The American envoy did not win recognition for his country, Spain signed no treaty of alliance, and her loans to the rebellious Colonies were piddling. Jay, as a neophyte, was in no position to match the experienced diplomats of Europe, and his lack of financial support frequently left him embarrassed. The Spanish ministers were unduly cautious and jealous and appear to have preferred a stalemate: Britain defeated and weakened, but the Colonies, under some guise, still a part of the British Empire. Yet the mission was not fruitless. Spain did declare war against England, though for no reason related to the American side of the war. Neither Spain nor the United States could comprehend the aims of the other, but the mission served as a vital link between the two countries when both fought and defeated a common foe. Based on primary sources and monographs; 79 notes.

T. B. Davis, Jr.

728. Smith, Paul H. SIR GUY CARLETON, PEACE NEGOTIATIONS, AND THE EVACUATION OF NEW YORK. *Can. Hist. R. 1969 50(3): 245-264.* The first detailed analysis of Carleton's conduct as commander in chief in America reveals his audacious attempt to reinforce New York, though ordered to evacuate it, in order to force Congress into peace negotiations with him. Inability to carry out the scheme led to his abrupt resignation and request to return to England in August 1782, after encountering repeated frustrations during a tenure of a mere 14 weeks in New York. Based on documents from the Public Records Office, the British Headquarters' Papers, the William Smith diary, and the correspondence of George III.

A

729. Van Alstyne, Richard W. THOMAS WALPOLE'S LETTERS TO THE DUKE OF GRAFTON ON AMERICAN AFFAIRS, 1776-1778. *Huntington Lib. Q. 1966 30(1): 17-33.* The merchant banker Thomas Walpole had excellent connections with America and France. A Whig hoping for reunion of the colonies with Great Britain, he was able to communicate with the opposition and, through the Duke of Grafton, with the Ministry. The letters here printed (nine from 1776, two from 1777, one from 1778) show how Walpole, particularly through contact with Dr. Edward Bancroft of Massachusetts, attempted to make use of his knowledge of American relations with France.

H. D. Jordan

730. Whitridge, Arnold. BEAUMARCHAIS AND THE AMERICAN REVO-
LUTION. *Hist. Today [Great Britain] 1967 17(2): 98-105.* A study of the financial and material aid organized by Caron de Beaumarchais for the American
colonists in the War of Independence, 1776-82. Beaumarchais, a French musi-
cian, playwright, financier, and secret agent, created a fictitious organization
called Roderigue Hortalez & Company and during the war shipped supplies to
the value of five million livres to the colonists. The Americans, because of the
insistence of Arthur Lee that the arms and supplies were gifts, refused to pay for
these valuable shipments. Not until 1835 did Congress assent to honor some of
the claims of the heirs of Beaumarchais.   L. A. Knafla

731. Young, Philip. THE NETHERLANDS AND THE UNITED STATES.
Halve Maen 1966 40(4): 7-8, 14. In 1780, at a crucial stage of the American
Revolution, John Adams was sent to the Netherlands by the new U.S. Government. His mission was to secure financial assistance for the American cause in
the continuing struggle with Great Britain. Adams found that the bankers of
Amsterdam were unwilling to risk the making of loans to the United States,
especially since the Dutch then still had an alliance with the British. Adams was
not greatly discouraged. If he could provoke a break between Britain and the
Netherlands, and persuade the Dutch to recognize the United States as an independent nation, he felt sure that he would be able to obtain the needed economic
aid. He therefore conducted a masterful press campaign, and ultimately convinced the Dutch people that the United States was going to win the war with
Britain. In February of 1782, the Council of Friesland voted to recognize the
United States, and the other provinces followed suit in the ensuing months. When
Adams was finally able to negotiate loans in Amsterdam, a permanent bond
developed between the United States and the Netherlands.
                                                                    B. T. Quinten

The Peace of Paris, 1783

732. Klingelhofer, Herbert E. MATTHEW RIDLEY'S DIARY DURING THE
PEACE NEGOITATIONS OF 1782. *William and Mary Q. 1963 20(1): 95-133.*
The text of the diary from 27 August to 13 December 1782, while Ridley, a
Maryland agent, was in Paris. Ridley was in close touch with the leading figures
of the time, was aware of the personal tensions and jockeying for position, and
in one case helped bring Adams and Franklin together. The diary "corroborates
other accounts of the negotiations and, at places, supplements them."
                                                                  E. Oberholzer, Jr.

733. Murphy, Orville T. THE COMTE DE VERGENNES, THE NEW-
FOUNDLAND FISHERIES AND THE PEACE NEGOTIATION OF 1783:
A RECONSIDERATION. *Can. Hist. R. 1965 46(1): 32-46.* Examines Ver-
gennes' policy towards the Newfoundland fisheries during the peace negotiations

of 1783. Vergennes did not attempt to deceive the Americans or deny them fishing rights. In the Treaty of 1778 France had agreed to guarantee American possessions, but Vergennes felt that the American claim to Newfoundland fisheries' rights was unfounded and he was not willing to prolong the war in order to obtain British cession of these rights. Furthermore, his own demand for "exclusive" rights was not an attempt to exclude Americans from the Newfoundland fisheries; it was a sincere attempt to avoid future conflict over the fisheries by establishing for the various powers specific areas where their fishermen would have "exclusive" rights, thereby avoiding the conflicts which had occurred in the past when French and English fishermen had fished in the same areas.   A

734. Smith, Dwight L. JOSIAH HARMAR, DIPLOMATIC COURIER. *Pennsylvania Mag. of Hist. and Biog. 1963 87(4): 420-430.* In 1783 Harmar was chosen to take to the American ministers in France a copy of the Treaty of Paris that Congress had finally secured a quorum to ratify. The author describes Harmar's trip to and stay in Paris. Based on the Harmar Papers and other manuscripts in the Clements Library, University of Michigan. 49 notes.
E. P. Stickney

735. Wolf, Edwin, II. THE AMERICAN PRINTINGS OF THE DEFINITIVE TREATY OF PEACE OF 1783 FREED OF OBFUSCATION. *Papers of the Biblio. Soc. of Am. 1971 65(3): 272-278.* Reviews and rejects assertions that John Dunlap of Annapolis issued the first American printing of the Definitive Treaty between Great Britain and the United States and that the U.S. Arms first appeared on a printed document when Philippe Denis Pierres printed the treaty in Paris in 1783. The first American printing of the Treaty was by William Ross of New York, while the Arms had been printed by Pierres earlier in 1783 on the *Constitutions des Treize Etats-Unis de l'Amérique.* Includes a checklist of American printings of the treaty in 1783 and 1784. Based on Franklin Papers and newspapers; 15 notes, appendix.
C. A. Newton

7

THE REVOLUTION & THE WEST: AN ERA OF DETACHED INVOLVEMENT

Indians & Indian Relations

736. Covington, James W. MIGRATION OF THE SEMINOLES INTO FLORIDA, 1700-1820. *Florida Hist. Q. 1968 46(4): 340-357.* The original Indian tribes of Florida, around 25 thousand Apalachee, Calusa, and Timucuan, were almost extinct when the Lower Creek began settlements on the peninsula. Relatively late arrivals to the Florida peninsula, the Seminole migrated in three distinct phases. In the first period, between 1700 and 1750, they made raids, as English allies, against the Spaniards and their Indian allies. In the second period, 1750-1812, several villages were settled in the northern part of Florida, while small groups explored the remainder of the peninsula. In the third period, 1812-20, pressure from white settlers in Georgia and Alabama pushed the Upper and Lower Creek tribes to move south into Florida. Available evidence indicates that prior to 1800, no Seminole villages were located south of Tampa Bay. As more of the Creek moved into Florida, where they were known as Seminole, they were welcomed by the Spanish. In the period 1812-20, around two thousand Upper and Lower Creek moved, seeking refuge in Spanish Florida following defeats in Alabama and Georgia. A compilation of Indian bands in Florida in 1822 listed only five (out of 35) bands at Tampa Bay or south of it. Within a short time after the signing of the 1823 Treaty of Moultrie Creek, a considerable number of Seminole migrated into central and southern Florida. Partly based on unpublished English records; 69 notes.   R. V. Calvert

737. Covington, James W. TRADE RELATIONS BETWEEN SOUTHWESTERN FLORIDA AND CUBA—1600-1840. *Florida Hist. Q. 1959 38(2): 114-128.* Enumerates the items of trade and describes the nature of commercial relations between the Indians (and later the white men) of Florida and the Spanish colonials of Cuba during the period 1600-1840. Based on U.S. State papers and on autobiographies, travel accounts, secondary works, and newspapers.   G. L. Lycan

738. DeVorsey, Louis, Jr. INDIAN BOUNDARIES IN COLONIAL GEORGIA. *Georgia Hist. Q. 1970 54(1): 63-78.* Describes the changing boundary dividing Indian territory from that settled by whites, and postulates the dual nature of the frontier (a frontier of whites advancing westward and a retreating Indian frontier). Four maps delineate Indian boundaries established by treaty-making process with the tribes, especially with the Creek and Cherokee Indians. Although the Indians lost territory at each stage, most of Georgia was still controlled by the tribes at the outbreak of the American Revolution. 25 notes.
R. A. Mohl

739. Fenton, William N. TOWARD THE GRADUAL CIVILIZATION OF THE INDIAN NATIVES: THE MISSIONARY AND LINGUISTIC WORK OF ASHER WRIGHT (1803-1875) AMONG THE SENECAS OF WESTERN NEW YORK. *Pro. of the Am. Phil. Soc. 1956 100(6): 567-581.* Describes changes in Seneca culture after Sullivan's raid in 1779 in terms of modern disaster-theory. The author discusses the cosmology, demography, and social and political organization of the Seneca, using the notes written in 1859 by Asher Wright, a Dartmouth graduate who learned the Seneca language and developed a written language for teaching. Fundamental in Seneca culture were the principles of unanimity in all tribal decisions, and land as common property. The author describes the disintegrating effect of the violation of these principles by the whites, and then gives an account of the reconstruction promoted by Wright and other Christian missionaries. One of their major efforts was the establishment in 1855 of the Thomas Indian School on the Cattaraugus Reservation. Illus.
N. Kurland

740. Goff, John H. THE PATH TO OAKFUSKEE: UPPER TRADING ROUTE IN GEORGIA TO THE CREEK INDIANS. *Georgia Hist. Q. 1955 39(1): 1-36, (2): 152-171.* A geographical and historical discussion of an important Indian trading route in eastern Georgia during the 18th and early 19th centuries.
C. F. Latour

741. Gold, Robert L. THE EAST FLORIDA INDIANS UNDER SPANISH AND ENGLISH CONTROL: 1763-1765. *Florida Hist. Q. 1965 44(1/2): 105-120.* One hundred and fifty Indians followed the Spaniards out of Florida when it was lost to the British in 1763. The English continued giving presents to the Indians in Florida to keep peace, but conditions were quite uneasy when the American Revolutionary War began. Based on state papers, private papers, secondary works, and periodical material.
G. L. Lycan

742. Gold, Robert L. THE SETTLEMENT OF THE PENSACOLA INDIANS IN NEW SPAIN, 1763-1770. *Hispanic Am. Hist. R. 1965 45(4): 567-576.* The transfer of Florida to Great Britain by the Treaty of Paris of 1763 saw the Spanish population of Florida leave the colony. Among the exiles were Christianized Indians. A group of Indians from Pensacola was resettled in a village called San Carlos, outside of Vera Cruz, New Spain (Mexico). The article traces the history of this Indian group from their departure from Florida through the evolution of a functioning settlement by 1770. 37 notes.
B. B. Solnick

743. Greening, W. E. HISTORIC ODANAK AND THE ABENAKI NATION. *Can. Geographical J. 1966 73(3): 92-97.* Traces the participation of the Abenaki Indians in American history and the growth of the town of Odanak, in Quebec. The Abenaki were first dealt with by French Roman Catholic priests. In the late 17th century they were driven north out of their homeland in Maine. The French settled them in towns along the Saint Francis River, the main colony at Odanak. They raided the English colonies for the French and took many white captives. In 1760 Lord Amherst sent Major Robert Rogers on his famous raid, which almost completely destroyed Odanak. In the Revolutionary War several Abenaki served the American cause. After the War of 1812 they settled down to farming and crafts. Illus.   W. A. Buckman

744. Handlin, Oscar and Mark, Irving, eds. CHIEF DANIEL NIMHAM VS. ROGER MORRIS, BEVERLY ROBINSON, AND PHILIP PHILIPSE—AN INDIAN LAND CASE IN COLONIAL NEW YORK, 1765-1767. *Ethnohistory 1964 11(3): 193-246.* Reprints and edits British Museum Lansdowne MSS., 707, fol. 24 ff., "A geographic, historical Narrative or Summary," which documents the editor's article, "Land Cases in Colonial New York, 1765-1767," in the *New York Law Quarterly Review,* 1942, vol. 19, 165-194. This deals with conflicts which resulted when "poor tenant farmers, settlers from New England, and civilized Wappinger Indians fought for their lands, in the courts and on the fields, against the great patentees who were striving to build up estates in Dutchess and Westchester Counties." The anonymous author was a Connecticut lawyer friendly to the Indian title and claimants. A sketch map shows the Beekman, Philipse, and Cortland Manor lands involved.   H. J. Graham

745. Hoffman, Bernard G. ANCIENT TRIBES REVISITED: A SUMMARY OF INDIAN DISTRIBUTION AND MOVEMENT IN THE NORTHEASTERN UNITED STATES FROM 1534 TO 1779. *Ethnohistory 1967 14(1/2): 1-46.* Outlines basic features of tribal distribution in the Colonial period. Based on contemporary primary sources; maps, tables, 8 notes, biblio.   R. S. Burns

746. Johnston, Charles M. JOSEPH BRANT, THE GRAND RIVER LANDS AND THE NORTHWEST CRISIS. *Ontario Hist. 1963 55(4): 267-282.* Joseph Brant claimed the Indians were a separate nation and were able to sell their Grand River lands without reference to the Crown. He faced the determined opposition of Lieutenant-Governor Simcoe. After Simcoe's withdrawal Brant was able to take advantage of a frontier crisis in 1797, the prospect of Franco-Spanish aggression in the Mississippi region and rumors of an Indian uprising in Ontario to extort from Peter Russell a confirmation of the land sales. The honesty of Brant's own financial dealings was often doubted, as the Six Nations appeared to gain little from the sale of the land. Based on the Powell Papers and various papers relating to the Six Nation Indians in the possession of the New-York Historical Society. 59 notes.   J. M. E. Usher

747. Johnston, Jean. MOLLY BRANT: MOHAWK MATRON. *Ontario Hist. 1964 56(2): 105-124.* In 1759 an upper class Mohawk, Molly Brant, became

housekeeper for Sir William Johnson, beloved British Indian agent living with the Iroquois. Molly managed Johnson's large household establishment well, and she bore Johnson nine children. When Johnson died in 1774, Molly and her brother Joseph inherited his influence with the Six Nations Indians. Molly proved influential in keeping the confederacy largely on the British side during the American Revolutionary War. In 1796 Molly died with doubts that her people, who had lost their ancestral lands in the war, could rest secure in their cultural identity among the European civilizations.   G. Emery

748. Kawashima, Yasu. LEGAL ORIGINS OF THE INDIAN RESERVATION IN COLONIAL MASSACHUSETTS. *Am. J. of Legal Hist. 1969 13(1): 45-56.* The Massachusetts Indian reservations developed in the 17th and 18th centuries into political, economic, and cultural centers. The probable original purpose of the reservations was to provide a means to assimilate the Indians into white society. By 1786, when the State reservation system was replaced by Federal reservation policy, the system "had virtually come to an end...." Based on government documents; 47 notes.   L. A. Knafla

749. Kelsay, Isabel T. JOSEPH BRANT: THE LEGEND AND THE MAN. *New York Hist. 1959 40(4): 368-379.* Discusses the difficulties of research on this prominent Iroquois leader, particularly the problem of separating legend from fact in the Revolutionary period. The author describes some of Brant's personal characteristics and certain facets of American Indian culture illustrated by his career.   A. B. Rollins

750. Knapp, David, Jr. THE CHICKAMAUGAS. *Georgia Hist. Q. 1967 51(2): 194-196.* A résumé of the history of the Chickamauga, a small segment of the Cherokee tribe that seceded from the parent group in 1777 under the leadership of Chief Chincobacina (Dragging Canoe). The Cherokee had previously allied with the British in colonial conflicts but remained neutral during the American Revolution. The Chickamauga, however, retained their British connections and launched a series of attacks on American settlements between 1777 and 1792. The death of Chincobacina in 1792 was followed by the reintegration of the Chickamauga into the Cherokee tribe. Documented; 2 notes.   R. A. Mohl

751. Kurtz, Henry. THE RELIEF OF FORT PITT, AUGUST 1763. *Hist. Today [Great Britain] 1963 13(11): 784-794.* The British defeat of the Pontiac Conspiracy stymied the Indian attempt to oust the British from their western frontier and, perhaps, to wrest all of North America from the white man.   L. A. Knafla

752. Lewin, Howard. A FRONTIER DIPLOMAT: ANDREW MONTOUR. *Pennsylvania Hist. 1966 33(2): 153-186.* Centers on Montour's services as diplomat and interpreter from 1742 to 1768. Excluding some success during Pontiac's Rebellion, Montour's activities as a soldier left something to be desired. Part Indian, he was trusted by Indians and was made a counselor by the Six Nations. As a diplomat, he served Virginia, Pennsylvania, and Indian Superintendent Sir

William Johnson. Montour's relations with George Washington, Conrad Weiser, and George Croghan are described in detail. Montour received large tracts of land for his services, but he lost most of these rewards and was frequently in debt. He was noted for his attachment to whiskey, but he managed to remain sober when his services were most needed. Based on a variety of primary sources. 128 notes.

D. C. Swift

753. Mahon, John K. ANGLO-AMERICAN METHODS OF INDIAN WARFARE, 1676-1794. *Mississippi Valley Hist. R. 1958 45(2): 254-275.* A review of tactics and weapons used by the Indians, and by American colonists, militia and British and American soldiers. The sharp-shooting frontiersmen were not as effective in fighting Indians as American folklore suggests. The soldiers in the ranks, well trained in the use of musket and bayonet, and applying tactics combining fire and movement, were most likely to win in encounters with the Indians. The Indians relied heavily on surprise and they usually succumbed when forced to make a stand. Based on published sources, among them contemporary diaries.

E. H. Boehm

754. Marshall, Peter. SIR WILLIAM JOHNSON AND THE TREATY OF FORT STANWIX, 1768. *J. of Am. Studies [Great Britain] 1967 1(2): 149-179.* Reinterprets the career of Sir William Johnson, New York land-speculator and superintendent of Indian affairs for the northern department. Johnson's effort at the Treaty of Fort Stanwix has been treated too simplistically and negatively by historians. A variety of political and material interests influenced his conduct. Moreover, he concluded a treaty which must be considered a success and "which incorporated those policies and assumptions reflected over the years in his official correspondence: the maintenance of imperial regulation of Indian affairs, the according of special position to the Iroquois, and the satisfaction of speculators' demands for additional land." The relationship between Johnson, royal officials in England, and other English and colonial figures—Thomas Penn, for example —are also discussed. Based on such published primary sources as *Documents Relative to the Colonial History of the State of New York* (Albany, 1853-58) and *The Papers of Sir William Johnson* (Albany, 1921-62).   D. J. Abramoske

755. O'Donnell, J. H. ALEXANDER MC GILLIVRAY: TRAINING FOR LEADERSHIP, 1777-1783. *Georgia Hist. Q. 1965 49(2): 172-186.* Traces the emergence of McGillivray as "Head Warrior" of the Creek Nation following the slaying of Euristisigus in 1782. It is problematical whether McGillivray would have been elevated to that position had it not been for the experience and influence he gained through his service in the British Indian Department during the American Revolution.   R. Lowitt

756. Orians, George H. PONTIAC IN LITERATURE. *Northwest Ohio Q. 1963 35(4): 144-163, 36(1): 31-53.* Part I, 1764-1915. Although he apparently alluded to Pontiac in his journals of 1760, Major Robert Rogers did not specifically identify him before his *Concise Account of North America* in 1765. Rogers also wrote a play about Pontiac in 1766, and Alexander Macomb used him as the central figure in a play written in 1835. *Wacousta,* by the Canadian John Rich-

ardson in 1832, was the first important novel to use Pontiac as a theme. Francis Parkman's *History of the Conspiracy of Pontiac* (1851) provided a classic account of his career. Historical material turned up since Parkman's day has corrected or supplemented his narrative without taking any luster off his penetrating study. Pontiac passed out of literature for several years, but at the turn of the century he returned as a theme in *A Spectre of Power* (1903) by Charles Egbert Craddock (Mary Noailles Murfree), *A Sword on the Old Frontier* (1903) by Randall Parrish, and *The Heroine of the Strait* (1902), by Mary Crowley. Based on secondary sources; illus., 15 notes. Part II, 1916-64. Although historical fiction revived him in 1925 after 20 years of submergence, Pontiac did not reappear as a significant figure until 1937. The author describes the post-1938 fiction in which Pontiac played a role, concentrating on those novels centering around affairs in Detroit and those based on events at Fort Pitt.

W. F. Zornow

757. Sosin, Jack M. THE BRITISH INDIAN DEPARTMENT AND DUNMORE'S WAR. *Virginia Mag. of Hist. and Biog. 1966 74(1): 34-50.* In 1774 many of the western Indian tribes were unhappy over the land cessions of the Treaties of Hard Labor (1770), Lochaber (1770), and Fort Stanwix (1768). Their animosities were chiefly directed against the Virginians who used some retaliatory Indian raids as a pretext to drive the tribes from western lands claimed by the colony. The ensuing Lord Dunmore's War forced the Indians to remain north of the Ohio River. Only intensive diplomacy by the British Indian Department kept other tribes from coming to the aid of the Shawnee and Delaware and attacking portions of the Virginia frontier denuded of protection by the campaign. Based on the Gage Papers in the William L. Clements Library, Ann Arbor, Michigan, and other contemporary sources, published and manuscript.

K. J. Bauer

758. Torok, C. H. THE TYENDINAGA MOHAWKS. *Ontario Hist. 1965 57(2): 69-77.* Studies the Iroquois confederacy during the period of the American Revolutionary War to show that the Iroquois tribes grew by groups splitting off from parent bodies to form fairly autonomous new villages. The example of the Tyendinaga Mohawk is used to support the thesis that the local village autonomy had been in uneasy balance with the centralized league authority ever since the league's creation. As the league grew old, the village autonomy reasserted itself and marginal factions broke away to form new tribes based on the village.

G. Emery

Spanish Colonial Administration

759. Armas Medina, Fernando de. LUISIANA Y FLORIDA EN EL REINADO DE CARLOS III [Louisiana and Florida in the reign of Charles III]. *Estudios Americanos [Spain] 1960 19(100): 67-92.* Historical summary which

studies the gestation and agreements of the Treaty of Paris (1763) with regard to the Gulf of Mexico, and the way it benefitted the English. Reference is made to western Louisiana, which was ceded to Spain during the era of its sovereignty, and was an administrative part of the Captaincy-General of Cuba; the geographical extension of Spanish Louisiana; the peace of Versailles (1783), by which Spain gained exclusive rights over the lands around the Gulf, the different situations in Louisiana before its cession to England and at the time of its restitution to Spain; and the independent government of Cuba, under one command, of Louisiana and both Floridas. Based on published and unpublished documents from the Archivo General de Indias in Seville; biblio.   B. T. (IHE 40649)

760. Arnade, Charles W. FLORIDA HISTORY IN SPANISH ARCHIVES. REPRODUCTIONS AT THE UNIVERSITY OF FLORIDA. *Florida Hist. Q. 1955 34(1): 36-50.* A survey of the vast amount of source materials for Florida history, especially the official Spanish documents, 1518 to 1820, and of writings based on them. Deplores the fact that historians have made slight use of these documents but predicts the papers will now come into more use because they have been made readily available in the P. K. Yonge Library of Florida History, University of Florida.   G. L. Lycan

761. Coker, William S. PETER BRYAN BRUIN OF BATH: SOLDIER, JUDGE AND FRONTIERSMAN. *West Virginia Hist. 1969 30(4): 579-585.* Reprints three letters by Peter (Pedro) Bryan Bruin (ca. 1754-1826) to Colonel Philip Pendleton concerning Bruin's efforts to repay debts. The first letter is from Bath (Berkeley Springs) in 1878, the second from New Orleans, Louisiana, in 1788, and the last from Bayou Pierre, Mississippi, in 1789. Provides a brief introduction to Bruin. 24 notes.   C. A. Newton

762. Coker, William S. and Holmes, Jack D. L. SOURCES FOR THE HISTORY OF THE SPANISH BORDERLANDS. *Florida Hist. Q. 1971 49(4): 380-393.* Approximately 140 thousand pages of material for Spanish Louisiana have been microfilmed, and an index is available from Loyola University, New Orleans. A guide to the microfilmed diocesan records of Louisiana and the Floridas, 1576-1803, is available from the University of Notre Dame. The Mississippi Department of Archives and History, Jackson, has the microfilm negative of the Natchez chancery court records of 1781-97. Microfilm copies of 20 thousand pages of documents relating to Spanish Alabama, 1780-1813, are available at the Universities of Alabama in Birmingham and Tuscaloosa; the University of West Florida, Pensacola; and the University of Florida, Gainesville. Photostats and typescripts from archives in Madrid relating to Tennessee and the Old Southwest are available at the Lawson McGhee Library, Knoxville, Tennessee. Memphis State University has microfilmed materials from Mexico City, Seville, Madrid, Cuba, and Santa Fe. Cabildo records of New Orleans, 1769-1803, are available on microfilm from the New Orleans Public Library. The Wisconsin Historical Society has copies of Spanish archival material for 1766-1805. In the Library of Congress are the Woodbury Lowery Collection for 1551-1660, the East and West Florida Papers, and the Jeannette Thurber Connor Papers. The most comprehensive collection of material from Spanish archives, 1565-1763, is at the

University of Florida. Information on copying of French materials can be obtained from the Coordination Center of the Manuscript Division, Library of Congress.   R. V. Calvert

763. Gold, Robert L. POLITICS AND PROPERTY DURING THE TRANSFER OF FLORIDA FROM SPANISH TO ENGLISH RULE, 1763-1764. *Florida Hist. Q. 1963 42(1): 16-34.* The treaty of 1763 transferring Florida from Spain to Britain stipulated that Spanish subjects should have 18 months in which to sell their real estate. Britain tended to ignore that provision, by prematurely granting to her soldiers land claimed by Spanish nationals; and the Spanish government and nationals violated the time limit by making fictitious "sales" to private British speculators who promised to sell the property later and give a part of the proceeds to the previous Spanish owners.   G. L. Lycan

764. Gold, Robert L. THE DEPARTURE OF SPANISH CATHOLICISM FROM FLORIDA, 1763-1765. *The Americas 1966 22(4): 377-388.* Following the loss of Florida in the Seven Years' War, the Spanish inhabitants (including the clergy) and certain Christianized Indians were evacuated to Cuba and Mexico. Religious objects were also taken to Cuba where they underwent both inventory and litigation, the latter to determine whether they belonged to the Crown or the Church. Church real estate left in Florida was taken as the property of the British government. The "departure of Spanish Catholicism" was, however, only the culmination of a gradual retreat which had been going on since early in the century. Based chiefly on photostated documents from Seville archives and other primary sources; 30 notes.   D. Bushnell

765. Gold, Robert L. THE SETTLEMENT OF THE EAST FLORIDA SPANIARDS IN CUBA, 1763-1766. *Florida Hist. Q. 1964 42(3): 216-231.* When Great Britain obtained Florida in 1763 the entire Spanish population of St. Augustine opted to move to Cuba. There they experienced dire hardships, and after Spanish reacquisition of Florida during the American Revolutionary War a remnant of the group accepted the Spanish king's invitation to return to St. Augustine.   G. L. Lycan

766. Holmes, Jack D. L. SOME IRISH OFFICERS IN SPANISH LOUISIANA. *Irish Sword [Ireland] 1964 6(25): 234-247.* Deals with six Spanish officers who were born in Ireland but served in Louisiana (or West Florida). They were Alexandro O'Reilly, Carlos Howard, Arturo O'Neill, Enrique White, Pedro Bryan Bruin and Mauricio O'Conor. Information on family background, troops they led, engagements in which they participated, positions held, actions taken while in military service and other biographic data is provided in sketches of each man. Based on unpublished material in the Archivo General de Indias as well as printed sources and articles.   H. L. Calkin

767. Holmes, Jack D. L. THREE EARLY MEMPHIS COMMANDANTS: BEAUREGARD, DEVILLE DEGOUTIN, AND FOLCH. *West Tennessee Hist. Soc. Papers 1964 18: 4-38.* Biographical studies of the three commandants

of San Fernando de las Barrancas, including their problems at the Spanish post (1795-97) on the Chickasaw Bluffs, site of Memphis. They were: Elias Beauregard (1759-1809); Vicente Folch y Juan (1754-1829); and Josef Deville Degoutin Bellechasse (1761-ca. 1829). 192 notes, many citing unpublished sources in the archives of Louisiana and Spain.   W. A. Klutts

768. Kleber, Louis C. SPAIN AND ENGLAND IN FLORIDA. *Hist. Today [Great Britain] 1969 19(1): 46-52.* Sketches miscellaneous events in Florida from around 1567 to 1819. The major topics discussed are wars and the interaction among the British, French, and Spanish. The thesis is that Spain failed to maintain her hold on Florida because she never encouraged more than a military presence, and that Florida revealed signs of development only when she entered into the orbit of British genius. Illus.   L. A. Knafla

769. Reges, Stephen G. A SPANISH GOVERNOR'S INVITATION TO MARYLAND CATHOLICS. *Maryland Hist. Mag. 1965 60(1): 93-98.* Describes Governor Antonio de Ulloa's plan during the years 1766-83 for settling Louisiana with Catholics who had suffered real or imagined hardships under Protestant British rule. However, the American Catholic influx never became a reality. Maryland Catholics were reluctant to give up the wealth and comfort they enjoyed even though deprived of religious liberty. It was not the British but the American frontiersmen in search of the ultimate western limit who were the real threat to European power in the mid-continent. 18 notes.   D. H. Swift

770. Ware, John D. SAINT AUGUSTINE, 1784: DECADENCE AND RE-PAIRS. *Florida Hist. Q. 1969 48(2): 180-187.* Gives translations of two letters dated 1784 from Vicente Manuel de Zéspedes y Velasco, first governor of Spanish East Florida, and two letters written by Mariano de la Rocque, commandant of engineers at Saint Augustine. The state of disrepair of the fortress, barracks, guardrooms, and the governor's house is revealed. Questions arise, on reading these letters, as to why no convicts seemed to be available to assist in the repair of the public buildings, as was the usual practice, and why there was no record of the repair work on the governor's residence (in the 1784 statement of expenses) although the work was apparently done in that year. Based partly on unpublished Library of Congress East Florida Papers; 20 notes.   R. V. Calvert

British Colonial Administration

771. Bragg, Marion B. BRITISH LAND GRANTS IN WARREN COUNTY, MISSISSIPPI. *J. of Mississippi Hist. 1964 26(3): 229-234.* Lists 17 British land grants of 1776-79 issued by Governor Peter Chester of West Florida in the area of the present Warren County, Mississippi. The grants were usually made to retired British naval officers with the acreage dependent upon rank. Few of the

grants were settled, but they did add further confusion to the already chaotic land-title situation in that region after the United States obtained the area in 1798. Based mainly on Mississippi Provincial Archives, English Dominion Manuscripts in the Mississippi Department of Archives and History.   D. C. James

772. Harrell, Laura D. S. COLONIAL MEDICAL PRACTICE IN BRITISH WEST FLORIDA. *Bull. of the Hist. of Medicine 1967 41(6): 539-558.* The practice of medicine in the province of British West Florida was restricted by problems of medical logistics. While the British ministry at Whitehall was responsive to requests for medical aid, the supplies which they sent were periodically lost in shipment. Hence, the supply of medicines, drugs, and equipment was inadequate. While the governors and military commanders of West Florida cooperated with the physicians, the physicians still worked under a severe handicap. Based on primary materials in the Public Record Office, London, England. Illus., 54 notes.   P. D. Thomas

773. Johnson, Cecil. WEST FLORIDA REVISITED. *J. of Mississippi Hist. 1966 28(2): 121-132.* Describes British administration of the province of West Florida after 1763, Spanish conquest of the area in 1779-81, and the role of the area in the peace negotiations of 1782-83. Concludes that "the efforts to defend West Florida from Spain may have weakened the British position militarily in the older colonies to the northeast"; that it is not clear whether the cession of West Florida to Spain was a direct consequence of her conquest of the area; that Britain was apparently willing "to cede both Floridas in order to avoid the greater or more significant loss of Gibraltar"; and that the transfer of the Floridas from England to Spain probably made it easier for the United States to acquire the area later. Undocumented.   J. W. Hillje

774. Rea, Robert R. A NAVAL VISITOR IN BRITISH WEST FLORIDA. *Florida Hist. Q. 1961 40(2): 142-153.* John Blankett, an officer in the British Navy, and George Johnstone, Governor of British West Florida, obtained official British support in 1764 to build a fort in British West Florida on the Mississippi River and to open a shipping channel from the Mississippi along the Iberville, so they could have access to the upper Mississippi without using the Spanish-controlled mouth of that river. The project seemed practical and useful, but failed due to inadequate support from Britain and Indian hostility. Based on extensive personal papers, official colonial records, and secondary works.

G. L. Lycan

775. Rea, Robert R. "GRAVEYARD FOR BRITONS," WEST FLORIDA, 1763-1781. *Florida Hist. Q. 1969 47(4): 345-364.* When British forces occupied West Florida late in 1763 following Spanish withdrawal, bark huts without fireplaces served as troop barracks in Pensacola, and crowded Mobile's Fort Condé (Charlotte) was in a neglected state. Appointed surgeon to the military hospitals, John Lorimer arrived in Pensacola in August 1765. With simultaneous epidemics of yellow fever, dysentery, and either typhus or typhoid, along with malaria, a single regiment in one month lost four officers, five officers' wives, and nearly a hundred men. Taking command in March 1767 Brigadier General

Frederick Haldimand immediately began improvements at Pensacola such as moving the stockade palisades farther away from the crowded barracks, planting vegetable gardens, building a hospital, beginning swamp drainage, and bringing in fresh drinking water. Despite Lorimer's recommendations for draining the area, and for erecting two-story barracks, Mobile remained a fever-ridden camp in the "graveyard for Britons" at the Spanish takeover in 1781. The penurious policy of the Government toward the American command resulted in shortage of medical supplies and hospital space and a lack of such basic necessities as a balanced diet to blankets for cold weather. Based partly on the Gage Papers in the William L. Clements Library and the Haldimand Papers in the Public Archives of Canada; 47 notes.   R. V. Calvert

776. Rea, Robert R. MILITARY DESERTERS FROM BRITISH WEST FLORIDA. *Louisiana Hist. 1968 9(2): 123-137.* Duty in British West Florida was undesirable and many soldiers deserted. Pensacola and Mobile offered few attractions to the exhausted veterans of the Havana campaign. Large-scale desertions prevented the British from accomplishing their exploratory and expansionist missions. The deserters generally went to New Orleans or other settlements in Louisiana, although they were unwelcome and often met misfortune there. Some deserters were recovered by the British. Based on the papers of the military commanders Thomas Gage and Frederick Haldimand; 51 notes.

R. L. Woodward

777. Rea, Robert R. REDCOATS AND REDSKINS ON THE LOWER MISSISSIPPI, 1763-1776: THE CAREER OF LT. JOHN THOMAS. *Louisiana Hist. 1970 11(1): 5-35.* British acquisition of West Florida increased British activity on the lower Mississippi, but at the same time exposed them to "the danger of redskinned highwaymen." To meet this threat, they established Fort Bute and Panmure and stationed Indian agents at the "critical juncture" of the Mississippi and Iberville Rivers. The most notable of these agents was Lieutenant John Thomas, "whose long association with Fort Bute and the lower Mississippi vividly illustrates the problems and conditions of Britain's southwestern frontier." The author traces Thomas' career there, with his frequent and unfortunate conflicts with the Spaniards and with his superiors. Based on manuscript sources from archives in the United States, Canada, and England; 40 notes.

R. L. Woodward

778. Rea, Robert R. THE KING'S AGENT FOR BRITISH WEST FLORIDA. *Alabama R. 1963 16(2): 141-153.* At the end of the Great War for Empire in 1763, British troops occupied Spanish Pensacola and French Mobile and "royal proclamation united them in the colony of West Florida." In addition to the usual administrative officials, a special officer, the king's agent, was appointed. He would reside in London and "distribute those funds voted by Parliament for the development of the province. The first occupant of this position was John Ellis, merchant, naturalist, and Fellow of the Royal Society." Ellis filled the office until his death in 1776. "Typical of the assistance which the king's agent rendered to the infant colony was the establishment of a regular communication between Gulf

ports and older Atlantic colonies." Ellis also attempted to assemble scientific data from the new province. He eventually received thousands of seeds, cuttings, etc. from officials in the province.   D. F. Henderson

779. Rea, Robert R. 1763—THE FORGOTTEN BICENTENNIAL. *Alabama Hist. Q. 1963 25(3/4): 287-293.* "The ever-recurring project of annexing West Florida to the state of Alabama" has been raised again, appropriately, in 1963. In 1763 the coastal strand was incorporated into the British province of West Florida. This British period of history lasted nearly 20 years. Alabama's historians have been "content to leave our British colonial history to other hands." A review of the literature concerning this period reveals that the textbooks lag far behind the work of scholarly research.   E. P. Stickney

780. Reibel, Daniel B. A KIND OF CITADEL: 1764-1805. *Michigan Hist. 1963 47(1): 47-71.* Traces the history of what passed for a citadel at Detroit from the time it was built by the British until its destruction by fire. Basing his analysis almost entirely on original sources, the author concludes that Detroit never had a bona fide citadel. What its design called "a kind of citadel" more nearly resembled a fortified barracks. Although frequently threatened with attack, the citadel's usual condition was one of disrepair, which neither British nor American commanders were able to correct.   J. K. Flack

The Westward Movement

781. Allen, Ben and Lawson, Dennis T. THE WATAUGANS AND THE "DANGEROUS EXAMPLE." *Tennessee Hist. Q. 1967 26(2): 137-147.* An account of the first trans-Appalachian settlements. After the conferences of Fort Stanwix and Hard Labor, immigrants began to settle by mistake on Cherokee lands along the Watauga River in Tennessee and North Carolina. Defying orders of the British to leave, they formed the Watauga Association to lease the land from the Indians. The royal governors of North Carolina and Virginia vetoed the purchase of the land from the Cherokee by the Transylvania Company. With the beginning of hostilities in 1776 the Wataugans threw their support with the rebels and fought well, especially against the Indian allies of the British. Representatives of the area were included as the delegates from Washington County in the North Carolina Constitutional Convention. The pioneers provided a "dangerous example" of defiance of royal power, helped hold the West against the Indians, and maintained American interests in the Ohio Valley against British and Spanish claims. Based on secondary sources; 20 notes.   C. F. Ogilvie

782. Blair, John L., ed. MRS. MARY DEWEES'S JOURNAL FROM PHILADELPHIA TO KENTUCKY. *Register of the Kentucky Hist. Soc. 1965 63(3): 195-218.* Presents a rather obscure diary which describes the scenes visited and

the difficulties encountered on a pioneer family's trip across the Alleghenies. The diary has appeared in print twice previously, but this is the first time it has been published from the original manuscript with lengthy explanatory notes. Documented.   J. F. Cook

783. Bonner, James C. THE OPEN RANGE LIVESTOCK INDUSTRY IN COLONIAL GEORGIA. *Georgia R. 1963 17(1): 85-92.* The west had its beginning in colonial America as cattle, hogs, goats, and geese roamed the back country. This article is a case study of the range conditions in Georgia during this period. Undocumented.   H. G. Earnhart

784. Born, John D., Jr. CHARLES STRACHAN IN MOBILE: THE FRONTIER ORDEAL OF A SCOTTISH FACTOR, 1765-1768. *Alabama Hist. Q. 1966 27(1/2): 23-42.* Describes the problems facing businessmen in the British colony at Mobile. The major problems were lack of trade agreements with the Spanish and the British and the failure of the British military to aid the merchants. The problem of collecting debts is given much detailed attention.
                                                                                            E. E. Eminhizer

785. Born, John D., Jr. JOHN FITZPATRICK OF MANCHAC: A SCOTTISH MERCHANT IN THE LOWER MISSISSIPPI TRADE PRIOR TO THE REVOLUTION. *J. of Mississippi Hist. 1970 32(2): 117-134.* Traces the economic activities of John Fitzpatrick, a Scottish merchant who worked in New Orleans in the years 1767-69. He "was forced out of the city by General Don Alejandro O'Reilly in 1769, and moved to Manchac in West Florida where he continued to buy and sell until February of 1784." Focusing largely on the period 1767-76, the author describes Fitzpatrick's trade with West Florida, his success until 1772 when "the English monopoly on the Mississippi River" ended as numbers of American traders entered Manchac and sold for low profits, and his Loyalism during the war, when he "lost his business and his savings." Based chiefly on a letterbook of Fitzpatrick deposited in the New York Public Library; 57 notes.
                                                                                            J. W. Hillje

786. Burgess, Charles E. JOHN RICE JONES, CITIZEN OF MANY TERRITORIES. *J. of the Illinois State Hist. Soc. 1968 61(1): 58-82.* Relates difficulties encountered in establishing a stable society in Kaskaskia and the surrounding areas after the Seven Years' War and during the American Revolution. Jones was a member of the militia organized at Louisville in 1786 under the command of George Rogers Clark and which operated that year in the vicinity of Vincennes. In 1787 Clark sent him to Kaskaskia to rally support for his expedition from the settlers in that area. The author describes the intricate maneuvers and negotiations which followed until Arthur St. Clair became governor of the Northwest Territory in 1790. In 1810 Jones moved across the Mississippi into Louisiana Territory.   S. L. Jones

787. Burghardt, Andrew F. THE ORIGIN AND DEVELOPMENT OF THE ROAD NETWORK OF THE NIAGARA PENINSULA, ONTARIO, 1770-

1851. *Ann. of the Assoc. of Am. Geographers 1969 59(3): 417-440.* "During the American Revolution, white settlers entered the Niagara Peninsula by way of the four entry points previously established by the Indians. The aboriginal trails served as the avenues of penetration, but with fuller settlement these trails were improved, abandoned, or extended according to the needs of the settlers. The river road became the most prevalent type of route because of the felt need for a juxtaposition of land and water transport. New roads were cut across the inherited network to tie remote areas to the administrative centers. With full settlement of the land the survey roads came to dominate. The analysis leads to the conclusions that the Indian trails did not predetermine the road alignments, that towns create roads rather than vice versa, that the true urban centers were the foci for six or more through routes, and that the sequence of development has been strongly at variance with the model suggested by Taaffe, Morrill, and Gould." J

788. Burton, Arthur G. and Stephenson, Richard W. JOHN BALLENDINE'S EIGHTEENTH-CENTURY MAP OF VIRGINIA. *Q. J. of the Lib. of Congress 1964 21(3): 172-178.* Describes and reproduces the 23 1/2 by 32 inch "Map of Potomack and James Rivers in North America showing their several Communications with the Navigable Waters of the New Province of the River Ohio" drawn about 1772 and used by John Ballendine, colonial and English agent for the Grand Ohio Company in discussed schemes for land and navigation promotion, 1774-75. Documented. H. J. Graham

789. Butler, Mann. DETAILS OF FRONTIER LIFE. *Register of the Kentucky Hist. Soc. 1964 62(3): 206-229.* Paints a general picture of the daily life of the settlers living on the frontier of Virginia, Pennsylvania, and Maryland during the Revolutionary period. It briefly describes several aspects of frontier life including: hunting, military duties, mechanic arts, marriages, sports, medicine, religion, and housebuilding. The article is excerpted from *Valley of the Ohio,* a work unfinished when the author died in 1855, and it commemorates the 180th anniversary of the author's birth. Documented. Biblio. J. F. Cook

790. Cartlidge, Anna M. COLONEL JOHN FLOYD: RELUCTANT ADVENTURER. *Register of the Kentucky Hist. Soc. 1968 66(4): 317-366.* A biographical account of Virginia-born Colonel James John Floyd who was one of the early pioneers in Kentucky. A surveyor by profession, Floyd also held a commission in the militia. Several of his adventures with Indians are recounted, one of which involved Daniel Boone. During the American Revolution Floyd sailed on a privateer, of which he was part owner; he was captured by the British, imprisoned, and later smuggled to France, where he was able to buy passage home. In Kentucky, Colonel Floyd held several important positions including trustee to lay out the town of Louisville, a trustee to establish the first college in Kentucky, and one of the first judges of the District Court of Kentucky County. He was killed in an Indian ambush near Clear Station, Kentucky, in 1783. Based on primary sources including contemporary journals, diaries, and Floyd's letters in the Draper Collection of the Wisconsin Historical Society; 168 notes. B. Wilkins

791. Cecil, L. Moffitt. SIMMS'S PORGY AS NATIONAL HERO. *Am. Litera-ture 1965 36(4): 475-484.* The struggle of William Simms' fictional character Captain Porgy to save his estate during the parlous times following the Revolutionary War is analogous to the struggling American Republic. In both, the frontier experience is crucial to the formulation of national character. 4 notes.
R. S. Burns

792. Farrell, David. SETTLEMENT ALONG THE DETROIT FRONTIER, 1760-1796. *Michigan Hist. 1968 52(2): 89-107.* Uses a variety of original and secondary sources to trace population growth and land distribution in Detroit under British rule. 6 illus., 72 notes.
J. K. Flack

793. Folmsbee, Stanley. THE JOURNAL OF JOHN COTTEN, THE "RELUCTANT PIONEER"—EVIDENCE OF ITS UNRELIABILITY. *Tennessee Hist. Q. 1969 28(1): 84-94.* Questions the authenticity of a journal purportedly kept by John Cotten from 1771 to 1811. Argues that the journal was either purposely falsified by Cotten or written by someone of a later generation, probably the latter. Evidences are presented that Cotten, in the journal an English officer who deserted to the Regulators at the Battle of Alamance (1771), was instead an American deserter. The author rejects the journal's account of Cotten's experiences in the Watauga settlements and on the trip with John Donelson to Nashville in 1779. Among the historical errors the journal perpetrates are a false chronology of the Watauga governments and misinformation about the activities of Daniel Boone and James Robertson. The most serious accusation is that a fictitious John Donelson is placed genealogically between the founder of Nashville and the brother-in-law of Andrew Jackson. An editorial note states that the owner of the journal, J. W. L. Matlock, who had previously published articles based upon it in the *Quarterly,* declines to enter a debate on its dependability or to permit examination of it. 5 notes.
C. F. Ogilvie

794. Gaines, William H., Jr. COURTHOUSES OF BRUNSWICK AND GREENSVILLE COUNTIES. *Virginia Cavalcade 1970 19(3): 37-41.* Brunswick County was established by the Virginia General Assembly in 1720 to encourage settlement of the territory between the fall line and the Blue Ridge mountains and thus secure the area from the encroachments of the Indians and, more especially, the French. Greensville County, named in honor of General Nathanael Greene (1742-86), was formed out of Brunswick County in 1780. Discusses reasons for the changing boundaries, settlement, and erection of courthouses. Records are extant from 1732. Illus.
N. L. Peterson

795. Gates, Paul W. TENANTS OF THE LOG CABIN. *Mississippi Valley Hist. R. 1962/63 49(1): 3-31.* During the 1780's most Kentuckians lived on acreage controlled by absentee landlords. With the separation from Virginia, these "tenants of the log cabin" strove for land policy which would be more beneficial to local owners. After 40 years of litigation and land title controversy, the land improvement rights of settlers had been secured through a series of occupancy laws. As the frontier moved westward occupancy laws were adopted in many of the States. Kentucky had set the pattern.
G. M. Gressley

796. Green, E. R. R. QUEENSBOROUGH TOWNSHIP: SCOTCH-IRISH EMIGRATION AND THE EXPANSION OF GEORGIA, 1763-1776. *William and Mary Q. 1960 17(2): 183-199.* Traces the unsuccessful effort to attract Scotch-Irish emigrants to a settlement on the Ogeechee River. Although Queensborough received but few settlers because of Indian raids and did not survive the Revolution, the effort is significant because of the attempt to settle the back country directly from Europe, and because it indicates the desire for territorial expansion.   E. Oberholzer, Jr.

797. Hagy, James W. THE FRONTIER AT CASTLE'S WOODS, 1769-1786. *Virginia Mag. of Hist. and Biog. 1967 75(4): 410-428.* The first permanent settlement in Russell County, Virginia, Castle's Woods attracted a heterogeneous group of early settlers including Daniel Boone. The settlement suffered severely during the so-called Lord Dunmore's War in 1774 and withstood attacks during the Revolution. As a case study of a frontier settlement, Castle's Woods "both supports and contradicts the ideas of the Turner school of historians." Based on manuscript and printed sources; 61 notes.   K. J. Bauer

798. Holmes, Jack D. L. INDIGO IN COLONIAL LOUISIANA AND THE FLORIDAS. *Louisiana Hist. 1967 8(4): 329-349.* Traces the indigo industry in colonial Louisiana and Florida, government encouragement of the crop, and its expansion from its beginnings in the early 18th century to its decline after 1795 owing to foreign competition and soil exhaustion. The author includes contemporary descriptions and statistics of indigo production in these colonies. Based on published documents and secondary sources, archival sources in France, Spain, and Louisiana; 118 notes.   R. L. Woodward

799. Jakle, John A. THE AMERICAN BISON AND THE HUMAN OCCUPANCE OF THE OHIO VALLEY. *Pro. of the Am. Phil. Soc. 1968 112(4): 299-305.* Analyzes the interaction and relationship between the buffalo and human inhabitants of the Ohio Valley, especially Kentucky. Many bison were enabled to move into the valley because of fires set by the Indians to flush game and to create prairie land which was attractive to the buffalo. The effect of these animals on the white settlements in the valley in the late 18th century and the influence of buffalo traces provided "an integral part of the Ohio Valley's initial settlement fabric and even set the pattern for urban growth in portions of the Valley." Based largely on secondary materials; 25 notes.   W. G. Morgan

800. Kay, M. L. M. AN ANALYSIS OF A BRITISH COLONY IN LATE EIGHTEENTH CENTURY AMERICA IN THE LIGHT OF CURRENT AMERICAN HISTORIOGRAPHICAL CONTROVERSY. *Australian J. of Pol. and Hist. 1965 11(2): 170-184.* By a close examination of the farmer's protest movement, known as the Regulators, in North Carolina in the years 1750 to 1772, the author disputes Louis Hartz's interpretation *The Liberal Tradition in America* (New York: Harcourt, Brace and World, 1955) that part of the uniqueness of American society was that it lacked feudalism. He maintains that "feudal institutions were there, if somewhat muted by the vastness of the continent and

the opportunities available to substantial portions of the population." Regulators felt themselves members of a "mistreated agricultural class." Based on colonial records of North Carolina and recent monographs.   W. D. McIntyre

801. Lunger, Irvin E. EDUCATION ON THE EARLY KENTUCKY FRONTIER: 1967 BOONE DAY ADDRESS. *Register of the Kentucky Hist. Soc. 1967 65(4): 261-270.* In this address, the speaker contrasts the slow development of elementary and secondary education with the early and progressive development of higher education in pioneer Kentucky. The main obstacles to elementary and secondary schools were the indifference, ignorance, and political expediency on the part of the early settlers and government officials. Higher education was a different story. Transylvania University, which was founded in 1780 had, by the 1820's under the leadership of Horace Holley, risen to national prominence. The school's medical and law departments were among the finest in the country. Conflict between State support and denominational control caused the school's decline. Undocumented.   B. Wilkins

802. Marshall, P. LORD HILLSBOROUGH, SAMUEL WHARTON AND THE OHIO GRANT, 1769-1775. *English Hist. R. [Great Britain] 1966 80(317): 717-739.* An account of the attempts of the Philadelphia trader Samuel Wharton to recuperate his financial losses on the frontier by gaining the British government's recognition of his acquisition of a large tract of Indian land in the Ohio Valley, already partly guaranteed by the Treaty of Fort Stanwix (1768) with the Iroquois. The new Secretary of State for America Lord Hillsborough was, however, hostile to the treaty, which extended the boundary of settlement so far west, and suspicious of the number of public and private grants it entailed. Hillsborough hoped to discourage Wharton and his associates by at first offering a grant of an impossibly large size (20 million acres), but when they eagerly accepted the grant, fell back on obstructive tactics, since delay meant financial ruin to Wharton. Wharton and his friends managed to convince a committee of council and eventually the cabinet to approve both the grant and plans for a new colony to be named Vandalia; Hillsborough resigned. Delays, the result of an indecisive ministry and cumbersome administrative machinery, proved fatal; the Boston Tea Party and the ensuing American crisis killed the Vandalia scheme. Documented, particularly from the Croghan Papers (Cadwallader Collection), Pennsylvania Historical Society; the Fetherstonhaugh Papers (in the possession of Paul Mellon); and Colonial Office Papers.   D. H. Murdoch

803. Martin, James Kirby. THE RETURN OF THE PAXTON BOYS AND THE HISTORICAL STATE OF THE PENNSYLVANIA FRONTIER, 1764-1774. *Pennsylvania Hist. 1971 38(2): 117-133.* Deals with the activities of the Paxton Boys after 1764. Challenges the contentions that they were democratic and allied with the proprietary forces. The Paxton Boys had a number of reasons to be dissatisfied with the rule of Governor John Penn. They opposed his efforts to collect quitrents in bad times and considered his method of selling lands in the Susquehannah Valley unfair. They also complained of the Removal Act of 1768, a measure designed to clear settlers from Indian territory, and the prosecution of Frederick Stump, a frontiersman who killed 10 Indians. In 1769, many of the

Paxton Boys agreed to move into the Wyoming Valley to support with force the claims of the Susquehannah Company of Connecticut. Because their "method was force, not rational discussion and debate," the Paxton Boys were not democratic. 42 notes.   D. C. Swift

804. Matlock, J. W. L. JOHN COTTEN: RELUCTANT PIONEER. *Tennessee Hist. Q. 1968 27(3): 277-286.* Relates the incidents that caused John Cotten, son of a wealthy, landed North Carolina family, to fight against his own militia in the Battle of Alamance ("a rebellion of the farmers of Orange County against the injustices of the royal Colonial Government of William Tyron, 16 May 1771"), to join settlers moving from North Carolina to the Tennessee wilderness, and finally to found a new family homestead outside what is now Nashville. The author, a great-great-great-grandson of Cotten, quotes from his ancestor's journal, a handwritten diary kept for 40 years (1771-1811). 24 notes.
                                                    M. W. Machan

805. Meeks, Harold A. AN ISOCHRONIC MAP OF VERMONT SETTLE-MENT. *Vermont Hist. 1970 38(2): 95-102.* Maps the advance of the frontier from 1760 to 1824, following Stanley D. Dodge's technique of drawing lines connecting points settled at the same time, but reducing the intervals to four years. Dates of the first settlement in each town are taken indirectly from Zadock Thompson's *Gazetteer* (1824). Settlement before the Revolution touched two tiers of towns in the Connecticut Valley, to Barnet and Peacham; and three tiers in the west, to Colchester and Jericho. Settlement during 1776-83 advanced as much as in the previous eight years, but had already started in the southern Champlain Valley. Except for such mountain towns as Goshen-Huntington and Mansfield-Woodbury, and the northern half of the northeast, Vermont was settled by 1791. The assumption that settlement followed military roads and riverways seems less significant than the relationship of settlement to topography. Map.
                                                    T. D. S. Bassett

806. Moor, Dean. THE PAXTON BOYS: PARKMAN'S FRONTIER HY-POTHESIS. *Mid-Am. 1954 36(4): 211-219.* Recounts and analyzes an incident described in Francis Parkman's *History of the Conspiracy of the Pontiac* (1851), and suggests that Parkman anticipated many of the ideas of Frederick Jackson Turner. Particular emphasis is placed upon Parkman's recognition that American development was an evolutionary process in which the environmental influences of the frontier played an important role.   R. F. Campbell

807. Moss, Roger W., Jr. ISAAC ZANE, JR., A "QUAKER FOR THE TIMES." *Virginia Mag. of Hist. and Biog. 1969 77(3): 291-306.* Isaac Zane, Jr., is important as an example of the individual back-country entrepreneur who helped open the colonial frontier. The son of a successful Philadelphia Quaker builder, he purchased an interest in the Marlboro Iron Works near Winchester, Virginia, in 1767 and became the sole proprietor the following year. A local political figure, he took an active if unspectacular part in the events leading to independence and turned his iron works into a war plant during the Revolution. He also took in a number of Quakers who had been expelled from Philadelphia

for being "inimical" to the American cause. Despite his frontier environment, he was a dilettante scientist and lived gracefully. Based on varied manuscript and printed sources; 72 notes.   K. J. Bauer

808. Painter, Levinus K. THE RISE AND DECLINE OF QUAKERISM IN THE MONONGAHELA VALLEY. *Bull. of Friends Hist. Assoc. 1956 45(1): 24-29.* Covers the period from the first organized Friends meeting west of the Allegheny Mountains in 1782, until the westward movement brought the closing of the last meeting in the Monongahela Valley before 1870.   N. Kurland

809. Siebert, Wilbur. THE EARLY SUGAR INDUSTRY IN FLORIDA. *Florida Hist. Q. 1956/57 35(4): 312-319.* A description of the hazardous, disappointing experiences of sugar manufacturers in Florida from 1776-1843. Based on deed books; *American State Papers,* Public Lands; and secondary works.   G. L. Lycan

810. Sifton, Paul G. THE WALKER-WASHINGTON MAP. *Lib. of Congress Q. J. 1967 24(2): 90-96.* The Library of Congress has received a map copied by George Washington from a map made by Thomas Walker in 1769 to accompany a memorandum from Walker to the Virginia House of Burgesses concerning the boundary between the western settlements and the Indians. It is believed that Washington added information to the map copied from Lewis Evans' map of 1755 and from his own personal knowledge. The Walker map has disappeared. The map was probably used by Washington on his mission to survey the lands between the Little and Great Kanawha Rivers in 1770. Illus., 2 maps, 26 notes.   H. E. Cox

811. Smith, Dwight L. ISRAEL ANGELL AND THE WEST IN 1788. *Rhode Island Hist. 1963 22(1): 1-15, (2): 39-50.* Part I. Briefly summarizes Angell's career and, particularly, his tour from Johnston, Rhode Island, to Marietta, Ohio. In addition to visiting members of the Society of the Cincinnati, Angell investigated his investments in the Ohio Company. Reproduces an edited version of Angell's unpublished journal for the period from 4 August 1788 to 3 September 1788, which is housed in the Rhode Island Historical Society. Part II. Reproduces the second portion of an edited version of Angell's unpublished journal for the period from 4 September to 9 October 1788 in which Angell described his return trip from Marietta, Ohio, to Johnston, Rhode Island.   P. J. Coleman

812. Stealey, John Edmund, III. FRENCH LICK AND THE CUMBERLAND COMPACT. *Tennessee Hist. Q. 1963 22(4): 323-334.* Reviews early settlements on the Cumberland River, at French Lick, which is today Nashville, from their beginning to the adoption of the Compact—"a typical social and economic document of the frontier"—1 May 1780. It was superseded by the organization of Davidson County in 1783. 33 notes, citing secondary sources, and the Draper manuscript, not otherwise identified.   W. A. Klutts

813. Stealey, John Edmund, III. GEORGE CLENDINEN AND THE GREAT KANAWHA VALLEY FRONTIER: A CASE STUDY OF THE FRONTIER DEVELOPMENT OF VIRGINIA. *West Virginia Hist. 1966 37(4): 278-296.* As was so often the case with land speculators, it was the expectation of profits, not the actual existence of them, that led George Clendinen to promote the settlement of western lands. Born in northern Ireland in 1746, he accompanied his parents to Virginia in the 1750's. After participating in Lord Dunmore's campaign of 1774 against the Ohio Indians, he served in the Virginia militia on the frontier during the Revolution. Elected from Greenbrier County to the Virginia Assembly in 1781, he served until 1789. In this office he promoted the interests of the West by championing internal improvements. He was also active in land speculation and in promoting western settlement. He was able to secure the establishment of Kanawha County in 1789 and during most of the period from 1791 through 1795 represented that county in the legislature. He was a typical frontiersman who used his political position to promote his personal interests. Based on published primary and secondary sources.

D. N. Brown

814. Watlington, Patricia. DISCONTENT IN FRONTIER KENTUCKY. *Register of the Kentucky Hist. Soc. 1967 65(2): 77-93.* Seeks to show Virginia defense policies and restrictive land titles as the two chief causes of discontent in Kentucky. Many conservative frontiersmen remained loyal to England believing England would provide a defense against the Indians. Others supported the Congressional claim, hoping that Congress would annul Virginia land titles and grant statehood to Kentucky. The author believes the same factors which produced a frontier liberalism could also produce a frontier conservatism as evidenced in Kentucky. Drawn from state government records and manuscript collections in several state historical societies, 77 notes.   B. Wilkins

815. Wells, Gordon M. BRITISH LAND GRANTS—WILLIAM WILTON MAP, 1774. *J. of Mississippi Hist. 1966 28(2): 152-160.* Lists 355 land grants in the years 1765-73 in the area which became the state of Mississippi. The list gives the number of acres, their location, the name of the person to whom granted, and the date of the grant. The author compiled the information from the William Winton map of 1774, a map in the British Public Record Office, and a document in the Mississippi Department of Archives and History. Copies of these documents are on file in the latter depository.   J. W. Hillje

816. Welter, Rush. THE FRONTIER WEST AS IMAGE OF AMERICAN SOCIETY 1776-1860. *Pacific Northwest Q. 1961 52(1): 1-6.* An examination of selected writings in eastern U.S. magazines and newspapers indicating thought and images of the developing western region of the United States.

C. C. Gorchels

817. Wolf, George D. THE BIG RUNAWAY OF 1778. *Pro. and Collections of the Wyoming Hist. and Geological Soc. 1970 23: 3-19.* In 1778 the "Big Runaway" occurred along the West Branch of the Susquehanna River. With the coming of independence the "Fair Play" settlers of that region faced potential

terror from Great Britain and the Indians. Describes the situation confronting these settlers and the events that led to a massacre. When news of the Wyoming Valley Massacre (3 July 1778) reached the area, panic reigned as people emptied the valley north of Sunbury, Pennsylvania. Many of the men remained at Fort Augusta (Sunbury) to help secure the frontier against any further encroachment to the south. 56 notes.   H. B. Powell

818. Wolf, George D. THE POLITICS OF FAIR PLAY. *Pennsylvania Hist. 1965 32(1): 8-24.* Discusses the people and politics of approximately one hundred families who settled near the present cities of Williamsport and Lock Haven, Pennsylvania, and established a community and a political organization known as the Fair Play system.   W. B. Miller

The War in the West

819. Appel, John C. COLONEL DANIEL BRODHEAD AND THE LURE OF DETROIT. *Pennsylvania Hist. 1971 38(3): 265-282.* Colonel (later Brigadier General) Daniel Brodhead (1736-1809) was stationed at Fort Pitt from 1778 to 1781. During his first year at the fort, Brodhead served under Brigadier General Lachlan McIntosh, who was removed due to Congressional dissatisfaction with his preparations for an assault upon Detroit. Brodhead replaced McIntosh as commandant and was charged with the duty of continuing preparations for an expedition against Detroit. Because his force was small and insufficiently supplied, Brodhead devoted his efforts to gathering reliable intelligence about Detroit and forwarding it to George Washington. Contemporaries and historians have charged Brodhead with causing the failure of George Rogers Clark's expedition to Detroit. The author maintains that Brodhead offered what supplies he could and that he lacked manpower to contribute to the effort. Washington removed Brodhead because he was charged with misfeasance and malfeasance in office. Washington apparently did not take seriously the charge that Brodhead obstructed Clark. In relation to all these charges, the author maintains that Brodhead was a victim of circumstances. 61 notes.   D. C. Swift

820. Bertin, Eugene P. FRONTIER FORTS ON THE SUSQUEHANNA. *Now and Then 1965 14(12): 376-393.* Describes the forts which were used by the settlers on the west branch of the Susquehanna River during the darkest days of the Revolutionary War in this region from 1777 to 1779. Most were erected by private individuals and are compared by the author to a modern bomb shelter. During periods of Indian attack, local citizens would take shelter there. The largest of these forts were built by the colony and were staffed with militia. Despite these precautions, an Indian and Tory attack depopulated the region during the summer of 1779. Illustrated with drawings, pictures, and maps of the forts described.   H. Ershkowitz

821. Fall, Ralph Emmett. CAPTAIN SAMUEL BRADY (1756-1795), CHIEF OF THE RANGERS, AND HIS KIN. *West Virginia Hist. 1968 29(3): 203-223.* A genealogical summary of the immediate family life of Samuel Brady. His father, John (1733-79), and several brothers served Washington in the Revolution, most of the time in Pennsylvania. After the war Samuel earned a savage reputation in Indian warfare but was formally exonerated. Based on published biographies and genealogies; 54 notes.   C. A. Newton

822. Ferrer-Llull, Francisco and Hefter, J. THE SPANISH LOUISIANA REGI-MENT IN THE FLORIDAS, 1779-1781. *Military Collector and Historian 1964 16(3): 79-81.* Describes the dress of the Regimiento de Infanteria de Louisiana which served as an ally of the American colonies from 1779 until 1781. Unpublished material at the Royal Academy of History in Madrid is cited. Illus., 6 notes.   C. L. Boyd

823. Ganyard, Robert L. THREAT FROM THE WEST: NORTH CAROLINA AND THE CHEROKEE, 1776-1778. *North Carolina Hist. R. 1968 45(1): 47-66.* In 1766 North Carolina faced two threats: a British invasion supported by local Tories, and an uprising of the Cherokee Indians, which was beginning just as the British were defeated. The Cherokee were stirred by westward expansion of the white man and their own young hotheads. There is no proof that either the Tories or the British encouraged them, and much evidence that attempts were made on the British side to dissuade the Indians from indiscriminate violence. North Carolina, with the assistance of militia from Virginia and South Carolina, dispersed the Indians and destroyed many villages and crops in the late summer of 1776. A peace treaty was made in 1777 which kept the Cherokee quiet until late in 1780. 53 notes.   J. M. Bumsted

824. Gerlach, Don. PHILIP SCHUYLER AND THE NEW YORK FRON-TIER IN 1781. *New-York Hist. Soc. Q. 1969 53(2): 148-181.* Although Major General Philip Schuyler filled no military position after his replacement by General Horatio Gates as commander of the Northern Department in 1777, he continued to be active in the cause of the Revolution. From his vantage point in Albany, he kept Washington informed of developments, sent spies into enemy-held territory, and assisted in obtaining supplies for the Army. An indication of the importance of his role was the attempt by the British to capture him in the summer of 1781. The author's conclusion is that, although Schuyler's activities were not of vital importance, they helped the American effort considerably. Primary and secondary sources; 2 illus., 58 notes.   C. L. Grant

825. Haarmann, Albert W. THE SIEGE OF PENSACOLA: AN ORDER OF BATTLE. *Florida Hist. Q. 1966 44(3): 193-199.* Britain tried to hold Pensacola in 1781 with about two thousand men from her army and naval units of Negroes, Indians, German mercenaries, and local militia. Spain took the city with an attacking force of some eight thousand men: army, navy, French, Irish, Negro, and mulatto. Based on primary and secondary sources.   G. L. Lycan

826. Haarmann, Albert W. THE SPANISH CONQUEST OF BRITISH WEST FLORIDA, 1779-1781. *Florida Hist. Q. 1960 39(2): 107-134.* A brief overall account of the methodical process by which the Spanish military leader Don Bernardo de Gálvez conquered West Florida from Britain, 1779-81. Based on Spanish and American State papers, collections of personal papers, and biographical and secondary works.   G. L. Lycan

827. Havighurst, Walter. A SWORD FOR GEORGE ROGERS CLARK. *Am. Heritage 1962 13(6): 56-64.* Recounts the story of George Rogers Clark's attacks and victories against the British forts, Kaskaskia, Cahokia, and Vincennes, north of the Ohio River. The author notes the roles of the French settlers, especially Father Pierre Gibault and Dr. Jean Laffont. He details the spectacular success against Vincennes against huge odds in 1778-79, and notes the consequences of this exploit. Undocumented; illus.   C. R. Allen, Jr.

828. Holmes, Jack D. L. ROBERT ROSS' PLAN FOR AN ENGLISH INVASION OF LOUISIANA IN 1782. *Louisiana Hist. 1964 5(2): 161-177.* Analyzes two letters written by Robert Ross, British merchant, to Governor Dunmore of the House of Lords, 3 and 8 March 1782. Ross was long active in trading in the lower Mississippi Valley, basing his operations at Natchez and New Orleans. The letters are significant for two reasons: 1) "British plans to invade Louisiana in 1796 and 1814 followed basically the pattern first established by Ross in 1782" in his suggestions to Dunmore, 2) they "shed interesting light on conditions in Louisiana and West Florida during a period of bustling, wartime activity." The letters are in the Chalmer Papers, New York Public Library.

D. C. James

829. Kennett, Lee. A FRENCH REPORT ON ST. AUGUSTINE IN THE 1770'S. *Florida Hist. Q. 1965 44(1/2): 133-135.* An espionage report of 1777 to the French government concerning ways to capture St. Augustine from the British. Based on secondary works and periodical material.   G. L. Lycan

830. Martinez Ortiz, José. UN VALENCIANO EN LA INDEPENDENCIA DE LOS ESTADOS UNIDOS [A Valencian in the independence of the United States]. *R. de Hist. de América [Mexico] 1960 50: 488-495.* Juan Miralles y Troillón, a native Spaniard and resident of Havana, came as a special agent of the Spanish Court to the Congress in Philadelphia. He kept the Spanish Court informed of American land claims in the Mississippi, in the Gulf area, and in Florida. He reported on American power potential in the area and predicted probable demands for free navigation of the Mississippi, and for maintenance of Pensacola as an open port. The Spanish representative arrived in January 1778 and died in Morristown, New Jersey, where Washington's army was quartered in April 1780.   T. B. Davis, Jr.

831. Massay, G. F. FORT HENRY IN THE AMERICAN REVOLUTION. *West Virginia Hist. 1962/63 24(3): 248-257.* Once the American Revolution materialized the West began to play a major role. The English and the Americans

recognized the importance of the Indians in the West and each sought to gain their support. Fort Henry, located in what is now Wheeling, was a ready target for the Indians. Describes several efforts made by the Indians to take the fort.
M. Kanin

832. McAdams, Donald R. THE SULLIVAN EXPEDITION: SUCCESS OR FAILURE. *New-York Hist. Soc. Q. 1970 54(1): 53-81.* In the late summer of 1779 Major General John Sullivan led an expedition against the Iroquois. The expedition was considered a success and has been so regarded by subsequent historians. Although more careful study raises several questions which need further research, one conclusion seems valid. In view of the Indian activities in the years following the expedition, the expedition did not break the power of the Iroquois. Thus, the expedition did not succeed in its major objective. Based on primary sources; 5 illus., 48 notes.
C. L. Grant

833. McLellan, Hugh, ed. CAPTAIN JOB WRIGHT'S COMPANY OF WIL- LETT'S LEVIES AT BALLSTON IN 1782. *New York Hist. 1969 50(4): Supplement, 13-21.* Reproduces from the scarce first issue of the *Quarterly Journal of the New York State Historical Association* (October 1919) the text of Captain Job Wright's correspondence with Governor George Clinton (1739-1812) and other officials concerning the disposition of New York State troops along the New York frontier during the closing days of the Revolutionary War.
G. Kurland

834. Murphy, W. S. THE IRISH BRIGADE OF SPAIN AT THE CAPTURE OF PENSACOLA, 1781. *Florida Hist. Q. 1960 38(3): 216-225.* Count Bernardo de Galvez, with a Spanish Army of more than 7,000 men, including 580 officers and men of the "Irish Brigade of Spain," besieged the British forces at Pensacola, Florida, for two months and captured them on 2 May 1781—at a critical time during the American Revolution.
G. L. Lycan

835. Scott, Kenneth, ed. BRITAIN LOSES NATCHEZ, 1779: AN UNPUB- LISHED LETTER. *J. of Mississippi Hist. 1964 26(1): 45-46.* Consists of a brief letter of October 1779 from 59 settlers at Natchez on the Mississippi River to a British lieutenant colonel, praising his valiant but vain efforts to defend British possessions along the Mississippi against the Spanish. The letter, which is in the British Public Record Office, Colonial Office Papers, 5:397, "is important be- cause it reveals many names of Natchez settlers" hitherto unknown.
D. C. James

836. Sosin, Jack M. THE USE OF INDIANS IN THE WAR OF THE AMERI- CAN REVOLUTION: A RE-ASSESSMENT OF RESPONSIBILITY. *Can. Hist. R. 1965 46(2): 101-121.* Examines American and British actions concerning the use of Indians. The decision to use them was precipitated on both sides by local groups. Due to a distaste for savage warfare by certain British officials,

Indians were not used until relatively late and then with little effect. Based primarily on unpublished manuscripts in the Clements Library and the Public Archives of Canada. A

837. Stanley, George F. G. THE SIX NATIONS AND THE AMERICAN REVOLUTION. *Ontario Hist. 1964 56(4): 217-232.* Having long occupied a buffer zone between competing colonial powers, the Iroquois were at last driven from their lands during the American Revolution when their old allies, the British, and the American colonies, had divided in civil war. Though their neutrality was early encouraged by both sides, first the British and then the Americans forced them to adopt a belligerent role. Because the main threat to their lands was the advancing American settlement, most fought with the British and gained by doing so. The Iroquois, already losing to American settlement, received new lands from Britain in reward for their military aid. G. Emery

838. Tanner, Helen Hornbeck. ZESPEDES AND THE SOUTHERN CONSPIRACIES. *Florida Hist. Q. 1959 38(1): 15-28.* Vicente Manuel de Zéspedes, Spanish Governor of East Florida, 1784 to 1790, steered warily through a morass of conspiracies involving nationals of the United States, Britain and Spain whose objectives were the acquisition of private lands in the Floridas, control of the fur trade with the Indians, free navigation of the Mississippi, or even a revolution against Spain aimed at creating a new republic on the Gulf of Mexico or annexation of the territory to the United States. Based on Spanish colonial records and secondary works. G. L. Lycan

8

THE LOYALISTS:
CHOICES & CONSEQUENCES

General

839. Anderson, James LaVerne. THE IMPACT OF THE AMERICAN REVO-
LUTION ON THE GOVERNOR'S COUNCILLORS. *Pennsylvania Hist. 1967*
34(2): 131-146. Studies the effects of the American Revolution on the last members of colonial Pennsylvania's council. Two members were Loyalists, one worked
energetically for the Patriot cause, and the rest took a "position of neutral
moderation leaning to the British side." Those assuming neutral positions suffered little other than loss of political power and a temporary economic setback
in economic status due to inflation and heavy taxation. Richard Penn lost quitrents and much of his land, and Tory Andrew Allen suffered confiscation of his
lands. After the revolution, former council members reestablished their fortunes
and moved along the fringes of elite society in revolutionary America. Two,
Benjamin Chew and Edward Shippen, Jr., even held respectively the posts of
President of the High Court of Appeals and Chief Justice of Pennsylvania. Their
rehabilitation was facilitated by personal and family connections as well as their
well-known lack of enthusiasm for crown rule. The children of these proprietary
councillors occupied prominent places in revolutionary society. Based on a variety of primary and secondary sources; 61 notes.   D. C. Swift

840. Bail, Hamilton Vaughan. ZADOCK WRIGHT: THAT "DEVILISH"
TORY OF HARTLAND. *Vermont Hist. 1968 36(4): 186-203.* Zadock Wright
of Northfield, Massachusetts, veteran of the French and Indian Wars, one of two
1761 grantees to settle Hartland, Vermont, owner of some 550 acres there and
local esquire, joined the Queen's Loyal Rangers under John Peters on 6 August
1777. His estate was confiscated and later sold to Roger Enos. He fought at
Bennington and Saratoga; he was captured while visiting Hartland in May 1778
and taken to Albany. While 18 months on parole, he was converted to Shakerism
by Mother Ann Lee. Released in August 1780, he returned to Hartland and from
1782 was a founder and business manager of the Shaker communities at Enfield
and Canterbury, New Hampshire. 20 notes.   T. D. S. Bassett

841. Becker, Carl. JOHN JAY AND PETER VAN SCHAACK. *New York Hist. 1969 50(4): Supplement, 1-12.* John Jay and Peter Van Schaack both made their first appearances in public life by serving as members of New York's Committee of 51, formed in 1774 in the wake of the Boston Port Act. Both were conservative in their politics, fearing independence, mob rule, and civil strife. Jay married a Livingston and Van Schaack married a De Lancey, giving both men access to New York's "best families." Yet, four years later, Jay had taken his place as a leader of the Patriot cause while Van Schaack was exiled as a Loyalist. In seeking to discover why one man became a revolutionary while another remained loyal to the Crown, the author emphasizes the psychological differences between the two men. Van Schaack, who lost two sons and the sight of one eye in this period, was more inclined to bow to fate than was the more optimistic Jay. The author concludes that the differences between Patriots and Loyalists were thin indeed. The article is reprinted from the first issue of the *Quarterly Journal of the New York State Historical Association* (October, 1919). Based on primary and secondary sources; 14 notes.　　　　　　　　　G. Kurland

842. Brown, Wallace. THE AMERICAN FARMER DURING THE REVOLUTION: REBEL OR LOYALIST? *Agric. Hist. 1968 42(4): 327-338.* While 90 percent of the colonial population was rural, the dynamism of opposition to the British was mainly located in urban areas. However, available evidence indicates that most country areas were neutral or Whig (prorevolution) and that far more farmers were Whig or neutral than loyal. The loyalty of many farmers was personal and particular. Farmers as farmers were not motivated by their occupation, except in that it tended to breed indifference.　　　　W. D. Rasmussen

843. Brown, Wallace. THE LOYALISTS AND THE AMERICAN REVOLUTION. *Hist. Today [Great Britain] 1962 12(3): 149-157.* Examines the Loyalist followers during the American Revolution and their plight in seeking new homes in England, Canada and the West Indies and the attempt of some to return to an independent United States.　　　　　　　　　L. D. Kasparian

844. Brown, Wallace. THE VIEW AT TWO HUNDRED YEARS: THE LOYALISTS OF THE AMERICAN REVOLUTION. *Pro. of the Am. Antiquarian Soc. 1970 80(1): 25-47.* Loyalists have generally been neglected by both American and English historians of the American Revolution, although such one-sidedness distorts history. "Better" college textbooks hardly mention the Loyalists. If seen in the context of the whole question of loyalty, from the 17th century to the present, the Tories can be considered more objectively. Scattered accounts of Loyalists need to be integrated into overall accounts of the Revolution. Comparative studies are needed, directed toward consideration of the Loyalists in Canada, the West Indies, Sierra Leone, Great Britain, and those who remained in the United States. A possible fruitful approach would be a comparison of all British colonies which did not rebel. More detailed studies are needed, including biographies, which might help explain the strange lack of organization and success of Loyalists. More study is needed on minorities—Negroes, Indians, and women and perhaps a Namier-style dictionary to help identify the Loyalists. Perhaps, if the story of Loyalist persecution is fully told, the American Revolution did have

a "terror" after all. There is need for both broad and narrow research on Loyalists in Canadian history. A renaissance in Loyalist studies is evident in recent years, so that by the time of the Revolutionary bicentennial, a much more objective picture of the Revolution should be available at both scholarly and popular levels. Based on secondary sources; 73 notes. R. V. Calvert

845. Calhoon, Robert M. "I HAVE DEDUCED YOUR RIGHTS": JOSEPH GALLOWAY'S CONCEPT OF HIS ROLE, 1774-1775. *Pennsylvania Hist. 1968 35(4): 356-378.* Centers on the theoretical underpinnings of Joseph Galloway's "Plan of Union." Particular stress is laid upon his doctrine of representation and subordination, and the difficulty inherent in reconciling them. The author approaches the topic through two neglected polemics: Galloway's *A Candid Examination of the Mutual Claims of Great Britain and the Colonies* (1775) and his *Reply* (1775) to attacks upon his position. Based on primary and secondary materials; 65 notes. D. C. Swift

846. Clark, Michael D. JONATHAN BOUCHER: THE MIRROR OF REACTION. *Huntington Lib. Q. 1969 33(1): 19-32.* Jonathan Boucher (1738-1804), who was born in England and became, somewhat fortuitously, an Anglican Priest in Maryland from 1770 to 1775, is well-known for his expression of traditionalist resistance to the American rebellion. Against the Lockean secular and contractualist view of government, he set the claims of "obedience for conscience' sake," defending Sir Robert Filmer's 17th-century patriarchal views and, like Burke, objecting to the sweeping aside of a proven establishment. He championed a stable, hierarchical society while claiming that of America was fluid and unstructured; thus, he came to occupy an intellectual blind alley. H. D. Jordan

847. Crary, Catherine S. THE HUMBLE IMMIGRANT AND THE AMERICAN DREAM: SOME CASE HISTORIES, 1746-1776. *Mississippi Valley Hist. R. 1959 46(1): 46-66.* A study of 30 Loyalist case histories which serve as a sampling of the economic opportunities and social upgrading of the humble immigrant to America just prior to the Revolution. Their stories, told to the British Crown as they applied for subsistence allowances, bear witness to the many avenues for self-advancement open to the industrious colonist, such as military bounties, the demand for gunsmiths, carpenters, and other labor, advantageous marriages, and land opportunities. Based primarily on the first eight volumes of the Loyalist Transcripts, the appeals for temporary support which preceded adjudication of claims for losses. Cases were selected which gave enough of the colonist's life story in America to evaluate the extent of economic and social advancement, if any, achieved through immigration to America. A

848. Evanson, Philip. JONATHAN BOUCHER: THE MIND OF AN AMERICAN LOYALIST. *Maryland Hist. Mag. 1963 58(2): 123-136.* Although he opposed the Stamp and Townshend Acts, Jonathan Boucher, an Anglican minister first in Virginia and later in Maryland, was an outspoken Loyalist during the American Revolution who had no use for the social compact theory of government or the tenets of republicanism and democracy. He returned to England in the fall of 1775. W. L. Fox

849. Fall, Ralph Emmett. THE REV. JONATHAN BOUCHER, TURBU-
LENT TORY (1738-1804). *Hist. Mag. of the Protestant Episcopal Church 1967
36(4): 323-356.* Sketches the English divine and philologist, with much attention
to his residence in Virginia and Maryland from 1759 to 1775. During this time
he served as tutor to John Parke Custis, stepson and ward of George Washington.
When the struggle between the Colonies and the mother country began, although
he felt much sympathy for the former, he opposed any resort to force. Compelled
to preach for six months in 1775 with loaded pistols in his pulpit, he finally bowed
to the growing hostility of his parishioners and sailed for England. In his final
sermon he vowed that no one should prevent him from praying and shouting
"God save the King." George III's government rewarded such loyalty with a
pension. In 1797 he published *A View of the Causes and Consequences of the
American Revolution* and dedicated it to George Washington, in the hope of
reconciling the two countries and the two former friends. Based on primary and
secondary sources, drawing upon Boucher's *Reminiscences of an American Loyalist, 1738-1789* (Port Washington, N.Y.: Kennkat Press, 1925), and his other
writings; 157 notes.   E. G. Roddy

850. Henderson, Patrick. SMALLPOX AND PATRIOTISM: THE NORFOLK
RIOTS, 1768-1769. *Virginia Mag. of Hist. and Biog. 1965 73(4): 413-424.* Argues
that the riots in Norfolk, Virginia, in 1768 and 1769 over smallpox inoculations
were "a convenient point of contention" between the Patriots (anti-inoculation-
ists) and Loyalists (pro-inoculationists). Documented.   K. J. Bauer

851. Keesey, Ruth M. LOYALISM IN BERGEN COUNTY, NEW JERSEY.
William and Mary Q. 1961 18(4): 558-576. An analysis of the prominent Tories
shows that the Loyalists were above the common level, but for the most part
neither large landholders nor public officials. The county's proximity to New
York and the natural inclination to maintain the status quo were incentives to
Loyalism. The confiscation of Loyalist estates did not democratize landholding
in Bergen County.   E. Oberholzer, Jr.

852. Launitz-Schurer, Leopold S., Jr. WHIG-LOYALISTS: THE DE LAN-
CEYS OF NEW YORK. *New-York Hist. Soc. Q. 1972 56(3): 178-198.* Because
they supported the unpopular side and left relatively few historical documents
(when compared with their more successful rivals, the Livingstons), the De
Lancey family has been neglected in studies of prerevolutionary New York.
During the disputes over the Stamp Act and later, the family was most prominent
and at times actually more influential than the Livingstons. However, the family
unsuccessfully attempted to oppose the First Continental Congress and lost support thereafter. When James De Lancey, leader of the family, left for England
in the spring of 1775, defeat of the family became obvious and most of its members
became active in opposition to the Revolution. Based largely on primary sources;
illus., 40 notes.   C. L. Grant   E. P. Stickney

853. Merritt, Bruce G. LOYALISM AND SOCIAL CONFLICT IN REVOLU-
TIONARY DEERFIELD, MASSACHUSETTS. *J. of Am. Hist. 1970 57(2):
277-289.* Finds social conflict to be the root difference between Revolutionary

Whigs and Loyalist Tories, but the conflict cannot be explained in terms of poor Whigs versus wealthy Tories. Rather, it was a case of agrarian Whigs versus commercial Tories. The Tory group contained a disproportionately small number of farmers, but its ranks included lowly artisans and successful professional men. The Revolutionary War adversely affected a number of the wealthy Tories, but also saw a financial decline of a number of prewar Whig leaders. Moreover, conservative political leaders were replaced by a "new breed of unheard citizens." The Williams family had dominated the county and town of Deerfield, benefitting from the power of Israel Williams. The power of this family had waned by the 1760's and the office-holding Tory elite was broken by the war. 38 notes.

K. B. West

854. Shelton, W. G. THE UNITED EMPIRE LOYALISTS: A RECONSIDER-ATION. *Dalhousie R. [Canada] 1965 45(1): 5-16.* The Loyalists have received little attention from serious historians. The formative period of their lives was spent in the American colonies and is regarded as part of U.S. history. Thus, the Loyalists who came to British North America are deprived of their past and much of their meaning. The result is a strange impression of one group called American Tories vanishing into well-deserved oblivion, and another group known as United Empire Loyalists suddenly emerging in the Canadian wilderness clutching their Union Jacks. Noted are the arguments of Loyalists during the American Revolution. The Loyalist was no more reactionary than the Whig but thought the dispute could be settled peacefully.

L. F. S. Upton

855. Williams, George H. WILLIAM EDDIS: WHAT THE SOURCES SAY. *Maryland Hist. Mag. 1965 60(2): 121-131.* A biographical account of the man who has given the best description of colonial and revolutionary Maryland. Eddis' most important work was *Letters from America, Historical and Descriptive; Comprising Occurrences from 1769 to 1777 Inclusive.* He served in several judicial and administrative posts for the British Government in Annapolis. The Revolution cut short his career and he returned to England. From 1780 to 1794 he petitioned the Royal Commission which was "charged with making a settlement of Loyalist claims." 47 notes.

D. H. Swift

856. Zimmer, Anne Young and Kelly, Alfred H. JONATHAN BOUCHER: CONSTITUTIONAL CONSERVATIVE. *J. of Am. Hist. 1972 58(4): 897-922.* Historians have depicted Boucher as an arch-reactionary, a divine-right Tory whose thought looked back to the 17th century. This does less than justice to his development from an ardent Virginia Whig to a lukewarm Conservative in Maryland to a high Tory in exile in England. This development may have taken place as a result of a change in his personal fortunes, but his real place in the development of American thought is as a legal conservative reminiscent of Edmund Burke. He venerated order and authority and repudiated rebellion, allowing only passive resistance to unjust laws. Boucher repudiated Locke's contract theory, but was in advance of his age in his more tolerant views on race and in his view of the state as a positive source of social progress. 115 notes.

K. B. West

857. —. [COPLEY'S PORTRAIT OF MRS. ROGER MORRIS]. *Winterthur Portfolio 1965 2: 1-26.*
Richardson, Edgar P. COPLEY'S PORTRAIT OF MRS. ROGER MORRIS I: COPLEY'S NEW YORK PORTRAITS, pp. 1-13. Covers ten Copley portraits completed during a six month visit to New York City, June to December 1771. The New York portraits of John Singleton Copley (1738-1815) have two major characteristics, "the portrait of elegance and the portrait of character." Copley's subjects in New York were from the upper aristrocratic class; many were to be Loyalists during the American Revolution. During the last six months of 1771 Copley was at the height of his powers. His grasp of character and economy of means of expression were never to be surpassed. The portraits give the viewer a feeling of personal acquaintance. Based on primary and secondary sources; 10 photos, 29 notes.
Simmons, Richard C. COPLEY'S PORTRAIT OF MRS. ROGER MORRIS II: MRS. MORRIS AND THE PHILIPSE FAMILY, AMERICAN LOYALISTS, pp. 14-26. The Philipse family, dating from 1653 or before, gained prominence in the Province of New York through large manorial holdings in Westchester County. Mary Philipse (1729-1825), once courted by George Washington, married Roger Morris, an English gentleman in the British Army in 1758. The Morrises played an active role in New York society until the Revolution. The Roger Morris Jumel Mansion (West 160th Street and Edgecombe Avenue) showed an advanced architectural taste for the pre-Revolutionary period. The mansion and Morris lands were confiscated as Tory property during the Revolution and later sold. Based on primary and secondary sources; 7 photos, 33 notes.

N. A. Kuntz

Posture & Role in the Revolution

858. Brown, Alan S. JAMES SIMPSON'S REPORTS ON THE CAROLINA LOYALISTS, 1779-1780. *J. of Southern Hist. 1955 21(4): 513-519.* Reproduces letters from Simpson to Lord George Germain, Secretary of State for American Development, and to Sir Henry Clinton, Commander-in-Chief of British Forces in America. These letters show what the British could expect from the inhabitants of the Carolinas if the British began a campaign to recover the Carolinas.

R. Kerley

859. Brown, Richard D. THE CONFISCATION AND DISPOSITION OF LOYALISTS' ESTATES IN SUFFOLK COUNTY, MASSACHUSETTS. *William and Mary Q. 1964 21(4): 534-550.* Attempts to examine the motivation and effects of the confiscation and disposition of Loyalist estates in Suffolk County, Massachusetts. Suffolk has special signifiance since the county lay in the heart of revolutionary activities. Indecision prevailed in regard to confiscation for several years after the first considerations in 1775. Confiscation bills were not

enacted until April 1779. The fiscal benefits of confiscation and disposition were of little consequence; the chief value was that of a political weapon to punish the Tories. H. M. Ward

860. Brown, Wallace. AMERICAN LOYALISTS IN BRITAIN. *Hist. Today [Great Britain] 1969 19(10): 672-678.* An account of the several thousand Loyalists who sought refuge in Britain during the American Revolution. Their reaction to Britain and in particular to London was ambivalent or disapproving. Overshadowed by disease, they formed emigrant communities, criticized the policies of George III and his ministers, and were ill at ease with the superciliousness, debauchery, and the class structure of British society. While some returned to America after the conclusion of the war, "those who remained had a negligible effect on English History." Portraits. L. A. Knafla

861. Cohen, Joel A. RHODE ISLAND LOYALISM AND THE AMERICAN REVOLUTION. *Rhode Island Hist. 1968 27(4): 97-112.* Describes the treatment of Loyalists, particularly the public and private pressures they endured from ostracism, loyalty oaths, and confiscation of property. Based on public records in the Rhode Island State Archives, and on town records, published documents, newspapers, and secondary accounts. P. J. Coleman

862. Coleman, John M. JOSEPH GALLOWAY AND THE BRITISH OCCUPATION OF PHILADELPHIA. *Pennsylvania Hist. 1963 30(3): 272-300.* Interprets Galloway's role as superintendent general in Philadelphia during the Revolutionary War. The central role of this office was commercial regulation to prevent the conveyance of "Necessaries to the Rebel Armies" and the misapplication of cargoes meant for the British forces. However, from the beginning, Galloway was more concerned with constitutional questions. A staunch Loyalist, he felt that constitutional union between America and the mother country could be achieved. When the British were forced to evacuate Philadelphia, Galloway and other Loyalists fled to England. His relationship with the British General Howe is discussed. Based on primary and secondary sources; 3 illus., 79 notes. M. J. McBaine

863. Crary, Catherine Snell. THE TORY AND THE SPY: THE DOUBLE LIFE OF JAMES RIVINGTON. *William and Mary Q. 1959 16(1): 61-72.* Relying chiefly on the memoirs of Allan McLane, an informant of George Washington, corroborates the statement in G. W. P. Custis' memoirs that Rivington was an American spy, furnishing DeGrasse (via McLane) with the code of the British fleet in time for the siege of Yorktown. After the evacuation of New York, Rivington continued to publish Tory propaganda as a cover for his espionage. E. Oberholzer, Jr.

864. Cuneo, John R. THE EARLY DAYS OF THE QUEEN'S RANGERS, AUGUST 1776—FEBRUARY 1777. *Military Affairs 1958 22(2): 65-74.* Describes the formation and early activities of the Loyalist "Queen's Rangers" under Major Robert Rogers, 1776-77. K. J. Bauer

865. Dean, David M., ed. THE END OF A SIEGE, A SILENT LOYALIST BECOMES A RELUCTANT PATRIOT: A LETTER FROM JOHN ANDREWS TO WILLIAM WHITE, DECEMBER 14, 1779. *Pennsylvania Hist. 1970 37(4): 381-386.* John Andrews (1746-1813), an Anglican minister, was rector of a parish and operated a school in Queen Anne's County, Maryland, when the American Revolution began. While he did not actively work against the Revolution, he refused to support it. Due to his Loyalist sentiments he eventually lost his parish and found it necessary to remove to York, Pennsylvania, where he opened a school. In this letter to Reverend William White, Andrews complained of the Pennsylvania Test Act and the difficulties he suffered due to his attachment to the British Crown. To avoid further persecution and to assure his ability to support his family, he reluctantly gave his allegiance to the Congress of the United States. The letter was found in White's correspondence, located in the Church Historical Society, Austin, Texas. 12 notes.   D. C. Swift

866. Gandy, Willard E. THE COLONISTS WHO WOULDN'T REBEL. *Social Educ. 1963 27(7): 385-389.* Briefly summarizes the history of the Loyalists during the American Revolution. Based exclusively on standard secondary sources.   M. Small

867. Klyberg, Albert T. ARMED LOYALISTS AS SEEN BY AMERICAN HISTORIANS. *New Jersey Hist. Soc. Pro. 1964 82(2): 101-108.* Understandably, the most pro-Loyalist position has been taken by the United Empire Loyalists. In 1895 Moses Coit Tyler compared the revolutionists to the Confederates and the Loyalists to the supporters of the Union. In 1901 Flick described in detail the Loyalists of New York, and in 1902 Van Tyne discussed the strengths and weaknesses of the Loyalists. Recently we have a group of historians who describe their military activities, previously overlooked. The definitive work in this category is a 1962 doctoral thesis by Paul H. Smith (University of Michigan) who explains much of the bitterness of the rebellion turned civil war. A review article which also cites the works of other historians.   E. P. Stickney

868. Lambert, Robert S. THE FLIGHT OF THE GEORGIA LOYALISTS. *Georgia R. 1963 17(4): 435-448.* Traces the plight, flight and efforts of the Georgia Loyalists to keep body and soul together during the American Revolution. Case studies are presented in several instances. Undocumented.   H. G. Earnhart

869. Lawson, John L. THE "REMARKABLE MYSTERY" OF JAMES RIVINGTON, "SPY." *Journalism Q. 1958 35(3): 317-323, 394.* Critically examines the myth that the Tory editor James Rivington was permitted to remain unpunished in New York after the close of the American Revolution because he had been a spy for George Washington. Scholars have failed to find any valid documentary evidence to support the myth. Some patriot spies gleaned information from Rivington's newspaper and possibly he was unwittingly used by Washington's espionage agents. The author suggests that it was probably the tradition of respect for newspaper editors that enabled Rivington and other Tory editors to get preferred treatment.   L. Gara

870. Lynd, Staughton. WHO SHOULD RULE AT HOME? DUTCHESS COUNTY, NEW YORK, IN THE AMERICAN REVOLUTION. *William and Mary Q. 1961 18(3): 330-359.* Shows that the contemporaries of the Revolution were aware that the Revolution also involved the question of rule at home. Pre-revolutionary Dutchess County was a hierarchical community favoring the rich. The confiscation and sale of Loyalist estates led to a redistribution of land, which was "the first major break-through of the independence struggle into social change" and culminated in the end of the feudal society.

E. Oberholzer, Jr.

871. Maguire, James H. "ELISIUM AND THE WILDS": A LOYALIST'S ACCOUNT OF EXPERIENCES IN AMERICA AT THE BEGINNING OF THE AMERICAN REVOLUTION. *Hist. New Hampshire 1971 26(4): 31-44.* Edward Parry came to Portsmouth, New Hampshire, in 1771 as mast agent for the British navy. In the spring of 1775 he was arrested as a Tory in Georgetown, Maine, and his land and logs all were confiscated eventually. He had jointed the "Tory Associators of Portsmouth" in January 1775 and had connections with Tory tea consignees and counterfeiters. Assigned to live with Capt. Timothy Parker of Sturbridge (25 August 1775 to 13 July 1776), he was paroled back to Portsmouth, shipped in January 1777 to Halifax in exchange for John Langdon's sister. He reached England on 23 August 1777. Selections from his 1775-77 journal show patriot opinion, family customs, and some of his Loyalist associations. 9 notes.

T. D. S. Bassett

872. Monahon, Clifford P. and Collins, Clarkson A., III, eds. A LETTER FROM WILLIAM ELLERY TO HENRY MARCHANT. *Rhode Island Hist. 1965 24(2): 49-54.* Describes the Tory domination of a Newport town meeting in November 1775. Original in the Rhode Island Historical Society, Providence.

P. J. Coleman

873. Nye, Wilbur S. AFTERMATH OF MOORE'S CREEK: PLIGHT OF THE TORIES. *Am. Hist. Illus. 1970 4(9): 16-19.* The Tories of North Carolina were for a time cowed. The Whigs gave them a hard time. Many Tories lost their property, and some lost their lives. Gives in full the claim of Alexander Morrison, a plantation owner, against the British Government, submitted in 1783 for reimbursement of property losses suffered by reason of service for the Crown. Illus.

E. P. Stickney

874. Olson, Gary D. THOMAS BROWN, LOYALIST PARTISAN, AND THE REVOLUTIONARY WAR IN GEORGIA, 1777-1782. *Georgia Hist. Q. 1970 54(1): 1-19, and 54(2): 183-208.* Part I. Details British efforts to defeat the rebellious Colonies in the South. To this end the British Governor of East Florida, Patrick Tonyn, directed the activities of a small provincial garrison, friendly Indians, and Loyalist refugees from Georgia and the Carolinas. Planter Thomas Brown became a leader of Tory exiles, worked closely with Tonyn, led "Brown's rangers" on border raids into Georgia, and made several efforts to organize backcountry Loyalists as a fighting force. He also gathered military intelligence for the British. These efforts generally had few positive

results, for overall British military strategy failed in the South and reports of Loyalist sympathies of the backcountry residents were mistaken. Based mainly on military correspondence; 44 notes. Part II. Details the British efforts to subdue the rebellious Southern Colonies. "Brown's Rangers" was composed of Loyalists and Creek and Cherokee Indians. After the surrender of Charlestown to the British, Brown was sent into Cumberland to stem the flow of western volunteers to the rebels. Returning, he assumed the defense of Savannah. Later, going to East Florida, he aided in the British evacuation and cession to Spain. An extreme Loyalist, Brown migrated to the Bahamas where he became a planter and was active in politics until his death in 1825. Documented from military correspondence and area histories; 67 notes.   R. A. Mohl

875. Reubens, Beatrice G. PRE-EMPTIVE RIGHTS IN THE DISPOSITION OF A CONFISCATED ESTATE: PHILIPSBURGH MANOR, NEW YORK. *William and Mary Q. 1965 22(3): 435-456.* Supports the theory that confiscation of Loyalist estates was a significant social reform set off by the American Revolution. The New York law of 1779 permitted attainted as well as patriot tenants on confiscatory lands to have the first right to purchase farms on which they resided. About 80 percent of the new owners of Philipsburgh Manor (Philipse Manor) were small farmers; most of these had been tenants. Land reform was not widespread because patriot manor lords could keep their estates intact. Statistical tables on purchasers of Philipsburgh Manor.   H. M. Ward

876. Riccards, Michael P. PATRIOTS AND PLUNDERERS: CONFISCATION OF LOYALIST LANDS IN NEW JERSEY 1776-1786. *New Jersey Hist. 1968 86(1): 14-28.* Discusses the history of laws aimed at confiscating Loyalist lands in New Jersey during 1776-86. The financial windfall expected from these lands never reached the State treasury due to corruption, inflation, and currency manipulation. Challenges the thesis of John Franklin Jameson's 1940 *The American Revolution Considered as A Social Movement* (Princeton, N.J.: Princeton U. Press) which states that "American social democracy was a result of confiscation." Other influences than land confiscation made New Jersey more democratic after the American Revolution. 65 notes.   T. H. Brown

877. Roberts, William I., III. THE LOSSES OF A LOYALIST MERCHANT IN GEORGIA DURING THE REVOLUTION. *Georgia Hist. Q. 1968 52(3): 270-276.* Reveals the disrupting influence of the American Revolution upon the normal course of colonial commerce. William Moss, agent and commission merchant in Savannah for Liverpool businessmen, established a prosperous business between 1772 and 1775. The imposition of the Continental Association brought a suspension of British and West Indian trade. Goods imported by Moss were confiscated, and the boycott prevented him from exporting remittances to his Liverpool correspondents. Similarly, radical control of the courts prevented new suits against debtors and executions of previous judgments; thus, many of Moss's customers refused to pay their debts. Moss abandoned the colony early in 1776 with total losses above 9,000 pounds. Based upon research in depositions and other documents filed with the Board of Commissioners on American Claims in 1787; 19 notes.   R. A. Mohl

878. Robertson, Heard. NOTES ON THE MUSTER ROLLS OF THE KING'S RANGERS. *Richmond County Hist. 1972 4(1): 5-15.* Studies a contingent of southern Loyalist soldiers during the American Revolution. The King's Rangers, first organized in 1776 as the East Florida Rangers, and later as the King's Carolina Rangers, served the British primarily in Florida and Georgia. Under the leadership of Lieutenant Colonel Thomas Brown, the King's Rangers twice captured Augusta, Georgia, first in 1779 and then in 1780. Reproduces Brown's muster-roll lists from 25 April to 24 June 1781. Based on recently discovered muster-roll lists in the Public Archives of Canada; illus., 21 notes.

H. R. Grant

879. Smith, Paul H. THE AMERICAN LOYALISTS: NOTES ON THEIR ORGANIZATION AND NUMERICAL STRENGTH. *William and Mary Q. 1968 24(2): 259-277.* Evaluates the problems of ascertaining the number of Loyalists during the Revolution. Muster rolls, military pay warrants, and other records are examined to determine the number of provincials serving as militia and regulars in the British Army. An estimated 19 thousand of 21 thousand men who saw service in provincial corps were Loyalists. Table, 27 notes.

H. M. Ward

880. Snoddy, Oliver. THE VOLUNTEERS OF IRELAND. *Irish Sword [Ireland] 1965 7(27): 147-159.* During the American Revolution, several hundred Irish in the colonies joined the Volunteers of Ireland founded by Sir Henry Clinton. Their participation in the Battle of Camden, problems of discipline, and the use of the volunteers by Charles Cornwallis are discussed. Biographic sketches of two officers, John Doyle and Welbore Ellis Doyle, are provided. Two rolls of the unit, one taken on Christmas 1778 and the second on 1 October 1782, are included.

H. L. Calkin

881. Teeter, Dwight L. "KING" SEARS, THE MOB AND FREEDOM OF THE PRESS IN NEW YORK, 1765-76. *Journalism Q. 1964 41(4): 539-544.* Isaac "King" Sears, a New York merchant and ship captain, led mob attacks on Tory newspaper offices on four different occasions, twice against the well-known printer, James Rivington (whom he ultimately forced out of business). He headed a mob which kidnaped a prominent Tory clergyman-pamphleteer, the Rev. Samuel Seabury. One of his attacks was upon the shop of Samuel Loudon, known in journalism history as a patriot printer, even though he printed a pamphlet in answer to Thomas Paine's *Common Sense.* Sears' activities suggest something of the power of the mob at the beginning of the American Revolution. He personified a thesis presented in Leonard W. Levy's *Legacy of Suppression* (Cambridge, Massachusetts, 1960) that the Revolution, instead of establishing freedom of the press, almost extinguished it.

S. E. Humphreys

882. Vernon-Jackson, H. O. A LOYALIST'S WIFE: LETTERS OF MRS. PHILIP VAN CORTLANDT, 1776-77. *Hist. Today [Great Britain] 1964 14(8): 574-580.* Extracts from four letters (without commentary) of a wife of a lieutenant-colonel in the New Jersey Brigade, December 1776-February 1777. The letters contain social tid-bits. The author is a descendant.

L. A. Knafla

Postwar Status:
Readjustment or Exodus

883. Baker, Donald S. CHARLES WESLEY AND THE AMERICAN LOY-ALISTS. *Pro. of the Wesley Hist. Soc. [Great Britain] 1965 35(1): 5-9.* Covers the period after the peace of 1783 and illustrates Wesley's attitude by reference to his poems "Hymns on Patriotism," in particular "The Testimony of the American Loyalists, 1783." Wesley was horrified at the seemingly callous treatment by the British Government of the American Loyalists, whose position after the peace of 1783 was at least difficult. During the political battle which ensued the fortunes of the Loyalists fluctuated with the changes in the tide of battle. Finally many Loyalists died and their cause was lost. Wesley's attitudes, colored by his High Church Toryism, whether right or wrong, emphasized the plight of those who suffered as a result of the struggle. 13 notes.   L. Brown

884. Butterfield, L. H. NEW LIGHT ON THE NORTH ATLANTIC TRIAN-GLE IN THE 1780'S. *William and Mary Q. 1964 21(4): 596-606.* A review article of *The Diary and Selected Papers of Chief Justice William Smith, 1784-1793. Volume I: The Diary, January 24, 1784 to October 5, 1785,* L. F. S. Upton, ed. (Toronto: The Champlain Society, 1963). This is a newly "recovered" diary of a New York Tory, later of Quebec, who left with the British evacuation of New York City by General Sir Guy Carleton. Under Carleton, Smith's mission was to urge the colonization of Canada by Tories and English settlers, with a hope of regaining the former colonies, now the United States, and to counter French influence. The diary sheds much light on Anglo-American diplomacy (especially concerning Smith's encounters with the American minister, John Adams) and English political and social life.   H. M. Ward

885. Crary, Catherine S. THE AMERICAN DREAM: JOHN TABOR KEM-PE'S RISE FROM POVERTY TO RICHES. *William and Mary Q. 1957 14(2): 176-195.* Attorney General Kempe of New York (1759-82) acquired 163,000 acres within a decade, most of it for a purely nominal consideration. Making the most of his position, Kempe had the information, the connections, and the influence to get what he wanted without going outside the law. His Loyalism, however, was disastrous, and he recovered from the British Government less than 10 percent of the value lost. Based on colonial records and Kempe's papers.
E. Oberholzer, Jr.

886. Fingard, Judith. THE ESTABLISHMENT OF THE FIRST COLONIAL EPISCOPATE. *Dalhousie R. [Canada] 1967 47(4): 475-491.* Examines the decision to establish the first English colonial episcopate in Nova Scotia in 1787. The American Revolution had shown how uncontrolled religious dissent could bolster political unrest and had convinced the British Government that a strong Church of England in the remaining British North American colonies would be a bulwark of authority. Further, the creation of Anglican bishops in the United States had

left the British North American colonies in a rather anomalous position without a bishop of their own. Charles Inglis, a Loyalist exile from New York, was consecrated the first Bishop of Nova Scotia whose diocese included all of British North America. The office was, however, shorn of all temporal or civil authority and limited strictly to ecclesiastical functions. 35 notes. L. F. S. Upton

887. Fingerhut, Eugene R. USES AND ABUSES OF THE AMERICAN LOY-ALISTS' CLAIMS: A CRITIQUE OF QUANTITATIVE ANALYSES. *William and Mary Q. 1968 24(2): 245-258.* Asserts that the transcripts of the manuscript books and papers of the British Parliament's Commission of Enquiry into the Losses and Services of the American Loyalists used in various histories are too limited for a quantitative study of Loyalist personnel. Many kinds of properties were not considered by the commission and petitions were not statistically representative of the Loyalists. Considering fraudulent claims, misrepresentation, and the many emigrants not applying for claims, this source does not yield valid quantitative data. 2 charts, 26 notes. H. M. Ward

888. Hoffman, Philip G. AUSTRALIA'S DEBT TO THE AMERICAN REVOLUTION. *Historian 1955 17(2): 143-156.* The outbreak of the American Revolution created two problems which led to the settlement of New South Wales, the nucleus of Australia. The need for a colony to receive convicts and displaced Loyalists led to British settlement at a time when the French were seriously considering Australian colonization. James Matra, an American Loyalist, is given credit for the colonization plan that was followed by the Pitt Ministry. E. C. Johnson

889. Lamb, J. William. WILLIAM LOSEE: ONTARIO'S PIONEER METHODIST MISSIONARY. *Bull. of the United Church of Can. 1969 (21): 28-47.* Discusses the missionary career of Losee (1757-1832), the first regularly appointed Methodist missionary to serve in Canada west of the Maritimes. A native of Dutchess County, New York, Losee supported the British during the American Revolution and went to Nova Scotia in 1783 as a United Empire Loyalist. While there he converted to Methodism. In 1789 the Methodist Episcopal Church sent him to the Lake Champlain circuit as a lay preacher. He soon crossed into Canada, however, and visited the Loyalist settlements along the St. Lawrence around Adolphustown, many of whose residents also came from Dutchess County. As a result he was allowed to form a circuit in Canada, and returned to the Adolphustown area in February 1791. Losee returned to New York after establishing Methodism in that area for four years. His departure was occasioned by a mental breakdown caused by his failure to win the hand of Elizabeth Detlor, who instead married Darius Dunham, Losee's assistant in Upper Canada. Based on primary and secondary sources; 51 notes. B. D. Tennyson

890. Lambert, Robert S. CONFISCATION OF LOYALIST PROPERTY IN GEORGIA, 1782-1786. *William and Mary Q. 1963 20(1): 80-94.* The confiscation law of 1778, designed to restore public finances, could not be executed until 1782, and then it proved difficult to dispose of the confiscated land. Once the law

was in effect, its harsher features were removed. Confiscation was no financial panacea for the state, and there is no evidence that it resulted in any significant redistribution of property to landless Whigs.   E. Oberholzer, Jr.

891. Lower, Arthur. LOYALIST CITIES. *Queen's Q. [Canada] 1966 72(4): 657-664.* Comparison between Saint John, New Brunswick, and Kingston, Ontario, as two cities founded in the same year for Loyalist refugees from the American Revolution and now of the same size and with a common deficiency in local pride. Kingston, less ingrown, is changing more rapidly.

M. Abrash

892. Norton, Mary Beth. JOHN RANDOLPH'S "PLAN OF ACCOMMODATIONS." *William and Mary Q. 1971 28(1): 103-120.* John Randolph (ca. 1727-84) of Virginia, a Loyalist, in 1780 proposed a plan for governing the Colonies after an anticipated British victory. Randolph recommended limiting the power of Parliament over the Colonies, abolishing the Board of Customs Commissioners, and allowing the Colonists free trade with Spanish America. Randolph suggested reorganization of the imperial system, and urged the British to encourage diversity in relations among the Colonies. Reproduces the plan. 28 notes.

H. M. Ward

893. Peters, Thelma. [LOYALISTS IN THE BAHAMA ISLANDS]. *Florida Hist. Q.*

THE LOYALIST MIGRATION FROM EAST FLORIDA TO THE BAHAMA ISLANDS, 1961 40(2): 123-141. During the American Revolution some twelve thousand new residents, mostly Loyalists, entered East Florida. The peace settlement in 1783 delivering Florida to Spain was to them a calamity, and some four to seven thousand of them migrated to the Bahama Islands with considerable assistance from Britain. Based on Spanish and British official records, genealogical records, personal papers, and secondary works.

THE AMERICAN LOYALISTS IN THE BAHAMA ISLANDS: WHO THEY WERE, 1962 40(3): 226-240. Discusses the Loyalists who went to Florida to escape the wrath of the American Patriots. When Spain acquired Florida in 1783 these Loyalists moved to the Bahama Islands, playing an important role in the government and economy of the islands. Based on British official records, genealogical records, personal papers, newspapers, and secondary works.

G. L. Lycan

894. Rawlyk, George A. THE GUYSBOROUGH NEGROES: A STUDY IN ISOLATION. *Dalhousie R. [Canada] 1968 48(1): 24-36.* The "Loyalist Negroes" who settled in Nova Scotia after the American Revolution, received poor land in remote areas and were subject to discrimination by whites, but by the second generation the survivors had come to grips with the Nova Scotia environment. A handful of leaders appeared, notably Thomas Brownspriggs, one of the original settlers at Tracadie, followed by Dempsey Jordan, both schoolteachers. The Negroes were largely ignored by the Roman Catholic Church and the Anglicans but became an object of concern for Methodists and Baptists. The census report

of 1871 is used to assess the position of the Negroes in Guysborough County, when their numbers stood at 747. The author comments on education provided for Negroes between 1790 and 1940. 19 notes.   L. F. S. Upton

895. Talman, James J. ONTARIO: A PRODUCT OF THE AMERICAN REV-OLUTION. *Hist. Mag. of the Protestant Episcopal Church 1968 37(2): 129-134.* Sketches the history of American "Loyalists" who crossed into Canada during or after the Revolutionary War. This was the main address at the meeting of the Corporate Communion of Anglican Historians held during the convention of the American Historical Association in Toronto 29 December 1967. 8 notes, primary and secondary.   E. G. Roddy

896. Wright, J. Leitch, Jr. LORD DUNMORE'S LOYALIST ASYLUM IN THE FLORIDAS. *Florida Hist. Q. 1971 49(4): 370-379.* Investigation into the motives of Lord John Murray (1732-1809), fourth Earl of Dunmore, in accepting the governorship of the Bahamas in 1787 sheds light on British policy after the American Revolution. Concerned over the fate of Loyalists, Dunmore attempted to gain British governmental authorization to launch a campaign against Spanish-held West Florida in 1782, so that a refuge for Loyalists might be established in the Floridas and Louisiana. Most active promoters of a campaign against the Spaniards were Dunmore's fellow land speculators. Some four million acres of land he claimed (most of it in the Ohio Valley) had been confiscated by the rebels. His reasoning was that a Loyalist colony in the lower Mississippi Valley could aid in gradually regaining the area from there to Canada for Britain. When the final peace treaty was signed, allowing Spain to retain West Florida, Dunmore decided to make the Bahamas his Loyalist base. As governor of the islands, he encouraged Loyalist expeditions to the mainland, the most outstanding of which was that by William Augustus Bowles. He also entertained and gave presents and commissions to various southern Indian delegations and attempted to trade di-rectly with these Indians without going through Spanish authorities. During the 1793-96 British-Spanish alliance, Dunmore's plea for special trading concessions was rejected by the Spanish, who had good reason for distrusting him. His recall in 1796 ended his scheme for setting up a Loyalist-Indian state in the Old Southwest. Based partly on unpublished letters and official documents; 23 notes.   R. V. Calvert

9

THE CONFEDERATION: UNDER THE FIRST CONSTITUTION

General

897. Bruce, James Wakefield. THE GREAT SEAL OF THE UNITED STATES. *Mankind 1969 2(1): 16-19.* The Great Seal, symbolic of American sovereignty, is used on state documents to certify official government acts. Seals date back to ancient times. On the day the Declaration of Independence was signed, Benjamin Franklin, John Adams, and Thomas Jefferson were appointed to name a seal for the new United States. This committee and two succeeding ones, however, failed to complete the task of finding an acceptable design. Finally Charles Thomson, the Secretary of Congress, prepared a design based on his study of all three reports. After some modifications his seal was accepted by Congress and written into law in 1782. Illus. A. H. Pfeiffer

898. Crane, Verner W. FRANKLIN'S "THE INTERNAL STATE OF AMERICA" (1786). *William and Mary Q. 1958 15(2): 214-227.* Following an introduction, presents the text of Benjamin Franklin's article. The significance of this statement, hitherto overlooked, is that it shows Franklin's optimistic appraisal of the "critical period." Its purpose was to remonstrate against the reports of the English press concerning economic dislocations in the post-Revolutionary period. E. Oberholzer, Jr.

899. Henderson, James H. CONSTITUTIONALISTS AND REPUBLICANS IN THE CONTINENTAL CONGRESS, 1778-1786. *Pennsylvania Hist. 1969 36(2): 119-144.* Using bloc analysis of the voting of the Pennsylvania delegations to the Continental Congress from 1778 to 1786, the author examines the interplay of State and national politics. Between 1778 and 1780, the delegation was dominated by the Constitutionalists who supported the radical State constitution of 1776. Conservatives (or Republicans) dominated the delegation for the next four years. The Constitutionalists recaptured the delegation in 1785-86. Constitutionalists tended to vote with New Englanders while Conservatives were inclined to

ally with the South. These shifts in voting patterns reveal that Pennsylvania had the most highly developed party system in the United States. While political patterns within the States influenced national politics, the author emphasizes the importance of ideological issues of national importance in determining voting behavior and alignments in Congress. Illus., 2 tables, 28 notes.

D. C. Swift

900. Hough, Samuel. CASTIGLIONI'S VISIT TO RHODE ISLAND. *Rhode Island Hist. 1967 26(2): 53-64.* An annotated translation of relevant sections of the two-volume work by Luigi Castiglioni, *Viaggio negli Stati Uniti dell'America Settentrionale fatto negli anni, 1785, 1786 e 1787...con alcune osservazioni sui vegetabili piu utili de quel paese* published in Milan in 1790. The volumes cover several individual States and the Federal Government. P. J. Coleman

901. Johnson, Herbert A. TOWARD A REAPPRAISAL OF THE "FED-ERAL" GOVERNMENT: 1783-1789. *Am. J. of Legal Hist. 1964 8(4): 314-325.* Criticizing the paucity and lack of thoroughness of the study of the constitutional development of the period of the Confederation, the author suggests areas of needed study and points out what he considers important developments in the period. His emphasis in this latter area is upon the organization of executive departments in 1781. N. Brockman

902. McColley, Robert. JEFFERSON'S RIVALS: THE SHIFTING CHARAC-TER OF THE FEDERALISTS. *MidContinent Am. Studies J. 1968 9(1): 23-33.* Traces the background of the Federalist Party by showing three phases of its history clearly marked by varying degrees of philosophy and contrasts in membership. The first period, 1785 to 1789, is referred to as the "nationalistic" period because the major concern of the Federalists at that time was foreign relations. The "Washingtonian Federalism," from 1789 to 1800, was highlighted by the superior political administration of George Washington in terms of his balanced approach to economic interdependence between the sections, and his positive neutralism in foreign affairs. From 1800 to 1815 "Reactionary Federalism" is the theme that epitomizes the sectional, elitist policies of the Federalists during their years of political decline. Many Federalists would, however, survive the demise of their party and contribute to the national interest as Republicans, Whigs, or moderates. Based on primary and secondary sources; 15 notes.

B. M. Morrison

903. Morris, Richard B. THE CONFEDERATION PERIOD AND THE AMERICAN HISTORIAN. *William and Mary Q. 1956 13(2): 139-156.* A historiographical and critical essay. The differences between the Federalist (Bancroft, Fiske, McMaster, and partly McLaughlin) and the anti-Federalist (J. A. Smith, Charles A. Beard, Merrill Jensen) schools of historiography hinge not so much on the interpretation of the "critical period" as on their views of the Revolution. The writer rejects the position that the Revolution was a democratic movement which was aborted by the Federalist triumph, but he believes that the adoption of Federalism was a more radical act than the winning of independence.

E. Oberholzer, Jr.

904. Nichols, Marie A. THE EVOLUTION OF THE ARTICLES OF CON-FEDERATION, 1775-1781. *Southern Q. 1964 2(4): 307-340.* The Articles developed from separate plans drawn by Benjamin Franklin and John Dickinson for a political union of the colonies. A draft of the Articles was presented to the Continental Congress in July 1776, was subjected to point-by-point scrutiny and underwent many changes before it was adopted in November 1777. Land speculation in the "landless" states played an important part in delaying ratification by the states until the lands north of the Ohio were ceded to Congress, which body would be easier to treat with than legislatures jealous of the interests of their own citizens in the western lands.   D. A. Stokes

905. Ola, Opeyemi. CONFEDERAL SYSTEMS: A COMPARATIVE ANAL-YSIS. *Civilisations [Belgium] 1968 18(2): 270-284.* A discussion of confederation in Germany, Switzerland, and the United States from 1774 to 1871. The author discusses the origins of these confederations, their structure and functions, operational problems, and the transition from confederation to federalism. 56 notes.
H. L. Calkin

906. Rorer, Henry S. JUDGE CYRUS GRIFFIN. *Virginia Cavalcade 1964 14(3): 22-27.* A biography of Cyrus Griffin, president of Congress under the Articles of Confederation and judge of the first national court. Illus.
R. B. Lange

907. Sifton, Paul G. OTTO'S MEMOIRE TO VERGENNES, 1785. *William and Mary Q. 1965 22(4): 626-645.* After six years of residence in the United States as secretary to the French minister to the United States, Chevalier Louis-Guillaume Otto describes diverse aspects of American life. Of particular interest are Otto's observations on the Confederation government, the need for a French commercial entente with the United States, and the problems of American expansion and sectionalism. He also comments on the relations of the United States with foreign countries in general. The *Mémoire* is reproduced here.
H. M. Ward

908. Treacy, Kenneth W. THE OLMSTEAD CASE, 1778-1809. *Western Pol. Q. 1957 10(3): 675-691.* Traces the history of one of the first legal battles over States' rights and Federal-State relations in the United States.   H. Kantor

Domestic Problems, Programs, & Affairs

909. Bjork, Gordon C. THE WEANING OF THE AMERICAN ECONOMY: INDEPENDENCE, MARKET CHANGES, AND ECONOMIC DEVELOPMENT. *J. of Econ. Hist. 1964 24(4): 541-566.* Sketches the U.S. economy during the Confederation period, but concentrates on the statistics of foreign commerce.

The author concludes that "the fortunes of the United States were 'less gloomy than has been imagined'; that there was a modest increase in the value of American exports in the postwar period and [that] the terms of trade were certainly much more favorable than they had been prior to the Revolution." Albert Fishlow, the discussant, comments on the author's statistical evidence and suggests the need for more work on the internal economy.   E. Feldman

910. Clark, William Bell. INSTRUCTIONS TO CAPTAIN JOHN GREEN, COMMANDER OF THE *EMPRESS OF CHINA,* FOR THE FIRST VOYAGE TO CHINA OF A SHIP CARRYING THE AMERICAN FLAG. *Am. Neptune 1954 14(4): 298-299.* The instructions, dated 25 January 1784, recently found, are in the handwriting of Daniel Parker and concern the pioneer trip to Canton. The instructions are printed here in full, and consist of general directives to the captain about provisions, port agents and supercargoes. The ship arrived in Macao on 23 August 1784.   J. Erickson

911. Coughlin, Sister Magdalen. THE ENTRANCE OF THE MASSACHUSETTS MERCHANT INTO THE PACIFIC. *Southern California Q. 1966 48(4): 327-352.* When Massachusetts merchants lost the British West Indian trade after the American Revolution, the base of their economy was struck and they desperately searched for new markets. The new government under the Articles of Confederation encouraged them to pursue commerce in the Orient. The sailing of the *Empress of China* from Boston in February 1784 represented this Yankee thrust into the China trade, although it was not actually the first penetration of Far Eastern commerce by Americans. There had been individual examples earlier. The new American-Chinese trade depended, however, upon Americans' finding something of value on the Oriental market to exchange for Chinese goods. This new demand drew Massachusetts merchants to the Northwest coast of North America where furs promised a solution to the problem. Boston merchants dominated this three-cornered trade in furs from the Northwest, Chinese goods, and merchandise from New England to exchange for furs. Later, the economic roots planted on the west coast by New Englanders led to diplomatic pressure and eventually to acquisition of the area. Based on primary and secondary sources; 104 notes.   W. L. Bowers

912. Cross, Francis E. NOOTKA SOUND: WINTER, 1788-89. *Am. Neptune 1955 15(3): 205-213.* The first American flag vessels to enter the Pacific Ocean were the ship *Columbia* and the sloop *Washington,* sailing from Boston, 1 October 1787. The voyage took them to Friendly Cove, Nootka Sound, where the Commodore decided to spend the winter, less for reasons of distress or inclement weather than from a wish to convert the sloop into a brigantine. By the spring, the converted *Washington* was ready to sail. Details of this stay are provided from comments and extracts from notes and journals.   J. Erickson

913. Dorsey, Rhoda M. THE PATTERN OF BALTIMORE COMMERCE DURING THE CONFEDERATION PERIOD. *Maryland Hist. Mag. 1967 62(2): 119-134.* Traces the growth of wheat and flour exports in Baltimore during the Confederation period. Lists all ships that entered and left the port between

1780 and 1787. Gives vessel names, captains, tonnage, size of crews, points of departure, places of registration, and cargoes. Despite the large amount of trading, Baltimore was still a small trading center compared to Philadelphia, New York, and Boston. Baltimore had close ties to Philadelphia banks and business firms. 27 notes.   D. H. Swift

914. Dos Passos, John. ROBERT MORRIS AND THE "ART MAGIC." *Am. Heritage 1956 7(6): 86-89, 113-115.* In 1781 Morris assumed control of American finances in a period of currency chaos which made bookkeeping nearly impossible. Such conditions inevitably gave rise to questions concerning Morris' integrity. Morris used his bank to stabilize the currency; notes on his bank were sounder than the Continental currency. His own finances were bound up with those of the American nation; manipulations had risen to tenuous heights, and postwar depression endangered Morris' own investments. By 1797 he was ruined and in danger of arrest. The next year he entered a debtor's prison and remained there until the passage of a bankruptcy law in 1801. Undocumented; illus.
C. R. Allen, Jr.

915. Holmes, Oliver W. SHALL STAGECOACHES CARRY THE MAIL?— A DEBATE OF THE CONFEDERATION PERIOD. *William and Mary Q. 1963 20(4): 555-573.* Shows that Congress decided to have stagecoaches carry the mails largely in order to encourage intercourse among sections. The British precedent of 1784 did not influence the decision which created friction between Congress and Postmaster General Ebenezer Hazard. Congress desired to serve the public interest, while Hazard sought to operate the post office in a businesslike manner. He found stagecoaches inexpedient and expensive.
E. Oberholzer, Jr.

916. Knight, Russell W. GENERAL GLOVER BATTLES A "TEMPORAL CURSE." *Essex Inst. Hist. Collections 1965 101(2): 116-120.* Outlines the various efforts of General John Glover of Marblehead, Massachusetts to restore his fortune and that of his town following the American Revolution. Reprints a letter dated 17 March 1783 from Glover to General Benjamin Lincoln. Glover's efforts were ultimately successful, and he recouped much of his loss.
J. M. Bumsted

917. Kohn, Richard H. THE INSIDE HISTORY OF THE NEWBURGH CONSPIRACY: AMERICA AND THE COUP D'ETAT. *William and Mary Q. 1970 27(2): 187-220.* Views the conspiracy as a nationalist intrigue. The plot was several years in the making, over discontent with Congress' handling of affairs relating to the military—especially over pay and delay in adoption of commutation. By carefully examining each stage in the development of the plot, responsibility is largely fixed on General Horatio Gates and nationalists in Congress; the Army was used as a tool. The plot itself did not aim at a coup d'etat but, if it had succeeded, it could have led to one. 100 notes.   H. M. Ward

918. Myer, Max W., Mrs. CHARLES GRATIOT'S LAND CLAIM PROB-LEMS. *Bull. of the Missouri Hist. Soc. 1965 21(3): 237-244.* Presents, through the problems of Gratiot, a merchant and leading citizen of St. Louis, the difficulties, obscurities, and dishonesty that characterized some of the land warrant business of the post-Revolution period. Gratiot took land warrants in payment for services to Virginia during the Revolution, warrants out of which he was subsequently cheated. An editorial introduction accompanies an 1815 letter from Gratiot to a Mr. Keen seeking to locate his missing warrants or the land grants based thereon. 24 notes. R. J. Hanks

919. Nash, Gary B. WILLIAM CHURCHILL HOUSTON PAPERS. *Princeton U. Lib. Chronicle 1965 26(2): 119-122.* Princeton University Library has received the papers of William Churchill Houston relating to his position as receiver of Continental taxes in New Jersey from 1782 to 1785. There are weekly reports to Robert Morris, accounts of county tax quotas and taxes collected, receipts, and miscellaneous letters. "Taken together, the materials provide...a rather exact picture of the fiscal operations by which the Continental Congress, at the conclusion of the war and during the first years of peace, attempted to brake the headlong decline of the national finances and restore equilibrium, both political and economic, to the exhausted and badly divided nation." D. Brockway

920. Olson, Gary D. THE SODERSTROM INCIDENT: A REFLECTION UPON FEDERAL-STATE RELATIONS UNDER THE ARTICLES OF CONFEDERATION. *New-York Hist. Soc. Q. 1971 55(2): 108-118.* The so-called Soderstrom incident of 1784-85 further suggests that the basic weakness of the government under the Articles of Confederation concerned the relationship between that government and the States. Duly commissioned by Sweden as consul in Massachusetts, Richard Soderstrom waited nearly five months for congressional recognition. In the meantime he received recognition from Massachusetts and exercised functions of his office. In his use of the incident to attempt to assert Federal authority, Secretary for Foreign Affairs John Jay became more convinced of the need for a stronger central government, as did others. Based on primary sources; 2 illus., 16 notes. C. L. Grant

921. Polishook, Irwin H. THE COLLINS-RICHARDSON FRACAS OF 1787: A PROBLEM IN STATE AND FEDERAL RELATIONS DURING THE CONFEDERATION ERA. *Rhode Island Hist. 1963 22(4): 117-121.* Analyzes the dispute about the legality of requiring U.S. officials (tax collectors and postmasters) to accept Rhode Island paper money. P. J. Coleman

922. Reed, John F. "TIS DEATH TO COUNTERFEIT." *Manuscripts 1968 20(3): 13-17.* Although it is becoming increasingly difficult to obtain manuscript materials from the period of the American Revolution, it is still possible for private collectors to obtain Continental and State currencies. The Continental Congress issued a total of 241,552,780 dollars in paper currency in eleven issues dating from 1775 to 1779. Nine of these issues are still readily collectible. Undocumented, illus., photos. P. D. Thomas

923. Rich, Myra L. SPECULATIONS ON THE SIGNIFICANCE OF DEBT: VIRGINIA, 1781-1789. *Virginia Mag. of Hist. and Biog. 1968 76(3): 301-317.* The Virginia economy in 1781-89 lacked a viable medium of exchange and had to rely on a network of private credit. The State did not develop domestic sources of capital but relied on British and Northern merchants for it. Thus she perpetuated her colonial economic dependency even after political independence. Based on manuscript and printed sources, monographs, and newspapers; 62 notes.

K. J. Bauer

924. Schaffer, Alan. VIRGINIA'S "CRITICAL PERIOD." *The Old Dominion: Essays for Thomas Perkins Abernethy (Charlottesville: The U. Press of Virginia, 1964), pp. 152-170.* Summarizes the varied views of historians on the period 1784-88 in Virginia. In reality, the state quickly rose from the depths of British devastation to pay 123,000 pounds into the coffers of the Continental government. Then, as abruptly, it descended again into the depths of depression. A detailed study shows that this depression in Virginia at the end of the Confederation period "...was not the result of government ineptitude, the weakness of the Confederation, enmity between the states, or change of national markets." Rather it was the outcome of a speculator's attempt to monopolize a considerable proportion of the state's major export trade in tobacco. Based on letters of Jefferson and others and on official documents; 77 notes.

E. P. Stickney

925. Tailby, Donald G. FOREIGN INTEREST REMITTANCES BY THE UNITED STATES, 1785-1787: A STORY OF MALFEASANCE. *Business Hist. R. 1967 41(2): 161-176.* A study of the policy of servicing the foreign-held debt of the United States by private businessmen during 1785-87. The author concludes that the use of private merchants as fiscal agents by the Treasury proved unsatisfactory as a policy of conducting public affairs.

J. H. Krenkel

926. Wilmerding, Lucius, Jr. THE UNITED STATES LOTTERY. *New-York Hist. Soc. Q. 1963 47(1): 5-39.* In 1776, the revolutionary government of the United States tried to solve some of its fiscal problems with an elaborate lottery scheme. The lottery was designed to supplement domestic borrowing with a device that would attract the funds of the lower classes. It was supposed to bring in about seven million dollars. Unfortunately, it failed to raise even a hundredth of the expected sum by the time it was liquidated in 1782. Nevertheless, it did provide an occasion for the Congress to deal with the question of paying its financial obligations. Congress chose to pay at an arbitrary rate which was higher than the current value of "Continentals," but not as high as the face value of the obligations—a prudent solution. Based on the published journals of Congress, the published papers of important figures as well as the manuscript papers of Congress and Robert Morris.

N. Varga

927. Zornow, William F. NEW YORK TARIFF POLICIES, 1775-1789. *New York Hist. 1956 37(1): 40-63.* A detailed examination of schedules and policies, with the general conclusion that New York had no significant discriminatory

regulations against other American states and that the contemporary arguments for a new Federal constitution to prevent interstate tariffs were defective, insofar as they were based on the case of this state.   A. B. Rollins

928. —. [HORATIO GATES AT NEWBURGH]. *William and Mary Q. 1972 29(1): 143-158.*
    Nelson, Paul David. HORATIO GATES AT NEWBURGH, 1783: A MISUNDERSTOOD ROLE, pp. 143-151. Takes issue with Richard H. Kohn's article "The Inside History of the Newburgh Conspiracy: America and the Coup d'Etat," *William and Mary Quarterly* 1970 27(2): 187-220 on the inside story of the Newburgh conspiracy involving Washington's officers in 1783. Does not agree that politicians were using Army discontent. Evidence does not show Gates as the treasonous officer raising mutiny. Gates only championed the interests of the soldiers as to pay and other issues. Gates did aid in writing and distributing the inflammatory sheets, but he was bent only upon developing a strong remonstrance. Disputes Kohn's evaluation of Gates' character.
    Kohn, Richard H. RICHARD H. KOHN'S REPLY, pp. 151-158. Denies the extreme position assigned him by Nelson, that he charged Gates with treason. Also, his evidence is admittedly circumstantial but is corroborated by other evidence. 23 notes.   H. M. Ward

Indians, Ordinances, & the West

929. Berkhofer, Robert F., Jr. JEFFERSON, THE ORDINANCE OF 1784, AND THE ORIGINS OF THE AMERICAN TERRITORIAL SYSTEM. *William and Mary Q. 1972 29(2): 231-262.* Federal land policy had its origins in the debates in Congress from 1776 on. Congress had already determined a territorial policy before Thomas Jefferson took his seat in 1783. Jefferson's contribution was mainly his proposal for the delineating of boundaries. Details the report of Jefferson's committee of 1784 and amendments by Congress. The Ordinance of 1787 (Northwest Ordinance) was an extension rather than repudiation of the Ordinance of 1784. Emphasizes the consistency of Congress. 81 notes.
                                      H. M. Ward

930. Bloom, John Porter. CONFERENCE ON THE HISTORY OF THE TERRITORIES OF THE UNITED STATES, NOVEMBER 3-4, 1969. *Prologue: J. of the Natl. Archives 1969 1(3): 43-50.* Held at the National Archives building under the direction of the author, present editor of *The Territorial Papers of the United States,* this meeting was the fifth in a series of conferences on various subjects sponsored by the National Archives and Records Service. At the opening session, Clarence Edwin Carter, late editor of the *Territorial Papers,* was honored through the presentation of reminiscences of him by Philip D. Jordan and Harold W. Ryan. The four sessions of scholarly papers centered on the 1787 Northwest Ordinance, relations between the U.S. Congress and the territories, territorial

courts of the Far West, and the territories in the 20th century. Authors and titles are mentioned and brief summaries of papers presented are given. The author concludes with the full text of the Jordan and Ryan tributes to Carter. 4 illus.

W. R. Griffin

931. Gerlach, Larry R. CONNECTICUT, THE CONTINENTAL CONGRESS, AND THE INDEPENDENCE OF VERMONT, 1777-1782. *Vermont Hist. 1966 34(3): 188-193.* Soil exhaustion and shortage of arable land pressed Connecticut population into Vermont during the last third of the 18th century. Connecticut favored Vermont's admission. Many Connecticut Yankees had invested in New Hampshire grants, and many more had settled there, with New Hampshire titles. Oliver Wolcott always favored the Vermont claim to admission, and Roger Sherman actively promoted it. Opponents charged that delegates were bribed with land grants, but evidence is lacking. Congress denied petitions of 1777 and 1779, but in 1781 it required only the repeal of Vermont's annexation of towns east of the Connecticut River as condition of admission. The dismemberment of New York through admission of Vermont was also intertwined with the western land issue. Failure to admit Vermont weakened Connecticut's land claim, defeated in 1782. Based on published and MS. correspondence, documents of the Continental Congress and Vermont State Papers.   T. D. S. Bassett

932. Gerlach, Larry R. FIRMNESS AND PRUDENCE: CONNECTICUT, THE CONTINENTAL CONGRESS, AND THE NATIONAL DOMAIN, 1776-1786. *Connecticut Hist. Soc. Bull. 1966 31(3): 65-75.* A shortage of agricultural land made Connecticut especially sensitive to the loss of western land claims, especially those in the Wyoming [Pennsylvania] Valley. The State opposed giving Congress authority to determine western boundaries and voted against Maryland's attempts to appoint commissioners to investigate claims. Because Maryland refused to ratify the articles, accommodation became necessary. After other states ceded their land and Congress applied pressure, Connecticut began to modify its position. After much maneuvering Congress accepted the State's modified cession, excluding a "Western Reserve" for its veterans. The affair demonstrated the "illiberalism and provincialism" in Connecticut as well as the State's "legitimate needs" for additional land. "Opportunism, perfect timing, and adroit political maneuvering" gave Connecticut an "advantageous settlement" despite great obstacles.   L. R. Murphy

933. Griffin, J. David. HISTORIANS AND THE SIXTH ARTICLE OF THE ORDINANCE OF 1787. *Ohio Hist. 1969 78(4): 252-260.* Surveys monographic and textbook treatment of the question of the motivations for the adoption of the antislavery article of the Ordinance of 1787 from Richard Hildreth's discussion of the matter in 1849 to a monographic study by Jack E. Eblen on territorial government published in 1968, entitled *The First and Second United States Empires. Governors and Territorial Government, 1784-1912* (Pittsburgh, 1968). The author concludes that no adequate analysis of the problem has appeared.

S. L. Jones

934. Horsman, Reginald. AMERICAN INDIAN POLICY IN THE OLD NORTHWEST, 1783-1812. *William and Mary Q. 1961 18(1): 35-53.* The consistent aim throughout this period was to acquire Indian land from the Ohio to the Mississippi. The view of Washington and Philip Schuyler, that land seizures were justified by the Indians' aid to the British, prevailed until 1787, at which time Henry Knox's policy of peace and absorption was substituted. Jefferson sought to encourage Indian agriculture and manufacturing, to release hunting land for settlers, transmuting acquisitiveness into "lofty moral purpose." The acquisition policy succeeded, but peace was not achieved, for "wholesale land acquisition and friendship with the Indians were incompatible." E. Oberholzer, Jr.

935. Jordan, Philip D. A DEDICATION TO THE MEMORY OF CLARENCE EDWIN CARTER, 1881-1961. *Arizona and the West 1968 10(4): 308-312.* While Wisconsin- and Illinois-educated Clarence Edwin Carter was a professor of history at Miami University in Ohio (1910-31), he established a reputation as a skilled editor, particularly in several volumes of *Collections* of the Illinois State Historical Society and of the correspondence of General Thomas Gage. In 1931, he was appointed editor of *The Territorial Papers of the United States.* In this capacity he produced 26 volumes in the next 30 years, sponsored at first by the Department of State and later by the National Archives, despite the fact that about one-fourth of his time was occupied in budget making and related activities necessary to keep the project alive. He was a meticulous editor with rigid standards, a master craftsman who demanded as much from others. Appended with a selected bibliography of his works. Illus. D. L. Smith

936. Lynd, Staughton. THE COMPROMISE OF 1787. *Pol. Sci. Q. 1966 81(2): 225-250.* Approaches the Northwest Ordinance adopted by the Continental Congress on 13 July 1787 as the product of sectional compromise; examines the problems of the Constitutional Convention which had, on 12 July 1787, adopted the three-fifths compromise; and submits that whether or not the ordinance was consciously intended to resolve the problems of the convention, it may have done so. The author sees the fugitive slave clause, unanimously adopted by both bodies, as a manifestation that the makers of both the ordinance and the Constitution were ready to compromise the concept that all men are equal. Documented. Sr. M. McAuley

937. Pattison, William D. THE SURVEY OF THE SEVEN RANGES. *Ohio Hist. Q. 1959 68(2): 115-140.* An account of the first subdivision of federal territory under the Land Act of 1785. Despite hope that at least 13 ranges (rows) of townships could be staked out in the summer of 1785, one each by a surveyor from one of the states, only seven ranges were complete by the summer of 1788. Progress was slowed principally by hostile Indians. Main immediate beneficiary of the surveying was the Ohio Company of Associates, whose representatives were allowed to reconnoiter lands and which gained a bridgehead to the lands finally chosen. As a trial of the American Rectangular Land Survey System, field work was a failure. Based on Hutchins Papers in Pennsylvania Historical Society, published collections, and records of the Continental Congress and of surveyors in the National Archives. A

938. Swan, William O. THE NORTHWEST ORDINANCES, SO-CALLED, AND CONFUSION. *Hist. of Educ. Q. 1965 5(4): 235-240.* Distinguishes and defines from original documents the Ordinance of 20 May 1785, the Ordinance of 13 July 1787, and the contract of 27 October 1787 between the Ohio Company of Associates and the Board of Treasury.　　　　　　　　J. Herbst

939. Taylor, Robert J. TRIAL AT TRENTON. *William and Mary Q. 1969 26(4): 521-547.* The controversy between Pennsylvania and Connecticut over disputed lands, originally granted to the Susquehanna Company, was settled in Pennsylvania's favor on 30 December 1782 by five commissioners acting under Article IX of the Articles of Confederation. The dispute is traced back to 1754. Light is shed on the legal machinery of both States, the overall problem of cession of western lands, private soil rights, Indian rights, and public land policy. Leading persons served as agents for both States in the preliminaries and at the proceedings of the commissioners. 89 notes.　　　　　　　　H. M. Ward

940. Tyler, Bruce. THE MISSISSIPPI RIVER TRADE, 1784-1788. *Louisiana Hist. 1971 12(3): 255-267.* The Spaniards, for defensive reasons, employed a number of measures to keep Anglo-Americans from trading on the Mississippi. Nevertheless, traffic upriver was spreading rapidly. New Orleans itself depended on some of this trade for supply, but Spanish officials continued to harass the traders, for they did not want to be overwhelmed by the "undesirable" Americans. A growing trade via the Gulf of Mexico with Philadelphia merchants helped to provide a temporary alternative to Spain's dilemma, but Spain could not forever stop the inevitable westward movement of the Anglo-Americans. Based on primary and secondary sources; 41 notes.　　　　　　　　R. L. Woodward

941. Vivian, Jean H. MILITARY LAND BOUNTIES DURING THE REVOLUTIONARY AND CONFEDERATION PERIODS. *Maryland Hist. Mag. 1966 61(3): 231-256.* A study of the land offers of Congress, the pressure of former military men for satisfaction of their land claims, and the policies adopted to implement the pledges of Congress. The exigencies of war favored the need for land bounties and money bounties to procure long periods of enlistment. The Land Ordinance (1785) provided for the allocation of a part of the public domain to retired officers and men. The Ohio Company Purchase (1787) and the Symmes Purchase (1788) constituted the sole means by which veterans of the Continental Army received land bounties during the Confederation period. 76 notes.　　　　　　　　D. H. Swift

942. Wright, J. Leitch, Jr. CREEK-AMERICAN TREATY OF 1790: ALEXANDER MC GILLIVRAY AND THE DIPLOMACY OF THE OLD SOUTHWEST. *Georgia Hist. Q. 1967 51(4): 379-400.* Traces the background of the Creek-American Treaty of New York City of 1790 and explains the reasons for its ineffectiveness. The treaty, signed by the supposed leader of the Creek, Alexander McGillivray, provided for permanent peace between the U.S. Government and the Southern Indians, stipulated the cession of Indian lands to the Americans, and placed the Creek under the protection of the national government rather than the State of Georgia or some foreign power. Secret clauses granted

McGillivray a monopoly of the Indian trade and a duty-free port for the importation of trading goods. But the treaty was ineffective. McGillivray did not represent all of the Southern Indians; the State of Georgia claimed sovereignty over the Indians and the land of the southern territory; and both Great Britain and Spain had important interests in the area. The failure of the U.S. negotiators, especially Secretary of War Henry Knox, to take account of their interests caused these four parties to work actively for the demise of the agreement. Thus the British stirred up the anti-McGillivray Indians, the Spanish weaned McGillivray from his bargain with the United States, and the terms of the treaty were never executed. Based on research in published and unpublished diplomatic manuscripts; 49 notes. R. A. Mohl

International Relations

943. Bolkhovitinov, N. N. NOVYE RABOTY O RUSSKO-AMERIKANSKOI TORGOVLE V XVIII-NACHALE XIX VEKA [New works about Russian-American trade in the 18th and the beginning of the 19th centuries]. *Novaia i Noveishaia Istoriia [USSR] 1967 11(4): 122-126.* Bibliography concerning the nature, volume, and significance of Russian-American trade. Based on Russian and American archival material; 23 notes. E. B. Richards

944. Boyd, Julian P. TWO DIPLOMATS BETWEEN REVOLUTIONS: JOHN JAY AND THOMAS JEFFERSON. *Virginia Mag. of Hist. and Biog. 1958 66(2): 131-146.* Between 1784 and 1789, John Jay was Secretary of Foreign Affairs and Thomas Jefferson was Minister to France. During this period, Jay sought to draw the United States into the British orbit, while Jefferson was attempting to pull her toward France. The cross-purpose at which the two men worked is demonstrated by examining the negotiations for a consular convention with France. Franklin succeeded in negotiating one in 1784, but Jay prevented its passage by Congress. In 1786 Jefferson secured a new convention which was ratified in 1788 despite Jay's opposition. Throughout the negotiations Jay played the role of an obstructionist and showed clearly that he objected to French consuls, but not to those of other countries. Based on letters, diplomatic documents, and congressional journals. D. Houston

945. Critoph, Gerald E. THE EVOLVING IMAGES OF THE UNITED STATES. *Mississippi Q. 1963 16(1): 3-14.* A general review of the changing images of America in the eyes of foreign observers. The author discusses effects some of these images have had on the attitudes of other nations toward the United States. To a degree, an analogy can be drawn between the behavior of nations and that of individuals. Certain traits can be discerned which basically influence foreign policy: 1) a nation's fighting strength, 2) its ability to attract strong friends and allies, and 3) the kindling temperature of a nation's inclination to fight. Europeans generally belittled the country under the Articles of Confederation,

thereby influencing the move toward a stronger central government. With a strong feeling of common traditions, Great Britain has often looked upon the United States in the manner of an indulgent relative, while France has held no such viewpoint. In 1914, three images of the United States were held which have become deeply imbedded: 1) the Latin American view of the "Colossus of the North," 2) the central and eastern European and Japanese image of an ambitious imperialist with bark but no bite, and 3) the British-Western European image of the growing pains of a young nation. 29 notes.   R. V. Calvert

946. Crosby, Alfred W., Jr. THE BEGINNINGS OF TRADE BETWEEN THE UNITED STATES AND RUSSIA. *Am. Neptune 1961 21(3): 207-215.* Traces development of trade to Russia in the 1780's. Exchange of Russian iron, sailcloth, linen, hemp, and cordage for colonial goods began even before 1700. The Westernization policies of Peter the Great allowed the introduction of tobacco, a major commodity, in American revolutionary trade. Rice, indigo, and sugar were also important. Until 1775 England acted as the entrepôt for this traffic. Direct trade to Russia began after the Revolution ended. Russian production of tobacco forced a concentration on sugar, indigo, rice, and dyewood, which were goods typical of a cargo to Russia for over a century. The first vessel arrived at St. Petersburg from Boston in 1783, under Daniel McNeil. By 1784 this trade pattern had been established.   J. G. Lydon

947. Godechot, Jacques. LES RELATIONS ECONOMIQUES ENTRE LA FRANCE ET LES ETATS-UNIS DE 1778 A 1789 [The economic relations between France and the United States from 1778 to 1789]. *French Hist. Studies 1958 1(1): 26-39.* France helped the United States to gain her freedom with the hope of finding a permanent ally against Great Britain and also developing close trade associations with the new country. France did not achieve either goal. The author, starting with the first contacts of the two countries, demonstrates that France could not and did not succeed in her commercial relations with the United States. French merchants continually complained that they were not doing enough business with the United States. He finds, from reports of French agents in the United States, that France was not catering to the commercial demands of the United States as did the British. This, combined with the American desire to open trade routes not only with Europe but with all parts of the world and the Napoleonic Wars, continued to keep the balance of trade between the two countries in favor of the United States.   J. Adelson

948. Griffiths, David M. AMERICAN COMMERCIAL DIPLOMACY IN RUSSIA, 1780 TO 1783. *William and Mary Q. 1970 27(3): 379-410.* The mission of Francis Dana to St. Petersburg (1781-83) was unfruitful. The author disputes the usual reason of Catherine II's dislike for American revolutionaries; Russian policy with the West was based instead on military considerations—with the United States having little to offer. Ineptitude of both the U. S. Congress and the diplomat impeded the mission. Cited are diplomatic pressures on Russia from other countries. Fear of European nations of America's potential inroads on world trade was also an impediment. The author discusses trade conditions in detail. 104 notes.   H. M. Ward

949. Johnson, Amandus. THE AMERICAN-SWEDISH TREATY OF 1783. *Am.-Scandinavian R. 1958 46(2): 152-156.* In 1782 King Gustavus III of Sweden asked his Ambassador in Paris, Count Gustav Philip Creutz, to propose to Benjamin Franklin a Treaty of Commerce and Friendship between the Thirteen States and Sweden. The treaty took a year to negotiate, and was concluded on 3 April 1783. It contained 27 articles and was to be in force for 15 years. It actually stood for 33 years before it was ratified, and most of the articles were retained. It was ahead of its time and included such principles as freedom of the seas, religious freedom and others which have still not been universally accepted.
M. Petrie

950. Levy, H. Phillip. JOHN ADAMS PRESENTS HIS CREDENTIALS. *Hist. Today [Great Britain] 1959 9(1): 59-63.* John Adams' ministry to England in 1785 as representative of the new United States can hardly be considered successful from the American point of view, or as a high point in his career, but it was a dramatic moment between a king and his former colonist, and on the whole it went far toward establishing peaceful relations between the two countries.
E. D. Johnson

951. Mayo, Lida. MISS ADAMS IN LOVE. *Am. Heritage 1965 16(2): 36-39, 80-89.* When John Adams became the first American minister to England he took his daughter Abigail to London with him and Mrs. Adams. The romances of the charming young lady were ended by her marriage to Colonel William Stephens Smith, the secretary to the legation who married the "boss's daughter." A 10-page portfolio on London accompanies the article.
J. D. Filipiak

952. Neel, Joanne. THE MARQUESS OF CARMARTHEN AND THE UNITED STATES, 1783-1791. *Hist. Today [Great Britain] 1963 13(2): 108-114.* Francis Osborne, Marquis of Carmarthen and Duke of Leeds, was the British foreign secretary who used his exquisite manners and schrewdness to reestablish Anglo-American relations. His efforts, which are seldom acknowledged, helped to make possible the exchange of diplomatic missions between the two countries in 1791.
L. A. Knafla

953. Palmer, R. R. THE DUBIOUS DEMOCRAT: THOMAS JEFFERSON IN BOURBON FRANCE. *Pol. Sci. Q. 1957 72(3): 388-404.* An analysis of Jefferson's reaction to the early stages of the French Revolution, up to his departure from France in September 1789. Lafayette's influence on Jefferson's appraisal of the situation is held accountable for his lack of appreciation of the privileged character of the Assembly of Notables. At that stage, John Adams rather than Jefferson was aware of the dangers of aristocracy and the usefulness of a strong executive for the cause of the people. Until his departure, there are no indications of visionary enthusiasm for the cause of "democracy." Jefferson lacked class-consciousness himself and was little aware of it in others.
G. Stourzh

954. Peterson, Merrill D. THOMAS JEFFERSON AND COMMERCIAL POLICY, 1783-1793. *William and Mary Q. 1965 22(4): 584-610.* To Thomas

Jefferson's agricultural point of view, foreign commerce was a necessity. Though he felt trade should be left to regulate itself, he favored strengthening the powers of the Confederacy to regulate foreign commerce in order to establish a counter-vailing system in the United States against European mercantilism. Jefferson sought an equal footing in trade through treaties. The record of attempting to secure full trade privileges and to use the commerce power under the Constitution as a weapon of coercion against Great Britain and France was, for Jefferson, as secretary of state, one of frustration and failure.   H. M. Ward

955. Ritcheson, Charles R. ANGLO-AMERICAN RELATIONS 1783-1794. *South Atlantic Q. 1959 58(3): 364-380.* Holds that the traditional American view of Anglo-American relations in the years 1783-94 is biased and one-sided, that the British were not always the villains of the peace. The author's purpose is "to invite attention" to this "critical period" and to make "certain suggestions about lines of inquiry and reappraisal." He describes in general terms the traditional American view of the problem, then notes seldom considered facts and events which indicate that America was as often at fault as Britain. Alexander Hamilton's view of England was not one of simple Anglophilia, but rather a realistic appreciation of the fact that the United States were still economic colonies. Undocumented.   C. R. Allen, Jr.

956. Vidalenc, Jean. UNE MISE AU POINT DE DIVERS PROBLEMES AN-TILLAIS: LES ETATS-UNIS ET LE MARCHE HAITIEN [A consideration of various problems of the Antilles: the United States and the Haitian market]. *R. d'Hist. Econ. et Sociale [France] 1957 35(1): 84-90.* Review article on Alain Tournier's *Les Etats-Unis et le marche haïtien* (Washington, 1955), tracing the relations between the United States and Haiti from 1784 to the present. The United States first contested for domination of the Haitian market with France, and then with Britain; now, after many years with no serious competition, with Japan and West Germany.   R. E. Cameron

10

THE CONSTITUTION:
ITS MAKING & RATIFICATION

General

957. Bradley, Harold. THE AMERICAN ADVENTURE IN FEDERALISM. *Current Hist. 39(228): 92-95 and 100.* Reviews the history of American federalism, from the experience of the 13 colonies through the Articles of Confederation and the Constitution, noting the various crises that stimulated the move toward a stronger federal union, and the different attempts made to weaken or destroy that union, from the nullification effort of South Carolina to the Civil War. The author insists, however, that the American "experiment in federalism...was conducted in a favorable environment," and that such environment is not present in the world as a whole today. Cultural diversity and strong nationalisms present insuperable obstacles to the formation of a world federation. Comparison of the origin of the federal union of the United States with that of the United Nations are useless unless this is taken into account. The best possible solution may lie in a series of regional federations based on common language, culture and political experience.   W. J. Schellings

958. Brogan, D. W. THE QUARREL OVER CHARLES AUSTIN BEARD AND THE AMERICAN CONSTITUTION. *Econ. Hist. R. [Great Britain] 1965 18(1): 199-223.* Surveys Beard's concepts concerning the American Constitution, and the reactions to them by his contemporaries and later historians. For all his shortcomings, Beard is crucial in American historiography, where there is "a pre-Beard and a post-Beard epoch."   B. L. Crapster

959. Bruchey, Stuart. THE FORCES BEHIND THE CONSTITUTION: A CRITICAL REVIEW OF THE FRAMEWORK OF E. JAMES FERGUSON'S *THE POWER OF THE PURSE*...WITH A REBUTTAL BY E. JAMES FERGUSON. *William and Mary Q. 1962 19(3): 429-438.* Examines "the thematic essay which encloses" E. James Ferguson's book, concluding that, certain disclaimers notwithstanding, it follows Charles Beard's economic interpretation.

The author suggests that Alexander Ramsey's work be considered in studying the motives of the Constitutional Convention. In rebuttal, Ferguson maintains that agreement with certain of Beard's points does not make one a Beardian and admits the existence of noneconomic causes.   E. Oberholzer, Jr.

960. Coleman, Peter J. BEARD, MC DONALD, AND ECONOMIC DETER-MINISM IN AMERICAN HISTORIOGRAPHY. *Business Hist. R. 1960 34(1): 113-121.* There were no detailed studies of Charles A. Beard's *An Economic Interpretation of the Constitution of the United States* (1913) for a full genera-tion. Recently, critical appraisals were made by Robert E. Brown, in *Charles A. Beard and the Constitution: A Critical Analysis of "An Economic Interpretation of the Constitution"* (Princeton, 1956), and by Forrest McDonald, in *We the People: The Economic Origins of the Constitution* (Chicago, 1958). The authors of both works conclude that the Beard thesis was faulty. "Brown rests his case primarily upon criticism of Beard's methodology,...McDonald although agreeing that Beard's methods were so faulty as to invalidate much of what he said, goes much further by challenging the assumption upon which Beard predicated his research." Coleman points out that if scholars produced a series of case studies on various themes in economic history, working from the particular to the gen-eral, more meaningful conclusions could be made, and there would not be a perpetuation of "the tendency to fill the vacuum with engaging but spurious generalizations which result from premature and irresponsible synthesis."
                                                        J. H. Krenkel

961. Commager, Henry Steele. THE CONSTITUTION: WAS IT AN ECO-NOMIC DOCUMENT? *Am. Heritage 1958 10(1): 58-61, 100-103.* Rejects the economic interpretation of the Constitution offered by Charles A. Beard and analyzes evidence to the contrary. Undocumented; illus.
                                                        C. R. Allen, Jr.

962. Elkins, Stanley and McKitrick, Eric. THE FOUNDING FATHERS: YOUNG MEN OF THE REVOLUTION. *Pol. Sci. Q. 1961 76(2): 181-216.* Discusses the theses of Charles Beard, R. E. Brown, and Forrest McDonald regarding the role of the men who formulated the Constitution of the United States. Much in line with the study of Merrill Jensen, *The New Nation* (New York: Knopf, 1950), the author advances the theory that the struggle for the Constitution was not fought on economic grounds; was not a matter of ideology; was not, in the fullest and most fundamental sense, even a struggle between nationalism and localism. The key struggle was between inertia and energy, the latter being embodied among the younger Federalist membership in the Constitu-tional Convention.   Sr. M. McAuley

963. Ferguson, E. James. [REVIEW OF] *E PLURIBUS UNUM: THE FORMA-TION OF THE AMERICAN REPUBLIC, 1776-1790* BY FORREST MC-DONALD. (BOSTON: HOUGHTON MIFFLIN COMPANY, 1965). *William and Mary Q. 1966 23(1): 148-155.* The author, McDonald, treats the movement for national government from the disputes over the Articles of Confederation to the ratification of the Constitution. According to Ferguson, he takes a Beardian

interpretation: those who wished to strengthen the Union wanted primarily the power of Congress to tax in order to pay the public debt. Questionable are McDonald's assertions that weak States favored the Constitution and that Connecticut agreed to delay Federal restriction of the slave trade for South Carolina's assistance in securing Senate and Supreme Court authority over land questions. In general, McDonald overdoes his attempt to reverse orthodox interpretations.

H. M. Ward

964. Francovich, Carlo. LA RIVOLUZIONE AMERICANA E IL PROGETTO DI COSTITUZIONE DEL GRANDUCA PIETRO LEOPOLDO [The American Revolution and Grand Duke Peter Leopold's project for a constitution]. *Rassegna Storica del Risorginento [Italy] 1954 41(2/3): 371-377.* Within the framework of his extensive reform projects, Grand Duke Peter Leopold of Tuscany (later Emperor Leopold II) planned as early as 1779 to give his country a constitution. This constitutional project was the subject of a book by J. Zimmermann, *Das Verfassungsprojekt des Grossherzogs Peter Leopold von Toscana* (Heidelberg, 1901). The author analyzes the projected constitution and finds analogies with the American Constitution. He also cites a letter from Benjamin Franklin to Philip Mazzei in which Franklin expressed his esteem for Grand Duke Leopold.

W. E. Heydendorff

965. Jordan, Philip H., Jr. CONNECTICUT ANTI-FEDERALISM ON THE EVE OF THE CONSTITUTIONAL CONVENTION: A LETTER FROM BENJAMIN GALE TO ERASTUS WOLCOTT, FEBRUARY 10, 1787. *Connecticut Hist. Soc. Bull. 1963 28(1): 14-21.* Excerpts from the letter of Benjamin Gale to Erastus Wolcott, 10 February 1787, in the possession of the Connecticut Historical Society. Wolcott had written a series of essays on taxation published in January and February 1787 in the *Connecticut Courant.* Dr. Benjamin Gale was opposed to the State's participation in the approaching Constitutional Convention. Wolcott declined to serve as a delegate to the convention in Philadelphia, but later was a member of the State convention at Hartford. Instructed by his town of East Windsor to approve the Constitution, he joined the majority in ratification.

E. P. Stickney

966. Krout, John A. ALEXANDER HAMILTON'S PLACE IN THE FOUNDING OF THE NATION. *Pro. of the Am. Phil. Soc. 1958 102(2): 124-128.* A discussion of Hamilton's contributions to the calling and success of the Constitutional Convention and the adoption of the Constitution. The importance of his economic theories is also noted.

N. Kurland

967. Lynd, Staughton. BEARD, JEFFERSON AND THE TREE OF LIBERTY. *MidContinent Am. Studies J. 1968 9(1): 8-22.* Attempts to show that Charles Beard's interpretation of the Constitution as a document formulated by special economic interests is incorrect because it was based on Jefferson's own conception of his time. The origin of this misconception may be found by investigating three phases of Jefferson's role in this misunderstanding. First, there is the split between Jefferson and Hamilton that was caused by sectional forces that Jefferson did not understand and of which Beard was completely unaware. Sec-

ond, Jefferson's own conception of this split, though unfounded, has influenced Charles Beard to see divisions of classes through Jefferson's eyes. Third, these errors are more readily perceivable if one understands the effect that 18th-century thought had on Jefferson. The contribution of Lord Bolingbroke to Jeffersonian democracy, for example, is a case in point as is Montesquieu, for they both stressed common themes that Jefferson came to associate with agrarianism and capitalism. In this sense, Charles Beard has adopted Jefferson's philosophy and imposed it on various phases of American history. Based on primary and secondary sources; 53 notes.   B. M. Morrison

968. Lynd, Staughton, ed. ABRAHAM YATES'S HISTORY OF THE MOVEMENT FOR THE UNITED STATES CONSTITUTION. *William and Mary Q. 1963 20(2): 223-245.* The text of Yates' manuscript, with an introduction by the editor. Yates (1724-96) combined the charges of conspiracy and aristocracy in his anti-Federalist history, regarded Robert Morris as the arch-enemy, and anticipated the views of Beard and Jensen.   E. Oberholzer, Jr.

969. Main, Jackson T. CHARLES A. BEARD AND THE CONSTITUTION: A CRITICAL REVIEW OF FORREST MC DONALD'S *WE THE PEOPLE,* WITH A REBUTTAL BY FORREST MC DONALD. *William and Mary Q. 1960 17(1): 86-110.* A defense of Beard against the attack by McDonald. Acknowledging McDonald's use of hitherto neglected primary sources, Main accuses him of an unfair selection of facts and of faulty interpretation. An effort to refute a thesis, Main notes, will not reveal the truth, for the conclusions are predetermined. In his rebuttal, McDonald accuses his critic of misreading the book, of faulty arithmetic, and of illogical conclusions: "My humble effort was directed at getting us back on the path. Apparently Mr. Main prefers the wilderness."   E. Oberholzer, Jr.

970. Malone, Dumas. TAPPING THE WISDOM OF THE FOUNDING FATHERS. *New York Times Mag. 1956 27(May): 25, 32, 34, 37, 39.* Refers to the many projects under way to publish the papers of the founding fathers of the American Republic, and suggests that we may find wisdom and enjoyment in exploring the ideas and activities of such men as George Washington, Alexander Hamilton, Thomas Jefferson, and John Adams.   R. F. Campbell

971. Schuyler, Robert Livingston. FORREST MC DONALD'S CRITIQUE OF THE BEARD THESIS. *J. of Southern Hist. 1961 27(1): 73-80.* Acting upon a suggestion made by the late Charles A. Beard in his *Economic Interpretation of the Constitution of the United States,* Forrest McDonald has done the research to determine the validity of Beard's hypothesis that the Constitution was an economic document drawn by a consolidated economic group, that the line of cleavage for and against it was between substantial personal property interests on the one hand and small farming and debtor interests on the other and that large security holders were a considerable or preponderating element in causing adoption of the Constitution. In a review article on McDonald's resultant *We the People: The Economic Origins of the Constitution* (Chicago: U. of Chicago Press,

1958), Schuyler finds that McDonald has overturned the Beard thesis and that details as found by McDonald do not substantiate Beard's assumptions.

S. E. Humphreys

972. Seed, Geoffrey. THE DEMOCRATIC IDEAS OF JAMES WILSON: A REAPPRAISAL. *British Assoc. for Am. Studies Bull. [Great Britain] 1965 (10): 3-30.* An examination of statements made by James Wilson during the Federal Convention of 1787, the Pennsylvania Ratifying Convention, and the Pennsylvania Constitutional Convention of 1789-90, provides considerable evidence to support the thesis that Wilson was a genuine democrat. Some of Wilson's contemporaries and historians have glibly assumed that Wilson advocated democratic ideas only to win support for the strengthening of the central government. But even during the Pennsylvania Constitutional Convention, Wilson voted with the radical leaders on most of the basic issues. Ninety notes cite Farrand's *Records of the Federal Convention,* manuscripts, and other sources.

D. J. Abramoske

973. Wehtje, Myron F. RUFUS KING AND THE FORMATION OF THE CONSTITUTION. *Studies in Hist. and Soc. 1969 1(2): 17-31.* Although King reflected the provincial views of New England, he nevertheless recognized the need for and advantages of a strong central government. As a delegate to the Constitutional Convention, he argued that a centralized government could best insure the rights and interests of both sections and States. Upon his return to Newburyport, Massachusetts, he was elected as a delegate to the Massachusetts ratifying convention. Like his role on the national level, King was active in preparing the way for the positive although close vote (187-168) by the Massachusetts delegates favoring ratification of the Constitution. Based on primary and secondary sources including the correspondence of Rufus King; 80 notes.

S. R. Sherter

974. Wilkins, Robert P. ORIN G. LIBBY: HIS PLACE IN THE HISTORIOGRAPHY OF THE CONSTITUTION. *North Dakota Q. 1969 37(3): 5-20.* Examines the influence of Orin Grant Libby's 1894 *The Geographical Distribution of the Votes of the Thirteen States on the Federal Constitution, 1787-1788* (New York: Burt Franklin). A student of Frederick Jackson Turner, Libby broke new ground in his assessment of the geographical distribution of Federalist and Anti-Federalist sentiment. His work has been a major influence on students from Algie M. Simons and Charles Austin Beard to Staughton Lynd and Jackson Turner Main. Libby's distinction between commercial (including export agriculture) and noncommercial interests more nearly reflects current views than Beard's "personality"-"reality" distinction. The remainder of the volume reproduces the text and maps of Libby's work. 60 notes.

J. F. Mahoney

Failures of the
Articles of Confederation

975. Feer, Robert A. GEORGE RICHARDS MINOT'S *HISTORY OF THE INSURRECTIONS:* HISTORY, PROPAGANDA, AND AUTOBIOGRAPHY. *New England Q. 1962 35(2): 203-228.* Pictures George Richards Minot, early American historian, as a person who was unduly concerned about his reputation, who preferred moderation to extremes, and who avoided controversy whenever possible. As the author of *History of the Insurrections* (1788) Minot tried to discuss Shays' Rebellion in such a way as to avoid antagonizing any of the groups or persons that had been involved. He pictured the Shaysites as men temporarily resorting to violence in order to rectify what they believed to be a very unjust situation. Among other considerations was Minot's concern that his history should depict representative government as strong rather than weak for any British readers his work might have. The result was a book noted for its objectivity even though its author had certain utilitarian functions in his mind at the time it was written.   L. Gara

976. Feer, Robert A. SHAYS'S REBELLION AND THE CONSTITUTION: A STUDY IN CAUSATION. *New England Q. 1969 42(3): 388-410.* Concludes that Shays's Rebellion (1786) was a decisive event neither in the calling of the Philadelphia Convention nor in the formation of the Constitution. George Washington, James Madison, Alexander Hamilton, James Wilson (1742-98) and Rufus King (1755-1827) were concerned about the event but had already decided that a radical revision of the Articles of Confederation was either desirable or inevitable. Other delegates were silent on the issue, while some Anti-Federalists, such as Elbridge Gerry and George Clinton (1739-1812), had opposed Shays. More decisive events were the refusal of New York to agree to a Federal import in 1786, the failure of the Annapolis Convention, and the continuous threat of paper money in Maryland, Virginia, and Rhode Island. Based on primary and secondary sources; 45 notes.   K. B. West

977. Ikemoto, Kōzō. IWAYURU "SHEIZU NO HANRAN" NO HAIKEI NI TSUITE [On the background of Shays' Rebellion in 1786-87]. *Seiyō Shigaku [Japan] 1958 37: 48-69.* Considers Shays' Rebellion to be the result of internal conflicts within the State of Massachusetts, caused by its financial policies and judicial system. The author also discusses the historiography of the period of the Articles of Confederation.   H. Imai

978. Manders, Eric and Snook, George A. SHAYS' REGULATORS, 1786-1787. *Military Collector and Historian 1963 15(3): 83, 85.* "It is certainly reasonable to assume that many of these Revolutionary War veterans [in Shays' Rebellion] wore their old uniforms while campaigning against what, to them, were the same, or worse injustices than they had suffered under the British Crown." Illus., 8 notes.   C. L. Boyd

979. Morgan, Edmund S. THE POLITICAL ESTABLISHMENTS OF THE UNITED STATES, 1784. *William and Mary Q. 1966 23(2): 286-308.* Published anonymously in 1784, *The Political Establishments of the United States of America* argues the need for a strong central government and the demolishment of the state governments. This document was probably written by a major political figure. It exposes the weaknesses of the Articles of Confederation and the dangers of divisive government. Strong national government would promote "disinterested patriotism," agriculture, and commerce. Confusion in governmental structure and authority imperils democracy. Pamphlet reproduced.   H. M. Ward

980. Nash, Vernon. THE LEAGUE OF NATIONS: ANOTHER ROPE OF SAND. *Current Hist. 1960 39(228): 82-86.* Reviews the history of the League of Nations and that of the United States under the Articles of Confederation. Both are found to have been ineffective, and Alexander Hamilton's essay in the *Federalist Papers,* No. 15, will supply the reasons why any such league of independent states must fail. The United Nations follows in the footsteps of the League, with just as little success. Action taken by any such international organization can be and has been beneficial, but only in those areas where voluntary cooperation can be secured. The question of the divisibility of sovereignty can be answered by placing it in the hands of the people, and allocating it to the various levels of national and world government, as in a federal system.

W. J. Schellings

981. Riley, Stephen T. DR. WILLIAM WHITING AND SHAYS' REBELLION. *Pro. of the Am. Antiquarian Soc. 1956 66(2): 119-166.* Discusses the role that William Whiting, a physician and Justice of the Peace, played in this Massachusetts rebellion of 1786 which was mainly due to the economic depression immediately after the war. Whiting favored the debtors' cause because he feared another lawless period. Under the pseudonym Gracchus, he wrote a pamphlet in their defense, which was later judged to be a seditious libel. The text of this pamphlet and correspondence related to it are printed in full.

D. van Arkel

982. Winston, Alexander. A MORE PERFECT UNION. *Hist. Today [Great Britain] 1966 16(6): 391-399.* A superficial sketch of the Philadelphia Convention from 14 May to 15 September 1787. The author centers his sketch on the alleged weaknesses of the Articles of Confederation, and the improbabilities of successfully revising them. Biblio.   L. A. Knafla

Intellectual Antecedents
of the Constitution

983. Albertini, Mario. CHE COSA E IL FEDERALISMO [What is federalism?]. *Politico [Italy] 1956 21(3): 580-597.* With *Le Fédéralisme,* a publication by the Centre de Sciences politiques de l'Institut d'Etudes juridiques de Nice, (Paris: Presses Universitaires de France, 1956), as his starting point, the author analyzes Alexander Hamilton's ideas on government as expressed at the Philadelphia Convention of 1788 and in the *Federalist* and tries to give a practical rather than a philosophical definition of federalism.   E. Füssl

984. Anderson, William. THE INTENTIONS OF THE FRAMERS. *Am. Pol. Sci. R. 1955 49(2): 340-352.* The intentions of the makers of the U.S. Constitution are reexamined. The author concludes that whatever their intentions may have been, they are largely irrelevant today. The Constitution is a living document and has been gradually and continually modified to suit modern conditions.
D. Houston

985. Bellot, H. Hale. COUNCIL AND CABINET IN THE MAINLAND COLONIES. *Tr. of the Royal Hist. Soc. [Great Britain] 1955 5: 161-176.* Examines the reasons why the position of the Cabinet developed differently in the United States than in Great Britain. The difference lies not only in the ill-defined position of the British Cabinet by 1783, but resulted largely from the circumstance that the constitutional practice of the British colonies differed from that of Britain. The roots of the American developments lie in the constitutional system of the mainland colonies, and particularly in the constitutional devices of the lower houses of the colonial legislatures.   J. A. S. Grenville

986. Brant, Irving. MADISON, THE "NORTH AMERICAN," ON FEDERAL POWER. *Am. Hist. R. 1954 60(1): 45-54.* In Volume VI of *The Papers of Thomas Jefferson* doubt is expressed regarding James Madison's authorship of *The North American No. 1* and *No. 2,* published anonymously in Philadelphia in 1783. The matter deserves serious study because the articles, unfriendly to the idea of State sovereignty, have additional significance if they really were written by Madison. Internal and circumstantial evidence confirm the author's view, expressed on earlier occasions, that the authorship of these statements can be assigned to Madison.   W. C. Langsam

987. DeConde, Alexander. WILLIAM VANS MURRAY'S *POLITICAL SKETCHES.* A DEFENSE OF THE AMERICAN EXPERIMENT. *Mississippi Valley Hist. R. 1955 41(4): 623-640.* First categorizes Murray as one of those "second-rate intellectuals," who, during the nation's formative years, made a contribution to political thought and to the actual functioning of government. In his *Sketches,* Murray is seen as an incisive commentator on the nature and

future of American democracy on the eve of the Federal Convention, and as a voice of the much underrated conservative political tradition of Alexander Hamilton and John Adams. Murray's volume dealt with government, politics, and religion in the American States. He defended representative democracy and denied that size, refinement, or luxury were incompatible with democracy. Lucid and readable, the *Sketches* reveal an admiration for the English Government, an intense American patriotism, and a desire for a stronger central government, and help the reader toward a more accurate definition of the conservative American political tradition. G. L. A. Reilly

988. Ferguson, E. James. THE NATIONALISTS OF 1781-1783 AND THE ECONOMIC INTERPRETATION OF THE CONSTITUTION. *J. of Am. Hist. 1969 56(2): 241-261.* In the last years of the Revolution, a desire to strengthen the central government animated a nationalist movement composed of army officers, merchants, public creditors, and elitists who were suspicious of democracy in the States. Led by financier Robert Morris (1734-1806), a program remarkably similar to that later pressed by Alexander Hamilton was proposed: a funded national debt, Federal taxation, establishment of a national bank, and assumption of the debts of the States. The program was a failure by 1786 after a proposed Federal import was defeated and States began to assume State debts. The movement was reinvigorated by Shays' Rebellion and was carried to triumph in the Constitutional Convention of 1787. It illustrates the organic connection between economic development and nationalism, which, for proponents, was inseparable. 55 notes. K. B. West

989. Fisher, Louis. THE EFFICIENCY SIDE OF SEPARATED POWERS. *J. of Am. Studies [Great Britain] 1971 5(2): 113-131.* Reviews the "separation of powers" doctrine, implicit in the U.S. Constitution, as viewed by six leading Americans—George Washington (1732-99), Alexander Hamilton (1757-1804), John Jay (1745-1829), Thomas Jefferson (1743-1826), John Adams (1745-1829), and James Madison (1751-1836). The experiences of these men in State governments and the Continental Congresses convinced them of the need to elaborate separate judicial, legislative, and executive powers in the Constitution. "Greater administrative efficiency and more reliable governmental machinery," they believed, were important results of "separation of powers." 76 notes. H. T. Lovin

990. Harrold, Frances. THE UPPER HOUSE IN JEFFERSONIAN POLITICAL THEORY. *Virginia Mag. of Hist. and Biog. 1970 78(3): 281-294.* Given the controversy surrounding the principle of bicameralism and the Jeffersonian faith in the people, questions why Jefferson consistently supported the need for an upper house. British and colonial precedent may have influenced Jefferson, but more influential were the historically well-documented examples of group tyranny. Popular passion, the meanness of self-interest, and the impracticality of schemes to elevate the aristocracy of talent to places of political leadership directed his hope that the Senate act as the keeper of a "mixed polity." Extensive notes. C. A. Newton

991. Hoffer, Peter C. THE CONSTITUTIONAL CRISIS AND THE RISE OF A NATIONALISTIC VIEW OF HISTORY IN AMERICA, 1786-1788. *New York Hist. 1971 52(3): 305-323.* America's leaders in 1775-1800 used history to justify the American Revolution and to win support for the Constitution. Whereas the Revolution was justified by using examples from ancient and modern European history, the Constitution was debated largely in terms of examples drawn from American history. Between 1786 and 1788 the idea developed that European historical experience did not apply to America, which was unique in the world and more moral, pious, and politically free than any other community. In turn, the Constitution became the unique cornerstone of a nationalistic interpretation of American history. Based on primary and secondary sources; illus., 29 notes.   G. Kurland

992. Hofstadter, Richard. A CONSTITUTION AGAINST PARTIES. *Government and Opposition [Great Britain] 1969 4(3): 345-366.* Discusses pluralistic, antiparty attitudes in the young Republic, featuring those of James Madison. Americans did not respect English parties of the 18th-century. American "pre-parties" practiced a vigorous, experience-yielding factionalism, but deferential Colonial politics (as in Virginia) elected men not for their proposals but for their reputation. Liberty, the basic value to the Founding Fathers, was to be protected by legislative checks since the checks of the political process were suspect. Ideally, two houses, rather than two parties, would check each other. In advocating the Constitution, antiparty thinkers such as Madison actually were establishing the major force in creating two great parties. Madison envisioned a pluralism among the parties rather than within them. He did not foresee parties as great, bland, enveloping coalitions. Because he feared the tyranny of a majority faction, Madison sought pluralism through a large republic and through majorities made up of weak, precarious coalitions. His view of pluralism owed much to his understanding of the liberties of religious dissent; parties were to resemble the multiplicity of sects. Based on primary and secondary sources; 29 notes.
                                                       H. Weisser

993. Hutchinson, William T. UNITE TO DIVIDE: DIVIDE TO UNITE; THE SHAPING OF AMERICAN FEDERALISM. *Mississippi Valley Hist. R. 1959 46(1): 3-18.* An interpretative essay about certain characteristics of England's policy toward the 13 American colonies and of the colonies' relations among themselves, which, after modification by experiences during the Revolutionary war and under the Articles of Confederation, served importantly to determine the form of the Federal union embodied in the Constitution of 1787. Special emphasis is given to the public domain in the West and to the territorial system of the United States as major influences upon the development of American federalism prior to about 1820.   A

994. Keller, Hans Gustav. DIE QUELLEN DER AMERIKANISCHEN VER-FASSUNG [Sources of the American Constitution]. *Schweizer Beiträge zur Allgemeinen Geschichte [Switzerland] 1958 16: 107-141.* An inquiry into the bases and elements out of which the American Constitutional Convention created the Federal Constitution of the United States. The "fathers" of the Constitution used

with prudence and care all that was offered them by the experience and knowledge of their generation, people, race and almost the whole Western world. They considered and used some of the constitutional designs submitted to them, the existing Articles of Confederation, the new constitutions of the constituent States and the political philosophy of the age. The examples of the federalist structure of the British Empire, various older plans for the formation of a union and the constitutional history of the American colonial period also had some influence on their work. Based mainly on source material concerning the history of the Constitutional Convention, and also on scholarly literature on the topic.   A

995. Riker, William H. DUTCH AND AMERICAN FEDERALISM. *J. of the Hist. of Ideas 1957 18(4): 495-521.* The framers of the American Constitution seem from their frequent references to the United Netherlands to have been influenced by Dutch federalism. There is solid historical evidence, however, for only a slight influence exerted by "inaccurate descriptions of the Dutch constitution," and by "poorly written histories of Dutch events." Moreover, the framers used this material "not as foreign experience from which they could learn, but as a metaphor for domestic experience from which they had *already* learned very much."   W. H. Coates

996. Schröder, Hans-Christoph. POLITISCHES DENKEN UND VERFASSUNGSGEBUNG IN DER FRÜHZEIT DER VEREINIGTEN STAATEN. EIN LITERATURBERICHT [Political thought and constitution-making in the early history of the United States. A bibliographical report]. *Jahrbuch für Amerikastudien [West Germany] 1969 14: 259-269.* Reviews 14 books published between 1961 and 1967 in England and America, including two biographies of John Quincy Adams (1767-1848) and one of Fisher Ames (1758-1808), with emphasis on such issues as: the importance of English political actions, traditions, and theories for the genesis of the American Revolution and the American constitutions; the egalitarian features of political representation, the style of campaigning and holding elections, and the growing polarization between the executive and legislative in prerevolutionary America; the similarities and differences between the concepts of checks and balances on the one hand and the separation of powers on the other hand; the extent of the ideological consensus between the Federalists and Anti-Federalists; and the relevance of the economic and social background for the ideological and constitutional changes. Undocumented.

G. P. Bassler

997. Shoemaker, Robert W. "DEMOCRACY" AND "REPUBLIC" AS UNDERSTOOD IN LATE 18TH CENTURY AMERICA. *Am. Speech 1966 41(2): 83-95.* Pointing out that the founding fathers generally condemned democracy while consistently praising republicanism, the author set out to find the differences between the two in the late 18th century. Much confusion existed, for sometimes the terms were used synonymously, although more often differently. The similarity arose from their both being the opposite of "monarchy" and their both positing sovereignty in the people. But here they separated. Democratic governments tried to get as close to the people as possible, to place maximum authority in their hands. Republican governments sought to extract from the

multitude the most capable members as representatives of the whole. By reducing or eliminating the powers of the executive and the judiciary in state governments of the Revolutionary period, democrats sought the concentration of powers in the portion of government closest to the people, the lower houses of the legislatures. Republicans, on the other hand, sought the separation of powers between equally balanced executive, legislative, and judicial branches as in the federal Constitution. Concentration or separation of powers was the acid test between a "democracy" and a "republic." Based on essays and books of late 18th-century political writers, 69 notes.   A

998. Simon, Paul L. THE APPOINTING POWERS OF THE PRESIDENT. *Cithara 1963 3(1): 41-55.* Analyzes the relevant debates at the Constitutional Convention, which centered on the judiciary, and during the period of ratification, in which the question was an issue in Virginia and North Carolina.
                                                                      D. M. Fahey

The Constitutional Convention

999. Banks, Margaret. DRAFTING THE AMERICAN CONSTITUTION— ATTITUDES IN THE PHILADELPHIA CONVENTION TOWARDS THE BRITISH SYSTEM OF GOVERNMENT. *Am. J. of Legal Hist. 1966 10(1): 15-33.* Arguing that the American colonists liked the British system of government, the author traces the reasons for the adoption of such a different system by the Constitutional Convention. Largely depending on James Madison's *Debates in the Federal Convention of 1787* (Athens: Ohio U. Press, 1966), the article cites comparable features of the British and U.S. systems.   N. Brockman

1000. Brown, Robert E. ECONOMIC DEMOCRACY BEFORE THE CONSTITUTION. *Am. Q. 1955 7(3): 257-274.* Historians appear to have accepted the view that people who came to America were accustomed to economic class differences in Europe and brought this social order to America with them where it continued until the frontier tended to equalize the economic differences. The author cites works of contemporary observers to show that in the period 1750-90, American society was an "economic democracy" in which man owned land, had political rights because he was a land owner, and his economic opportunities were unlimited. These observers were British, European, and American. Even the debates in the Constitutional Convention 1787 show the prevalence of land owners when the delegates were debating the government for the future when men would not all be property owners.   R. Kerley

1001. Burke, Joseph C. MAX FARRAND REVISITED: A NEW LOOK AT SOUTHERN SECTIONALISM AND SLAVERY IN THE FEDERAL CONVENTION. *Duquesne R. 1967 12(1): 1-21.* Attempts to show that the records of the American Constitutional Convention of 1787 which Max Farrand edited (published 1911-37) contradict the conclusions reached by Farrand the historian. Farrand's conclusion that the issue of Western lands rather than the issue of slavery was the great concern of the convention reflected the viewpoint of his contemporaries rather than the viewpoint of the participants of the convention. 111 notes. L. V. Eid

1002. Corwin, Edward Samuel. FRANKLIN AND THE CONSTITUTION. *Pro. of the Am. Phil. Soc. 1956 100(4): 283-288.* Benjamin Franklin's contribution to the U.S. Constitutional Convention was of small value, except in three instances: 1) he opposed a long residence requirement preliminary to naturalization; 2) he opposed limiting suffrage in national elections to freeholders, and 3) when dissension threatened to disrupt the Convention, he moved that sessions be opened with prayers, and when a text was agreed upon he urged its adoption even though he had reservations. The author denies the authenticity of a derogatory prophecy concerning Jews allegedly made in the Convention by Franklin and first published in 1934 in a pro-Nazi publication. Documented. N. Kurland

1003. Feerick, John T. THE ELECTORAL COLLEGE: WHY IT WAS CREATED. *Am. Bar Assoc. J. 1968 54(3): 249-255.* The manner of selecting a President was hotly debated at the Constitutional Convention, and various alternatives were suggested. The establishment of the electoral college system was a response both to objections to legislative election of an executive and to doubts as to the ability of the people to adequately select a President. 49 notes. J. M. McCarthy

1004. Holcombe, Arthur N. THE ROLE OF WASHINGTON IN THE FRAMING OF THE CONSTITUTION. *Huntington Lib. Q. 1955/56 19(4): 317-334.* The usual view that George Washington's importance lay in his presence and encouragement at, rather than in influence on, the actual framing of the Constitution needs revision. Carefully considered, there are many indications that his weight was felt at a number of important points and that he should be regarded not only as the standard bearer in the struggle for a more vigorous government but as one of the chief compromisers who made it possible. H. D. Jordan

1005. Keller, Hans Gustav. UNITARISMUS UND FOEDERALISMUS IM WERK DER AMERIKANISCHEN VERFASSUNGS-GEBENDEN VERSAMMLUNG [Centralism and federalism in the work of the American Constitutional Convention]. *Zeitschrift für Politik [West Germany] 1958 5(3): 214-219.* Views the Constitution of the United States as a document designed to meet immediate and practical needs, not as an expression of political ideals. The author concludes that the Constitutional Convention created a new form of government by forming a strong union but no centralized system. E. Ziemke

1006. Nadelmann, Kurt. ON THE ORIGIN OF THE BANKRUPTCY CLAUSE. *Am. J. of Legal Hist. 1957 1(3): 215-228.* History of the Bankruptcy

Clause in the U.S. Constitution. Using the documents of the Federal Convention of 1787, the debates on the clause are put in the context of contemporary colonial practice.   N. Brockman

1007. Ohline, Howard A. REPUBLICANISM AND SLAVERY: ORIGINS OF THE THREE-FIFTHS CLAUSE IN THE UNITED STATES CONSTITU-TION. *William and Mary Q. 1971 28(4): 563-584.* The three-fifths clause did not derive from a sectional swap, as southern historians contend, or from a rejection of Revolutionary ideas, as the Progressive historians say. The clause instead resulted in a compromise of two political positions—those who wanted legislative supremacy and those who considered the people sovereign. Cites evidence that support of the three-fifths clause did not mean endorsement of slavery. Mentions writings of various nationalists and Anti-Federalists. 72 notes.   H. M. Ward

1008. Rosenberg, Leonard B. WILLIAM PATERSON: NEW JERSEY'S NA-TION-MAKER. *New Jersey Hist. 1967 85(1): 7-40.* William Paterson, after his graduation from the College of New Jersey in 1763, entered the practice of law and became the first State Attorney General. In 1790 he was elected governor of New Jersey. From his work at the Federal Convention at Philadelphia in 1787 to his death in 1806 Paterson exerted "considerable influence on those events and ideas that were giving shape to the nation's political life." He introduced the New Jersey plan at the convention, from it were derived the "supremacy clause," the Supreme Court, and the recognition of the equality of the states in the Senate. As U.S. Senator (1787-90) he was largely responsible for the inclusion in the Judiciary Act of 1789 of authorization of writs of error to the Supreme Court on judgments of state courts. As governor of New Jersey (1790-93) he codified and revised the state's legal system. During his years as a Supreme Court Justice he was the first to enunciate clearly the principle of judicial review. 116 notes.
E. P. Stickney

1009. Tokushi, Yoshibumi. SHIHŌKEN YŪETSU-SEI TO 1787-NEN NO KEMPŌ KAIGI [Judicial supremacy and the Constitutional Convention of 1787]. *Seiyō Shigaku [Japan] 1957 (34): 59-72.* A commentary on and criticism of Charles Beard's and Thomas Corwin's theories. The author argues that they misunderstood or minimized the role which James Madison played in developing the idea of judicial review in the Convention, although they recognized Madison's great contribution to the making of the Constitution.   H. Imai

1010. Ulmer, S. Sidney. SUB-GROUP FORMATION IN THE CONSTITU-TIONAL CONVENTION. *Midwest J. of Pol. Sci. 1966 10(3): 288-303.* After some introductory remarks about the attempts to analyze the forces that pro-duced the U.S. Constitution, with particular emphasis upon the work of Charles Beard, Forrest McDonald, Lee Benson, and Robert Brown, the author suggests the use of bloc analysis in understanding the voting behavior of representatives to the convention. The author concludes that there were cohesive blocs, upon which issue variation had little effect; and that distribution of property, economic interests of the delegates, and large state-small state dichotomy cannot account for the voting groups revealed. The investment in slavery could have been a contributing factor in the grouping of particular states. Suggests further research into this area, using the new quantitative techniques. 7 tables, 22 notes.

J. W. Thacker, Jr.

1011. Ulmer, S. Sidney. THE ROLE OF PIERCE BUTLER IN THE CONSTI-TUTIONAL CONVENTION. *R. of Pol. 1960 22(3): 361-374.* Depicts Butler's role as that of a man strong for State sovereignty and a relatively weak central government with an almost pathological fear of executive abuse. Butler proposed the mode for election of the President as adopted by the Constitutional Convention. Otherwise, his efforts as a member of the Convention were negative and defensive, concerned with maintaining state power, controlling executive power and protecting the interests of the propertied class. Between 1787 and 1793, however, Butler's receptiveness to certain "republican" ideals suggests a philosophical evolution. Based on the correspondence of Pierce Butler and Weedon Butler Manuscript in the British Museum.

Sr. M. McAuley

1012. Unsigned. HAMILTON'S PLAN FOR A CONSTITUTION. *Freedom and Union 1957 12(6): 15-18.* Excerpts from a speech by Alexander Hamilton at the Federal Convention in Philadelphia on 18 June 1787, taken from the notes of Robert Gates, a delegate from New York State. Hamilton proposed the establishment of a strong, centralized governnent which would have virtually abolished all powers of the States. Though the Convention considered this plan too drastic for adoption, the discussion thereof resulted in the compromise solution which left certain powers to the States.

R. Mueller

Ratification of the Constitution

1013. Adair, Douglass. "THAT POLITICS MAY BE REDUCED TO A SCIENCE:" DAVID HUME, JAMES MADISON AND THE TENTH *FEDERALIST. Huntington Lib. Q. 1956/57 20(4): 343-360.* Moral philosophy, and in particular the researches and conclusions of the 18th-century Scottish school, had for Americans of the Revolutionary period much of the authority that scientific knowledge now has. The Constitution of 1787 owed a great deal to the conviction that there was a genuine science of politics. A most illuminating example is that of James Madison's famous and surprising forecast that an "extended republic" of great size and variety of interests could use these very qualities to produce stability and justice. Careful comparison shows that in developing this idea in *Federalist* No. 10, Madison owed much, even in vocabulary, to certain essays of David Hume, whose scattered axioms he selected and welded into his own cogent and closeknit argument.

H. D. Jordan

1014. Adair, Douglass. *THE FEDERALIST PAPERS. William and Mary Q. 1965 22(1): 131-139.* A review article comparing four editions of *The Federalist* published in 1961. The author examines especially the detective work by the editors to determine the authorship of certain of the *Federalist* essays, with emphasis on statistical "odds." The Jacob E. Cooke, Clinton Rossiter, Roy P. Fairfield, and Benjamin F. Wright editions are discussed.			H. M. Ward

1015. Aly, Bower. HOW HAMILTON, OUTVOTED 2 TO 1, WON NEW YORK FOR FEDERAL UNION. *Freedom and Union 1957 12(7/8): 15-22.* Excerpts from speeches by Alexander Hamilton before the New York Convention during July 1788, urging the delegates to ratify the U.S. Constitution. The author credits Hamilton's rhetorical skill and directness of diction, and the clarity with which he set forth his arguments, for his eventual success in gaining acceptance of the Constitution by two-thirds of the Convention delegates who had initially opposed it.			R. Mueller

1016. Benton, William A. PENNSYLVANIA REVOLUTIONARY OFFICERS AND THE FEDERAL CONSTITUTION. *Pennsylvania Hist. 1964 31(4): 419-435.* Surveys the attitudes of the Revolutionary officers of Pennsylvania toward the Constitution. Examines the part they took in the ratification struggle in Pennsylvania, and the possibility that the issue of a standing army versus the militia system affected their judgments. Federalists and Anti-Federalists split on this issue: Federalists preferred a standing army and the Anti-Federalists preferred a state militia system. The officers' attitudes showed that economic, religious, and geography factors were of no significant value. 41 notes.
			D. H. Swift

1017. Brant, Irving. SETTLING THE AUTHORSHIP OF *THE FEDERALIST. Am. Hist. R. 1961 67(1): 71-75.* Most scholars now agree in assigning the authorship of *Federalist* Numbers 49-58 to James Madison rather than Alexander Hamilton, but they still leave the authorship of Numbers 62 and 63 in doubt. An analysis of the evidence used to assign 49 through 58 to Madison indicates that numbers 62 and 63 should also be assigned to him.			M. Berman

1018. Brooks, Robin. ALEXANDER HAMILTON, MELANCTON SMITH, AND THE RATIFICATION OF THE CONSTITUTION IN NEW YORK. *William and Mary Q. 1967 24(3): 339-358.* Deflates Hamilton's influence on the New York ratifying convention and compares standard interpretive works on Hamilton's role. Melancton Smith, a willing compromiser, was a leading figure. Ratification would have been almost impossible without Smith, who, as the only New York City resident on the "anti" side, became convinced—via Madison's argument rather than Hamilton's persuasion—that the only alternative to probable rebelliousness in the city was unconditional acceptance of the Constitution. 50 notes.			H. M. Ward

1019. Carson, Jane. THE FAT MAJOR OF THE F.H.C. *The Old Dominion: Essays for Thomas Perkins Abernethy (Charlottesville: The U. Press of Virginia, 1964), pp. 79-95.* Describes the activities and attitudes of a group of students at the College of William and Mary in the 1770's, led by James Innes, whom they referred to as their "fat Major." F.H.C. (meaning never divulged) was the first college fraternity in British America. Innes is now remembered in Virginia history as the speaker in the Convention of 1788 where he was chosen by friends of the Federal Constitution to make the final pleas for its adoption. Though neither a planter nor son of a planter, he was accepted for leadership within the gentry. Based in part on the Jefferson Papers. 39 notes.   E. P. Stickney

1020. Crane, Elaine F. PUBLIUS IN THE PROVINCES: WHERE WAS *THE FEDERALIST* REPRINTED OUTSIDE NEW YORK CITY? *William and Mary Q. 1964 21(4): 589-592.* These essays were carried only by a relatively few newspapers during the ratification contest, and only about 20 of the essays appeared in newspapers in states where ratification was in question. Local journals, with hometown writers, performed most of the persuasive service.
H. M. Ward

1021. Hamilton, Nancy S. WHEN PATRICK HENRY FOUGHT THE FEDERAL CONSTITUTION. *Freedom and Union 1955 10(6): 6-13.* Reprint of excerpts of speeches made in June 1788 during the debates at Richmond on the ratification by Virginia of the federal Constitution. Among those quoted are James Madison, Edmund Randolph, John Marshall *(pro)* and Patrick Henry, Benjamin Harrison, John Tyler, James Monroe, and George Mason *(con)*.
R. Mueller

1022. Katz, Judith M. CONNECTICUT NEWSPAPERS AND THE CONSTITUTION, 1786-1788. *Connecticut Hist. Soc. Bull. 1965 30(2): 33-44.* Examines the editorial and news content of 10 Connecticut newspapers regarding the writing and ratification of the U.S. Constitution. The author found that all 10 printers wanted "a strong central government" and, despite the lack of accurate information, strongly supported the work of the Philadelphia convention. Once copies of the document were available, they enthusiastically advocated its ratification. Evidence as to how much influence the journalists had is inconclusive, although "they probably exerted greater authority than their counterparts today."
L. R. Murphy

1023. Kenyon, Cecilia M. MEN OF LITTLE FAITH: ANTI-FEDERALISTS ON THE NATURE OF REPRESENTATIVE GOVERNMENT. *William and Mary Q. 1955 12(1): 3-43.* Influenced by Montesquieu and Rousseau, the Anti-Federalists of 1787-88 opposed the ratification of the Constitution because of their distrust in man's ability to use power wisely. They were not democrats and had no faith in representative government on a large scale. They lacked the faith and vision needed to apply their principles on a nationwide scale.
E. Oberholzer, Jr.

1024. McDonald, Forrest. THE ANTI-FEDERALISTS. *Wisconsin Mag. of Hist. 1963 46(3): 206-214.* A discussion of the reasons, political and socioeconomic, which caused people to take either the Federalist or anti-Federalist viewpoint concerning the Constitution. Resources include election returns of the time, contemporary newspapers, and published biographies and diaries.

W. F. Peterson

1025. O'Brien, William, ed. JUSTICE CUSHING'S UNDELIVERED SPEECH ON THE FEDERAL CONSTITUTION. *William and Mary Q. 1958 15(1): 74-94.* Following an introduction, presents the text of Justice William Cushing's speech. Elevated to the chair during the first part of the Massachusetts ratifying convention by John Hancock's illness, Cushing remained silent but upon Hancock's return prepared a speech for delivery on the day before the final vote. The speech remained undelivered, probably because Hancock, a "prima donna," did not wish to share the glory with another major speaker and also because Cushing opposed the conciliatory amendments, notably a Bill of Rights, which Hancock advocated.

E. Oberholzer, Jr.

1026. Parramore, Thomas C. A YEAR IN HERTFORD COUNTY WITH ELKANAH WATSON. *North Carolina Hist. R. 1964 41(4): 448-463.* Describes the stay in North Carolina of the Massachusetts merchant and travel-writer Elkanah Watson. He purchased a plantation in eastern North Carolina in connection with efforts to establish an export-import enterprise in the area. He also vigorously fought a losing battle for ratification of the U.S. Constitution by North Carolina. Documented from the Watson collection in the New York State Library and materials from the North Carolina State Archives.

L. R. Harlan

1027. Pittman, R. Carter. JASPER YEATES'S NOTES ON THE PENNSYLVANIA RATIFYING CONVENTION, 1787. *William and Mary Q. 1965 22(2): 301-318.* The notes of Federalist Jasper Yeates at the Pennsylvania Ratifying Convention begin where the notes of Alexander Dallas leave off. They are a valuable addition to the printed notes on the convention in J. B. McMaster and F. D. Stone, *Pennsylvania and the Federal Constitution, 1787-88* (Philadelphia, 1888) and the brief notes of Anthony Wayne in *Manuscripts* 1964 16(1): 18-21. The document is reproduced.

H. M. Ward

1028. Polishook, Irwin H. AN INDEPENDENCE DAY CELEBRATION IN RHODE ISLAND, 1788. *Huntington Lib. Q. 1966 30(1): 85-93.* Independence Day in 1788 came soon after news that New Hampshire, the ninth State, had ratified the Federal Constitution. The greatly outnumbered Federalists of Rhode Island, trying to keep their flag flying, planned an outdoor feast and celebration to honor independence and ratification jointly. On the previous night, however, anti-Federalist crowds, converging on Providence from the countryside, threatened violence, which was averted only by a hasty agreement in which the promoters agreed to omit overt honor to the new Constitution. The three accounts of this episode printed here are from contemporary newspapers.

H. D. Jordan

1029. Roll, Charles, Jr. WE, SOME OF THE PEOPLE: APPORTIONMENT IN THE THIRTEEN STATE CONVENTIONS RATIFYING THE CONSTITUTION. *J. of Am. Hist. 1969 56(1): 21-40.* Applying the recent Supreme Court injunction of "one man-one vote" as a principle of legislative representation to the State conventions ratifying the Federal Constitution, the author finds grossly inequitable distribution of representation, especially in the key State of South Carolina. Theoretically, representation was so skewed as to make possible ratification by delegates representing only 14.7 percent of the white population or blocking its ratification by delegates representing 4 percent of the white people. In fact, when the required nine States had ratified, they represented only about 40 percent. The malapportionment benefited the proponents of the Constitution and was also skewed to favor commercial and coastal areas, thus giving some support to the views of Charles A. Beard, Forrest McDonald, and Lee Benson. 12 tables, 27 notes. K. B. West

1030. Rotella, Salvatore G. MONTESQUIEU AND THE *FEDERALIST*. A RESEARCH NOTE ON *FEDERALIST 47*. *Il Politico [Italy] 1967 32(4): 825-832.* In the plan of *The Federalist Papers,* numbers 47-51 stand as a well-defined unit. From number 47 the internal structure of the power of the Federal Government is discussed. Yet number 52 begins with the statement, "In the last four papers..." Why not five? Probably because number 47 gives theory in an attempt to present Montesquieu's true meaning of the separation of powers. Numbers 48-51, on the other hand, deal with practice. The conclusion to be reached is that the Constitution must be accepted on its own merits and not because it is or is not consistent with Montesquieu's political philosophy. Undocumented. Sr. M. P. Trauth

1031. Scanlan, James P. THE *FEDERALIST* AND HUMAN NATURE. *R. of Pol. 1959 21(4): 657-677.* Close examination of the *Federalist* essays (1788), written to promote acceptance of the Constitution of the United States, reveals a fully developed theory of human nature—that the strongest motives affecting human actions are antagonistic passions and immediate and personal interest. Only rarely are individuals or states guided by the weaker motives of amicable passion, true and common interest, and reason or virtue. Awareness of this underlying theory helps explain the necessity for repeated demonstrations of how the proposed Constitution would "institutionalize" the stronger motives and reinforce the weaker to promote the public good. The theory also explains the manner in which arguments were directed at the immediate and personal interest of politically powerful groups. D. R. Millar

1032. Straus, Lawrence Guy. REACTIONS OF SUPPORTERS OF THE CONSTITUTION TO THE ADJOURNMENT OF THE NEW HAMPSHIRE RATIFICATION CONVENTION—1788. *Hist. New Hampshire 1968 23(3): 37-50.* After a majority of five voted on 22 February 1788 to adjourn the Exeter convention, a four-month campaign achieved a 10-vote majority for ratification of the Constitution 21 June in Concord. All five New Hampshire weeklies were Federalist, but much of the backcountry was anti-Federalist. Six states had ratified by February; Maryland and South Carolina ratified in April and May.

Privately pessimistic, Federalists publicly used bandwagon psychology and called their opponents Tories or Shaysites. This article won the Cincinnati essay prize at Exeter in 1967. 71 notes to newspapers, published correspondence, and state papers.																			T. D. S. Bassett

1033. Swindler, William F. THE LETTERS OF PUBLIUS. *Am. Heritage 1961 12(4): 4-7 and 92-97.* A survey of the hasty writing of the *Federalist Papers* (1787-88) by Alexander Hamilton, James Madison and John Jay to support ratifications of the U.S. Constitution. The continuing importance of the *Papers,* still regarded as the classic exposition of the American federal system, is shown by the numerous reissues and new editions. The contents of the *Papers* is reviewed in the light of the contemporary pressures which helped produce it. Undocumented.																			C. R. Allen, Jr.

1034. —. [RATIFICATION OF THE UNITED STATES CONSTITUTION BY THE STATE OF NEW JERSEY]. *J. of the Rutgers U. Lib. 1959/60 23(1): 1-8, 10-32.*
	Brennan, William J., Jr. NEW JERSEY'S RATIFIED COPY OF THE FEDERAL CONSTITUTION, pp. 1-3.
	McCormick, Richard P. THE UNANIMOUS STATE, pp. 4-7.
	A LIST OF MEMBERS OF THE STATE CONVENTION, pp. 8.
	MINUTES OF THE CONVENTION OF THE STATE OF NEW JERSEY (1787), pp. 10-32.
	The ratification of the Constitution of the United States by New Jersey on 19 December 1787 brought that State formally into the Federal union and was vital to the establishment of the new, united nation. The occasion of the return of the copy of the Constitution, together with the ratification document, to Rutgers University is recorded, and an account of the ratification proceedings at Trenton is given. A list of convening members and the Minutes of the Convention are appended.																			B. Waldstein

11

REVOLUTIONARY SOCIETY: ERA OF THE REVOLUTION

General

1035. Blunt, Ruth H. SARAH HENRY AT WINTON. *Virginia Cavalcade 1965 15(2): 34-37.* An account of the life of Sarah Henry, the mother of Patrick Henry. Illus.   R. B. Lange

1036. Coddington, John Insley. ANCESTORS AND DESCENDANTS OF LADY CHRISTINA STUART (1741-1807) WIFE OF THE HON. CYRUS GRIFFIN OF VIRGINIA. *Natl. Geneal. Soc. Q. 1964 52(1): 25-36.* A genealogical account of the ancestors and descendants of Lady Christina Stuart, who was born at Traquair House, Peebles County, Scotland, in 1741. Lady Christina eloped with Cyrus Griffin (1748-1810), a young Virginian who was studying law in Edinburgh. They were married in Edinburgh on 29 April 1770. A few months later they moved to London, where Griffin became a law student at the Middle Temple. The couple settled in Virginia late in 1773. "During much of his later life, Cyrus Griffin and his family lived in 'Griffin House,' on the corner of Queen and Nicholson Streets, Williamsburg, Va., and there Lady Christina Griffin presumably died, 8 Oct. 1807." 127 notes.   D. D. Cameron

1037. Coleman, Kenneth. COLONIAL GEORGIA: NEEDS AND OPPORTU-NITIES. *Georgia Hist. Q. 1969 53(2): 184-191.* A historiographical survey of major writings on colonial Georgia, noting areas of needed research. The Trustee period (1733-54) has been most thoroughly studied by historians. The greatest need is for a more balanced picture of the less well-known Royal period (1754-75). Specialized areas for new research might include: land granting and settlement process, evaluation of wealth, trade and commerce, laboring and dependent classes, institutional development, Indian affairs, and biographies of leading Georgia figures. The author is writing a single-volume general study of colonial Georgia. Undocumented.   R. A. Mohl

1038. Heffernan, John B. THE INFLUENCE OF NAVAL AND MARITIME DEVELOPMENTS ON THE HISTORY OF GEORGIA. *Georgia Hist. Q. 1955 39(3): 240-252.* Discusses various events of naval significance in the 18th and early 19th centuries, which in some way affected the history and development of Georgia.   C. F. Latour

1039. Jackson, Harry F. CONTRIBUTIONS TO AMERICA OF THE DUTCH PATRIOT FRANCIS ADRIAN VAN DER KEMP (1752-1829). *New York Hist. 1962 43(4): 371-384.* Describes the life of a significant political, religious and intellectual pioneer in Herkimer and Oneida Counties.

                                                                A. B. Rollins

1040. Marshall, Peter. TRAVELLERS AND THE COLONIAL SCENE. *Bull. of the Brisith Assoc. for Am. Studies 1963 (7): 5-28.* Describes the reactions of British, French, and American travelers during the 18th century to the 13 colonies. Such topics as the Southern colonies, agriculture, religion, urban life, slavery, and the West are discussed. Based on secondary sources and published travel accounts.   D. J. Abramoske

1041. McLoughlin, William G. OLNEY WINSOR'S "MEMORANDUM" OF THE PHENOMENAL "DARK DAY" OF MAY 19, 1780. *Rhode Island Hist. 1967 26(3): 88-90.* Reproduces and discusses four accounts of this phenomenon, presumably caused by smoke from fires in northern New England. Originals in the possession of Robert S. Preston of East Providence.   P. J. Coleman

1042. Paul, Charles L. COLONIAL BEAUFORT. *North Carolina Hist. R. 1965 42(2): 139-152.* Settlement in the Core Sound region of North Carolina began in the early part of the 18th century, and Beaufort, laid out in 1713 and incorporated in 1723, was its center. The town grew very slowly, but it had a variety of merchant and artisan residents. Beaufort had no resident minister or church in the colonial period, but it did acquire a school just before the American Revolution. 93 notes.   J. M. Bumsted

1043. Sherman, Constance D. THROUGH AN EIGHTEENTH-CENTURY LOOKING GLASS. *New England Q. 1954 27(4): 515-521.* Describes political, social and economic conditions in New England at the time when Jean Joseph Marie Toscan was appointed French vice consul in Boston (1781). Prints Toscan's report to the French Court in 1789 in which he enlarged on his own poor financial situation and recorded his impressions of New England and the character of Americans. Based on publications and the Toscan papers in the New Hampshire Historical Society.   S

1044. Stoney, Samuel G. THE GREAT FIRE OF 1778 SEEN THROUGH CONTEMPORARY LETTERS. *South Carolina Hist. Mag. 1963 64(1): 23-26.* A letter from Gabriel Manigault to his grandson in Europe describes a fire in Charleston which began 15 January. He lists houses which were burned and saved in the Old City, including his stores. A street-by-street inventory of houses and occupants is enumerated. A letter from John Lewis Gervais to a friend, 19 April, tells of the chief commodity losses.   V. O. Bardsley

1045. Unsigned. BRITISH RECORDS RELATING TO AMERICA ON MI-CROFILM. *Can. Assoc. for Am. Studies Bull. 1967 2(1): 40-41.* A series edited for the British Association for American Studies by Walter E. Minichinton includes as new items the letters of Joseph Priestley, 1766-1803; the American correspondence of James Bryce from 1871 to 1922; the John Sparling and William Bolden letterbooks, 1788-99 (Liverpool merchants who returned from Virginia in the 1760's); material from the Dalhousie Muniments including reports and letters of colonial officials James Glen and John Forbes; and Reports on the Cotton Market, 1848-63.   D. J. O'Brien

1046. Weaver, Bettie Woodson. MARY JEFFERSON AND EPPINGTON. *Virginia Cavalcade 1969 19(2): 30-35.* A biographical sketch of Thomas Jefferson's younger daughter Mary (1778-1804), who upon the death of her mother in 1782, was placed under the care of Elizabeth and Francis Eppes at their plantation, Eppington, in Chesterfield County. She remained there until 1787 when her father, then in France as minister plenipotentiary, sent for her. In 1797 Mary Jefferson married John Wayles Eppes, son of Elizabeth and Francis, and spent much of her brief married life at Eppington. Her great affection for the plantation is stressed. The article includes information on the architecture of Eppington. Undocumented, illus.   N. L. Peterson

State & Local Politics

1047. Abbot, William W. THE STRUCTURE OF POLITICS IN GEORGIA: 1782-1789. *William and Mary Q. 1957 14(1): 47-65.* During this period the legislature dominated the State government. Although the upcountry members had a majority of seats from the beginning, the tidewater planters controlled politics until 1785. Nineteen men of exceptional ability held two-thirds of all committee posts and dominated the assembly of over 300 members. Using common sense in dealing with practical problems, they prepared Georgia for statehood in the Union. Voting qualifications and eligibility for office are also discussed.   E. Oberholzer, Jr.

1048. Barnes, Raymond P. GEORGE HANCOCK. *Virginia Cavalcade 1970 20(2): 34-39.* Biographical sketch of George Hancock (1754-1820), prominent citizen of Botetourt County. He was a member of the Virginia General Assembly from 1784 to 1787, and again in 1792, and of the Congress of the United States from 1793 to 1797. Describes his large house, Santillane, on the southern outskirts of Fincastle. William Clark (1770-1838) of the Lewis and Clark expedition married Julia Hancock, daughter of George Hancock, in June 1808. Undocumented; illus.　　　　　　　　　　　　　　　　　　　　　　　N. L. Peterson

1049. Bellot, H. H. THE LEIGHS OF SOUTH CAROLINA. *Tr. of the Royal Hist. Soc. [Great Britain] 1956 (6): 161-187.* The history of Peter Leigh (1711-59), who was chief justice of South Carolina from 1753 to 1759, and of his son, Egerton Leigh (1733-81), attorney-general of South Carolina from 1765 to 1781.　　　　　　　　　　　　　　　　　　　　　　　J. A. S. Grenville

1050. Berkeley, Edmund and Berkeley, Dorothy S. "THE ABLEST CLERK IN THE U.S.", JOHN JAMES BECKLEY. *Virginia Mag. of Hist. and Biog. 1962 70(4): 434-446.* John Clayton, attorney general of Virginia, sent for Beckley who sailed from London in 1769 and remained with the Clayton family until Clayton's death in 1774, becoming a member of the family after Clayton's death. Describes his early clerical career in Virginia and later in the House of Representatives, where he continued his clerical activity until his death in 1807.　　　　　　　　　　　　　　　　　　　　　　　J. H. Boykin

1051. Bernstein, David. A GLIMPSE AT NEW JERSEY COLONIAL POLITICS. *J. of the Rutgers U. Lib. 1967 30(2): 53-59.* Discusses the contents of an election broadside of March 1772, from Cumberland County, New Jersey. Stresses the importance of this unique document as a source for investigating and understanding the characteristics of local political warfare and their relationships to colonial political life. 10 notes.　　　　　　　　　　　　　　M. Kroeger

1052. Blaustein, Albert P. NEW YORK BAR ASSOCIATIONS PRIOR TO 1870. *Am. J. of Legal Hist. 1968 12(1): 50-57.* An outline of the trends to form associations in the New York bar prior to 1870. The earliest association was formed in the 1740's and carried on activities until 1770. Little is known about it except that it reached its height of influence in the 1760's and was a victim of the struggle between the De Lancey and Livingston families for control of the Colonial Legislature in 1768. In 1770 a club called The Moot was founded and lasted until 1775. After the Revolution, the bar declined generally and was not to reemerge as a powerfully organized entity until after the Civil War. During this interim, however, New York's oldest active legal group, the New York Law Institute, was founded in 1828. The institute was never an active bar association in the modern sense. The only other significant attempt to organize the New York bar came in 1835 when the Legal Alliance was attempted. The movement failed, however, and the bar remained disorganized and powerless until 1869. Based on records of the Association of the Bar of the City of New York, histories of the American bar, and scholarly journals; 28 notes.　　　　　　　G. P. Smith

1053. Bonomi, Patricia. POLITICAL PATTERNS IN COLONIAL NEW YORK CITY: THE GENERAL ASSEMBLY ELECTION OF 1768. *Pol. Sci. Q. 1966 81(3): 432-447.* Attempts, by comparing a list of 126 names culled from wills drawn within approximately one year after the March 1768 election in New

York City with the poll of that election, to make a judicious estimate of the importance of apathy, and finds that approximately 40 percent of those eligible to vote did not do so. Since the ratio of gentlemen, merchants, and lawyers was far higher than would be present in an average cross section of the population, this suggests that in the future apathy must be given proportionally far greater attention in explaining discrepancies between the actual vote and the total adult white male population. The author points out the apparent fallacy in studying voting patterns of automatically assuming that nonvoting can be attributed to an exclusive franchise or that the ordinary citizens of New York City were chafing under the strictures of "aristocratic" rule. The possibility that the electorate "were content to accept leadership from wealthy men who had the leisure time to work for legislation usually very much in harmony with the views of their constituents" is noted. Documented from published sources, as well as from the William Smith Papers, New York Public Library, and material in the New York Historical Society Collection. Annotated list of Participation in New York City Election of 1768.   Sr. M. McAuley

1054. Boyd, Julian P. A NEW GUIDE TO THE INDISPENSABLE SOURCES OF VIRGINIA HISTORY. *William and Mary Q. 1958 15(1): 3-13.* Describes the work of the Virginia Colonial Records Project, designed to furnish "a definitive guide to the vast resources for the history of...Virginia...from 1580 to 1780," and notes its superiority over Charles M. Andrew's work with respect to the Colonial Office Paper (C. O. 5 series). The author pleads for the support of "impractical men" who strive to make documentary sources available.
E. Oberholzer, Jr.

1055. Bridenbaugh, Carl. VIOLENCE AND VIRTUE IN VIRGINIA, 1766: OR THE IMPORTANCE OF THE TRIVIAL. *Pro. of the Massachusetts Hist. Soc. 1964 76: 3-29.* Describes the murder in June 1766 of Robert Routledge, a prominent merchant of Prince Edward County, Virginia, by Col. John Chiswell, a leader of the colony's aristocracy. The significance of the incident lies in the intensely hostile reaction of the press and the public to attempts by the aristocracy to shield Chiswell. Many were led to question "the governing of Virginia in the interests of a class by a small faction of the class." Based largely on Virginia newspapers, colonial documents and manuscript sources, the article reproduces the "first American murder diagram." 46 notes.   J. B. Duff

1056. Champagne, Roger. FAMILY POLITICS VERSUS CONSTITUTIONAL PRINCIPLES: THE NEW YORK ASSEMBLY ELECTIONS OF 1768 AND 1769. *William and Mary Q. 1963 20(1): 57-79.* Contrary to Carl Becker's thesis of over half a century ago, *The History of Political Parties in the Province of New York 1760-1776* (1909), the struggle in New York as to who should rule at home before 1776 was not between the privileged and unprivileged but rather between two groups within the ruling aristocracy. From 1765 to 1775 the Livingstons and the De Lanceys exploited popular agitation of imperial issues for local political purposes. If Becker had had available the manuscript papers of the political leaders and had made greater use of legislative journals he would have reached a different conclusion. 69 notes.   E. P. Stickney

1057. Childs, J. Rives. FRENCH CONSUL MARTIN OSTER REPORTS ON VIRGINIA 1784-1796. *Virginia Mag. of Hist. and Biog. 1968 76(1): 27-40.* Oster served as French vice-consul at Richmond and Norfolk from 1784 to 1796. His reports deal largely with his difficulties in settling disputes among the unruly French nationals in Virginia and getting the local courts to recognize his official position. Occasionally, political news is included. Oster continued to represent France at Norfolk as late as 1806 when he appears as a commissary of commercial relations. Based primarily on Oster's reports in the French National Archives; 24 notes.   K. J. Bauer

1058. Cohen, Joel A. DEMOCRACY IN REVOLUTIONARY RHODE IS-LAND: A STATISTICAL ANALYSIS. *Rhode Island Hist. 1970 29(1/2): 3-16.* Traces the history of the suffrage from the beginnings of the Colony. Calculates from tax records that most adult males who wished to vote in the Revolutionary era could do so. Concludes from an analysis of the economic standing of elected officials in 14 towns, 1775-84, that those who had a stake in society controlled local affairs. Based on manuscript records in the Rhode Island State Archives, in the Rhode Island Historical Society, and in the offices of town clerks, and on published records and secondary accounts.   P. J. Coleman

1059. Coleman, John M. THOMAS MC KEAN AND THE ORIGINS OF AN INDEPENDENT JUDICIARY. *Pennsylvania Hist. 1967 34(2): 111-130.* Considers Thomas McKean's career as Chief Justice of Pennsylvania (1777-99) in relation to the emergence of an independent judiciary in the commonwealth. As Pennsylvania's first constitution made no provision for executive and judicial independence, the task of moving toward judicial independence was a formidable one and should be evaluated in that light. Although the assembly did overrule decisions of the court, evidence of progress toward judicial independence is found in the court's granting of fair trials to those under attainder who wanted to clear themselves of charges of disloyalty. The author finds further evidence in the assembly's respect for the court's advisory opinions. Much attention is given to McKean's dual role as Pennsylvania's chief justice and the delegate to the Continental Congress from Delaware. McKean and the court came to personify the conservative reaction of the post-Revolutionary years. Based on a variety of primary sources; illus., 71 notes.   D. C. Swift

1060. Coleman, Kenneth. RESTORED COLONIAL GEORGIA (1779-1782). *Georgia Hist. Q. 1956 40(1): 1-20.* Georgia was the only one of the areas under British control during the Revolutionary War in which all branches of colonial civil government were restored after British recapture. This experience met with little success because of the hostility of the Whig back country.
                                                                                      C. F. Latour

1061. Coleman, Peter J. THE INSOLVENT DEBTOR IN RHODE ISLAND, 1745-1828. *William and Mary Q. 1965 22(3): 413-434.* Examines Rhode Island's insolvency law of 1745 and its subsequent amendments. This was the only debtor relief law in the colonies to survive the Revolution and the adoption of a national bankruptcy law in 1800. Relief was primarily temporary, permitting stays of execution (thus postponing imprisonment). Relates to state and federal court decisions on contracts and bankruptcy. Considers social aspects of indebtedness, particularly its causes. Statistical tables on the determination of insolvency petitions (1756-1828) included.   H. M. Ward

1062. Conley, Patrick T. RHODE ISLAND CONSTITUTIONAL DEVELOP-MENT, 1636-1775: A SURVEY. *Rhode Island Hist. 1968 27(2): 49-63 and (3): 74-94.* Part I. Analyzes the theological basis of Roger Williams' belief in the separation of church and state, his role in obtaining a charter in 1663, the legislative implementation of its general directives, and the overwhelming approval of it by the colonists. Part II. Emphasizes the principal constitutional issues, including civil and religious liberties, the evolution of the court system, the creation of a bicameral legislature, and suffrage. Based on records in the Rhode Island State Archives and the John Carter Brown Library, published and unpublished documents, and secondary accounts.   P. J. Coleman

1063. Conley, Patrick T. RHODE ISLAND'S PAPER MONEY ISSUE AND *TREVETT* V. *WEEDEN* (1786). *Rhode Island Hist. 1971 30(3): 95-108.* Analyzes the debt and tax problems that prompted the Rhode Island General Assembly to issue 100 thousand pounds in paper money in 1786, the propaganda attack against the emission, and the force acts of June and August 1786, which were enacted to require the acceptance of paper money. Historians have misread *Trevett* v. *Weeden,* mistakenly seeing it as an early manifestation of judicial review. Reexamines the court record and argues that the judiciary did not nullify the force act of August 1786, but rather refused to enforce the law on the technical grounds that it lacked jurisdiction. Based on town records, documents in the Rhode Island State Archives, Providence, and in the Newport Historical Society, and on secondary sources.   P. J. Coleman

1064. Coulter, E. Merton. DAVID MERIWETHER OF VIRGINIA AND GEORGIA. *Georgia Hist. Q. 1970 54(3): 320-338.* A brief biographical sketch of Meriwether (1755-1822). He was born in Virginia, served in the Revolutionary War, and became a friend of Washington and Jefferson. Moving to Georgia after the war, Meriwether served as State legislator, congressman, and as an Indian Commissioner, in which function he was instrumental in removing the Cherokee from Georgia. Among his other accomplishments, Meriwether helped found the University of Georgia. A brief account of Meriwether's immediate family is also included. Based largely on State, local, and genealogical records; 80 notes.
R. A. Mohl

1065. Crouse, Maurice A., ed. PAPERS OF GABRIEL MANIGAULT, 1771-1784. *South Carolina Hist. Mag. 1963 64(1): 1-13.* Gabriel Manigault (son of Peter Manigault, speaker of the Commons House of Assembly, 1765-72), was an architect and lawyer, educated at Geneva and Lincoln's Inn. The letters and the portion of a diary cover the years 1771-82. Prominent among the figures mentioned are Henry Laurens, John Rutledge, Arthur Middleton.
V. O. Bardsley

1066. De Pauw, Linda Grant. E. WILDER SPAULDING AND NEW YORK HISTORY. *New York Hist. 1968 49(2): 142-155.* Spaulding's *New York in the Critical Period* (1932) remains the standard work on its subject. After decades of shifting interpretations, Spaulding's study has withstood the test of time and must be considered as the starting point for all research into New York State history in the period from 1783 to 1789. While following the Progressive interpretation, Spaulding did not emphasize his historiographical position to the exclusion of a factual re-creation of the period, and the great value of his work rests upon the wealth of factual material he uncovered. While dated in its interpretation, Spaulding's work is a classic. 45 notes.   G. Kurland

1067. Evans, Emory G. THE RISE AND DECLINE OF THE VIRGINIA ARISTOCRACY IN THE EIGHTEENTH CENTURY: THE NELSONS. *The Old Dominion: Essays for Thomas Perkins Abernethy (Charlottesville: The U. Press of Virginia, 1964), pp. 62-78.* The founders of the most important families of 18th-century Virginia were of prosperous middle-class origins who arrived with financial backing and gradually rose to prominence by combining official position with planting. The Nelson family is an exception to this pattern; their fortune was established through commerce. The second generation did exceptionally well and until 1772 represented the strongest single-family influence in Virginia politics. Thomas Nelson (third generation) played an active part in the Revolution and succeeded Thomas Jefferson as governor. After 1740, however, the indebtedness of Virginians to citizens of Great Britain increased tremendously. Thomas Nelson was among those who were in serious financial difficulties before the American Revolution began and like other third generation families, he lost wealth, power, and position. Based on the author's doctoral dissertation, University of Virginia, 1957. 36 notes.   E. P. Stickney

1068. Flaherty, David H. A SELECT GUIDE TO THE MANUSCRIPT COURT RECORDS OF COLONIAL NEW ENGLAND. *Am. J. of Legal Hist. 1967 11(2): 107-126.* A compilation of some of the extant manuscript records for colonial Massachusetts, Connecticut, and Rhode Island with special emphasis on the period prior to 1776. The emphasis is on the basic corpus of existing legal materials. They are organized by state, county, and courts within the county. Not included are such records as dockets, executions, and probate materials. Based primarily on manuscript sources with references to major printed sources; 7 notes.   G. P. Smith

1069. Friedman, Bernard. THE NEW YORK ASSEMBLY ELECTIONS OF 1768 AND 1769. *New York Hist. 1965 46(1): 3-24.* Reexamines, from contemporary manuscript and news sources, the New York Assembly elections of 1768 and 1769. Replying to a thesis previously proposed by Roger Champagne in "Family Politics versus Constitutional Principles: The New York Assembly Elections of 1768 and 1769" *(William and Mary Quarterly, 20(1): 5779),* Friedman argues that the "sound and fury" was a sign of the weakness, rather than the success of the old families; and that the activities of 1768 and 1769 were a "watershed" which marked the passing of family politics as a dominant force. Stresses the role of the "radicals" and the substantive revolutionary issues.   A. B. Rollins

1070. Friedman, Bernard. THE SHAPING OF THE RADICAL CONSCIOUS-NESS IN PROVINCIAL NEW YORK. *J. of Am. Hist. 1970 56(4): 781-801.* It would be wrong to see class conflict as the basis for a conservative-radical dichotomy in New York politics. The radical consciousness was formed most strongly among farmers and mechanics who were strongly committed to an acquisitive economy and middle-class values. They protested insecure land tenure, unfair building regulations, and cheap imported labor. They based their politics on self-interest and a broad equalitarianism in opposition to a rationalist ethic that appealed to an allegedly disinterested aristocratic gentry ruling for the public good and through the deference of the "inferior classes." The radicals urged a degree of self-determination in the colony that was unacceptable to the gentry as early as 1765. They saw in the British connection a strong support for the gentry whose rule they came to oppose. 81 notes. K. B. West

1071. Gaines, William H., Jr. COURTHOUSES OF PRINCE EDWARD AND NOTTOWAY COUNTIES. *Virginia Cavalcade 1970 20(2): 40-46.* Describes the creation of two additional counties (Prince Edward in 1753 and Nottoway in 1788) by divisions of Amelia County. Supplies the histories of the courthouses. Two centuries of Prince Edward County records are intact. Undocumented, illus. N. L. Peterson

1072. Ganyard, Robert L. RADICALS AND CONSERVATIVES IN REVO-LUTIONARY NORTH CAROLINA: A POINT AT ISSUE, THE OCTOBER ELECTION, 1776. *William and Mary Q. 1967 24(4): 568-587.* The election of the Fifth Congress was of special significance because it was to act as a constitutional convention. The traditional view that the election was a triumph for the radicals is disputed. The author analyzes the contested elections in Orange, Chowan, and Guilford counties and also a sampling of the elected delegates. Actually the election was a moderate-conservative victory. The sources and interpretations of some historians of North Carolina are criticized. 28 notes. H. M. Ward

1073. Gertney, Kenneth. JAMES READ—OBSCURE PUBLIC SERVANT. *Hist. R. of Berks County 1970 36(1): 7-10, 33.* Read (1718-93) was born into the Philadelphia upper class. He was trained as a lawyer. He migrated to Reading upon establishment of the Berks County courts. Among the civil positions he held were clerk of the orphan's court, clerk of the court of common pleas, clerk of the court of quarter sessions, prothonotary, and recorder of deeds. Several of these positions he held simultaneously for long periods. He ranks as one of the earliest and most prominent public servants in the early history of Berks County. At the State level he belonged to the Radical or Constitutional Party, and served on the Council of Censors in 1783 and the Supreme Executive Council from 1787 to 1790. Illus., 17 notes. H. B. Powell

1074. Gibson, George H. "STOP THIEF!" CONSTITUTION AND MINUTES OF THE FRIENDS TO JUSTICE, 1786-1794. *Delaware Hist. 1964 11(2): 91-110.* Publishes the constitution, the list of members, and the minutes of America's first known mutual protection society, established in Wilmington in 1786 to supplement local law enforcement. Marauding vagrants from the Revolutionary Army, discharged convicts from Philadelphia who traveled south to spread their terror, and a general scourge of lawlessness in Delaware after the American Revolution prompted leading members of the city to establish a vigilante group. The primary function of the society was to sound an alarm in cases of theft and then ride out on prearranged routes in the hope of apprehending the culprit and recovering the stolen goods. The minutes reveal that the society responded to call on only three occasions. For undetermined reasons, the society declined rapidly. Based on primary and secondary sources; illus., 17 notes.   R. M. Miller

1075. Greene, Jack P. FOUNDATIONS OF POLITICAL POWER IN THE VIRGINIA HOUSE OF BURGESSES, 1720-1776. *William and Mary Q. 1959 16(4): 485-506.* An analysis of the role of 630 burgesses. Only 110 members had significant influence, but no one section had a monopoly on power. The leaders were drawn from among the wealthy planters and lawyers with economic interests. Most of them had family connections, educational advantages, and experience on the parish or county levels. Note, biblio.   E. Oberholzer, Jr.

1076. Greene, Jack P. THE NORTH CAROLINA LOWER HOUSE AND THE POWER TO APPOINT PUBLIC TREASURERS, 1711-1775. *North Carolina Hist. R. 1963 40(1): 37-53.* Describes the processes of nominating and appointing public treasurers in the Lower House of the Assembly of North Carolina. The Crown and the colonial legislature disputed whose authority this power rested in. By assuming an important share of executive duties, the North Carolina Lower House extended its authority beyond that of the British House of Commons. The Governors of North Carolina between 1730 and 1775 never were able to remove from the Lower House the power to appoint public treasurers. 35 notes.   D. H. Swift

1077. Greene, Jack P. VIRGINIA POLITICAL CULTURE IN THE ERA OF THE AMERICAN REVOLUTION. *Virginia Q. R. 1968 44(2): 302-310.* A review of *The Letters and Papers of Edmund Pendleton,1734-1803,* collected and edited by David John Mays in two volumes (Charlottesville: U. Press of Virginia, 1967). These volumes reflect the political culture of colonial and Revolutionary Virginia. This political culture was concerned with maintaining order, ensuring that justice prevailed, preserving the ideal of government by the virtuous and enlightened, and keeping an open society where a man might rise as high as his ability, resources, and opportunities allowed.
                O. H. Zabel

1078. Harkins, William J. THE ORIGIN AND DEVELOPMENT OF THE OFFICE OF SECRETARY OF STATE OF GEORGIA. *Georgia Hist. Q. 1969 53(4): 455-462.* Traces State bureaucracy to colonial origins. The original office of Secretary of State evolved from the colonial position entitled "Secretary of the Trustees," a personal representative of the Georgia Trustees who gathered reports from colonial officers and furnished instructions from England. With the transition to Royal government in Georgia in 1754, the Secretary of the Trustees became Secretary of the Colony, retaining old record-keeping and reporting duties, with additional new duties concerning colonial elections. He also became custodian of official records of the Colony. With the establishment of State government in 1777, these functions were assumed by the office of Secretary of State, although the position was not officially recognized until 1798. The secretary's official duties were expanded throughout the antebellum years. Based on research in published State records; 40 notes.   R. A. Mohl

1079. Harlow, Thompson R. THE MOSES PARK MAP, 1766. *Connecticut Hist. Soc. Bull. 1963 28(2): 33-37.* The Moses Park map was acquired from the Anson Phelps Stokes Collection in 1963. It is the first of four maps published before 1800 based on original surveys. The Moses Park survey was instigated at the request of George Montagu Dunk, the 2nd Earl of Halifax, Secretary of State in His Majesty's Service, who was trying to improve the postal service in North America. For this purpose a more accurate map of Connecticut was needed. No mention was made of westward lands, with the ironic result that this map was used in 1774 against the claims of Connecticut to lands in Pennsylvania. Illus.
E. P. Stickney

1080. Harrison, Lowell H. A YOUNG VIRGINIAN: JOHN BRECKIN-RIDGE. *Virginia Mag. of Hist. and Biography 1963 71(1): 19-34.* Breckinridge studied for a law career but pursued the dual career of farmer and lawyer. Believing firmly in local self-government and freedom of religion, he also felt that no state had the right to dissolve the Confederation without the consent of the other twelve. The article explains colonial conditions that resulted in abundant litigation to keep lawyers busy.   J. H. Boykin

1081. Hawes, Lilla Mills. SOME PAPERS OF THE GOVERNOR AND COUNCIL OF GEORGIA, 1780-1781. *Georgia Hist. Q. 1962 46(3): 280-296, (4): 395-417.* Presents aspects of the royal government of Georgia during the American Revolution in 1780-81.   R. Lowitt

1082. Hecht, Arthur. UNITED STATES-CANADIAN POSTAL RELATIONS OF THE EIGHTEENTH CENTURY. *New York Hist. 1957 38(3): 233-256.* Detailed discussion of the routes, methods of travel, rates and financial problems of the early postal system between New York and Canada, 1755-98. Based on newly inventoried correspondence and postal records in the National Archives.   A. B. Rollins

1083. Hendricks, Nathaniel. A NEW LOOK AT THE RATIFICATION OF THE VERMONT CONSTITUTION OF 1777. *Vermont Hist. 1966 34(2): 136-140.* After quoting historians' statements that the first Vermont constitution was never ratified, the author argues that Thomas Chittenden's letter of 6 February 1778 suggests that freemen approve the constitution by electing representatives to the General Assembly. He further cites the actions of three towns opposing and four supporting the 1777 constitution.   T. D. S. Bassett

1084. Hendricks, Nathaniel. THE EXPERIMENT IN VERMONT CONSTITUTIONAL GOVERNMENT. *Vermont Hist. 1966 34(1): 63-65.* The records of seven towns are cited to show that "legally warned town meetings" were held in 1777 to choose delegates to two Windsor conventions for the purpose of forming a state constitution.   R. S. Burke

1085. Johnson, Edward G. AN UNKNOWN MARYLAND IMPRINT OF THE EIGHTEENTH CENTURY. *Papers of the Biblio. Soc. of Am. 1969 63(3): 200-203.* Describes *A Rational Enquiry Into...Civil Government,* written by the Reverend Isaac Campbell (d. 1784). The book has been hitherto unrecorded in basic bibliographies. Advertised in October 1784 in *The Maryland Gazette,* it was in press in July 1785, and probably appeared later in the year. The one copy, located in the Archives of the Diocese of Maryland, is mutilated. 2 notes.
                                                                                        C. A. Newton

1086. Johnson, Herbert A. CIVIL PROCEDURE IN JOHN JAY'S NEW YORK. *Am. J. of Legal Hist. 1967 11(1): 69-80.* Generalizations concerning procedure in the civil court of New York during the period of John Jay's practice. The author surveys civil procedure in the county courts of common pleas and the Mayor's Courts of Albany, New York, and Westchester Borough. He then sketches steps necessary to prosecute a suit in the New York Court of Chancery and in the Court of Vice-Admiralty. The appellate structure of New York's courts is also touched upon. The New York civil procedure was fairly close to the English pattern, both in common law and equity courts during the last decade of the colonial period and remained basically unchanged until the enactment of the New York procedural codes in 1848. Based on court records, state codes, and scholarly articles; 38 notes.   G. P. Smith

1087. Johnson, Herbert A. GEORGE HARRISON'S PROTEST: NEW LIGHT ON *FORSEY* VERSUS *CUNNINGHAM*. *New York Hist. 1969 50(1): 61-82.* Reproduces the text of George Harrison's appeal to New York Governor Cadwallader Colden in the case of *Forsey* v. *Cunningham* (1764). Wounded in a duel with Cunningham, Thomas Forsey was awarded a judgment of 50 pounds by a common law jury. However, Waddel Cunningham appealed the jury's decision to Governor Colden on the ground that the award was excessive. Under common law, the Governor could hear appeals from the verdicts of common law juries only under Writs of Error, the facts of the case could not be appealed. But, as his instructions from the King placed no limits on his appellate powers, Colden accepted Cunningham's appeal and ordered a stay of proceedings. The bench and bar of New York vigorously condemned Colden's action as undermining the powers of common law juries. Colden, on the other hand, held that appeals by Writs of Error alone subjected the people to the tyranny of judges. The Privy Council in 1765 decided to allow Colden to hear Cunningham's appeal but declared that all subsequent appeals were to be by Writ of Error only. The case was a landmark in colonial constitutional history. Based on primary and secondary sources; 2 illus., 39 notes.   G. Kurland

1088. Kay, Marvin L. Michael. PROVINCIAL TAXES IN NORTH CAROLINA DURING THE ADMINISTRATIONS OF DOBBS AND TRYON. *North Carolina Hist. R. 1965 42(4): 440-453.* The tax structure of colonial North Carolina was highly inequitable, based on the poll tax and liquor import duties. Administration was inefficient and corrupt, partly because of the practice of paying officials by fees and commissions, but largely because the financial structure reflected the general governmental and power relationships. A small number of individuals controlled both local and provincial governments. Efficient, honest administration demanded that the provincial treasurer oversee the activities of the county sheriffs and other collectors, but instead, collusion between these officials was endemic and the governors were unable to effect reform. "The choices of this period seem to have been between provincial control which was oligarchic and corrupt and imperial control with a promise of honesty." Documented largely from published records. J. M. Bumsted

1089. Kay, Marvin L. Michael. THE PAYMENT OF PROVINCIAL AND LOCAL TAXES IN NORTH CAROLINA, 1748-1771. *William and Mary Q. 1969 26(2): 218-240.* Demonstrates that North Carolinians carried an increasingly heavy burden of taxes, secured through multitudinous duties. The poll and liquor taxes were the chief means of provincial finance. Discussed are taxes at all levels—colony, county, and parish—with instances of overlapping taxation. Excluding imperial dues and levies, quitrents, etc., the taxes paid by North Carolinians were much higher than in previous estimates. The inequitable tax structure and narrow fiscal policies contributed to demands for imperial currency reform and relief from colonial local taxes. 62 notes. H. M. Ward

1090. Keim, C. Ray. PRIMOGENITURE AND ENTAIL IN COLONIAL VIRGINIA. *William and Mary Q. 1968 25(4): 545-586.* Disagrees with traditional assumptions that primogeniture and entail followed along English lines in Virginia and discusses 125 special legislative acts docking entails before 1774. The conditions of a frontier society and availability of land contributed to the evasion of entail. Custom against entail had been so developed by 1785 that all sons could inherit equally in cases of intestacy. Most land in Virginia was never held in entail. Based on legislative records and court file documents; 112 notes. H. M. Ward

1091. Kenney, Alice P. DUTCH PATRICIANS IN COLONIAL ALBANY. *New York Hist. 1968 49(3): 249-283.* Organized as a trading center, Albany was ruled by its more prominent mercantile families, who were more concerned with the preservation of their privileges than with the welfare of the colony as a whole. Until the American Revolution, Dutch was the preferred language of Albanians, and though in the midst of an English colony, they retained their Dutch institutions. Albany's social and political life was dominated by about a dozen families, the more important being the Schuylers, Lansings, Rosebooms, and Wendels. Political divisions tended to follow family lines and to reflect family rivalries and squabbles. Based on primary and secondary sources; 14 illus., 41 notes. G. Kurland

1092. Lee, Charles E. DOCUMENTARY REPRODUCTION: LETTERPRESS PUBLICATION—WHY? WHAT? HOW? *Am. Archivist 1965 28(3): 351-365.* Analyzes the publication program of South Carolina Archives under J. Harold

Easterby, archivist from 1948 to 1960, comparing it to the work of his predecessor A. S. Salley, who had published 80 volumes of select documents. With cramped quarters and only a third of the records in custody, Easterby's new series of colonial and State records dramatized the needs of the program and eventually resulted in a new building completed after his death. Gifts of space allowed for centralization of old records of the State prior to 1900, and losses of records in wars proved not as serious as thought. Secretary of State records are complete from 1671 to 1903, and legislative records are under control from 1671 to 1775. Undocumented.   D. C. Duniway

1093. Levy, Leonard W. and Leder, Lawrence H. "EXOTIC FRUIT": THE RIGHT AGAINST COMPULSORY SELF-INCRIMINATION IN COLO-NIAL NEW YORK. *William and Mary Q. 1963 20(1): 3-32.* A refutation of the allegation of Julius Goebel and T. Raymond Naughton, *Law Enforcement in Colonial New York: A Study in Criminal Procedure* (New York, 1944), that the privilege from self-incrimination was unknown in colonial New York. The authors trace the development of the principle from the reign of Elizabeth through Coke and the Restoration period. The principle was found in the law books used in colonial New York and was applied in the courts. Although the New York Constitution of 1777 contained no bill of rights, it continued the common law, which comprehended the privilege. The Poughkeepsie Convention of 1788 recommended the inclusion of the right in the Federal Constitution.

E. Oberholzer, Jr.

1094. Main, Jackson Turner. POLITICAL PARTIES IN REVOLUTIONARY MARYLAND, 1780-1787. *Maryland Hist. Mag. 1967 62(1): 1-27.* Discusses the composition of parties in the Maryland House of Delegates. Follows three lines of investigation: the constituencies which the men represented, the characteristics of the delegates, and the nature of the issues which divided them. Political alignments are explained primarily by analyzing the economic and social environment, with particular attention to the needs and objectives of geographical areas, and of social and occupational groups. 5 graphs, 54 notes.   D. H. Swift

1095. Main, Jackson Turner. SECTIONS AND POLITICS IN VIRGINIA, 1781-1787. *William and Mary Q. 1955 12(1): 96-112.* An analysis of the counties' attitudes on political matters in relation to their socioeconomic characteristics. Not the Fall Line, separating the Tidewater and Piedmont areas, but the James River, separating the Northern Neck from the Southside, was the dividing line. Still more meaningful is the division between counties with access to navigable rivers and those removed from these streams. Based on tax lists and voting records.   E. Oberholzer, Jr.

1096. Main, Jackson Turner. SOCIAL ORIGINS OF A POLITICAL ELITE: THE UPPER HOUSE IN THE REVOLUTIONARY ERA. *Huntington Lib. Q. 1964 27(2): 147-158.* Analysis of the social origins of members of the colonial councils (1763-66) shows them to have been largely the social and economic elite of each colony. The new and larger senates which followed had a great infusion of new men, some of the established middle class, many who as individuals had risen rapidly to economic power. The strongholds of the old elites had been democratized. Further lines of investigation should be pursued to understand the relations between the new leaders and political alignments.   H. D. Jordan

1097. Pole, J. R. SUFFRAGE AND REPRESENTATION IN MASSACHU-SETTS: A STATISTICAL NOTE. *William and Mary Q. 1957 14(4): 560-596.* Analyzes voting trends and requirements for officeholding, 1780-1860. The property qualifications for voters in the constitution of 1780 were largely ignored, and an effort to disfranchise the Shaysites was reversed by the next legislature. By the time of the convention of 1820, suffrage reform was no longer a material issue and after 1821 all adult males, except paupers, were enfranchised. Property qualifications for legislators continued until 1840, thus creating a social distinction between voters and their representatives.   E. Oberholzer, Jr.

1098. Polishook, Irvin H. PETER EDES'S REPORT OF THE PROCEED-INGS OF THE RHODE ISLAND GENERAL ASSEMBLY, 1787-1790. *Rhode Island Hist. 1966 25(2): 33-42, (3): 87-97, (4): 117-129, 26(1): 15-31.* A summary of the career and political attitudes of Peter Edes, a Boston printer, who established the controversial *Newport Herald* in 1787. Reproduced are Edes' reports, with annotations, of the sessions of the Rhode Island General Assembly in October 1787, February, March, June, October, and December 1788, March, May, June, September, and October 1789, and January 1790.
P. J. Coleman

1099. Rankin, Hugh F. CRIMINAL TRIAL PROCEEDINGS IN THE GEN-ERAL COURT OF VIRGINIA. *Virginia Mag. of Hist. and Biog. 1964 72(1): 50-74.* Discusses the sometimes crude criminal proceedings before the highest court of colonial Virginia.   K. J. Bauer

1100. Reed, H. Clay and Palermo, Joseph A. JUSTICES OF THE PEACE IN EARLY DELAWARE. *Delaware Hist. 1971 14(4): 223-237.* The office of justice of the peace, widely sought after in England and colonial Delaware as recognition of social prominence within the county, retained its vital role in local government in Delaware until the American Revolution. The Delaware constitutions of 1776 and 1792 stripped the justice of his administrative and highly judicial functions, reducing him to minor status in the judicial system. Justices did not, however, suffer for lack of work. In addition to the traditional duties of taking recognizances, settling small debt claims, and binding individuals over to court, the justices took on such new tasks as poor relief, toll road fines, and the enforcement of Sabbath laws. While the prestige of the office declined in the 19th century, the office still attracted men of worth and standing, many of whom boasted those same qualities of good sense and at least casual acquaintance with the law which sustained colonial justices. 55 notes.   R. M. Miller

1101. Riley, Edward M. THE VIRGINIA COLONIAL RECORDS PROJECT. *Natl. Geneal. Soc. Q. 1963 51(2): 81-89.* Establishment of the Virginia Colonial Records Project in 1955 was necessary because the records kept at Jamestown and Williamsburg, Virginia, were either lost or destroyed during the wars fought on Virginia soil. Other than the few abstracts acquired in the 1860's, and the text for the journals, Virginia had previously made no effort to secure and publish the colonial records kept by the Public Record Office in London, England, and by 12 other institutions in the London area. "The aim of the Virginia Colonial Records Project is to find, to examine, and to make reports upon manuscript material relating to the Colony and to procure copies of that material on microfilm, or if microfilm is not available, by other photographic processes. The chronological range of the project is, at the extremes, about 1585 to 1785, which is to say from the period of the earliest attempts at settlement in North America, till the early years of the Commonwealth of Virginia." Although it has become evident that it is impossible to survey all of the city and county archives in Great Britain, the project has brought about a renaissance in the study of colonial Virginia's history.   D. D. Cameron

1102. Rowe, G. S. A VALUABLE ACQUISITION IN CONGRESS: THOMAS MC KEAN, DELEGATE FROM DELAWARE TO THE CONTINENTAL CONGRESS, 1774-1783. *Pennsylvania Hist. 1971 38(3): 225-264.* McKean represented Delaware in the Continental Congress from 1774 to 1783, excepting one year. In 1777 McKean, a Pennsylvania resident, was president of Delaware and he served in that State's assembly until 1779. In addition to these duties, McKean served as Pennsylvania's chief justice after 1777. There was considerable opposition in Pennsylvania to his plural office-holding. In Delaware, however, there was a tradition of pluralism, and whatever opposition McKean faced there was based neither upon the place of his residence nor his practice of holding several offices. Focuses on McKean's belief that a good representative "should create opinion, then direct it." Despite instructions from the Delaware legislature, McKean pushed the State toward independence and later toward accepting the Articles of Confederation. McKean followed a similar course in adopting strong nationalist positions in the Continental Congress. Based on the McKean Papers at the Historical Society of Pennsylvania, *Journals of the Continental Congress,* and other primary sources; 90 notes.   D. C. Swift

1103. Sanchez-Saavedra, E. M. "WE HAVE ONLY TO LAMENT BEING CONCERNED IN THIS BUSINESS...." *Virginia Cavalcade 1971 20(3): 34-38.* Describes the attempt in 1779-80 by groups under the direction of Thomas Walker of Virginia and Richard Henderson of North Carolina to settle the boundary dispute between the two States. Based on the journal of Daniel Smith, a member of the surveying party; 6 illus.   N. L. Peterson

1104. Sheehan, Bernard W. THE QUEST FOR INDIAN ORIGINS IN THE THOUGHT OF THE JEFFERSONIAN ERA. *MidContinent Am. Studies J. 1968 9(1): 34-51.* Discusses the interest of Jefferson and his contemporaries in the derivation of the American Indian. Varied theories expounded by numerous intellectuals of Jefferson's generation are cited, and the latter's investigation of Indian languages is surveyed at length, as are a number of weird explanations set forth by others. The majority of observers, however, manifested good judgment and a scientific approach and through their efforts helped to bring about a positive delineation of the Indian's place in the closed order of 18th-century society. Based on primary and secondary sources; 38 notes.   B. M. Morrison

1105. Surrency, Erwin C. THE COURTS IN THE AMERICAN COLONIES. *Am. J. of Legal Hist. 1967 11(3): 253-276.* A study of the origin of American courts seeking to solve historical problems arising from the fact that colonial courts exercised similar jurisdiction in different colonies under different titles. Colonial court growth was left to circumstance, but the original courts in most colonies were created by executive action of the royal governor. Gradually the general assemblies came to legislate on procedure and other matters. The colonial judicial systems were strikingly similar. Generally, each colony had civil and criminal courts of limited jurisdiction, presided over by justices of the peace. The governor and his council constituted a trial court of general jurisdiction and exercised appellate powers over the justice of the peace courts. Few chancery courts were established permanently in the colonies. Separate probate courts were not established in any of the colonies except Maryland. Based on court records, journal articles, and secondary sources; 77 notes.   G. P. Smith

1106. Swindler, William F. JOHN MARSHALL; PREPARATION FOR THE BAR—SOME OBSERVATIONS ON HIS LAW NOTES. *Am. J. of Legal Hist. 1967 11(2): 207-213.* Illustrates the significance for legal history of the nature and function of John Marshall's (1755-1835) law notes, taken during the months he studied for the bar. Several entries on abatement are excerpted and annotations are made in footnotes. Based on the law notes, legal sources cited therein, and biographical sources; 17 notes.   G. P. Smith

1107. Syrett, David. TOWNMEETING POLITICS IN MASSACHUSETTS, 1776-1786. *William and Mary Q. 1964 21(3): 352-366.* From a study of town meetings, concludes that in form there was "a kind of majority rule that approached pure democracy," but in actuality, the meetings often were dominated by the minority and by officials willing to break the rules. The frequency of meetings caused sparse attendances; notification often was poor; local officials had wide latitude in interpreting the voting qualifications; and voting procedure could be irregular.   E. Oberholzer, Jr.

1108. Unsigned. A DOCUMENT OF JULY 4, 1776. *J. of the Presbyterian Hist. Soc. 1960 38(3): 191-192.* An appeal from the people of the counties of Westmoreland and West Augusta, claimed by both Virginia and Pennsylvania, to the Second Continental Congress of the United States, for relief from the conflicting jurisdiction of the two States. The manuscript is in the papers of the Presbyterian Historical Society. It contains no signatures, and it is not clear whether it is a draft for the signed copy, or a copy of the original.   W. D. Metz

1109. Walker, Leola O. OFFICIALS IN THE CITY GOVERNMENT OF COLONIAL WILLIAMSBURG. *Virginia Mag. of Hist. and Biog. 1967 75(1): 35-51.* Attempts to reconstruct a list of city officials of Williamsburg from a series

of oaths of allegiance sworn in 1738-52 and 1768-74. The material is from the Library of Congress and a wide range of other contemporary sources. 27 notes.
                                                                          K. J. Bauer

1110. Warden, G. B. THE CAUCUS AND DEMOCRACY IN COLONIAL BOSTON. *New England Q. 1970 43(1): 19-45.* The existence of a small secretive group controlling the elections of Boston's representatives to the General Court as well as local office has long been suspected but perhaps can never be fully proved. However, the continuity in a variety of offices, the interconnectedness of certain prominent leaders in economic and familial ties, social clubs, militia, fire companies, churches, and trades suggests that such a caucus was in existence since, ca. 1719. Directed by Elisha Cooke until 1737 and financed by John Hancock after 1764, the group seems not to have been able to use liquor and personal wealth to lubricate political machinery in the intervening years. However, tax abatements and financial juggling may have been used to influence votes. The caucus does not seem to have been incompatible with democratic political operations, especially in the Boston town meeting, and was consistently motivated by an antiroyalist animus. 47 notes.   K. B. West

1111. Weir, Robert M. "THE HARMONY WE WERE FAMOUS FOR": AN INTERPRETATION OF PRE-REVOLUTIONARY SOUTH CAROLINA POLITICS. *William and Mary Q. 1969 26(4): 473-501.* South Carolinians had shaped a definite ideology concerning politics. The context of freedom under the British and South Carolina constitutional system was delineated. Absence of factions assured that the politician was checked at every turn by individual citizens. Affecting attitudes toward politics were economic prosperity, geographic location, Negrophobia, emulation of English ways, and religious dissent. The author's thesis simply is that Carolinians were developing "a country ideology" which transformed the character of local politics. There is comment on some of the particulars in the confrontation between "outsiders" (British placemen) and the representatives of internal interests. 62 notes.   H. M. Ward

1112. Wilkenfeld, Bruce M. THE NEW YORK CITY COMMON COUNCIL, 1689-1800. *New York Hist. 1971 52(3): 249-273.* Studies the backgrounds and tenure of members of the New York City Common Council, 1689-1800. In 1689-1733, the average length of tenure was 4.4 years; 56 percent of the council came from the city's artisan class, while 44 percent came from the mercantile elite. Except for the lowest classes, the council was fairly representative of New York's general population. Rotation in office was the rule. In 1734-75, average length of tenure increased to 5.8 years, and 50 percent of the members came from the elite mercantile and legal communities. Before the Revolution, merchants and lawyers dominated the council. In 1784-1800, the average length of tenure dropped to 3.6 years, and 59 percent of the council came from the artisan class. New York City politics was never monolithic and bears out Jackson Turner Main's conclusions about the structure of colonial political life. Based on primary and secondary sources; 6 illus., 42 notes.   G. Kurland

1113. Williams, John A. and Breer, Kay. ORIGINS OF THE "TEN-YEAR TIME-LOCK" IN THE VERMONT CONSTITUTION. *Vermont Hist. 1969 37(2): 132-147.* Lists 11 constitutional conventions (1777-1870) with dates of convening, proportion of proposals adopted, and substance of some of the 26 amendments. Minority and majority reports to the 1869 Council of Censors and samples of the amendment procedure (1959-64) are printed. The conventions of 1777, 1786, and 1793 adopted new constitutions. Of 106 proposals at eight conventions (1814-70), 25 percent were adopted. Of 94 proposals (1880-1960), 19 percent were adopted. T. D. S. Bassett

1114. Williams, John A. and Wallace, Marlene. VERMONT STATE PAPERS: RICH SOURCES FOR THE STUDY OF VERMONT HISTORY. *Vermont Hist. 1970 38(3): 214-249.* A serial description of 82 volumes of manuscripts in the Secretary of State's vaults (from 1778 to 1877, mostly before 1837), indexed by Mary Greene Nye. Henry Stevens, Sr., of Barnet, collected volumes 1-42 (1778-1800). Includes his transcripts relating to the New Hampshire-New York land controversy and the Haldimand negotiations, and 43 volumes of Surveyor-General's Papers, partly transcripts (indexed in *Vermont State Papers,* vol. 1). Reports on legislative, executive and financial, judicial, and local records. T. D. S. Bassett

1115. Wyllie, John C., ed. THE SECOND MRS. WAYLAND, AN UNPUB-LISHED JEFFERSON OPINION ON A CASE IN EQUITY. *Am. J. of Legal Hist. 1965 9(1): 64-68.* Prints, with brief commentary, a certified copy of an opinion by Thomas Jefferson written for a widow on her rights of inheritance. The original has been lost. N. Brockman

1116. Zornow, William F. THE SANDY HOOK LIGHTHOUSE INCIDENT OF 1787. *J. of Econ. Hist. 1954 14(3): 261-266.* Shows that, contrary to a number of noted authorities, the act of 1787 by the New York legislature, to which New Jersey reacted by taxing the Sandy Hook lighthouse, actually moderated the charges on New Jersey ships. F. L. Nussbaum

1117. Zuckerman, Michael D. THE SOCIAL CONTEXT OF DEMOCRACY IN MASSACHUSETTS. *William and Mary Q. 1968 25(4): 523-544.* Looks into the larger question of the franchise in Massachusetts, in its social context rather than simply quantification. The author finds homogeneity and harmony in voting patterns with the argument that no conflict or dissent obtained an opposition party status. Town meetings were governed by consensus and avoided controversial issues. The franchise, therefore, was inclusive—a "democracy without demo-crats." The author takes issue with the implications of Robert E. Brown, *Middle-Class Democracy and the Revolution in Massachusetts, 1691-1780* (New York: Russell & Russell, 1955). 38 notes. H. M. Ward

1118. —. [THE SMALL FARMER IN EIGHTEENTH-CENTURY VIR-GINIA POLITICS]. *Agric. Hist. 1969 43(1): 91-105.*

Williams, D. Alan. THE SMALL FARMER IN EIGHTEENTH-CEN-
TURY VIRGINIA POLITICS, pp. 91-101. Extensive popular political participation at the local level and the relative ease with which land could be acquired
tended to deter attacks on the leadership of Virginia's gentry. Political opportunity, economic prosperity, and the maturation of plantation society produced an
equilibrium in Virginia politics at mid-century. Based mainly on Virginia county
records; 31 notes.

    Riley, Edward M. COMMENTARY ON THE SMALL FARMER IN
POLITICS, pp. 103-105. Williams is correct in investigating the local situation
in Virginia, but he unnecessarily diminishes the importance of the Burgess and
neglects the House of Burgess' journals. The paper is marred by factual errors
and too many generalizations. Williams' explanation of Virginians' motives for
serving in government is also open to some question. Based on published sources;
9 notes.   D. E. Brewster

Economic & Business Activity

1119. Alden, Dauril. YANKEE SPERM WHALERS IN BRAZILIAN WA-
TERS, AND THE DECLINE OF THE PORTUGUESE WHALE FISHERY
(1773-1801). *The Americas 1964 20(3): 267-288.* Although the commercial whaling industry in Brazil dated from the early 17th century, until 1773 colonial
whalers hunted only the smaller whales that frequented coastal waters. In that
year, the Brazilian whalers began to hunt the larger and more valuable sperm
whales, applying techniques learned from captured members of a New England
whaling ship. A considerable expansion of Brazilian whaling activities followed,
but permanent decline set in by the end of the century as increased whaling by
British and North American fleets depleted the catch in the vicinity of Brazil.
Based on Brazilian private and public archival sources.   D. Bushnell

1120. Beck, Herbert H. ELIZABETH FURNACE PLANTATION. *J. of the
Lancaster County Hist. Soc. 1965 69(1): 25-41.* An account of the charcoal iron
furnace plantation built and operated by Henry William Stiegel and later Robert
Coleman. It was the site of Stiegel's first glassmaking venture. The business
history of the furnace is related in detail. A description is given of a mansion
building which survives. Illus., map.   J(J. W. W. Loose)

1121. Beeson, Kenneth, H., Jr. INDIGO PRODUCTION IN THE EIGH-
TEENTH CENTURY. *Hispanic Am. Hist. R. 1964 44(2): 214-218.* Employing
Bernard Romans' *Natural History of East and West Florida* (New York, 1775),
reports the details of indigo manufacture in British Florida.
                                           B. B. Solnick

1122. Belden, Louise Conway. HUMPHRY MARSHALL'S TRADE IN PLANTS OF THE NEW WORLD FOR GARDENS AND FORESTS OF THE OLD WORLD. *Winterthur Portfolio 1965 2: 107-126.* Marshall (1722-1802) turned his interest in plants into a profitable business. He collected, studied, and shipped to England and France numerous plants, seeds, and animals. European buyers such as Sir Joseph Banks (1743-1820) were interested in North American plants for study, and, on occasion, for profit. Growing North American vegetation was somewhat a status symbol for English gardeners. In 1785 Marshall cataloged American trees and published his findings under the title of *Arbustrum Americanum.* This was the first publication on American trees written by an American and published in America. By combining the enthusiasm of an amateur botanist with the knowledge of a professional nurseryman, Marshall made a living and enhanced the reputation of his country in Europe. Based on primary and secondary sources; 8 photos, 42 notes.   N. A. Kuntz

1123. Berry, Thomas S. THE RISE OF FLOUR MILLING IN RICHMOND. *Virginia Mag. of Hist. and Biog. 1970 78(4): 387-408.* A detailed summary of milling and its leading entrepreneurs during the four chief periods of its growth, 1772-97, 1798-1818, 1819-48, and 1849-61. The first era saw slow, erratic beginnings and heavy speculation by leaders. Stronger businessmen with a more concentrated concern for their businesses (such as Joseph Gallego) dominated the second era. Their dependence on the world market caused major dislocations as a result of the 1818 panic. The third period began and ended in depression, yet entrepreneurs expanded the scope of their business interests. During the middle years, milling gained substantial security along with modest growth. The last period opened with, and maintained until 1860-61, tremendous expansion in Richmond production; at its close, with the cessation of formerly profitable trade outlets, collapse loomed. 7 photos, 64 notes.   C. A. Newton

1124. Bruchey, Stuart. SUCCESS AND FAILURE FACTORS: AMERICAN MERCHANTS IN FOREIGN TRADE IN THE EIGHTEENTH AND EARLY NINETEENTH CENTURIES. *Business Hist. R. 1958 32(3): 272-292.* Analyzes the many factors which contributed to the success or failure of a number of 18th- and 19th-century American merchants engaged in foreign trade and provides a summary of some of the more important business practices of the times.   V. P. Carosso

1125. Buhler, Kathryn C. THREE TEAPOTS WITH SOME ACCESSORIES. *Boston Mus. Bull. 1963 61(324): 53-63.* Describes a teapot by Nathaniel Hurd (1729/30-78; Massachusetts goldsmith); two teapots by Zachariah Brigden (1734-87); a teapot, stand, ladle, sugar urn, and coffee urn by Paul Revere (1735-1818); and a creampot by Thomas Revere (1739/40-1817, brother of Paul Revere). Based in part on Paul Revere's Daybook, a page of which is reproduced here; illus.   J. M. Hawes

1126. Chamberlain, Narcissa G. THE NEIGHBORS OF JEREMIAH LEE AND THE BOUNDARIES OF HIS PROPERTY. *Essex Inst. Hist. Collections 1969 105(2): 124-136.* Traces the history of the boundaries of the merchant town house of Jeremiah Lee built in Marblehead in 1768, showing that the boundaries of the present property have changed very little. Illus., 4 figs.

J. M. Bumsted

1127. Chyet, Stanley F. AARON LOPEZ: A STUDY IN BUEBAFAMA. *Am. Jewish Hist. Q. 1963 52(4): 295-310.* Contemporary comments, both Jewish and non-Jewish, concerning the character and personality of Aaron Lopez, one of New England's leading merchant shippers of the 1770's. Ezra Stiles, for instance, compared him to Socrates and Pope Clement XIV.   F. Rosenthal

1128. Cullen, Joseph P. INDENTURED SERVANTS. *Am. Hist. Illus. 1967 2(1): 32-38.* The shortage of labor in colonial America led the colonists to resort to slaves and indentured servants. The indenture system is described as accounting for "over 60 percent of all immigrants into the colonies down to 1776." The variation in length of service is described as are other related practices, such as providing the servant with 50 acres once his indenture had been completed. A brief comment is also made on the effects of slave labor on the indenture system.

J. D. Filipiak

1129. Dallett, Francis James. A COLONIAL BINDING AN ENGRAVING DISCOVERY: THE COLLEGE LEDGER OF 1769. *Princeton U. Lib. Chronicle 1970 31(2): 122-128.* The only Colonial binding on any official records of Princeton University is "The Ledger of the Trustees of the College of New Jersey, 1 May 1769." The binding, according to the bookbinder's trade card, was by John Dean of Philadelphia, whose history is related. The trade card was engraved by Dunlap Adams who also may have done the first engraved college diploma. Illus., 22 notes.   D. Brockway

1130. Davison, Robert. THE REPUTATION OF A QUAKER BUSINESSMAN. *Bull. of Friends Hist. Assoc. 1958 47(2): 73-79.* Quakers have generally been concerned about the moral dangers of business employment. However, a Quaker merchant in New York, Isaac Hicks (1767-1820), had a reputation among Quakers for conducting his business on Quaker principles and providing a proper religious and moral atmosphere for his young apprentices. The author gives several examples of solicitations for employment of young boys under Hicks in which the main concern was with the opportunity for proper moral training and protection. Documented.   N. Kurland

1131. Destler, Chester McArthur. THE GENTLEMAN FARMER AND THE NEW AGRICULTURE: JEREMIAH WADSWORTH. *Agric. Hist. 1972 46(1): 135-153.* Examines Wadsworth's agricultural activities between the mid-1770's and his death in 1804. A Connecticut merchant as well as a farmer, Wadsworth belonged to the group of Atlantic seaboard gentry who, among their other interests, wanted to introduce the English agricultural revolution of the late 18th century into the United States. Wadsworth's special concern was improving

U.S. livestock and introducing new crop varieties. Based primarily on the Jeremiah Wadsworth Papers in the Connecticut Historical Society; 65 notes.

D. E. Brewster

1132. Dyke, Samuel E. THE BACHMAN FAMILY OF CABINETMAKERS: 1766-1897. *J. of the Lancaster County Hist. Soc. 1965 69(3): 168-180.* A history of the Bachman family, French Huguenots who settled in Lancaster County in 1766, and the fine cabinetmaking produced by five Bachmans during the years cited. Craftsmanship and design are analyzed and compared with the 18th-century work of the Philadelphia School. Illus. with examples of desks, highboys, and details of the art. J(J. W. W. Loose)

1133. Ellsworth, Lucius F. THE PHILADELPHIA SOCIETY FOR THE PROMOTION OF AGRICULTURE AND AGRICULTURAL REFORM, 1785-1793. *Agric. Hist. 1968 42(3): 189-199.* The Philadelphia Society for the Promotion of Agriculture was organized on 1 March 1785, largely through the efforts of John Beale Bordley, John Cadwalader, and Samuel Powel. Most of the new techniques advocated by the society were for intensive farming at a time when extensive farming was the most economically advantageous for many farmers. The members emphasized English practices. For several reasons, the society came to an end in 1793. However, it had focused attention on four topics: ways of overcoming soil exhaustion, methods of increasing crop production, means of improving livestock, and plans for laying out farmyards. Based upon the minutes of the society. W. D. Rasmussen

1134. Ernst, Joseph Albert. THE ROBINSON SCANDAL REDIVIVUS: MONEY, DEBTS, AND POLITICS IN REVOLUTIONARY VIRGINIA. *Virginia Mag. of Hist. and Biog. 1969 77(2): 146-173.* A restudy of the embezzlement of a hundred thousand pounds by John Robinson from the Colony of Virginia in 1756-66 "helps to clarify the intricate relationship among paper money, debts, and politics in revolutionary Virginia." The expanding Virginia economy of the 1750's, which was largely an outgrowth of increased British investment, collapsed in the following decade. Under these conditions Robinson's loan of the hundred thousand pounds to businessmen and entrepreneurs "was a move which shrewdly anticipated a revival of the economy and repayment of the loans" and provided the economy with some badly needed currency. Based on private papers, public documents, and monographs; 2 tables, 87 notes.

K. J. Bauer

1135. Ewing, Joseph S. THE CORRESPONDENCE OF ARCHIBALD MC-CALL AND GEORGE MC CALL, 1777-1783. *Virginia Mag. of Hist. and Biog. 1965 73(3): 313-353, (4): 425-454.* Reprints, with introduction and notes, 13 letters between Archibald McCall, a Virginia merchant in Glasgow, Scotland, and his cousin and business associate in Tappahannock, Virginia, 1777-83. They mostly contain comments on business and social matters. Includes also Archibald McCall's petition for admission to Virginia citizenship and three letters written after his return home. K. J. Bauer

1136. Fairbanks, Jonathan L. THE HOUSE OF THOMAS SHIPLEY "MILLER AT THE TIDE" ON THE BRANDYWINE CREEK. *Winterthur Portfolio 1965 2: 142-159.* Discusses the Thomas Shipley (1718-89) house, built between 1759 and 1788 in Wilmington. The house reflected the Quaker tastes of its owner. The house was destroyed in 1957, but parts have been reconstructed in the Winterthur Museum. Shipley began as a small merchant, moving to Wilmington in 1756. In the following years Shipley took interest in a grist mill and garnered, with his partners, a monopoly on one of the most prosperous milling centers in America. Shipley's house and his business habits reflect the Quaker sense of practicality and good order. Gives the names of the Shipley family and indicates the owners of the house. Based on primary and secondary sources; 13 photos, chart, 52 notes.   N. A. Kuntz

1137. Fales, Martha Gandy. DANIEL ROGERS, IPSWICH GOLDSMITH (THE CASE OF THE DOUBLE IDENTITY). *Essex Inst. Hist. Collections 1965 101(1): 40-49.* Attributes the origin of a number of pieces of silver of Essex County, Massachusetts, to the craftsman Daniel Rogers (1735-1816) of Ipswich (in Essex County) instead of to Daniel Rogers (1753-92) of Newport, Rhode Island. The Ipswich silversmith's mark was D. ROGERS. At present, evidence for this attribution is circumstantial. It is known, however, that there was an Ipswich craftsman named Daniel Rogers, and many works marked with his name have no connection with Newport but do have many connections with the Essex area. Illus.   J. M. Bumsted

1138. Fales, Martha Gandy. THE SHORTS, NEWBURYPORT CABINET-MAKERS. *Essex Inst. Hist. Collections 1966 102(3): 224-240.* Biographical information and attribution of works for a number (seven or possibly eight) of cabinetmaking Shorts. An analysis is made of account books and other papers relative to these artisans, including the complete inventory of the stock of Sewall Short (1735-75), showing "not only his personal estate but also...the materials necessary to his trade—brasses, locks, squares of glass; maple, mahogany, walnut, pine, and cedar boards; various kinds of tools—and...the furniture, both finished and unfinished, on hand in his shop." Illus.   J. M. Bumsted

1139. Farnie, D. A. THE COMMERCIAL EMPIRE OF THE ATLANTIC, 1607-1783. *Econ. Hist. R. [Great Britain] 1962 15(2): 205-218.* A synthesis of the state of Atlantic trade in the light of recent research (listed in an appended bibliography) which aims at fostering "discussion of the role of England in the growth of Atlantic trade during the two formative centuries." This is part of a great frontier movement, which found not gold but soil for the production of staples. The Dutch War of 1664-67 is "being seen as a turning point in history for it established English control over a complex of Atlantic trade." Sections are devoted to the nature and trends in the trade in cod and furs, tobacco, sugar, and slaves. The "Cisatlantic response" was the Americanization of English commerce and the development of a secular, commercial tradition. The revolt of the American colonies showed the dangers of settler-participation and of over-dependence on the American market.   B. L. Crapster

1140. Farris, Sara Guertler. WILMINGTON'S MARITIME COMMERCE 1775-1807. *Delaware Hist. 1970 14(1): 22-51.* Between 1775 and 1807 Wilmington emerged as an important distributing and marketing center for local products drawn from the surrounding countryside and from the coasting traffic and for international trade. Wilmington's favorable location and Delaware's mild tariff laws gave Wilmington merchants a decided advantage over their Philadelphia competitors. Despite British restrictions, before and after the Revolution, the small vessels employed in the West Indian trade regularly evaded British authority and carried North American foodstuffs and supplies to the sugar islands, returning home with sugar products. Also important was the Irish trade. The Philadelphia-Wilmington merchants exchanged flaxseed, potash, and especially flour, for Irish linens. While the bulk of the Wilmington foreign commerce went to the West Indies and Ireland, Wilmington merchants, after the American Revolution, boldly sought out new markets. Ships owned by Wilmington merchants such as the Hemphill family found their way to France, Holland, and even the Orient. Between 1807 and 1815, however, Wilmington's commerce experienced a decline as British and French incursions, when tied to the trade restraints imposed by the U.S., British, and French governments, discouraged international trade for some. As a consequence, merchants found alternate areas for investment, and were especially attracted to the manufacturing enterprises growing up along the Brandywine. Although commerce enjoyed a revival after the war, Wilmington capital remained largely committed to manufactures, and commerce never again rose to dominate the economic life of the city. 75 notes.

R. M. Miller

1141. Fingerhut, Eugene R. FROM SCOTS TO AMERICANS: RYEGATE'S IMMIGRANTS IN THE 1770'S. *Vermont Hist. 1967 35(4): 186-207.* The Scots-American Company, organized 5 February 1773, intended to reproduce a Scottish farming community in America, except that the Scots would be owners, not tenants. Their agents, who had inspected lands from North Carolina to northern New York, chose the southern half of Ryegate, Vermont, because of its Presbyterian owner (John Witherspoon) and Congregational neighbors, its river or road transportation to the coast, its freedom from Indian enemies, its relatively safe title, and familiar topography. In November 1773 they contracted for over ten thousand acres at 1,186 New York pounds but did not receive their deed until October 1775 after John Church, the previous proprietor under New Hampshire title, had also received a New York patent. Some 30 households reached Ryegate by 1775. Many, arriving on the New England coast after the Revolution started, never got there. By 1784 Ryegate was an Upper Connecticut Valley town with Scottish ties. Documented from emigrant company records, published state archives, and the Vermont Historical Society Papers of James Whitelaw, principal agent who stayed in Vermont.

T. D. S. Bassett

1142. French, Hannah D. CALEB BUGLASS, BINDER OF THE PROPOSED BOOK OF COMMON PRAYER, PHILADELPHIA, 1786. *Winterthur Portfolio 1970 6: 15-32.* Buglass (ca. 1738-97) was the binder of the Book of Common Prayer. The proposed book was to be for the new Protestant Episcopal Church, and was designed to please the remnant of churchmen who had sided with the patriots in the American Revolution. The book was printed but never adopted.

The author used 44 bindings, 12 from the Prayer Books, to show that Buglass was the binder. Born in England, Buglass came to Philadelphia in 1774 and established a bindery. He established himself as a master craftsman. The binding of the Book of Common Prayer came at the height of his career. Based on primary and secondary sources; 11 photos, 35 notes.   N. A. Kuntz

1143. Gill, Harold. COLONIAL SILVER AND SILVERSMITHS. *Virginia Cavalcade 1970 19(3): 5-13.* An account of silversmiths in Colonial Virginia, at least 19 of whom worked in Williamsburg between 1699 and 1775. The best-known silversmiths were James Geddy (1731-1809) and his brother-in-law William Wadill, also an engraver. Although colonists preferred English-made silver, a large quantity of silver was produced in Virginia. Only a few pieces, however, have survived, and the fate of Virginia silver remains a mystery. Undocumented, illus.   N. L. Peterson

1144. Goyne, Nancy A. THE BUREAU TABLE IN AMERICA. *Winterthur Portfolio 1967 3: 24-36.* The bureau table, introduced in England in the early 1720's, was popular in America throughout the latter part of the 18th century. The basic design is that of a dressing table with drawers and a hinged looking glass. It was popular in the urban areas of the eastern coast, particularly in Boston, Massachusetts, Philadelphia, Pennsylvania, and Charleston, South Carolina. Mainly purchased by people of means, it stood in a bedroom and was generally used as a dressing table. The cabinetmakers of Philadelphia are discussed, with particular emphasis on David Evans and Jonathan Gostelowe. These craftsmen generally sold a bureau table for about five pounds. Based on primary and secondary sources; 7 illus., 50 notes.   M. J. McBaine

1145. Gwyn, Julian. MONEY LENDING IN NEW ENGLAND: THE CASE OF SIR PETER WARREN AND HIS HEIRS 1739-1805. *New England Q. 1971 44(1): 117-134.* Analyzes money lending by Captain Peter Warren, a naval officer connected by marriage with the De Lancey family of New York. Warren had a considerable fortune by the time of his death in 1752. He lent out several thousand pounds sterling to friends in New England, including prominent figures in the political and commercial community. His heirs found some difficulty in collecting the debts after his death, and the efforts continued until 1805. He lost relatively little on unmortgaged bad debts and one can conclude that private money lending was a profitable and secure form of investment, though debtors were often remiss in meeting interest payments. Warren and his agents were reluctant to press lawsuits because his clients were prominent men. It appears that the money borrowed was used for consumption, not investment, though more needs to be known of New England money lending generally. Based on MS. sources; 63 notes.   K. B. West

1146. Hackensmith, Charles William. JOHN FITCH, A PIONEER IN THE DEVELOPMENT OF THE STEAMBOAT. *Register of the Kentucky Hist. Soc. 1967 65(3): 187-211.* The evidence that John Fitch was the originator of steam navigation in the United States and that he may have invented the earliest steam locomotive (ca. 1790's) is presented. As early as 1786, Fitch successfully built and operated a steamboat of his own design. Because of this, he was granted exclusive right to operate steamboats within the boundaries of New Jersey, Delaware, New York, Pennsylvania, and Virginia, by each State's legislature. There is good reason to believe that Robert Fulton benefited directly from Fitch's work. Further biographical data is given besides a brief history of early steam navigation. Sources include early books about Fitch, articles in scholarly journals, newspapers, and state records; 24 notes.   B. Wilkins

1147. Hamilton, Suzanne. THE PEWTER OF WILLIAM WILL: A CHECK-LIST. *Winterthur Portfolio 1971 7: 129-160.* William Will (1742-98) has long been recognized as the outstanding pewterer of 18th-century America. Fine workmanship, ambitious design, and impressive variety of forms contribute to the high esteem in which he is held today. Lists 197 pieces attributed to Will. Mentions each piece, the date of creation, and current owner, and gives a bibliographical reference. Based on primary and secondary sources; 29 photos, 10 notes.   N. A. Kuntz

1148. Henratta, James A. ECONOMIC DEVELOPMENT AND SOCIAL STRUCTURE IN COLONIAL BOSTON. *William and Mary Q. 1965 22(1): 75-92.* Using a statistical analysis, the author shows that Boston, with the emergence of trade and industry from 1750 to 1775, underwent a social transformation from a landed to a maritime society. A stratified social order appeared: at one end of the spectrum were the elite "merchant princes" and at the other the mobile "proletarians."   H. M. Ward

1149. Herndon, G. Melvin. HEMP IN COLONIAL VIRGINIA. *Agric. Hist. 1963 37(2): 86-93.* A detailed account of the cultivation of hemp and the three most common methods of processing it, as well as a description of hemp-breaks and mills. By the mid-18th century it became a commercial crop equal to about one-fourth the value of the tobacco crop, both as to acreage and market value. The culture of hemp in Virginia reached its apex during the Revolution and deteriorated soon afterwards.   W. D. Rasmussen

1150. Herndon, G. Melvin. THE DIARY OF SAMUEL EDWARD BUTLER, 1784-1786, AND THE INVENTORY AND APPRAISEMENT OF HIS ESTATE. *Georgia Hist. Q. 1968 52(2): 203-220.* Butler was a Virginia tobacco planter who migrated to the virgin soil of upper Georgia after the American Revolution. His diary recounts his journey to Georgia with two other planters in 1784 to acquire land, as well as a second trip in 1786 to secure additional acreage. He kept a record of expenses, which reveals the cost of food, lodging, and other necessaries. A list of coins in his possession shows the variety of money, foreign and American, which circulated in the post-Revolutionary period. Also included is an inventory and appraisal of Butler's estate at his death in 1809.   R. A. Mohl

1151. Hindes, Ruthanna. DELAWARE SILVERSMITHS 1700-1850. *Delaware Hist. 1967 12(4): 247-308.* Presents biographical sketches of 51 silversmiths and apprentices who worked or studied in Delaware during 1700-1850. The large number of silversmiths suggests the healthy condition of crafts in Delaware in this period. Because a definite level of wealth and urbanization was necessary to sustain specialized crafts, most Delaware silversmiths worked in Wilmington. Still, most Delaware smiths were only able to maintain themselves by practicing multiple occupations or by diversifying their business interests. Although affected by the larger urban centers of Baltimore and Philadelphia, Delaware silver was "in no way provincial in style, or inferior in workmanship." Delaware styles generally followed American trends in style, but Delaware smiths developed along with Philadelphia and Baltimore smiths a particular regional style such as the pierced or gallery rim. Probably because of the large numbers of Quaker smiths in the area, Delaware styles were often less ornate than those from other areas. Notes examples of coin silver spoons to illustrate Delaware styles and trends. Based largely on primary sources; 54 illus., 326 notes.

R. M. Miller

1152. Hupp, James L. WEST VIRGINIANS TO THE RESCUE: JAMES RUM-SEY'S MEMORIAL IN LONDON. *West Virginia Hist. 1969 30(2): 506-509.* Sketches the 1953 success of an eighth-grade project that resulted in the dedication of a memorial at the London grave of James Rumsey (1743-92), who in 1787 demonstrated his steamboat on the Potomac River. Note.   C. A. Newton

1153. Jones, Alice Hanson. LA FORTUNE PRIVEE EN PENNSYLVANIE, NEW JERSEY, DELAWARE 1774 [The private fortune in Pennsylvania, New Jersey, and Delaware, 1774]. *Ann. Economies, Soc., Civilisations [France] 1969 24(2): 235-249.* The level of American life in 1774 was high, in absolute as well as relative terms. This is partially explained by the relatively favorable proportion between manual and farm work and by the abundance of wood. The colonists represented a dynamic population. In general it appears that Americans lived better than their European counterparts. It also appears that the growth in capital exceeded 2 percent per year, a remarkable exploit in a country in the process of development. Based on printed sources and on the author's unpublished doctoral thesis at the University of Chicago; 2 tables.   R. Howell

1154. Jones, Alice Hanson. WEALTH ESTIMATES FOR THE AMERICAN MIDDLE COLONIES, 1774. *Econ. Development and Cultural Change 1970 18(4, pt. 2): 1-172.* Estimates the private wealth of Pennsylvania, New Jersey and Delaware in 1774 by examination of the detailed inventories in probate records and other materials, and by use of a sample, classified by age. Only five counties —Philadelphia, Northampton, and Westmoreland, Pennsylvania; Burlington, New Jersey; Kent, Delaware—are examined in detail. Comparing the data obtained to later periods in American history, the author believes that Americans were well-off in 1774 (better off than the average European) and that there was an ostensible decline in wealth from 1774 to 1805. The author also concludes that "the average annual growth of real per capita private wealth from 1774 to 1966 was 1.26 per cent." 4 illus., 56 tables, 94 notes, biblio., appendix.

J. W. Thacker, Jr.

1155. Jones, Newton B. WEIGHTS, MEASURES, AND MERCANTILISM: THE INSPECTION OF EXPORTS IN VIRGINIA, 1742-1820. *The Old Dominion: Essays for Thomas Perkins Abernethy (Charlottesville: The U. Press of Virginia, 1964), pp. 122-134.* Mercantilism was an integral part of the life of Virginians and other colonists. After 1776 the existing laws were not only continued in force, but by 1820 four additional products had been added as subject to inspection. During the Revolution, Virginians accepted the mercantilistic regulation; only the misuse of controls, of which examples are given, was to be resisted. After 1820 the trend was away from compulsory inspection. Based on Virginia Statutes, 35 notes.   E. P. Stickney

1156. Kihn, Phyllis. JEREMIAH WADSWORTH'S COACH. *Connecticut Hist. Soc. Bull. 1963 28(2): 42-44.* Gives the history of the coach imported from England in 1784 by Jeremiah Wadsworth, commissary general to the American troops, 1778-79. It was damaged on shipboard but repaired and redecorated in New York. After Jeremiah Wadsworth's death, the coach became the property of his son, Daniel, who valued it at 250 dollars. A description of the coach appeared in some reminiscent articles in the *Connecticut Post,* 1883-86. The detailed receipt for the purchase of the coach is given. Based on manuscripts in the Connecticut Historical Society's collections.   E. P. Stickney

1157. Klingaman, David C. THE DEVELOPMENT OF THE COASTWISE TRADE OF VIRGINIA IN THE LATER COLONIAL PERIOD. *Virginia Mag. of Hist. and Biog. 1969 77(1): 26-45.* A quantitative study of Virginia's coastal trade in 1768-72 based upon statistics derived from the naval lists. These suggest that trade among the American colonies flourished during the period and that the pace of growth of Virginia's trade was exceptional. The major exports were corn and wheat, and the chief coastwise imports were sugar and rum. 10 tables, 19 notes.   K. J. Bauer

1158. Kulikoff, Allan. THE PROGRESS OF INEQUALITY IN REVOLUTIONARY BOSTON. *William and Mary Q. 1971 28(3): 375-412.* Discusses whether there was increasingly greater equality in occupations, distribution of wealth and status, and political power, 1771-90. Finds that a hardening social inequality was in the making. The proportion of wealth held by poor and middle classes decreased. In postwar Boston the opportunity to migrate and the chance, though limited, of moderate economic success, deterred social conflict. Map, 15 tables, 66 notes.   H. M. Ward

1159. Lacy, Harriet S. EMERY FAMILY ACCOUNT BOOKS. *Hist. New Hampshire 1966 21(2): 45-48.* Describes seven surviving volumes of the accounts of an Exeter, New Hampshire, family of merchants and lawyers. One of the Emerys operated two privateers out of Newburyport, Massachusetts, 1777-79; another recorded his fees as clerk of the Court of Common Pleas, 1783-1801.
                                                    T. D. S. Bassett

1160. Land, Aubrey C. ECONOMIC BEHAVIOR IN A PLANTING SOCI-
ETY: THE EIGHTEENTH CENTURY CHESAPEAKE. *J. of Southern Hist.*
1967 33(4): 469-485. Using various sources, but chiefly county records, the
author analyzes the agricultural spectrum in pre-Revolutionary Maryland and
Virginia and then seeks to find the basis for the opulence of the fortunate few.
These few rose to dominant positions by types of enterprise more often associated
with a business community than with the leisured routine of the field crop,
tobacco. They provided services for an agrarian society as merchants, moneylend-
ers, and land dealers. As manufacturers and processors they supplied some con-
sumer goods. Clearly they saw in community needs economic opportunities, and
their estates show the consequences of their perception. They possessed the
chattels and adornments of the good life, and they owned the obligations—the
paper—of a debtor society. Yet neither their activities as businessmen nor their
wealth divorced them from their social milieu, the vast body of the poor and the
moderately endowed. 36 notes.   S. E. Humphreys

1161. Lemon, James T. HOUSEHOLD CONSUMPTION IN EIGHTEENTH-
CENTURY AMERICA AND ITS RELATIONSHIP TO PRODUCTION
AND TRADE: THE SITUATION AMONG FARMERS IN SOUTHEAST-
ERN PENNSYLVANIA. *Agric. Hist. 1967 41(1): 59-70.* Each person in a farm
family of average or better than average standard of living in southeastern Pennsylvania consumed each year about 150 pounds of meat, dairy products from one
or two cows, 10 to 15 bushels of grain, the production of a garden plot and six
or seven fruit trees, and the fleece of two sheep or the equivalent. A family of five
would need about 75 acres of cleared land to produce these necessities. Most
farms were larger than this, and it can be estimated that as many as 80 percent
of the farmers were involved in selling in the market. Based on 159 wills and other
contemporary documents.   W. D. Rasmussen

1162. Lenik, Edward J. BLOOMINGDALE FURNACE: AN ANCIENT
IRONWORKS REVISITED. *New Jersey Hist. Soc. Pro. 1964 82(3): 180-184.*
The New York, Susquehanna and Western Railroad now passes over the high
bank on the Pequannock River, rediscovered by the author in 1962 as the site of
the Bloomingdale Furnace, first mentioned in 1767. Excavations begun in the
spring of 1963 revealed the casting arch as measuring 14 feet across at its widest
point. Further excavations are planned. The North New Jersey Highlands Historical Society desires that the furnace be preserved as a historic industrial landmark.
Map.   E. P. Stickney

1163. Lenik, Edward J. THE TUXEDO-RINGWOOD CANAL. *Pro. of the*
New Jersey Hist. Soc. 1966 84(4): 271-273. The small canal (three miles long,
three feet deep, with a channel seven and one-half feet wide) running from Tuxedo
Lake, Orange County, New York, in a southwesterly direction to the Ringwood
River, was built around 1765 by Peter Hasenclever. The Tuxedo-Ringwood Canal
exerted considerable influence on the economic development of the North Jersey
area. Hasenclever, a German, headed a London syndicate which formed a corporation, The American Iron Company. In his first year in America, he brought
over 535 Germans who built bridges, forges, furnaces, reservoirs, and mills. He

developed ironworks at Ringwood, Charlotteburg, and Long Pond in New Jersey and at Haverstraw and Cortlandt in New York. A description of Tuxedo Lake and the canal to Ringwood is given in a report by four appraisers to Governor William Franklin of New Jersey in 1769. Hasenclever intended to float charcoal on the canal to the furnaces and forges to save the expense of cartage.

E. P. Stickney

1164. Lobdell, Jared C. SOME EVIDENCE OF PRICE INFLATION ON LONG ISLAND, 1770-1782, FROM THE PAPERS OF RICHARD JACKSON, JUNIOR. *J. of Long Island Hist. 1968 8(2): 39-43.* A single table comparing prices paid for four commodities (sugar, rum, molasses, and tea) by Richard Jackson, Jr. of Hempstead indicates price rises in each commodity for the 12 years. Using 1770 for an index of 1.00, in 1782 sugar was at 2.07 per loaf and 1.85 per barrel; rum, at 3.27; molasses, at 4.04; and tea, at 1.26. The inflationary index is generally a little lower than for Philadelphia. Notes.

C. A. Newton

1165. Lockridge, Kenneth. LAND POPULATION AND THE EVOLUTION OF NEW ENGLAND SOCIETY, 1630-1790. *Past and Present [Great Britain] 1968 (39): 62-80.* Contrary to the customary view that early America was invariably a land of room and opportunity, the growth of population and the practice of partible inheritance combined to produce a marked decline in the average size of landholdings in New England during the colonial period. A process of economic polarization was under way, and this produced rising land prices and a widening social and economic gap between rich and poor. Historians who present colonial America as a middle-class democracy fail to note this evolutionary deterioration in the later 18th century, a process that exacerbated prerevolutionary fears of the "Europeanization" of America. The author appeals for more research into this problem and the reasons why colonial settlers were reluctant to move West.

A. W. Coats

1166. Lovett, Robert W. A TIDEWATER MERCHANT IN NEW HAMPSHIRE. *Business Hist. R. 1959 33(1): 60-72.* An account of the business enterprises of the Frost family of Durham, New Hampshire (1770-1884), especially of George Frost (1765-1841). The author calls attention to a typical "Yankee trader," who was the focal point for scores of enterprises, but whose nonspecialized adventures became progressively restricted with changing times. Based on records in Baker Library, Harvard Business School, and on interviews with members of the family.

A

1167. Lydon, James G. FISH AND FLOUR FOR GOLD: SOUTHERN EUROPE AND THE COLONIAL AMERICAN BALANCE OF TRADE. *Business Hist. R. 1965 39(2): 171-183.* Historians have underemphasized the importance of the trade between southern Europe and the English colonies of North America. "Perhaps a third or more of the adverse balance of payments was covered" by the southern European markets.

J. H. Krenkel

1168. MacMaster, Richard K. and Skaggs, David C., eds. [ALEXANDER HAMILTON, PISCATAWAY FACTOR]. *Maryland Hist. Mag.* THE LETTERBOOKS OF ALEXANDER HAMILTON, PISCATA-WAY FACTOR, 1774-1776, 1966 61(2): 146-165, 61(4): 305-328. 1967 62(2): 135-169. Part I. Covers the year 1774. Consists of letter samples from the large collection of ledgers and journals comprising 132 volumes that make up the John Glassford and Company Papers in the Library of Congress. The letters offer a contemporary account of the economic and political situation in Maryland, from the viewpoint of a Scottish factor in the tobacco trade. Hamilton's correspondence deals mainly with business matters and the fear of loss at sea which made it necessary to send the same information by different ships. 85 notes. Part II. Covers the years 1774-75. A description of Alexander Hamilton (d. 1799) and of the problems he encountered in operating his establishment in the latter part of 1774 and early 1775. Recounts the old problems of collecting debts, of adequately stocking items, and of giving a proper price for tobacco. The epistles illustrate examples of social frustration caused by economic problems and the growing trend toward independence. The Scottish factor appeared sympathetic to the colonial cause. 80 notes. Part III. Reproduces letters written to James Brown and Company of Glasgow concerning the state of the company stores at Bladensburg, Lower Marlboro, and Piscataway. Reports primarily the debts owed the firm by various Maryland planters. Hamilton's sole concern was for some means to insure that the firm's liabilities would be recovered. He constantly remarked that the disputes between Britain and her Colonies prevented collections. Hamilton did not leave the Potomac Valley until 1778, and then only temporarily, partly because of an inheritance to an iron forge and flour mills on Occoquan Creek, Prince William County, Virginia. 94 notes.

POST-REVOLUTIONARY LETTERS OF ALEXANDER HAMILTON, PISCATAWAY MERCHANT. JANUARY-JUNE 1784, 1968 63(1): 22-54. Hamilton's (d. 1799) position as a factor for Scottish merchants was jeopardized by: 1) the growing influx of American factors into the tobacco trade replacing the traditional British firms, 2) commercial development away from places such as Piscataway to more urbanized trading communities, and 3) the Scottish tobacco lords, who, as a result of the American War of Independence, reduced their investments with the former colonies. Hamilton's business problems were complicated by personal financial obligations. Reproduces 16 letters, which are now in the Manuscripts Division of the Library of Congress.

E. P. Stickney

1169. Main, Jackson Turner. THE DISTRIBUTION OF PROPERTY IN POST-REVOLUTIONARY VIRGINIA. *Mississippi Valley Hist. R. 1954 41(2): 241-258.* Shows that a majority of the adult white males were not landowners, though the proportion of landless was not the same everywhere. Of the landowners, most were small farmers, 80 percent holding 200 acres or less. The distribution of slaves also varied greatly by section and the Fall Line, not the Tidewater, was the region of the largest estates. The physiography of Virginia was in a state of flux in the 1780's and 1790's. Based on annual compilations by the State of Virginia, begun in the years immediately following the close of the American Revolution.	G. L. A. Reilly

1170. Main, Jackson Turner. THE ONE HUNDRED. *William and Mary Q. 1954 11(3): 355-384.* A study of Virginia's hundred wealthiest men in the 1780's. These "one hundred" controlled only six percent of the land and six and one-half percent of the slaves. Large plantations were beginning to be divided. Entail and primogeniture, if ever frequently practiced, seem to have had little effect on landholding. Based on tax records; tables. E. Oberholzer, Jr.

1171. Marzio, Peter C. CARPENTRY IN THE SOUTHERN COLONIES DURING THE EIGHTEENTH CENTURY WITH EMPHASIS ON MARY-LAND AND VIRGINIA. *Winterthur Portfolio 1972 7: 229-250.* In general, the carpenters in Virginia and Maryland from 1700 to 1780 were either independent and itinerant craftsmen, or master builders. The independent craftsman normally divided his time between farming and his trade. The lack of a well-developed apprenticeship-guild system prevented the craft from providing high quality work. The term "master builder" was merely a generic name for prosperous carpenters working in the southern colonies. The southerners tried to attract skilled carpenters, but when one did arrive, he found personal abuse and unemployment. The vastness of the land, individual self-sufficiency, slavery, and the pedantry of gentlemen combined to make most areas of the South hostile toward sophisticated craftsmen. As a result buildings were poorly constructed, in terms of both materials and craftsmanship. Based on primary and secondary sources; 15 photos, 87 notes. N. A. Kuntz

1172. McCormick, R. P. THE ROYAL SOCIETY, THE GRAPE, AND NEW JERSEY. *New Jersey Hist. Soc. Pro. 1963 81(2): 75-84.* The Royal Society offered a premium for the planting of vineyards in the colonies. Two New Jersey men were winners: Edward Antill received the largest individual premium ever awarded by the Society to an American, and another, William Alexander, was honored with a gold medal. Antill's essay, republished in the *Transactions of the American Philosophical Society,* vol. I, was the first publication by any American on fruit. The work remained the authoritative work on the subject for more than half a century. It was a monument to failure: no colonial viticulturist could successfully cultivate the European grape *vitis vinifera.* But "the encouragement that he, and many others, received from the Society was instrumental in producing the knowledge that was at last to make possible the effective exploitation of the American grape." Documented. E. P. Stickney

1173. Minchinton, Walter E. RICHARD CHAMPION, NICHOLAS PO-COCK, AND THE CAROLINA TRADE. *South Carolina Hist. Mag. 1964 65(2):87-97.* Among other items the author delves into the fascinating relationship between 18th-century English porcelain makers and South Carolina, a sometime source of kaolin. Letters, ships' manifests, and other primary sources are used. A map of the route of the ship *Lloyd* from Bristol to Charleston is included. V. O. Bardsley

1174. Monahon, Eleanore Bradford. PROVIDENCE CABINETMAKERS. *Rhode Island Hist. 1964 23(1): 1-22.* An illustrated, descriptive catalogue of various pieces of furniture produced by Providence craftsmen from about 1740 to 1840 and now mainly in the collections of the Rhode Island Historical Society. Based on newspaper, manuscript, and archival records.   P. J. Coleman

1175. Morris, Richard B. AMERICAN LABOR HISTORY PRIOR TO THE CIVIL WAR: SOURCES AND OPPORTUNITIES FOR RESEARCH. *Labor Hist. 1960 1(3): 308-318.* The historian who undertakes a study of American labor in the colonial, Revolutionary, and early national eras is confronted with a lack of trade-union archives and published source materials which are so plentiful for the period since the Civil War. For American labor history prior to the Civil War the researcher must "turn to unorthodox sources, such as court records and other legal papers, petitions for legislative relief, the records of business firms, and local newspapers." The author cites specific examples from areas which he has explored. The court records which are especially valuable are widely scattered in county courthouses. In Connecticut and Maryland, however, the colonial county court records have been transferred to the State archives. In many cases files of local newspapers can be found only in the town in which they were published. Mention is made of several repositories of industrial records. The business firms with the most systematically preserved records in the pre-Civil War period are the railroads. The author concludes that although the materials for American labor history prior to the Civil War are widely scattered and often difficult to locate, the scholar will be well compensated for his searching by unusual "opportunities for original and penetrating insights."
J. H. Krenkel

1176. Prager, Frank D. A SCREW PROPELLER DRAWING OF THE FITCH PERIOD. *Am. Neptune 1963 23(3): 204-211.* Discusses this drawing in relation to earlier suggestions for screw propulsion and Fitch's steamboat interests. The drawing includes a steam engine as motive power. Fitch may well have communicated this idea to John Stevens and other Americans who began to experiment in this area five or six years later. Sources are the Fitch papers in the Library of Congress.   J. G. Lydon

1177. Prager, Frank D. AN EARLY STEAMBOAT PLAN OF JOHN FITCH. *Pennsylvania Mag. of Hist. and Biog. 1955 79(1): 63-81.* The plans here reproduced are for a paddle-wheel steamboat drawn by John Fitch of Philadelphia in 1785-86. Fitch's contributions to the development of the steamboat were more significant than previously thought. It is evident that his work cleared sufficient errors to make Fulton's success possible.   D. Houston

1178. Price, Jacob M. THE BEGINNINGS OF TOBACCO MANUFACTURE IN VIRGINIA. *Virginia Mag. of Hist. and Biog. 1956 64(1): 3-29.* Studies the early days of Virginian tobacco manufacture in the colonial and post-Revolutionary period. Based on letters written in the 1780's by Stephen Mitchell VI, a young Scottish artisan working in Virginia.   C. F. Latour

1179. Roach, Benner R. THOMAS NEVEL (1721-1797) CARPENTER, EDUCATOR, PATRIOT. *J. of the Soc. of Architectural Historians 1965 24(2): 153-164.* An account of the life of a Philadelphia carpenter, who started the first school of architectural drawing in the city, executed military work during the War of Independence, and played a modest part in postwar civic life. Based on Pennsylvania archives, deed books and letters of the Carpenter's Company. 3 illus.   W. D. McIntyre

1180. Roberts, William I., III. SAMUEL STORKE: AN EIGHTEENTH-CENTURY LONDON MERCHANT TRADING TO THE AMERICAN COLONIES. *Business Hist. R. 1965 39(2): 147-170.* Numerous studies have been made on the contributions of American merchants to colonial trade, but the role played by the English merchants has generally been ignored. In this study of Samuel Storke, it is suggested that the English merchants may have been much more important in the development of transatlantic colonial trade than has generally been assumed.   J. H. Krenkel

1181. Rosenblatt, Samuel M. MERCHANT-PLANTER RELATIONS IN THE TOBACCO CONSIGNMENT TRADE: JOHN NORTON AND ROBERT CARTER NICHOLAS. *Virginia Mag. of Hist. and Biog. 1964 72(4): 454-470.* Norton, a London consignment merchant, was a close personal and business friend of Nicholas. Nicholas informed Norton of conditions in Virginia and solicited business for him while the merchant acted as London agent and banker for the planter. Norton also served as Virginia's London fiscal agent during Nicholas' term as treasurer of the colony. Based on the Norton and Nicholas Papers at Colonial Williamsburg.   K. J. Bauer

1182. Scott, Kenneth. SAMUEL CASEY, PLATERO Y FALSARIO [Samuel Casey, silversmith and forger]. *Numisma [Spain] 1954 4(11): 35-40.* History of the forgeries of a New York silversmith who lived in the second half of the 18th century. Casey counterfeited some Spanish money, particularly 18th-century duros.   J. Lluís y Navas (IHE 18545)

1183. Scott, Kenneth. THE CRUISE OF THE WHALER *NIGHTINGALE* IN 1768. *Am. Neptune 1963 23(1): 22-28.* Traces the day by day occurrences of this vessel's whaling cruise in the waters off the eastern coast of Canada between April and October 1768. Based on the diary of Dr. Samuel Adams (1745-1819) of Sandwich, Massachusetts, who acted as ship's doctor aboard the sloop *Nightingale.* Cold weather, ice, and lack of prey caused Captain Seth Folger to turn for better hunting to the waters farther off shore, after cruising from early May to early July in the Straits of Belle-Isle. Apparently much of the crew's food was obtained by hunting and fishing. Wood was gathered ashore for drying the catch. Competition was abundant. A large number of other whalers are noted, with the amount of oil taken. Two whales were struck and taken, two discovered stranded, and the carcass of another salvaged. The cruise produced more than 60 barrels of oil, a mediocre voyage. Dr. Adams' diary is in the New-York Historical Society archives.   J. G. Lydon

1184. Scott, Kenneth. THE SANDY HOOK LIGHTHOUSE. *Am. Neptune 1965 25(2): 123-127.* Examines the background leading to the erection of this aid to navigation, including problems of financing and maintenance through the period of the Revolution. Dimensions of the original structure are included. Illus.
J. G. Lydon

1185. Shaner, Richard H. ARCHAEOLOGICAL EXCAVATION AT OLEY FORGE. *Hist. R. of Berks County 1971 36(2): 55-58, 77-79.* The author describes a course for advanced history students he is conducting at Oley Valley High School. His archaeological field research class is limited to 10 students who spend a double class period each week, plus their own time on Saturdays, excavating two sites at Oley Forge. The forge was founded in 1744 by John Lesher and continued to produce iron during the American Revolution. Because servants often buried broken dishes and other objects in privies, the researchers selected an old stone privy as one site. The second site was a purported slave dwelling. The privy proved to be the most interesting site, yielding bottles, glasses, plates, dishes, and a toothbrush. Similar projects would enrich history at the high school level as it did for these students. 5 photos, 5 notes.
H. B. Powell

1186. Snow, Sinclair. NAVAL STORES IN COLONIAL VIRGINIA. *Virginia Mag. of Hist. and Biog. 1964 72(1): 75-93.* Tar was exported from Virginia as early as 1608, but too frequently it was of low quality. By the time of the Revolution, Virginia was rapidly falling behind the Carolinas as a source of naval stores.
K. J. Bauer

1187. Spawn, William and Spawn, Carol M. FRANCIS SKINNER, BOOKBINDER OF NEWPORT: AN EIGHTEENTH-CENTURY CRAFTSMAN IDENTIFIED BY HIS TOOLS. *Winterthur Portfolio 1965 2: 47-61.* Historians and collectors have long neglected American bookbinders, but a new method, taking rubbings from tool bindings for comparison, allows identification of the work of one man, and the study of a man's tools make relatively easy the establishment and pursuit of the career of one man or a group. Skinner (ca. 1708-85), a skilled craftsman, had the longest career of any known American bookbinder of the 18th century. His style was nevertheless provincial, showing the lack of outside influence and competition. Based on primary and secondary sources; 6 photos, 20 notes.
N. A. Kuntz

1188. Sprowls, R. Clay. A HISTORICAL ANALYSIS OF LOTTERY TERMS. *Can. J. of Econ. and Pol. Sci. 1954 20(3): 347-356.* Two features of lotteries are studied: 1) the inequality of prize distribution, and 2) the actuarial value of the gamble (i.e., the ratio of the value of prizes distributed to the total revenue derived from the sale of tickets). Representative lotteries of four countries are treated: England and the United States in the period 1740-1840, and modern lotteries in Spain and France in the years 1947-49. It was found that prize distributions varied between and within countries, depending on the market. Generally, the actuarial value was found to be approximately 0.6, although some U.S. lotteries were as high as 0.9.
C. R. Spurgin

1189. Taylor, George R. AMERICAN ECONOMIC GROWTH BEFORE 1840: AN EXPLORATORY ESSAY. *J. of Econ. Hist. 1964 24(4): 427-444.* Proposes the hypothesis that until about 1710 economic growth in colonial America was slow and irregular; that from 1710 to 1775 it "was relatively rapid for a preindustrial economy...and that from 1775 until 1840... *average* per capita production showed very little if any increase." The essay is based on recent studies of American economic history.   E. Feldman

1190. Taylor, Overton Hume. THE "FREE ENTERPRISE" IDEOLOGY AND AMERICAN IDEALS AND INSTITUTIONS. *Daedalus 1963 92(3): 415-432.* Traces the historical growth of laissez-faire ideology of John Locke, the 18th-century French philosophes of the Enlightenment, and the American founding fathers, especially Thomas Jefferson. "Authoritarian systems...rest upon the utterly pessimistic premise that were the people as the governed 'let alone,' they would do each other and society in, completely....To some extent, libertarian-and-democratic systems tend to involve the opposite, optimistic premise...." Originally, the majority of Americans favored the optimistic view; only certain urban classes urged passage of restrictive economic laws. Later, and now, the majority tends toward the pessimistic, "statist" view (as judged by the activities of their elected representatives); economic restrictions proliferate with no end in sight. The author suggests that, although the free enterprise ideal is presently unworkable, a standard must be found to limit governmental interference, for the good of individuals and that of society as a whole. Undocumented.
M. J. McBaine

1191. Thayer, Theodore. AN EIGHTEENTH-CENTURY FARMER AND PIONEER: SYLVANUS SEELY'S EARLY LIFE IN PENNSYLVANIA. *Pennsylvania Hist. 1968 35(1): 45-63.* An account of the life of an 18th-century farmer-pioneer based on the diary of Sylvanus Seely. In 1768 he managed the 700-acre farm of his uncle in Berks County, Pennsylvania. Considerable attention is given to the details of farm management. In the next year, the farm was sold and Sylvanus moved to the Lackawaxen River valley, where his uncle owned 10 thousand acres. There Seely, his three brothers, and two slaves settled at Blooming Grove. Sylvanus' travels and involvement in the fur trade are discussed at length. In 1771 he and his family left his brothers at Blooming Grove and took residence in a house in Chatham, New Jersey.   D. C. Swift

1192. Thomson, Robert Polk. THE TOBACCO EXPORT OF THE UPPER JAMES RIVER NAVAL DISTRICT, 1773-1775. *William and Mary Q. 1961 18(3): 393-407.* From an analysis of a naval officer's manifest book, the author shows that, during the years covered by the study, Glasgow, rather than London, was the principal market for Virginia tobacco, and that the bulk of the tobacco was shipped by factors rather than consignment agents. Tables.
E. Oberholzer, Jr.

1193. Walton, Gary M. A MEASURE OF PRODUCTIVITY CHANGE IN AMERICAN COLONIAL SHIPPING. *Econ. Hist. R. [Great Britain] 1968 21(2): 268-282.* Demonstrates the productivity change which occurred in shipping engaged in American colonial waters 1675-1775. Available evidence clearly indicates that substantial improvements were taking place. Despite variation in rates among commodity routes, the general trend is unmistakably downward. The uncompounded increase per annum in shipping productivity ranged between .6 percent and 3.1 percent by commodity route, with a general index suggesting an overall increase of approximately 1.35 percent per annum. Based on various unpublished freight rate sources from the Public Record Office (London) and from American libraries.   B. L. Crapster

1194. Walton, Gary M. OBSTACLES TO TECHNICAL DIFFUSION IN OCEAN SHIPPING, 1675-1775. *Explorations in Econ. Hist. 1970 8(2): 123-140.* Discusses changes in the technology of ocean shipping, 1765-1775, and examines variations between technical feasibility and actual practice. Improved market arrangement and reduction of dangers from pirates and privateers caused most of the improvement. The outcome was imitation of the Dutch flyboat—not the adoption of a new development, but the spread of an old development. Based mainly on colonial Naval Office Lists; 5 tables, 35 notes.   S

1195. Walton, Gary M. SOURCES OF PRODUCITIVTY CHANGE IN AMERICAN COLONIAL SHIPPING, 1675-1775. *Econ. Hist. R. [Great Britain] 1967 20(1): 67-78.* Most of the improvement is attributable to gains in economic organization and reduced uncertainties associated with pirates, privateering, and similar hazards. Reduction in size of crews and diminution of armaments cut costs. Time spent in port was reduced because of better organization of the market and no need to await convoys. Technological change was only a minor factor. The reciprocal of freight rate indexes is used as a measure of productivity change. Uses a variety of unpublished material in the Public Record Office (London) and in the possession of London insurance companies to describe size of vessels, armament, crews, port times, and speed of ships entering ports in continental America, Jamaica, and Barbados.   B. L. Crapster

1196. Wilkins, Barratt. A VIEW OF SAVANNAH ON THE EVE OF THE REVOLUTION. *Georgia Hist. Q. 1970 54(4): 577-584.* Describes Savannah, Georgia, in 1774, examining its growth in comparison to Charleston, South Carolina. Discusses business and residential patterns and describes wharves, churches, schools, and middle-class living standards. Local government lay in the hands of the parish vestry and the colonial assembly. By the Revolution, Savannah showed signs of economic maturity and urban sophistication. Part of the city's growth can be explained by its rapid commercial expansion into Charleston's large trade area. Based on primary and secondary sources; 16 notes.
                                                              R. A. Mohl

1197. Wilson, Kenneth M. SERENDIPITY AND AN AMELUNG TUMBLER. *Connecticut Hist. Soc. Bull. 1964 29(2): 33-42.* Tells how the Amelung tumbler was "discovered" by chance in the Connecticut Historical Society's glass collection. It is compared with other typical Amelung free-blown glass in the possession of other museums. John Frederick Amelung landed in Baltimore in 1784 bringing with him 68 glassworkers and appurtenances for outfitting a glass factory which he opened in 1785. Only about two dozen pieces are known which were produced by Amelung, the maker of the best American glass of the 18th century. 10 illus., 12 notes. E. P. Stickney

1198. Zirkle, Conway. PLANT HYBRIDIZATION AND PLANT BREEDING IN EIGHTEENTH-CENTURY AMERICAN AGRICULTURE. *Agric. Hist. 1969 43(1): 25-38.* A survey of 18th-century American plant breeding. The author emphasizes corn in his discussion because of the availability of records, the intentional crossing and selection efforts made with corn, and because of the crop's importance in the New World. Plants have spontaneously hybridized themselves for thousands of years, but in the 18th century we began to understand the process and to experiment with it. Based on printed sources; biblio.
D. E. Brewster

1199. —. [ARTHUR YOUNG AND AMERICAN AGRICULTURE]. *Agric. Hist. 1969 43(1): 43-67.*
Loehr, Rodney C. ARTHUR YOUNG AND AMERICAN AGRICULTURE, pp. 43-56. Discusses the influence of British agriculture on American farming, especially in the late 18th century, and of Arthur Young's importance. The author notes that most Americans who kept in touch with farming developments in England were not practicing farmers. After the War of 1812, British influence declined because of weakening cultural ties and the peculiarities of the American agricultural situation. America failed to adopt English farming methods, but benefited from the attempt. Based on printed sources; 49 notes.
Woodward, Carl R. A DISCUSSION OF ARTHUR YOUNG AND AMERICAN AGRICULTURE, pp. 57-67. Discusses Young's American correspondence, his contacts with American agricultural societies, and his presumed authorship of *American Husbandry.* The author notes that other British writers had prepared the way for Young's popularity in America. Based on published sources; 29 notes. D. E. Brewster

1200. —. [LANDSCAPE ARCHITECTURE AND HORTICULTURE IN 18TH-CENTURY AMERICA]. *Agric. Hist. 1969 43(1): 149-167.*
Senn, T. L. FARM AND GARDEN: LANDSCAPE ARCHITECTURE AND HORTICULTURE IN EIGHTEENTH-CENTURY AMERICA, pp. 149-157. Discusses the early and continued colonial interest in horticulture and landscape gardening. The 18th century was a great century for horticulture due to the variety of developments in farming and gardening, to the exploration of the New World, and to the discovery of large numbers of hitherto unknown plants. Based on secondary sources; 15 notes.
Horsfall, Frank, Jr. HORTICULTURE IN EIGHTEENTH-CENTURY AMERICA, pp. 159-167. Except among the landed aristocracy, horticulture was stagnant in colonial America and was intended primarily to provide supplemental

foods. Those who had enough money, land, and labor, however, developed gardens not only for food but also as status symbols. Horticulture and landscape gardening were most developed in the South. Based on secondary sources; 16 notes.   D. E. Brewster

1201. —. [SILK CULTURE IN COLONIAL GEORGIA]. *Agric. Hist. 1969 43(1): 120-147.*

Ewan, Joseph. SILK CULTURE IN THE COLONIES WITH PARTIC-ULAR REFERENCE TO THE EBENEZER COLONY AND THE FIRST LOCAL FLORA OF GEORGIA, pp. 129-141. Discusses silk production up to the Revolution, concentrating on the botanical aspects and the natural history of the subject. Discusses a number of contemporary writings on silk production. An appendix gives a list of plants mentioned in the anonymous publication, "Nachrichten und Anmerkungen aus dem Pflanzenreiche in Goergien, von einem Prediger der Colonie Ebenezer, 1752" ["Report and remarks on the plant kingdom in Georgia by a preacher of the Ebenezer Colony, 1752"], which the author attributes to John Martin Bolzius. Based mainly on published contemporary literature; 37 notes.

Bonner, James C. SILK GROWING IN THE GEORGIA COLONY, pp. 143-147. Supplements Ewan's article with a brief discussion of the practical aspects of Georgia silk production during the 1730's-60's. Based on published materials; 18 notes.   D. E. Brewster

1202. —. [TOBACCO PLANTERS' PROBLEMS]. *Agric. Hist. 1969 43(1): 69-89.*

Land, Aubrey C. THE TOBACCO STAPLE AND THE PLANTER'S PROBLEMS: TECHNOLOGY, LABOR, AND CROPS, pp. 69-81. Discusses tobacco growing in Maryland and Virginia, ca. 1720-70. The Chesapeake planter, usually a small grower, had established a system of production by the early 18th century that gave him a modest return. In response to an expanding market, those planters who had cash or credit increased their labor supply rather than witness a change in their technology. Those who could not buy slaves continued in traditional ways, making a marginal living. The author indicates that the great planters of tobacco's golden age drew much of their wealth from nonfarm interests. Based largely on Maryland and Virginia inventories of estates and accounts of probate. 2 tables. 31 notes.

Jordan, Weymouth T. SOME PROBLEMS OF COLONIAL TOBACCO PLANTERS: A CRITIQUE, pp. 83-86. Summarizes Land's article and suggests that he examine wills and court records, though they will probably substantiate his conclusions. Calls for further examination of American indebtedness to British creditors, for a close study of the conditions of slavery, and for a history of tobacco cultivation from 1614 to 1860. Historians should not go much further in applying sampling techniques.

Zirkle, Conway. TO PLOW OR NOT TO PLOW: COMMENT ON THE PLANTERS' PROBLEMS, pp. 87-89. Colonial farming technology developed to deal with the unusual conditions in America. Plowing was often impractical in the colonies, and in many cases would have meant more rapid depletion of the soil.   D. E. Brewster

Slavery

1203. Babuscio, Jack. CREVECOEUR IN CHARLES TOWN: THE NEGRO IN THE CAGE. *J. of Hist. Studies 1969 2(4): 283-286.* Crèvecoeur's *Letters from an American Farmer,* published in 1782, picture a new nation in a new world having a new social system whose laws were those of a natural order and in which men were free and society was uninstitutionalized. But Letter IX describes Crèvecoeur's encounter with a Negro caged in a tree and being pecked to death by birds as punishment for a crime against the whites. Babuscio points out that the difference between social fact and ideal such as that which shocked Crèvecoeur ought also to shock today's romantics who conceive of democracy as a form of anarchic relationships.   N. W. Moen

1204. Bruns, Roger. ANTHONY BENEZET'S ASSERTION OF NEGRO EQUALITY. *J. of Negro Hist. 1971 56(3): 230-238.* Anthony Benezet (1713-84) was a Quaker schoolteacher who became the most prolific antislavery propagandist during the period of the American Revolution. He based his arguments against slavery on the unequivocal assertion that Negroes were biologically, morally, and intellectually equal to all other people. Some of his ideas about black culture, especially that in Africa, were simplistic and overdrawn, but it must be remembered that most opponents of slavery in his day still considered Negroes inherently inferior in almost every respect. 33 notes.   R. S. Melamed

1205. Buxbaum, Melvin H. CYRUS BUSTILL ADDRESSES THE BLACKS OF PHILADELPHIA. *William and Mary Q. 1972 29(1): 99-108.* Reproduces an address of a free Christian Negro to a group of slaves in Philadelphia in 1787. Provides a biography of the speaker, Bustill, who was born a slave. Bustill's passiveness indicates that black abolitionists during the period worked within the context of Christian submissiveness. Only through complete deference to divine will would slaves ever be free. 22 notes.   H. M. Ward

1206. Cole, Wilford. HENRY DAWKINS AND THE QUAKER COMET. *Winterthur Portfolio 1968 4: 34-46.* Traces a late 18th-century print of Benjamin Lay (1677-1759) etched and engraved by Henry Dawkins (fl. 1753-80). Lay was a Philadelphian and one of the first Quakers to object to slavery on moral and humanitarian grounds. The original painting was by English-born William Williams (fl. 1747-90), a leading Philadelphia painter. The author traces the evolution of the original painting through six copies, all lacking the qualities of great art. The value of the works is in their message. Based on an early biography of Lay and various antislavery tracts; 10 photos, 52 notes.   N. A. Kuntz

1207. Higgins, W. Robert. CHARLES TOWN MERCHANTS AND FACTORS IN THE EXTERNAL NEGRO TRADE, 1735-1775. *South Carolina*

Hist. Mag. 1964 65(4): 205-217. Lists 405 merchants, giving year of trading, number of cargoes, duty paid. Sources are drawn from "Treasurer's Journals, Duties" in South Carolina Archives.   V. O. Bardsley

1208. Holmes, Edward A. GEORGE LIELE: NEGRO SLAVERY'S PROPHET OF DELIVERANCE. *Baptist Q. [Great Britain] 1964 20(8): 340-351, 361.* Discusses the influence of George Liele on Negro Baptists in America and Jamaica. Liele was the first Negro to be ordained in the United States as a Baptist minister and formed the first Negro Baptist Church near Augusta, Georgia. Liele's life in the United States is surveyed. Following his removal to Jamaica in 1783, his activity among the slaves and his influence on the British Baptists in getting their aid are discussed. The reasons for his success in Jamaica are listed.   E. E. Eminhizer

1209. Lovejoy, David S. SAMUEL HOPKINS: RELIGION, SLAVERY AND THE REVOLUTION. *New England Q. 1967 40(2): 227-243.* Hopkins, minister at Great Barrington, Massachusetts (1743-ca.1770), and then in Newport, Rhode Island (1770-1803), opposed slavery vigorously. As with many others, his opposition to slavery was grounded on the principles of the Declaration of Independence, but Hopkins' opposition was also based on long-held religious convictions. A "new light" preacher influenced greatly by the work of Jonathan Edwards, he believed slavery contrary to the principles of "disinterested benevolence" put forward by Edwards in his *The Nature of True Virtue* (1775). He also pressed the well-established idea of a covenant between God and the nation, a covenant which was broken by the continued toleration of slavery. 23 notes.   K. B. West

1210. MacEacheren, Elaine. EMANCIPATION OF SLAVERY IN MASSA-CHUSETTS: A REEXAMINATION, 1770-1790. *J. of Negro Hist. 1970 55(4): 289-306.* Slavery was obscurely instituted in Massachusetts Bay a few years after the Colony was established, and its demise was equally obscure more than one hundred years later. It is still not clear why the Federal Census of 1790 failed to record any slaves in Massachusetts. The judicial and economic arguments of historians fail to provide a satisfactory answer to the problem; any solution must be found in local studies of the period. Concludes that evidence now indicates that the "peculiar institution" disintegrated in Boston because of the individual actions of both masters and slaves, and that the provisions of the Massachusetts Constitution of 1780 may have played a more important role than has been previously thought. 53 notes.   R. S. Melamed

1211. MacMaster, Richard K. ARTHUR LEE'S "ADDRESS ON SLAVERY": AN ASPECT OF VIRGINIA'S STRUGGLE TO END THE SLAVE TRADE, 1765-1774. *Virginia Mag. of Hist. and Biog. 1972 80(2): 141-157.* Reviews the colony-wide controversy over the slave trade in the 1760's. Various arguments for restrictions on or the cessation of the slave trade were commonplace. Arthur Lee (1740-92) was among the more persistent advocates of abolition of the trade. His key arguments were that slavery was indefensible and adversely affected white culture and society. Such arguments contributed to the end of the slave trade by the Virginia Association in 1774. Reproduces the original Lee "Address on Slavery." 61 notes. C. A. Newton

1212. Macmaster, Richard K. LIBERTY OR PROPERTY? THE METHOD-IST PETITION FOR EMANCIPATION IN VIRGINIA, 1785. *Methodist Hist. 1971 10(1): 44-55.* Virginia Methodists petitioned the Virginia General Assembly in 1785 for the emancipation of all slaves in Virginia. Provides background on the attitudes toward slavery and attempts from 1775 to 1785 by Methodists to have slaves freed, and reproduces the petition of 1785, presumably drawn up by Thomas Coke. Itinerant Methodist preachers carried copies of the petition in their saddlebags throughout the State. At the same time, counter-petitions were circulated. The petitions were presented to the Assembly; they were debated, but no legislative action was taken. 29 notes. H. L. Calkin

1213. McManus, Edgar J. ANTI-SLAVERY LEGISLATION IN NEW YORK. *J. of Negro Hist. 1961 46(4): 207-216.* The American Revolution encouraged efforts to abolish slavery in New York. The New York Constitutional Convention of 1777 resolved that the legislature should take steps to abolish domestic slavery. Although in 1785 a majority of the legislators favored some kind of emancipation, their inability to agree on the question of suffrage for the freedmen made enactment of an emancipation measure impossible. Laws prohibiting the slave trade and encouraging private manumission were passed, and in 1799 the legislature added a *Gradual Manumission Act* to the State's statutes. In 1817 it enacted a general emancipation law to be effective in 1827. The New York movement for emancipation reflected the spirit of the times and cut across party and class lines. L. Gara

1214. Ruchames, Louis. THE SOURCES OF RACIAL THOUGHT IN COLO-NIAL AMERICA. *J. of Negro Hist. 1967 52(4): 251-272.* Racial thought in the English colonies in America was rooted in a long heritage of European racial thinking, ethnocentrism, and a history of slavery involving both Europeans and Africans. The author rejects Carl Degler's theory that racial prejudice led Englishmen to practice discrimination and that discrimination led to slavery. Rather it was the English experience with the slave trade, based on the assumption that Negroes were inferior creatures fit only for enslavement, that formed the English settlers' attitudes toward Africans in American colonies. Documented mostly by writings of other historians, 66 notes. L. Gara

1215. Spector, Robert M. THE QUOCK WALKER CASES (1781-83)—SLAV-ERY, ITS ABOLITION, AND NEGRO CITIZENSHIP IN EARLY MASSA-CHUSETTS. *J. of Negro Hist. 1968 53(1): 12-32.* Argues that the Quock Walker cases in the Massachusetts courts were a part of a series of court decisions which brought about a "common law" of abolition rather than a new departure from legal tradition. Despite Section 91 of the Massachusetts *Body of Liberties* (1641) which prohibited slavery, economic considerations led to a growth of the institution in the colonial period. The Quock cases—*Walker vs. Jennison, Jennison vs.*

Caldwell, and *Commonwealth vs. Jennison*—did not end discrimination against Negroes, which took numerous forms. Based on legal records, manuscript and published materials; 101 notes.   L. Gara

1216. Swift, David E. SAMUEL HOPKINS: CALVINIST SOCIAL CONCERN IN EIGHTEENTH CENTURY NEW ENGLAND. *J. of Presbyterian Hist. 1969 47(1): 31-54.* Examines the antislavery activities of Samuel Hopkins (1721-1803) during and after the American Revolution. A student of Jonathan Edwards, Hopkins' earliest social concern was for fair treatment of Indians living near his parish. He argued for this on the basis that Christian compassion and expediency dictated fairness. When he transferred from a frontier to an urban parish, his concern for Negro slaves was similarly animated. In gaining an antislavery reputation during the Revolution, Hopkins exerted a great influence on his fellow clergymen, showing them the moral significance of the slave system. He was a leader in movements to send Negroes back to Africa while he educated some Negroes to be Christian missionaries there. The author uses some of Hopkins' writings and biographies about his subject. 52 notes.   D. M. Furman

1217. Unsigned. A SLAVE MUTINY, 1764. *Connecticut Hist. Soc. Bull. 1966 31(1): 30-32.* Reprints two descriptions of a slave revolt aboard the brig *Hope* out of New London off the African coast in 1764. On 15 May 45 slaves mutinied, killed the captain, and took control of the vessel. The remaining whites soon suppressed the slaves, but the brig and its cargo were subsequently confiscated by Spanish officials in the West Indies.   L. R. Murphy

1218. Wax, Darold D. GEORGIA AND THE NEGRO BEFORE THE AMERICAN REVOLUTION. *Georgia Hist. Q. 1967 51(1): 63-77.* Although British merchants and the imperial government have long been thought responsible for promotion of the American slave trade, the author contends that in the case of Georgia the colony's trustees enjoyed a free hand for two decades in fashioning a colonial establishment based solely upon white labor. Despite petitions from Georgia settlers and complaints in Parliament, the trustees enforced a ban on slavery, a policy embodied in legislation of 1735. Local advocates of slavery emphasized the necessity of Negro laborers in advancing the colony economically, while opponents focused upon the inhumanity of the institution and the dangers of slave revolts and conspiracies. The economic argument won out and the trustees authorized legislation of 1750 repealing the prohibition on slavery, which rapidly became an established institution in pre-Revolutionary Georgia. 44 notes.   R. A. Mohl

1219. Wax, Darold D. THE IMAGE OF THE NEGRO IN THE *MARYLAND GAZETTE,* 1745-75. *Journalism Q. 1969 46(1): 73-80.* To shed light on colonial attitudes toward the Negro, all the known issues of the *Maryland Gazette* from 1745 through 1775 were examined to see the kind of Negro described. In the plantation economy Negro slaves were important. In the *Gazette* the Negro was seen as a form of property and a possessor of skills. With this was the image of a recalcitrant with a propensity for violence and social disruption: this is seen in sales announcements and new items. Remarks portrayed blacks as significantly different from whites, inferior and generally undesirable. On the one hand the Negro was inadequate by white standards, being childlike in behavior; on the other, the Negro was often described as sly, crafty, and deceitful, one who bore watching. The total image is complex, and indicates that patterns of race prejudice and discrimination are deeply set in the Nation's past. Based on primary sources; 22 notes.   K. J. Puffer

Education & Intellectual Life

1220. Andrews, Stuart. THOMAS JEFFERSON, AMERICAN ENCYCLOPAEDIST. *Hist. Today [Great Britain] 1967 17(8): 501-509.* Thomas Jefferson was an encyclopaedist who kept alive the ideas of the French encyclopaedists in America. The author discusses Jefferson's education, library, and ideas. He is chiefly interested in Jefferson's *A Summary View of the Rights of British America* (1774) and *Notes on Virginia* (1785). There are also observations on Jefferson's interests in university education, meteorology, Unitarianism, and Indian vocabularies. Illus.   L. A. Knafla

1221. Baskin, M. P. VYDAIUSHCHIISIA AMERIKANSKII MYSLITEL' [An outstanding American philosopher]. *Voprosy Filosofii [USSR] 1955 (6): 70-80.* On the 250th anniversary of the birth of Benjamin Franklin, surveys his activity as a philosopher, stressing his anti-theological attitude, which was probably also anti-religious to some extent, and his sociological views.   G. Lovas

1222. Bayles, Ernest E. SKETCH FOR A STUDY OF THE GROWTH OF AMERICAN EDUCATIONAL THOUGHT AND PRACTICE. *Hist. of Educ. Q. 1961 1(3): 43-49.* This outline of a course in the history of American education proposes to weld "the thought and the deed," to discuss how "each line of [educational] thought is reflected in a line of events." For the period 1630-1750 the author recognizes the Puritan thought of education as discipline and the goal of universal literacy. The period 1750-1860 is characterized by the thought of John Locke, implemented in Franklin's Academy, and of Johann Heinrich Pestalozzi implemented by Horace Mann and Henry Barnard. From 1860 to 1930 the lines go from Locke to Johann Friedrich Herbart to Ashley Thorndike, and from Jean Jacques Rousseau to Friedrich Froebel to William Kilpatrick. For the period after 1930 John Dewey's principle of "interaction" serves best as organizing concept.   J. Herbst

1223. Belok, Michael V. THE COURTESY TRADITION AND EARLY SCHOOLBOOKS. *Hist. of Educ. Q. 1968 8(3): 306-318.* Early American school books (from about 1710 to 1810) were adaptations of courtesy books, designed to develop republican gentlemen. From the courtesy books, schoolbook authors had inherited the assumption that a gentleman's education can be planned, that it is to stress virtue as the basis of gentlemanly character, and that the basis of virtue is sound religion. 27 notes.   J. Herbst

1224. Bier, Jesse. WEBERISM, FRANKLIN, AND THE TRANSCENDEN-TAL STYLE. *New England Q. 1970 43(2): 179-192.* "...certain elements of the Transcendental style represent the last clear literary reflex of the Protestant ethic and the spirit of capitalism, as described by Max Weber....I mean to focus upon Benjamin Franklin as the quintessential ethical capitalist in Weber's view and as the functional historic model for both Emerson and Thoreau. In this way we may see that certain leading and expansive features of Transcendental style are developments away from a strict Franklinian pragmatism and a narrow cost-analysis of experience to a higher and broader expression of Protestant economy and moral ledgerism." For Emerson God was a sublime accountant rewarding virtue with prosperity or with higher rewards. Emerson was more worldly and utilitarian than Thoreau, who scorned material success as destructive of basic human values such as happiness. Thoreau too, however, sometimes used a "cost-analysis" style and accepted basic traditional values such as hard work. Both, along with Franklin, shared a rather simplistic denial of the moral complexities of life and today seem shallower in their perceptions than figures such as Hawthorne or Melville. 32 notes.   K. B. West and S

1225. Cantor, Milton. JOEL BARLOW, YALE UNDERGRADUATE. *New-England Galaxy 1963 5(2): 3-13.* Examines the collegiate career of Joel Barlow (1754-1812) at Yale College during the American Revolution. These years provided the stuff of intellectual self-assurance for Barlow, but the conservatism of New Haven did not hammer him into its archetypal form, possibly because of the numerous interruptions of the war.   T. J. Farnham

1226. Carrell, William D. AMERICAN COLLEGE PROFESSORS: 1750-1800. *Hist. of Educ. Q. 1968 8(3): 289-305.* From a statistical evaluation of some two hundred college professors in the American colonies, the author concludes that American college professors were part of the scholarly community of Europe, that their American training was recognized as equal to that given in Europe's universities, and that as ministers they belonged in most instances to the liberal wing of American Protestantism. As liberal Protestants they stressed rationality in religion and order and stability in society, and constituted a minority in late 18th-century America. The author also suggests that the length and permanency of individual teaching careers indicate that "college teaching was viewed with an esteem previously unsuspected by educational historians." 10 notes.
                                                              J. Herbst

1227. Carrell, William D. BIOGRAPHICAL LIST OF AMERICAN COLLEGE PROFESSORS TO 1800. *Hist. of Educ. Q. 1968 8(3): 358-374.* Includes 142 men positively identified as professors and 80 additional names for whom no biographical data could be found. The listing is nearly complete, except for missing data from Washington College, Maryland, Washington College, Tennessee, and the College of William and Mary.   J. Herbst

1228. Chiel, Arthur A. EZRA STILES—THE EDUCATION OF AN "HEBRI-CIAN." *Am. Jewish Hist. Q. 1971 60(3): 235-241.* Ezra Stiles (1727-95), with his wide interest in all branches of learning, became a serious student of Hebrew in his 40th year, a decade before being called to the presidency of Yale (then a college). Isaac Touro, chazzan of the Newport Synagogue, became his tutor; Stiles acquired the necessary grammatical and rabbinic texts and rapidly made his way through the Hebrew text of the Bible. By 1772 he felt ready to plunge into Hebrew mysticism, as his purchase of a 1684 edition of the Zohar shows. The numerous notes and comments in his *Diaries* indicate that his concern with Hebrew lore grew from his desire to explore "ancient Christian truths...."

F. Rosenthal

1229. Chiel, Arthur A. THE RABBIS AND EZRA STILES. *Am. Jewish Hist. Q. 1972 61(4): 294-312.* Ezra Stiles' "Oration Upon the Hebrew Literature," delivered at Yale University in 1781, contains a reference to five rabbis who became his teachers in Newport. Various entries in Stiles' "Literary Diary," the 15 volumes of which in the Beinecke Rare Book and Manuscript Library of Yale University were examined by the author, were used to reconstruct the visits of these five men and their associations with Stiles, 1759-74. Stiles was eager to deepen his Hebrew knowledge, and especially to learn more about Jewish mystical literature. 58 notes.

F. Rosenthal

1230. Chitty, Arthur Ben. COLLEGE OF CHARLESTON: EPISCOPAL CLAIMS QUESTIONED, 1785-. *Hist. Mag. of the Protestant Episcopal Church 1968 37(4): 413-416.* A study of the growth of the College of Charleston, a nonsectarian school with Episcopal origins. Beginnning with a 1748 library society and chartered in 1770, controversy nevertheless delayed the school's opening until after the Revolution. The first principal, Episcopalian Rev. Robert Smith, used his wealth and prestige to the advantage of the college, but the school returned to the high school level in 1795. Neglect kept it small and insecure, the presidency being vacant from 1810 to 1823. A tremendous revival began in 1823 and, despite deaths and squabbles, the college became the first municipal institution of higher learning in America. The school prospered, and title was vested in the city council by 1838. Assets mounted. In 1918 it went coed, and in 1920 free tuition for city and later county students was introduced.

E. G. Roddy

1231. Cohen, Sheldon S. THE PARNASSUS ARTICLES. *Hist. of Educ. Q. 1965 5(3): 174-186.* A series of articles under the penname Parnassus appeared in the *Connecticut Courant* early in 1783, attacking the government of Yale College as outmoded, aristocratic, and sectarian, and asking for the addition of secular officers, particularly state legislators, to the Yale Corporation. The author maintains that Parnassus gave expression to a new nationalistic spirit which was shared by Noah Webster and the New Hampshire legislature when it sought to alter the charter of Dartmouth College, and that the anonymous author probably was Timothy Dwight, who became Yale's president in 1795. J. Herbst

1232. Conlon, Noel P. THE COLLEGE SCENE IN PROVIDENCE, 1786-
1787. *Rhode Island Hist. 1968 27(3): 65-71.* Part of an 18th-century political
statement found in the Carter-Danforth Papers of the Rhode Island Historical
Society Library. The statement refers, in a pseudobiblical form, to dissension in
the nation over economic and religious differences. Based on secondary biographical sources and the Carter-Danforth Papers.   P. J. Coleman

1233. Crane, Verner W. THE CLUB OF HONEST WHIGS: FRIENDS OF
SCIENCE AND LIBERTY. *William and Mary Q. 1966 23(2): 210-233.* This
club was a philosophical and political coterie, a London coffee house which
Benjamin Franklin and other "greats" of the age patronized. Though dissenters
dominated the group, discussions turned on science, moral philosophy, and politics. Discussed are the roles and contributions of such prominent members as
Josiah Quincy, Jr., Joseph Priestley, James Boswell, and Richard Price. Franklin,
hoping to perserve both the empire and American rights, found in the club a
means of promoting good will and sense among middle-class Englishmen.
                                                                      H. M. Ward

1234. Crowe, Charles. THE REVEREND JAMES MADISON IN WILLIAMS-
BURG AND LONDON, 1768-1771. *West Virginia Hist. 1964 25(4): 270-278.*
An account of James Madison, cousin of the future president, educated at Williamsburg and later a professor of natural philosophy and mathematics at that
college. He thought religion and science, politics, and humanitarianism were
intertwined and sought to explore the threads connecting them. He was a founder
of the Williamsburg Asylum, a member of the Royal Humane Society, and an
organizer of the Society for the Advancement of Useful Knowledge. In 1775
Madison went to England where he studied philosophy and was ordained a
deacon in the Anglican Church. His return to America in 1776 was hastened by
his sympathy for the colonial cause. Emphasis is on the years covered in the title
but biographical material is included beyond the stated dates. Documented.
                                                                      D. N. Brown

1235. Davis, Richard Beale. THE INTELLECTUAL GOLDEN AGE IN THE
COLONIAL CHESAPEAKE BAY COUNTRY. *Virginia Mag. of Hist. and
Biog. 1970 78(2): 131-143.* A major segment among the two generations in
Virginia and Maryland prior to American independence placed matters of reason
above those of emotion and will. They thereby earn the distinction for their time
and place as an intellectual golden age. There were plentiful opportunities for
quality education. Graceful architecture, ingenious landscape designs, and count-
less concerts and theatricals, both public and private, attest to the appreciation
of the fine arts. Religions and theological thinking held a high place (though lowly
by New England standards), as is evident in such works as the sermon book of
Robert Paxton, and the five volumes of James Blair's discourses. Belletristic
writing had quality practitioners—Ebenezer Cook, the Annapolis Tuesday Club,
and others. Political writings by Thomas Jefferson, Edmund Pendelton, George
Mason, Edmund Randolph, Daniel Dulany, Charles Carroll, and James Madison
highlighted the era.   C. A. Newton

1236. Duveen, Denis I. and Klickstein, Herbert S. ALEXANDRE-MARIE QUESNAY DE BEAUREPAIRE'S *MEMOIRE ET PROSPECTUS, CON-CERNANT L'ACADEMIE DES SCIENCES ET BEAUX ARTS DES ETATS-UNIS DE L'AMERIQUE, ETABLIE A RICHMOND, 1778.* [Alexander-Marie Quesnay de Beaurepaire's *Memoir and prospectus, concerning the Academy of Sciences and Fine Arts established in America at Richmond, 1788].* *Virginia Mag. of Hist. and Biog. 1955 63(3): 280-285.* Describes a memoir by the Chevalier de Beaurepaire, an idealistic young Frenchman who proposed to establish an American Academy patterned after the Académie Française. Although supported by the French Crown, de Beaurepaire's project never progressed beyond the building stage. C. F. Latour

1237. Fischer, David Hackett. JOHN BEALE BORDLEY, DANIEL BOOR-STIN, AND THE AMERICAN ENLIGHTENMENT. *J. of Southern Hist. 1962 28(3): 326-342.* Disagrees with a thesis by Daniel J. Boorstin that there was little or no parallel in America to the Enlightenment of 18th-century Europe. Fischer bases his argument upon the facts of the life of John Beale Bordley (1727-1804), a Maryland planter and agricultural reformer greatly influenced by European ideas, as one example of an Enlightenment thinker in America parallel to that of Europe. He asserts that in upper-class American society of the period, there was a very close intellectual influence from Europe and argues that Boorstin errs in having "over-homogenized" American culture of the period. S. E. Humphreys

1238. Hanley, Thomas O'Brien. YOUNG MR. CARROLL AND THE MON-TESQUIEU. *Maryland Hist. Mag. 1967 62(4): 394-418.* A study of the French college days of Charles Carroll of Carrollton, his encounter with the theories of Montesquieu, his intellectual environment, and his distinctive points of view. Montesquieu's *The Spirit of the Laws* summed up for Carroll the insights of the age and related them to the stream of Western thought and experience from the times of the Roman Republic. Virtue (the spirit of the law of the republic, connoting love of country) was the spirit with which Carroll entered the Revolution. Later, Carroll successfully opposed the double tax measure in Maryland by a compromise on the true spirit of English laws. 52 notes. D. H. Swift

1239. Hienton, Louise Joyner. SIDELIGHTS: THE FREE SCHOOL IN PRINCE GEORGES COUNTY, 1723-1774. *Maryland Hist. Mag. 1964 59(4): 380-391.* In 1723 an act of the General Assembly established a free school in every county in Maryland. After a long period of struggling with schoolmasters and especially with funds, the General Assembly in 1774 passed an act to unite the free schools of St. Marys, Charles, and Prince Georges Counties. 69 notes. E. P. Stickney

1240. Jackson, Sidney L. THE *ENCYCLOPEDIE METHODIQUE:* A JEFF-ERSON ADDENDUM. *Virginia Mag. of Hist. and Biog. 1965 73(3): 303-311.* Describes Thomas Jefferson's activities as the agent for various Americans in securing subscriptions to Charles Joseph Panckoucke's *Encyclopédie Méthodique.* Based on the published Jefferson papers. K. J. Bauer

1241. Ketcham, Ralph. JAMES MADISON AT PRINCETON. *Princeton U. Lib. Chronicle 1966 28(1): 24-54.* In 1769 James Madison traveled to Princeton to enter the College of New Jersey as a sophomore. The curriculum was relatively progressive and stimulating, allowing for the reading and discussing of thinkers who were considered revolutionary in outlook at the time. Madison generally followed the prescribed student routine. He made friends with many men who later became famous. The political atmosphere was strongly inclined toward freedom and resistance of the British. Madison received a foundation of learning in the classical tradition, the Christian tradition, Locke, and the polite writers about manners and civilizations.   D. Brockway

1242. Kohlbrenner, Bernard J. RELIGION AND HIGHER EDUCATION: AN HISTORICAL PERSPECTIVE. *Hist. of Educ. Q. 1961 1(2): 45-56.* American colonial colleges showed a strong influence of religion in their curricula and in the later professional activities of their students. By 1860, 175 of 182 permanently established colleges were under denominational control, and many owed their existence to missionary activities in the West. Catholic colleges declared the education of the laity and preparation of the clergy to be their double aims. Secular forces made their home in the State universities which received their greatest stimulus with the Morrill Act of 1862. The First and Fourteenth Amendments were interpreted to eliminate public support for religious educational institutions, and German influences tended to exclude religion as a university subject. Today the trend toward secularism is checked by the increasing student interest in religion.   J. Herbst

1243. McAnear, Beverly. COLLEGE FOUNDING IN THE AMERICAN COLONIES, 1745-1775. *Mississippi Valley Hist. R. 1955 42(1): 24-44.* Between 1745 and 1775 seven new colleges were founded in British North America. Such a development coincided both with a growth of the spirit of nationalism and with the persistence of sectarian discussion, such as the Old Light-New Light controversy. Years of prosperity also fostered such foundations. College promoters became interested in advancing higher education through affiliation with either a library company or a church. British-trained products were sought by the trustees as prospective presidents. The greatest problem of administrators was that of getting the money necessary to keep the college open. As the colonial era closed some Americans were priding themselves that they had achieved educational self-reliance.   G. L. A. Reilly

1244. McCormick, Richard P. DUTCH ORIGINS OF RUTGERS, THE STATE UNIVERSITY. *Halve Maen 1966 41(3): 7-8, 15, 1967 41(4): 11-12.* Part I. In pursuit of autonomy from its European parent, the Dutch Reformed Church in 18th-century North America enjoyed only limited success, especially once New York City members withdrew support in order to join the Anglicans in founding nonsectarian King's College (1754). Roused by this act, the church's majority founded Queen's College in New Brunswick, New Jersey (1766), as a strictly Dutch seminary. Illus. Part II. Under the recast charter of 1770, the college was situated at New Brunswick, a president, Frederick Frelinghauysen, chosen, and a building acquired. At the same time the rift in the Dutch Reformed Church in

America was healed by creating a General Assembly all but independent of the Amsterdam Classis. Thus, on the eve of revolution, Coetus and Conferentie factions alike had colleges (Rutgers and Queens) and cooperated in their support.
G. L. Owen

1245. Middlekauff, Robert. A PERSISTENT TRADITION: THE CLASSICAL CURRICULUM IN EIGHTEENTH-CENTURY NEW ENGLAND. *William and Mary Q. 1961 18(1): 54-67.* A detailed analysis of the classics in the curricula of New England schools and colleges. The Revolution brought criticisms of the classical curriculum, but the public took little interest in the matter, and the schools continued in the old traditions.
E. Oberholzer, Jr.

1246. Reinhold, Meyer. OPPONENTS OF CLASSICAL LEARNING IN AMERICA DURING THE REVOLUTIONARY PERIOD. *Pro. of the Am. Phil. Soc. 1968 112(4): 221-234.* Traces the opposition to the classical curriculum in America before, during, and after the Revolution. The author examines the men who served in the vanguard of the anticlassical movement—including Benjamin Franklin, Thomas Paine, Noah Webster, Benjamin Rush—and their tactics. The opponents of the educational status quo argued that classical studies were superfluous in and irrelevant to a society which needed practical knowledge. In noting the critics' failure, the author disagrees with them and makes a brief statement in favor of the utility of the classics. Based essentially on printed source works of the period in question; 86 notes.
W. G. Morgan

1247. Renwick, John. *BELISAIRE* IN SOUTH CAROLINA, 1768. *J. of Am. Studies [Great Britain] 1970 4(1): 19-38.* In the French "literary invasion" of North America after 1763, *Bélisaire* (1767) by Jean François Marmontel (1723-99) had the greatest impact in South Carolina. Marmontel attacked the French Government and described political disquiet, malaise that beset the French monarchy and ruling classes, and intolerance practiced against the Huguenots. The Huguenot minority in South Carolina understood and responded to the theses set forth in Marontel's novel. Other Carolinians, too, saw in the novel "American implications" and accordingly responded to the parallels that appeared to exist between Louis XV's France and colonial South Carolina. Based on French and English editions of *Bélisaire* that were available in 1768 and a few letters and writings of colonial Carolinians; 37 notes.
H. T. Lovin

1248. Rezneck, Samuel. AMOS EATON, "THE OLD SCHOOLMASTER," IN PRECEPT AND DEED. *New York Hist. 1958 39(2): 165-178.* Describes the career and contributions of Amos Eaton (1776-1842), an upstate New York "universal genius," who followed in the tradition of Benjamin Franklin and Thomas Jefferson. As an itinerant lecturer, author and master of the Rensselaer School, he experimented constantly with educational methods. He promoted an emphasis on motivating the student, on broad liberal education and on educating the sons of "the merchant, the mechanic and the manufacturer."
A. B. Rollins

1249. Sellers, Charles Grier, Jr. JOHN BLAIR SMITH. *J. of the Presbyterian Hist. Soc. 1956 34(4): 201-225.* Biographical sketch of Smith (1756-99), graduate of Princeton, Presbyterian minister, second president of Hampden-Sidney College (Prince Edward County, Virginia), first president of Union College (Schenectady, New York), and leading figure in the assessment controversy in Virginia, 1784-85.

W. D. Metz

1250. Sensabaugh, George F. MILTON IN EARLY AMERICAN SCHOOLS. *Huntington Lib. Q. 1955/56 19(4): 353-383.* From the Revolution to about 1825 many textbooks, of both British and American origin, were used in instruction in writing, reading and speaking. Some of them, such as Lindley Murray's *English Grammar,* enjoyed tremendous currency, and all drew from a common tradition. The role of John Milton in these works was greater than that of any other author, and in this way much of his writing moved into the fabric of American culture.

H. D. Jordan

1251. Spiller, Robert E. FRANKLIN ON THE ART OF BEING HUMAN. *Pro. of the Am. Phil. Soc. 1956 100(4): 304-315.* A defense of the validity, greatness and contemporary relevance of Benjamin Franklin as a humanist and moral philosopher. Franklin's romantic and anti-intellectualist critics misjudged him because the value assumptions from which they proceeded differed from his. As the 20th century has renewed interest in 18th-century values, interest in, and correct interpretation of, Franklin has increased. The author discusses the consistency and reasonableness of Franklin's ideas to show that as a moral philosopher he displays the same intellectual detachment, faith in empirical procedure, and belief that the purpose of acquiring knowledge is its application to the improvement of man, that he reveals as a natural philosopher. Franklin is the artist of the good life. Documented.

N. Kurland

1252. Straub, Jean S. ANTHONY BENEZET: TEACHER AND ABOLITIONIST OF THE EIGHTEENTH CENTURY. *Quaker Hist. 1968 57(1): 3-16.* Of a Huguenot family which moved from France to Holland, England, and America, Benezet spent over 40 years teaching in what became Penn Charter School and his own girls school in Philadelphia. He kept order without corporal punishment. In 1778 he published *The Pennsylvania Spelling Book* and a primer, and with the second editions in 1782 an essay on grammar. He disapproved of studying Latin, except for medicine, because of the Romans' heathen and militarist spirit. Lectures on useful sciences were to be copied into a bound notebook for permanent reference. He wrote several tracts against slavery, taught blacks in Philadelphia, and opposed recolonization in Africa.

T. D. S. Bassett

1253. Straub, Jean S. MAGAZINES IN THE FRIENDS LATIN SCHOOL OF PHILADELPHIA IN THE 1770'S. *Quaker Hist. 1966 55(1): 38-45.* Extensive quotations from a collection of MSS. periodicals by students at what became William Penn Charter School. They show transient editors, shifting titles, and articles on nature, morals, personalities, hazing, and recreation.

T. D. S. Bassett

1254. Thomson, Robert Polk. COLLEGES IN THE REVOLUTIONARY SOUTH: THE SHAPING OF A TRADITION. *Hist. of Educ. Q. 1970 10(4): 399-412.* Explores the failure of many new colleges to survive in the post-Revolutionary South. The American Revolution shattered the bases of educational support even though the Revolution itself had encouraged the formation of new colleges by the removal of British restrictions. The cores of Southern higher education had been religion, the classical gentlemen's education, and the liberal educational dreams of reformers such as Thomas Jefferson. Uses William and Mary College as a partial test case and shows how the new colleges could not contain the "cores" and therefore could not attract the necessary financial and public support. In addition, the South failed to create a sense of nationalism or a sense of community purpose to effectively support public institutions of higher learning in the period. Based partially on archival research; 42 notes.

L. C. Smith

1255. Tyack, David. EDUCATION AS ARTIFACT: BENJAMIN FRANKLIN AND INSTRUCTION OF "A RISING PEOPLE." *Hist. of Educ. Q. 1966 6(1): 3-15.* The experience of change and discontinuity in Franklin's own life is here seen as providing the impetus for his rejection of academic custom and religious orthodoxy and for his construction of the Academy for the Education of Youth in Philadelphia. With the academy, the author argues, Franklin sought to systematize his own self-education. Utility of subject matter for the students becomes the keynote of the proposal which made history and English the central subjects, and stressed behavior rather than doctrine as the central concern of the teacher. Franklin, Tyack feels, viewed schooling as the avenue of social and occupational advance in an age of change.

J. Herbst

1256. Wolf, Edwin, II. EVIDENCE INDICATING THE NEED FOR SOME BIBLIOGRAPHICAL ANALYSIS OF AMERICAN-PRINTED HISTORICAL WORKS. *Papers of the Biblio. Soc. of Am. 1969 63(4): 261-277.* Presents "haphazard findings made in the course of collating by eye-scanning presumptive duplicates in the Library Company of Philadelphia" to demonstrate the need for systematic textual comparison of variant copies of American-printed historical works. Comparisons of variant copies of such items as Jacob Duché *The American Vine* (1775) and Israel Pernberton et al., *Address to the Inhabitants of Pennsylvania* (1777) are included. Many examples of variants are given.

C. A. Newton

1257. Wolf, Edwin, II. THE DISPERSAL OF THE LIBRARY OF WILLIAM BYRD OF WESTOVER. *Pro. of the Am. Antiquarian Soc. 1958 68(1): 19-106.* The library of William Byrd III (1728-77), built largely by his father and grandfather, was one of the largest and finest libraries in colonial America, "a carefully balanced collection of the best literature and learning of the day." A catalogue made about 1750 lists 2,345 titles in 3,513 volumes. The author traces the dispersal of the library by sale between 1778 and 1803 and the subsequent history of various segments of it. Approximately four hundred volumes have been identified and located.

W. D. Metz

1258. Wolf, Edwin, II. THE LIBRARY OF EDWARD LLOYD IV OF WYE HOUSE. *Winterthur Portfolio 1969 5: 87-121.* Examines the largest library in 18th-century Maryland, that of Edward Lloyd, IV (1744-96). The library held more than 700 titles, excluding duplicates, and numbered more than 2,500 volumes. The present inventory was based on earlier ones dating back to 1796. After deciphering poorly written or misspelled titles, the author can give a clear picture of the literary holdings of a prominent Maryland family. The library held works primarily on history, biography, science, and the arts. Interestingly, the Lloyds lacked the classics in the original tongue. Gives the complete inventory of the Lloyd library. Based on primary and secondary sources; 20 notes, appendix.

                                                   N. A. Kuntz

1259. Wright, Louis B. INTELLECTUAL HISTORY AND THE COLONIAL SOUTH. *William and Mary Q. 1959 16(2): 214-227.* A plea for the study of the intellectual history of the colonial South. The author urges the use of newspapers, private correspondence, and official documents as sources. Good biography should replace interested genealogical accounts; the history of education, Christianity, and the arts also needs attention.   E. Oberholzer, Jr.

Social & Cultural Developments

1260. Anderson, Jack Sandy. THE LEVI SHINN HOUSE. *West Virginia Hist. 1968 29(2): 138-140.* Discusses the history of the house and the lives of its builder Levi Shinn (1748-1807) and his descendants. Shinn built the house on the southern edge of Shinnston, Harrison County, during the Revolution in 1778. He disposed of the most valuable of his lands in 1793 and, in 1819, that land was "laid off into lots and sold...thereby laying the foundation" for the town of Shinnston. Photo.   C. A. Newton

1261. Archdeacon, Thomas. EARLY AMERICAN SOCIAL STRUCTURE: CHANGING VIEWS AND EMPHASIS. *New England Social Studies Bull. 1968 25(1): 12-16.* Studies of American colonial society have suffered from inadequate statistical information. This deficiency is being corrected for the upper echelons of society, as evidenced by Jackson T. Main's *The Social Structure of Revolutionary America* (Princeton: Princeton U. Press, 1965). This procedure must be extended to all strata of society and must include the analysis of all available records.   C. Thibault

1262. Berkeley, Edmund, Jr. QUOITS, THE SPORT OF GENTLEMEN. *Virginia Cavalcade 1965 15(1): 11-21.* Describes the activities of the Buchanan Spring Quoit Club of Richmond, Virginia, whose membership, including Chief Justice John Marshall, enjoyed feasting and playing quoits on Saturday afternoons.   R. B. Lange

1263. Bethke, Robert D. CHESTER COUNTY WIDOW WILLS (1714-1800): A FOLKLIFE SOURCE. *Pennsylvania Folklife 1968 18(1): 16-20.* The wills recorded in Will Books A (1714) through J (1800) have been examined to determine the kinds of information they give about Pennsylvania ways. Numerous excerpts from the provisions demonstrate the kinds of property, including slaves, which the widows held. Clothes, beds, and saddles seem to be most important. Discusses funeral arrangements. 60 notes, biblio. F. L. Harrold

1264. Britt, Albert Sidney, Jr. THE SOCIETY OF THE CINCINNATI IN THE STATE OF GEORGIA. *Georgia Hist. Q. 1970 54(4): 553-562.* Sketches the history of the Society of the Cincinnati, emphasizing its activities in Georgia. American Revolutionary officers founded the organization in 1783 in an effort to perpetuate the ideals of the Revolution. Early conflict arose over the motives of the group; opponents feared the beginnings of an American nobility. The society faded in the mid-19th century as the original members died. The society in Georgia was also founded in 1783, but lost records prevent reconstruction of the chapter's progress and demise. Reorganized in 1902, the society now enrolls descendants of the original members and actively supports the principles set in 1783. Based largely on society publications; 18 notes. R. A. Mohl

1265. Bryan, Mary Givens. GEORGIA'S COLONIAL WILLS. *Am. Archivist 1963 26(1): 51-54.* A slightly edited version of the author's introduction to *Abstracts of Colonial Wills of the State of Georgia, 1733-77* (Atlanta, 1962). The scope of the publication is outlined, and hope expressed that it will stimulate a series of publications of colonial documents in state archives. The wills and other records are said to tell much about the lives of the early settlers, their problems, and how they solved them. R. E. Wilson

1266. Coblentz, David H. COLONIAL REVOLUTIONARY PERIOD. *Manuscripts 1968 20(2): 32-35.* As prices continually advance on the autograph market, collectors are finding new items of interest which can be purchased by modest collectors. Colonial recipes, indentures, and bills of lading can still be obtained for moderate sums. Examples of these materials are reproduced and a brief explanation of each of them is given. Photo. P. D. Thomas

1267. Cook, Edward M., Jr. SOCIAL BEHAVIOR AND CHANGING VALUES IN DEDHAM, MASSACHUSETTS, 1700 TO 1775. *William and Mary Q. 1970 27(4): 546-580.* Discerns the operational values (as distinct from ideal values) through behavior, as revealed in local records. As the town of Dedham grew, people took a more active role in town meetings, support of the church ceased to be voluntary and became a general tax, and institutions of the town veered toward "social paralysis." Disputes among precincts and churches lessened social control. Despite decline of economic opportunity, people were reluctant to leave Dedham because of family ties. Interests after 1700, such as the quest for status, were tied more to the Colony than to the local community. Map, 2 tables, 63 notes. H. M. Ward

1268. Dell, Robert M. and Huguenin, Charles A. VERMONT'S ROYALL TY-
LER IN NEW YORK'S JOHN STREET THEATRE: A THEATRICAL
HOAX EXPLODED. *Vermont Hist. 1970 38(2): 103-112.* The John Street
Theatre (1767-98) in New York, where Royall Tyler's *The Contrast* was first
performed, was a red wooden building with gallery, pit, boxes, and aristocratic
audiences. The theater seated perhaps a thousand people. The British garrison
patronized and acted in the theater from 1777 to 1783. A woodcut by James H.
Richardson, supposedly showing the interior in 1791, has too small a stage and
pit, no boxes, the wrong kind of curtain, implausible graffiti, and anachronistic
gas light brackets, as well as the bustle on the actress.
                                                            T. D. S. Bassett

1269. Doud, Richard K. JOHN HESSELIUS, MARYLAND LIMNER. *Win-
terthur Portfolio 1969 5: 129-153.* Sketches the life, personality, and painting of
John Hesselius (1728-78). The son of Gustavus Hesselius (1682-1755), also a
painter, John Hesselius confined his work to portraiture, and reflected the late
English baroque and English rococo traditions. He is one of the few artists
working in the middle Colonies whose training and background were exclusively
American. In terms of style, Hesselius shows the influence of Robert Feke and
John Wollaston. Although not a genius, he was a competent painter and a
respected member of Maryland society. Based on primary and secondary sources;
12 photos, 45 notes, 4 appendixes.   N. A. Kuntz

1270. Doud, Richard K. THE FITZHUGH PORTRAITS BY JOHN HES-
SELIUS. *Virginia Mag. of Hist. and Biog. 1967 75(2): 159-173.* Discusses the 13
portraits of members of the Fitzhugh family of Stafford County, Virginia, painted
from 1751 to 1771 by John Hesselius of Annapolis, Maryland. Based on printed
and manuscript sources; catalog, illus., 8 notes.   K. J. Bauer

1271. Dunbar, Gary S. DEER-KEEPING IN EARLY SOUTH CAROLINA.
Agric. Hist. 1962 36(2): 108-109. The keeping of deer as pets was common in
South Carolina until after the Revolutionary War.   W. D. Rasmussen

1272. Elder, William V., III. THE ADAMS-KILTY HOUSE IN ANNAPOLIS.
Maryland Hist. Mag. 1965 60(3): 314-324. Describes one of the more important
examples of late 18th-century architecture in the Annapolis tradition. William
Buckland built the Adams-Kilty house in 1773. The house resembles the Ham-
mond-Harwood and Chase-Lloyd homes, also designed by Buckland. Discusses
the inner designs, as well as various changes made during the 19th century.
During the present century the building was divided by temporary partitions to
accommodate two separate dwellings. 5 illus., 23 notes.   D. H. Swift

1273. Fales, Martha Gandy. THE EARLY AMERICAN WAY OF DEATH.
Essex Inst. Hist. Collections 1964 100(2): 75-84. Discusses the extravagances at
funerals in the colonial period, particularly the presenting of mourning rings—

of gold, marked with the name and initials of the deceased, the date of his death, and his age—to the minister and close friends. The rings were frequently ornamented. Illus. J. M. Bumsted

1274. Farnham, Charles W. GLOCESTER, RHODE ISLAND, VITAL RECORDS. *Rhode Island Hist. 1967 26(3): 91-96.* Lists births, deaths, and marriages from 1768 to 1882 drawn from a store account book in the possession of Ella Hopkins of Chepachet, Rhode Island. P. J. Coleman

1275. Fody, Edward S. JOHN WITHERSPOON: ADVISOR TO THE LOVE-LORN. *Pro. of the New Jersey Hist. Soc. 1966 84(4): 239-249.* Analyzes three letters by John Witherspoon, president of Princeton University, to the *Pennsylvania Magazine* (1775-76) on the subject of marriage. They show that the Puritan patriarchal concept of family life was no longer dominant but had given way to the "common sense" philosophy which emanated from Scotland and which satisfied the American urge for the practical. A conclusion discusses sources and modern works on Scottish realism, a topic which appears to have been neglected by American historians. E. P. Stickney

1276. Harrigan, Anthony. THE CHARLESTON TRADITION. *Am. Heritage 1958 9(2): 48-61, 88-93.* Sketches the culture and society of Low Country South Carolina from the 17th century to the Civil War, during which time English and Huguenot planters produced a unique culture. Undocumented; illus. C. R. Allen, Jr.

1277. Harris, P. M. G. THE SOCIAL ORIGINS OF AMERICAN LEADERS: THE DEMOGRAPHIC FOUNDATIONS. *Perspectives in Am. Hist. 1969 3: 159-344.* Demonstrates "that differences in the degree to which America was an open society between 1750 and 1760, or, for example, 1840 and 1850, were greater in certain crucial respects than those between 1750 and 1850. Over and over again, fairly predictable patterned changes within the span of a decade or so exceeded the effect of trends lasting a century or more." The significant differences in opportunity that have existed at various times throughout American history have been due to relatively short-term demographic and economic processes. There was no "grand, sweeping, overall conversion from an overwhelmingly class-dominated model to an image of the open society. Nor was there a long-term regression to a closed society." Variation in the social backgrounds of our national leadership—in politics, education, business, the arts, and other professions—"occurred not as a consequence of great events like the American Revolution or major processes like the advent of industrialism or the closing of the frontier, but at fairly regular intervals of just over twenty years on the average." Scholars have simply failed to cope with what seems to have been the essentially cyclical nature of opportunity. It is evident that for two or three centuries "the temporal relationships of population growth, internal migration, immigration, community formation, institutional expansion, economic development and retrenchment, the number of particular types of leadership openings, and the breadth of the social base from which they were filled all display surprisingly consistent chronological patterns of a comparable cyclical nature." The essence of American social structure "has always reflected, and re-created, cyclical fluctuations in the rate of expansion of our population." Based on published sources; tables, charts.   D. J. Abramoske

1278. Harte, Thomas J. SOCIAL ORIGINS OF THE BRANDYWINE POPULATION. *Phylon 1963 24(4): 369-378.* The author examined the public and parish records as well as conducting personal interviews among the Brandywine population of southern Maryland. He concluded that the Brandywines, a triracial, isolated population, originated in Charles County prior to 1778 and probably in socially-disapproved interracial unions.   S. C. Pearson, Jr.

1279. Jensen, Oliver. THE PEALES. *Am. Heritage 1955 6(3): 41-51, 97-101.* Provides a general survey of the ideas and activities of Charles Willson Peale, one of the "universal men" of 18th-century America. As soldier, patriot, scientist and painter, Peale seemed to embody the "American spirit in all the joy and optimism of its youth." In his activities he sought to exemplify the unity of science, art and morality; in his ideas, he was a disciple of the Age of Reason. Illus.
                                                                    A. W. Thompson

1280. Jones, George F. COLONIAL GEORGIA'S SECOND LANGUAGE. *Georgia R. 1967 21(1): 87-100.* Discusses German, the second-most-common language in 18th-century Georgia. Residents of the town of Ebenezer at first spoke the Upper German of Salzburg, but in the 1780's the influence of Pastor Johann Martin Boltzius (1703-65) and his East Middle German modified this. Later a Swabian influence modified it again. General James Edward Oglethorpe (1696-1785) spoke German. "During Ebenezer's brief prosperity, the German language was firmly enough entrenched to absorb other languages," but, "although German was a vigorous and growing language in Georgia in 1775, a half century later it was almost dead." This was partly due to the effects of the Revolution, and partly to the Germans' aptitude in learning English.
                                                                    T. M. Condon

1281. Lacy, Harriet S., ed. EPHRAIM ROBERTS—MEMORANDUM BOOK. *Hist. New Hampshire 1969 24(3): 20-33.* In 1773 the Roberts family sold its farm for 6,365 pounds and moved to what became Alton at the south end of Lake Winnepesaukee. When New Durham Gore (as it was then called) was organized into a town in 1777, Joseph Roberts was first selectman. The teenager's diary (in the Society library) reflects the first two years' settlement: raisings, clearing and burning, frolicks, bears and livestock, household industry, and trips to Dover. Also, there is brief reference to two tours of military duty.
                                                                    T. D. S. Bassett

1282. Mackey, Howard. SOCIAL WELFARE IN COLONIAL VIRGINIA: THE IMPORTANCE OF THE ENGLISH OLD POOR LAW. *Hist. Mag. of the Protestant Episcopal Church 1967 36(4): 357-382.* A study of colonial vestry records which indicates that while the Old Dominion could hardly be called a Welfare State, she took an ecclesiastical and paternalistic attitude toward her less fortunate subjects. The author suggests that further research is needed to more fully evaluate the influence of the English Old Poor Law in Virginia, but notes that it furthered internal peace during the colonial period and that it contributed to lower-class loyalty to Virginia authority during the Revolution. Tables, 27 notes, drawn mostly from primary vestry and parish records.

E. G. Roddy

1283. Malone, Dumas. THE WILLIAMSBURG SPIRIT LIVES ON. *New York Times Mag. 1955 4(December): 26-27, 30, 32, 34.* A sketch of the cultural and political life of 18th-century Williamsburg (Virginia). R. F. Campbell

1284. Mappen, Marc A. THE PAUPERS OF SOMERSET COUNTY: 1760-1800. *J. of the Rutgers U. Lib. 1970 33(2): 33-45.* Examines the problem of poverty in colonial society by studying 71 paupers in the townships of Franklin and Hillsborough in Somerset County who received assistance from 1760 to 1800. Investigates the community in which they lived and institutions established for their care. Concludes that "the image of an extended family caring for the welfare of its members does not hold true for the indigent of Franklin and Hillsborough." Based on primary sources; 5 tables, 40 notes. M. Kroeger

1285. Mattfield, Mary S. JOURNEY TO THE WILDERNESS: TWO TRAV-ELERS IN FLORIDA, 1696-1774. *Florida Hist. Q. 1967 45(4): 327-351.* Jonathan Dickinson's *Journal* (1699) and William Bartram's *Travels through North and South Carolina, Georgia, East and West Florida* (1791) have literary merit beyond that of good travel narratives. Analysis of the two would perhaps aid in understanding the development of American literature, since each reflects a dominant viewpoint of the century in which it was written. Dickinson's account of his struggle in the northeastern Florida wilderness, while he and his shipwrecked family and companions were half-starved captives of Indians, is that of a devout 17th-century traveler interpreting his experience in the light of the working of Divine Providence. Originally regarding both the pagan Indians and primitive nature as decivilizing influences, Dickinson gradually recognized nature as his chief enemy. On the other hand, traveler-naturalist Bartram, traveling in the vicinity almost a century later, viewed nature as a challenge to his curiosity, seeking to study nature for the purpose of both admiring the Almighty Creator's work and finding unknown natural specimens of use to society. Bartram's romanticism, then, was modified with practicality so that nature, the Indian, and civilization were all composites of both good and evil. 33 notes.

R. V. Calvert

1286. Mohl, Raymond A. THE HUMANE SOCIETY AND URBAN REFORM IN EARLY NEW YORK, 1787-1831. *New-York Hist. Soc. Q. 1970 54(1): 30-52.* The most important of the voluntary relief organizations in New York City during the post-Revolutionary period was the Humane Society of New York City, founded in 1787. It began as an agency that was concerned with the penal system and that was opposed to impressment of debtors, but it eventually assisted in all types of relief work. Its major goal was finally achieved in 1831 with the passage of legislation abolishing imprisonment for debt. Its widespread activities and the support it gained reflected the great concern of many Americans for the conditions existing at that time. Based on primary sources, 6 illus., 43 notes.

C. L. Grant

1287. Moyne, Ernest J. JOHN HAZLITT, MINIATURIST AND PORTRAIT PAINTER IN AMERICA, 1783-1787. *Winterthur Portfolio 1970 6: 33-40.* The career of Hazlitt (1767-1837) in America has never been accurately summarized. Hazlitt arrived in New York in 1783 and traveled with his father. Hazlitt began painting portraits before he was 18 years old. He painted miniatures of some of the leading ministers of Massachusetts. Hazlitt returned to England in 1787 where he became recognized as "a miniaturist of the highest rank." He began his career at an early age and under anything but favorable circumstances. He deserves to be remembered as a competent miniaturist and portrait painter. Based on primary and secondary sources; 4 photos, 34 notes.

N. A. Kuntz

1288. Richardson, Edgar P. CHARLES WILLSON PEALE'S ENGRAVINGS IN THE YEAR OF NATIONAL CRISIS, 1787. Charles Willson Peale's pioneer effort to establish printmaking in Philadelphia failed only because it was ahead of its time; prints to be framed and hung on the wall did not become profitable until after the War of 1812. Reproduced are portraits of Benjamin Franklin, the Marquis de Lafayette, and George Washington, engravings of the State House in Philadelphia as well as several other scenes. 12 illus., 31 notes.

E. P. Stickney

1289. Roth, Cecil, ed. A DESCRIPTION OF AMERICA, 1785. *Am. Jewish Arch. 1965 17(1): 27-33.* A letter, January 1785, from a recent immigrant to Charleston, South Carolina, Joseph Salvador (1716-86) to Emanuel Mendes Da Costa (1717-91) of London. He is highly critical of both the raw countryside and the wild, uncivilized population.

A. B. Rollins

1290. Sands, Oliver Jackson. THE SOCIETY OF THE CINCINNATI IN THE STATE OF VIRGINIA. *Virginia Cavalcade 1963 13(1): 35-41.* Traces the Virginia chapter of the Society of the Cincinnati (named after the patriot citizen-soldier of Rome and made up of officers who like Cincinnatus returned to civilian life following the Revolution) from its founding through its decline and eventual rejuvenation as a result of reversing its position and accepting the principle of hereditary membership.

R. B. Lange

1291. Sherwin, Oscar. MADAN'S CUREALL. *Am. J. of Econ. and Sociol. 1963 22(3): 427-443.* A detailed examination of Reverend Martin Madan's *THELPH-THORA; or a Treatise on Female Ruin in Its Causes, Effects, Consequences, Prevention, and Remedy; considered on the basis of the Divine Law: under the following heads, viz. Marriage, Whoredom, and Fornication, Adultery, Polygamy, Divorce; with many other incidental matters; particularly including an Examination of the Principles and Tendency of Stat. 26 Geo. II. C. 33. commonly called the Marriage Act. In two volumes.*

B. E. Swanson

1292. Simons, Harriet P. and Simons, Albert. THE WILLIAM BURROWS HOUSE OF CHARLESTON. *Winterthur Portfolio 1967 3: 172-203.* Discusses the history of the William Burrows house in Charleston, South Carolina. It was built between 1772 and 1774 and is "worthy of attention in assessing the architecture and life of Charleston in the colonial period." The history of the property is given, with particular attention to the owners. After the death of William Burrows (ca. 1783) the ownership of the house passed from the Burrows family. In 1784 the house was sold at public auction and, by 1809, it had become a boarding house owned by Jehu Jones. After Jones's death the house had many negligent owners and began to deteriorate. It was razed in 1928. The Burrows house drawing room, however, was preserved and is kept today in the Winterthur Museum. 29 illus., 135 notes. M. J. McBaine

1293. Smith, Helen Burr and Moore, Elizabeth V. JOHN MARE: A COMPOSITE PORTRAIT. *North Carolina Hist. R. 1967 44(1): 18-52.* The details of John Mare's life in New York through 1774 were assembled by Helen Burr Smith of New York City and of his later life by Elizabeth V. Moore in Edenton, North Carolina. Until the two biographies were put together nothing was known in Edenton of his having been a painter. His known portraits are listed, 12 in all; all are signed and dated and unquestionably authentic. In Edenton, Mare was a well-known merchant and politician. Why he stopped painting when he left New York remains a mystery as well as how he learned his art. Based on court, state, and local records; 222 notes. E. P. Stickney

1294. South, Stanley A. "RUSSELLBOROUGH": TWO ROYAL GOVERNORS' MANSION AT BRUNSWICK TOWN. *North Carolina Hist. R. 1967 44(4): 360-372.* Description of the governors' mansion at Brunswick, North Carolina, built in the late 1750's and burnt to the ground in 1776, based on historical records and archaeological excavations begun in May 1966. The burning of the mansion sealed and preserved a large quantity of artifacts, which are now being cataloged, processed, and restored. Illus., 27 notes. J. M. Bumsted

1295. Stein, Roger B. ROYALL TYLER AND THE QUESTION OF OUR SPEECH. *New England Q. 1965 38(4): 454-474.* A central critical problem of Tyler's play *The Contrast* inheres in the dialogue. This was the second play and the first comedy written by a native American. It was produced by a professional company in New York in 1787. Speech patterns of different characters are presented, as is also the speech of individual characters, as they appear at different times. Banter, word play, vocal sounds, and speech as a mask are illustrated repeatedly. The speech is important in the plot. Based on published works; 23 notes. A. Turner

1296. Stimson, Frederick S. WILLIAM ROBERTSON'S INFLUENCE ON EARLY AMERICAN LITERATURE. *Americas 1957 14(1): 37-43.* Cites evidence of the influence (to 1831) of Robertson's *History of America* (1777) on U.S. prose and poetry concerning Spanish America. Robertson was an important source of factual data, and contributed also to the spread of popular "fancies" about Spanish iniquity (the "Black Legend") and the noble savage.

D. Bushnell

1297. Stoddard, Roger E. NOTES ON AMERICAN PLAY PUBLISHING, 1765-1865. *Pro. of the Am. Antiquarian Soc. 1971 81(1): 161-190.* American plays as well as British ones were published without regard for any copyright before 1790, the date of the U.S. copyright act. Between 1765 and 1800 the American press published at least 254 editions of plays. Over 100 publishers in 21 cities in 10 States were publishing plays in the 18th century. The theater determined the market for a play, since the theater audience provided the purchasers for the published play. The first play to be published in the American colonies was an untried five-act blank-verse tragedy by Thomas Godfrey of Philadelphia (1765). Banned in 1774 by the Continental Congress, the theater resumed in the mid-1780's to enthusiastic audiences and was flourishing by the 1790's. Although only 65 plays were published between 1765 and 1789, 189 editions of British and American plays were published in the 1790's. Although American publishers considered printing an established play too big a risk in 1765, the growing respectability and popularity of the theater by 1865 assured the profitability of publishing even amateur plays by beginning playwrights. Includes a chronological index of American printed plays to 1800, a list of dramatic copyrights to 1800, and an index of American plays to 1865. Based partly on primary sources; 50 notes.   R. V. Calvert

1298. Tinkcom, Margaret B. CLIVEDEN: THE BUILDING OF A PHILA-DELPHIA COUNTRYSEAT, 1763-1767. *Pennsylvania Mag. of Hist. and Biog. 1964 88(1): 3-36.* Describes, with floor plans, the building of a country house by Attorney General Benjamin Chew at Germantown. Based on the family papers at Cliveden; illus., 66 notes.   E. P. Stickney

1299. Wolfgang, Marvin E. JOHN MELISH, AN EARLY AMERICAN DEMOGRAPHER. *Pennsylvania Mag. of Hist. and Biog. 1958 82(1): 65-81.* Considers the work of Melish (1771-1822), a Philadelphia merchant, importer and author "whose works on geography and population analysis have received little attention from historians and political economists."   H. W. Currie

1300. Wood, Charles B., III. A SURVEY AND BIBLIOGRAPHY OF WRIT-ING ON ENGLISH AND AMERICAN ARCHITECTURAL BOOKS PUB-LISHED BEFORE 1895. *Winterthur Portfolio 1965 2: 127-137.* There is no comprehensive list of influential works on English or American architecture. Discusses some of the more pertinent works and the influence of architectural books issued before 1895. "List of Architectural Books Available in America before the Revolution," an article of Helen Park in the *Journal of the Society of Architectural Historians* (October 1961), is the most useful for a list of English pattern books in America before the Revolution. Bibliographical information on English works is available only in scattered sources. The need for comprehensive studies is obvious. Suggests further study leading to the formation of a list of European architectural books available in the United States before 1876. Moreover, there is a need for monographic studies on influential American architectural authors. Based on primary and secondary sources; 6 notes, biblio.

N. A. Kuntz

1301. Wright, Louis B. ANTIDOTE TO ROMANTIC CONCEPTS OF COLONIAL VIRGINIA. *Virginia Q. R. 1966 42(1): 137-141.* A review essay of *The Diary of Colonel Landon Carter of Sabine Hall, 1752-1778,* edited by Jack P. Greene, (Charlottesville: U. Press of Virginia, 1964). A detailed social history of the daily life of a prominent Virginia aristocrat, it presents a remarkably complete picture of 18th-century Virginia agriculture, and describes intimate details of family life, slavery, and treatment of illnesses. While this 1,150-page diary is gloomy and pessimistic, it provides an antidote to romantic notions of ease, luxury and comfort surrounding 18th-century Virginia aristocrats. "A major contribution to the social history of the period."

O. H. Zabel

Religion

1302. Albaugh, Gaylord P. AMERICAN PRESBYTERIAN PERIODICALS AND NEWSPAPERS, 1752-1830, WITH LIBRARY LOCATIONS. (ALSO SUBSEQUENT TITULAR HISTORIES TO DATES OF DISCONTINUANCE BUT WITHOUT LOCATIONS AFTER 1830). *J. of Presbyterian Hist. Part I: A-C. 1963 41(3): 165-187; Part II: D-N. (4). 243-262; Part III: O-R. 1962 42 (1): 54-67; Part IV: S-Y. (2): 124-144.* This listing is a separated portion of a much more comprehensive interdenominational study under the title: "A History and Annotated Bibliography of American Religious Periodicals and Newspaper, 1730-1830, with Library Locations." New England journals are not included. Cites 49 titles. An appendix includes additional titles proposed through 1830.

W. D. Metz

1303. Albright, Raymond W. CONCILIARISM IN ANGLICANISM. *Church Hist. 1964 33(1): 3-22.* Traces the development of canon law in England contending that, from its foundation, the Church of England recognized the same ecclesiastical law as did the rest of Christendom though modifying and interpreting it to accommodate English circumstances. "Changes in the canon law of the church in England in the sixteenth and subsequent centuries were not an abrogation but an attempt to adapt the commonly accepted Corpus Juris Canonici to the new situation and needs in England." Although acts of 1534 and 1543 reaffirmed the continuation of the portions of medieval canon law approved by use and custom, their authority was understood to derive from the fact that "they were appropriate and applicable and had long been observed in England and through such observance had come to acquire the force of English common law." Recodified in 1603, the canons are again being restudied by an Archbishops' Commission on Canon Law. In a section on the American Church the author traces the creation out of colonial antecedents of the Protestant Episcopal Church in the

United States of America in the years 1784 to 1789, emphasizing its continuity with the Church of England in episcopal government and conciliar procedure. In its formation "and in its subsequent legislation through the last 175 years this church, like the Church of England, has respected its heritage, has recognized its common background, and has stood in the conciliar tradition dependent on the canon law and constitutions adopted from the beginning of conciliar proceedings."   S. C. Pearson, Jr.

1304. Aldrich, James M. SOUTHAMPTON CALLS A NEW PASTOR. *Long Island Forum 1971 34(10): 214-222.* On 31 December 1784 the Southampton Presbyterian Church hired Joshua Williams as its new pastor. Williams kept a journal, here reproduced, recording the vital statistics of his parish which constitutes an important primary source on the development of Southampton, Long Island. The journal was kept until 1789 when Williams left the parish for reasons unknown. 21 notes.   G. Kurland

1305. Baker, Frank. AMERICAN METHODISM: BEGINNINGS AND ENDS. *Methodist Hist. 1968 6(3): 3-15.* The beginnings of Methodism in America were characterized by seven purposes or elements. The first characteristic of the religion introduced into Georgia by John and Charles Wesley was piety. From the first the Methodist movement stood for evangelism. Devout worship was another hallmark. Fellowship was another element in early American Methodism. Living by rules or discipline was a familiar feature; lay leadership and community service were other important aspects. 22 notes.   H. L. Calkin

1306. Baker, Frank. EARLY AMERICAN METHODISM: A KEY DOCUMENT. *Methodist Hist. 1965 3(2): 3-15.* Thomas Taylor wrote to John Wesley in 1768 regarding the rise of Methodism in New York. The letter is reproduced here with an introduction and 74 notes.   H. L. Calkin

1307. Baker, Frank. THE BEGINNINGS OF AMERICAN METHODISM. *Methodist Hist. 1963 2(1): 1-15.* Methodism went through three phases in its development—as a movement, a society and a church. It was started as a movement by John Wesley in Georgia in 1736. It became a church in Baltimore, Maryland, in 1784. Methodist societies of a kind existed in 1736 and remained a feature of the Methodist movement, although subject to much fluctuation and little proof of real continuity in any area. Methodism was kept alive by scattered evangelical leaders, foremost of whom was George Whitefield, whose labors of consolidation were taken over by Captain Thomas Webb in 1766.
H. L. Calkin

1308. Beachy, Alvin J. THE AMISH SETTLEMENT IN SOMERSET COUNTY, PENNSYLVANIA. *Mennonite Q. R. 1954 28(4): 263-292.* A description of the cultural development of the Amish communities in western Pennsylvania between 1744 and 1840. Reprint of two chapters of the author's dissertation.   S

1309. Boller, Paul F., Jr. WASHINGTON'S RELIGIOUS OPINIONS. *Southwest R. 1963 48(1): 48-61.* Analyzes Washington's statements for their religious content or implication. Numerous long excerpts from Washington's writings are included. The author concludes that Washington could be classed as a deist. Washington's "allusions to religion are almost totally lacking in depths of feeling." D. F. Henderson

1310. Bradley, David H. FRANCIS ASBURY AND THE DEVELOPMENT OF AFRICAN CHURCHES IN AMERICA. *Methodist Hist. 1971 10(1): 3-29.* An account of the early development of various African Methodist churches in America. Reviews the basic intent and convictions of Bishop Francis Asbury regarding Negroes and analyzes the changes and compromises that took place in his principles from 1771 until his death in 1816. These are related to the peculiar features of American Methodism in that period. Based in part on Asbury's journal, diaries and letters of his contemporaries, and Methodist church records; 103 notes. H. L. Calkin

1311. Bunting, Samuel J., Jr. GENERAL FRANCISCO DE MIRANDA AND THE QUAKERS. *Bull. of Friends Hist. Assoc. 1959 48(2): 128-130.* Presents the description of Quaker meetings in the United States in the diary of General Francisco de Miranda, the hero of Venezuela, in 1783 and 1784. Miranda visited a Quaker meeting in Philadelphia in December 1783 and one in Newport in September 1784. In regard to the former he commented on a sermon of an hour and a half "in the style of our pompous friar preachers." With respect to the latter he mentioned that not a single word had been uttered in a meeting of two hours. Miranda noted the simplicity and neatness of both congregations, but he was unfavorably impressed by the neglect, tastelessness, and lack of cleanliness evident in their meeting houses. T. L. Moir

1312. Burr, Nelson R. THE CRITICAL PERIOD OF THE EPISCOPAL CHURCH IN NEW JERSEY. *Hist. Mag. of the Protestant Episcopal Church 1960 29(2): 139-144.* Examines the influence of the Church in New Jersey from 1784 to 1790. Under the leadership of the Reverend Abraham Beach, the Episcopalians of New Jersey took a middle ground between Samuel Seabury and William White, following the former on episcopacy and liturgy, and the latter on lay participation in church government. Beach headed the committee which, opposing the liberal wing's deviations from Anglican norms, secured the rejection of the proposed prayer book of 1785. E. Oberholzer, Jr.

1313. Buxbaum, Melvin H. FRANKLIN LOOKS FOR A RECTOR: "POOR RICHARD'S" HOSTILITY TO PRESBYTERIANS. *J. of Presbyterian Hist. 1970 48(3): 176-188.* Traces the efforts of Benjamin Franklin to obtain for the Academy and College of Philadelphia a rector who would be philosophically compatible with the goals envisioned for a school of practical education. Franklin desired that the rector be a religious man who possessed a liberal mind and would encourage morality rather than piety and emphasize the value of practical education. Rejecting Congregational and Presbyterian clergy as too bigoted, Calvinist, irrational, and politically oriented, Franklin concentrated on securing an Anglican. The Anglican Church appeared to Franklin as more rational by virtue of its adoption of a doctrine of liberal moralism. Additionally Franklin had been favorably impressed by Anglicanism while in England. David Martin, the first Anglican whom Franklin approached, accepted only on a temporary basis. Franklin desired Samuel Johnson to succeed Martin, but Johnson refused all of Franklin's overtures. At this point Franklin could have secured Francis Alison, but Franklin's bias against Presbyterians would not permit him to examine this candidate who was, in fact, closest to Franklin in philosophy. Another Anglican, William Smith, was chosen for the post. Smith, however, proved to be the willing instrument of the proprietary party and engaged in politics to the detriment of the welfare of the academy. As a result, Franklin lost control of the school which he had founded and resigned from his position as trustee. Based largely on secondary sources; 58 notes.　　　　　　　　　　　　　　　　　　　　S. C. Pearson, Jr.

1314. Cadbury, Henry Joel. A MAP OF 1782 SHOWING FRIENDS MEETINGS IN NEW ENGLAND, RECENTLY ACQUIRED BY THE JOHN CARTER BROWN LIBRARY, BROWN UNIVERSITY. *Quaker Hist. 1963 52(1): 3-5.* The map described is reproduced as the frontispiece of this issue of *Quaker History.* The original is mounted on the same kind of heavy linen as military maps of the period; it was a road map that the minister could consult to find out the location of the various meetings and the distances between them. Nearly a hundred local meetings are located.　　　　　　　　　　E. P. Stickney

1315. Cadbury, Henry Joel. A WOOLMAN MANUSCRIPT. *Quaker Hist. 1968 57(1): 35-41.* Reports finding a stitched book of 42 pp. quarto by Abner Woolman, with a covering letter of 1772 to the Philadelphia Meeting for Sufferings by his elder brother John, in the archives of the Philadelphia Yearly Meeting of Friends. It shows the same concerns against slavery, excessive drinking, and paying war taxes which John expressed. The author quotes samples and adds details of the family history from a dozen Quaker sources especially for 1770-72, a period for which we have no journal of John Woolman.
　　　　　　　　　　　　　　　　　　　　　　　　　　　　　T. D. S. Bassett

1316. Cadbury, Henry Joel. ANOTHER WOOLMAN MANUSCRIPT. *Quaker Hist. 1972 61(1): 16-23.* Identifies and gives partial provenance of "A Word of Remembrance and Caution to the Rich," a manuscript in the Haverford College Library, as written by John Woolman. The author, on scrutiny of other manuscript copies and editions, concludes that this was Woolman's original title, not "A plea for the poor," and that it was probably written in America. No evidence explains why it was omitted from the 1774 edition of Woolman's *Journal,* or why it was first published in Dublin in 1793. 19 notes.　　　　T. D. S. Bassett

1317. Carroll, Kenneth L. THE NICHOLITES BECOME QUAKERS: AN EXAMPLE OF UNITY IN DISUNION. *Bull. of Friends Hist. Assoc. 1958 47(1): 3-19.* An account of the process by which the followers of Joseph Nichols (died 1773 or 1774) gradually merged with the Quakers in Maryland and North Carolina during the last quarter of the 18th century. In principles and practices

the two groups were similar, differing only in matters of discipline, as, for example, in the case of the Nicholite insistence on plainness. Based on Quaker records.
N. Kurland

1318. Case, Leland D. ORIGINS OF METHODIST PUBLISHING IN AMERICA. *Papers of the Biblio. Soc. of Am. 1965 59(1): 12-27.* Although 1789 is the traditional beginning of American Methodist publishing, in 1737 a copy of John Wesley's, *A Collection of Psalms and Hymns* appeared, printed by Lewis Timothy in Charleston, South Carolina. With George Whitefield's arrival in 1740, this hymnal probably enjoyed modest distribution. When the Methodist movement spread to America in the 1760's it built upon this meager foundation and continued to heed its founder's injunction to ministers to dispense with readings as well as sermons. By 1789, when John Dickins founded the Methodist Book Concern, "book writing, editing, manufacturing, promotion, accounting, sales, and distribution were fused functionally" into Methodism.
C. A. Newton

1319. Chyet, Stanley F. A SYNAGOGUE IN NEWPORT. *Am. Jewish Arch. 1964 16(1): 41-50.* Documents the activities of the Jewish community in Newport, Rhode Island, in the 1750's and 1760's and the formation of their congregation.
A. B. Rollins

1320. Chyet, Stanley F. THE POLITICAL RIGHTS OF THE JEWS IN THE UNITED STATES: 1776-1840. *Am. Jewish Arch. 1958 10(1): 14-75.* Demonstrates the substantial freedom of religion established at the national level by the Constitution, the Declaration of Independence and the Northwest Ordinance. The author documents in detail State Constitutional discriminations against Jews after the Revolution.
A. B. Rollins

1321. Clem, Alan L. THE VESTRIES AND LOCAL GOVERNMENT IN COLONIAL MARYLAND. *Hist. Mag. of the Protestant Episcopal Church 1962 31(3): 219-229.* Traces the secular and religious functions of the vestry in the colonial period. State functions terminated with the Revolution, at which time the vestries' right to choose the parish priest was recognized.
E. Oberholzer, Jr.

1322. Corre, Alan D., ed. and compiler. THE RECORD BOOK OF THE REVEREND JACOB RAPHAEL COHEN. *Am. Jewish Hist. Q. 1969 59(1): 23-76.* Jacob Raphael Cohen, hazzan of Congregation Mikveh Israel, Philadelphia, from 1784 to 1811, kept a record book which spans the period from 1776 to 1843, having been continued by others after Cohen's death. The manuscript, listing memorial prayers, circumcisions, marriages, and deaths, contains over 500 names. The record book is translated and annotated. 227 notes.
F. Rosenthal

1323. Cushing, John D. NOTES ON DISESTABLISHMENT IN MASSACHUSETTS, 1780-1833. *William and Mary Q. 1969 26(2): 169-190.* Discusses the "dual corporation" status of town and church, citing the case of *John Murray vs. Inhabitants of the First Parish* in Gloucester. It concerned a suit by a Universalist preacher (heard on appeal by the Supreme Judicial Court) that was decided in favor of rights of dissenters but afforded no relief for "religious societies." Eventually, the Massachusetts courts accepted the legality of Catholic and dissenter ordination. The author comments on the rising attack on support of churches in their political corporate status. 54 notes.   H. M. Ward

1324. Fabian, Bernhard. JEFFERSON'S *NOTES ON VIRGINIA:* THE GENESIS OF QUERY XVII, "THE DIFFERENT RELIGIONS RECEIVED INTO THAT STATE." *William and Mary Q. 1955 12(1): 124-138.* Compares Thomas Jefferson's discussion of religious liberty in the *Notes* with his recently published *Outline of Argument* used in 1776 in the discussion on disestablishment. The *Outline* formed the basis of this part of the *Notes.* Jefferson's *Outline,* in turn, was influenced by John Locke's *Letter Concerning Toleration* and Shaftesbury's *Letter Concerning Enthusiasm.*   E. Oberholzer, Jr.

1325. Fanning, Samuel J. PHILIP EMBURY, FOUNDER OF METHODISM IN NEW YORK. *Methodist Hist. 1965 3(2): 16-25.* Philip Embury established Methodism in New York in 1766. The author provides background information on the Palatines in Ireland, from which Embury came, as well as information on the growth of Methodism in Ireland. Biographical details are provided on Embury's life and activities in Ireland and New York.   H. L. Calkin

1326. Freeman, Stephen A. PURITANS IN RUTLAND, VERMONT 1770-1818. *Vermont Hist. 1965 33(2): 342-348.* Sketches Congregationalist history in West Rutland (1773-87) under the leadership of Benajah Roots, a New Light exponent from Simsbury, Connecticut, and (1788-1818) under Lemuel Haynes, mulatto evangelist; and in East Rutland (1789-95) under Samuel Williams, former Harvard professor, and (1797-1821) under Heman Ball. Uses contemporary sermons and records, in the framework of C. C. Goen's *Revivalism and Separatism in New England: 1740-1962* (New Haven: Yale U. Press).
        T. D. S. Bassett

1327. Guthrie, Dwight R. JOHN MC MILLAN. *J. of the Presbyterian Hist. Soc. 1955 33(2): 63-85.* A sympathetic biographical sketch of John McMillan (1752-1833), minister and founder of various Presbyterian congregations in Western Pennsylvania.   R. Mueller

1328. Hamilton, Kenneth G. SALEM IN WACHOVIA: AN EXAMPLE OF MORAVIAN COLONIZING GENIUS. *Moravian Hist. Soc. Tr. 1966 21(1): 53-75.* The bicentennial of the founding of Winston-Salem, North Carolina, emphasises Salem, the older portion of the city established in 1766.
        J. G. Pennington

1329. Hamilton, Kenneth G. THE MORAVIAN ARCHIVES AT BETHLEHEM, PENNSYLVANIA. *Am. Archivist 1961 24(4): 415-423.* The Moravian archives contain 500,000 manuscript items, plus music, painting and library collections of a significant size. A unique historical record is the Bethlehem Diary, 1742-1871, which was a daily record (33,352 pages) compiled by individual congregations and sent to the main church office. The personal papers of individual leaders, and the files of missionaries among both the Indians and the German immigrants enrich the Moravian archives. G. M. Gressley

1330. Hartdagen, Gerald E. VESTRY AND CLERGY IN THE ANGLICAN CHURCH OF COLONIAL MARYLAND. *Hist. Mag. of the Protestant Episcopal Church 1968 37(4): 371-396.* Discusses the continual vestry-clergy conflicts in colonial Maryland. During the frequent ministerial vacancies, parishes were allowed either to appoint a reader or hire temporary replacements; the governor, however, retained the right of permanent appointment. The vestries' attempts to influence the choices did not often succeed, though in the later 18th century they did begin to assert their rights over clergy at the expense of both governor and proprietor. Effective clergy control had, moreover, been lacking. Courts, bishops, commissaries, intervention from London had all failed. But by 1771, the clergy were made subject to law. Immorality and neglect had grown, as the chronic shortage of ministers and the importance of connections made it relatively simple for unqualified or immoral clergy to obtain even a rich parish. Constant disagreements thus arose between vestry and clergy over such matters as income. Primary sources, 40 notes. E. G. Roddy

1331. Hiner, Ray, Jr. SAMUEL HENLEY AND THOMAS GWATKIN; PARTNERS IN PROTEST. *Hist. Mag. of the Protestant Episcopal Church 1968 37(1): 39-50.* Sketch of two Anglican divines who migrated to Virginia in 1770, became professors at the College of William and Mary, and contributed to that volatile social, religious, and political climate of which colonial Williamsburg was a part. Although both were Tories, they opposed the idea of an American episcopate much to the annoyance of their coreligionists in the northern colonies. 48 notes, mostly primary and drawing heavily on the *Virginia Gazette.*
E. G. Roddy

1332. Hood, Fred J. REVOLUTION AND RELIGIOUS LIBERTY: THE CONSERVATION OF THE THEOCRATIC CONCEPT IN VIRGINIA. *Church Hist. 1971 40(2): 170-181.* Argues "that conservative Protestants, as represented by a majority of the Presbyterians in Virginia, conceived of religious liberty as a religious dogma compatible with an established religion and that the legal separation of church and state did not alter that belief or its influence." Freedom of conscience was idealized by Presbyterians, but state support for a Protestant Christianity was seen as necessary for the preservation of society. Between 1776 and 1779 Presbyterians opposed favored status for Episcopalianism, but after 1779 they argued not against state support to religion but rather against the establishment of a specific sect. The survival of a theocratic concept is reflected in Presbytery of Hanover memorials to the Virginia Assembly in 1776 and 1777 and in Presbyterian reactions to the general assessment bill of 1779 which provided for a multiple establishment. Only in 1785 under pressure from its western laity and in jealous fear of Episcopalianism did Virginia Presbyterianism declare for full disestablishment, still hoping for the establishment of a "theocratic society of the millennium" in America. Based mainly on secondary sources; 41 notes. S. C. Pearson, Jr.

1333. Kessner, Thomas. GERSHOM MENDES SEIXAS: HIS RELIGIOUS "CALLING," OUTLOOK AND COMPETENCE. *Am. Jewish Hist. Q. 1969 58(4): 445-471.* Gershom Mendes Seixas (1745-1815) served as hazzan (cantor and preceptor) at Congregation Shearith Israel in New York City from 1768 until his death in 1815. During this long period Seixas served as the spokesman and representative of New York Jewry and performed ever wider functions as cantor, teacher, preacher, and rabbinic authority. His philosophy was a blend of Jewish traditionalism and 18th-century enlightenment. Based on materials in the Seixas Collection in the American Jewish Historical Society Library; illus., 97 notes. F. Rosenthal

1334. Lacy, Harriet S. AN EIGHTEENTH-CENTURY DIARIST IDENTIFIED: SAMUEL PARKER'S JOURNAL FOR 1771. *Hist. New Hampshire 1970 25(2): 2-44.* Parker (1744-1804) graduated from Harvard University in 1764, taught school in Greenland and Portsmouth, New Hampshire, and did some legal work. He became assistant rector of Trinity Church in 1773, married, and shortly before his death was elected Bishop of the Eastern Diocese of the Protestant Episcopal Church. His diary records a turning point in his life. Apparently wavering between careers as a lawyer or Congregational minister, in August 1771 he moved to the provincial capital, a center of Anglican society. Contrapuntal to memoranda of religious and business meetings in his diary are party notes of wining and dining, dancing, singing, play-acting, chess and checkers, and tea and travel with a large, upper-class circle about the taverns and mansions of coastal New Hampshire. 3 illus., map, appendix. T. D. S. Bassett

1335. Lewis, Andrew W., ed. HENRY MUHLENBERG'S GEORGIA CORRESPONDENCE. *Georgia Hist. Q. 1965 49(4): 424-454.* Letters to Reverend Henry Melchior Mühlenberg from 1777 to 1784 commenting on factions and strife in the Ebenezer community of (German Lutheran) Salzburgers owing to internal financial and religious bickerings and Revolutionary War depredations. R. Lowitt

1336. Libby, Robert Meridith Gabler. ANGLICAN-LUTHERAN ECUMENISM IN EARLY AMERICAN HISTORY. *Hist. Mag. of the Protestant Episcopal Church 1967 36(3): 211-231.* Random selections illustrating the close and cordial relationship between Lutherans and Anglicans in colonial, Revolutionary, and early national years. Lutherans tended to join in the services of the Anglican Church in areas where they did not have churches of their own. Gradually, however, Lutherans came to oppose the idea of union of the two churches. By 1821 the General Synod of Lutheran Churches formed and thus put an end to this early ecumenical movement. Based mainly on secondary sources; 58 notes. E. G. Roddy

1337. Madden, Richard C. CATHOLICS IN COLONIAL SOUTH CAROLINA. *Records of the Am. Catholic Hist. Soc. of Philadelphia 1962 73(1/2): 10-44.* A carefully detailed study of Catholics in South Carolina in the 17th and 18th centuries, demonstrating that there were many more of these than historians have generally noted. Persecution of Catholics in the colony is documented.   C. G. Hamilton

1338. Marcus, Jacob Rader. THE HANDSOME YOUNG PRIEST IN THE BLACK GOWN: THE PERSONAL WORLD OF GERSHOM SEIXAS. *Hebrew Union Coll. Annual 1970 40/41: 409-467.* Gershom Mendes Seixas (1746-1816) was America's first native Jewish clergyman and was completely receptive to the colonial influences of the period with its emphasis on enlightened rationalism and the Protestant ethic. He found no conflict between his fundamental Judaism and the application of these principles to the contemporary situation. Seixas was originally employed as the hazzan (reader and teacher) of the New York Shearith Israel congregation (1768/69) and he held the post until his death in 1816, with one 8-year break as a result of the Revolutionary War. He also achieved recognition as a preacher, rabbi, and spokesman for the Jewish community. 111 notes.   F. Rosenthal

1339. Marcus, Jacob Rader. THE THEME IN AMERICAN JEWISH HISTORY. *Pub. of the Am. Jewish Hist. Soc. 1959 48(3): 141-146.* Maintains that even in as short a time span as that of American Jewish history, a definite number of themes can be ascertained: 1) 1654-1776: the synagogue as the central and only agency in Jewish life; 2) 1776-1840's: diminishing interest in religious matters and appearance of confraternities; 3) 1840's-1880: nationalism and federalism, or the urge to greater unity; 4) 1880-1903: a time of chaos, indicating the emergence of East European leadership, and 5) since 1903: unification of all Jews through their accommodation to American life and culture; creation of nationwide agencies. At present there exists the problem of accommodating these nationwide agencies to the actuality of strong individual congregations and communities.
                                                                 F. Rosenthal

1340. Martin, Howard H. PURITAN PREACHING: NOTES ON AMERICAN COLONIAL RHETORIC. *Q. J. of Speech 1964 50(3): 285-292.* A summary of prescriptive comments on the rhetoric of the sermon as found in ordination sermons before the American Revolution. Puritan preachers most consistently recommended that the preacher: 1) speak to the rational capacities of the audience; 2) avoid emotionalism; 3) prepare thoroughly; 4) adapt to the emotional and mental states of the audience; 5) speak plainly, honestly, and courageously, in a clear and unaffected style; and 6) make little use of notes. "Men need to be frightened and not be pleased" advised the colonial Puritan preacher. Sources consist primarily of 50 pre-Revolutionary ordination sermons, examined in the Henry E. Huntington Library and the Houghton and the Andover-Harvard Library of Harvard University, 50 notes.   M. A. Hayes

1341. Maser, Frederick. ROBERT STRAWBRIDGE, FOUNDER OF METHODISM IN MARYLAND. *Methodist Hist. 1966 4(2): 3-21.* A biographical sketch of Robert Strawbridge with emphasis on his organization of Methodist societies and his ministry in Maryland, Virginia, New Jersey, and Pennsylvania from 1766 to 1774. Other topics discussed are his early life in Ireland, his role in the controversy over administering the sacraments and as a property owner.

H. L. Calkin

1342. McLoughlin, William G. ISAAC BACKUS AND THE SEPARATION OF CHURCH AND STATE IN AMERICA. *Am. Hist. R. 1968 73(5): 1392-1413.* As the leading spokesman of the Baptists in the American colonies during the Revolutionary Era, Isaac Backus (1724-1806) played a significant role in the formulation of the American tradition of separation of church and state. The difference between the evangelical theory of Separationism for which Backus spoke and the more deistic, rationalistic theory of Jefferson and Madison is defined. Further, it is pointed out that the views of Roger Williams had little influence upon the formulation of this tradition in the Revolutionary Era and that they are quite distinct both from those of Jefferson and Madison and of Backus. Since the evangelical version of Separationism dominated American life from the Revolution until well into the 20th century, historians should give more attention to the work of Backus. At the same time they should note that these views did not spring full-blown from Baptist theological principles but they evolved slowly and pragmatically over the generation following the First Great Awakening.

A

1343. McLoughlin, William G. THE BALKCOM CASE (1782) AND THE PIETISTIC THEORY OF SEPARATION OF CHURCH AND STATE. *William and Mary Q. 1967 24(2): 267-283.* This case in effect disestablished the church in Massachusetts, even though it was not until the 1830's that the official ties with the State were severed. Baptists made a test case, in the suit of Elijah Balkcom against the tax collectors, of the constitutionality of the certificate system. The role of Isaac Backus is stressed. Comparisons are made with various views of religious freedom. 2 appendixes: a summary account in the Inferior Court of Common Pleas, Bristol County Court House; and shorthand notes of the trial from the papers of Robert Treat Paine. 17 notes.   H. M. Ward

1344. McLouglin, William G. THE FIRST CALVINISTIC BAPTIST ASSOCIATION IN NEW ENGLAND, 1754?-1767. *Church Hist. 1967 36(4): 410-418.* Traces the history of the Six Principle Calvinistic Baptist Association of New England which preceded the Warren Association of 1767. Though no official records of the association are known to survive, there are several references to it in the unpublished papers of Isaac Backus. The association marks an important phase in the transition from the earlier Six Principle Arminian tradition to the Five Principle Calvinist tradition among New England Baptists. Backus, who was pastor of a Baptist church in Middleborough, Massachusetts, worked among neighboring Arminian Baptists with success for the Five Principle Calvinist cause. Becoming aware of the Six Principle Calvinistic Baptist Association, he drew its member churches into fellowship. In 1766 the Six Principle Baptists agreed to continue practicing the sixth principle (laying on of hands for church membership) but not to hold this principle a bar to communion with others. After the formation of the Warren Association most of these churches joined it. A chart indicating member churches, pastors, and related data is provided. The entries in the Backus Papers from 1763 to 1767 which refer to the association are published. Based on the Backus Papers at Andover Newton Theological School; 13 notes. S. C. Pearson, Jr.

1345. Mead, S. A. FROM COERCION TO PERSUASION: ANOTHER LOOK AT THE RISE OF RELIGIOUS LIBERTY AND THE EMERGENCE OF DENOMINATIONALISM. *Church Hist. 1956 25(4): 317-337.* An examination of the causes of the constitutional provisions for religious freedom, in the light of Philip Schaff's thesis that Congress was "shut up to this course by...the actual conditions of things" in 1787. The Great Awakenings created confusion and compromise in which "right" and "left" wing Protestantism, and "sect" and "church" were fused; the result was the "denomination." By 1787 the distinction between these groups was meaningless, and no church was strong enough to make a bid for establishment. The churches "placed their feet unwittingly on the road to religious freedom,...grudgingly and of necessity."
E. Oberholzer, Jr.

1346. Mills, Frederick V. ANGLICAN EXPANSION IN COLONIAL AMERICA 1761-1775. *Hist. Mag. of the Protestant Episcopal Church 1970 39(3): 315-324.* Examines the "remarkable development" of the Anglican Church just prior to the War of Independence. The vitality of Anglicanism was reflected in three areas of church activity: new construction, ministerial enlistments, and clerical education. The fact that local parishes, in the absence of any bishops in America, became centers of power contributed to the polity of the post-Revolution independent Episcopal Church. Based on Episcopal Church archives, colonial archives, and secondary sources; charts, 36 notes. A. J. Stifflear

1347. Moore, LeRoy, Jr. RELIGIOUS LIBERTY: ROGER WILLIAMS AND THE REVOLUTIONARY ERA. *Church Hist. 1965 34(1): 57-76.* Sketches Williams' views of religious liberty and compares and contrasts them with ideas of religious liberty prominent in the latter years of the 18th century. Williams' ideas on liberty grew out of his Puritanism, and the key to his thought is his allegiance to divine sovereignty which he believed to be qualified in some measure by every form of church order. He sought a "wall of separation" between church and state to protect the church and divine sovereignty. John Locke, who informed the minds of the Revolutionary Era, drew upon the same Puritan milieu which shaped Williams, but he shifted the argument from a theocentric to an anthropocentric base—from concern for a state which would not restrict God to a concern for one which would allow men full freedom in the exercise of inalienable rights. The writings of both Jefferson and Madison reflect the Lockean orientation. Among dissenters supporting religious freedom, John Leland overlooked the role of Roger Williams and Isaac Backus, while suggesting the significance of Williams' contribution in his *History of New England.* He appealed to Enlightenment figures in his political pamphlets supporting separation. Thus the Revolutionary Era was virtually unaware of Williams and of his theological defense of religious freedom. S. C. Pearson, Jr.

1348. Moyne, Ernest J. THE HAZLITT'S JEWISH NEIGHBORS IN EIGH-
TEENTH CENTURY PHILADELPHIA. *Am. Jewish Hist. Q. 1967 56(4):
452-456.* On their way from England to Boston, this Unitarian minister and his
family spent a year in Philadelphia (June 1783-August 1784). Their Jewish neigh-
bor "Mr. Gomez" has been identified as Moses Daniel Gomez in whose house
lived two boys and two girls, the orphaned children of his sister Rachel. Hazlitt's
daughter Margaret refers to these Jewish friends in her diary, written shortly
before her death.   F. Rosenthal

1349. Musser, Edgar A. OLD ST. MARY'S OF LANCASTER, PA.: THE
JESUIT PERIOD, 1741-1785. *J. of the Lancaster County Hist. Soc. 1967 71(2):
69-136.* Traces the line of sovereignty of English vicars-apostolic over the American Colonies from 1623 to 1784, and the line of American Bishops in the Mary-
land-Pennsylvania areas from 1784 to 1935. Lists pastors of St. Mary's Church,
Lancaster County, from 1741 to 1966. Describes Jesuit relations with the Cones-
toga Indians, and the formation of the Maryland Mission and the Catholic
Church in Pennsylvania. Examines the pastoral offices of Joseph Greaton, S.J.
(1679-1753), Henry Neale, S.J. (d. 1748), William Wappeler, S.J. (1711-81),
Richard Molyneux, S.J. (1696-1766), Theodore Schneider, S.J. (1703-64), Ferdi-
nand Farmer, S.J. (1720-86), James Pellentz, S.J. (ca. 1727-1800), James A.
Frambach, S.J. (ca. 1718-91), and Luke Geissler, S.J. (1735-86), and the support
of the missions by Sir John James (a layman and convert). Undocumented, 7
illus., 2 maps, biblio.   J. S. Pula

1350. Pilcher, George William. THE PAMPHLET WAR ON THE PROPOSED
VIRGINIA ANGLICAN EPISCOPATE, 1767-1775. *Hist. Mag. of the Protes-
tant Episcopal Church 1961 30(4): 266-279.* Surveys the pamphlet war between
the advocates of a colonial episcopate, led by the SPG's Thomas Bradbury
Chandler, and the opposition. This war terminated with the outbreak of the
American Revolution and Chandler's departure for England.
                                                          E. Oberholzer, Jr.

1351. Rabe, Harry G. THE REVEREND DEVEREAUX JARRATT AND
THE VIRGINIA SOCIAL ORDER. *Hist. Mag. of the Protestant Episcopal
Church 1964 33(4): 299-336.* This 18th-century Virginian's *Autobiography* sup-
plies much of the evidence upon which this study is based. The Rev. Devereaux
Jarratt rose from the yeoman class to the gentry, eventually taking orders in the
Anglican Church. For 38 years he served as pastor of Bath in Dinwiddie County,
Virginia. Although a product of the "New Awakening," he contributed nothing
original to theology. His working agreement with the Virginia Methodists collapsed when they broke with Anglicanism and organized the Methodist Episcopal
Church in America. His attitude toward the War for Independence, the separation of church and state and the "leveling" of Virginia's social classes was typical
of a man of his background and beliefs. Augustinian in his view of history,
Jarratt's conservatism comes through in his writings. Convincing proof is offered
that he was himself a slaveowner (and defender of slavery on Biblical grounds)
despite his denials. The article is based on a master's thesis, Claremont College.
Documented.   E. G. Roddy

1352. Rhodes, Irwin S. EARLY LEGAL RECORDS OF JEWS OF LANCAS-
TER COUNTY, PENNSYLVANIA. *Am. Jewish Arch. 1960 12(1): 96-108.*
Abstracts of documents collected at the Archives, largely deeds and wills running
from the 1740's to the 1880's, but mostly from the second half of the 18th century.
A. B. Rollins

1353. Richardson, Robert. DOCUMENTARY HISTORY OF THE AMERI-
CAN CHURCH: SIX LETTERS OF THOMAS BRADBURY CHANDLER.
Hist. Mag. of the Protestant Episcopal Church 1963 32(4): 371-391. Six letters
by Chandler (1726-90), dated 1776-77, in connection with the movement for an
American episcopate, with a biographical sketch of Chandler.
E. Oberholzer, Jr.

1354. Schell, Edwin. METHODIST TRAVELING PREACHERS IN AMER-
ICA, 1773-1799. *Methodist Hist. 1964 2(2): 51-67.* A compilation of 850 persons
who served as traveling Methodist preachers in America from 1773 to 1799.
Where available, the years of appointment, receiving on trial, receiving in full
connection, ordination and termination are provided. H. L. Calkin

1355. Schrag, Martin H. INFLUENCES CONTRIBUTING TO AN EARLY
RIVER BRETHREN CONFESSION OF FAITH. *Mennonite Q. R. 1964 38(4):
344-353.* From old English translations of nonextant German documents is
revealed the influence of Pietism and of the Church of the Brethren in Lancaster
County, Pennsylvania, and its environs, between 1770 and 1798. Most noticeable
is the acceptance of the crisis experience of conversion, which was not part of
Mennonite or of earlier Brethren thinking. These influences may have come from
abroad or may have developed from local Pietistic organizations, especially during the Great Awakening. The tolerance of infant baptism where the parents
desire it showed a Pietistic tendency to work with Lutheran and Reformed sects,
which was never part of the Mennonite tradition. This explains the sources which
contributed to the earlier stages of the movement which culminated in the organization of the River Brethren who could not feel at home in any established
religious group in the Lancaster area. C. G. Hamilton

1356. Smith, Timothy L. CONGREGATION, STATE, AND DENOMINA-
TION: THE FORMING OF THE AMERICAN RELIGIOUS STRUCTURE.
William and Mary Q. 1968 24(2): 155-176. Considers the rise of Protestant
denominations as a result of mobility making for voluntary association. Loneli-
ness and danger and the need to reconstruct communities out of fragmentized
family life were factors in searching for religious solidarity. The development of
an American tradition of state control over religious and cultural matters and the
roles of the various colonial churches are examined. 60 notes. H. M. Ward

1357. Smith, Warren Thomas. ATTEMPTS AT METHODIST AND
MORAVIAN UNION. *Methodist Hist. 1970 8(2): 36-48.* The relationship between Methodists and Moravians began well in 1728, but deteriorated to the point
that John Wesley (1703-91) called Moravian doctrine "flatly contrary to the

Word of God," and ended their association. In 1785, however, Wesley's brother Charles (1707-88) attempted to oppose his separatism (especially with regard to the American branch of the society) by renewing discussion of union with the Moravians, who were committed to the framework of the existing church. To this end Charles opened contacts with Benjamin La Trobe, head of the Moravians in England. Major obstacles to union proved to be John Wesley's tendencies toward formation of an independent denomination; his ordination of ministers without Anglican sanction; the individual and intense nature of the Moravian group; and most especially Thomas Coke (1747-1814), superintendent of the American Methodists, whom the Moravians distrusted for his advocacy of national churches and his wish to form a new denomination. Talks continued, however, and many objections were satisfied, until 1786 when La Trobe died and a scheduled meeting with John Wesley could not take place. The discussions show the involved processes that church union conversations often require. 75 notes.

P. M. Olson

1358. Smith, Warren Thomas. THE CHRISTMAS CONFERENCE. *Methodist Hist. 1968 6(4): 3-27.* An account of events prior to, during, and subsequent to the Christmas Conference held in Baltimore, Maryland, in 1784 at which the Methodist Episcopal Church was established in the United States. The author discusses John Wesley's reasons for sending Thomas Coke, Richard Whatcoat and Thomas Vasey to America; the decision to hold a conference; the roles of Coke and Francis Asbury; the adoption of a liturgy and a discipline; the naming of the church; ordinations; and the results of the conference. Based largely on journals of Coke and Asbury; 96 notes.

H. L. Calkin

1359. Stern, Malcolm H. TWO JEWISH FUNCTIONAIRES IN COLONIAL PENNSYLVANIA. *Am. Jewish Hist. Q. 1967 57(1): 24-51.* Reconstructs the religious and communal functions of two men: Barnard Jacobs, ritual circumciser between 1757 and 1790, and Mordecai Moses Mordecai (1727-1809), circumciser and marriage performer to Jews in colonial Pennsylvania, at a time when proper rabbinic leadership was frequently not available. Sources used include Barnard Jacobs' list of 33 circumcisions performed prior to 1790 and various pieces of correspondence involving Mordecai's relation with the Mikveh Israel Congregation of Philadelphia. Based on available public records and archival materials. Illus., 115 notes, appendix.

F. Rosenthal

1360. Stoltzfus, Grant M. HISTORY OF THE FIRST AMISH MENNONITE COMMUNITIES IN AMERICA. *Mennonite Q. R. 1954 28(4): 235-262.* A description of the development of the various Amish communities in Pennsylvania between 1750 and 1845. The article is an extract from the author's dissertation.

S

1361. Tarver, Jerry L. BAPTIST PREACHING FROM VIRGINIA JAILS, 1768-1778. *Southern Speech J. 1964 30(2): 139-148.* The established Episcopal Church in Virginia successfully restricted religious activities by other Protestant groups. Zealous preaching by Baptists brought them into conflict with laws designed to protect the established church. Often imprisoned, Baptist ministers spoke from their jail cells, demanding freedom of religion and speech. Presidents Washington, Madison, and Jefferson were sympathetic to the Baptist cause. 42 notes. H. G. Stelzner

1362. Taussig, Harold E. DEISM IN PHILADELPHIA DURING THE AGE OF FRANKLIN. *Pennsylvania Hist. 1970 37(3): 217-236.* Surveys the religious thought of 48 members of the American Philosophical Society in 1768, including Benjamin Franklin, John Dickinson, David Rittenhouse, Benjamin Rush, William Smith, John Bartram, and James Logan. With some notable exceptions, membership in the American Philosophical Society was more an indication of social standing and attachment to the proprietary party in Pennsylvania than a sign of interest or accomplishment in science. While many members of the urban upper class held deistic beliefs, "Christianity was much more than a vestige" among these aristocrats. Rather, many of them retained traditional religious beliefs and blended them with certain tenets of deism. Desim probably had few adherents among the lower classes. 82 notes. D. C. Swift

1363. Tresch, John W., Jr. THE RECEPTION ACCORDED GEORGE WHITEFIELD IN THE SOUTHERN COLONIES. *Methodist Hist. 1968 6(2): 17-26.* George Whitefield came to America from England on seven preaching missions between 1736 and 1770. Throughout his ministry he was drawn more to the South than to the North in the American colonies. The nature of his preaching, his reception by the people, his personal viewpoints on slavery and liquor, the opposition to him, and his general popularity are described. 90 notes. H. L. Calkin

1364. Trueblood, Roy W. UNION NEGOTIATIONS BETWEEN BLACK METHODISTS IN AMERICA. *Methodist Hist. 1970 8(4): 18-29.* Negroes have been a part of Methodist history in America since 1766. As early as 1787 they desired to have their own church organizations with black leadership. As a result, the African Methodist Episcopal Church, the African Methodist Episcopal Zion Church, and the Christian Methodist Episcopal Church were established. During the past 100 years repeated efforts have been made to unite the three into a single church. Structural differences, personal pride and ambition, and failure to take the negotiations seriously are among the reasons union has not been accomplished. 22 notes. H. L. Calkin

1365. Unsigned. THE EXCOMMUNICATION OF REVEREND JOHN BAPTIST CAUSSE: AN UNPUBLISHED SERMON BY BISHOP JOHN CARROLL OF BALTIMORE. *Records of the Am. Catholic Hist. Soc. of Philadelphia 1970 81(1): 42-56.* An ecclesiastical fortune-seeker, Causse arrived in Philadelphia in August 1785 after leaving his European convent and wandering in the New World. For a time he ministered to Germans in western Pennsylvania. In 1791 he was jailed briefly following a bizarre episode of extortion and fraud, and took over a circus called "Jerusalem." Suspended and stripped of his faculties, he went to Baltimore and rallied some German supporters. Presents the text of Bishop Carroll's sermon excommunicating Causse. 23 notes. J. M. McCarthy

1366. Vickers, John A. LAMBETH PALACE LIBRARY. *Methodist Hist. 1971 9(4): 22-29.* Discusses the Fulham Papers in the library of Lambeth Palace, London, insofar as they pertain to items of Methodist interest in America before the War of Independence, particularly in relation to George Whitefield, John Wesley, and Joseph Pilmore. 11 notes.   H. L. Calkin

1367. Walden, Daniel. BENJAMIN FRANKLIN'S DEISM: A PHASE. *Historian 1964 26(3): 350-361.* Reveals Franklin as a "practical, prudent deist who in his search for authenticity was also one of the first of a new breed of existential Americans." Documented.   Sr. M. McAuley

1368. Washington, George. GEORGE WASHINGTON'S LETTER TO THE LUTHERANS AT PHILADELPHIA. *Concordia Hist. Inst. Q. 1965 38(3): 154-155.* George Washington thanked the German Lutheran Congregation at Philadelphia for its "kind address" of confidence, praised the American Lutheran community, and asked for continued support. The letter is reprinted from Paul F. Boller, Jr., *George Washington and Religion* (Dallas: Southern Methodist U., 1963), pp. 168, 169.   D. J. Abramoske

1369. Wiener, Theodore. JEWISH COMMUNAL ACTIVITY IN THE UNITED STATES, A BIBLIOGRAPHY OF INSTITUTIONS BEFORE THE CIVIL WAR. *Studies in Biblio. and Booklore 1961 5: 122-136.* "Culled from earlier lists," the 165 chronologically arranged (1760-1860) publications described were issued by 29 congregations, 27 fraternal and philanthropic organizations, and 14 educational or literary societies. New York and Philadelphia Jewish communities predominate, but there are also entries for Rhode Island, Savannah, Charleston, New Orleans, Baltimore, Ohio, Richmond (Virginia), Louisville (Kentucky), San Francisco, and Chicago.   J. C. Wyllie

Science & Medicine

1370. Beard, Eva, ed. DOCTOR NATURALIST ON TOUR 1783-1784. *Am.-German R. 1958 25(1): 27-29.* Publishes a report of Dr. Johann David Schoepf concerning his travels in the American Confederation. Schoepf, former chief surgeon with the Ansbach troops sent to aid the British army in the American Revolution, was well acquainted with the scientific knowledge of his day and made a broad range of observations.   G. H. Davis

1371. Bell, Whitfield J., Jr. JOHN REDMAN, MEDICAL PRECEPTOR, 1722-1808. *Pennsylvania Mag. of Hist. and Biog. 1957 81(2): 157-169.* An analysis of the career, education, and religious beliefs of John Redman, an important Philadelphia doctor and onetime president of the College of Physicians and Surgeons.   D. Houston

1372. Bell, Whitfield J., Jr. NICHOLAS COLLIN'S APPEAL TO AMERICAN SCIENTISTS. *William and Mary Q. 1956 13(4): 519-550.* The text of Collin's address to the American Philosophical Society (1789), suggesting topics for investigation: medicine, rural economics, agriculture, navigation, land surveys, botany, zoology and meteorology. In the introduction the editor observes that Collin made no original contribution to scientific knowledge.

E. Oberholzer, Jr.

1373. Berkeley, Edmund and Berkeley, Dorothy S. JOHN CLAYTON, SCIENTIST. *Virginia Cavalcade 1964 13(4): 36-41.* Traces the life of John Clayton, a botanist of colonial Virginia whose correspondence, specimens, and descriptions of American plants enabled Johann F. Gronovius to publish his *Flora Virginica.* Undocumented.

R. B. Lange

1374. Bolhouse, Gladys E. ABRAHAM REDWOOD, PHILANTHROPIST, BOTANIST. *Newport Hist. 1972 45(2): 17-35.* Relates the ideas and career of Abraham Redwood, Jr., founder of the Redwood Library. Redwood was born in 1709 or 1710, and lived as a young boy in Newport. He received most of his education in Philadelphia, as was natural for many Quakers of the day. He married Martha Coggeshall at the age of 18 and visited his inherited plantation on Antigua in 1730 or 1731. While there, he became interested in rare plants and botany while expanding his plantation and slave holdings. Redwood's civic career coincided with the "Golden Age" of Newport history during the 1740's and 1750's. In the 1770's, he refused to give up his slaves at the urging of the Quaker meeting, and was dismissed from the Fellowship. During the Revolutionary era, he moved to Mendon, Massachusetts, and died there in 1788. He was remembered as one of the wealthy benefactors of colonial Newport society.

D. P. Peltier

1375. Botti, Priscilla Smith. ELIZABETH WHITMORE: MIDWIFE OF MARLBORO. *Vermont Hist. 1971 39(2): 98-100.* From family and D.A.R. sources and the town history, traces the migration of Elizabeth Whitmore (1727-1814), a tinker's wife from Middletown, Connecticut, to Vermont in 1763. She had learned midwifery in Middletown and supported the family on two dollar delivery fees while her husband traveled, cleared the farm, fought in the Revolution, and represented the town at political conventions.

T. D. S. Bassett

1376. Chinard, Gilbert. ANDRE AND FRANÇOIS-ANDRE MICHAUX AND THEIR PREDECESSORS. AN ESSAY ON EARLY BOTANICAL EXCHANGES BETWEEN AMERICA AND FRANCE. *Pro. of the Am. Phil. Soc. 1957 101(4): 344-361.* Deals with exchanges of botanical ideas, and of seeds and plants, from the settlement of the first French colonists in Canada through the beginning of the 19th century. The author describes the activities of early missionaries and travelers, particularly Pierre de Charlevoix (1682-1761). The development of royal nurseries in France increased the demand for specimens, and this was one of the reasons for sending André Michaux to America in 1785. His primary task was to find suitable trees for the replenishment of depleted

French forests which supplied naval stores. The author gives a detailed account of the activities of André, the father (1746-1802), and François-André, the son (1770-1855). François René de Chateaubriand, Thomas Jefferson, and Benjamin Franklin also played important parts in the exchange, which reflects the 18th-century attitude on science and the diffusion of knowledge. Documented.

N. Kurland

1377. Compton, Arthur H. THE WORLD OF SCIENCE IN THE LATE EIGHTEENTH CENTURY AND TODAY. *Pro. of the Am. Phil. Soc. 1956 100(4): 296-303.* A summary and interpretation of Benjamin Franklin's contributions to the understanding of electrical phenomena, and a discussion of the development of Newtonian mechanics and its effect on 18th-century conceptions of the role of God.

N. Kurland

1378. Cowen, David L. A STORE MIXT, VARIOUS, UNIVERSAL. *J. of the Rutgers U. Lib. 1961 25(1): 1-9.* A printed broadside circulated 11 October 1784, advertising the materia medica and related items offered for sale by Smith, Moore and Co., New York, has recently come into possession of the Rutgers University Library. The document is of literary, historical and scientific interest. Written in amusing and ingenious verse, it lists 120 medical products in use at the time, illustrating the alacrity with which Britain had resumed trade with her former colonies, the availability of herbs and drugs from all over the world, and the trends in materia medica at the time, revealing a definite move away from dependence on animal materials, a preponderance of vegetable materials, and the beginning of the use of minerals, indicating that the practice was beginning to become more scientifically empirical than hitherto.

R. E. Wilson

1379. Crump, Stuart F. JOSEPH BROWN, ASTRONOMER. *Rhode Island Hist. 1968 27(1): 1-12.* Sketches the life of Joseph Brown with particular emphasis on his role as an astronomer. There is a detailed account of Brown's observation of the 1769 transit of Venus. Based on primary and secondary sources.

P. J. Coleman

1380. D'Elia, Donald J. DR. BENJAMIN RUSH AND THE AMERICAN MEDICAL REVOLUTION. *Pro. of the Am. Phil. Soc. 1966 110(4): 227-234.* Discusses the theories of Dr. Benjamin Rush (1745-1813) and his influence upon American medical practice during Revolutionary and post-Revolutionary years, from about 1769 to 1813. Rush's acceptance of republicanism disorganized all his opinions and produced his American medical system, a scientific counterpart to the political and social revolution. The yellow fever epidemic in Philadelphia in 1793 helped give definite form to Rush's concept of the nature of disease: all illness is caused by a fundamental fever relating to the blood. This view led logically to his practice of therapeutic blood-letting and purging. Thus did Rush launch the overthrow of the old regime in medicine, simplifying the cause and treatment of disease to one. Spurred by his equalitarian ideals, he also made a notable impact on the development of hospitals and of attitudes toward the insane, as well as on American medical training and the general view of medicine's role in the broad scope of human existence. Based primarily on printed sources. 67 notes. W. G. Morgan

1381. Duveen, Denis I. and Klickstein, Herbert S. [FRANKLIN AND LAVOISIER]. *Ann. of Sci. [Great Britain].* BENJAMIN FRANKLIN (1706-1790) AND ANTOINE LAURENT LAVOISIER (1743-1794). PART I. FRANKLIN AND THE NEW CHEMISTRY, 1955 11(2): 103-128. Through correspondence and personal contact with the two scientists, Franklin was acquainted with both the phlogistic school of chemistry by Joseph Priestly and the anti-phlogistic school by Lavoisier. He never publicly abandoned Priestley's views, though this may have been due to a reluctance to enter into polemics.
BENJAMIN FRANKLIN (1706-1790) AND ANTOINE LAURENT LAVOISIER (1743-1794). PART II. JOINT INVESTIGATIONS, 1955 11(4): 271-308. At the outbreak of the American Revolution, America was threatened with a shortage of gunpowder. Franklin was in touch with Lavoisier after the Régie des Poudres was established on the latter's initiative, and passed on information to the Colonies. The two men collaborated on two reports to the Académie Royale des Sciences on the construction of gunpowder magazines. Other subjects on which they collaborated were aeronautics and animal magnetism. R. S. Smith

1382. Duveen, Denis I. and Klickstein, Herbert S. THE "AMERICAN" EDITION OF LAVOISIER'S *L'ART DE FABRIQUER LE SALIN ET LA POTASSE. William and Mary Q. 1956 13(4): 493-498.* An examination of the paper and type of the "American" edition of Charles Williamos's translation, supposedly published in Philadelphia in the early 19th century, indicates that it was printed in France in 1784 or 1785. The translation is accurate. The translator's motive was to gain recognition in America, to which he hoped to return. E. Oberholzer, Jr.

1383. Gerlach, Larry R. SMALLPOX INOCULATION IN COLONIAL NEW JERSEY: A CONTEMPORARY ACCOUNT. *J. of the Rutgers U. Lib. 1967 31(1): 21-28.* Discusses the state of medical science in early America, with emphasis on smallpox, especially in New Jersey. Describes the several methods of inoculation. Reproduces the complete text of the pamphlet, "The General Method of Enoculation as now Practiced." This description of 18th-century inoculation procedures, published between 1760 and 1790, is the only known account of variolization in colonial New Jersey. The pamphlet now is found in the Hendrickson Family Papers in the Special Collection Department of the Rutgers University Library. 20 notes. M. Kroeger

1384. Gorman, Mel. GASSENDI IN AMERICA. *Isis 1964 55(4): 409-417.* Copies of editions of Pierre Gassendi's (1592-1655) writings, dated and autographed by identifiable Harvard and Yale students, one as early as 1675-76, indicate that Gassendi was read in the colonial period. Because Gassendi's writings included an exposition of the astronomical theories of Galileo and Johannes

Kepler, his readers found a ready source "of celestial information to interpret their almanacs and especially to understand the preaching of their spiritual and intellectual leaders." Documented, biographical data on the owners of dated copies of Gassendi's writings.   J. Stannard

1385. Kaiser, Leo M. ON MUSSI'S "IN VIRGAM FRANKLINIANAM." *William and Mary Q. 1967 24(2): 288-291.* This Latin ode, honoring Benjamin Franklin, was written by Antonio Mussi, professor of philosophy at the University of Milan and later director of the Ambrosian Library. The occasion for the poem was the installation of lightning rods on the Royal Brera Gymnasium. Several printed texts of the poem are compared. The poem is reproduced only in Latin.   H. M. Ward

1386. Kunitz, Stephen J. BENJAMIN RUSH ON SAVAGISM AND PROGRESS. *Ethnohistory 1970 (1/2): 31-42.* "Benjamin Rush, one of the signers of the Declaration of Independence and the most influential physician of the Revolutionary period, delivered a lengthy address concerning the natural history of medicine among North American Indians. The text of this lecture is analyzed to demonstrate how basic cultural assumptions and values affect our view of truth and, more specifically, how Rush's medical opinions were colored by the then-current notions of savagism and progress."   J

1387. Labaree, Leonard W. BENJAMIN FRANKLIN'S BRITISH FRIEND-SHIPS. *Pro. of the Am. Phil. Soc. 1964 108(5): 423-428.* Comments on the variety of distinguished acquaintances acquired by Franklin during the 15 years he lived in the British Isles as a colonial agent. The article refers to at least 22 prominent British friends, largely gained through the Royal Society and an informal organization—the Club of Honest Whigs. They followed many occupations, but generally had strong interests in science and medicine, and were sometimes drawn from the dissenting clergy. Franklin's education was significantly advanced by these contacts which helped to prepare him for his subsequent career in diplomacy. 32 notes referring to both primary and secondary material.
                                                              R. G. Comegys

1388. Lopez, Claude A. SALTPETRE, TIN AND GUNPOWDER: ADDENDA TO THE CORRESPONDENCE OF LAVOISIER AND FRANKLIN. *Ann. of Sci. [Great Britain] 1960 16: 83-94.* After a short introduction describing some of the personal contacts between Antoine Lavoisier and Benjamin Franklin, the author gives several letters relevant to the contacts between the two men, drawn from the mass documents assembled at Yale University for the publication of the Franklin Papers under the editorship of L. W. Labaree.
                                                              N. Rescher

1389. Radovskii, M. I. RUSSKO-AMERIKANSKIE NAUCHNYE SVIAZI V 18-19 VV. PO MATERIALAM ARKHIVA AN SSSR [Russian-American scientific relations in the 18th and 19th century. According to archival material of the Academy of Sciences of the USSR]. *Vestnik Istorii Mirovoi Kul'tury*

[USSR] 1957 (2): 100-106. The name of Benjamin Franklin, with whom the article mainly deals, first appeared in Russia in the year 1752 in the publications of the Petersburg Academy of Sciences. After that he appeared constantly in the press, in scholarly periodicals and on official occasions at the Academy. Important contributions to the theory of electricity in the 1750's were made by Academy members, including G. V. Rikhman, Mikail Lomonosov, and Franz Aepinas, who concerned himself particularly with the dissemination of Franklin's scientific achievements in Russia. In 1789 Franklin became an honorary member of the Academy, whose director, Princess Ekaterina Dashkova, he personally knew.   E. Wollert

1390. Robins, William J. and Howson, Mary Christine. ANDRE MICHAUX'S NEW JERSEY GARDEN AND PIERRE PAUL SAUNIER, JOURNEYMAN GARDENER. *Pro. of the Am. Phil. Soc. 1958 102(4): 351-370.* A detailed account of the establishment and operation of a garden in New Jersey designed to supply France with specimens and information relating to American flora. André Michaux (1746-1803) arrived in the United States for this purpose in November 1785, and purchased land for a garden in Bergen County, New Jersey in March 1786. While Michaux traveled, the garden was maintained by his assistant, Pierre Paul Saunier (1751-1818), who inherited and extended the garden after Michaux's death. This garden played an important part in familiarizing Europe with American horticulture. Documented; illus., biblio., appendix.   N. Kurland

1391. Smith, C. Earle, Jr. HENRY MUHLENBERG—BOTANICAL PIONEER. *Pro. of the Am. Phil. Soc. 1962/63 106(5): 443-460.* Contains biographical information concerning Reverend G. H. E. Muhlenberg (1753-1815), Pennsylvania clergyman and botanist; discusses his methods of classification and briefly describes the Muhlenberg herbarium now in the possession of the Academy of Natural Sciences of Philadelphia.   R. G. Comegys

1392. Stookey, Byron. SAMUEL CLOSSY, A.B., M.D., F.R.C.P. OF IRELAND—FIRST PROFESSOR OF ANATOMY, KING'S COLLEGE (COLUMBIA), NEW YORK. *Bull. of the Hist. of Medicine 1964 38(2): 153-167.* Arriving in New York in 1763 from Trinity College, Dublin, Samuel Clossy (1724-1786) became in 1765 professor of Natural Philosophy at King's College. Two years later, while continuing as professor of Natural Philosophy at King's, he became professor of Anatomy in the new medical school. The author of this article regards Clossy "as the foremost medical scholar in the colonies in the 1760's," one of the distinguished members of the colonial New York medical guild that included Cadwallader Colden, John Jones, and Peter Middleton.   W. L. Fox

1393. Thomson, Elizabeth H. THE ROLE OF PHYSICIANS IN THE HUMANE SOCIETIES OF THE EIGHTEENTH CENTURY. *Bull. of the Hist. of Medicine 1963 37(1): 43-51.* The latter half of the 18th century witnessed the founding of several humane societies in Europe, England, and America. The English and American organizations, the physicians involved in them, and their interest in artificial respiration are the subject of this article.   W. L. Fox

Journalism

1394. Brigham, Clarence S. ADDITIONS AND CORRECTIONS TO *HISTORY AND BIBLIOGRAPHY OF AMERICAN NEWSPAPERS, 1690-1820. Pro. of the Am. Antiquarian Soc. 1961 71(1): 15-62.* Presents additions and corrections to the parent work, published in 1947 in two volumes. Included are nine new titles; the article is otherwise devoted to corrections and to additional biographical and historical information. Twenty-six states and the District of Columbia are covered.   W. D. Metz

1395. Hixson, Richard F. "FAITHFUL GUARDIAN" OF PRESS FREEDOM. *Pro. of the New Jersey Hist. Soc. 1963 81(3): 155-163.* Isaac Collins founded New Jersey's first permanent newspaper, the *New-Jersey Gazette,* in December 1777 with legislative support. Parts of letters between Collins and Governor William Livingston discussing Collins' stand on the freedom of the press are given with background information. "Collins' courteous yet forceful refusal to concede to outside pressure, including legislative, stand as early declarations for the untrammeled liberty of the press." His stand for truth as a defense against libel, balanced reporting for both sides, and protection of anonymous authors contributed to the freedom of the press in both New Jersey and the United States.   B. B. Swift

1396. Hoffman, Ronald. THE PRESS IN MERCANTILE MARYLAND: A QUESTION OF UTILITY. *Journalism Q. 1969 46(3): 536-544.* The five newspapers serving the Maryland merchant community 1760-85 reflect the development of the upper Chesapeake region. Their role in this expansion was one of assistance. Primarily, the merchant employed the newspapers as a retailing agent. Details the functions of the newspapers and the services they provided. During the period no significant new commercial services were introduced and offered to the public. The newspapers did not really serve Maryland's vital centers of trade. Retailers from Annapolis flooded the newspapers with advertising, but ports other than Annapolis were the principal locations serving Maryland's tobacco and wheat trade. The majority of merchants conducted their business away from Annapolis and did not use the press. They had not required a press in order to prosper in a market country. Based on primary sources; 47 notes.

K. J. Puffer

1397. Merritt, Richard L. PUBLIC OPINION IN COLONIAL AMERICA: CONTENT-ANALYZING THE COLONIAL PRESS. *Public Opinion Q. 1963 27(3): 356-371.* Discusses the application of the methods of content analysis to the press of colonial America. B. E. Swanson

1398. Miller, C. William. BENJAMIN FRANKLIN'S WAY TO WEALTH. *Papers of the Biblio. Soc. of Am. 1969 63(4): 231-246.* Following a concise summary of the author's progress in preparing a bibliography of Franklin imprints, reviews "the means Franklin used to elbow his way to preeminence as a printer-publisher." The source of his success was his newspaper, although his magazine contributed modestly. The reason these ventures proved profitable was Franklin's literary abilities, his font of smaller letters than his rivals owned, use of the least expensive paper available, the free franking allowed a postmaster, and advertising income. Franklin's issues of books earned him prestige, not money. Based on primary sources; notes. C. A. Newton

1399. Parker, Peter J. THE PHILADELPHIA PRINTER: A STUDY OF AN EIGHTEENTH-CENTURY BUSINESSMAN. *Business Hist. R. 1966 40(1): 24-46.* Presents a composite picture of the 18th-century Philadelphia printers and shows the type of business in which they engaged. The printer in colonial America represented a "unique mixture of businessman and publicist." J. H. Krenkel

1400. Teeter, Dwight L. PRESS FREEDOM AND THE PUBLIC PRINTING: PENNSYLVANIA, 1775-83. *Journalism Q. 1968 45(3): 445-451.* Suggests some of the reasons Pennsylvania newspapers were able to sharply criticize the government and go unpunished, 1775-83. First, the printers were also petty merchants and were not completely dependent on government printing orders. Second, the government needed the printers for the great quantity of official printing, and the politicians thought newspapers, pamphlets, and handbills important aids to winning the war. Third, the governmental power was pluralistic in nature, with strong factions. Political essays were usually written by politicians whose political power protected the printers. When Thomas Paine lost his position with Congress because of a letter he wrote to John Dunlap's *Pennsylvania Packet,* the Pennsylvania Assembly, which was often at odds with Congress, soon hired him. Political maneuverings protected the printers. Different levels of government, each with its own financial resources, ensured that if one printing job was lost, another might soon be found. With their freedom, the printers developed a framework of principle from which to operate. Based on primary and secondary sources; 38 notes. K. J. Puffer

1401. Teeter, Dwight L. THE PRINTER AND THE CHIEF JUSTICE: SEDITIOUS LIBEL IN 1782-83. *Journalism Q. 1968 45(2): 235-242.* In 1782, printer Eleazer Oswald moved to Philadelphia from Baltimore; he was known as a man who loved a fight. He quickly made an enemy of Chief Justice Thomas McKean (1734-1817) by printing stinging complaints in his newspaper, the *Independent Gazetteer,* about fines levied against two army officers in September 1782. McKean saw to it that the Philadelphia grand jury, meeting in December, would hear charges of libel. Oswald opened his newspaper's columns to attacks on McKean and his court, and to arguments against the use of the law of seditious libel. Discusses the ideas presented. The controversy was rooted in Pennsylvania's politics. Oswald was arrested twice; he did nothing to diminish bitter partisan feelings. The grand jury finally voted 17-2 against indicting him. The controversy brought long discussion of the proper roles of grand juries, which was of some interest outside Pennsylvania. Based on primary and secondary sources; 56 notes.

K. J. Puffer

REFERENCE MATTER

INDEX

This is a combined index of author, biographical, geographical, and subject entries. Biographical entries are followed by an asterisk. Autobiographical entries are followed by two asterisks. Personal names without asterisks are authors of articles.

A

Abbot, William W. 1047
Abernethy, Thomas J. 499
Abnaki 522 743
Abolitionists 1204-6 1212 1216 1252
Aboville, François Marie d', Colonel* 609
Academy for the Education of Youth (Philadelphia) 1255 1313
Adair, Douglass 337 1013-4
Adams (family)* 304 306 310
Adams, Abigail (Mrs. William Stephens Smith)* 951
Adams, Dunlap* 1129
Adams, John* 89 302-3 305 307-9 380 477 712 722 731 884 897 950-1 989
Adams, John Quincy* 60 531 712 996
Adams, Samuel (physician)* 1183
Adams, Samuel* 72 264 380 468 531
Adams, Thomas R. 478
Adams, Willi Paul 1
Addison, Joseph* 124

Adolphus, John Leycester* 29
African Methodists 1310 1364
Agents, colonial 104 378 390 427 431 443 446-7 451 467 476 778
Agriculture 51 171 368 379 1133 1160-1 1191 1198-200
  Connecticut 1131
  Florida 798 1121
  Georgia 1201
  Maryland 1202
  New Jersey 1172
  Pennsylvania 452 1133 1161 1191
  Virginia 368 1118 1149 1181 1202. *See also* Tobacco
Aitchison, William* 218
Akers, Charles W. 132
Alabama 784
Alamance (battle) 793 804
Albany (battle) 606
Albany, New York 1091
Albaugh, Gaylord P. 1302
Albertini, Mario 983
Albright, Raymond W. 1303
Alden, Dauril 1119

Alden, John Richard* 2 7 12
Aldrich, James M. 1304
Aldridge, Alfred Owen 311-3
Alexander, John* 153
Alexander, John K. 172-3 268 461 608
Alexander, William (known as Lord Stirling)* 259
Alexander, William* 1172
Alfred (vessel) 195
Allan, Thomas (Lord Nash)* 294
Allen, Andrew* 839
Allen, Ben 781
Allen, Ethan* 501 504-5 511 284
Allen, Ira* 717
Allen, John* 243
Alliance (vessel) 668
Aly, Bower 1015
Amacher, Richard E. 314
Amelung, John Frederick* 1197
American Iron Company 1163
American Philosophical Society 258 330 1362 1372
American Revolution 220
  causes 4 11-12 14 16 23

339

LIST OF PERIODICALS

This list contains the titles of the periodicals surveyed for abstracts in ERA OF THE AMERICAN REVOLUTION. The titles are arranged in alphabetical order by journal title.

The frequency of publication, years of coverage, and the code of the country of publication follow the title of the periodical.

Example:

Alabama Historical Quarterly	Q	1963-	US
Cithara	SA	1963-	US
History Today	M	1954-	GB
Numisma	Q	1958-	SP

Abbreviations and explanation:

A	annual		Q	quarterly
B	biennial		SA	semiannual
BM	bimonthly		SM	semimonthly
BW	biweekly		3	3 times a year
I	irregular		T	triennial
M	monthly		W	weekly

Persons interested in further information concerning the journals are referred to HISTORICAL PERIODICALS (Santa Barbara: Clio Press, 1961) and ULRICH'S INTERNATIONAL PERIODICALS DIRECTORY 1969/70, thirteenth edition (New York: R. R. Bowker, 1969).

Alphabetical list of country codes and countries:

AA	Austria	IR	Ireland
AR	Argentina	IT	Italy
AU	Australia	JA	Japan
BE	Belgium	NO	Norway
CA	Canada	SP	Spain
CU	Cuba	SU	Union of Soviet Socialist Republics
DE	Denmark	SZ	Switzerland
EG	East Germany	US	United States
FR	France	VZ	Venezuela
GB	Great Britain	WG	West Germany

A

Agricultural History	Q	1954-	US
Alabama Historical Quarterly	Q	1963-	US
Alabama Review	Q	1963-	US
American Archivist	Q	1954-	US
American Bar Association Journal	M	1967-74	US
American Book Collector	8	1963-	US
American Heritage	BM	1955-	US
American Historical Review	5	1954-	US
American History Illustrated	10	1966-	US
American Jewish Archives	SA	1954-	US
American Jewish Historical Quarterly	Q	1954-	US
American Journal of Economics and Sociology	Q	1963-	US
American Journal of Legal History	Q	1957-	US
American Literature	Q	1963-	US
American Neptune	Q	1954-	US
American Political Science Review	Q	1954-	US
American Quarterly	Q	1954-	US
American Scholar	Q	1963-	US
American Speech	Q	1963-	US
American West	BM	1964-	US
American-German Review	S	1955-	US
American-Scandinavian Review	Q	1954-	US
Americas, The	Q	1954-	US
Annales: Économies, Sociétés, Civilisations	BM	1954-	FR
Annales Historiques de la Révolution Française	Q	1954-57	FR
Annales of Science	BM	1955-	GB
Annales of the Association of American Geographers	Q	1963-	US
Anuario de Estudios Americanos	A	1953-	SP
Arizona and the West	Q	1963-	US
Army Quarterly and Defence Journal	Q	1963-	GB
Aussenpolitik	Q	1954-	WG
Australian Journal of Politics and History	3	1956-	AU

B

Baptist Quarterly	Q	1955-	GB
Boston Museum Bulletin	Q	1963-73	US

British Association for American Studies Bulletin			GB
(old title, see Journal of American Studies)			
Bulletin of Friends Historical Association			US
(old title, see Quaker History)			
Bulletin of the History of Medicine	BM	1963-	US
Bulletin of the Institute of Historical Research	SA	1954-	GB
Bulletin of the Irish Committee of Historical Science	Q	1955-59	IR
Bulletin of the Military Historical Society	Q	1955-62	GB
Bulletin of the United Church of Canada	I	1963-	CA
Business History Review	Q	1954-	US

C

Cahiers des Dix (ceased pub)		1963-	CA
Canadian Association for American Studies Bulletin		1965-68	CA
(ceased pub 1969)			
Canadian Geographical Journal	M	1963-	CA
Canadian Historical Review	Q	1954-	CA
Canadian Journal of Economics and Political Science	Q	1954-	CA
Canadian Journal of History	3	1966-	CA
Canadian Review of American Studies	SA	1970-	CA
Centennial Review	Q	1963-	US
Church History	Q	1954-	US
Cincinnati Historical Society Bulletin	Q	1964-73	US
Cithara	SA	1963-	US
Civilisations	Q	1955-	BE
Concordia Historical Institute Quarterly	Q	1962-	US
Connecticut Historical Society Bulletin	Q	1963-	US
Contemporary Review	M	1954-	GB
Cornell Library Journal (ceased pub 1972)	I	1966-72	US
Current History	M	1955-	US

D

Daedalus	Q	1963-	US
Dalhousie Review	Q	1954-	CA
Daughters of the American Revolution Magazine	M	1971-	US
Delaware History	SA	1968-	US
Deutsche Rundschau (ceased pub 1963)	M	1954-63	WG
Duquesne Review	SA	1962-	US
Durham University Journal	3	1954-	GB

E

Early American Literature	3	1971-	US
Economic Development and Cultural Change	Q	1966-	US
Economic Historical Review	3	1954-	GB
English Historical Review	Q	1954-	GB
Essex Institute Historical Collections	Q	1963-	US
Estudios Americanos (ceased pub 1961)	Q	1955-61	SP
Ethnohistory	Q	1963-	US
Etudes	M	1955-	FR
Explorations in Economic History	Q	1955-	US

F

Florida Historical Quarterly	Q	1954-	US
Freedom and Union		1955-57	US
Freeman	M	1970-	US
French Historical Studies	Q	1958-	US

G

Georgia Historical Quarterly	Q	1955-	US
Gids, De	M	1955-	NO
Government and Opposition	Q	1966-	GB

H

Halve Maen	Q	1963-	US
Hebrew Union College Annual	A	1955-	US
Hispania	Q	1954-	SP
Hispanic American Historical Review	Q	1954-	SP
Historia	I	1955-	AR
Historia	M	1955-56	FR
Historian	Q	1954-	US
Historic Preservation	Q	1964-	US
Historical Journal	Q	1954-	GB
Historical Magazine of the Protestant Episcopal Church	Q	1954-	US
Historical New Hampshire	Q	1963-	US
Historical Review of Berks County	Q	1969-70	US
Historical Studies	SA	1954-	AU
Historische Zeitschrift	3	1954-	WG
Historisk Tidsscrift	3	1954-	DE
History	3	1954-	GB
History and Theory	3	1961-	US
History of Education Quarterly	Q	1954-	US
History Teacher	Q	1968-	US
History Today	M	1954-	US
Huntington Library Quarterly	Q	1954-	US

I

Indiana History Bulletin	M	1968-	US
Irish Sword	SA	1955-	IR
Isis	Q	1954-	US
Istoricheskii Arkhiv (ceased pub 1962)	BM	1955-62	SU

J

Jahrbuch für Amerikastudien	A	1959-	WG
Journal of American History	Q	1964-	US
Journal of American Studies	3	1960-	GB
Journal of British Studies	SA	1962-	US
Journal of Church and State	3	1963-	US
Journal of Economic History	Q	1954-	US
Journal of Historical Studies (ceased pub 1970)	Q	1967-70	US

Journal of Human Relations (ceased pub 1973)	Q	1963-73	US
Journal of Interamerican Studies and World Affairs	Q	1959-	US
Journal of Interdisciplinary History	Q	1970-	US
Journal of Long Island History	SA	1963-	US
Journal of Mississippi History	Q	1963-	US
Journal of Negro History	Q	1954-	US
Journal of Politics	Q	1954-	US
Journal of Presbyterian History	Q	1954-	US
Journal of Southern History	Q	1954-	US
Journal of the Arms and Armour Society	Q	1956-65	GB
Journal of the History of Ideas	Q	1954-	US
Journal of the History of Medicine and Allied Sciences	Q	1954-	US
Journal of the Illinois State Historical Society	Q	1963-	US
Journal of the Lancaster County Historical Society	Q	1963-73	US
Journal of the Presbyterian Historical Society	Q	1954-	US
Journal of the Rutgers University Library	SA	1955-74	US
Journal of the Society for Army Historical Research	3	1955-	GB
Journal of the Society of Architectural Historians	Q	1963-	US
Journalism Quarterly	Q	1954-	US

L

Labor History	Q	1960-	US
Library of Congress Quarterly Journal	Q	1963-	US
Long Island Forum	M	1969-	US
Louisiana History	Q	1955-	US

M

Mankind	BM	1967-	US
Manuscripts	Q	1963-	US
Marine Corps Gazette	M	1955-60	US
Mariner's Mirror	Q	1955-	GB
Maryland Historical Magazine	Q	1963-	US
Massachusetts Historical Society Proceedings	A	1953-	US
Memoirs and Proceedings of the Manchester Literary and Philosophical Society	A	1954-	GB
Mennonite Quarterly Review	Q	1954-	US
Methodist History	Q	1962-	US
Michigan History	Q	1963-	US
Mid-America	Q	1954-	US
Midcontinent American Studies Journal	SA	1963-	US
Midwest Journal of Political Science	Q	1954-	US
Militär Politisches Forum	M	1954-59	WG
Military Affairs	Q	1955-	US
Military Collector and Historian	Q	1963-	US
Military Review	M	1963-	US
Miroir de l'Histoire	M	1954-63	FR
Mississippi Quarterly	Q	1963-	US
Mississippi Valley Historical Review (old title, see Journal of American History)			US
Montana	Q	1955-	US
Moravian Historical Society Transactions	A	1963-	US

N

National Genealogical Society Quarterly	Q	1963-	US
Nautical Research Journal	Q	1965-	US
New England Quarterly	Q	1954-	US
New England Social Studies Bulletin	A	1954-	US
New-England Galaxy	Q	1963-	US
New Jersey Historical Society Proceedings			US
(old title, see New Jersey History)			
New Jersey History	Q	1963-	US
New York Historical Society Quarterly	Q	1963-	US
New York History	Q	1955-	US
New York Times Magazine	W	1954-61	US
Newport History	Q	1969-73	US
Nineteenth-Century Fiction	Q	1964-	US
North Carolina Historical Review	Q	1963-	US
North Dakota Quarterly	Q	1963-	US
Northwest Ohio Quarterly	Q	1963-	US
Notes and Queries	M	1955-	GB
Notes and Records of the Royal Society of London	SA	1964-	GB
Novaia I Noveishaia Istoriia	BM	1957-	SU
Now and Then	Q	1962-	US
Numisma	Q	1958-	SP

O

Ohio History	Q	1958-	US
Ontario History	Q	1963-	CA

P

Pacific Northwest Quarterly	Q	1955-	US
Papers of the Bibliographical Society of America	Q	1963-	US
Parliamentary Affairs	Q	1954-	GB
Past and Present	I	1954-	GB
Pennsylvania Folklife	Q	1963-	US
Pennsylvania History	Q	1963-	US
Pennsylvania Magazine of History and Biography	Q	1955-	US
Perspectives in American History	A	1967-	US
Phylon	Q	1954-	US
Political Science Quarterly	Q	1954-	US
Polish Review	Q	1956-	US
Politico	Q	1954-	IT
Ponte	M	1954-	IT
Princeton University Library Chronical	3	1963-	US
Proceedings and Collections of the Wyoming Historical and Geological Society	I	1970-	US
Proceedings of the American Antiquarian Society	SA	1954-	US
Proceedings of the American Philosophical Society	BM	1955-	US
Proceedings of the Massachusetts Historical Society	A	1953-	US
Proceedings of the New Jersey Historical Society			US
(old title, see New Jersey History)			
Proceedings of the South Carolina Historical Association	A	1963-	US

Proceedings of the Wesley Historical Society	Q	1955-	GB
Prologue: Journal of the National Archives	3	1963-	US
Publications of the American Jewish Historical Society (old title, see American Jewish Historical Quarterly)			
Public Opinion Quarterly	Q	1963-	US

Q

Quaker History	SA	1954-	US
Quarterly Journal of Speech	Q	1964-	US
Quarterly Journal of the Library of Congress	Q	1963-	US
Queen's Quarterly	Q	1954-	CA

R

Radford Review (ceased pub 1972)	Q	1966-72	US
Rassegna Storica del Risorgimento	Q	1954-	IT
Records of the American Catholic Historical Society of Philadelphia	Q	1954-	US
Register of the Kentucky Historical Society	Q	1963-	US
Review of Politics	Q	1954-	US
Revista Cubana		1957-	CU
Revista de Historia	I	1960-	VZ
Revista de Historia de América	SA	1955-	MX
Revue d'Histoire Diplomatique	Q	1954-	FR
Revue d'Histoire Économique et Sociale	Q	1954-	FR
Revue de l'Université d'Ottawa	Q	1963-	CA
Revue de l'Université Laval (ceased pub 1966)		1963-66	CA
Revue de Paris (ceased pub 1970)	M	1954-70	FR
Revue Historique de l'Armée	Q	1954-	FR
Revue Maritime	M	1963-	FR
Rhode Island History	Q	1963-	US
Richmond Country History	SA	1971-73	US
Rocky Mountain Social Science Journal	SA	1966-	US
Royal United Service Institute Journal	Q	1955-	GB
Russian Review	Q	1954-	US

S

Scholarly Publishing	Q	1969-	CA
Schweizer Beiträge zur Allgemeinen Geschichte	A	1954-58	SZ
Seijō Shigaku	I	1968-	JA
Shien	BM	1955-	JA
Shirin	BM	1955-	JA
Slavic Review	Q	1954-	US
Slovakia	A	1954-	US
Social Education	Q	1963-	US
Social Science	Q	1963-	US
Social Studies	7	1963-	US
Societas: A Review of Social History	Q	1971-	US
South Atlantic Quarterly	Q	1954-	US
South Carolina Historical Magazine	Q	1963-	US
Southern California Quarterly	Q	1962-	US

Southern Quarterly	Q	1963-	US
Southern Speech Journal	Q	1963-	US
Southwest Review	Q	1963-	US
Speech Monographs	Q	1965-	US
Storia e Politica	Q	1962-	IT
Studi Storici	Q	1959-	IT
Studies in Bibliography and Booklore	I	1954-	US
Studies in History and Society	I	1968-	US

T

Tagebuch	M	1954-	AA
Teki Historyczne	A	1954-	GB
Tennessee Historical Quarterly	Q	1963-	US
Transactions of the Royal Historical Society	A	1954-	GB
Transactions of the Royal Society of Canada	A	1954-	CA

U

Ukrainian Quarterly	Q	1954-	US
United States Naval Institute Proceedings	M	1954-	US
University of Toronto Quarterly	Q	1963-	CA

V

Vermont History	Q	1963-	US
Vestnik Istorii Mirovoi Kul'tury	I	1957-	SU
Virginia Cavalcade	Q	1963-	US
Virginia Magazine of History and Biography	Q	1955-	US
Virginia Quarterly Review	Q	1954-	US
Voprosy Filosofii	M	1954-	SU

W

West Tennessee Historical Society Papers	A	1963-	US
West Virginia History	Q	1963-	US
Western Political Quarterly	Q	1955-	US
William and Mary Quarterly	Q	1954-	US
Winterthur Portfolio	A	1964-	US
Wisconsin Magazine of History	Q	1962-	US
Wissenschaftliche Zeitschrift der Humboldt-Universität zu Berlin	I	1954-	EG

Y

Yale University Library Gazette	Q	1965-	US

Z

Zeitschrift für Politik	Q	1954-	WG

FESTSCHRIFTS

Essays on American Literature in Honor of Jay B. Hubbell (Durham: Duke U. Press, 1967).

The Old Dominion: Essays for Thomas Perkins Abernethy (Charlottesville: The U. Press of Virginia, 1964).

Writing Southern History: Essays in Historiography in Honor of Fletcher M. Green (Baton Rouge, La.: Louisiana State U. Press, 1967).

LIST OF ABSTRACTERS

A

D. J. Abramoske
M. Abrash
H. M. Adams
J. Adelson
C. J. Allard
C. R. Allen Jr.
D. van Arkel
W. M. Armstrong
L. L. Athey

B

V. O. Bardsley
T. D. S. Bassett
G. P. Bassler
K. J. Bauer
G. D. Bearce
M. Berman
A. Birkos
A. Blumberg
E. H. Boehm
J. D. Born, Jr.
W. L. Bowers
C. L. Boyd
J. H. Boykin
D. E. Brewster
N. Brockman
D. Brockway
D. N. Brown
L. Brown
T. H. Brown

W. A. Buckman
J. M. Bumsted
R. S. Burke
R. S. Burns
D. Bushnell

C

H. L. Calkin
N. Callahan
R. V. Calvert
D. D. Cameron
R. E. Cameron
R. F. Campbell
V. P. Carosso
J. A. Casada
J. A. Clarke
W. H. Coates
A. W. Coats
P. J. Coleman
R. G. Comegys
T. M. Condon
J. F. Cook
H. E. Cox
B. L. Crapster
H. W. Currie

D

T. B. Davis, Jr.
D. Davis
G. H. Davis
K. P. Davis

T. B. Davis
R. C. Delk
C. F. Delzell
D. Dodd
J. B. Duff
D. C. Duniway

E

H. G. Earnhart
C. L. Eichelberger
L. V. Eid
G. Emery
E. E. Eminhizer
D. C. Engler
J. Erickson
H. Ershkowitz
K. Eubank
D. H. Eyman

F

E. Füssl
D. M. Fahey
T. J. Farnham
E. Feldman
J. D. Filipiak
J. K. Flack
W. L. Fox
W. C. Frank
D. M. Furman

G

J. Gagliardo
D. P. Gallagher
L. Gara
A. N. Garland
J. S. Gassner
J. G. Gazley
R. I. Giesberg
C. C. Gorchels
H. J. Gordon, Jr.
H. J. Graham
C. L. Grant
H. R. Grant
J. A. S. Grenville
G. M. Gressley
W. R. Griffin
G. N. Grob

H

C. G. Hamilton
R. J. Hanks
P. H. Hardacre
L. R. Harlan
F. L. Harrold
J. M. Hawes
M. A. Hayes
D. F. Henderson
J. Herbst
W. E. Heydendorff
J. W. Hillje
F. B. M. Hollyday
D. Houston
R. Howell
S. E. Humphreys
W. Hunsberger

I

H. Imai

J

D. C. James
K. James

J. H. Jensen
E. C. Johnson
E. D. Johnson
S. L. Jones
H. D. Jordan
C. B. Joynt
J. Judd

K

T. Kage
M. Kanin
H. Kantor
L. D. Kasparian
P. W. Kennedy
R. Kerley
W. A. Klutts
L. A. Knafla
J. H. Krenkel
M. Kroeger
N. A. Kuntz
G. Kurland
N. Kurland

L

R. B. Lange
W. C. Langsam
C. F. Latour
A. H. Lawrence
C. A. LeGuin
R. E. Lindgren
J. Loose
G. Lovas
H. T. Lovin
R. Lowitt
G. L. Lycan
J. G. Lydon

M

M. W. Machan
H. M. Madden
J. F. Mahoney
R. J. Marion

Sr. M. McAuley
M. J. McBaine
R. V. McBaine
J. M. McCarthy
F. J. McDonald
W. D. McIntyre
R. S. Melamed
W. D. Metz
D. R. Millar
R. M. Miller
W. B. Miller
T. Miyake
N. W. Moen
R. A. Mohl
T. L. Moir
H. Monteagle
W. G. Morgan
B. M. Morrison
R. Mueller
G. A. Mugge
D. H. Murdoch
L. R. Murphy

N

H. O. Nelli
L. G. Nelson
C. A. Newton
C. M. Nowak
F. L. Nussbaum

O

D. J. O'Brien
E. Oberholzer, Jr.
C. F. Ogilvie
D. C. Oliver
P. M. Olson
B. W. Onstine
G. L. Owen

P

S. C. Pearson, Jr.
D. P. Peltier
J. G. Pennington

N. L. Peterson
W. F. Peterson
M. Petrie
A. H. Pfeiffer
R. S. Pickett
S. R. Pliska
H. B. Powell
S. Prisco
K. J. Puffer
J. S. Pula
C. J. Pusateri

Q

B. T. Quinten

R

R. C. Raack
L. Raife
W. D. Rasmussen
G. Rehder
G. L. A. Reilly
N. Rescher
M. B. Rex
E. B. Richards
D. R. Richardson
E. G. Roddy
A. B. Rollins
H. M. Rosen
F. Rosenthal
H. K. Rosenthal
D. F. Rossi
F. Rotondaro

S

P. L. Saltsman
R. G. Schafer
W. J. Schellings

G. Schoebe
S. R. Sherter
L. D. Silveri
H. J. Silverman
W. M. Simon
Y. Slavutych
D. A. Sloan
M. Small
D. L. Smith
G. P. Smith
L. C. Smith
R. S. Smith
G. E. Snow
B. B. Solnick
C. R. Spurgin
F. J. Stachowski
J. Stannard
G. J. Stansfield
H. G. Stelzner
E. P. Stickney
A. J. Stifflear
A. R. Stoesen
D. A. Stokes
G. Stourzh
M. R. Strausbaugh
M. Svanevik
B. E. Swanson
B. B. Swift
D. C. Swift
D. H. Swift

T

R. D. Tallman
B. D. Tennyson
J. W. Thacker, Jr.
C. Thibault
J. R. Thomas
P. D. Thomas
A. W. Thompson
Sr. M. P. Trauth
A. Turner

U

L. F. S. Upton
J. M. E. Usher

V

R. B. Valliant
N. Varga
J. R. Vignery
D. Visser

W

B. Waldstein
H. M. Ward
D. F. Warner
H. Weisser
K. B. West
D. P. Wharton
W. E. Wight
B. Wilkins
M. M. Williamson
R. E. Wilson
E. Wollert
R. L. Woodward
J. C. Wyllie

Y

D. A. Yanchisin
A. P. Young

Z

O. H. Zabel
E. Ziemke
W. F. Zornow